LIMITATION OF ACTIONS

LLOYD'S COMMERCIAL LAW LIBRARY

Arbitration Law
by Robert Merkin
(looseleaf)

Interests in Goods
by Norman Palmer and
Ewan McKendrick
(1993)

The Law of Insurance Contracts
second edition
by Malcolm A. Clarke
(1994)

The Law of Insurance Contracts
first supplement
by Malcolm A. Clarke
(1996)

EC Banking Law
second edition
by Marc Dassesse, Stuart Isaacs QC
and Graham Penn
(1994)

*The Law and Practice Relating to
Appeals from Arbitration Awards*
by D. Rhidian Thomas
(1994)

Force Majeure and Frustration of Contract
second edition
Edited by Ewan McKendrick
(1995)

*The Practice and Procedure
of the Commercial Court*
fourth edition
by The Hon. Sir Anthony Colman
and Victor Lyon
(1995)

*Professional Liability:
Law and Insurance*
by Ray Hodgin
(1996)

Arbitration Act 1996
by Robert Merkin
(1996)

Civil Jurisdiction and Judgments
second edition
by Adrian Briggs
and Peter Rees
(1997)

*The Practice and Procedure of
the Companies Court*
edited by Alan Boyle QC
and Philip Marshall
(1997)

*Arbitration Practice and Procedure:
Interlocutory and Hearing Problems*
second edition
by D. Mark Cato
(1997)

LIMITATION OF ACTIONS

BY

DAVID W. OUGHTON
Professor of Commercial Law
De Montfort University, Leicester

JOHN P. LOWRY
Associate Director of the Centre for Consumer
and Commercial Law Research, Brunel University
Visiting Fellow, Fairleigh-Dickinson University,
New Jersey, USA

ROBERT M. MERKIN
Professor of Commercial Law, Cardiff Law School
Consultant, Wilde Sapte, Solicitors

|L|L|P|

LONDON   HONG KONG
1998

LLP Reference Publishing
69–77 Paul Street
London EC2A 4LQ

SOUTH EAST ASIA
LLP Asia Limited
Room 1101, Hollywood Centre
233 Hollywood Road
Hong Kong

First published 1998

British Library Cataloguing in Publication Data
A catalogue record for this book
is available from the
British Library

ISBN 1-85978-128-4

Are you satisfied with our customer service?

These telephone numbers are your service hot lines for questions and queries:

Delivery: +44 (0) 1206 772866
Payment/invoices/renewals: +44 (0) 1206 772114
LLP Products & Services: +44 (0) 1206 772113
e-mail: Publications@LLPLimited.com or fax us on +44 (0) 1206 772771

*We welcome your views and comments in order to ease any problems
and answer any queries you may have.*

LLP Limited, Colchester CO3 3LP, U.K.

Text set in 10/12pt Times
by Interactive Sciences Ltd
Gloucester
Printed in Great Britain by
MPG Books Ltd,
Bodmin, Cornwall

FOREWORD

BY THE HONOURABLE MR JUSTICE LIGHTMAN

The law of limitations reflects a compromise between what is and what is not an excusable delay and an excusable reason for delay in commencing proceedings. It is undesirable to require a potential claimant to commence proceedings precipitately when (as matters may turn out) there may be no need to occasion the cost and other undesirable consequences. But the cloud over a person's life of a claim which may or may not materialise into a lawsuit has to be experienced to be understood. The law reflects a balance between these two conflicting considerations.

The law of limitations is a purely statutory creation. The statutory rules are detailed and (with limited exceptions) rigid and inflexible and on occasion produce unreasonable results. The Court has limited scope under the guise of statutory construction to blunt the inevitable rough edges and fill the *lacunæ*: the task has to be handed back to the legislature for a fresh layer of legislation—small comfort for the litigant in the case where the legislation is found wanting. The contrast is with the approach of the Court of Chancery which has developed the established body of principles in the field of Equity which allows the Court to grant or refuse relief according as to whether the delay renders its grant inequitable. The rules of Equity founded on considerations of justice and conscience ought never to produce injustice.[1]

Questions of limitation constantly arise in the daily round of legal practitioners and judges. It is an area of the greatest practical importance. The product of legislative activity and judicial commentary on legislation is complex and bulky. Few areas of law have over recent years developed so fast. The time has been reached when there is a vital need for fundamental rethinking as to the principles underlying the modern law of limitations and an examination of the stage now reached in its development. This exercise requires research and detailed study, a challenge academic lawyers of the quality of the authors of this work are peculiarly well-equipped to meet. The authors have undertaken this exercise and produced a comprehensive restatement of the current law. A totally new work, rather than a revised or re-worked edition of an earlier work, is more likely to have and exercise the freedom to survey the field afresh, unencumbered by baggage from the past. Fresh thinking is the mark of this work. A glance at the index reveals the width of the field examined.

---

1. Compare Lord Reid in *Cartledge v. E Jopling & Sons* [1963] AC 758 at 772: "[Unlike the provisions of the Limitation Act] the common law ought never to produce a wholly unreasonable result".

The Woolf Report and its philosophy that litigation shall be conducted economically and expeditiously require that the legal component in proceedings shall be served by books such as this. This book should find its place in any well-stocked library, and will certainly be in mine.

THE HONOURABLE MR JUSTICE LIGHTMAN
Royal Courts of Justice
London

PREFACE

The law of limitation of actions has long been contentious, not least because it attempts to strike a balance between the conflicting interests of plaintiffs and defendants. Since 1936 there have been four statutes to amend and reform the law of limitation of actions, and no fewer than six official bodies have reviewed English law in this respect and reported their findings to Parliament. In considering the purpose served by limitation periods, the *Twentieth Report, Interim Report of the Law Reform Committee on Limitation of Actions in Personal Injury Claims*[1] observed:

"In the first place, it is intended to protect defendants from being vexed by stale claims relating to long-past incidents about which their records may no longer be in existence and as to which their witnesses, even if they are still available, may well have no accurate recollection. Secondly, we apprehend that the law of limitation is designed to encourage plaintiffs not to go to sleep on their rights, but to institute proceedings as soon as it is reasonably possible for them to do so . . . Thirdly, the law is intended to ensure that a person may with confidence feel that after a given time he may treat as being finally closed an incident which may have led to a claim against him . . . ."

In attempting to achieve justice as between the parties to an action, the law has, of necessity, reached a compromise solution. The Law Reform Committee recognised that "the idea of a single uniform period applicable to every cause of action is plainly unattainable".[2] It therefore endorsed the notion that the running of time must generally depend on the *terminus a quo*, which is the date of accrual of the plaintiff's cause of action. The Committee's proposals were enacted in the Limitation Act 1980—a consolidating statute. However, that Act did little to solve the complexities associated with a system of limitation of actions which had developed along piecemeal lines during the twentieth century. Despite various criticisms of English law in this respect, it has been held by the European Court of Human Rights to be proportionate to the aims sought to be achieved by the relevant legislation,[3] however, proportionate though it may be, one cannot help but feel that on occasions the results achieved by the law seem to operate in an arbitrary fashion.

  The debate surrounding the justice of the rules of limitation of actions will no doubt continue with increasing vigour. It is therefore noteworthy that in June 1995, the Law Commission was moved to announce that it intended to undertake a comprehensive review of the law of limitation of actions.[4] Overall in terms of civil litigation generally,

1. Cmnd 5630, 1974.
2. *Final Report,* Cmnd 6923, 1977, para 1.10.
3. *Stubbings* v. *United Kingdom* (36–37/1995/542–543/628–629).
4. Sixth Programme of Law Reform, Law Commission Report No 234, item 3.

much is afoot. The publication of the Woolf Report,[5] if taken together with the work of the Law Commission, may provide the necessary impetus which will herald a root and branch reform. However, the pace of law reform in this area is necessarily ponderous and is rightly marked by cautious, measured steps. Consequently, although little is likely to emerge in the immediate future, the horizon looks promising.

In recent times the subject of limitation of actions has spawned a substantial quantity of published work. This text itself has some of its origins in *Latent Damage*, a short work by the last-named author, published in 1987 in the wake of the Latent Damage Act 1986. In adding to the titles in the catalogues we have sought to provide an exhaustive and critical analysis of the law which nevertheless seeks to inject some order into what is seemingly a disparate body of rules. As far as possible, we have chosen to structure our work into sections which reflect a fairly broad, albeit traditional, classification of substantive law: the law of contract, including commercial law (Part II); the law of tort (Part III); and equity, trusts, personal representatives and real property (Part IV). Before embarking upon each of these substantive areas, Part I examines general matters such as the relationship between statutes of limitation and equitable principles on the matter of delay in instituting proceedings, the generalities of accrual of a cause of action, the symbiotic relationship between limitation periods and rules of pleading and procedure and the postponement and extension of limitation periods. Since these issues are critical to the mechanism of rules in respect of limitation of actions, in so far as they operate and impact on all branches of civil litigation, it is thought that they warrant separate and discrete treatment. Those miscellaneous rules which transcend our classification are considered in Part V.

Inevitably with a work of this kind areas of overlap may be found. In our defence we plead, somewhat expediently, for their retention on the ground of necessity. The busy practitioner or academic is better aided by self-contained chapters rather than interminable cross-referencing.

The study of the law of limitation of actions has been a Herculean task, and the work of those who have trodden the path before us is gratefully acknowledged. More specifically, David Oughton would like to express his gratitude to Martin Davis for helpful discussions on aspects of contract law and the law relating to debt. John Lowry expresses his gratitude to Rod Edmunds and James Penner for their encouragement and typically incisive comments on the chapters on equity and real property. The vigilance of Rod Edmunds in monitoring the outflow of new limitation cases deserves special thanks. Needless to say, responsibility for all infelicities remains with the authors alone. The support of all our colleagues who have endured our obsession with this project during its protracted gestation period is also gratefully acknowledged, as is the help of the librarians at our respective universities and the Institute of Advanced Legal Studies. The chapters on Arbitration and Insurance have to some extent drawn upon material previously published by Rob Merkin.[6]

---

5. *Access to Civil Justice, Final Report to the Lord Chancellor on Civil Justice in England and Wales,* July 1996.
6. Respectively, *Arbitration Law* (LLP Limited, looseleaf); *Insurance Contract Law* (Kluwer Publishing Limited, looseleaf).

This book is dedicated to our families who have lived with our physical and mental absences with grace and forbearance over the last year. We are especially grateful for the help provided by Sue Oughton in assisting with the tedious task of proof-reading.

Finally, thanks are accorded to all at LLP Limited who have moved this book through the publication process. We are particularly indebted to our editor who tolerated our delays with good humour and patience going beyond that which should be decently expected.

Our intention has been to state the law as at 1 August 1997, although we have managed to incorporate such later material as could be accommodated at proof stage.

DAVID OUGHTON
Hailsham, East Sussex

JOHN LOWRY
Scaynes Hill, West Sussex

ROBERT MERKIN
Aylesbeare, Devon

CONTENTS

PART III—TORT

PART V—MISCELLANEOUS LIMITATION PERIODS

24 MISCELLANEOUS LIMITATION PERIODS 403

APPENDICES

TABLE OF CASES

Decisions of the European Court of Justice and the European Court of First Instance are listed below numerically. These decisions are also included in the preceding alphabetical table.

TABLE OF LEGISLATION

PART I

GENERAL PRINCIPLES

CHAPTER 1

THE HISTORY AND POLICY OF LIMITATION OF ACTIONS

INTRODUCTION

The essential purpose of a statute of limitation is to place time limits on the period within which a person may commence legal proceedings or, in some instances, to require notice of a claim to be given to the other party to potential legal proceedings. Although this is highly relevant to actions at common law, it should be observed from the outset that any imposition of a limitation period upon the bringing of an action is done by way of statutory intervention, since there is no principle of limitation at common law.

Since the matter of limitation of actions is one which is beyond the scope of common law rules, the courts have no option but to interpret the relevant statutory provision and apply it so as to give effect to the intention of Parliament. Accordingly, whether a particular judge agrees with a policy of limitation of actions does not really matter. However, this has not prevented individual judges from passing an opinion on the matter with the result that there may be instances in which a litigant's action has been held to be time barred much to the displeasure of the members of the court hearing the case.[1]

The classic statement of principle concerning what is to be regarded as a statute of limitation is to be found in *Gregory* v. *Torquay Corporation*[2] in which it was stated that a statute of limitation is any statute which imposes a limit of time upon an *existing* right of action.[3] It may be argued that this statement is technically inaccurate in the sense that there may be statutory limitations upon the time within which proceedings may be brought in respect of rights of action which are not existing rights. For example, new statutory torts may be created from time to time which create a new cause of action and, at the same time, Parliament may provide for a limitation period applicable to the newly created tort. For example, the Consumer Protection Act 1987 imposes a variety of strict liability on the producer of a defective product, but at the same time introduces a strict cut-off period on all actions under Part I of the Act which runs for 10 years from the date on which a product was last supplied by someone to whom the Act applies[4] in addition to specific rules of limitation which apply to individual actions.

---

1. See *Reeves* v. *Butcher* [1891] 2 QB 509 at 511 *per* Fry LJ: "We do not have to determine whether the defence here set up is handsome or conscientious but whether it is good in law." Cf *Green* v. *Rivett* (1702) 2 Salk 421 "the Statute of Limitations, on which the security of all men depends, is to be favoured".
2. [1911] 2 KB 556.
3. *Ibid* at 559 *per* Pickford J. Emphasis added.
4. Limitation Act 1980, s 11A and see also Ch 21.

THE POLICIES UNDERLYING THE IMPOSITION OF LIMITATION PERIODS

The broad policies which underlie the law on limitation of actions were set out in the report of the Edmund Davies Committee, entitled *Limitation of Actions in Cases of Personal Injury*,[5] in which it was observed:

"In considering what recommendations we should make . . . we have constantly borne in mind what we conceive to be the accepted function of the law of limitation. In the first place, it is intended to protect defendants from being vexed by stale claims relating to long-past incidents about which their records may no longer be in existence and as to which their witnesses, even if they are still available, may well have no accurate recollection. Secondly, we apprehend that the law of limitation is designed to encourage plaintiffs not to go to sleep on their rights but to institute proceedings as soon as it is reasonably possible for them to do so . . . Thirdly, the law is intended to ensure that the person may with confidence feel that after a given time he may treat as being finally closed an incident which might have led to a claim against him."[6]

Accordingly, the three broad considerations are the protection of the defendant from stale claims, the encouragement of plaintiffs to bring proceedings as swiftly as is reasonably possible and allowing defendants to "close the ledger" on events long past.

So far as stale claims are concerned, it has been said that a statute of limitation is an "act of peace"[7] which is intended to prevent defendants from living in perpetual fear of the risk of a legal action being brought. It is said that "litigation is not an intrinsically desirable activity"[8] and that the law is fully conscious of the evil of protracted litigation, which cannot be allowed to go on indefinitely.[9] Thus it has also been said that "The primary purpose of the limitation period is to protect a defendant from the injustice of having to face a stale claim, that is a claim with which he never expected to have to deal".[10]

Accordingly, although generally the purpose of litigation is to establish the truth, there are times when the quest for the truth must give way to other considerations in the public interest. This public interest against the evil of protracted litigation may, on occasions, give way to another public interest in ensuring that justice is done in appropriate cases. Thus there are circumstances in which it is just to allow a plaintiff to proceed with his case despite the expiry of a relevant limitation period. For example it will be seen that a court has a discretion to disapply a limitation period in cases of disability, fraud, concealment or mistake[11] and there are special rules on the exercise of discretion applicable to cases of personal injury and death.[12]

On the basis of a defendant perspective and the policy underlying rules on limitation of actions, it has been observed that "Christianity forbids us to attempt enforcing the payment of a debt which time and misfortune have rendered the debtor unable to discharge"[13]

---

5. Cmnd 1829, 1962.

6. *Ibid* at para 17. See also Law Reform Committee, *Final Report on Limitation of Actions*, Cmnd 6923, 1977, para 1.7.

7. *A'Court* v. *Cross* (1825) 3 Bing 329 at 332 *per* Best CJ.

8. *Ampthill Peerage Case* [1977] AC 547 at 575 *per* Lord Simon.

9. *Ibid*. As Lord Simon observes, Charles Dickens' fictional case of *Jarndyce* v. *Jarndyce* in *Bleak House*, depicting the effects of a drawn-out and ruinous law suit on Miss Flite, is based on fact.

10. *Donovan* v. *Gwentoys Ltd* [1990] 1 All ER 1018 at 1024 *per* Lord Griffiths.

11. See Ch 6.

12. See Ch 19.

13. *A'Court* v. *Cross* (1825) 3 Bing 329 at 333 *per* Best CJ.

and that if there has been a delay of sufficient magnitude, "some good excuse for non-payment might be presumed".[14]

As has been observed above, the purpose of a statute of limitations is not merely to do justice from the potential defendant's point of view, it is also said to benefit the plaintiff, in the sense that the existence of a limitation period, in a particular case, encourages the plaintiff to bring proceedings promptly while matters are still fresh in the memory of witnesses and relevant documents remain readily available.[15] The difficulty with actions brought long after the cause has accrued is that important witnesses may be dead or not traceable and even those who can be traced will probably have only a limited recollection of the events to be considered by the court. However, against this it should also be noted that while the courts will discourage delay in seeking redress, they do not seek to encourage precipitate litigation, since it is undesirable for plaintiffs to be "encouraged to keep their eyes on the courts".[16] Rules on limitation of actions may also be regarded as a reflection upon the conduct of the dilatory plaintiff, in the sense that if a plaintiff has failed to enforce his rights within a certain period of time, he has only got himself to blame if he loses his right to proceed with the action. For example, in *Board of Trade* v. *Cayzer Irvine & Co*[17] it was observed that:

"The whole purpose of ... [the] Limitation Act is to apply to persons who have good causes of action which they could, if so disposed, enforce, and to deprive them of the power of enforcing them after they have lain by for the number of years respectively and omitted to enforce them. They are thus deprived of the remedy which they have omitted to use."[18]

It will be seen below that in terms of historical development, the earliest general Statute of Limitations[19] applied only to actions at common law, with the result that it had no application to actions in equity. However, the equitable doctrine of laches[20] provided similar protection against stale claims, albeit subject to a range of equitable discretions, with the result that it was observed in *Smith* v. *Clay*[21] that "Equity aids the vigilant, not the indolent".[22] Accordingly, for the purposes of seeking equitable relief, a plaintiff was required to come to court as quickly as was reasonably possible in order to avoid application of the principle that "delay defeats equity" since it was quite likely that delay could be taken to indicate affirmation.[23]

Since the Judicature Acts 1873–75, courts have been able to give both common law and equitable remedies, but the division between statutory rules of limitation and the doctrine of laches continues. However, despite the fact that many of the time limits laid down by the Limitation Act 1980 do not apply to claims for equitable relief,[24] it is provided in the 1980 Act that statutory limitation periods may be "applied by the court by analogy in like manner as the corresponding time limit under any enactment repealed by the Limitation

14. *Ibid.*
15. See *R.B. Policies at Lloyd's* v. *Butler* [1950] 1 KB 76.
16. *Cartledge* v. *E Jopling & Sons Ltd* [1962] 1 QB 189 at 195 *per* Sellers LJ.
17. [1927] AC 610.
18. *Ibid* at 628 *per* Lord Atkinson.
19. Statute of Limitations 1623, 21 Jac 1, c 16.
20. See Ch 3.
21. (1767) 3 Bro CC 639n.
22. *Ibid* at 640n *per* Lord Camden LC. ("*Vigilantibus non dormientibus subvenit aequitas*").
23. See *Lindsay Petroleum Co* v. *Hurd* (1874) LR 5 PC 221; *Erlanger* v. *New Sombrero Phosphate Co* (1878) 3 App Cas 1218; *Clough* v. *London & North Western Railway* (1871) LR 7 Ex 26 at 35.
24. Limitation Act 1980 s 36(1) and see Ch 3.

Act 1939 was applied before 1st July 1940". Accordingly, it is possible for a court of equity to adopt a statutory rule in order to assist its discretion[25] but the statutory rule does not bind the court absolutely. The wording of section 36(1) is important, however, since its language suggests that the application of a statutory limitation period in an action for equitable relief will apply only where the court could have acted in a like manner before the Limitation Act 1939 was enacted. It would seem to follow from this that the recent introduction of statutory longstop provisions will not fall within section 36(1), as such time limits were not heard of at the relevant time.

THE HISTORY OF TIME LIMITS ON CIVIL CLAIMS

Although the principal means by which the time within which a civil claim must be prosecuted is now the Statute of Limitations and other statutory measures which prevent claims from being brought out of time, there are other devices which have operated in a similar fashion. For example, in relation to the ownership and possession of land, the device of fixing a date representing the limit to legal memory operates in the same way as a limitation period. Accordingly, since 1275[26] Parliament has fixed the limits of legal memory (or time immemorial) as the commencement of the reign of Richard I in 1189.

Although the earliest formal and general provision dealing with the matter of limitation of actions is said to be the Statute of Limitations 1623[27] the first statutory limitation period was to be found in a statute of 1540, which concerned only actions for the recovery of property.[28] The Act of 1623 laid down a general limitation period which required that all common law actions had to be commenced and sued upon within six years of their accrual. This simple provision, albeit producing harsh results in some cases, lasted without substantial amendment for a period of over 300 years.[29] However, twentieth-century legislators have discovered pitfalls, which has resulted in a comparative flurry of legislative activity resulting in changes to the law in 1939, 1954, 1963, 1972, 1975 and 1980. Even since the most recent consolidation in the form of the Limitation Act 1980, there has been no halt to the changes in the law. For example, perceived defects in the law relating to latent damage resulted in the amendment of the 1980 Act by the Latent Damage Act 1986 and the introduction of a new statutory regime concerning strict liability for defective products has brought with it new and complex rules on limitation of actions in such cases by virtue of the provisions of the Consumer Protection Act 1987.

Given that there has been so much legislative activity in this area of the law, it might be thought that Parliament might have sorted out most of the difficulties associated with the earlier legislation. However, in many respects, recent changes have served only to complicate the law of limitation of actions still further, especially in view of the fact that most of the recent changes in the law have resulted in new limitation periods being

25. *Brooksbank* v. *Smith* (1836) 2 Y & C Ex 58 at 60 *per* Alderson B.
26. Statute of Westminster I, 1275, 3 Edw. I, St. I, c. 8. See also Prescription Act 1832 (c. 71), Preamble.
27. 21 Jac 1, c 16.
28. 32 Hen. VIII, c. 2 (Prescription).
29. Certain changes were made as a result of the Civil Procedure Act 1833, the Real Property Limitation Acts 1833 and 1874 and the Public Authorities Protection Act 1893, all of which were consolidated, with amendments, in the Limitation Act 1939.

superimposed on existing periods of limitation, applicable in marginally different circumstances. Because of this process of superimposition, it is possible for nine different limitation periods to be identified as arising out of the same set of facts, according to whether the action is one for breach of a tortious obligation, breach of contract or breach of statutory duty.

The impetus for reform in each case was generally based upon the perceived lacunae and deficiencies of the previous legislation. These difficulties could be said to arise from a number of different sources. For example, on occasion, the blame could be laid squarely at the door of the legislators who had done their job so badly that the current legislation was almost impossible to interpret. For example, the Limitation Act 1963 had the misfortune to be described as having a strong claim to be regarded as the worst-drafted Act on the statute book.[30] In other cases, the reason for law reform was that the earlier statutory provision had become so complex that changes became essential. For example, in relation to the provisions of the Limitation Act 1939, s 26, regarding the position of a bona fide purchaser it was once remarked that it was unnecessary and undesirable to expand on the meaning of the relevant provision because it was impossible to understand its scope and meaning.[31]

In other instances, change has been manufactured by virtue of a high level judicial decision pointing out the injustice which may follow from the application of a particular rule. Thus at one time the relevant provisions on limitation of actions drew no distinction between claims in respect of personal injury and other claims in contract or in tort, the relevant limitation period running for six years from the date of accrual of the cause of action. Subsequently, it was recommended that in personal injury cases, the limitation period should be reduced to one of two years from the date of accrual of the cause of action, subject to a judicial discretion to extend the period, provided this did not extend to cover actions commenced more than six years from the date on which the cause of action accrued.[32] However, subsequent legislative changes ignored the advice given by the Tucker Committee, preferring instead to impose a limitation period which ran for three years from the date of accrual of the cause of action, but which provided for no discretion to extend that period in appropriate cases. The effect of this was to allow time to start running against a plaintiff who, at the time, was unaware that he had suffered any material damage in respect of which he might sue. This was particularly so in cases of latent personal injury, as was graphically illustrated by the House of Lords' decision in *Cartledge* v. *E Jopling & Sons Ltd*[33] in which the plaintiff contracted pneumoconiosis as a result of his employers' breach of duty at a time well before 1950. This had resulted in serious lung damage, which the plaintiff discovered after 1950, but writs were not issued until 1956 by which time the plaintiff was out of time. At the time, no regard could be had to the question whether the plaintiff could reasonably have discovered that he had suffered damage with the result that the plaintiff was out of time before he even knew that he was able to bring an action against his employers. As was observed at the time, this unpalatable result was a necessary consequence of the way in which the Limitation Act 1939, s 2 was worded:

30. *Central Asbestos Co Ltd* v. *Dodd* [1973] AC 518 at 529 *per* Lord Reid.
31. *Eddis* v. *Chichester Constable* [1969] 2 Ch 345 at 362 *per* Winn LJ.
32. *Report of the Committee on the Limitation of Actions* (Tucker Committee) Cmnd 7740, 1949.
33. [1963] AC 758.

"It appears to me to be unreasonable and unjustifiable in principle that a cause of action should be held to accrue before it is possible to discover any injury and, therefore, before it is possible to raise any action. If this were a matter governed by the common law I would hold that a cause of action ought not to be held to accrue until either the injured person has discovered the injury or it would be possible for him to discover it if he took such steps as were reasonable in the circumstances. The common law ought never to produce a wholly unreasonable result."[34]

The unfairness referred to by Lord Reid in *Cartledge* v. *E Jopling & Sons Ltd* is not the only consideration in cases of this kind. It has already been observed that, in terms of policy, rules on limitation of actions are concerned with a number of issues including the protection of defendants from stale claims, encouraging plaintiffs to institute proceedings without unreasonable delay so that the most effective use may be made of evidence and allowing a defendant to feel confident that a possible claim against him is finally closed after the expiry of a specified period of time. The problem with the emphasis on justice to the plaintiff in personal injury and latent damage cases is that the certainty associated with strict limitation periods is lost, with the result that it is possible for a defendant to be dragged into court to face an allegation of negligence long after he has retired and maybe long after his professional indemnity insurance has lapsed. However, despite this, the Edmund Davies Committee[35] recommended that where a person suffers personal injury, his claim should not be barred by the three-year limitation period if he could not reasonably have been expected to know of his injury during that period, provided action was commenced within 12 months of discovering the injury.[36]

While it may be argued that the introduction of limitation periods based on the notion of discoverability tends towards uncertainty in the law, the same development reveals another policy issue which underlies these changes. It has been seen above that one of the principal reasons for statutory limitation periods is that a defendant ought to be allowed to close the book on the possibility of being sued after the expiry of a certain period of time. This justification for strict limitation periods may well be justified where the law operates a system of individual fault. However, the effective defendant in the majority of modern personal injury cases is an insurance company rather than an individual tortfeasor. Accordingly, the effect of the private insurance system is such that even if a tortfeasor is found to be "at fault" it is still his insurer who ends up paying the bill. In these circumstances, the pressure to insist on strict limitation periods in order to prevent individual wrongdoers from indeterminate personal financial liability inevitably abates in favour of a policy which prefers to emphasise the need of the plaintiff to recover compensation from a defendant backed by an insurer who is paid to spread the risk of loss amongst its policyholders.

THE COMMON LAW AND LIMITATION OF ACTIONS

It has been observed above that Lord Reid in *Cartledge* v. *E Jopling & Sons* remarked that if the matter of limitation of actions was subject to the common law it would have been

---

34. *Ibid* at 772 *per* Lord Reid. See also *Pirelli General Cable Works* v. *Oscar Faber & Partners* [1983] 2 AC 1 for similar views on undiscoverable latent property damage which ultimately led to the enactment of the Latent Damage Act 1986.

35. *Report of the Committee on Limitation of Actions in Cases of Personal Injury*, Cmnd 1829, 1962.

36. Given effect by the Limitation Act 1963 s 7. The 12-month period was extended to three years by the Law Reform (Miscellaneous Provisions) Act 1971, s 1(1).

possible for the court to introduce a rule based upon reasonable discoverability of damage.[37] However, the problem was one which could not be sorted out by reference to any common law rule since the concept of limitation of actions had no place at common law. Accordingly, the matter of limitation of actions is a statutory creation based upon the various policies considered above.

Generally, where a statutory provision creates a limitation period, it will do so through the use of words to the effect that no action shall be brought after the expiry of three, six or twelve years from the date on which the cause of action accrued. What this normally means is that, subject to exceptional cases, if the time limit has expired, the plaintiff's remedy is barred, but the question also arises whether there is any jurisdiction to dismiss an action before the expiry of a statutory limitation period. It would appear that there may be highly exceptional circumstances in which a court is prepared to dismiss an action for a remedy at common law on the ground that there has been inordinate and inexcusable delay, despite the fact that the statutory period of limitation has not yet expired.[38] Since these exceptional cases cannot be explained on the basis that any statutory provision allows the court to act in this way, it would appear that there is some common law jurisdiction which allows dismissal for want of prosecution by the court where it is no longer possible to ensure that there is a fair trial of the issues because of that delay.

Moreover, there may be circumstances in which an action will never become time barred under present rules. In these wholly exceptional circumstances, it may be possible to strike out the plaintiff's action due to inordinate delay in issuing a writ. In *Hogg* v. *Hamilton & Northumberland Health Authority*[39] the plaintiff was under a disability as a result of undergoing a surgical operation. The disability was one which was unlikely ever to be reversed, with the result that the plaintiff's action would never become time barred. One writ had been issued, but was not proceeded with. Subsequently after much delay a second writ was issued, but given the likelihood that this too would be abandoned in due course, the Court of Appeal struck out the action as an abuse of process.

It can be seen from the comments above that there may be some limited common law jurisdiction in relation to matters of limitation of actions, in order to ensure that the judicial process is conducted fairly. However, if there is some omission on the part of the legislators, such as a failure to provide for a limitation period in a given set of circumstances, it will not be possible for this omission to be made good through the application of any common law principle. For example, in *Bray* v. *Stuart A West & Co*[40] the plaintiff sought an order to the effect that a solicitor should honour an undertaking made some seven years earlier. The solicitor concerned argued that no order could be made, on the basis that the plaintiff's action was time barred. In the event, Warner J considered that the Limitation Act 1980 contained no provision applicable to an action of this kind. In the event, it was held on the facts that the solicitor could be ordered to fulfil his undertaking despite the delay.

Strictly, in these circumstances, if there is no relevant limitation period, the logical and literal conclusion should be that there is no relevant limitation period at all, in which case the action ought to be allowed to continue regardless of the passage of time. However,

37. See above fn 34 and associated text.
38. See *Birkett* v. *James* [1978] AC 297; *Department of Transport* v. *Chris Smaller (Transport) Ltd* [1989] 1 All ER 897.
39. [1993] 4 Med LR 369.
40. (1989) 139 New Law Jo 753.

there are ways round this problem. For example in *Bray* Warner J considered that, since the making of the order sought was a matter of discretion, the court could take account of any delay in deciding whether to exercise that discretion. Moreover, the court could also take account of any delay in equity through an application of the doctrine of laches. In other instances, despite an apparent omission on the part of the draftsmen of legislation, it may be possible for the court to stretch existing rules to fit the circumstances of a case which is strictly not covered by the relevant legislation.[41]

41. See e.g. *Kleinwort Benson Ltd v. South Tyneside Metropolitan Borough Council* [1994] 4 All ER 972.

CHAPTER 2

APPLICATION OF THE LIMITATION ACT 1980

As will be emphasised on numerous occasions throughout this book, the matter of limitation of actions is something which is entirely based on statutory principles, since there is no notion of limiting the time within which an action may be brought at common law. A brief historical survey of the relevant Statutes of Limitations is provided in the previous chapter, but the present law is now to be found in the Limitation Act 1980, supplemented by other provisions specific to particular areas of law.

THE LAYOUT OF THE 1980 ACT

In fairly broad terms the 1980 Act takes on board a number of principles: (I) a multiplicity of different limitation periods, applicable to different causes of action, is generally undesirable and where possible, a single period covering as many forms of action as possible should be applied.[1] (II) The limitation period should always run from the date on which the cause of action accrued.[2] (III) The basic principle underlying the scheme of any legislation should be one of limitation in the sense of barring a remedy, rather than prescription, in the form of extinguishing a right of action, otherwise than where exceptional circumstances prevail.[3]

The general scheme of the Limitation Act, considered in detail in later chapters, is briefly set out below. Part I of the Act makes provision for a range of different time limits applicable to different causes of action covering matters such as actions in tort, actions founded upon a simple contract, actions on a specialty, actions for sums recoverable by statute, actions in respect of wrongs causing personal injuries or death, actions to recover land and rent, actions to recover money secured by a mortgage or charge or to recover proceeds of the sale of land, actions in respect of trust property or the personal estate of deceased persons, actions for an account, and other miscellaneous limitation periods not covered by any of the previously stated categories.

Despite the aspiration of the Law Revision Committee that there should be as few different limitation periods as possible, it is clear from the wide variety of different rules that different circumstances require different considerations. Thus in one case, the relevant limitation period for actions in respect of contribution is as short as two years from the date of accrual of the cause of action,[4] yet in the case of certain actions initiated by the

1. Law Revision Committee, *Fifth Interim Report* (1936, Cmnd 5334) para 5.
2. *Ibid*, para 7.
3. *Ibid*, para 24.
4. See Ch 25.

11

Crown for the recovery of land, the relevant period can be as long as 60 years.[5] In between a general period of six years tends to be applied to common law actions in tort[6] and contract,[7] although in each case that period runs from the date on which the cause of action accrued, which in tort actions, generally, means the date on which damage is caused. The problem of identifying the date of damage has led, in some cases, to the introduction of a limitation period based upon the knowledge of the plaintiff, which has the capacity for extending the date on which time starts to run for a substantial period. In actions which relate to real property and specialties, a slightly longer period of 12 years applies.[8] Moreover, many of these limitation periods may be postponed or extended by virtue of other provisions of the 1980 Act.

Part II of the Act, indeed, makes special provision for circumstances in which a limitation period may be extended or excluded, as the case may be. The main grounds for extension are to be found in actions based on a simple contract where there has been an acknowledgement of liability or a debt or part payment of a debt.[9] Furthermore, the general grounds of disability, fraud, deliberate concealment and mistake[10] automatically prevent time from running against the plaintiff until such time as the plaintiff becomes aware of the relevant circumstance. In addition to these general rules which are capable of extending a limitation period, there are also circumstances in which a court has a discretion to allow an action in respect of a personal injury action or one for defamation to be allowed to proceed out of time, through the exercise of judicial discretion, thereby effectively ignoring the primary limitation period, where justice so demands.[11] Part III of the 1980 Act contains a number of supplementary provisions, dealing specifically with arbitration awards,[12] procedural matters,[13] including counterclaims, and third-party claims amongst other matters.

TRANSITIONAL PROVISIONS

As will be seen below, the nature of some of the limitation periods applicable to certain types of action can be relatively lengthy. Because of this it has been necessary to make arrangements for some quite elaborate transitional provisions, especially in cases where there have been marked changes in the law relating to limitation of actions resulting in substantial differences of approach over a period of time. This is especially the case where there have been changes which result in a particular type of action becoming time barred when, under previous legislation, the same type of action would not have been subject to a time bar. This explains why the transitional provisions contained in the Limitation Act 1980 and the Latent Damage Act 1986[14] are fairly detailed. In contrast other changes in the law have not necessitated the same degree of provision for transitional arrangements.

5. See Ch 4.
6. See Ch 18.
7. See Ch 8.
8. See Ch 15.
9. See Ch 9.
10. See Ch 6.
11. See Chs 19 and 22.
12. See Ch 11.
13. See Ch 7.
14. See Ch 20.

In particular, the Consumer Protection Act 1987 did not need detailed transitional arrangements since the action introduced by that Act was entirely new, with the result that there was no pre-existing set of provisions in respect of the matter of limitation of actions with which the new rules could be confused.

(a) The main transitional arrangements in the Limitation Act 1980

Schedule 2 of the 1980 Act details the transitional arrangements, the most important of which are considered briefly below. In relation to a claim for contribution[15] by one tortfeasor against another, where the damage in respect of which contribution is sought occurred before 1 January 1979[16] the provisions of the Law Reform (Married Women and Tortfeasors) Act 1935 and the Limitation Act 1963, s 4 are stated to remain in force after the date on which the 1980 Act itself came into force.[17] So far as the matter of acknowledgment[18] and part payment[19] is concerned, where necessary, the Limitation Act 1939, s 23 is to remain in force in respect of any acknowledgment or part payment made before 1 August 1980, on which date section 6 of the 1980 Act came into force.[20] Where there is an action for set-off or counterclaim which falls outside the provisions of the Limitation Act 1980, s 35[21] it is provided that the Limitation Act 1980, s 28 is to continue to apply, "as originally enacted".[22]

(b) Can the Limitation Act operate retrospectively?

Given that there have been repeated changes to the law in respect of limitation of actions over a period of time, the problem can arise whether the most recent legislation can operate retrospectively so as to render an action in time, despite the fact that under the previous law, the action in question would have been time barred. The point is most likely to arise in cases in which a new set of rules on limitation of actions is introduced, based on the plaintiff's knowledge of relevant facts,[23] or where a statutory discretion allows the court to permit an action to proceed out of time.[24] The question of retrospectivity also turns on the precise effect of a statute such as the Limitation Act 1980. As a general rule, it is said that where a statute is substantive, in the sense that it deals with rights of action, it is to be presumed that an existing right of action will not be taken away, in the absence of an express provision in the statute to the contrary. However, where the statute deals with procedural matters only, then in the absence of an express statement to the contrary, it will

15. See Ch 25.
16. The date on which the Civil Liability (Contribution) Act 1978 came into force, replacing the somewhat different provisions in respect of contribution contained in the Law Reform (Married Women and Tortfeasors) Act 1935.
17. Limitation Act 1980, Sch 2, para 1.
18. See Chs 9 and 23.
19. See Ch 9.
20. Limitation Act 1980, Sch 2, para 5.
21. See Ch 7.
22. Limitation Act 1980, Sch 2, para 6.
23. As in the case of latent damage and personal injury actions, as to which see Chs 20 and 19 respectively.
24. See Limitation Act 1980, s 33, discussed in Ch 19.

be presumed that its provisions apply to all actions, whether past, present or future.[25] Generally, statutes of limitation are regarded as procedural matters, but they cease to be so once the limitation period has expired[26] since on expiry, the defendant is able to plead the limitation defence and, as such, has acquired a substantive right to assume that he is no longer in a position to be sued by the plaintiff and may dispose of documents and other evidence relating to the possible claim.

The effect of changes in the law was sharply in point in *Arnold v. Central Electricity Generating Board*[27] in which the plaintiff sued the defendants in their capacity as successors of a public authority with electricity-generating powers. Her action was in respect of latent personal injury suffered by her now deceased husband resulting from the asbestos-contaminated conditions in which he had been required to work. Although the court would, ordinarily, have been able to exercise its discretion in favour of the plaintiff, the particular hurdle she faced was that under previous legislation, an action against a public authority became time barred within 12 months of the date on which the cause of action accrued.[28] However, the provision relied upon had subsequently been repealed by the Law Reform (Limitation of Actions) Act 1954, which itself had been replaced in turn by the Limitation Act 1963 and the Limitation Act 1980 by the time the action came to be heard. However, the problem facing the plaintiff was that her husband last worked for the defendants in 1943 and that, applying the 12-months limitation period, any action he could have brought would have been time barred in 1944, one year after leaving the defendants' employment, unless it could be said that later limitation provisions operated retrospectively.

One of the arguments pressed strongly for the plaintiff was that changes in the law of limitation of actions in the Limitation Act 1963 were intended to remedy the injustice caused by the rule in *Cartledge v. E Jopling & Sons Ltd,*[29] namely, that in cases of latent personal injury, existing rules on limitation of action allowed a person to become time barred before he even realised that he was able to sue in respect of the injury he had suffered. However, in expressing the unanimous opinion of the House of Lords, Lord Bridge in *Arnold* remained unpersuaded that this was a sufficient argument for treating a limitation statute as having a retrospective effect.

A second line of argument pressed on the House of Lords, this time by the defendants, was that the relevant law should be strictly construed according to the language used by Parliament. On this approach, it was argued, the Law Reform (Limitation of Actions) Act 1954 applied a three-year limitation period to actions against public authorities in respect of personal injuries, with the result that even if the newer law operated retrospectively, the plaintiff was still well out of time before the date on which proceedings were commenced in the early 1980s. Moreover, even the Limitation Act 1963, which introduced a limitation period based on discoverability by the plaintiff of the facts relevant to the cause of action, did not contain any specific provisions to deal with damage which occurred before 4 June 1954,[30] which was a date some 10 years after the date on which the plaintiff's husband's cause of action accrued under the older legislation.

---

25. *The Ydun* [1899] P 236.
26. *Maxwell v. Murphy* (1957) 96 CLR 261.
27. [1988] AC 228.
28. Limitation Act 1939, s 21.
29. [1963] AC 758. Discussed in Chs 18 and 19.
30. The date on which the Law Reform (Limitation of Actions) Act 1954 came into force.

On a strict interpretation approach, Lord Bridge in *Arnold* opined that since there were no specific provisions in the 1963 Act to deal with events occurring before 1954, then it followed that the 1963 Act could not be back-dated to cover events which occurred at least 10 years earlier.

Finally, a further argument which worked in favour of the defendants was that under the provisions of the Interpretation Act 1889, s 38(2)[31] it is stated that "the repeal of an enactment does not, unless the contrary intention appears . . . (c) affect any right, privilege, obligation or liability acquired, accrued or incurred under that enactment". Since there appeared to be no contrary intention expressed in any of the legislation which followed that in force at the time the plaintiff's cause of action accrued, it had to be assumed that a cause of action which had become time barred before the date on which later legislation came into force remained time barred.

31. Now the Interpretation Act 1978, s 16(1).

CHAPTER 3

LIMITATION AND RELATED ISSUES

LACHES AND ACQUIESCENCE—THE EQUITABLE MAXIMS

Equity acts *in personam*. This arises from the axiom that the jurisdiction of equity is premised upon the conscience[1] and conduct of the individual. Through the centuries, the Chancellors of the Chancery Court would decide cases in accordance with their own particular concept of justice. The unpredictability which resulted from this *ad hoc* approach to the administration of justice led Selden to observe that equity varied with the length of the Chancellor's foot. However, the so-called maxims of equity provided the unifying threads which injected cohesiveness into the equitable jurisdiction. Most appeared in their present form during the eighteenth century although their origins stretch back in time long before that.[2] Within the context of limitations, the maxim *vigilantibus, non dormientibus, aequitas subvenit* (equity assists the diligent, not the tardy) which is now encompassed by the doctrines of laches and acquiescence, is of obvious importance. In *Erlanger* v. *New Sombrero Phosphate Co*[3] Lord Blackburn summarised the position in the following terms: "A court of equity requires that those who come to it to ask its active interposition to give them relief should use due diligence, after there has been such notice or knowledge as to make it inequitable to lie by . . . "[4]

The interrelationship between laches and acquiescence

Unless the plaintiff seeking equitable relief has instituted proceedings with promptitude, he may be refused the remedy sought, on the basis of the equitable defence of laches.[5]

---

1. See, for example, the speech of Lord Browne-Wilkinson in *Westdeutsche Landesbank Girozentrale* v. *Islington London Borough Council* [1996] 2 All ER 961 at 988 in which he observed: "In the case of a trust, the conscience of the legal owner requires him to carry out the purposes for which the property was vested in him (express or implied trust) or which the law imposes on him by reason of his unconscionable conduct (constructive trust)."

2. Richard Francis, *Maxims of Equity* (London, 1728). See also, the comments of Professor Yale in the Selden's Society's edition of *Lord Nottingham's Chancery Cases* at p lviii, Vol 1.

3. (1878) 3 App Cas 1218.

4. *Ibid* at 1279. See also *Smith* v. *Clay* (1767) 3 Bro CC 639n where Lord Camden stated: "Equity aids the vigilant, not the indolent." His Lordship explained the theoretical basis underlying laches in the following terms: "A Court of Equity, which is never active in relief against conscience, or public convenience, has always refused its aid to stale demands, where the party has slept upon his right and acquiesced for a great length of time. Nothing can call forth this Court into activity, but conscience, good faith, and reasonable diligence; where these are wanting, the Court is passive and does nothing." See further, McLean, "Limitation of Actions in Restitution", [1989] CLJ 472.

5. It was stated in *Re Sharpe* [1892] 1 Ch 154 at 168 that delay in bringing proceedings "may furnish a defence in equity to an equitable claim".

Primarily, the defence is concerned with preventing the defendant being prejudiced by the plaintiff's dilatoriness in bringing the action. The governing principle here would appear to be that the defence is available whenever it would be *unjust* to allow the plaintiff's claim for equitable relief to proceed. The "definitive"[6] statement encapsulating the doctrine of laches is to be found in the speech of Lord Selborne in *Lindsay Petroleum Co* v. *Hurd*[7] where he said:

"Where it would be practically unjust to give a remedy, either because the party has, by his conduct, done that which might fairly be regarded as a waiver of it, or where by his conduct or neglect he has, though perhaps not waiving that remedy, yet put the other party in a situation in which it would not be reasonable to place him if the remedy were afterwards to be asserted, in either of these cases lapse of time and delay are not material. But in every case, if an argument against relief, which otherwise would be just, is founded upon mere delay, that delay of course not amounting to a bar by any statute of limitations, the validity of that defence must be tried upon principles substantially equitable. Two circumstances, always important in such cases, are, the length of the delay and the nature of the acts done during the interval, which might affect either party and cause a balance of justice or injustice in taking the one course or the other, so far as relates to the remedy."[8]

The terms "laches" and "acquiescence", as used by the judges, are not capable of precise definition since they are confusingly used to fit the facts of the particular case in issue. In *Nelson* v. *Rye*[9] Laddie J, referring to Lord Selborne's remarks, observed that:

"It can be misleading to approach the equitable defences of laches and acquiescence as if they consisted of a series of precisely defined hurdles over each of which a litigant must struggle before the defence is made out . . . The courts have indicated over the years some of the factors which must be taken into consideration in deciding whether the defence runs. Those factors include the period of delay, the extent to which the defendant's position has been prejudiced by the delay, and the extent to which that prejudice was caused by the actions of the plaintiff. I accept that mere delay alone will almost never suffice, but the court has to look at all the circumstances . . . and then decide whether the balance of justice or injustice is in favour of granting the remedy or withholding it. If substantial prejudice will be suffered by the defendant, it is not necessary for the defendant to prove that it was caused by the delay. On the other hand, the plaintiff's knowledge that the delay will cause such prejudice is a factor to be taken into account."[10]

For simplicity's sake, it can be stated that the defendant may successfully raise the defences if it can be established that the plaintiff, by failing to institute proceedings expeditiously, can be deemed to have either:

> (i) acquiesced in the defendant's conduct and thereby sanctioned it (estoppel),[11] or
>
> (ii) knowing that some right has been infringed by the defendant's conduct, fails to bring suit (negligent inactivity).[12]

---

6. Lord Blackburn in *Erlanger* v. *New Sombrero Phosphate Co* (1878) 3 App Cas 1218 at 1279.

7. (1874) LR 5 PC 221.

8. *Ibid* at 239–240. See also *Weld* v. *Petre* [1929] 1 Ch 33, at 51–52; *Holder* v. *Holder* [1968] Ch 353; *Orr* v. *Ford* (1989) 167 CLR 316 at 341.

9. [1996] 2 All ER 186. Noted (1996) 17 Co Law 218.

10. *Ibid* at 200–201. See also, *Al–Fayed* v. *Emanouel Antiques Ltd*, *The Times* 22 August 1997, CA (Roch LJ).

11. *Duke of Leeds* v. *Earl of Amherst* (1846) 2 Ph 117 at 123.

12. In *Glasson* v. *Fuller* [1922] SASR 148, Poole J defined "acquiescence" as carrying *two* meanings: "If one stands by while he sees the violation of his right in progress, and takes no steps to interfere, he is said to acquiesce in the violation, and he may be thereby debarred from his remedy in respect of it. This is acquiescence in the true sense, but its effect has nothing to do with the lapse of time, and it has no relation to laches. In another

The first, or primary, sense covers the situation where a plaintiff stands by and does not take any action to prevent the infringement of his rights so that the defendant is led to believe that his conduct in question is sanctioned by the plaintiff. This has been described as estoppel by words or conduct, so that it would be inequitable to allow the plaintiff to proceed against the defendant.[13] Typically, the defendant or third parties would have changed their position in reliance on the plaintiff's delay.[14] For example, in *Duke of Leeds* v. *Earl of Amherst*[15] the action was for an account of equitable waste committed by the plaintiff's father while in possession of the family estates as a tenant for life. The father had demolished the family mansion-house and had cut a quantity of the ornamental trees in the parkland. Lord Cottenham LC stressed that:

"This Court looks with great jealousy at claims postponed until they cannot be as effectually resisted as if they had been made sooner; and this is a case in which the Court ought to be peculiarly tenacious of that principle; for if the acts of waste complained of were done . . . in the exercise of a sound discretion and for the benefit of the estate, it is highly probable that the party who committed them would, from the same motive, although only tenant for life, have expended sums in the permanent improvement of the estate . . . "[16]

Similarly, in *Lamshed* v. *Lamshed*[17] the plaintiff, having initiated a claim for specific performance, did nothing for six years during which time the defendant had contracted to resell the land to a third party. The High Court of Australia refused the decree on the basis that the plaintiff's delay rendered it inequitable to grant the relief claimed. Kitto J explained that the case is one:

"[I]n which a defendant, not precipitately but at length, in circumstances which made it not altogether unreasonable to do so, has prejudiced his position; and it is a case in which third parties, not shown to be in any way at fault and not being warned by any caveat on the title, have acquired interests which will be defeated if a decree for specific performance should now be made."[18]

The secondary sense ascribed to the term "acquiescence" for the purposes of the doctrine of laches is where the plaintiff, with knowledge that some right is being or has

sense, acquiescence is used to denote that some equitable right of A has been violated, as where he has been induced to make a gift by undue influence, or where there is a *cestui que trust*, and his trustee has purchased the trust property, and that after the influence has ceased or the violation has been brought to his knowledge he assents to the continuance of the state of affairs resulting from the violation, to the retention of the gift by the donee, or of the property by the trustee. The lapse of time without proceedings being taken by A is evident of such assent, and upon acquiescence of this latter kind the doctrine of laches is based. Acquiescence in the strict sense implies either that the party acquiescing has abandoned his right, or that he is estopped from asserting it. Acquiescence in this sense is no more than an instance of estoppel by words or conduct. Laches, acquiescence in the second sense, is no defence if there is a Statute of Limitations in operation, unless it exceeds the period allowed by the Statute."

13. *De Bussche* v. *Alt* (1878) 8 Ch D 286 at 314.

14. *Watson* v. *Commercial Bank of Australia* (1879) 5 VLR (M) 36; *Re Scottish Petroleum Co* (1882) 23 Ch D 413; *Civil Service Co-operative Society of Victoria Ltd* v. *Blyth* (1914) 17 CLR 601; *Agbeyegbe* v. *Ikomi* [1953] 1 WLR 263; in *Erlanger* v. *New Sombrero Phosphate Co* (1878) 3 App Cas 1218 Lord Cairns LC expressed the view that "it would be contrary to the principles of equity to give to the company the relief which, at an earlier period, they might have obtained"; *Weld* v. *Petre* [1929] 1 Ch 33. In *Taylor Fashions Ltd* v. *Liverpool Victoria Friendly Society* [1982] 1 QB 133 at 151, Oliver J stated that "it would be unconscionable for a party to be permitted to deny that which, knowingly or unknowingly, he has allowed or encouraged another to assume to his detriment". See also, *Film Investors Overseas Services SA* v. *Home Video Channel Ltd, t/a The Adult Channel, The Times,* 2 December 1996.

15. (1846) 2 Ph 117.

16. *Ibid* at 121–122.

17. (1963) 109 CLR 440.

18. *Ibid* at 455.

been violated by the defendant, fails to initiate proceedings against him to vindicate the infringement of that right, so that the plaintiff's inactivity can be regarded as *acquiescence* in the state of affairs created by the defendant. The position here was summarised by Lord Cottenham LC in *Duke of Leeds* v. *Earl of Amherst*[19] who said: "If a party having rights stands by and sees another dealing with the property in a manner inconsistent with that right, and makes no objection while the act is in progress he cannot afterwards complain. That is the proper sense of the word 'acquiescence' . . . "[20] However, where a statutory limitation period does apply to the plaintiff's action, then the doctrine of laches as defined in its secondary sense will not afford a defence until after the expiration of the limitation period.[21] In determining whether the plaintiff has acquiesced, the length of delay between the defendant's wrongful act and the initiation of proceedings is therefore a material factor.[22] A primary consideration here is that evidence supporting the defence may be lost or witnesses may die.[23] The point was eloquently put by Lord Campbell LC in *Bright* v. *Legerton*[24] who said:

"A Court of Equity will not allow a dormant claim to be set up when the means of resisting it, if unfounded, have perished . . . it has been beautifully remarked with respect to the emblem of Time, who is depicted as carrying a scythe and an hour glass, that while with the one he cuts down the evidence which might protect innocence, with the other he metes out a period when innocence can no longer be assailed."[25]

The effect of the passage of time upon the ability of a defendant to recall reliable evidence was considered in *Nelson* v. *Rye*.[26] The plaintiff, a musician, sued his business manager, Rye, for an account of the monies received by him during the 10-year period, 1980–90, during which he had managed the plaintiff's career. The defendant had overseen the plaintiff's financial affairs, including the receipt of all income due, in return for 20 per cent of the income. The defendant was to account to the plaintiff at regular intervals. However, no account was ever requested or provided. The defendant argued that the duty to account for the period prior to 1985 was time barred by virtue of the Limitation Act 1980, ss 5 and 23. The plaintiff contended that his claim was not contractual but based on a breach of fiduciary duty and therefore outside the scope of the 1980 Act; or alternatively that it was an action for breach of trust, and the Act exempted claims by a beneficiary of

19. (1846) 2 Ph 117.

20. *Ibid* at 123.

21. In *Archbold* v. *Scully* (1861) 9 HLC 360, Lord Wensleydale said at 383: " I take it that where there is a Statute of Limitations the objection of simple laches does not apply until the expiration of the time allowed by the Statute. But acquiescence is a different thing; it means more than laches. If a party, who could object, lies by and knowingly permits another to incur an expense in doing an act under the belief that it would not be objected to, and so a kind of permission may be said to be given to another to alter his condition, he may be said to acquiesce; but the fact of simply neglecting to enforce a claim for the period during which the law permits him to delay without losing his right, I conceive cannot be any equitable bar." See also, *Moors* v. *Marriott* (1878) 7 Ch D 543; *Re Birch* (1884) 27 Ch D 622; *Glasson* v. *Fuller, supra*, fn 12.

22. *Rundell* v. *Murray* (1821) Jac 311; *Boyns* v. *Lackey* (1958) 58 SR (NSW) 395.

23. In *Watt* v. *Assets Co* [1905] AC 317 at 329, Lord Halsbury LC commented: "It appears to me that the matter rests, not upon any question of technical law, but upon broad common sense, and especially upon these two principles—that at this distance of time every intendment should be made in favour of what has been done as being lawfully and properly done, and that the persons who are now insisting upon these rights have lain asleep upon their rights so long that as a matter of fact we know that witnesses have perished, and the opportunities which might have been had if the question had been earlier raised have passed away."

24. (1861) 2 De GF & J 606.

25. *Ibid* at 616–617.

26. *Supra*, fn 9.

a trust to recover trust property from a trustee from being time barred. In the alternative, the defendant pleaded the plaintiff's laches. Laddie J held that that the cause of action at issue was breach of fiduciary duty, not breach of contract, even though the fiduciary relationship in question had its origins in contract. Consequently, the limitation period applicable to a claim in contract did not apply to the plaintiff's action for an account. However, the learned judge went on to hold that the plaintiff's claim was caught by the doctrine of laches with the result that his claim was disallowed for the period 1980–85. Laddie J stated that:

"Mr Rye is particularly anxious that he will find it impossible to recall the minutiae of what expenses, including many very small ones, were incurred on what date and for what purpose. The court should bear in mind that a party may be inclined to understate his powers of recall when it is in his interests to do so. Nevertheless I am satisfied that Mr Rye's fears are justified. We are not here considering major events in Mr Rye's life but the comparative trivia of the day-to-day movements of funds in a small business."[27]

The effect of acquiescence can be seen in *Mitchell* v. *Homfray*[28] where a patient had given a series of gifts to the defendant, his doctor, in circumstances in which the gifts in question could be impeached on the ground of undue influence. After the undue influence had ceased the patient, with knowledge that the transactions were voidable, did not bring proceedings against the defendant. The Court of Appeal held that the patient's delay during his lifetime constituted conduct which affirmed the gifts so that his executors could not now seek to have them set aside. The approach adopted by the court tends to substantiate the view that mere delay, without more, is not decisive in defeating a claim. This can also be seen in *Allcard* v. *Skinner*[29] which also involved the granting of gifts under undue influence, and where the plaintiff waited for some six years before attempting to have the gifts set aside. The defence of laches succeeded but not merely on the ground of delay. Lindley LJ explained that: "The case by no means rests on mere lapse of time. There is far more than inactivity and delay on the part of the plaintiff. There is conduct amounting to confirmation of her gift."[30]

Whether the defendant is relying on laches or upon acquiescence *simpliciter*, the defences are personal and available only against the conduct of the particular plaintiff. In consequence, the defences cannot be raised in respect of the conduct of the plaintiff's predecessors in title. In *Nwakobi* v. *Nzekwu*[31] the Privy Council drew the distinction between the doctrine of laches and estoppel implied by conduct or words. The latter, (estoppel *in pais*), operates from the time the defendant changed his position in reliance on the conduct or words in question and continues to operate through the successors in title. Laches, on the other hand, is

"a personal disqualification on the part of the particular plaintiff: it cannot be treated as a stigma on the title to land which, once impressed, necessarily descends with the title . . . it can be relied on only when account has been taken of all the circumstances that affect both the immediate plaintiff and the immediate defendant. Lapse of time is always one of these circumstances . . . "[32]

---

27. *Ibid* at 204.
28. (1881) 8 QBD 587.
29. (1887) 36 Ch D 145.
30. *Ibid* at 186.
31. [1964] 1 WLR 1019.
32. *Ibid* at 1024 (*per* Viscount Radcliffe).

The Board did go on to recognise, however, that the acquiescence of a predecessor in title will be a relevant consideration when assessing the defendant's equity, and will be particularly material where such acquiescence constitutes estoppel.

Triggering statutory limitation periods by analogy

The defences considered above only operate against claims for equitable relief;[33] they do not arise from the statutory limitation periods which, in the main, are generally restricted to *legal* remedies.[34] Nevertheless, the doctrine of laches and acquiescence are expressly preserved by the 1980 Act,[35] but will only operate where the plaintiff's claim is not time barred whether by virtue of express statutory provision or by equity acting by analogy.[36]

Although section 36(1) excludes claims for specific performance of a contract, injunctions and other equitable remedies from the statutory limitation period, it goes on to recognise the notion of equity applying the limitation period by "analogy." This accords with the maxim that "equity follows the law", for, as observed by Lord Westbury in *Knox* v. *Gye*,[37] "[W]here the remedy in equity is correspondent to the remedy at law, and the latter is subject to a limit in point of time by the Statute of Limitations, a court of Equity acts by analogy to the statute, and imposes on the remedy it affords the same limitation".[38] In consequence, if the court considers the plaintiff's delay in bringing proceedings to be unjustified, and the delay in question exceeds the statutory limitation period, the claim for relief will be rejected by analogy to the statute on the basis that it is conscionable to bar the action. In *Metropolitan Bank* v. *Heiron*[39] a bank sought to recover payments of commission made by a debtor to one of its directors. The action failed, since a period exceeding six years had elapsed since the bank had first discovered the director's breach. James LJ approached the issue from the standpoint of an equitable debt arising between the defaulting director and the bank. The Court of Appeal reasoned that the action against the fiduciary to account for the bribes was analogous to the common law action for money had and received, and therefore an equivalent six-year limitation period should operate from the time when the bank discovered the director's breach of duty. James LJ said:

33. Equitable remedies are those dispensed by a court of equity before the Judicature Acts 1873–75, for example, injunctions and specific performance, but should now include Mareva injunctions and Anton Piller orders.

34. However, the scope of the doctrine has been limited so that the six-year limitation period now applies against a beneficiary's claim against a trustee for breach of trust: see the Limitation Act 1980, s 21(3), discussed *infra*.

35. Section 36(2) provides that "nothing in the Act shall affect any equitable jurisdiction to refuse relief on the ground of acquiescence or otherwise". The phrase "or otherwise" is generally thought to refer to laches.

36. *Re Pauling's Settlement Trusts; Younghusband* v. *Coutts & Co* [1962] 1 WLR 86 at 115 (*per* Wilberforce J).

37. (1872) LR 5 HL 656. See further, Spry, *Principles of Equitable Remedies*, 4th ed (London: Sweet and Maxwell, 1990), at pp 399–414.

38. *Ibid* at 674. In *Brooksbank* v. *Smith* (1836) 2 Y & C Ex 58 at 60 Alderson B commented that "the Statute does not absolutely bind the Courts of Equity, but they adopt it as a rule to assist their discretion". See also, *White* v. *Ewer* (1670) 2 Vent 340; *Bonney* v. *Ridgard* (1784) 1 Cox Eq Ca 145; *Bond* v. *Hopkins* (1802) 1 Sch & Lef 143 at 149; *Beckford* v. *Wade* (1805) 17 Ves 87 at 97; *Marquis of Cholmondeley* v. *Lord Clinton* (1821) 4 Bli 1 at 119; *McDonnell* v. *White* (1865) 11 HLC 570; *Thomson* v. *Eastwood* (1877) 2 App Cas 215; *Gibbs* v. *Guild* (1882) 8 QBD 296; *Allcard* v. *Skinner* (1887) 36 Ch D 145; *Molloy* v. *Mutual Reserve Life Insurance Co* (1906) 94 LT 756.

39. (1880) 5 Ex D 319.

"If a man receives money by way of a bribe for misconduct against a company or *cestui que trust,* or any person or body towards whom he stands in a fiduciary position, he is liable to have that money taken from him by his principal or *cestui que trust.* But it must be borne in mind that the liability is a debt only differing from ordinary debts in the fact that it is merely equitable, and in dealing with equitable debts of such a nature Courts of Equity have always followed by analogy the provisions of the Statute of Limitations . . . "[40]

In *Re Robinson*[41] the plaintiff, who was a beneficiary under a trust, brought an action to recover money wrongly paid to another beneficiary by the trustee who, at the time of payment, was acting under a common mistake of fact. It was held, applying the Limitation Act by analogy, that since the claim was in the nature of a common law action for money had and received, it was time barred. Warrington J said:

"The present case resolves itself into this—that although, owing to the fact that the plaintiff is not the person who paid the money, the action is one which could not have been maintained at common law, it is in substance a mere money demand to which a Court of Equity, acting by analogy to the statute, would apply the same period of limitation."[42]

It therefore appears that in order for a statutory limitation to be applied by analogy, the equitable relief sought must have a legal analogue.[43] Thus, in *Seagram* v. *Knight*[44] it was held that, in a case where a tenant for life is liable for waste having wrongfully cut timber, time began running from the moment the cutting commenced just as if those entitled to the remainder had sought compensatory damages in trover.[45] The point was made in *Re Diplock*[46] that although an action against the beneficiaries against whom it was sought to recover monies wrongly distributed was analogous to the common law action for money had and received, it was also an action "in respect of a claim to the personal estate of a deceased person". For this, section 20 of the Limitation Act 1939 applied (now section 22 of the 1980 Act) whereby the limitation period was 12 years "from the date on which the right to receive the share or interest accrued". Accordingly, no other period could be applied by analogy.

Concealed fraud, fraud and mistake

The doctrine of applying limitation periods by analogy was never extended to cases involving the equitable concept of "concealed fraud", fraud or mistake and the doctrine of laches was not available by way of a defence. The position in equity was summarised by Lord James in *Bulli Coal Mining* v. *Osbourne,*[47] who said:

---

40. *Ibid* at 323. See also *Tito* v. *Waddell (No 2)* [1977] Ch 106 at 250–52; *AG* v. *Cocke* [1988] Ch 414. See now, *Attorney General for Hong Kong* v. *Reid* [1994] 1 AC 324 in which the distinction between bribes and secret profits was unequivocally laid to rest by the Privy Council. Lord Templeman stated at p 331: "As soon as the bribe was received . . . the false fiduciary held the bribe on a constructive trust for the person injured." Accordingly, the dichotomy between "ownership" which gives rise to a proprietary remedy and "obligation" where the remedy lies in debt, now appears to have been fused. See further, Cowan, Edmunds and Lowry, "*Lister & Co v. Stubbs*—Who Profits?" [1996] JBL 22.
41. [1911] 1 Ch 502.
42. *Ibid* at 513. This would now be decided in accordance with s 21(3) of the Limitation Act 1980.
43. *Ibid* See also, *Urquhard* v. *McPherson* (1880) 6 VLR (E) 17; cf *Cohen* v. *Cohen* (1929) 42 CLR 91.
44. (1867) LR 2 Ch App 628.
45. (1846) 2 Ph 117. See also, *Duke of Leeds* v. *Earl of Amherst* (1846) 2 Ph 117 (*supra*); *Re Lady Hastings* (1880) 35 Ch D 94 at 105; *Motor Terms Co Pty Ltd* v. *Liberty Insurance Ltd* (1967) 116 CLR 177.
46. [1948] Ch 465 at 502–516.
47. [1899] AC 351.

"It has always been a principle of equity that no length of time is a bar to relief in a case of fraud, in the absence of laches on the part of the person defrauded. There is therefore no room for the application of the statute in the case of concealed fraud, so long as the party defrauded remains in ignorance without any fault of his own".[48]

This has now been given statutory effect by section 32(1) of the 1980 Act.[49] This provides, *inter alia,* for the postponement of the limitation period where either:

"(a) the action is based upon the fraud of the defendant; or
(b) any fact relevant to the plaintiff's right of action has been deliberately concealed from him by the defendant; or
(c) the action is for relief from the consequences of a mistake;
until the plaintiff has discovered the fraud, concealment or mistake . . . or could with reasonable diligence have discovered it."[50]

In the circumstances listed, the plaintiff's delay in instituting proceedings will not operate to prejudice his claim. Thus in *Kershaw* v. *Whelan (No 2)*[51] the plaintiff's father died in 1979 leaving some £45,000 in trust to be distributed by the trustees in their absolute discretion. The trustees distributed £40,000 to the plaintiff's stepmother, and the balance to the plaintiff and his sister. In March 1991 the plaintiff brought proceedings in the alternative for negligence and breach of fiduciary duty against his stepmother's solicitor, claiming that he had improperly influenced the trustees. The claim arose from a letter sent by the defendant to the trustees in June 1979, which contained information about the plaintiff which he claimed was untrue or highly misleading, and which suggested that the stepmother should benefit from the trust fund to the exclusion of the plaintiff. The defendant had deliberately concealed the letter from the plaintiff and his advisers until 1983 when its existence became known. It was held that the common law claim was statute barred as time started to run in 1983; but the alternative claim for breach of fiduciary duty had to be considered separately in accordance with *Nelson* v. *Rye*.[52] Accordingly, the court had to balance the unconscionable conduct of the defendant in concealing the letter against the possibility that a real injustice had been done to the plaintiff. Given that the defendant had failed to establish laches and that the plaintiff's claim for breach of fiduciary duty was not barred by analogy with the Limitation Act, it could, therefore, proceed.

It has been observed that the meaning of "fraud" as used in this context is wider than that attributed to the term at common law.[53] Lord Denning has explained its meaning in the following terms:

"It is used in the equitable sense to denote conduct by the defendant . . . such that it would be against conscience for him to avail himself of the lapse of time . . . The cases show that if a man *knowingly* commits a wrong (such as digging underground another man's coal), or a breach of contract (such as putting in a bad foundation to a house), in such circumstances that it is unlikely to be found out

48. *Ibid* at 363.
49. Before the Limitations Act 1939, an action for fraud originated in equity.
50. Section 32(3) provides that the plaintiff's remedy is exercisable against any party claiming through the defendant except a bona fide purchaser for value without notice.
51. *The Times*, 10 February 1997. See also, *Tunbridge* v. *Buss Merton & Co, The Times*, 8 April 1997.
52. *Supra*, fn 9.
53. In *Tito* v. *Waddell (No 2)* [1977] Ch 106, Megarry V-C stated at 245 "any unconscionable failure to reveal is enough". See, also, *Clark* v. *Woor* [1965] 2 All ER 353, in which Lawton J stated at 356: "fraud does not necessarily mean deceit in the sense in which it is known in common law . . . the type of conduct which amounts to fraud is the type of conduct which was known in the Chancery Court as equitable fraud."

for many a long day, he cannot rely on the Statute of Limitations as a bar to the claim. . . . In order to show that he 'concealed' the right of action 'by fraud', it is not necessary to show that he took active steps to conceal the wrong-doing or breach of contract. It is sufficient that he *knowingly* committed it and did not tell the owner about it . . . To this word 'knowingly' there must be added 'recklessly' . . . Like the man who turns a blind eye, he is aware that what he is doing may well be wrong, or a breach of contract, but he takes the risk of it being so . . . "[54]

The notion of recklessness can be traced to the Court of Appeal's decision in *Beaman* v. *ARTS Ltd*.[55] The defendants, in breach of their duty as bailees, disposed of the plaintiff's goods without first informing her of their proposed course of action. The plaintiff commenced proceedings more than six years after the disposal of her property, claiming damages for conversion. The defendants argued that the action was time barred. The plaintiff successfully counterclaimed relying on section 26 of the Limitation Act 1939, now section 32(1) of the 1980 Act. The Court of Appeal held that the defendants' failure to obtain the plaintiff's consent to the sale constituted a reckless "concealment by fraud" of the right of action within paragraph (b) of the section. Lord Greene MR found the defendants' conduct to be "reckless . . . furtive and surreptitious".[56] He went on to state that:

"They recklessly and without taking the least trouble to verify the facts assumed (what was false and on a simple examination of the records would have been shown to be false) that the plaintiff had not troubled about her goods . . . I am of opinion that the conduct of the defendants, by the very manner in which they converted the plaintiff's chattels in breach of the confidence reposed in them, and in circumstances calculated to keep her in ignorance of the wrong that they committed amounted to a fraudulent concealment of the cause of action."[57]

The term "concealed fraud" therefore covers conduct which falls short of its common law meaning and is wider in scope than its ordinary use in language.[58] It is evident that given the equitable origins of "fraud" in this context, it focuses upon the degree of culpability attributable to the defendant's behaviour so that he will be guilty of concealed fraud where his conduct is "unconscionable".[59] This would seem to mean that the defendant's concealment must be perpetrated deliberately, so that he must be aware that he was committing a wrong, and "knowingly" suppressed it. For example, in *Bartlett* v. *Barclays Bank Trust Co Ltd*[60] the bank, as professional trustee of the Bartlett trust, held 99.8 per cent of the shares in a property company. The bank did not attend board meetings nor did it monitor the activities of the company beyond the information provided to it as a shareholder. When

---

54. *King* v. *Victor Parsons & Co* [1973] 1 WLR 29 at 33. See also, the first instance judgment of Denning J in *Beaman* v. *ARTS Ltd* [1949] 1 KB 550, discussed *infra*. In *Shaw* v. *Shaw* [1954] 2 QB 429, at 442 Denning LJ, as he then was, said that fraud requires more than "moral turpitude".

55. [1949] 1 KB 550.

56. *Ibid* at 565–66.

57. *Ibid*.

58. *Kitchen* v. *Royal Air Forces Association* [1958] 1 WLR 563.

59. The Law Reform Committee, *Final Report on Limitation of Actions* (1977, Cmnd 6923) states at para 2.22: "The essential feature of the concealed fraud approach (as distinct from the date of knowledge approach) is that it operates on some degree of blameworthiness on the part of the defendant beyond his mere failure to comply with his legal obligations; the traditional expression is 'unconscionable conduct' . . . ".

60. [1980] Ch 515. See, also, *Re Lands Allotment Co* [1894] 1 Ch 616, in which it was held that where company directors had made a series of unauthorised investments, they can, in the absence of fraud, rely on the Statute of Limitations. Kay LJ stated at 640: "I have no doubt that the directors at the time . . . believed, as they say they believed, that this was a perfectly valid and proper transaction, and they had no ground whatever for concealing it, and in order to bind them by a false statement of this kind . . . I should require it to be proved very clearly that they thoroughly apprehended the falseness of the statement that was made . . . "

the company embarked upon a series of highly speculative developments which proved disastrous, the trust suffered a large loss for which the trustee was held liable. The bank had not concealed the activities of the company from the beneficiaries. Brightman J, in reasoning that "fraud" in this context connotes behaviour that is unconscionable, adopted the definition formulated by Lord Denning MR in *Applegate* v. *Moss*[61]: "The section applies whenever the conduct of the defendant or his agent has been such as to hide from the plaintiff the existence of his right of action, in such circumstances that it would be inequitable to allow the defendant to rely on the lapse of time as a bar to the claim."[62] However, because the bank was not aware of its having committed a breach of trust, it was held that the bank could rely on the statutory limitation period.

Turning to the question of concealment of the plaintiff's cause of action, it is not sufficient that the defendant "ought to have known facts" which were material, but rather that the defendant must have *actually* known of such facts *and* deliberately concealed them. In this regard, Megaw LJ said in *King* v. *Victor Parsons & Co*[63] that:

"The judge was prepared to hold that 'ought to know' was sufficient to establish concealment by fraud, within the meaning given to that phrase by past decisions of the courts for the purpose of section 26 of the Act of 1939.[64] Accordingly he rejected the defence of limitation and gave judgment for the plaintiff. The defendants say that 'ought to know' is not enough. I agree. I do not think that the cases go so far; or that, at least as a general principle and in the absence of very special circumstances, the meaning of 'concealed fraud' should be extended to cover a case where the defendant, whether himself or by persons whose knowledge should be treated as his knowledge, did not know the fact or facts which constituted the cause of action against him."[65]

Where the defendant is an expert, it is not unreasonable for the plaintiff to rely on his special skill and knowledge, so that if the defendant deliberately withholds information from the plaintiff, that will constitute "concealment" for the purposes of the Act. In *Clark* v. *Woor*[66] the defendant, a builder, contracted with the plaintiffs to build a bungalow. The contract specified that certain high grade bricks were to be used in its construction. The defendant knew at the time of the contract that he would be unable to obtain the necessary bricks within the time period stipulated. He did not inform the plaintiffs of this, but went ahead and ordered lower quality bricks which proved unfit for the plaintiffs' purposes. Eight years after the building was completed the bricks began to flake. It was held that the defendant had concealed the plaintiffs' right of action, and given the special relationship which existed between the parties, the defendant's conduct was unconscionable and amounted to "fraudulent concealment". The action was not, therefore, time barred. Lawton J observed that the defendant was guilty of unconscionable behaviour amounting to fraud knowing "that the building owners were relying on him to perform his contract and treat them in a decent, honest way".[67]

For the purposes of section 32(1) above, the court will draw an inference of deliberate concealment where the defendant deliberately commits a breach of duty in circumstances

---

61. [1971] 1 All ER 747.
62. *Ibid* at 750.
63. [1973] 1 WLR 29.
64. Replaced by s 32 of the 1980 Act.
65. [1973] 1 WLR 29 at 33.
66. [1965] 2 All ER 353.
67. *Ibid* at 356.

in which the breach is unlikely to be discovered for some time.[68] This gives statutory effect to the decision in *Beaman* v. *ARTS Ltd.*[69]

NEGOTIATION BETWEEN PARTIES

A defendant is not precluded from pleading the Act merely because on-going negotiations between the parties led to the delay. In such circumstances the plaintiff's solicitor may be liable in negligence if he allows the claim to become time barred. In *Fletcher & Son* v. *Jubb, Booth & Helliwell*[70] the claim arose from a road traffic accident in which a driver of a tramcar operated by Bradford Corporation negligently collided with a vehicle belonging to the plaintiffs. The parties entered into negotiations to settle out of court, the plaintiffs having claimed £75.00. The Corporation did not dispute the issue of negligence, but did dispute the question of quantum and offered to settle at £20.00. When the plaintiffs commenced the county court action the Corporation successfully pleaded by way of defence that the claim was time barred. The plaintiffs therefore sued the defendant solicitors alleging negligence for their failure to initiate proceedings before the expiration of the limitation period. The Court of Appeal held that the solicitors were negligent and Bankes LJ summarised their duty in the following terms: "Now solicitors are under an obligation to bring to the discharge of their duty as solicitors reasonable care and skill and knowledge of the practice of the Court whose process they invoke on behalf of a client."[71]

However, a defendant may be precluded from pleading the limitation period where the parties have contracted out of the statute. In *Lubovsky* v. *Snelling*[72] the plaintiff's executrix claimed damages under the Fatal Accidents Act 1846 for the death of her husband which had been caused by the negligent driving of the defendant. The defendant's insurers admitted liability but contested quantum. A writ was duly issued within the limitation period, but was later withdrawn because the plaintiff had not, at that time, taken out letters of administration. By the time this was corrected a new writ was issued more than 12 months after the death.[73] The defendant pleaded that the claim was time barred. The Court of Appeal rejected the defence, holding that the admission of liability constituted an agreement not to plead section 3 of the 1846 Act. Scott LJ stated:

"I have no doubt that the plea was not so open, and to take the point was, in my opinion, discreditable, if not dishonest, on the part of the society [the insurers]. The plain meaning of the agreement . . . was that liability in damages to the plaintiff's cause of action for the money loss resulting to the dead man's dependants was once and for all definitely accepted by both the defendant and his insurers, and both of them were thereafter precluded from putting forward any

---

68. Section 32 (2).

69. *Supra.* See also the judgment of Lord Denning in *King* v. *Victor Parsons & Co, supra,* fn 63.

70. [1920] 1 KB 275.

71. *Ibid* at 279, citing Tindal CJ in *Godefroy* v. *Dalton* (1830) 6 Bing 460 at 468 who said: "a solicitor is liable for the consequences of ignorance or non-observance of the rules of practice of this Court; for the want of care in the preparation of the cause for trial; or of attendance thereon of his witnesses: and for the mismanagement of so much of the conduct of a cause as is usually and ordinarily allotted to his department of the profession. Whilst on the other hand, he is not answerable for error in judgment upon points of new occurrence, or of nice or doubtful construction, or of such as are usually intrusted to men in the higher branch of the profession of the law."

72. [1944] 1 KB 44.

73. By s 3 of the Fatal Accidents Act 1846, an action under the statute must be commenced within 12 calendar months after the death of the deceased.

defence whatever which would impeach that liability. It was just as much a contract not to plead s. 3 of the Act, as if that undertaking had been put in words . . . "[74]

In reaching their conclusions both Scott and Goddard LJJ (who delivered the principal judgments, Mackinnon LJ concurring) agreed that the case fell squarely within its decision in *Wright* v. *John Bagnall & Sons Ltd*[75] which concerned a claim brought under the Workmen's Compensation Act 1897, which prescribed a limitation period of six months. Here the employers had agreed to pay compensation, although the parties reserved the right to go to court to determine the issue of quantum. Collins LJ found there to be an agreement that compensation was to be fixed with the result that the defendants were "debarred from raising the point that the statutory limitation applied".[76] Accordingly, the time limit could be extended expressly or inferentially from the parties' conduct. Given the tenor of the language adopted by the judges, particularly the words used by Scott LJ in prefacing his approach in *Lubovsky*, it seems that on general equitable grounds the courts will not be loth to find that an admission of liability is tantamount to an agreement not to plead the statute.[77]

The parties to a contract may expressly agree that any action for breach should be commenced within a specified period which may, of course, be shorter than the statutory six years. In this regard, however, such terms may be caught by the Unfair Contract Terms Act 1977. For example under section 2(i) it is no longer possible for a contracting party to exclude or restrict his liability in negligence for death or personal injuries by reference to any contract terms or to a notice given to persons generally or to particular persons.[78] In the case of other loss or damage, section 2(ii) provides that the validity of such a term will be measured by reference to the requirement of reasonableness.[79]

Election, in so far as the term can be distinguished from estoppel or waiver,[80] may also operate to disentitle a defendant from pleading a time bar. At its core, the distinction between the terms is that "election" focuses upon what a party does and is effective when made and communicated, whereas estoppel is concerned with what one party causes the other to do.[81] In *Kammins Ballrooms Co Ltd* v. *Zenith Investments (Torquay) Ltd*[82] the tenants of business premises requested a new tenancy before the statutory two-month

74. [1944] 1 KB 44, at 46. See also, *Abouchalache* v. *Hilton International Hotels (UK) Ltd* (1992) 126 Sol J 857.

75. [1900] 2 QB 240.

76. *Ibid* at 244.

77. It is our view that the decisions are illustrative of the courts exercising their general equitable jurisdiction to deny an unconscionable defendant a defence based upon expediency. Put simply, it is tenable to conclude that these decisions fall within the doctrine of estoppel. See also, *Rendall* v. *Hill's Dry Docks and Engineering Co* [1900] 2 QB 245, (CA) and *The Sauria* [1957] 1 Lloyd's Rep 396 (CA).

78. See also s 3 and s 6 which cover terms limiting liability to consumers or other customers.

79. Section 11 and Sch 2.

80. On this there has been some confusion, see *Craine* v. *Colonial Mutual Fire Insurance Co Ltd* (1920) 28 CLR 305 at 325–28; *BP Exploration Co (Libya) Ltd.* v. *Hunt (No 2)* [1982] 1 All ER 925 at 946–47; cf *Proctor & Gamble Philippine Manufacturing Corp* v. *Peter Cremer GmbH & Co* [1988] 3 All ER 843 at 852. In *Beatty* v. *Guggenheim*, 122 NE 378 (1919) Cardozo J stated at 381 that: "Much of the trouble comes from the use of the misleading word 'waiver' . . . It is made to stand for many things—sometimes for estoppel, sometimes for contract, sometimes for election." Whether or not "waiver" is merely a synonym for estoppel and election or is, in fact, a separate and distinct doctrine in its own right is far from clear.

81. *Khoury* v. *Government Insurance Office of New South Wales* (1984) 165 CLR 622 at 633 *per* Mason, Brennan, Deane and Dawson JJ.

82. [1971] AC 850.

period from the service of the notice to quit had elapsed.[83] The House of Lords recognised that a landlord could "waive" (in the sense of an election) this formality but that on the facts, and by a bare majority, it was held that there had been no such waiver since the landlord had not taken any steps which would debar the subsequent assertion of his rights. Viscount Dilhorne commented that:

"Even if it had been established—which in my opinion is not the case—that the respondents were aware of the breach before then, I do not see how their conduct can be held to amount to an election between two courses of action open to them. They did not, in my opinion, do anything which precluded them from taking the point that the application was bad."[84]

Finally, a party may be estopped from pleading the Act where it can be shown that:

(a) an unequivocal representation was made, either by words or conduct or by the omission to act, which

(b) produced the belief or expectation in the mind of the representee,

(iii) that the limitation period would be extended.[85]

---

83. The Landlord and Tenant Act 1954 lays down a minimum as well as a maximum time limit for the bringing of certain actions. Section 29(3) of the Act provides that: "No application under section 24(1) of this Act shall be entertained unless it is made not less than two nor more than four months after the giving of the landlord's notice under section 25 of this Act or, as the case may be, after the making of the tenant's request for a new tenancy."

84. *Ibid* at 873.

85. *K Lokumal & Sons (London) Ltd* v. *Lotte Shipping Co Pte Ltd (The August Leonhardt)* [1985] 2 Lloyd's Rep 28; *Kaliszewska* v. *J Clague & Partners* (1984) 5 Con LR 62.

CHAPTER 4

PARTIES

THE CROWN AND ELEEMOSYNARY CORPORATIONS SOLE

While the provisions of the Limitation Act apply generally, nevertheless specific rules are modified as a consequence of the special status enjoyed by the Crown throughout its history. Up until 1947 private suits could not be instituted against the Crown directly, but rather, such actions could only be brought by means of the antiquated petition of right. This was a petition by a subject which the Crown referred voluntarily to a court of law having signified its consent by the Attorney-General endorsing the petition "Let Right be Done".[1] Subject to two exceptions,[2] this form of petition was abolished by the Crown Proceedings Act 1947 which removed the immunity enjoyed by the Crown. Further, in actions brought by the Crown or a spiritual or eleemosynary corporation sole, the limitation periods are modified.

"The Crown" is defined as including the Duchy of Lancaster, the Duke of Cornwall, any Government department or officer of the Crown as such and any person acting on behalf of the Crown.[3] The word "eleemosynary" is not defined in the 1980 Act, but has been described as a formal word meaning charitable and which is related etymologically to the word "alms".[4] In *Re Armitages WT*[5] Goulding J subjected the meaning of the term "eleemosynary charity" to extensive consideration. The issue before the court was whether a bequest to the Norwich and Sheringham Town Councils of "equal annual payments of £200 or £300 to nursing homes for elderly women" was defeated by section 268(3) of the Local Government Act 1933 which prohibited local authorities accepting property in trust for an eleemosynary charity. The learned judge said:

"The particular term 'eleemosynary charity' is not a term of art with a judicially established definition . . . How then am I to ascertain the proper and natural meaning of the adjective in its place? I must have regard to the etymological origin of the word. It is an adjective derived from the Greek word which, through Latin, has come into our language as 'alms' . . . Having, as I have said, had regard to the derivation of the word and to the way in which it has been used in the judgments that have been cited, [*Attorney-General* v. *Calvert* (1857) 23 Beav 248; *Attorney-General* v. *St*

---

1. See further, the *Bankers' Case* (1690–1700) 14 How St 1; *Thomas* v. *The Queen* (1874) LR 10 QB 31; *Dyson* v. *A-G* [1911] 1 KB 410; *Churchward* v. *R* (1865) LR 1 QB 173; *A-G* v. *Great Southern and Eastern Rly Co of Ireland* [1925] AC 754; *New South Wales* v. *Bardolph* (1934) 52 CLR 455.
2. First, an action brought against the Sovereign in a personal capacity and secondly, for an action against the Crown with respect to matters arising outside the UK: s 40(2)(b) of the Crown Proceedings Act 1947. Section 37(5) of the Limitation Act 1980 provides that proceedings by way of petition of right shall be treated as being commenced on the date on which the petition is presented. See *Franklin* v. *Att-Gen* [1974] QB 185.
3. The Limitation Act 1980, s 37(3).
4. Garner, *A Dictionary of Modern Legal Usage* (Oxford: Oxford University Press, 1987).
5. [1972] 1 Ch 438.

John's Hospital, Bath (1876) 2 Ch D 554 and *In re Ross' Charity* [1899] 1 Ch 21] and looking at the context, I come to the conclusion that the term "eleemosynary charity" covers all charities directed to the relief of individual distress, whether due to poverty, age, sickness or other similar individual afflictions."[6]

With respect to corporation sole, the point has been made *obiter* by the Court of Appeal that the term covers the rector of a parish,[7] and a dean in right of his deanery.[8] Other examples include archbishops, bishops and vicars. The modified time periods are inapplicable to corporations aggregate, for example the Church Commissioners, and in this respect Lord Selborne commented in *Ecclesiastical Commrs of England and Wales* v. *Rowe*[9] that:

"The principle . . . was to prevent the negligence of one or two particular incumbents, each of whom would be in substance a mere tenant for life, from becoming a bar to the rights of their successors. That principle could have no permanent application after the transfer of title to a corporation aggregate, in which there is no such succession, and to which the Legislature has thought fit in all other cases to apply the shorter term of limitation."[10]

The modifications favouring the Crown

(1) Actions to recover land

Where the action relates to the recovery of land, section 15(1) of the 1980 Act[11] provides a limitation period of 12 years from the date on which the right of action accrued to the plaintiff. However, section 15(7) goes on to incorporate the modifications to the limitation period contained in Part II of Schedule 1 of the Act with respect to actions brought by, or by a person claiming through, the Crown and any spiritual or eleemosynary corporation sole. In favour of such plaintiffs, the limitation period is extended to 30 years.[12] Section 15(1) is further modified by Schedule 1, paragraph 11 which states that an action to recover foreshore may be commenced by the Crown within 60 years from the date on which the right of action accrued. All foreshore is prima facie owned by the Crown.[13] "Foreshore" is defined in paragraph 11(3) as meaning "the shore and bed of the sea and of any tidal water, below the line of the medium high tide between the spring tides and neap tides". However, where the land has ceased to be foreshore after an action has accrued to the Crown, but it nevertheless remains in its ownership, any right of action to recover such land may be brought before the expiration of the first of the following periods to expire, namely: (a) 60 years from the date of accrual of the right of action; or (b) 30 years from the date when the land ceased to be foreshore.[14]

Temporary encroachments of the foreshore by a third party will not necessarily destroy exclusive possession. In *Fowley Marine (Emsworth) Ltd* v. *Gafford*[15] the plaintiffs

---

6. *Ibid* at 444–45.
7. *Hayward* v. *Chaloner* [1968] 1 QB 107.
8. *Ecclesiastical Commrs of England and Wales* v. *Rowe* (1880) 5 App Cas 736 at 744 (*per* Lord Selborne LC).
9. *Supra*, fn 8.
10. *Ibid* at 744.
11. See further, Part IV, *infra.*
12. Sch 1, Part II, para 10.
13. *Fowley Marine (Emsworth) Ltd* v. *Gafford* [1968] 2 QB 618.
14. Sch 1 Part II, para 11(2).
15. [1968] 2 QB 618.

claimed ownership of Fowley Rythe, a small tidal creek used by pleasure boats for mooring. It was argued that their title derived from being in actual possession of the Rythe and, also, that their title derived from an ancient grant by the Crown together with conveyances, or alternatively, from a possessory title acquired against the Crown. When the plaintiffs demanded payment of an annual rent from all those using permanent moorings, the defendants refused to pay. The plaintiffs therefore claimed damages for trespass. The defendants contended that the action for trespass must fail since the plaintiffs lacked exclusive possession sufficient to establish ownership on the basis that their acts in maintaining permanent moorings amounted to "equivalent acts of concurrent possession". The Court of Appeal held that the plaintiffs had established exclusive possession which was not displaced by the acts of the defendants in laying moorings without permission, since in the absence of evidence that they were done *animo possidendi,* such acts must be regarded as wholly different in quality from those of the plaintiffs. Russell LJ stated that:

"I consider that there is a greater significance in the paper title, in that it attaches to the activities of those claiming under it a quality of acts of possession of the Rythe, whether the actual laying of moorings, or the granting of permission to others to lay moorings . . . In so far as others may have laid moorings, they can have done so only because they considered that, whoever might be in possession of the Rythe, they were entitled to lay moorings as incidental to the right of navigation, or pursuant to some other general right, or that whoever was in possession would not object; their activities were not, therefore, acts of possession or occupation of the Rythe, and they cannot be described as concurrent occupiers or possessors."[16]

Where the action to recover land is brought by a person claiming through the Crown or a spiritual or eleemosynary corporation sole, but the right of action first accrued to the Crown or such corporation sole, the action will become time barred upon the expiration of the shorter of the following two periods: (a) the period during which the action could have been brought by the Crown or the corporation sole; or (b) 12 years from the date on which the right of action accrued to some person other than the Crown or the corporation sole.[17]

(2) Payment of rent to a landlord wrongfully claiming the reversion

Schedule 1, paragraph 6[18] is framed to govern the situation where a tenant is in possession of land under a lease in writing whereby a rent of not less than £10.00 per annum[19] is reserved and the rent is received by a person wrongfully claiming to be entitled to the reversion. In this case, it is provided that the right of action to recover the land vested in the person rightfully entitled to it shall be treated as having accrued on the date when the rent was first received by the wrongful landlord and not on the date of the determination of the lease.[20] Accordingly, receipt of the rent is deemed to constitute adverse possession of the reversion,[21] and after 12 years the reversion will be extinguished.

16. *Ibid* at 630.
17. Sch 1, Part II, para 12.
18. See further, Part IV, *infra.*
19. The sum of £10.00 was increased from £1.00 per annum by the 1980 Act : Sch 2, para 8.
20. See *Williams* v. *Pott* (1871) LR 12 Eq 149, which held that a person claiming, without any real title to land is a person "wrongfully" claiming the reversion even though such claim may be mistaken and without any improper intention to deprive others of their property.
21. See Sch 1, Part I, para 8(3)(b).

Any lease granted by the Crown is exempted from this provision by virtue of paragraph 6(2). Therefore, where the lease is granted by the Crown the cause of action will be treated as having accrued on the date when the lease determines. In effect, where a tenant remains in possession without paying rent to the Crown, the running of time is postponed until the end of the tenancy, at which point the tenant at will no longer has adverse possession.

(3) Conveyance to the Crown or corporations sole

Where the land in question is conveyed to the Crown or a corporation sole at a point in time after the cause of action has accrued, time will start to run from the accrual of the action and not from the date of the conveyance. One effect of this rule is that a subsequent conveyance to the Crown or a corporation sole will not revive a cause of action which is already time barred. For example, if the cause of action to recover Blackacre accrues to A on 1 January 1985 it will become time barred on 1 January 1997 (s 15(1)). If on 2 January 1997, A conveys Blackacre to the Crown, no title will pass given that the action is time barred at that time. Further, the limitation period of 30 years which favours the Crown will not trigger, since once an action is statute barred it cannot be revived.

(4) General exemptions favouring the Crown

While section 37(1) of the 1980 Act lays down the general principle that the statute binds the Crown in the same way as it applies to proceedings between subjects, the section goes on to list a range of exceptions. It should be noted that section 37(3) provides that proceedings by or against the Crown include:

- (i) proceedings by or against Her Majesty in right of the Duchy of Lancaster;
- (ii) proceedings by or against any Government department or any officer of the Crown as such, or any person acting on behalf of the Crown; and
- (iii) proceedings by or against the Duke of Cornwall.

The proceedings by the Crown which are exempted from the ambit of the Act include actions for the recovery of any tax or duty or interest on any tax or duty; any forfeiture proceedings under the Customs and Excise Acts (within the meaning of the Customs and Excise Management Act 1979); or any proceedings in respect of the forfeiture of a ship. "Duty" is defined as including any debt due to Her Majesty under section 16 of the Tithe Act 1936, and "ship" as including every description of vessel used in navigation not propelled by oars.[22]

(5) Advowsons

Section 25 of the 1980 Act provided that the limitation period governing actions to enforce a right to present to or bestow any ecclesiastical benefice as patron of that benefice is the longer of the following two periods: (a) a period during which three clerks in succession have held adversely to the right of the patron, or someone through whom the patron

---

22. Limitation Act 1980, s 37(2).

claims; or, (b) 60 years of possession adverse to the patron's right. This was subject to a 100-year "long-stop" period.[23]

The Law Reform Committee[24] observed that:

"We have not . . . thought it necessary to examine this complex provision in any detail because such claims are of no practical importance in modern conditions. Moreover, it seems likely that, within the fairly near future, the General Synod will promote legislation to abolish (or greatly to modify) existing rights of private patronage and, if such legislation is enacted, [this section], already obsolescent, seems likely to be entirely obsolete."[25]

In fact section 25 was repealed by the Patronage (Benefices) Measure 1986,[26] ss 1(2) and 4(3) which provide for a register of patrons to be kept by the registrar of each diocese.

(6) The Royal prerogative

The prerogative power of the Crown is part of the common law, but while throughout early history the Crown enjoyed extensive powers over its subjects, its scope has been steadily eroded since about the seventeenth century. The nature of the Royal prerogative has been the subject of extensive debate both among academic commentators and the judiciary alike. For example Blackstone noted that the term:

" . . . signifies, in its etymology (from *prae* and *rogo*) something that is required or demanded before, or in preference to, all others. And hence it follows, that it must be in its nature singular and eccentrical; that it can only be applied to those rights and capacities which the king enjoys alone, in contradistinction to others, and not to those which he enjoys in common with any of his subjects; for if once any one prerogative of the crown could be held in common with the subject, it would cease to be prerogative any longer."[27]

For the purposes of limitations, section 37(6) of the 1980 Act provides that nothing in the Act shall affect the prerogative right of Her Majesty (whether in the right of the Crown or of the Duchy of Lancaster) or of the Duke of Cornwall to any gold or silver mine. In effect, no limitation period applies to proceedings by the Crown in respect of such rights.

(7) The Foreign Limitation Periods Act 1984[28]

Following the policy of the Limitations Act 1980, the 1984 statute applies to actions to which the Crown is a party in the same way as it applies to proceedings between subjects. For the purposes of the statute, the definition of the "Crown" as contained in section 37 of the 1980 Act is adopted.

---

23. Limitation Act 1980, s 25(1)(b).

24. LRC 21st Report, *Final Report on Limitation of Actions*, Cmnd 6923, 1977.

25. *Ibid* para 3.43.

26. See the Patronage (Benefice) Rules 1987, (SI 1987 No 773), which came into force on 1 October, 1987 and the Patronage (Appeals) Rules 1988, (SI 1988 No 1980), which came into force on 1 January, 1989.

27. Bl Comm 1.239. See, *Case of Proclamations* (1611) 12 Co Rep 74; *A-G v. De Keyser's Royal Hotel* [1920] AC 508; *Re Ferdinand, Ex-Tsar of Bulgaria* [1921] 1 Ch 107; *Burmah Oil Co v. Lord Advocate* [1965] AC 75. See also, [1973] CLJ (B Markesinis); HWR Wade & CF Forsyth *Administrative Law,* 7th ed (Clarendon Press: Oxford, 1994) at p 247 *et seq.*

28. Considered further *infra.*

PUBLIC AUTHORITIES

Prior to the enactment of the Law Reform (Limitation of Actions, etc) Act 1954, public authorities enjoyed the benefit of very short statutory time periods within which actions against them had to be commenced. For example, a limitation period of only six months was laid down by the Public Authorities Protection Act 1893 which governed "any action, prosecution, or other proceeding" against any person for "any act done in pursuance, or execution, or intended execution of any Act of Parliament, or of any public duty or authority, or in respect of any alleged neglect or default in the execution of any such Act, duty, or authority".

This statutory period was increased to one year by the Limitation Act 1939,[29] however, the special status enjoyed by public authorities was abolished by the 1954 Act.[30] Henceforth, the limitation period for actions against public authorities and their servants or agents was brought into conformity with that governing actions against private individuals.

JUDICIAL REVIEW

Judicial review is the process by which the High Court exercises its supervisory jurisdiction over inferior courts, tribunals and other public bodies. The court exercises its control by virtue of the three prerogative orders: certiorari; prohibition; mandamus. Further, since 1977 an applicant for judicial review may be awarded a declaration and/or injunction in addition to, or *in lieu* of, the prerogative orders. In *Council Of Civil Service Unions* v. *Minister for the Civil Service*[31] Lord Diplock classified the grounds for judicial review into three distinct heads. He said: "The first ground I would call 'illegality', the second 'irrationality' and the third 'procedural impropriety'. That is not to say that further development on a case by case basis may not in course of time add further grounds."[32]

Judicial review is governed by its own specific procedure contained in sections 29–31 and 43 of the Supreme Court Act 1981 and Order 53 of the Rules of the Supreme Court. Other rules are, expressly or impliedly, incorporated into Order 53.[33] Applications for judicial review together with supporting documents must be filed with the Crown Office, which is also responsible for listing.

An application for judicial review must undergo two separate stages. First, the applicant must apply *ex parte* to a judge of the High Court for leave to move for judicial review.[34] Secondly, if leave is granted, the substantive application can be heard by a divisional court, although normally it will be heard by a single judge. At the initial stage, the applicant

29. Section 21.

30. The Law Reform (Limitation of Actions, etc) Act 1954, s 1 which came into force on 4 June 1954. Causes of action which were time barred on 4 June 1954 remained barred (s 7(1)). See *Arnold* v. *Central Electricity Generating Board* [1988] AC 228.

31. [1985] AC 374 (the GCHQ case).

32. *Ibid* at 410. See, also, Lord Roskill at 414 and 415. See further, *R* v. *Secretary of State for the Environment, ex parte Nottinghamshire CC* [1986] AC 240, Lord Scarman at 249; *R* v. *Secretary of State for the Home Department, ex parte Brind* [1991] AC 484, Lord Roskill at 750. For an excellent analysis of the procedural and substantive law governing judicial review see Gordon, *Judicial Review*, 2nd ed. (London: Sweet & Maxwell, 1996).

33. See Ord 53, r 8.

34. Ord 53, r 3(1).

must establish prima facie grounds for relief. Such an application must be made "promptly" and, in any event, within three months from the date when the grounds for the application first arose, unless the court considers that there is good reason for extending the period within which the application shall be made.[35] However, it should be noted that the fact that an application is made within three months is not conclusive of it having been made promptly.[36] Further, section 31(6) of the Supreme Court Act 1981 provides that where the court considers that there has been undue delay in applying for judicial review, it may refuse to grant leave to make the application for the relief sought, if it considers that "the granting of the relief . . . would be likely to cause substantial hardship to, or substantially prejudice the rights of, any person or would be detrimental to good administration". Section 31(7) goes on to state that subsection (6) is without prejudice to any Act or rule of the court which limits the time within which an application for judicial review must be made, while Order 53, rule 4(3) provides that the preceding paragraphs "are without prejudice to any statutory provision which has the effect of limiting the time within which an application for judicial review may be made". It has been observed that these provisions are difficult to reconcile.[37] However, the House of Lords in *R* v. *Dairy Produce Quotas Tribunal, ex parte Caswell*[38] subjected the various provisions to extensive examination and laid down a series of principles designed to clarify their operation. Lord Goff stated that: "the combined effect of s 31(7) and r 4(1) is that there is undue delay for the purposes of s 31(6) whenever the application for leave to apply is not made promptly and in any event within three months from the relevant date".[39]

Where the applicant shows good reason, the judge may grant an extension.[40] However, the judge may still nevertheless refuse leave if he is of the view that the granting of relief would be likely to cause substantial hardship or be prejudicial or detrimental to good administration since, in the view of Lord Goff "section 31(6) simply contains particular grounds for refusing leave or substantive relief, not referred to in rule 4(1), to which the court is bound to give effect, independently of any rule of court".[41]

Furthermore, the point was also made that the judge should normally grant leave where good reason is shown under rule 4(1), and leave questions of hardship or prejudice or detriment arising under section 31(6) to be argued at the substantive application. The House of Lords found that it was not possible to adequately define the term "detriment to good administration" so as to provide a definitive test. However, it was accepted that there must be foreseeable positive harm to good administration and affirmative evidence of detriment or at the minimum evidence from which detriment may be inferred. Lord Goff stated that:

---

35. Ord 53, r 4(1).

36. *R* v. *Stratford on Avon DC, ex parte Jackson* [1985] 1 WLR 1319; *R* v. *Greenwich LBC ex parte Cedar Transport Group Ltd* [1983] RA 173. See also, *R* v. *Swale BC, ex parte Royal Society for the Protection of Birds* [1990] COD 263; *R* v. *Secretary of State for Health, ex parte Alcohol Recovery Project* [1993] COD 344.

37. Gordon, *op cit, supra*, fn 32 at p 48.

38. [1990] 2 AC 738. The Court of Appeal was of the view that r 4(3) and s 31(7) lead to a *"circulus inextricabilis"*.

39. *Ibid* at 746.

40. Ord 53, r 4. In *R* v. *Home Secretary, ex parte Ruddock* [1987] 1 WLR 1482, it was held that the importance of the point of law in issue was good reason to extend time. Similarly, in *R* v. *Stratford on Avon DC, ex parte Jackson* [1985] 1 WLR 1319, the time taken to obtain a legal aid order was held to be good reason.

41. [1990] 2 AC 738 at 747.

"I do not consider that it would be wise to attempt to formulate any precise definition or description of what constitutes detriment to good administration. This is because applications for judicial review may occur in many different situations, and the need for finality may be greater in one context than in another. But it is of importance to observe that section 31(6) recognises that there is an interest in good administration independently of hardship, or prejudice to the rights of third parties, and that the harm suffered by the applicant by reason of the decision which has been impugned is a matter which can be taken into account by the court when deciding whether or not to exercise its discretion under section 31(6) to refuse the relief sought by the applicant. In asking the question whether the grant of such relief would be detrimental to good administration, the court is at that stage looking at the interest in good administration independently of matters such as these. In the present context, that interest lies essentially in a regular flow of consistent decisions, made and published with reasonable dispatch; in citizens knowing where they stand, and how they can order their affairs in the light of the relevant decision. Matters of particular importance, apart from the length of time itself, will be the extent of the effect of the relevant decision, and the impact which would be felt if it were re-opened."[42]

Finally, the fact that an alternative remedy is available to the applicant will not, in itself, be a ground for refusing an extension of time although the court will generally be reluctant to exercise its discretion in favour of the applicant.[43] The point is that no general principle can be stated which accurately summarises the approach of the courts to the issue of delay or to the grounds for refusing relief contained in section 31(6). It is clear, however, that the courts retain the widest possible discretion,[44] and are entitled to take the issue of delay of their own motion.[45]

EUROPEAN DIRECTIVES

As a result of the UK's membership of the European Union, obligations are imposed by the EC Treaty, Regulations, Directives and Decisions issued by the EC Council and the Commission. The European Court of Justice has held that all national legislation must, so far as is possible, be interpreted by national courts so as to ensure conformity with any relevant Directive.[46] This has been construed by the House of Lords in *Webb* v. *EMO Air Cargo (UK) Ltd*[47] as imposing a general obligation on English courts.

For the purposes of limitation periods, time does not begin to run under RSC Order 53, rule 4 until a Directive has been correctly implemented into national law.[48] The rationale here is to avoid any uncertainty as to the extent of the rights conferred by the Directive in question during the period in which it has not been implemented. Thus, it was held in Case C–208/90 *Theresa Emmott* v. *Minister for Social Welfare*[49] that where a Directive conferring rights on individuals has not been implemented into national law, the Member

42. *Ibid* at 749–50.

43. *R* v. *Elmbridge BC, ex parte Health Care Corp Ltd* [1991] 3 PLR 63. Cf *R* v. *Paddington Valuation Officers, ex parte Peachey Property Corp* [1966] 1 QB 380; *R* v. *Devon CC, ex parte Baker* [1993] COD 253; *R* v. *Bristol Magistrates' Court, ex parte Rowles* [1994] COD 137.

44. See the judgment of Popplewell J in *Caswell, The Times,* 7 December, 1988.

45. *R* v. *Dairy Produce Quotas Tribunal, ex parte Wynne-Jones* (1987) 283 EG 643.

46. Case C–106/89 *Marleasing SA* v. *La Comercial Internacional de Alimentacion SA* [1990] ECR I–4135.

47. [1993] 1 WLR 49 at 59: " . . . it is for a United Kingdom court to construe domestic legislation in any field covered by a Community Directive so as to accord with the interpretation of the Directive as laid down by the European Court of Justice . . . " (*per* Lord Keith).

48. *Cannon* v. *Barnsley Metropolitan Borough Council* [1992] 2 CMLR 795, EAT.

49. [1991] 3 CMLR 894. See also the decision of the appeal tribunal in *Cannon, ibid.*

State cannot rely on an individual's delay in bringing proceedings under the Directive, and any time bar laid down by national law will not apply. The European Court of Justice stated in judgment that:

"[22] Only the proper transposition of the directive will bring that state of uncertainty to an end and it is only upon that transposition that the legal certainty which must exist if individuals are to be required to assert their rights is created.

[23] It follows that, until such time as a directive has been properly transposed, a defaulting Member-State may not rely on an individual's delay in initiating proceedings against it in order to protect rights conferred upon him by the provisions of the directive and that a period laid down by national law within which proceedings must be initiated cannot begin to run before that time."[50]

THE EUROPEAN COURT OF JUSTICE

The procedural rules governing actions in the European Court of Justice are laid down in the Rules of Procedure of the ECJ. The various Treaties[51] of the Community specify limitation periods, and in general provide that time starts to run on or from the occurrence of a particular event. This is subject to two qualifications contained in the Rules of Procedure. First, that the day during which the event or action from which the period is to run occurs shall be excluded when reckoning any period of time prescribed by the Treaties, the Statutes or the Rules of Procedure themselves.[52] Secondly, that the time for commencing proceedings against a measure adopted by an institution runs from the day following receipt of notification of it or "where the measure is published, from the fifteenth day after publication has been described in the *Official Journal*".[53] It is apparent, therefore, that *knowledge* of the occurrence of the event in question is the material factor rather than merely its occurrence.[54] Publication in the *Official Journal* is notice to the world at large and it is no defence that the applicant did not read the *Official Journal*. The test seems to be whether the applicant either had actual notice, or should, by exercising due diligence, have had the requisite knowledge. Further, in Cases 358/85 and 51/86 *France* v. *European Parliament*[55] the Advocate General stressed that where the applicant has full knowledge of the contested act before it is published in the *Official Journal*, time runs from the acquisition of knowledge and not from publication.[56]

The prescribed time limits can be extended to take account of postal delays. This varies according to the particular Member State within which the individual litigant is resident. For UK residents the extension period for postal delays is 10 days.[57] The period of grace is calculated by reference to the place where the party concerned, not his or her legal representative, is habitually resident.[58] It is provided that if a period "would otherwise end

50. *Ibid* at 916.
51. The Statutes of the European Coal and Steel Community (ECSC); the European Economic Community; the European Atomic Energy Community (Euratom).
52. Rules of Procedure of the European Court of Justice r 80(1)(a).
53. *Ibid*, r 81(1).
54. See, Case 88/76 *Société pour l'Exportation des Sucres SA* v. *Commission of the European Communities* [1977] ECR 709 at 731 (Advocate General Reischl).
55. [1988] ECR 4821. See also, *Karl Könecke Fleischwarenfabrik GmbH & Co KG* v. *Commission of the European Communities* [1980] ECR 665.
56. *Ibid* at 4838–39 (*per* Advocate General Mancini).
57. Annex II to the Rules of Procedure of the European Court of Justice.
58. Case 28/65 *Fonzi* v. *Euratom Commission* [1966] ECR 477 at 491.

on a Saturday, Sunday or an official holiday, it shall be extended until the end of the first following working day".[59] Proceedings are deemed to commence when the necessary documents are lodged with the Court.[60] Where the applicant chooses to enter into negotiations with the relevant Community institution with the object of settling the issue, the running of time will be suspended. If, however, the negotiations fail to achieve a settlement, the applicant must commence proceedings expeditiously if advantage is to be taken of the suspension, for otherwise time will be deemed to have continued running.

The Court also has discretion to grant extensions to take account of unforeseeable circumstances.[61] It has been held that this discretion will not be exercised merely because the plaintiff has experienced some difficulty in bringing proceedings.[62] However, the limitation period may be extended where the plaintiff can show the existence of unusual circumstances which were beyond his or her control. In *SIMET and FERAM* v. *High Authority*[63] Advocate General Gand held that "unforeseeable circumstances" and "*force majeure*" are "external events beyond the control of the person under the obligation, of a kind which that person could not foresee and the consequences of which he could not imagine".[64] The running of time will also be suspended where an application is made for legal aid, and will resume running from the date of notification to the applicant of the order granting legal aid.[65]

The limitation periods for actions which relate to European legislation are, in the main, relatively short. The reason for this is clear: lengthy time limits would lead to uncertainty surrounding legislative acts.[66] Legal certainty in this regard is therefore the overriding consideration. Thus, where no limitation period is laid down, the Commission will not delay indefinitely in exercising its power to impose fines.[67] Further, in contrast to English law where it is for the defendant to raise the issue of time bar by way of defence, the Court may take the point of its own motion.[68]

---

59. Rules of Procedure of the European Court of Justice, rr 80(2) and 101(2). The official holidays are listed in Annex I of the Rules of Procedure. They are: New Year's Day; Easter Monday; 1 May; Ascension Day; Whit Monday; 23 June (or 24, where the 23 is a Sunday); 15 August; 1 November; 25 and 26 December. It should be noted that time does continue to run during official holidays, weekends and vacations including holidays in the Member States, see Case 209/83, *Ferriera Valsabbia SpA* v. *Commission of the European Communities* [1984] ECR 3089, para 12.

60. See the decision in *SIMET and FERAM*, *infra*, fn 62.

61. Court of Justice Protocol, Art 42(2) provides that "no right shall be prejudiced in consequence of the expiry of a time limit if the party concerned proves the existence of unforeseeable circumstances or of *force majeure*".

62. Case 209/83 *Ferriera Valsabbia SpA* v. *Commission of the European Communities* [1984] ECR 3089 in which the plaintiff alleged that he could not find a lawyer and the local law libraries were closed for holidays. See also, Case 224/83 *Ferriera Vittoria* v. *Commission of the European Communities* [1984] ECR 2349; Case 42/85 *Cockerill-Sambre SA* v. *Commission of the European Communities* [1985] ECR 3749.

63. [1967] ECR 33.

64. *Ibid* at 50. In Case 284/82 *Acciaierie & Ferriere Busseni* v. *Commission of the European Communities* [1984] ECR 557 at 570–72, Advocate General Reischl took the view that "*force majeure*" covers external circumstances which make it impossible for the required action to be taken before the expiry of the limitation period; even if it does not presuppose absolute impossibility, there must still be abnormal difficulties which (i) are independent of the will of the person concerned and (ii) appear inevitable even if every useful precaution is taken.

65. Case T–92/92AJ *Lallemand-Zeller* v. *Commission of the European Communities* [1993] ECR II–31.

66. See, for example, Case 24/69 *Nebe* v. *Commission of the European Communities* [1970] ECR 145.

67. Case 48/69 *Imperial Chemical Industries Ltd* v. *Commission of the European Communities* [1972] ECR 619.

68. Case 33/72 *Gunnella* v. *Commission of the European Communities* [1973] ECR 475.

To illustrate the above provisions by way of an example. It is provided that an action to annul a Commission Decision under Article 173 of the Treaty of Rome must be commenced within two months of the Decision being notified to the applicant. This period will be extended by 10 days to take account of the residency of the applicant in the UK. Further, the day on which notification of the Decision took place (the event which caused time to start running) is excluded from the calculation. Calculation of the two-month period is carried out by reference to calendar months rather than set periods of 31 days, and ends at midnight on the relevant date. To this, account must be paid to any holidays, for example 25 and 26 December, lest the action be time barred by falling on such a date. Thus, the limitation period in the following illustration would be calculated as follows:

> Commission decision notified to X, a UK resident at 2pm on Friday, 1 November 1996. The period begins to run at midnight on 1 November 1996 (i.e. 00.00 hours 2 November). The two-month period expires at midnight on 1 January 1997 (or 00.00 hours 2 January). To this must be added 10 days, the period of grace granted on account of distance, which brings the period to 12 January 1997 (a Sunday). The limitation period will therefore expire on the next working day, Monday, 13 January at midnight.

With respect to legal proceedings for damages arising from non-contract liability (e.g. tortious),[69] the ECSC Statute, art 40, the EC Statute, art 43 and the Euratom Statute, art 44, provide that such actions "shall be barred after a period of five years from the occurrence of the event giving rise thereto". The event in question will be the occurrence of the damage flowing from a wrongful act. Accordingly, it has been held that the limitation period cannot start to run "before the date on which the injurious effects of the unlawful measures adopted by the Community were produced", rather than the dates on which the measures entered into force and were published.[70] The contractual liability of the European Communities and the institutions is governed by the law applicable to the particular contract.[71] For the purposes of determining the relevant limitation period the Contracts (Applicable Law) Act 1990 provides that the applicable law will govern the prescription and limitation of actions.[72] Accordingly, where the contract is governed by law other than that of England, that law will determine the limitation period.[73]

---

69. Art 215(2) provides that: "In the case of non-contractual liability, the Community shall, in accordance with the general principles common to the laws of the Member States, make good any damage caused by its institutions or by its servants in the performance of their duties." See further, TC Hartley, *The Foundations of European Community Law* (Oxford: Clarendon Press, 1994), pp 475–6; HG Schermers, T Heukels, and P Mead (eds), *Non-Contractual Liability of the European Communities* (Martinus Nijhoff, 1988) Chs 3 and 6.

70. Cases 256, 257, 265, 267/80 and 5/81 *Birra Wüher SpA* v. *Council and Commission of the European Communities* [1982] ECR 85.

71. EC Statute, Art 215(1). The Commission always inserts a "choice of law" clause in its contracts and it was held in Case 318/81 *Commission of the European Communities* v. *CODEMI* [1985] ECR 3693, that this clause prevails irrespective of any ensuing arguments that the contract was more closely connected with a country different from that specified in the clause.

72. Sch 1 of the Act incorporating Art 10(1)(d) of the Rome Convention.

73. See also, the Foreign Limitation Periods Act 1984.

CHAPTER 5

THE RUNNING OF TIME

THE CAUSE OF ACTION

It will be seen below that the concept of the cause of action is central to every aspect of limitation of actions, since it is the date on which the cause of action accrues that frequently sets the date from which time will run against the plaintiff, although this is not always the only date from which time is to run. However, nowhere in the Limitation Act 1980 or any of its predecessors is there to be found a definition of what constitutes a cause of action, although there is a definition of the word "action" in the 1980 Act, s 38(1) which states that an action includes any proceedings in a court of law, including an ecclesiastical court. Moreover, there is also express provision for arbitration to the extent that it is provided that the 1980 Act will apply in the same way to arbitrations as it applies to an action in the High Court.[1] Accordingly, the word action is, in effect, redefined so as to include both proceedings and arbitrations, with the result that it is probably more accurate to say that the concept of the cause of action should be read as a "cause of proceeding".[2]

Accordingly, in *China* v. *Harrow Urban District Council*[3] it was held that a claim by a local authority for arrears of rates could be regarded as an action for the purposes of the Limitation Act 1939, since there was no doubt that it involved proceedings in the sense that the cause of the proceeding was the ratepayer's failure to comply with his legal obligation to pay as required on demand by the local authority.

In addition to proceedings and arbitrations, it is also clear from the scheme of the 1980 Act that proceedings brought on a judgment will amount to an action within the legislation, but it has been held that the enforcement of a judgment debt is not to be regarded as proceedings for the purposes of the 1980 Act.[4]

In broad terms, what makes up a cause of action is "Every fact which it would be necessary for the plaintiff to prove, if traversed, in order to support his right to the judgment of the court".[5] The difficulty with this definition is that it emphasises only the plaintiff's role in relation to matters of proof, but it should also be appreciated that the defendant must also be in a position to be able to satisfactorily defend himself against the plaintiff's action. As a result, an alternative definition of a cause of action was given in

---

1. Limitation Act 1980, s 34(1).
2. See *China* v. *Harrow Urban District Council* [1954] 1 QB 178 at 185 *per* Lord Goddard CJ.
3. *Ibid.*
4. *WT Lamb & Sons* v. *Rider* [1948] 2 KB 331 and see also Ch 9.
5. *Read* v. *Brown* (1888) 22 QBD 128 at 131 *per* Lord Esher MR.

Hernaman v. *Smith*[6] in which it was said that, "A cause of action means all those things necessary to give a right of action, whether they be done by the plaintiff or a third person".[7]

From this, it follows that a whole range of considerations need to be taken into account in order to determine whether a cause of action exists, so that time may start to run against the plaintiff. Perhaps the most complete definition of a cause of action should take on board not just the problems of proof facing the plaintiff but also other factors as well. Thus in *Cooke* v. *Gill*[8] Brett J emphasised the position of both the plaintiff and the defendant when he said, "Cause of action has been held from the earliest time to mean every fact which is material to be proved to entitle the plaintiff to succeed—every fact which the defendant would have a right to traverse".[9]

Once all relevant facts are in place, it generally follows that time may begin to run against a plaintiff, and, in the absence of statutory intervention, time may even run against the plaintiff in cases in which he is unaware that the relevant facts exist which would allow him to commence proceedings against the defendant.

In the context of an action for damages for negligence[10] the definition of a cause of action means that all the facts relevant to the existence of a duty of care and a breach of that duty must be in place so that the plaintiff is theoretically able to prove that a duty was owed to him by the defendant and that the defendant is in breach of that duty. Moreover, since negligence is a tort which is dependent on proof of damage, it will also be necessary for the plaintiff to establish that the defendant's breach of duty is the legal and factual cause of the harm in respect of which compensation is sought.[11]

The principal difficulty associated with the definition of a cause of action is to ascertain when all the elements of the definition have been satisfied so that the cause of action may be said to have accrued. Different types of action raise different problems in relation to this issue, which are dealt with in more detail in the following chapters of this book.

In determining whether time will run against the plaintiff, regard also must be had to the legal competence of the parties to the action. In other words, there must be a plaintiff who is legally capable of succeeding in the action he brings and a legally capable defendant against whom the action may be brought. Where this is not the case, no cause of action can accrue. Special provision is made for the problem of legal disability, so far as it affects the plaintiff, with the result that until the disability no longer affects the plaintiff, time cannot run against him.[12] Most frequently, the problem of disability will arise in the context of an action in respect of the administration of the estate of a deceased person, or in some cases actions against corporate bodies which have been dissolved prior to the date on which the action is commenced.[13] However, as will be seen elsewhere this last matter is now covered by specific legislation which allows the restoration of a dissolved company to the register of companies for certain purposes.[14] In other contexts,

6. (1855) 10 Exch 659.
7. *Ibid* at 665 *per* Parke B.
8. (1873) LR 8 CP 107.
9. *Ibid* at 116. Cited with approval in *Coburn* v. *Colledge* [1897] 1 QB 702 at 706 *per* Lord Esher MR.
10. See Ch 18.
11. In the case of torts actionable *per se*, such as some forms of trespass, the need to prove damage is not necessary. See further Chs 18 and 22.
12. Limitation Act 1980, s 28 and see Ch 6.
13. See *Re Russo-Asiatic Bank* [1934] Ch 720.
14. See Ch 9.

the problem whether there is a defendant to be sued can arise where the defendant in a given case is able to hide behind the screen of diplomatic immunity with the result that the plaintiff's cause of action is not complete.[15]

THE CONTINUITY OF LIMITATION PERIODS

As a general rule, once time starts to run against a plaintiff, it will run continuously. For example, in *Prideaux* v. *Webber*[16] a cause of action accrued prior to the establishment of the Commonwealth, with the result that time started to run against the plaintiff. Subsequently, the King's law was suspended during the period of the Commonwealth, but this suspension had no effect on the plaintiff's action, since the position under the relevant Statute of Limitations was that once time started to run, it could not be interrupted in the absence of an express statutory exception.

There are, however, a number of recognised exceptions to this rule. In particular, under the 1980 Act s 34(5), where the High Court exercises its power to set aside an arbitration award or to order that an arbitration agreement has no effect, it may also order that the limitation period in respect of the award or agreement should cease to have effect and that any time which has elapsed, in the meantime, may be discounted for the purposes of any proceedings which may be commenced at a later stage.[17] Furthermore, special rules on the running of time apply to personal injury actions[18] and to defamation proceedings,[19] under both of which there is a judicial discretion to allow an action to proceed out of time despite the fact that the primary limitation period has expired. Under these provisions, special regard may be had to any disability suffered by the plaintiff and the prejudice which would be suffered by both the plaintiff and the defendant if the court were to decide to exercise its discretion or not, as the case may be.

Other exceptional provisions contained in Part II of the 1980 Act go further still in suspending the running of time altogether. Thus in the case of a plaintiff under a legal disability, such as infancy or unsoundness of mind, time does not start to run against the plaintiff until such time as he is free of that disability.[20] Moreover, where the defendant is guilty of fraud or deliberate concealment and in cases in which the plaintiff has been misled as a result of a mistake, time will not start to run against the plaintiff until such time as he is aware of the mistake, the fraud or the deliberate concealment.[21]

ONCE BARRED ALWAYS BARRED

The general effect of the expiry of time is that once the plaintiff has become time barred, that will remain the case. In *Arnold* v. *Central Electricity Generating Board*[22] the plaintiff

---

15. See *Musurus Bey* v. *Gadban* [1894] 2 QB 352.
16. (1661) 1 Lev 31.
17. See also Ch 11 on arbitration generally.
18. Limitation Act 1980, s 33 and see Ch 19.
19. Limitation Act 1980, s 32A as amended by the Defamation Act 1996, s 5(4) and see Ch 22.
20. See Ch 6.
21. See Ch 6.
22. [1988] AC 228.

was the widow of a man employed by the defendants' predecessor, Birmingham Corporation, from 1938 until 1943. On nationalisation, the responsibilities of the Corporation were taken over by the CEGB, with the result that the Board became the defendant in the present proceedings. The gist of the plaintiff's claim against the defendants was that her husband had contracted the fatal disease mesothelioma as a result of being employed in working conditions which exposed him to high levels of asbestos dust, which it was alleged amounted to either negligence or a breach of statutory duty, or both. Because of the slow development of the disease from which the plaintiff's husband suffered, his condition was not diagnosed until October 1981 and death did not ensue until May 1982. It was argued for the defendants that the plaintiff's claim under the Fatal Accidents Act 1976 was time barred on the basis that in the case of actions against a public authority, the Limitation Act 1939, s 21 applied a limitation period of only 12 months running from the date of accrual of the cause of action. Despite the fact that there had been several statutory amendments to the law in relation to the position of a plaintiff in an action for damages for personal injuries, which would ordinarily have allowed the court to permit an action to be heard out of time, the fact remained that if the limitation period had expired and if later statutory provisions did not operate retrospectively, the rule that once an action had become time barred it remained so barred had to be applied in favour of the defendants.

THE RUNNING OF TIME

As has been stated above, once time starts to run, it does so continuously from the date of accrual unless there is some special rule which indicates otherwise. Time stops running as soon as the plaintiff commences legal proceedings in respect of his cause of action, but only does so in respect of the action in respect of which proceedings are brought. Thus if a plaintiff has two possible, but distinct, actions arising out of the same set of facts and brings proceedings in respect of one of these, time will continue to run in respect of the other.[23] Thus in *Lefevre* v. *White*[24] the plaintiff successfully sued a tortfeasor in respect of personal injuries suffered by him, but it later transpired that the defendant was bankrupt. The plaintiff then sought to recover the amount of the judgment debt against the defendant's liability insurers under the Third Parties (Rights against Insurers) Act 1930. Unfortunately for the plaintiff, the writ was issued against the insurers more than six years after the date on which injury was suffered, with the result that the action against the insurers was out of time, despite the fact that the initial action against the defendant was well within the limitation period. It was accepted by Popplewell J that the writ issued against the first defendant could have no effect on the running of time against the insurers.

The same principle also seems to apply to cases in which the plaintiff seeks to enforce the same claim against more than one defendant. Thus if the plaintiff commences proceedings against one of a number of possible defendants, but later seeks to add a further defendant after the date on which the limitation period has expired, the application to add the second defendant will fail on the ground that the running of time is not suspended

23. *Manby* v. *Manby* (1876) 3 Ch 101.
24. [1990] 1 Lloyd's Rep 569.

merely by virtue of the fact that proceedings were commenced in time in relation to the first defendant.[25]

THE COMPUTATION OF TIME

If rules are to be laid down which specify that an action is to be time barred, there must also be rules which determine exactly when that period of time expires. So far as the commencement of proceedings is concerned, the general rule is that time will stop running when a writ is issued, with the result that the date of service makes no difference.[26]

The first of the general rules on the computation of time is that only whole days are to be counted in computing the precise limitation period. However, this rule is not as clear as might, at first sight, appear to be the case. In *Radcliffe* v. *Bartholomew*[27] the relevant statutory provision stated that an action in respect of cruelty to an animal could be commenced within one month of the wrong giving rise to the cause of action. The wrong in question occurred on 30 May and the action was commenced on 30 June. Since the remainder of the day on which the wrong took place, namely 30 May could be ignored, this meant that the action was in time, in that no more than one month had elapsed from the date on which, legally, the wrong was deemed to have occurred.

In contrast to the decisions considered immediately above, there appear to be exceptional cases. In *Gelmini* v. *Moriggia*[28] the defendant had signed a promissory note which provided for payment on 22 September 1906. The plaintiff's writ was issued on 23 September 1912 and the question arose whether this was in time. Channell J held that the cause of action was complete at the beginning of 23 September 1906, since applying ordinary rules on the accrual of the cause of action, that was the earliest date on which the plaintiff's action was complete, and from that time onwards, it would have been possible to commence proceedings against the defendant. This remained the case despite the fact that at 12.00 midnight between 22 and 23 September, no court official would have entertained an application to issue a writ in respect of the promissory note!

The day on which time would ordinarily expire is also an important consideration in the computation of the limitation period. For example, it is quite possible that the last day of the limitation period falls on a Saturday, Sunday or public holiday, in which case the court office will not be open and the plaintiff will not be able to arrange the necessary paperwork in order to allow for the issue and service of the writ. Some older cases tended to ignore the problems caused by court office closure, holding that a plaintiff could be considered time barred despite the fact that it was not possible to make the necessary arrangements on the last day of the limitation period.[29] However, later cases have tended to take a more sympathetic stance. For example in *Hodgson* v. *Armstrong*[30] it was held that in the case of a statutory provision which required the plaintiff to give notice to the court

25. *Virgo Steamship Co SA* v. *Skaarup Shipping Corporation* [1988] 1 Lloyd's Rep 352. See also the effect of the Limitation Act 1980, s 35, discussed in Ch 7.
26. RSC Ords 5 and 6.
27. [1892] 1 QB 161. See also *Marren* v. *Dawson, Bentley & Co Ltd* [1961] 2 QB 135 in relation to personal injuries in which an accident occurred at 1.30 p.m., but time did not begin to run until 12.00 midnight of the following day, some $10\frac{1}{2}$ hours later.
28. [1913] 2 KB 549.
29. See *Morris* v. *Richards* (1881) 45 LT 210; *Gelmini* v. *Moriggia* [1913] 2 KB 549.
30. [1967] QB 299.

by a specified date and the court office was not open on that date, then time could be extended to the next day on which the court office was open. The earlier cases to the contrary were distinguished on the basis that the court was required, actively, to do something[31]; however, it is equally true that in the case of issuing a writ, officials in the court office are also required, actively, to do something in order to arrange for issue of the writ. Accordingly, the distinction is a little uneasy at best. Subsequently, the Court of Appeal in *Pritam Kaur* v. *S Russell & Sons Ltd*[32] decided the matter along the lines adopted in *Hodgson,* preferring not to follow the line of reasoning in the older cases that since there was no rule in the Limitation Act to the effect that days on which the court office was closed should be ignored, then time had to be regarded as running continuously, it should expire on the last day regardless of the inconvenience this might cause to the plaintiff. The basis of the decision in *Pritam Kaur* to allow the plaintiff's action to proceed where the writ was issued on Monday 7 September when the limitation period had actually expired on Saturday 5 September was that it would be unfair to the plaintiff. However, there is also the counter-argument that the decision in that case was also unfair to the defendant.

THE EFFECT OF THE EXPIRATION OF TIME

Generally, it is said that when time expires against the plaintiff, his remedy is barred, but his right is not extinguished. Thus, in an action on a simple contract, or in an action for breach of a tortious duty all the plaintiff loses is his right to a remedy in the event of breach on the part of the defendant.[33] However, there are exceptions to this rule under which not just the remedy is barred, but the substantive right of the plaintiff's is extinguished altogether.

The new rules which now apply to acts of conversion by virtue of the Limitation Act 1980, s 4 stipulate that when the limitation period expires in respect of an action for conversion or theft, the property rights of the original owner are to be extinguished and any judicial remedy in favour of that person will also be barred.[34] Furthermore, both the Latent Damage Act 1986[35] and the Consumer Protection Act 1987[36] contain provisions which extinguish rights of action after the expiration of a specified period of time.[37]

The importance of the distinction between the barring of a remedy and the extinction of a right of action can be quite significant. In the first place, the limitation defence must be expressly pleaded by the defendant,[38] with the result that if he fails to do so and the

31. A distinction can be drawn with cases in which the active participation of a court official is not required, for example where the statutory provision requires a complaint to be "presented" to a tribunal, since presentation can be effected by putting something in a letterbox: *Swainston* v. *Hetton Victory Club Ltd* [1983] 1 All ER 1179.

32. [1973] QB 336. See also *Hartley* v. *Birmingham City District Council* [1992] 2 All ER 213.

33. See *Royal Norwegian Government* v. *Constant & Constant* [1960] 2 Lloyd's Rep 431 (contract); *C & M Matthews Ltd* v. *Marsden Building Society* [1951] Ch 758 (tort).

34. See Ch 22.

35. See Ch 20.

36. See Ch 21.

37. See Limitation Act 1980, ss 11A(3) (defective products) and 14B(2) (latent damage), both of which introduce long-stop provisions which are expressed to extinguish the right of action in favour of the plaintiff.

38. RSC Ord 18, r 8. Where there is a plea of limitation, the plaintiff's remedy will be regarded as time barred only from that date: *Kennett* v. *Brown* [1988] 1 WLR 582. See also Unger, 4 MLR 45 at 50.

plaintiff's right of action still survives, there will be nothing to prevent the court from adjudicating on the matter in the absence of a plea of limitation of actions.

A second consequence of the distinction is that it may be possible for a plaintiff to pursue his right by means other than seeking a judicial remedy. Although the plaintiff's right to the remedy is barred by the expiration, the same is not true of his right. Thus if the plaintiff can lawfully pursue a self-help remedy, such as abating a nuisance, there will be nothing, in law, to prevent him from doing so.[39] Similarly in the field of contract and commercial law, an unpaid seller of goods, in some circumstances, may have a lien over goods in his possession as security for the price, which can be exercised without the need to resort to court assistance.[40] Similarly, there are certain rights in favour of a personal representative of an estate, such as the right to deduct from a legacy the amount of a statute-barred debt owed by the legatee to the estate[41] or the right to deduct the amount of a statute-barred debt owed to himself.[42]

39. *C & M Matthews Ltd* v. *Marsden Building Society* [1951] Ch 758.
40. See Sale of Goods Act 1979, s 41. On the matter of possessory liens generally, see *Spears* v. *Hartley* (1800) 3 Esp 81; *Courtenay* v. *Williams* (1844) 3 Hare 539; *Re Lloyd* [1903] 1 Ch 385.
41. *Re Taylor* [1894] 1 Ch 671; *Turner* v. *Turner* [1911] 1 Ch 716.
42. *Hill* v. *Walker* (1858) 4 K & J 166.

CHAPTER 6

THE EXTENSION OF TIME

CIRCUMSTANCES IN WHICH TIME MAY BE EXTENDED

The limitation periods set out in the Limitation Act 1980 are for the most part fixed and not capable of extension, although the exceptional discretion to permit an action out of time for personal injuries is discussed elsewhere.[1] Nevertheless there are two general situations recognised in the 1980 Act which successive Limitation Acts have thought deserving of fixed-term extensions to the ordinary limitation periods. These are, first, where the plaintiff was under a legal disability, consisting of either minority or unsoundness of mind,[2] during or after the limitation period which prevented him from bringing an action and, secondly, where the plaintiff was defrauded by the defendant, under a mistake or had had the true facts which might have induced him to commence proceedings deliberately concealed from him. To the statutory list might be added a third common law exception which has been recently recognised: the possibility that the defendant is estopped from pleading a limitation defence. These exceptional cases will be considered below.

PLAINTIFFS UNDER A LEGAL DISABILITY[3]

(a) The legal framework

The Limitation Act 1980, s 28 provides as follows:

"(1) Subject to the following provisions of this section, if on the date when any right of action accrued for which a period of limitation is prescribed by this Act, the person to whom it accrued was under a disability, the action may be brought at any time before the expiration of six years from the date when he ceased to be under a disability or died (whichever first occurred) notwithstanding that the period of limitation has expired.

(2) This section shall not affect any case where the right of action first accrued to some person (not under a disability) through whom the person under a disability claims.

(3) When a right of action which has accrued to a person under a disability accrues, on the death of that person while still under a disability, to another person under a disability, no further extension of time shall be allowed by reason of the disability of the second person.

---

1. See Ch 19.
2. Limitation Act 1980, s 38(2).
3. See Jones, "Limitation Periods and Plaintiffs under a Disability—A Zealous Protection?" (1995) 14 CJQ 258.

(4) No action to recover land or money charged on land shall be brought by virtue of this section by any person after the expiration of thirty years from the date on which the right of action accrued to that person or some person through whom he claims.

(4A) If the action is one to which section 4A of this Act applies, subsection (1) above shall have effect as if for the words from 'at any time' to 'occurred)' there were substituted the words 'by him at any time before the expiration of three years from the date when he ceased to be under a disability'.

(5) If the action is one to which section 10 of this Act applies, subsection (1) above shall have effect as if for the words 'six years' there were substituted the words 'two years'.

(6) If the action is one to which section 11 or 12(2) of this Act applies, subsection (1) above shall have effect as if for the words 'six years' there were substituted the words 'three years'.

(7) If the action is one to which section 11A of this Act applies or one by virtue of section 6(1)(a) of the Consumer Protection Act 1987 (death caused by defective product), subsection (1) above—

(a) shall not apply to the time limit prescribed by subsection (3) of the said section 11A or to that time limit as applied by virtue of section 12(1) of this Act; and
(b) in relation to any other time limit prescribed by this Act shall have effect as if for the words 'six years' there were substituted the words 'three years'."

For the purposes of the special provisions under the Limitation Act 1980, s 14A(4) based on the plaintiff's knowledge of relevant facts resulting from the provisions of the Latent Damage Act 1986, the Limitation Act 1980, s 28A provides:

"(1) subject to subsection (2) below, if in the case of any action for which a period of limitation is prescribed by section 14A of this Act—

(a) the period applicable in accordance with subsection (4) of that section is the period mentioned in paragraph (b) of that subsection;
(b) on the date which is for the purposes of that section the starting date for reckoning that period the person by reference to whose knowledge that date fell to be determined under subsection (5) of that section was under a disability; and
(c) section 28 of this Act does not apply to the action;

the action may be brought at any time before the expiration of three years from the date when he ceased to be under a disability or died (whichever first occurred) notwithstanding that the period mentioned above has expired.

(2) An action may not be brought by virtue of subsection (1) above after the end of the period of limitation prescribed by section 14B of this Act."

The key provision is section 28(1). A number of the features of the operation of this provision are worthy of note. In the first place, the section applies only where the plaintiff was under a disability when the action accrued.[4] Accordingly, the time-bar extension does not cover the case in which a plaintiff was not under a disability at that date but subsequently came under a disability which prevented him from bringing an action in the limitation period.[5] This can cause particular difficulties where, for example, the defendant's negligence results in the plaintiff's mental disability. If the unsoundness of mind occurs immediately, the effect is that time does not begin to run against the plaintiff,[6] but if the unsoundness of mind is delayed in its onset, time may have started to run against

---

4. *Purnell* v. *Roche* [1927] 2 Ch 142.
5. We are necessarily concerned here only with the case in which the plaintiff has become of unsound mind.
6. *Kirby* v. *Leather* [1965] 2 QB 367.

the plaintiff, in which case he is caught by the rule on subsequent disability.[7] However, as has been seen already, section 33 expressly contemplates the discretionary extension of time in personal injury cases where there is a disability subsequent to the accrual of the plaintiff's cause of action.[8] Moreover, the requirement that the plaintiff, in latent damage cases of all classes, must have knowledge of the material facts concerning his claim, failing which the alternative limitation periods contained in the Limitation Act 1980, ss 11(4)(b) in relation to personal injuries, 11A(4)(b) in relation to defective products and 14A(4)(b) in relation to all other forms of latent damage, will not commence, will often come to the plaintiff's rescue, particularly where the reason for the disability was unsoundness of mind, even where section 28 does not apply. The combined effect of the provisions concerning disability and the "date of knowledge" test therefore means that in the case of an infant, there is an indefeasible right to bring an action for personal injuries at any time up to the age of 21, since section 28 means that time cannot start to run, in any event, until the infant achieves the age of majority and the three-year date of knowledge test allows an action to be commenced within the three years following his eighteenth birthday.[9]

Secondly, the six-year extension of time from the date on which the plaintiff ceased to be under a disability cannot itself be extended by further disability, either of the plaintiff himself or of any person claiming through him. The former proposition is apparent from the wording of section 28(1) itself and the latter is expressly provided for by section 28(2). This principle is extended by section 28(3) to the perhaps unlikely case in which the plaintiff was under a disability at the date of the accrual of his cause of action and who died while still under the disability, the action then vesting in a second person under a disability. In such circumstances a second extension is not available and time will run from the date of the plaintiff's death. Thirdly, a disability for the purposes of the 1980 Act is either infancy or unsoundness of mind.[10]

Fourthly, nothing in section 28 prevents a plaintiff with a disability from commencing proceedings before his disability has been overcome. Even if he is able to do so, however, section 28 will presume that he cannot, and will continue to benefit him for six years following the end of his disability.

These principles are applicable in cases of latent damage, although they are modified and operate somewhat differently as between the various classes of latent damage that may arise.

Section 28 raises a number of public policy issues concerned with the limitation defence. It has been seen already that the principal policy issue arising under rules on limitation of actions is that a defendant should not be required to face a stale claim when the recollection of witnesses may have dimmed and the availability of evidence, generally, may be adversely affected.[11] To the contrary, there is also a strong policy argument to the

7. See *Boot* v. *Boot* (1991) unreported, CA.
8. See Ch 19.
9. *Tolley* v. *Morris* [1979] 2 All ER 561.
10. Limitation Act 1980, s 38(3). The Act does not define the phrase, "unsound mind", although s 38(4) states that unsoundness of mind may be conclusively presumed if the plaintiff is either detained under the Mental Health Act 1983 or receiving treatment as an in-patient at any hospital or nursing home.
11. See Ch 1.

effect that the disadvantaged must be given a substantial period within which they are able to sue in respect of harm suffered by them.[12]

(b) Application to personal injury claims

(i) Cases to which section 28 applies

Extension under section 28 is available where the plaintiff has suffered personal injury,[13] whether or not his disability is attributable to that injury, although the additional period of time allowed is, for the sake of consistency with section 11, reduced to three years as opposed to the normal six years.[14] Perhaps the most interesting question is the relationship between sections 28 and 33 in personal injury cases. Under section 33,[15] the court has a discretion to allow an action in respect of personal injuries to proceed out of time where the plaintiff has been prejudiced by the operation of section 11. On this wording, it might be argued that it is not possible to extend time under section 33 where a plaintiff, under a disability at the date at which his action accrued, and out of time under section 11, has ceased to be under a disability, but has not brought an action in time under section 28. In such a case it might be said that it is the section 28 period rather than the section 11 period which has created the prejudice. This point has yet to be tested, and in most mental incapacity cases will be academic, given the existence of the alternative starting date for limitation purposes of the date of the plaintiff's knowledge, which would normally be after his recovery of soundness of mind. Conversely, the problem might well arise in minority cases, where the infant plaintiff was well aware of the facts but could not sue until coming of age.

(ii) Cases to which section 28 does not apply

It is clear from the express wording of section 28 that, if the plaintiff's disability arises after the accrual of his action, he cannot benefit from section 28 and must rely on section 33 alone for any extension of time under section 11. It is on this basis that one of the elements to be taken into account by the court in determining whether or not to exercise its discretion under section 33 is the duration of any disability of the plaintiff arising after the date of the accrual of the cause of action.[16]

Given that section 28 extends time only where the plaintiff was under a disability at the date of the accrual of his cause of action, that provision cannot assist a plaintiff who subsequently becomes of unsound mind. However, a plaintiff who becomes of unsound mind after the accrual of his cause of action but before he has acquired knowledge of the relevant facts listed in section 14, so as to trigger the alternative date of knowledge

---

12. See *Bull* v. *Devon Area Health Authority* [1993] 4 Med LR 117, CA. This policy ground will be especially strong in cases like *Bull* where the plaintiff was a child injured at birth, with the result that he was under a double disability.

13. This excludes injury caused as a result of the supply of a defective product where the plaintiff's action is brought under the Consumer Protection Act 1987: see Limitation Act 1980, s 28(7). But the s 28 extension is available to dependants who bring an action under the Fatal Accidents Act 1976 following the death of the victim: Limitation Act 1980, s 12(3).

14. Limitation Act 1980, s 28(6).

15. See Ch 19.

16. Limitation Act 1980, s 33(3)(d), discussed in Ch 19.

limitation period in section 11(4)(b), will presumably not face the possibility of time running against him until he has ceased to be under a disability[17] and has acquired knowledge of the necessary facts. It should be noted, in particular, that a plaintiff with an unsound mind cannot be deprived of the benefit of section 11(4)(b) on the basis of the constructive knowledge provisions of section 14(3), since although the test for the acquiring of knowledge is objective, it relates to the knowledge that might have been possessed by the plaintiff in question, namely, one with an unsound mind, and not a notional plaintiff of full mental capacity.

(iii) Illustrations

The following examples may illustrate the working of these provisions.

(1) Plaintiff (P) is negligently injured by defendant (D), and suffers damage in year 1, at a time when he was of unsound mind. On purely objective grounds his injuries would have been discoverable in year 3. His disability comes to an end in year 5, and he commences proceedings in year 7. This is precisely the case that section 28 is aimed at, and its effect is to start time running in year 5 despite the fact that under section 11(4)(b) his action accrued in year 1. If P's disability was such as to prevent him from acquiring knowledge under section 14 until year 5, the running of time under both limbs of section 11(4) will be identical. It is, however, possible to contemplate cases in which P was capable of ascertaining the relevant section 14 facts despite his disability; say, in the example above, in year 4. It would nevertheless appear that P is entitled to the benefit of section 28.

(2) The facts are as in (1) above, except that P does not bring his action until year 12. He is here time barred under both limbs of section 11(4), and the concession granted to him by section 28 has expired. He must thus seek the discretionary indulgence of the court under section 33.

(3) P is negligently injured by D and suffers damage in year 1, at a time when he was not under any legal disability. P becomes subject to a disability in year 2 but recovers in year 5. The facts listed in section 14 concerning his injury would have become discoverable on purely objective grounds in year 3, but are discovered by P in year 5, on his recovery from the disability. P brings an action in year 7. In such a case, section 28 can never come into play, so that time runs under section 11(4)(a) in year 1. However, time does not begin to run under section 11(4)(b) until the date of his knowledge, in year 5, so that his action is not time barred.

(4) The facts are as in (3) above, except that P does not commence proceedings until year 10. On these facts, he must again seek to satisfy the court of the justice of a discretionary extension of time in his favour under section 33.

---

17. Assuming, of course, that the nature of his disability is such as to prevent him from appreciating the necessary facts.

(c) Application to claims under the Latent Damage Act 1986

(i) Cases to which section 28 applies

Section 28 of the Limitation Act 1980 is equally applicable to actions which may be brought by virtue of the time limits contained in section 14A of the Act as inserted by the Latent Damage Act 1986, although the plaintiff is here entitled to the full six-year extension granted by section 28, consistent with his normal rights on the accrual of an action as conferred by section 14A(4)(a). Rather controversially, the extension of time under section 28 is not stated to be subject to the 15-year long-stop which normally applies to actions for latent damage which do not involve personal injury. The consequences of this may be illustrated thus.

> (1) P's building suffers damage in year 1, at a time when P is under a legal disability. P's disability comes to an end in year 8 and an action is brought in year 13. This is a classic illustration of a section 28 action, under which time does not run until year 8, and P has until year 14 to sue.
> (2) The facts are as in (1) above except that P's disability comes to an end in year 11 and P sues in year 18. Once again P is in time, as the 15-year long-stop does not operate against him. The position would be the same if P's disability had not come to an end until year 16; the long-stop does not prevent an extension under section 28 even if the action does not accrue until the long-stop has expired.

The alternative date in section 14A(4)(b) for the commencement of the limitation period, the date of the plaintiff's knowledge, is unlikely to extend the limitation period beyond that produced by a combination of section 14A(4)(a) and section 28, as it allows only three years from the date of the plaintiff's knowledge, as opposed to the six years granted from the end of the plaintiff's disability.

(ii) Cases to which section 28 does not apply

Section 2 of the Latent Damage Act 1986, which inserts a new section 28A into the Limitation Act 1980, makes express provision for cases in which the plaintiff's disability commenced after the date at which his action accrued under section 14A(4) (a). The effect of section 28A(1) is that such a plaintiff is given three years from the date at which his disability came to an end to bring his action, if that date is earlier than the date at which he ought to have acquired the relevant knowledge under section 14A(6)–(8). As a result, then, the plaintiff is given an extension, not to the period under section 14A(4) (a), but to the period under section 14A(4) (b). However, any such extension is, by virtue of section 28A(2), subject to the normal 15-year long-stop laid down by section 14B of the Limitation Act 1980.

(d) Claims under the Consumer Protection Act 1987

Claims under the Consumer Protection Act 1987, whether for personal injuries or for damage to property, fall within the general provisions of section 28. There are, however, two modifications introduced by the Act, which are incorporated into the Limitation Act 1980 as the new section 28(7). First, the period of six years contained in section 28(1) is reduced to three years, in line with the period allowed for actions under the Act. Secondly, the 10-year long-stop inserted into the Limitation Act 1980 by the Consumer Protection Act as section 11A(3) overrides any possible extension under section 28. This approach is by way of contrast to that taken under the Latent Damage Act 1986.

(e) Applications in respect of actions to recover land

Under section 28(4), in actions to recover land,[18] there is a long-stop provision which means that rules on disability cannot be employed in such cases after the expiry of 30 years from the date on which the cause of action first accrued.

(f) Disability and want of prosecution

It has been observed that where a plaintiff under a disability commences an action, it would be wrong to grant such a person an indefinite right to delay in bringing the matter to trial and it is questionable whether, in such circumstances, the court would be prepared to allow a fresh action to be started if the first action was dismissed for want of prosecution.[19] However, there may be circumstances in which this general principle is departed from.[20]

FRAUD, DELIBERATE CONCEALMENT AND MISTAKE

(a) The statutory provisions

The Limitation Act 1980, s 32 provides,

"(1) Subject to subsections (3) and (4A) below, where in the case of any action for which a period of limitation is prescribed by this Act, either—

(a) the action is based upon the fraud of the defendant; or
(b) any fact relevant to the plaintiff's right of action has been deliberately concealed from him by the defendant; or
(c) the action is for relief from the consequences of a mistake;

the period of limitation shall not begin to run until the plaintiff has discovered the fraud, concealment or mistake (as the case may be) or could with reasonable diligence have discovered it.

References in this subsection to the defendant include references to the defendant's agent and to any person through whom the defendant claims and his agent.

(2) For the purposes of subsection (1) above, deliberate commission of a breach of duty in circumstances in which it is unlikely to be discovered for some time amounts to deliberate concealment of the facts involved in that breach of duty.

(3) Nothing in this section shall enable any action—

(a) to recover, or recover the value of, any property; or
(b) to enforce any charge against, or set aside any transaction affecting, any property;

to be brought against the purchaser of the property or any person claiming through him in any case where the property has been purchased for valuable consideration by an innocent third party since

---

18. Within the extended meaning of such actions as defined in the Limitation Act 1980, s 38(7).
19. *Turner* v. *W H Malcolm Ltd* (1992) 15 BMLR 40 at 48 *per* Staughton LJ. See also *Tolley* v. *Morris* [1979] 2 All ER 561.
20. See *Hogg* v. *Hamilton & Northumberland Health Authority* [1993] 4 Med LR 369.

the fraud or concealment or (as the case may be) the transaction in which the mistake was made took place.

(4) A purchaser is an innocent third party for the purposes of this section—

    (a) in the case of fraud or concealment of any fact relevant to the plaintiff's right of action, if he was not a party to the fraud or (as the case may be) to the concealment of that fact and did not at the time of purchase know or have reason to believe that the fraud or concealment had taken place; and

    (b) in the case of a mistake, if he did not at the time of the purchase know or have reason to believe that the mistake had been made.

(4A) Subsection (1) above shall not apply in relation to any time limit prescribed by section 11A(3) of this Act or in relation to that time limit as applied by virtue of section 12(1) of this Act.

(5) Sections 14A and 14B of this Act shall not apply to any action to which subsection (1)(b) above applies (and accordingly the period of limitation referred to in that subsection, in any case to which either of those sections would otherwise apply, is the period applicable under section 2 of this Act)."

Accordingly, there are three exceptional cases in which the ordinary limitation periods laid down by the Act are suspended. These are:

    (a) the action is based upon the fraud of the defendant; or

    (b) any fact relevant to the plaintiff's right of action has been deliberately concealed from him by the defendant; or

    (c) the action is for relief from the consequences of a mistake.

In all such cases the period of limitation does not begin to run until the plaintiff has discovered the fraud, concealment or mistake or could with reasonable diligence have discovered it.

(b) Relationship between latent damage provisions and section 32

In all cases of latent damage the plaintiff is granted an alternative date to that of the occurrence of damage for the running of time, that date being the time of his actual or constructive knowledge of a series of material facts concerning his right to commence proceedings.[21] Moreover, since the alternative commencement dates set out in sections 11(4)(b) and 14A(4)(b) apply whether or not the true facts have been deliberately concealed by the plaintiff, it is enough that the plaintiff is not aware of them. Prima facie, then, in latent damage cases section 32 would appear not to have any independent effect but is subsumed by the general requirement of knowledge. Indeed, in one respect section 32 is narrower than the knowledge provisions, for in a case in which material fact A has been deliberately concealed by the defendant but in which the plaintiff was independently unaware of another material fact B, his discovery of the concealment of material fact A will set time running under section 32 but will not trigger the alternative knowledge limitation period until he has become aware of material fact B.

Nevertheless, there are two situations in which section 32 will have an independent effect in latent damage cases. First, it will be noted that under section 32(1) time begins to run only when the concealment was or ought to have been discovered, whereas under

---

21. See Ch 20.

the alternative commencement dates based on knowledge time begins to run from the date on which the plaintiff knew or ought to have known of the facts specified in section 14. Consequently a plaintiff who discovers the facts before he discovers that they had been deliberately withheld from him may take advantage of the later starting date established by section 32, although admittedly the additional time gained will in all probability in most cases be marginal.

Second, and more significant, is the relationship between section 32 and the long-stops laid down by the Latent Damage Act (Limitation Act 1980, s 14B) and the Consumer Protection Act (Limitation Act 1980, s 11A(3)). In both cases the long-stops override both the accrual of action and the alternative date of knowledge starting points for the relevant limitation periods, and it is thus apparent that section 32 becomes independently important if it can override the long-stops. The position is not, however, consistent. Under the Consumer Protection Act the 10-year long-stop is absolute, so that even in the event of deliberate concealment which cannot be discovered until after the expiry of 10 years from the date of the first supply of the defective product the plaintiff's action is nevertheless extinguished at the end of the 10-year period. This is the effect of the insertion into section 32 of the Limitation Act 1980 of a new subsection (4A) by the Consumer Protection Act. However, as far as claims under the Latent Damage Act 1986 are concerned, section 32(5) of the Limitation Act, as inserted by section 2(2) of the Latent Damage Act, provides that in the case of deliberate concealment the periods laid down by sections 14A and 14B (i.e., both the general limitation periods and the 15-year long-stop) cease to apply, and that a six-year time period starts to run either from when the damage occurred or from when the concealment could have been discovered, whichever date is later. The overriding of the long-stop for Latent Damage Act claims was recommended by the Law Reform Committee in its 1984 Report, and was defended passionately by the Lord Chancellor during the debates on the Bill, on the ground that a wrongdoer should not be permitted to take advantage of his own fraud. However, there is much to be said for the alternative view, voiced during the debates, that the real effect of permitting the long-stop to be overridden is not to satisfy moral indignation but to disrupt the settled insurance arrangements of the parties by increasing uncertainty.

To summarise, then, section 32 is likely to be of marginal impact only in latent damage claims for personal injuries and in claims under the Consumer Protection Act for defective products which cause personal injury or damage to property. However, as regards latent damage cases involving buildings and professional advice, and those for defective products which can be brought at common law rather than under the Consumer Protection Act 1987, section 32 overrides the 15-year long-stop and is thus likely to be of some significance. It is for this reason that the elements and operation of section 32 must now be examined.

(c) Diligence

Section 32(1) provides that the running of time will be postponed until such time as the plaintiff has discovered the fraud, concealment or mistake, or "could with reasonable diligence have discovered it". For these purposes, it appears that the plaintiff does not have to do everything possible to discover the fraud, concealment or mistake, but merely to do what a reasonable person would do, having regard to the particular circumstances of the case.[22] This raises the question whether there are circumstances in which patently obvious negligence on the part of the defendant will preclude the operation of section 32 on the ground that it is patent, even to a layman, that there has been a serious breach of duty, giving rise to a cause of action in the plaintiff's favour.

(d) Fraud

The meaning of the term fraud was considered by the Court of Appeal in *Beaman* v. *ARTS Ltd*[23] in which the plaintiff entrusted property to the defendants for safe-keeping. During the Second World War, the defendants believed that they would be unable to trace the plaintiff and gave the goods away because they feared for their safety during the Blitz. Subsequently, the plaintiff reappeared and asked for the return of her property. It was argued on the plaintiff's behalf that the defendants' actions in giving away the property amounted to fraud with the result that the otherwise time-barred action for conversion might still succeed despite the expiry of the primary limitation period for such actions. Denning J approached the case on the basis that since the defendants had acted honestly and in good faith, there was no fraud on their part, in which case, what is now section 32(1)(a) could not apply. The Court of Appeal, while confirming the result arrived at by Denning J, approached the matter in a slightly different way, holding that since the defendants honestly believed that the plaintiff had consented to the disposal, or that she would have done so had she been traceable, there could be no fraud. For the purposes of section 32(1)(a) it was considered that an action would only be based on fraud if fraud were an essential element in the plaintiff's claim.[24] It followed, therefore, that since an allegation of fraud is not essential in an action for conversion, what is now section 32(1)(a) could not apply. Accordingly, if an allegation of fraud is the essence of the plaintiff's claim against the defendant, it is possible that section 32(1)(a) may be used to prevent the running of time until the fraud is discovered or could reasonably have been discovered. For example, in *GL Baker Ltd* v. *Medway Building & Supplies Ltd*[25] funds were fraudulently transferred by a director of the defendant company from the plaintiff's account to that of the defendant company. In such circumstances, the essence of the plaintiff's claim against the defendant was one of fraud, in which case the special rules on limitation of actions came into play.

For the purposes of section 32(1)(a) it is the fraud which must be undiscoverable rather than the damage suffered by the plaintiff. For example, in the context of an application for postponement of the running of time under what is now section 32(1)(a), in *RB Policies at Lloyd's* v. *Butler*[26] a thief obtained a car from its owner by fraud and sold it to an innocent third party. Exercising their right of subrogation, the plaintiff insurers sought to recover the vehicle from that third party some 12 years after the original theft, having had problems tracing the vehicle in the meantime. It was held that the special rule on fraud had no application, since it was not the fraud which was undiscoverable, but simply the whereabouts of the stolen car.

---

22. *Peco Arts Inc* v. *Hazlitt Gallery Ltd* [1983] 1 WLR 1315.
23. [1949] 1 All ER 465, affirming the decision of Denning J [1949] 1 KB 550.
24. Consistent with the approach to s 32(1)(c) in relation to mistake: *Phillips-Higgins* v. *Harper* [1954] 1 QB 411.
25. [1958] 1 WLR 1216.
26. [1950] 1 KB 76.

(e) Deliberate concealment

The immediate predecessor of section 32(1)(b) of the Limitation Act 1980, section 26(b) of the Limitation Act 1939, referred not to deliberate concealment but to facts "concealed by the fraud" of the defendant. However, a series of cases established that the word "fraud" there used was wider than fraud in its common law sense and referred to "conduct unconscionable having regard to the relationship between the parties", and it is apparent that section 32(1)(b) was drafted to take in that view.[27] It is also settled that deliberate conduct encompasses recklessness.[28]

The concept of concealment is also a wide one. The primary meaning of the wording is undoubtedly to catch cases in which the defendant, aware of a breach of a duty by him, seeks to hide that fact.[29] However, many of the cases decided under the section or its predecessor have involved a deliberate breach of contract which, by its nature, is not readily discoverable. This is made clear by section 32(2),[30] which provides that, " . . . deliberate commission of a breach of duty in circumstances in which it is unlikely to be discovered for some time amounts to deliberate concealment of the facts involved in that breach of duty".

An example of this is *Beaman* v. *ARTS Ltd*,[31] in which the defendant bailees converted to their own use the plaintiff's goods while aware of the fact that the plaintiff would be unable for some time to check up on their whereabouts. For the purposes of what is now section 32(1)(b), it was held that there was no need for the plaintiff to prove fraud on the part of the defendants, so long as the plaintiff's action was "based on" fraud. Accordingly, it was considered that there had been fraudulent concealment and it was not necessary to show that the defendants had taken active steps to hide the existence of the cause of action from the plaintiff.

Decisions similar to that in *Beaman* v. *ARTS Ltd* have been reached in a series of building cases in which negligently constructed foundations were deliberately filled in before examination was possible or negligent advice was provided; these are discussed below. In this type of case, however, mere initial negligence which is unintentionally disguised will not bring section 32(1)(b) into operation: examples in the specific contexts of professional advice and building contracts are discussed below.

For the purposes of any defence to the limitation bar, the standard of proof applied requires the plaintiff alleging deliberate concealment to establish more than merely knowledge on the part of the defendant that there has been a concealment of relevant facts. Instead, particulars of the facts concealed have to be given either in the pleadings or in separate particulars. Accordingly in *Tunbridge* v. *Buss Merton & Co*[32] the plaintiff had alleged that the defendants had failed to reconsider the drafting of a debenture, which had it been reconsidered, a reasonably competent solicitor would have realised that a mistake

---

27. *Bartlett* v. *Barclays Bank Trust Co Ltd* [1980] 1 All ER 139 at 154 *per* Brightman J. See also *Applegate* v. *Moss* [1971] 1 QB 406 at 413; *Kitchen* v. *Royal Air Forces Association* [1958] 3 All ER 241; *King* v. *Victor Parsons Ltd* [1973] 1 All ER 206 at 209.
28. *Beaman* v. *ARTS Ltd* [1949] 1 KB 550; *King* v. *Victor Parsons Ltd* [1972] 2 All ER 625.
29. Unfortunately, there is some dispute as to the applicability of s 32(1)(b) in these circumstances. See below.
30. This subsection gives statutory effect to a number of decisions under the 1939 Act, notably the decision of the Court of Appeal in *King* v. *Victor Parsons Ltd* [1973] 1 All ER 206.
31. [1949] 1 KB 550.
32. (1997) *The Times*, 8 April, Laddie J, Ch D.

had been made. As a result of the defendants' negligence, the plaintiff suffered loss when the company in respect of which the debenture was secured became insolvent. The plaintiff's appeal was allowed on the ground that since a reasonably competent solicitor would have reconsidered the debenture, there was evidence of a failure to take reasonable care on the part of the defendant, in which case it would not be right to strike out the plaintiff's action.

(i) The role of agents

The rider to section 32(1) rather inelegantly states that all references in that section are to include "references to the defendant's agent and to any person through whom the defendant claims and his agent".[33] The courts have interpreted this phrase widely, and have permitted the extension of time against a defendant whose independent contractor had been guilty of concealed fraud.[34] However, the question of whether the extended time provided for by section 32 ceases to run once the plaintiff's agent, as opposed to the plaintiff, had or ought to have had knowledge of the deliberate concealment, is not in terms dealt with. The express reference to the agents of the defendant in section 32(1) would appear to indicate that the section does not cover the actual or constructive knowledge of the plaintiff's agents, and in *Peco Arts Inc* v. *Hazlitt Gallery Ltd*[35] Webster J tentatively endorsed that view. However, *dicta* in building cases decided under the marginally different wording of section 26(b) of the Limitation Act 1939 assume the contrary, and the point awaits final decision.[36]

Whether or not an agent acting on behalf of the defendant can be personally liable for their concealment on behalf of the defendant was considered in *King* v. *Victor Parsons Ltd*,[37] in which houses had been built on top of an infilled chalk-pit. The defendants in this action were the estate agents acting on behalf of the builders. With some reservations, it was considered, at first instance,[38] that the estate agents could be personally liable and that section 32(1)(b) could apply to them for limitation purposes, even though the plaintiff was only able to show that the agents had constructive, as opposed to actual, knowledge of the undisclosed facts. Subsequently, the Court of Appeal held that Thesiger J had gone too far in arriving at that conclusion, but were able to avoid having to restate the position due to their findings on the facts. In the event, the Court of Appeal was of the view that there had been fraud, in the sense that their knowledge could be regarded as actual rather than constructive.

(ii) Subsequent concealment

It was pointed out by Megarry V-C in *Tito* v. *Waddell (No 2)*[39] that the wording of section 26(b) of the Limitation Act 1939 appeared to confine its operation to cases in which the

---

33. For an application of this section see *Eddis* v. *Chichester Constable* [1969] 2 Ch 345.

34. *Applegate* v. *Moss* [1971] 1 QB 406. See also *Greater London Council* v. *Thomas McInerney & Sons Ltd* 1983 (unreported), in which the Court of Appeal held it to be arguable that a manufacturer of allegedly defective bricks was the agent of their supplier for the purpose of imputing knowledge to the supplier of those defects.

35. [1983] 1 WLR 1315.

36. *Lewisham London Borough Council* v. *Leslie & Co* (1978) 12 Build LR 22; *William Hill Organisation Ltd* v. *Bernard Sunley & Sons Ltd* (1983) 22 Build LR 1.

37. [1973] 1 All ER 206.

38. [1972] 1 All ER 625 at 626 *per* Thesiger J.

39. [1977] Ch 106 at 245.

deliberate concealment predated the accrual of the plaintiff's action. Section 32(1), by stating that "time shall not begin to run" until the plaintiff discovers the concealment, similarly indicates that once time has begun to run, any act of deliberate concealment by the defendant is to be disregarded. If this is correct, it is a significant limitation on the effectiveness of section 32, and it may well operate arbitrarily in latent damage cases where the damage does not occur until some time after the initial breach of duty by the defendant, for it becomes necessary to determine the precise date at which damage occurred in order to determine whether the defendant's subsequent act of concealment fell before or after that date. In practice, however, no decision has turned upon this point, which appears never to have been taken. Moreover, as will be seen below, in both construction and professional advice negligence suits the problem may be overcome by alternative analysis.

(iii) Application in building disputes

DISGUISED DEFECTIVE WORK

The building cases decided under section 32 and its immediate predecessor have for the most part involved either the laying of inadequate foundations by the contractor which have been covered up by him or the use by the contractor of incorrect building materials, the defects in which are not apparent or are hidden by a further process in the construction. The question has thus become whether the covering up was deliberately designed to hide the defect or whether the entire course of conduct was simply negligent. This is purely a question of fact. In *Applegate* v. *Moss*[40] and *King* v. *Victor Parsons & Co Ltd*[41] the courts were persuaded that there had been fraud by the builder in his covering up of defective foundations; in the former, the wholly inadequate nature of the foundations was the conclusive factor, while in the latter the finding of unconscionable behaviour was based on the failure by the builder to accept the advice of an architect. Again, in *Clark* v. *Woor*,[42] the deliberate use of underbaked bricks which began to crumble some nine years after the completion of the plaintiff's bungalow was held to be unconscionable conduct by the defendant builder, given the extent to which the plaintiff had relied upon the defendant's judgement. By contrast, in *William Hill Organisation Ltd* v. *Bernard Sunley & Sons Ltd*[43] the Court of Appeal found that the contractors had merely been negligent in their fixing of stone cladding, and that there was no fraudulent concealment simply because the cladding had been covered over.

It is impossible to lay down any hard and fast rules from these cases, although two generalisations may be put forward for guidance. First, the mere fact that negligent work has been covered up is not *per se* enough to produce a presumption that the defendant's conduct amounted to legal or equitable fraud. This emerges clearly from the decision of the Court of Appeal in *William Hill*, in which the argument that a builder is guilty of equitable fraud simply by getting on with the job after having committed a negligent act, was rejected. Further evidence of concealment is thus needed. Secondly, the relationship between the parties may be of importance. *Clark* v. *Woor* demonstrates that a plaintiff who

40. [1971] 1 All ER 747.
41. [1973] 1 All ER 206.
42. [1965] 1 WLR 650.
43. (1983) 22 Build LR 1.

employs a builder for domestic work is likely to be in a stronger position than a commercial purchaser, as his degree of reliance is greater. However, the Court of Appeal has denied that equality of power, sophistication or technical knowledge as between a builder or contractor and his employer must inevitably lead to the conclusion that there is no possibility of the contractor being able to perpetrate a legal or equitable fraud.

Lord Denning has put the matter thus[44]:

"It only requires a little imagination to think of circumstances in which workmen may do their work badly, leaving defects which the architect or supervisor would not discover, even by using reasonable diligence . . . It is all very well to talk about the council having its own architects and supervisors. But these gentlemen may have been misled by the contractors. The bad work may have been done when they were away, or their backs were turned for some good reason. The architects and supervisors may even have turned a blind eye to the defects: for some reward paid by the contractors . . . there are still people about who have an 'itching palm' . . . "

SUBSEQUENT DELIBERATE CONCEALMENT

All the cases discussed above involved fraudulent or negligent conduct concealed by the defendant during the building process. That situation does not give rise to the difficulty highlighted by Megarry V-C in *Tito* v. *Waddell (No 2)*,[45] namely, that a deliberate attempt by the defendant to conceal his breach of duty once time has started to run falls outside section 32(1)(b).[46] However, it is not difficult to contemplate circumstances in which that rule causes difficulty. Consider, for example, the facts of *Kaliszewska* v. *John Clague & Partners*.[47] In this case the plaintiff had engaged the defendant architect to design a bungalow, the building of which was completed in 1970. In 1974 cracks began to appear in the walls and the defendant returned to inspect the property. He gave reassuring advice to the plaintiff, on the strength of which purely cosmetic repairs were effected. By 1978 the cracking had reached worrying proportions, and on taking independent advice the plaintiff discovered that the bungalow's foundations were inadequate for the type of soil on which it had been built. Proceedings were commenced in March 1982. The defendant pleaded a limitation defence, arguing that the plaintiff's action had accrued at the latest in 1974, the date of the damage, or possibly even earlier on the strength of the "doomed from the start" doctrine.[48] Judge White accepted that the plaintiff's action had accrued in 1970 and was prima facie time barred, and he also accepted that the original design by the architect had been negligent but that he had not sought in any way to conceal facts from the plaintiff. It followed from this finding that section 32(1)(b) was not applicable to the original breach of duty, and it is significant to note that the subsection appears not to have been pleaded in relation to the subsequent reassuring visit, presumably on the strength of the doubts expressed in *Tito* v. *Waddell (No 2)*.[49]

On these facts it might have been possible to find that the defendant's visit and reassurance in 1974 amounted to an independent breach of duty by the defendant, which set in motion a new cause of action for misrepresentation; the plaintiff's loss would have

---

44. *Lewisham London Borough Council* v. *Leslie & Co* (1978) 12 Build LR 22 at 28.

45. [1977] Ch 106 at 245.

46. But see now the decision of the House of Lords in *Sheldon* v. *RHM Outhwaite (Underwriting Agencies) Ltd* [1995] 2 All ER 558, considered below in relation to professional negligence cases.

47. (1984) 5 Con LR 62.

48. On this aspect of the case see Ch 18.

49. [1977] Ch 106.

been her reliance on the false statement and thus the deprivation of her opportunity to commence proceedings within the limitation period. Indeed, if common law fraud could have been shown, section 32(1)(a) would have operated to postpone the limitation period until the fraud had been discovered or was discoverable with reasonable diligence. However, fraud within section 32(1)(a) was not alleged. A further possibility in these circumstances might have been that the false statement made in 1974 amounted to a negligent misrepresentation upon which the plaintiff had relied and had suffered loss. However, on the precise facts that line would not have benefited the plaintiff, as the new limitation period for the second cause of action would have expired in 1980 and proceedings were not commenced until 1982.

Presumably for these reasons, the plaintiff argued not that a new cause of action had accrued in 1974 but that the defendant was estopped by his conduct in 1974 from pleading a limitation defence. Judge White, applying the traditional elements of common law estoppel, held that the plaintiff was able to succeed on this ground since there had been a representation of fact that the foundations were sound; the maker of the statement, the architect, had intended that it should be relied upon; and the plaintiff had relied upon it and acted to her detriment by not seeking independent advice and by not commencing proceedings within the limitation period. Consequently, the defendant was estopped from relying upon the limitation defence. It follows from the reasoning adopted that, had the defendant's representation been outside the limitation period, the plaintiff could not have pleaded estoppel as she would not have been able to prove detrimental reliance.

The use of estoppel in these circumstances is novel and by no means free from difficulty. The most important unresolved question is the duration of the estoppel. It will be seen from the very facts of the case that the estoppel operated not just to override the limitation period running from the accrual of the original cause of action, but also permitted an action more than six years after the date of the statement giving rise to the estoppel. On principle it would appear clear that the defendant's inability to rely upon limitation would have come to an end once the plaintiff had discovered the true facts concerning the foundations of her bungalow. Judge White conceded this to be the case, but added that the plaintiff would thereafter have a further full limitation period in which to commence proceedings. This would appear to be generous, given that a substantial part of the limitation period had run prior to the statement giving rise to the estoppel. A further difficulty is whether the estoppel would have come to an end when the plaintiff ought to have discovered the truth; this is a question to which *Kaliszewska* does not provide an answer.

ILLUSTRATIONS

The interrelationship of the Latent Damage Act 1986, the deliberate concealment doctrine in section 32(1)(b) of the Limitation Act 1980 and the common law principle of estoppel may be demonstrated by the following example:

> Builder D knowingly erects a building with defective foundations in year 1. Damage occurs in year 12 and cracks appear in the walls of the building in year 14. Employer P summons the builder who assures him that the cracks are superficial only. The damage becomes objectively ascertainable in year 16 but P only becomes aware of it in year 17, when proceedings are commenced.

It is apparent that the 15-year long-stop in section 14B of the Limitation Act 1980 will bar any action under section 14A(4)(a) and (b) unless section 32(1)(b) can be brought into play. The reassurance by D in year 14 is outside section 32(1)(b) as time had commenced to run in year 12 by virtue of section 14A(4)(b), so if section 32(1)(b) is to operate P must seek to rely upon a plea that there was deliberate concealment in year 1. If this can be established, time will not run until year 16, the date at which the concealment had become apparent, and the limitation period is thereafter a further six years under section 32(5), and it is unnecessary for estoppel to be pleaded. However, if the plea of deliberate concealment cannot be made out, P may then rely upon the estoppel principle, the effect of which will be to give him a further six years from the date either of his discovery of the damage in year 17 or the date at which he ought to have discovered the damage in year 16; which of these possibilities is the proper starting date is far from clear.

(iv) Application in professional negligence cases

INITIAL NEGLIGENCE

The issue here is the extent to which section 32(1)(b) of the Limitation Act 1980 applies to cases in which a professional adviser negligently gives incorrect advice which is then not corrected by him. The simplest case is where the adviser did not at any stage discover the truth before the plaintiff suffered loss. Here the initial negligence is not to be regarded as deliberate concealment and, leaving aside any problem arising from the *Tito* v. *Waddell (No 2)*[50] principle, any subsequent acts of mere negligence do not fall within section 32(1)(b). In *Kitchen* v. *Royal Air Forces Association*[51] solicitors negligently failed to inform the plaintiff that she might have a right to sue under the Fatal Accidents Acts, and they did not become aware of the true position until after the limitation period had expired. The Court of Appeal held that the predecessor of section 32(1)(b), section 26(b) of the Limitation Act 1939, could not apply to those facts. Again, in *Costa* v. *Georghiou*,[52] the plaintiff's solicitors negligently failed to insert a rent review clause into a tenancy agreement to which he was a party, with the result that he could not claim an increased rent from his tenant. The Court of Appeal here ruled that the initial act was one of negligence only, and was not fraudulent concealment. An additional problem arising in this case was that the solicitors, having noted the blank space but not having appreciated its significance, inserted figures into the plaintiff's copy of the agreement, thereby indicating to him that all was well with the original. The evidence demonstrated that this subsequent act had not been fraudulent but merely a further example of negligence, so that section 32(1)(b) once again did not apply.[53]

---

50. *Ibid.*
51. [1958] 3 All ER 241.
52. (1984) unreported.
53. It is of interest to note that O'Connor LJ expressly confined his decision on this point to the wording of s 26(b) of the 1939 Act, and noted that the position might be different under s 32(1)(b) of the 1980 Act. This reservation appears to have been based on the fact that the word fraud does not appear in the current wording. However, there would appear to be no difference between the 1939 concept of fraudulent concealment and the 1980 wording of deliberate concealment, and O'Connor LJ may merely have been overcautious. Continuing incompetence would appear not to amount to deliberate conduct of any sort.

SUBSEQUENT CONCEALMENT

The difficulty in applying section 32(1)(b) arises in cases in which the defendant has discovered the truth but does nothing to correct the plaintiff's false impression. Here an immediate problem arises under *Tito* v. *Waddell (No 2)*,[54] namely that if time has begun to run, the defendant's failure to correct his negligent advice cannot fall within section 32(1)(b). This issue may not arise frequently in professional liability cases, for two reasons. First, time does not begin to run in such cases until a comparatively late stage.[55] Secondly, there is generally a fiduciary relationship between professional advisers and their clients, so that when the adviser becomes aware of the true facts he is under a duty to disclose them to the client; failure to do so amounts to an independent breach of duty which is capable of founding an action for damages.[56]

In *Sheldon* v. *RHM Outhwaite (Underwriting Agencies) Ltd*[57] the issue of subsequent concealment arose directly for consideration and by a 3 to 2 majority, the House of Lords held that section 32 was capable of applying after the date on which the plaintiff's cause of action has accrued, with the result that the normal limitation period was superseded, to be replaced by a fresh limitation period under section 32. In earlier cases, the issue directly before the House of Lords had been avoided on the basis that the deliberate concealment amounted to a fresh breach of duty, thereby avoiding the problem. For example, in *Kitchen* v. *Royal Air Forces Association*,[58] discussed above, the defendant solicitors, having become aware that their conduct had led to the plaintiff's action being statute barred, did not inform the plaintiff of an offer of compensation from the opposing party for fear of alerting the plaintiff to the possibility that she might have had an action under the Fatal Accidents Act. She did not discover the true facts until the limitation period against the solicitors had expired. It is apparent that the plaintiff's action in negligence against the solicitors had accrued at the point at which information was withheld from her, so that she was technically not entitled to rely upon section 26(b) of the Limitation Act 1939. The Court of Appeal nevertheless unanimously held that it applied to the case, and that the fraudulent concealment was enough to extend the limitation period. There is no satisfactory explanation of the point in the judgments of Lord Evershed MR and Parker LJ, but the most plausible principle emerges from the assertion of Sellers LJ that the defendants' failure to disclose the offer was "a further breach of duty".[59] There is, then, a distinction between a later act of negligence of the *Costa* v. *Georghiou* type, where the defendant was unaware that he had initially broken any duty and thus cannot be said to be intending to cover anything up,[60] and a breach of fiduciary duty.

The same principle appears to have been applied in *UBAF Ltd* v. *European American Banking Corporation*.[61] Here the plaintiffs alleged that they had been induced by the defendants' negligent misrepresentations to become party to a syndicated loan to a debtor

---

54. [1977] Ch 106.
55. See Ch 18.
56. On the recovery of damages for failure to disclose see *Banque Financière de la Cité* v. *Westgate Insurance Ltd* [1989] 2 All ER 952, CA.
57. [1995] 2 All ER 558.
58. [1958] 3 All ER 241.
59. *Ibid* at 253.
60. See also *Bartlett* v. *Barclays Bank Trust Co Ltd* [1980] 1 All ER 139.
61. [1984] 2 All ER 226. See also Ch 18.

who, unknown to them, was a bad risk. The plaintiffs, faced with the argument that time had run against them, pleaded that the defendants had subsequently become aware of the true facts and had failed to disclose them. The Court of Appeal, without pausing to consider whether the plaintiffs' action had accrued before the defendants had become aware of the information and had failed to disclose it, simply held that section 32(1)(b) governed the case, since the defendants had been under a continuing fiduciary duty, so that any failure by them to disclose material facts which they had subsequently discovered amounted to a fresh breach of duty.

It is necessary to make two comments on these cases. The first is that if each failure to disclose is a breach of fiduciary duty, there is no need to pray in aid section 32(1)(b) at all; it must simply be the case that a fresh limitation period begins to run. However, the reasoning in *Kitchen* and *UBAF* seems to assume that each breach of duty takes effect not as a new cause of action but rather as additional damage. It is nevertheless obvious that the *Tito* problem has been sidestepped and glossed over rather than rationalised in terms of the wording of section 32(1)(b). Secondly, if *UBAF* is correct, it would seem to follow that the solicitors in *Kitchen* were in breach of duty not only by failing to disclose the offer to the plaintiff, but in failing to admit to their mistake when they discovered the true facts themselves. It probably suffices to say that the courts have yet to work out the true relationship between post-accrual concealment and the wording of section 32(1)(b).

In *Sheldon* v. *RHM Outhwaite (Underwriting Agencies) Ltd*[62] Lloyd's Names started proceedings in 1992 against a firm of member agents, alleging negligence which had occurred in 1982. Accordingly, on any application of ordinary principles of limitation of actions, those proceedings were out of time. However, it was also alleged that members of the firm of members agents, in 1984, had deliberately concealed important facts relating to its conduct after the date of the alleged act of initial negligence. It was further argued that since the Names had commenced their action as soon as they were aware of the concealment, their action was therefore within the new limitation period created by section 32.

The majority[63] in *Sheldon* held that where there had been deliberate concealment at any stage, the limitation period would not begin to run, even if it would otherwise have commenced at an earlier stage, until the defendants' concealment was discovered or could reasonably have been discovered by the plaintiff. The basis of the decision seems to be policy driven rather than being based upon the strict wording of section 32 itself, as is evident from the reasoning of the minority[64] in the same case. What is apparent from the reasoning of the majority is that section 32 should be interpreted on the basis that it is there to protect the plaintiff against the defendant being able to cover up his wrong-doing by subsequent conduct. According to Lord Keith, the view expressed by Megarry V-C in *Tito* v. *Waddell (No 2)* that section 32(1)(b) cannot operate to prevent time from running once the cause of action has accrued was based on the slightly different wording of the Limitation Act 1939, s 1 which referred to the extension of time limits by virtue of the operation of rules on fraud, concealment and mistake. In contrast, the Limitation Act

62. [1995] 2 All ER 558. See McGee [1995] 111 LQR 580.
63. Lords Keith, Nicholls and Browne-Wilkinson.
64. Lords Lloyd and Mustill.

1980, s 1(2) allows for the "extension or exclusion" of ordinary time limits in accordance with the provisions of Part II of the Act.[65] According to Lord Keith[66]:

"It is clear enough that in so far as paras. (a) and (c) of sub-s (1) are concerned, the ordinary time limits are . . . completely excluded. I am of the opinion that these time limits are similarly excluded in any situation which is covered by the language of para (b), including the situation where the concealment does not take place until after the accrual of the cause of action. The introduction of a time limit commencing at the discovery or imputed discovery of the concealment necessarily involves that time cannot be treated as having started to run from accrual of the cause of action. Sections 2 and 5 are to that extent rendered inapplicable."

The difficulty with this interpretation is that section 32(1)(b) will serve to exclude the primary limitation period whether the concealment occurs one day or 5 years and 11 months after the date on which the primary limitation period would otherwise have cut in. Moreover, applying the logic of Lord Keith's argument, as he admits himself, if the effect of concealment is to *exclude* the primary limitation period, surely an act of concealment some 20 years after the initial damage caused by the breach of duty ought also to exclude the primary limitation period. Although as Lord Keith points out, " . . . it is not conceivable that a defendant would set out to conceal facts relevant to a cause of action when more than six years has elapsed since its accrual".[67]

In similar vein Lord Browne-Wilkinson also thought that an act of subsequent concealment falls within the literal meaning of section 32(1)(b), so that the primary limitation period is "excluded" by virtue of the effect of section 1(2). From this it follows that there is only one limitation period, namely that in section 32.[68]

All this may be very well in terms of desirable policy, but as Lord Lloyd pointed out in his dissenting judgment, the majority in *Sheldon* did not have very close regard to the precise wording of section 32(1)(b). As Lord Lloyd observes, section 28 is concerned with *extending* time limits in the case of disability, as does section 34 in relation to arbitration and section 33 is even more emphatic when dealing with the matter of the court's discretion and giving it the power to order that the special time limits under sections 11 and 13 are *excluded altogether.*[69] In contrast, section 32 refers only to *postponement* of a limitation period, which by definition can only be effected by prior concealment rather than subsequent concealment of relevant facts. As Lord Lloyd notes, had it been the intention of Parliament to allow for subsequent events, they could have used the language employed in section 29(5) when dealing with subsequent acts such as the part payment or acknowledgement of a debt, but Parliament did not do this.[70]

(f) Mistake

Under section 32(1)(c) the ordinary limitation period can be lengthened by reason of a mistake. Unlike the expansive interpretation given to section 32(1)(c) in *Sheldon* v. *Outhwaite*, considered in the previous section, it is clear that what is referred to here is a

---

65. [1995] 2 All ER 558 at 564. See also Lord Nicholls at 576 who opines that the words "shall not begin to run" in s 32(1)(b) should be read as "shall not run".
66. *Ibid.*
67. *Ibid.*
68. *Ibid* at 565.
69. *Ibid* at 569.
70. *Ibid* at 570.

mistake which is the basis of the cause of action itself. In *Phillips-Higgins* v. *Harper*[71] the plaintiff and the defendant were both solicitors who had connections with a legal practice run by the defendant, but from which the plaintiff was entitled to a share of profits. The plaintiff's action arose out of a dispute as to the plaintiff's entitlement to that share of profits. The plaintiff sued for an account, but ordinarily part of the period covered by the account would have fallen foul of the primary limitation period. However, the plaintiff argued that she was mistaken as to the amount of the profits to which she was entitled. Pearson J held that section 32(1)(c) was inapplicable on the ground that the type of mistake envisaged by paragraph (c) was no more than a mistake which formed an essential ingredient in the cause of action. Accordingly, the types of mistake which will suffice will include an operative mistake of fact which renders a contract void or a mistake which allows for restitutionary recovery of moneys paid. In *Phillips-Higgins* v. *Harper* the reason why the mistake was irrelevant was that the action was one for sums due and it did not matter whether there was a mistake or not. As was observed by Pearson J about the operation of what is now section 32(1)(c),[72]

"The right of action is for relief from the consequences of a mistake. It seems to me that this wording is carefully chosen to indicate a class of actions where a mistake has been made which has certain consequences and the plaintiff seeks to be relieved from those consequences . . .

In my opinion the mere operation of the Limitation Act unless excluded by the operation of this section is not a relevant consequence for the purposes of this section. If it were, then any concealment of a right of action from the plaintiff would be intended to be covered by this section and the provision (b) in respect of fraud [now deliberate concealment] should have been applied to mistake also."

Phillips-Higgins v. *Harper* has been the subject of quite strong criticism,[73] especially on the ground that there is much in the decision in *Re Diplock*[74] which militates against the decision arrived at by Pearson J. In *Re Diplock* the Court of Appeal seemed content to assume that a mistake on the part of a personal representative in distributing the estate of the deceased could postpone the running of time against the next of kin. It was clear from the judgments that mistake was not an essential ingredient in the cause of action since the action was based on receipt of property to which the recipients of the estate were not entitled. Sadly, the comments made in this context[75] were *obiter* since, in the event, the action was regarded as one in respect of the administration of personal estates[76] rather than one in respect of moneys had and received.[77]

While an operative mistake which renders a contract void at common law is undoubtedly covered by section 32(1)(c), it also has to be appreciated that the effect of a mistake in equity is to render a contract voidable. What is now section 32(1)(c) was intended as an attempt to codify the position in equity in relation to actionable mistakes. For these purposes, it was held in *Baker* v. *Courage & Co*[78] that a distinction must be drawn between cases in which both parties are mistaken and cases of unilateral mistake.

---

71. [1954] 1 QB 411.

72. *Ibid* at 418. See also *Singer* v. *Harrison Clark (a firm)* (1987) unreported: mistake not an ingredient in an action for professional negligence in causing a client to lose the benefit of an option to renew a lease.

73. See Goff & Jones, *The Law of Restitution,* 4th ed, 1993, p 769.

74. [1948] Ch 465.

75. *Ibid* at 514–16.

76. Covered by the Limitation Act 1980, s 22.

77. Covered by the Limitation Act 1980, s 5.

78. [1910] 1 KB 56.

According to Hamilton J, in cases of common and mutual mistake, where both parties are mistaken, time will run as soon as the mistake is operative. Thus in cases in which money is paid under a mistake, time will run as from the date of payment. In the case of a unilateral mistake, typically a mistake induced by the actions or words of the defendant, time will not run against the plaintiff until he is aware of the mistake.

It should be emphasised that this analysis was provided in 1910 and that the law might have changed for the purposes of the Limitation Act 1980, since there is no reference in section 32(1)(c) to different classes of mistake. All that paragraph (c) requires is that the mistake has been discovered or should have been discovered, at which point time begins to run against the plaintiff.

At this point, it might be considered whether the law in respect of mistake is really moving in the right direction. In one respect, the Limitation Act 1980 is out of date, in that sections 2 and 5 deal specifically with actions based on breach of a tortious duty and actions for breach of contract, but neither makes specific reference to the third branch of the common (and equitable) law of obligations, namely, the law of restitution.[79] Since the law of restitution has only recently been officially recognised[80] it is understandable that there is no specific provision for what, properly, should be regarded as restitutionary remedies in the 1980 Act: but it is perhaps time that relevant provision should be made.

It is important to emphasise that since the law of restitution is concerned with the restoration to the plaintiff of benefits which the defendant is not, in conscience, entitled to receive, there is a difference between restitutionary claims and those founded in tort and contract law. So far as tortious and contractual claims are concerned, the principal issue is one of compensation for damage suffered, losses caused or gains prevented.

If the principal issue in a restitutionary claim is concerned with the wrongful retention of a benefit resulting from a mistake, then it would seem to follow that time should not run against the plaintiff until he is, or ought to be, aware of the fact of the enrichment. On this basis, simple receipt of a benefit by the defendant should be irrelevant, despite the fact that the decision in *Maskell* v. *Horner*[81] decides otherwise, even in the face of very prompt action as soon as it was discovered by the plaintiff that the defendant had no right to levy toll charges at the market at which he had worked for a period of 12 years. Because the contractual limitation period was applied, all the plaintiff was able to recover were the payments made in the six years preceding the date on which the writ was issued. Had the case been dealt with by reference to the equitable doctrine of laches,[82] time would not have started to run against the plaintiff until such time as the plaintiff was free of any undue influence exercised by the defendant. But this was an action at common law and what were effectively contractual principles came to be applied.

In terms of the development of equitable principles, there seems to have been almost slavish obedience to rules contained in successive Limitation Acts so far as the issue of fraud is concerned, but the same is not true of cases of mistake outside a purely contractual

---

79. See McLean, "Limitation of Actions in Restitution" (1989) 48 CLJ 472, especially at 479–81 and 494–95.
80. *Lipkin Gorman* v. *Karpnale* [1991] 2 AC 548.
81. [1915] 3 KB 106.
82. See Ch 3.

context.[83] However, the same could not be said of mistake in the context of a contractual relationship.[84]

In a restitutionary claim, the injustice of allowing the defendant to retain the benefit he has received remains intact so long as the plaintiff is unaware of the mistake which keeps him in the dark about the state of affairs, especially where the mistake is responsible for depriving the plaintiff of the relevant facts and it is a mistake in respect of which he bears no fault.

The most detailed analysis of the effect of section 32(1)(c) is to be found in *Peco Arts Inc* v. *Hazlitt Gallery Ltd*[85] where the principal issue was whether the plaintiff could with reasonable diligence have been aware of a mistake as to the history of a work of art purchased from the defendant. It was common ground that both parties believed the drawing was an original by Ingres. On the basis of the analysis in *Baker* v. *Courage & Co Ltd*, considered above, time would run from the date when the common mistake became operative. However, Webster J made a number of comments, *obiter*, which reflected upon the types of mistake which might fall within the provisions of section 32(1)(c) which seem to limit the scope of its operation, perhaps with a view to providing peace of mind to those who work in the art world in the light of the decision at which he eventually arrived. The fact that the plaintiff could not reasonably have discovered the mistake meant that she was entitled to rescission of the contract. However Webster J opined that this did not mean that every mistaken attribution of a painting is caught by section 32(1)(c). The reason for this is that if there is a condition or a warranty as to attribution, only the seller is mistaken, in which case, the buyer has not paid money under a mistake.[86] Moreover, there is even an implication in Webster J's judgment to the effect that any form of mistaken, but bona fide, attribution which constitutes a term of the contract will not be covered by section 32.[87] This last suggestion seems difficult to accept since if there is a remedy for breach of contract, there seems to be no reason why section 32 should not apply to the limitation period in section 5.

So far as section 32(1)(c) is concerned, it is important to emphasise that the ground on which the running of time is extended is that of mistake, rather than any other particular conduct on the part of the defendant. Thus in *Ridyard* v. *Hoath*[88] it was argued for the plaintiff that wilful delay on the part of the defendant which induced the plaintiff to delay the commencement of proceedings fell within section 32. However, Lloyd LJ held that the language of section 32 must be read literally and that since there is no reference to wilful delay on the part of the defendant, this is not a matter which can be considered when determining whether the limitation period can be extended in favour of the plaintiff.

A particular problem which may arise in relation to mistakes is that, in the event of a transfer of property to a third party, that third party may acquire an interest in goods or land as a consequence of the mistake. Clearly this is a matter which requires attention, since the exercise of the power to extend a limitation period under section 32 will have adverse conseqences so far as the third party is concerned.

---

83. See *Randall* v. *Errington* (1805) 10 Ves 423.
84. See *Re Robinson* [1911] 1 Ch 502.
85. [1983] 1 WLR 1315.
86. *Ibid* at 1327.
87. *Ibid*.
88. (1987) (unreported).

Sections 32(3) and 32(4) deal with the situation in which an innocent third party has purchased property in good faith and for value. For these purposes, an innocent party is defined differently according to whether the court is concerned with the issue of fraud or concealment on the one hand or mistake on the other. For the purposes of cases of fraud or deliberate concealment, an innocent party is someone who is not a party to the fraud or concealment and who, at the time of purchase, has neither actual nor constructive knowledge of the fraud or concealment.[89] For the purposes of cases of mistake, an innocent party is one who has, at the time of purchase, no knowledge or reason to believe that the mistake had been made.[90]

The effect of section 32(3) is that section 32 will not work in favour of the plaintiff so as to allow the recovery of any property or the value of that property or to enforce any charge against property, or set aside any transaction affecting property, as against a *bona fide* purchaser for value.

One matter not specifically referred to in section 32(3) is whether a personal action for damages for conversion remains a possibility. However, it has since been confirmed that the wording of section 32(3) is sufficiently broad to encompass such an action, which is also barred where third party rights have accrued.[91]

---

89. Limitation Act 1980, s 32(4)(a).
90. Limitation Act 1980, s 32(4)(b).
91. *Eddis* v. *Chichester Constable* [1969] 2 Ch 345.

CHAPTER 7

PLEADING AND PROCEDURE

THE BURDEN OF PROOF ON THE PARTIES

A cardinal principle governing limitation of actions is that the court will not of its own motion strike out an action which is time barred. In general, it is for the defendant to raise the limitation issue by way of defence. The point was emphatically stated by Lord Cairns LC in *Dawkins* v. *Penrhyn (Lord)*[1] that: "It cannot be predicated, that the defendant will appeal to the Statute of Limitations for his protection; many people, or some people at all events, do not do so; therefore you must wait to hear from the defendant whether he desires to avail himself of the defence of the Statute of Limitations or not."[2]

The rationale here is that rather than being prescriptive in effect,[3] the statute merely operates to bar a plaintiff's remedy rather than the cause of action itself. It might be supposed that in initiating an action, the plaintiff would ordinarily seek determination of the limitation issue from the outset as part of the statement of claim since it is a corner-stone of the English law of evidence that he who alleges must prove.[4] It would seemingly follow, therefore, that bringing a time barred action is tantamount to bringing no action at all.[5] However, in *Ronex Properties Ltd* v. *John Laing Construction Ltd*[6] the Court of Appeal held that where there is a defence under the Limitation Act, the defendant can

---

1. (1878) 4 App Cas 51. See also, *Thursby* v. *Warren* (1628) Cro Car 159; *Stile* v. *Finch* (1634) Cro Car 384; *Hawkings* v. *Billhead* (1635) Cro Car 404; *Holland* v. *Yates Building Co Ltd, The Times,* 16 November 1989, CA. See further, RSC Ord 18, r 8(1) which states that it is for the defendant to plead the Act specifically.

2. *Ibid* at 59. Applied by the Court of Appeal in *Dismore* v. *Milton* [1938] 3 All ER 762, in which Greer LJ said at 763: "It may well be desirable to put an early end to actions which perhaps never ought to have been brought, but, as the law stands, the plaintiff may wait for the defendant to plead the statute of limitations, and, if the latter does so, he may be able in his reply to show that the case comes within one of the exceptions." In *Walkley* v. *Precision Forgings Ltd* [1979] 2 All ER 548 at 558, Lord Diplock stated that: "Despite the phraseology 'an action shall not be brought', it is trite law that technically a Limitation Act does not prevent the commencement of an action by the plaintiff after the limitation period has expired. What it does is to provide the defendant with a cast-iron defence if he chooses to avail himself of it; which he may do either by pleading it, or in a case where the action is indisputably statute-barred, by taking out a summons to have it dismissed as vexatious."

3. Subject to exceptions, see for example, conversion: s 3(2) of the Limitation Act 1980 (*infra,* Ch 22); the 10-year long-stop period introduced by s 11A of the Consumer Protection Act 1987 (*infra,* Ch 21); title to land: s 17 of the Limitation Act 1980 (*infra,* Ch 23). In cases of land, the expiry of the limitation period operates to extinguish the plaintiff's title to the land in question.

4. In *Robins* v. *National Trust Co* [1927] AC 515 at 520 Viscount Dunedin stated the principle thus: "Onus is always on a person who asserts a proposition or fact which is not self evident." See, also, *Crocker* v. *British Coal Corporation, The Times,* 5 July 1995. See further, Cross and Tapper, *Evidence,* (London: Butterworths, 1995) at 115 *et seq*; Phipson, *Evidence* 14th ed (London: Sweet & Maxwell, 1990) at para 4–02.

5. This certainly seems to have been the contention of the defendant in *Dismore* v. *Milton* [1938] 3 All ER 762, CA; see also, *Dawkins* v. *Penrhyn, supra,* fn 1.

6. [1983] 1 QB 398; [1982] 3 All ER 961.

either plead that defence and seek the trial of a preliminary issue or, in a very clear case, he or she can seek to strike out the claim on the ground that it is frivolous, vexatious and an abuse of the process of the court and support his or her claim with evidence.[7] But in no circumstances can the defendant seek to strike out on the ground that no cause of action is disclosed.[8] Donaldson LJ stated that:

"Authority apart, I would have thought that it was absurd to contend that a writ or third party notice could be struck out as disclosing no cause of action merely because the defendant may have a defence under the Limitation Acts. Whilst it is possible to have a contractual provision whereby the effluxion of time eliminates a cause of action and there are some provisions of foreign law that can have that effect, it is trite law that the English Limitation Acts bar the remedy and not the right, and furthermore that they do not even have this effect unless and until pleaded."[9]

Accordingly, when the defendant pleads the 1980 Act, the burden of proof shifts to the plaintiff who must demonstrate why the action is not in fact time barred.[10] The plaintiff must therefore show that the cause of action accrued within the time period in question. This issue may sometimes give rise to difficulties. For example, in *Darley Main Colliery Company* v. *Mitchell*[11] the plaintiff's land suffered subsidence and consequent damage was caused to his cottages as a result of the defendants' coal mining operations. This occurred in 1868 and the defendants, having admitted liability, repaired the damaged buildings. The defendants did not work the coal again after 1868, but in 1882, as a result of coal mining operations being carried out in the next adjoining land by a third party, a further subsidence occurred which again resulted in damage to the cottages. The defendants admitted that if the coal under the plaintiff's land had not been excavated in the first place, or if they had left sufficient support under the plaintiff's land, then the later coal mining operations would not have caused damage. However, the defendants contended that the cause of action in respect of the subsequent subsidence accrued in 1868 and was therefore time barred on the basis that in 1868 the plaintiff could and ought to have insisted on recovering once and for all any damage that might arise prospectively. Rejecting this contention, the House of Lords held that time did not begin to run against the plaintiff until the subsequent subsidence occurred. He could therefore maintain his action

7. Under RSC Ord 18, r 19(1) the power to strike out any pleading or the indorsement of any writ in the action or anything contained therein is exercisable: "on the ground that—(a) it discloses no reasonable cause of action or defence, as the case may be; or (b) it is scandalous, frivolous or vexatious; or (c) it may prejudice, embarrass or delay the fair trial of the action; or (d) it is otherwise an abuse of the process of the court . . . ".
8. See also, *F* v. *Wirral Metropolitan Borough Council and Liverpool City Council* [1991] 2 WLR 1132, CA. Cf *Wilby* v. *Henman* (1834) 2 Cr & M 658 and *Barclays Bank* v. *Walters*, *The Times*, 20 October 1988, CA.
9. *Supra*, fn 6, at 965. It should be noted, however, that *Kennett* v. *Brown* has since been overruled, see *Welsh Development Agency* v. *Redpath Dorman Long Ltd* [1994] 4 All ER 10.
10. *Cartledge* v. *E Jopling & Sons Ltd* [1963] AC 758; *London Congregational Union Inc* v. *Harriss & Harriss* [1988] 1 All ER 15.
11. (1886) 11 App Cas 127. Similarly, in *Ketteman* v. *Hansel Properties Ltd* [1985] 1 All ER 352 the principal question before the Court of Appeal was formulated by Lawton LJ at 356 as being: "When a building has faulty foundations due to negligence, giving rise either to subsequent structural damage or the need to take remedial action to avoid such damage, when does the cause of action accrue?" It was held that the cause of action accrued when the physical damage occurred, which was when the cracks in the walls appeared (on the facts, within the six year limitation period). Accordingly, the defendants' contention that the houses were "doomed from the start" (i.e. the date when they were transferred), and that this should be taken as the date when the cause of action accrued, was rejected. In *Pirelli General Cable Works Ltd* v. *Oscar Faber & Partners* [1983] 2 AC 1 at 18 Lord Fraser, commenting on the "doomed from the start" argument, observed that: "Such cases, if they exist, would be exceptional".

even though more than six years had passed since the last mining operations had been carried out by the defendants. Lord FitzGerald stated that:

"There was a complete cause of action in 1868, in respect of which compensation was given, but there was a liability to further disturbance. The defendants permitted the state of things to continue without taking any steps to prevent the occurrence of any future injury. A fresh subsidence took place, causing a new and further disturbance of the plaintiff's enjoyment, which gave him a new and distinct cause of action . . . it follows that the cause of action now insisted on by the plaintiff is not the same cause of action as that of 1868, but in point of law, as it is physically, a new and independent cause of action arising in 1882, and to which the defence of the Statute of Limitations is not applicable."[12]

Similarly, in *London Congregational Union Inc* v. *Harriss & Harriss*[13] the plaintiffs employed the defendants, a firm of architects, to design and supervise the construction of a church hall. Practical completion took place in January 1970 and final completion by the end of 1970. In August 1971 the hall was damaged by flooding during a storm which had caused the sewer in the street adjacent to the building to overflow. Further, damage was caused to the hall's interior plaster because the defendants had failed to install a damp-proof course. By mid-1975 flooding had occurred on 11 separate occasions and the plaintiffs stopped using the hall after August 1978. The plaintiffs sued the defendants claiming damages for negligence in the design of the drainage system and failure to install a damp-proof course. The defendants denied negligence and pleaded that the building was "doomed from the start" so that the plaintiffs' cause of action accrued when the building was erected, which was more than six years before the action was brought. The Court of Appeal held that where the consequences arising from a building defect were not immediately effective, the plaintiffs' cause of action did not accrue until the damage actually occurred. The court reasoned that the defect in the drainage design was latent and therefore distinct from the subsequent physical damage which gave rise to the cause of action.

However, in *Driscoll-Varley* v. *Parkside Health Authority*[14] the plaintiff, who had been assaulted by her husband, received medical treatment which she contended had aggravated her condition. She therefore brought an action in negligence, and the issue was whether the three-year time limit which starts to run from the later of the dates when the cause of action accrues and the date of knowledge (if later), as laid down by section 11(4) of the 1980 Act, had expired. She argued that it was only at a late stage of the treatment that she realised her condition was getting worse. It was held that the plaintiff should establish at the outset that the cause of action accrued within three years, so that thereafter the burden of proof shifted to the defendant to rebut this. It is submitted that this approach is correct where the limitation period is prescriptive in its effect.[15] Further, where it can be sensibly anticipated that the statute will be pleaded by way of defence, it is tactically efficient to pre-empt the plea by disposing of the issue in the statement of claim. However, the question of which party bears the burden of proof may of course depend upon the particular limitation period in issue as where, for example, the plaintiff seeks the exercise

12. *Ibid* at 151. Lord Blackburn, dissenting, found that the plaintiff had failed to establish that the cause of action accrued within the requisite time period. His Lordship, at p 139, rejected the notion "that there are fresh causes of action at each fresh subsidence arising from the old disturbance of the strata occasioning fresh damage to the same property".

13. *Supra*, fn 10.

14. [1991] 2 Med LR 346.

15. See fn 3, *supra*, and associated text.

of judicial discretion. Thus in *Beer* v. *London Borough of Waltham Forest*,[16] which involved an application under section 33 of the 1980 Act[17] for the court to exercise its discretion to "disapply" sections 11 and 12,[18] Hodgson J opined that the plaintiff should bear the burden of proof. This is examined further below.

SECTION 33[19] AND PRE-TRIAL DISCOVERY: PROCEDURAL ISSUES

As seen above, section 33 of the 1980 Act gives the court discretion in personal injury claims to exclude the time limits imposed by sections 11 and 12, where "it appears to the court that it would equitable to allow an action to proceed . . . "[20] In the exercise of its discretion the court is directed to have regard to the degree to which the three-year limitation period would prejudice the plaintiff, or any person whom he represents, and the prejudice which might be caused to the defendant, or any person whom he represents, by the exclusion of the time limits.[21]

This section should be read in the context of section 33(2) of the Supreme Court Act 1981 which allows a would-be plaintiff who is contemplating instituting proceedings in respect of personal injuries to apply for pre-trial discovery.[22] The interrelationship between section 33 of the Limitation Act 1980 and section 33(2) of the 1981 Act was considered by the Court of Appeal in *Harris* v. *Newcastle-Upon-Tyne Health Authority*.[23] In 1961 and 1965 the plaintiff underwent eye operations to correct a squint, in hospitals administered by the defendants. The surgery apparently left her eyelid partially closed and increasingly painful. In 1987 she had a medical examination in the course of which it was suggested to her that the problem with her eyelid was not of natural origin. She therefore considered bringing proceedings against the defendants and sought disclosure of her medical records. The defendants resisted her application for pre-action discovery on the basis that any prospective claim would be defeated by their proposed defence under the Limitation Act 1980. It was held that "ill-founded, irresponsible and speculative allegations or allegations based merely on hope would not provide a reasonable basis for an intended claim in subsequent proceedings".[24] However, the court concluded that where it was satisfied that facts material to such an action might emerge on discovery which would

16. 16 December, 1987, unreported.

17. See fn 20 *infra*, and associated text.

18. Sections 11 and 12 specify a three-year time limit within which proceedings which consist of or include an action in respect of personal injuries or death must be brought. The sections specify the date from which time is to run for the purposes of calculating the three-year time limit. See Ch 19.

19. This provision is examined further in Ch 19.

20. Section 33(1).

21. Section 33(1)(a) and (b). See *Hodgson* v. *Stockton Casting Co Ltd* [1997] 8 CL 67.

22. Section 33(2) of the Supreme Court Act 1981 provides: "On the application, in accordance with the rules of court, of a person who appears to the High Court to be likely to be a party to subsequent proceedings in that court in which a claim in respect of personal injuries to a person . . . is likely to be made, the High Court shall, in such circumstances as may be specified in the rules, have power to order a person who appears to the court to be likely to be a party to the proceedings and to be likely to have or to have had in his possession, custody or power any documents which are relevant to an issue arising or likely to arise out of that claim—(a) to disclose whether those documents are in his possession, custody or power; and (b) to produce such of those documents . . . ".

23. [1989] 1 WLR 96.

24. *Ibid* at 99, *per* Kerr LJ, citing James LJ in *Dunning* v. *United Liverpool Hospitals' Board of Governors* [1973] 1 WLR 586 at 593.

be also be relevant to the court in exercising its discretion under section 33 of the 1980 Act to disapply the relevant limitation period, the prospective action could not be described as doomed to failure. Accordingly, the plaintiff's application was allowed. The general principle to be applied was stated by Kerr LJ, who said:

" . . . since section 33 of the Limitation Act 1980 applies to all personal injury actions and is therefore always a longstop to a plea of limitation in such actions, and since applications for pre-trial discovery can also only be made in claims for personal injury, apart from death, one must obviously take account of section 33 before one can conclude that an action is so clearly bound to be defeated by plea of limitation as to be within the kind of situation which James LJ envisaged in that passage."[25]

DETERMINATION OF THE LIMITATION ISSUE

The rules governing the determination of whether or not a judgment or order is to be treated as final or interlocutory are contained in RSC, Order 59, rule 1A which provides, in so far as is relevant to limitation of actions:

"(1) For all purposes connected with appeals to the Court of Appeal, a judgment or order shall be treated as final or interlocutory in accordance with the following provisions of this rule . . .

(3) A judgment or order shall be treated as final if the entire cause or matter would (subject only to any possible appeal) have been finally determined whichever way the court below had decided the issues before it.

(4) For the purposes of paragraph (3), where the final hearing or the trial of a cause or matter is divided into parts, a judgment or order made at the end of any part shall be treated as if made at the end of the complete hearing or trial . . .

(6) Notwithstanding anything in paragraph 3 . . . the following judgments and orders shall be treated as interlocutory—[paragraphs (a)–(e) are not relevant for present purposes]

(ff) an order determining an issue as to limitation of actions other than as part of a final judgment or order within the meaning of paragraph (3)."

Consequently, the determination of the date of accrual of the cause of action is deemed to be interlocutory, unless part of the final judgment. However, an application to disapply the relevant limitation period pursuant to section 33 of the 1980 Act will be treated as final.[26] The practical implications of this rule were considered in *Hughes* v. *Jones*,[27] in which the plaintiff, who had suffered personal injuries in a motor accident, failed to institute proceedings within the three-year limitation period. It was accepted that this was due largely to the somewhat desultory correspondence which had been passing between the parties. The plaintiff's application under section 33 to the district judge to "disapply" the limitation period was rejected and her appeal to the county court was unsuccessful. On appeal to the Court of Appeal, it was observed that both parties, and the district judge in question, had apparently proceeded on the basis that the issue was an interlocutory matter. Henry LJ noted the apparent divergence between the law as laid down in binding authorities,[28] and the practice of county courts throughout England and Wales of treating section 33 applications as interlocutory, which carried the consequence that large numbers of

25. *Ibid* at 101–102.
26. *White* v. *Brunton* [1984] 1 QB 570; *Dale* v. *British Coal Corporation* [1992] 1 WLR 964.
27. *The Times*, 18 July 1996, CA.
28. *Supra*, fn 26.

district judges had been acting without jurisdiction. In holding that the case should be remitted back to the county court judge for directions, the court went on to reaffirm that such applications were final so that judge, when making such an order:

" . . . must, having regard to the significance that is attached to his exercise of discretion, set out clearly the reasons why he has exercised the discretion, both dealing with the matters that he took into account, and those he was statutorily required to take into account . . . The bare note of his reasons did not seem to satisfy that requirement. It followed that the plaintiff did not have a proper final hearing."[29]

DISPOSING OF THE LIMITATION PLEA

(a) Preliminary issues

Generally, after close of pleadings either party can apply on the summons for directions for an order that the limitation defence be tried as a preliminary issue.[30] The defendant is likely to adopt this approach where it is considered that the defence is well founded. Whether or not such an order is made is within the discretion of the court, and a preliminary issue will not be granted unless it is clear that this is the most advantageous means of expediting the issue having regard to the facts and circumstances of the case.[31]

On the trial of a preliminary issue the court can only proceed on the basis of the facts pleaded with the consequence that there may be insufficient evidence to resolve the limitation issue. Thus, in *National Bank of Commerce* v. *National Westminster Bank*[32] Webster J stressed that:

"It may well be that a limitations point can only be conveniently tried as a preliminary issue where the only cause or causes of action upon which the plaintiff can rely appear clearly on the face of the pleadings and where the question whether a whole or part of the action is statute barred can be decided without any reference to evidence or the history of the relationship between the parties."[33]

(b) The trial

Where the success of the defence is doubtful, the defendant may, exceptionally, choose to leave the issue for consideration at the full trial. This is less desirable than having the limitation point tried as a separate issue as it will certainly impact adversely on the issue of costs. The point was made by Lord Wilberforce in *Walkley* v. *Precision Forgings Ltd*[34] that: "[T]he predominant interest in these matters (all the more when the plaintiff is, as

---

29. *Supra*, fn 27, *per* Henry LJ.
30. See *Ronex Properties Ltd* v. *John Laing Construction Ltd* [1983] 1 QB 398. In an action in respect of personal injuries, where the directions of Ord 25, r 8 apply instead of the summons for directions, a separate application has to be made.
31. *Chelmsford District Council* v. *Evers* (1983) 25 Build LR 99.
32. [1990] 2 Lloyd's Rep 514.
33. *Ibid* at 519.
34. [1979] 2 All ER 548.

here, legally aided) is to dispose of any issue under the Limitation Act as expeditiously as possible."[35]

(c) Closing speeches

The defence of limitation should be pleaded expeditiously. Consequently, leaving it until closing speeches may result in the judge disallowing the plea. In this respect, it has been held by the Court of Appeal that whether or not leave will be granted to enter a late plea lies within the judge's discretion.[36] In *Ketteman* v. *Hansel Properties Ltd*[37] the defendant argued that a judge was bound to allow an amendment no matter how late it was, provided the other party could be properly compensated by an award of costs.[38] However, Lord Griffiths emphatically rejected this contention, and held that if a defendant wishes to plead that an action is time barred, this should be pleaded in the defence. He said:

" ... today it is not the practice invariably to allow a defence which is wholly different from that pleaded to be raised by amendment at the end of the trial even on terms that an adjournment is granted and that the defendant pays all the costs thrown away ... But justice cannot always be measured in terms of money ... Furthermore to allow an amendment before a trial begins is quite different from allowing it at the end of the trial to give an apparently unsuccessful defendant an opportunity to renew the fight on an entirely different defence."[39]

THE WRIT

Failure to serve the writ in time—RSC Order 6, rule 8

Order 6, rule 8(1)(c) provides that a writ is valid for a period of four months from the date of its issue and must be served on the defendant at any time during that period.[40] The issue of a writ operates to suspend the relevant limitation period for the duration of its validity. For the purposes of calculating time, the date on which the writ is issued is taken into account. Rule 8 confers on the court discretion to extend the validity of a writ for an additional period of four months and in this regard, successive extensions may be granted by the court. An application for extension can be made before or after the writ's validity has expired.

The scope of the court's discretion under Order 6, rule 8 was subjected to detailed scrutiny by the House of Lords in *Kleinwort Benson Ltd* v. *Barbrak Ltd, The Myrto (No 3)*.[41] The plaintiff bank was the mortgagee of a ship and brought proceedings *in rem*

---

35. *Ibid* at 551.
36. *Lewis* v. *Hackney London Borough Council*, 9 April, 1990, unreported.
37. [1987] 1 AC 189.
38. See *Clarapede & Co* v. *Commercial Union Association* (1883) 32 WR 262.
39. *Supra*, fn 37, at 220. Cf *Easton* v. *Ford Motor Co Ltd* [1993] 1 WLR 1511 CA.
40. For writs to be served out of jurisdiction, the validity period is extended to six months (RSC (Amendment No 4) 1989 No 2427).
41. [1987] AC 597, HL. See also, *Jones* v. *Jones* [1970] 2 QB 576. See further, the judgment of Lord Denning MR in *Baker* v. *Bowketts Cakes Ltd* [1966] 1 WLR 861 at 866. See also *Waddon* v. *Whitecroft-Scovill Ltd* [1988] 1 WLR 309, HL.

against the ship to enforce its security and arrested it. The bank had unsuccessfully attempted to reach a settlement with the 141 owners of the ship's cargo in respect of the costs incurred by the bank in unloading the vessel so that it could be sold. It therefore brought a test action against the largest cargo owner to establish the principle that all of the cargo owners were liable to meet the unloading costs. Since this action would not come to trial until after the bank's claim against the other cargo owners would be time barred, the plaintiff bank subsequently issued an omnibus writ against the other owners, their insurers or guarantors. To save costs, this writ was not served. An extension was therefore granted to the plaintiff, *ex parte*. After judgment was given in favour of the plaintiff in its test case brought against the largest cargo owner, it was granted a further extension of the writ for three months to allow time for the bank to calculate the exact amount due from each cargo owner (the defendants in the omnibus writ). The bank then served the writ. The respondents, who were four of the cargo owners, applied to the court to have the two extensions of the validity of the writ set aside. The Admiralty Registrar and the Admiralty judge dismissed their application. The respondents appealed successfully to the Court of Appeal which set aside the service of the writ on the ground that there had been no difficulty in serving it and therefore the writ could not be validly extended. The bank appealed successfully to the House of Lords.

It was held that the power to extend the validity of a writ under Order 6, rule 8 was not limited to exceptional cases only, but could be exercised if, having balanced the hardship caused to the plaintiff were an extension to be refused against the hardship caused to the defendant were it to be granted, there was good reason to do so. Further, where an application is made for an extension after the writ had ceased to be valid and the relevant limitation period had expired, the applicant must give a satisfactory explanation of his failure to apply during the currency of the writ. In the present case, since the extensions in question saved unnecessary proceedings and costs without occasioning prejudice to the respondents, they should not be set aside.

Lord Brandon identified three main categories of cases where a writ which has been issued before the relevant limitation period has expired is then subject to an application to the court for an extension of its validity. The three categories are:

(1) Cases where the application for extension is made at a time when the writ is still valid and before the limitation period has expired.
(2) Cases where the application for extension is made at a time when the writ is still valid but the relevant limitation period has expired.
(3) Cases where the application for extension is made at a time when the writ has ceased to be valid and the relevant limitation period has expired.

His Lordship noted that in cases falling within categories (1) and (2) it is still possible for the plaintiff to serve the writ before its validity expires, and the defendant will not be able to rely on a defence of limitation. Also, in category (1) cases but not category (2) cases, it is possible for the plaintiff to issue a fresh writ before the original writ ceases to be valid so that time will begin to run again. In cases falling within category (3) it is not possible for the plaintiff to serve the writ effectively unless its validity is first retrospectively extended. Further, in cases falling within this final category, the defendant will have an accrued right of limitation and therefore the court's discretion will only be exercised where the plaintiff satisfies the court that there was good reason why he failed to seek an extension during the period of the writ's validity.[42] However, Lord Brandon said that the fact that a defendant has an accrued right of limitation at the time when an application is made to the court to extend the writ's validity should not be regarded as the only significant factor in relation to such an extension.

In construing Order 6, rule 8 Lord Brandon observed that its predecessor (Order 8, rule 1, replaced by the current rule in 1962) made the exercise by the court of its power to renew a writ conditional on the court being satisfied that "reasonable efforts have been made to serve the [writ] or for other good reason, it should be renewed". His Lordship, having reviewed the authorities,[43] concluded that:

"I consider, therefore, that there must be implied in the new rule, as a matter of construction, a condition that the power to extend shall only be exercised for good reason . . . I think on the whole that it has been unhelpful to put the condition for extension as high as 'exceptional circumstances', an expression which conveys to my mind at any rate a large degree of stringency. The old rule in force until 1962 referred to 'any other good reason', and I think that the new rule should be interpreted as requiring 'good reason' and no more . . . Whether there is or is not good reason in any particular case must depend on all the circumstances of that case, and must therefore be left to the judgment of the judge who deals either with an *ex parte* application by a plaintiff for the grant of an extension, or with an *inter partes* application by a defendant to set aside an extension previously granted *ex parte*."[44]

Obvious examples of "good reason" for granting an extension of the validity of the writ would be where the defendant has been avoiding service or where his or her address is unknown.[45] Clearly, no definitive categorisation can be made of the grounds constituting "good reason". However, the fact that the parties have been engaged in pre-trial settlement negotiations will not in itself be a good reason even though there may have been an implied agreement between the parties deferring service of the writ.[46]

PROCEDURAL DELAYS

(a) Amending the writ or pleadings—RSC Order 20, rule 5 and section 35 of the Limitation Act 1980

Substantive and procedural issues arise where the plaintiff wishes to amend the writ, or where either party wishes to amend the subsequent pleadings. Although the writ may be amended once before it has been served on the defendant without the need to obtain the court's leave, any subsequent amendments must be made in accordance with RSC Order 20, rule 5(1), which provides:

---

42. In *Waddon* v. *Whitecroft-Scovill Ltd* [1988] 1 WLR 309, Lord Brandon rejected the plaintiff's contention that the fact that he applied for the extension prior to the writ's expiry should be counted in his favour. His Lordship said that the failure to seek an extension before the writ's expiry merely placed an additional hurdle against the plaintiff. In *Rogers* v. *Messrs Trethowans*, 23 February 1989, CA, unreported, the Court of Appeal expressed the view that category (1) cases should be treated with greater leniency when considering the issue of "good reason". See also, *Portico Housing Association Ltd* v. *Brian Moorehead and Partners* (1985) 1 Const LJ 226, CA.
43. See fn 41, *supra*. See also, *Battersby* v. *Anglo-American Oil Co Ltd* [1945] KB 23, CA.
44. *Supra*, fn 41 at 309–10.
45. *Battersby* v. *Anglo-American Oil Co Ltd*, *supra*, fn 43 at 32–33 *per* Lord Goddard CJ.
46. *The Mouna* [1991] 2 Lloyd's Rep 221, CA.

" . . . the Court may at any stage of the proceedings allow the plaintiff to amend his writ, or any party to amend his pleading, on such terms as to costs or otherwise as may be just and in such manner (if any) as it may direct."

This confers a wide discretion on the court to permit further amendments, the guiding principle being that this should be allowed wherever it is necessary in order to do justice between the parties by permitting the real issues in the case to be raised by the pleadings.[47] The basis upon which the court will proceed in deciding an application to amend the writ was summarised by Bowen LJ in *Cropper* v. *Smith*,[48] who said:

"[I] think it is a well established principle that the object of Courts is to decide the rights of the parties, and not to punish them for mistakes they make in the conduct of their cases by deciding otherwise than in accordance with their rights . . . I know of no kind of error or mistake which, if not fraudulent or intended to overreach, the Court ought not to correct, if it can be done without injustice to the other party. Courts do not exist for the sake of discipline, but for the sake of deciding matters in controversy, and I do not regard such amendment as a matter of favour or of grace . . . It seems to me that as soon as it appears that the way in which a party has framed his case will not lead to a decision of the real matter in controversy, it is as much a matter of right on his part to have it corrected, if it can be done without injustice, as anything else in the case is a matter of right . . . The question seems to me to be this: Can you by the imposition of any terms place the other side in as good a position for the purpose of having the question of right determined as they were in at the time when the mistake of judgment was committed? It does not seem to me material to consider whether the mistake of judgment was accidental or not, if not intended to overreach. There is no rule that only slips or accidental errors are to be corrected."[49]

In the exercise of its discretion, the court will seek to compensate the other party by an appropriate order as to costs.[50] As a matter of interpretation, Lord Denning MR observed in *Sterman* v. *EW & WJ Moore*[51] that the court should give rule 5(1) its full width, and should not reduce the scope of the discretion conferred by reference to sub-rules (2), (3), (4) and (5). He said:

"The new rules, it is said, have cut down the power to amend. You can only amend a writ, it is said, so as to avoid the Statute of Limitations, if the case can be brought expressly within Ord. 20, r. 5, sub-rr. (2), (3), (4) and (5)[52]: and that otherwise it is a strict rule of the court that no amendment can be allowed which would deprive a defendant of the benefit of the Statute of Limitations. Support for this interpretation of Ord. 20, r. 5 is given by the recent case in this court of *Braniff* v. *Holland & Hannen and Cubitts (Southern) Ltd* [1969] 1 W.L.R. 1533. But I must say that I cannot agree with it. If this restrictive interpretation were given to Ord. 20, r. 5, we should be once again allowing

---

47. In *GL Baker Ltd* v. *Medway Building & Supplies Ltd* [1958] 3 All ER 540 Jenkins LJ said at 546, that: "there is no doubt whatever that the granting or refusal of an application for such leave is eminently a matter for the discretion of the learned judge with which this court should not in ordinary circumstances interfere unless satisfied that the learned judge has applied a wrong principle or can be said to have reached a conclusion which would work a manifest injustice between the parties." He went on to add that all such amendments ought to be made "for the purpose of determining the real question in controversy between the parties to any proceedings or of correcting any defect or error in any proceedings".

48. (1883) 26 Ch D 700.

49. *Ibid* at 710–11.

50. *Ibid*. See further, *Tildesley* v. *Harper* (1876) 10 Ch D 393; *Weldon* v. *Neal* (1887) 19 QBD 394; *Australian Steam Navigation Co* v. *Smith* (1889) 14 App Cas 318; *Hunt* v. *Rice & Son* (1937) 53 TLR 931; *Indigo Co* v. *Ogilvy* [1891] 2 Ch 39; *Steward* v. *North Metropolitan Tramways Co* (1886) 16 QBD 178; *Kurtz* v. *Spence* (1888) 36 Ch D 774. In *Clarapede* v. *Commercial Union Association* (1883) 32 WR 262 at 263, Brett MR said: "However negligent or careless may have been the first omission, and however late the proposed amendment, the amendment should be allowed if it can be made without injustice to the other side. There is no injustice if the other side can be compensated by costs."

51. [1970] 1 QB 596.

52. *Infra*.

genuine claims to be defeated by technical defects. I think we should give full effect to the wide words of Ord. 20, r. 5(1). We should not cut them down by reference to sub-rules (2), (3), (4) and (5) . . . ."[53]

Order 20, rule 5 must be read in conjunction with the procedural requirements contained in section 35 of the 1980 Act, which provides for the addition of new claims in pending actions. In effect, although no new claims are allowed under section 35(1)(b) after the expiration of the limitation period if, by virtue of section 35(3), that would constitute "a new action to enforce that claim", there are exceptions to this general prohibition. These arise where, for example, the plaintiff wishes to add a new party or extend the scope of the action, or, where a defendant chooses to counterclaim or to claim against a co-defendant or third party.

Section 35(1) provides that any new claim made in the course of any action is deemed to be a "separate action". For the purposes of this provision, a "new claim" is defined as including:

(i) a claim made in or by way of third party proceedings (s 35(1)(a));
(ii) any claim made by way of set-off or counterclaim (s 35(2));
(iii) any claim involving the addition or substitution of a new cause of action (s 35(2)(a));
(iv) any claim involving the addition or substitution of a new party (s 35(2)(b)).

Categories (iii) and (iv) therefore cover any type of joinder (considered further, below).[54]

(i) Third party proceedings[55]

Third party proceedings arise whenever, in the course of any action, a claim is brought by the plaintiff or defendant against a new party (including fourth and subsequent parties), not previously a party to the action, "other than proceedings brought by joining any such person as defendant to any claim already made in the original action by the party bringing the proceedings".[56] The claim is treated as a separate action, but one which is deemed to have been commenced on the date when the third party proceedings commenced—i.e. such claims do not have retrospective effect.[57] This proviso adds a substantial qualification to this exception, so that the only real exception falling within section 35(1)(b) is an original set-off or counterclaim. Accordingly, although a third party notice can be issued outside the relevant limitation period it can be defeated by a limitation plea in the normal way.

Although the commencement of third party proceedings is not defined by the Act, it seems that such proceedings are commenced on the date of issue of the third party notice,

---

53. [1970] 1 QB 596 at 604. RSC Ord 20, r 5(2), (3), (4) and (5) are discussed *infra*.
54. See RSC Order 15, *infra*.
55. See the Law Reform Committee Report 1977, para 5.2 which states, by way of example, that: "The essential features of these proceedings are that a party who is being sued is trying to 'off-load' the whole or part of his liability on to someone else against whom he himself has (or claims to have) a cause of action and that rules of court permit him to do so without requiring him to institute separate proceedings".
56. Section 35(2).
57. Section 35(1)(a). RSC Ord 16 regulates the conduct of third party proceedings. In *Ronex* v. *John Laing Construction Ltd, supra*, fn 6, it was held that a defendant may seek to strike out third party proceedings on the basis that they are frivolous, vexatious and an abuse of the process of the court.

or if leave is required, the date on which the *ex parte* affidavit is lodged with the court.[58] A defendant must commence "third party proceedings" within the primary limitation periods as prescribed by the 1980 Act. Thus, where the plaintiff's action is commenced close to the expiry of the relevant limitation period, the defendant must act quickly if he or she is to institute proceedings and avoid the relevant time bar.[59] In this regard, given that the new claim is to be treated as a separate action, a defendant will be regarded as a "plaintiff" so that in appropriate circumstances, i.e. a personal injury claim, the defendant could apply to the court under section 33 to disapply the prescribed limitation period.[60]

(ii) Set-off and counterclaim

It was seen above that a claim by way of set-off or counterclaim against an existing party is treated as a separate action commenced on the same date as the original action or third party proceedings (where the claim is made in the course of third party proceedings).[61] Further, the effect of section 35(3) is that a party who has not previously made any claim in the action does not need to obtain leave to make what is, therefore, an original claim by way of set-off or to make an original counterclaim, even though the limitation period has expired. A defendant who has pleaded a set-off cannot later seek to raise a counterclaim after the limitation period has passed, although it seems that if the defendant has not made a previous claim, he may do so.[62]

(b) Amending the writ after expiry of the limitation period

Where the applicable limitation period has expired, Order 20, rule 5(2) states that providing the court considers it just to do so, a party may amend the writ in accordance with subrules (3), (4) and (5).[63] In *Chatsworth Investments Ltd* v. *Cussins (Contractors) Ltd* [64] Lord Denning MR said that the effect of this rule "has specifically overruled a series of cases which worked injustice . . . The courts should give Ord. 20, r. 5(1) its full width.

---

58. See *The Supreme Court Practice* in notes to s 35(1)(a). See also, *College Street Market Gardens* v. *Short*, 5 October 1989, unreported.
59. See the judgment of Nicholls LJ in *Howe* v. *David Brown Tractors (Retail) Ltd* [1991] 4 All ER 30 at 41–43; *Welsh Development Agency* v. *Redpath Dorman Long Ltd* [1994] 4 All ER 10, CA.
60. *Supreme Court Practice.*
61. Section 35(1)(b).
62. *Supreme Court Practice 1997*, vol 2, para 6163. Note *Ernst & Young* v. *Butte Mining plc (No 2)* [1997] 2 All ER 471, in which Lightman J observed, at 482, that: "So long as a successful application may be made under Order 15, r 5(2), a defendant's entitlement to proceed with a counterclaim and, accordingly, with the benefit of s 35 can be provisional only. Unilaterally by making a counterclaim, a defendant can put his foot in the door, but this is always subject to the right of the defendant to the counterclaim under Order 15, r 5(2) at an *inter partes* hearing to seek an order to have him ejected. Order 15, r 2(1) is not intended to afford to defendants in all cases a lifeline enabling them by means of service of a counterclaim to obtain a reprieve for the subject matter of such counterclaim from the ordinary consequences of the limitation period. This would involve a misuse of r 2(1) as well as an injustice to the defendants to counterclaim. There can only be a vested right if the subject matter of the counterclaim is not one which ought to be tried in a separate action. If the counterclaim is one which ought to be tried in a separate action, then the future of the counterclaim (and with it the potential saving by s 35 from the consequences of the Act) is a matter for the discretion of the court and, in the absence of its discretion, in any ordinary case procedural convenience is the primary consideration and limitation consequences are at best only a secondary consideration." On the facts, it was held that it would be unjust for the counterclaim to be used as a vehicle to defeat the Limitation Act.
63. See *infra.*
64. [1969] 1 WLR 1.

They should allow an amendment whenever it is just so to do, even though it may deprive the defendant of a defence under the Statute of Limitations".[65]

Rule 5(3) provides for amendments to be made in order to correct the name of a party.[66] Such an application may be allowed where the court is satisfied that the mistake is genuine, even though the mistake in question arose from the plaintiff's own carelessness or that of his advisers.[67] Further, section 35(7) of the 1980 Act and Order 20, rule 5(4)[68] permit amendments to alter the capacity in which a party sues provided the court considers it just to do so. Thus in *Beswick* v. *Beswick*,[69] it was held that a widow, suing in her personal capacity in respect of her husband's death, is entitled to amend the writ once letters of administration have been granted so as to claim as administratrix of the estate.

Sections 35(3) and 35(4) of the 1980 Act provide for rules of court to allow for the addition of new claims, "other than an original set-off or counterclaim", after the expiry of any time limit under the Act provided two conditions laid down by section 35(5) are satisfied.[70] The first requirement, as laid down by rule 5(5) is that upon an application to add a new cause of action, it must be demonstrated that the new cause of action arises out of the "same facts or substantially the same facts as a cause of action in respect of which relief has already been claimed in the action by the party applying for leave to make the amendment". This condition is restrictive, and the court will not permit a new cause of action to be raised unless substantially all the facts necessary to support it have been already pleaded in the original action. For example, in *Lloyds Bank plc* v. *Rogers*[71] the

65. *Ibid* at 5. See also *Sterman* v. *EW & WJ Moore, supra*, fn 50; *Brickfield Properties Ltd* v. *Newton* [1971] 1 WLR 862; *Rodriguez* v. *Parker* [1967] 1 QB 116.

66. RSC Ord 20, r 5(3). An amendment to correct a party's name may be allowed even though the effect will be to substitute a new party: r 5(2)(3).

67. *Katzenstein Adler Industries* v. *Borchard Lines Ltd, The Gladys* [1988] 2 Lloyd's Rep 274. In *Mitchell* v. *Harris Engineering Co Ltd* [1967] 2 QB 703 (discussed *infra*, see fn 88 and associated text) it was held, *inter alia*, that "mistake" should not be so restrictively construed as to mean only error without fault. Russell LJ observed, at 721, that: "It is suggested that mistake here means error without fault; but I do not see why the word should be so narrowly construed." Lord Denning MR noted, at 719, that where the court permits an amendment, its effect is retrospective to the date when the writ was issued.

68. This should be read together with s 35(2) and (4).

69. [1968] AC 58 at 73: "the respondent in her personal capacity has no right to sue, but she has a right as administratrix of her husband's estate to require the appellant to perform his obligation under the agreement." (*per* Lord Reid). See also, *Robinson* v. *Unicos Property Corp Ltd* [1962] 1 WLR 520, in which the approach adopted towards allowing an amendment under sub-r (4) was stated by Holroyd Pearce LJ at 525–26: "Here the plaintiffs' original claim was for damages for breach of a contract made by the third plaintiff with the defendants and they claimed that it had been made on behalf of the first and second plaintiffs. By their amendment the plaintiffs still wish to claim the same damages in respect of the same contract made with the defendants through the person of the third plaintiff, but they wish to claim as equitable assignees of the benefit which the then principals had in 1938. Thus they are claiming the same relief, but they are amending their title, namely, the intervening facts which entitle them to the benefit of the contract. In no sense is the nature of the action altered. The plaintiffs still wish to claim that which they claimed in the beginning. Nor are they suing in a different capacity. Although they now wish to claim by virtue of their right as equitable assignees of the benefits of the principal to the original contract, they still sue in their personal capacity as principals through the same agency on the contract albeit through an assignment on the benefit to them."

70. Section 35(5) substantially replicates the wording of sub-r (5) but is wider in so far as the section provides for amendment if the new cause of action arises out of the same or substantially the same facts as are already in issue "on any claim previously made in the original action". In this respect, see s 35(4) which proceeds on the basis that r 5(5) is the governing provision.

71. *The Times*, 24 March 1997. See also, *Elliott* v. *Chief Constable of Wiltshire, The Times*, 5 December 1996; *Fannon* v. *Backhouse, The Times*, 22 August 1987, CA; *Welsh Development Agency* v. *Redpath Dorman Long* [1994] 4 All ER 10, CA; and *Tabarrok* v. *EDC Lord & Co, The Times*, 14 February 1997, CA.

Court of Appeal held that the policy of section 35 of the 1980 Act was that, if factual issues were in any event going to be litigated between the parties, the parties should be able to rely upon any cause of action which substantially arose from those facts. Any relevant prejudice to the party opposing the amendment could be taken into account in the exercise of the court's discretion. The case arose out of a claim for breach of contract, in which the bank conceded that it had overcharged the customer. Due to the size of the interest and overdraft charges on the customer's account, the bank had dishonoured certain cheques and direct debits. By the time the customer determined what the state of his account would have been had the bank not levied excessive charges, the limitation period for the libel action had expired. The customer therefore sought leave to amend his pleadings. Hobhouse LJ said:

"Now that the whole question of the bank's dishonouring of the cheques and debit instructions and the justification for it and the damage to Mr. Rogers and his business was going to be before the court, there was no adequate reason why if part of what he was entitled to complain of amounted to the tort of libel he should not be allowed to include claims under that head as well."

The approach to be taken by the court when considering an application under rule 5 (5) was explained by Staughton LJ in *Hancock Shipping Co Ltd* v. *Kawasaki Heavy Industries Ltd*.[72] He said that the judge should not endeavour to predict the plaintiff's chances of success with or without the amendment. However, he went on to add four provisos to this proposition:

"(1) If the plaintiff's existing claim is bound to fail, that may possibly be relevant to what justice requires. (2) If it is bound to succeed, that could conceivably be relevant in deciding whether to allow a different cause of action leading to the same remedy but requiring much further investigation to be pleaded ... (3) If the new claim is bound to fail, leave should be refused on ordinary principles. (4) If the new claim is bound to succeed, that may affect the justice of the case. It must be rare that any of these situations will arise. In other cases, provided that the new claim is fairly arguable, it does not seem to me that any investigation of the need to amend is appropriate."[73]

Brickfield Properties Ltd v. *Newton*[74] is a paradigm case. The issue was whether an architect's alleged negligence in design constituted a different cause of action from his alleged negligence in supervising the construction of the building in question. The writ issued against the defendant claimed "damages for negligence and breach of duty by the defendant as an architect employed by the plaintiffs in supervising the building of six blocks of flats ... " The statement of claim, however, alleged as particulars of negligence that the defendant had "so negligently designed the buildings and superintended their setting out and/or erection that the same were defective ... "

Earlier correspondence between the parties made it clear that negligence in respect both of design and of supervision was being alleged. The defendant denied the allegations of negligent design and applied to strike out the allegations. At first instance, Milmo J struck out the allegations relating to negligent design and refused leave to the plaintiffs to amend their writ. The Court of Appeal held, *inter alia*, that the allegation of negligence against the defendant in the *design* of a building arose out of "the same facts or substantially the

72. [1992] 1 WLR 1025.
73. *Ibid* at 1031.
74. [1971] 1 WLR 862. See also, *Collins* v. *Herts CC* [1947] KB 598; *Dornan* v. *JW Ellis & Co Ltd* [1962] 1 QB 583; *Robinson* v. *Unicos Property Corp Ltd*, *supra*, fn 69; *Chatsworth Investments Ltd* v. *Cussins (Contractors) Ltd*, *supra*, fn 64; *Sorata Ltd* v. *Gardex Ltd* [1984] RPC 317; *Sion* v. *Hampstead Health Authority, The Times*, 10 June 1994, CA.

same facts" as an allegation of negligence against him in the *supervision* of the building and that therefore the writ could be amended after the expiry of the relevant limitation period by virtue of rule 5(5). Sachs LJ reasoned:

"Legal proceedings are serious matters in which the parties seek and are entitled to justice; so far as possible they should not be treated as a minuet or game in which the courts are astute to exclude a party from the floor or field by reason of a technically false step taken through a genuine and excusable mistake by their advisers . . . The design has inevitably to be closely examined even if the designs are, as is alleged here, experimental or such as need amplification as the construction progresses. The architect is under a continuing duty to check that his design will work in practice and to correct any errors which may emerge. It savours of the ridiculous for the architect to be able to say . . . 'true, my design was faulty, but, of course, I saw to it that the contractors followed it faithfully' and be enabled on that ground to succeed in the action. The same—or substantially the same—set of facts falls to be investigated in relation to the design claim and the superintendence claim. The plans and specifications and ancillary documents are relevant to the superintendence claim as well as to the design claim . . . Accordingly, the 'new cause of action' falls within the ambit of R.S.C., Ord. 20, r. 5(5), and is one which the court has jurisdiction to permit to be pursued."[75]

Similarly, in *Circle Thirty Three Housing Trust Ltd* v. *Fairview Estates (Housing) Ltd*[76] the plaintiff employed the defendant to design and a build a housing development. Defects appeared and the plaintiff issued a writ and served a statement of claim on the defendant alleging only defective workmanship. Subsequently, the plaintiff applied to amend the statement of claim to plead defective design. The defendant argued that it would add a new cause of action to the existing writ after the expiry of the limitation period. The Court of Appeal held that although the allegation of defective design was a different cause of action from that of defective workmanship, the amendment should be allowed since it arose out of the same or substantially the same facts as the existing pleaded cause of action.

Whether or not the amendment would result in a new cause of action for the purpose of section 35(5)(a) is a mixed question of law and fact.[77] In *Idyll Limited* v. *Dinerman Davison and Hillman*[78] it was alleged that the brickwork of a block of maisonettes had developed substantial defects which were due, *inter alia*, to breach of contract, negligence, defective design, and lack of supervision on the part of the defendants. The writ was issued in September 1966, and the statement of claim was delivered in April 1967. In April 1970 the plaintiff's solicitors wrote to one of the defendant's solicitors complaining of a further fault, namely that the roofs of the maisonettes had been so constructed that water was lying on them and that the waste waterpipe from the roof was too high and could not, therefore, carry away the water. In November they sought leave to amend their

75. [1971] 1 WLR 862 at 872–73.
76. (1985) 4 Const LJ 282 CA. See also, *Dickerson* v. *Lowery* 23 March, 1990, unreported; *Murray Film Finances* v. *Films Finances Ltd* 19 May, 1994, CA, unreported. Cf *Perestrello e Companhia Limitada* v. *United Paint Co Ltd* [1969] 1 WLR 570; *Balfour Beatty Construction* v. *Parsons Brown and Newton* (1991) 7 Const LJ 205, CA.
77. *Steamship Mutual Underwriting Association Ltd* v. *Trollope & Colls (City) Ltd* (1986) 33 Build LR 77 at 99 *per* May LJ; *Crown Estate Commissioners* v. *Whitfield Partners* 30 March, 1990, CA, unreported. In *Hydrocarbons Great Britain Ltd* v. *Cammell Laird Shipbuilders Ltd*, 58 BLR 123, an application to amend the statement of claim to allege negligent misstatement was disallowed. The original allegation pleaded negligent act, and the proposed amendment was in respect of a new cause of action which did not arise out of the "same facts or substantially the same facts" as the cause of action pleaded. Accordingly, there was no jurisdiction under s 35 of the 1980 Act or Ord 20, r 5(5) to allow the amendment.
78. (1985) 4 Const LJ 294, CA.

statement of claim. The official referee allowed the amendment and the defendants unsuccessfully appealed to the Court of Appeal. The difficulties encountered in attempting to predict the outcome of an application to amend were explained by Megaw LJ, who said:

"In some cases it is perfectly clear that a proposed amendment does involve the addition or substitution of a new cause of action. In some cases it is clear that it does not do so. In other cases there is a somewhat undefined borderline. In cases falling within the borderline it is, I think, a question of degree. I do not accept the proposition . . . that it is not, and cannot be, a question of degree."[79]

The effect of section 35 of the Limitation Act 1980 was recently subjected to detailed consideration by the Court of Appeal in *Welsh Development Agency* v. *Redpath Dorman Long*,[80] which concerned the addition of claims giving rise to new causes of action between the existing parties. The relevant limitation period was still running when the summons for leave to amend was taken out, but had expired at the time of the hearing. On its particular facts, it was found that certain proposed amendments to the plaintiff's pleadings involved new claims within section 35 which did not arise out of substantially the same facts as the causes of action already pleaded. To avoid the plaintiff gaining an unfair advantage through the retrospective effect of section 35(1), the addition of the new claims in issue was refused on the basis that the application was caught by section 35(3) of the 1980 Act. Glidewell LJ, who delivered the only judgment, affirmed the decision of the trial judge, and held that leave should be refused unless the plaintiff could show that the defendant did not have reasonable grounds to found a plea of limitation which would be prejudiced by the addition of the new claim.[81] The court therefore adopted a literal interpretation of section 35 with the result that if a party fails to oppose an application to amend, any limitation defence accruing after the commencement of the action will be lost. It would appear to follow that since amendments have retrospective effect, any limitation plea will fail unless the new claim was time barred at the date of the writ.[82]

The interrelationship between section 14A (introduced by the Latent Damage Act 1986, s 1[83]) and section 35 of the Limitation Act 1980 in a case where the plaintiff seeks to add an additional defendant after the expiry of the primary limitation period but within the further three year period starting from the plaintiff's date of knowledge, was considered by the Court of Appeal in *Busby* v. *Cooper*.[84] It was held that given that the primary objective of the Latent Damage Act 1986 was to extend the limitation period in cases of

79. *Ibid.*

80. [1994] 4 All ER 10. The case was a decision on an interlocutory matter.

81. In so finding, the Court of Appeal applied the test formulated by Purchas LJ in *Grimsby Cold Stores Ltd* v. *Jenkins and Potter* (1985) 1 Const LJ 362. Glidewell LJ distinguished *Leicester Wholesale Fruit Market* v. *Grundy* [1990] 1 WLR 107, CA, in which it was held that the proper test under RSC Ord 15, r 6(2)(a), *supra*, was whether, if a fresh action had been brought against the new defendant, he could have it struck out as an abuse of process of the court under RSC Ord 18, r 19(1), (see fn 7, *supra*). Glidewell LJ considered that any limitation defence in the *Leicester* decision would have accrued before the date of the writ so that s 35(1) would not have operated to the advantage of the plaintiffs. The decision in *Kennett* v. *Brown* [1988] 1 WLR 582, to the effect that amendments introducing a new claim should not be disallowed merely on the ground that the relevant limitation period had expired, was overruled. It should be noted that Schiemann LJ, in *Busby* v. *Cooper* [1996] CLC 1425 at 1433, stated that he "was not persuaded by the criticisms of *Kennett* v. *Brown* which [the *Welsh Development Agency*] case contains".

82. For a comprehensive analysis of the implications of the decision in *Welsh Development Agency* v. *Redpath Dorman Long*, see, R James, "New Claims and Limitation Periods", [1995] CJQ 42.

83. See Ch 20.

84. [1996] CLC 1425.

latent damage, the Act would be frustrated if it was construed as debarring the plaintiff from joining a defendant after the expiration of the primary limitation period. Thus, section 14A should be viewed as connoting an overall time limit, that is the primary limitation period as extended, where applicable, by the latent damage period. Further, until leave to amend was formally granted, there was no substantive amendment and consequently no relation back to the date of the writ as provided by section 35(1) of the 1980 Act and therefore no disadvantage to the defendant under section 35(3). Where the court orders the trial of a preliminary issue on the date of knowledge question, then leave to amend would not be granted until that issue had been resolved.[85]

The second condition, as laid down by section 35(5)(b), is that in the case of a claim involving a new party, "the addition or substitution of the new party [must be] necessary for the determination of the original action". Section 35(6) provides that an addition or substitution is only necessary where a mistake was made concerning the name of the original party,[86] or, the original claim made in the original action cannot be maintained unless the new party is joined or substituted as plaintiff or defendant.[87] In *Mitchell* v. *Harris Engineering Co Ltd*[88] the plaintiff suffered injury at work. His solicitors claimed damages from his employers, HE Co Ltd, a company registered in Northern Ireland with a London address at the registered office of an associated English company, HE Co (Leeds) Ltd. Both companies had the same secretary and the same directors. The writ was issued within three weeks of the expiration of the three-year limitation period. It was indorsed with the claim for damages for injuries sustained at the company's factory in Kent. However, the defendant named on the face of the writ was the English "Leeds" company. The error had been made by a junior clerk who had added the word "Leeds" because upon conducting a search of the English Companies Register, he had not found "HE Co Ltd", although he found HE Co (Leeds) Ltd with the same address. The writ was served, with the statement of claim, after the limitation period had expired. The defendant's solicitors pleaded that the wrong defendant had been sued. Accordingly, the plaintiff applied under Order 20, r 5 for leave to amend the writ by substituting "HE Co Ltd" for "HE Co (Leeds) Ltd".

The Court of Appeal held, *inter alia*, that the amendment fell within sub-rule (3) and should be allowed. The mistake was genuine and did not mislead the true defendants. Lord Denning MR also took the opportunity to discuss the nature and operation of the rule. He said:

"In my opinion, whenever a writ has been issued within the permitted time, but is found to be defective, the defendant has no right to have it remain defective. The court can permit the defect to be cured by amendment: and whether it should do so depends on the practice of the court. It is a matter of practice and procedure ... It is a most beneficial provision which enables the courts to

---

85. On this point the court distinguished *Welsh Development Agency* v. *Redpath Dorman Long Ltd, supra*, and applied *Davies* v. *Reed Stock & Co Ltd*, unreported, 26 July 1984, CA.
86. Section 35(6)(a); rr 5(2) and (3).
87. Section 35(6)(b); rr 5(2) and (3).
88. [1967] 2 QB 703. See also, *Evans Constuctions Co Ltd* v. *Charrington & Co Ltd and Bass Holdings Ltd* [1983] QB 810 in which Griffiths LJ stated at 825: "Is the rule to be limited to mere mis-spelling or some other slip such as leaving out one word in the long title of a company so that looking at the name on the proceedings the nature of the mistake can readily be seen; or is it to be more liberally construed so that it will cover the case when entirely the wrong name has been used? I see no reason why it should not include a case where entirely the wrong name has been used, provided it was not misleading, or such as to cause any reasonable doubt as to the identity of the person intended to be sued."

amend proceedings whenever the justice of the case so requires. The amendment relates back to the date of the issue of the writ."[89]

However, a stricter approach was adopted towards the issue in *Beardmore Motors Ltd v. Birch Bros (Properties) Ltd.*[90] In 1932 the applicants took an assignment of a lease expiring in December 1957. The lessors were Birch Brothers Ltd. In 1947, the freehold reversion was assigned by the lessors to Birch Brothers (Properties) Ltd. The latter company was not a subsidiary of Birch Brothers Ltd, although the two companies did share the same office and had the same secretary and directors. When Birch Brothers (Properties) Ltd served a notice terminating the tenancy as from the date when the lease expired, the applicants issued a summons applying for a new tenancy, naming Birch Brothers Ltd as respondents. This was served on the secretary to both companies. The master granted the applicants leave to amend the summons by correcting the respondents' name, and the respondents applied to have the amendment struck out. It was held that the mistake was more than a mere misnomer. Harman J said:

"The applicants knew that there were two such companies; they also knew that Birch Brothers (Properties) Ltd. were their landlords, but they chose to sue Birch Brothers Ltd. I cannot say that they intended, when they used the one title, to use the other. It is not as if the other title were that of a non-existing person, or that they were under any misapprehension. They simply gave the name of an existing company which they knew, and knew as not being their landlords, as respondents to the summons. It is not, in those circumstances, open to me to say that this was a mere misnomer. I can only assume that they intended to sue Birch Brothers Ltd., of whom they knew and who, indeed, were the original freeholders of this property, when they issued the summons in the way they did."[91]

It is suggested that the preferred approach is that adopted by the Court of Appeal in *Mitchell* v. *Harris Engineering Co Ltd*, and that Harman J's views have been superseded by the greater flexibility clearly apparent in more recent appellate judicial pronouncements as epitomised by Lord Denning's judgment.[92]

(c) Joinder of parties—RSC Order 15, rules 6 and 7

Once an action has begun a party to it may wish to add new parties. The position is governed by Order 15, rule 6(5) which provides that no person shall be added or substituted as a party after the expiry of any relevant period of limitation[93] unless the following two conditions are satisfied:

"(a) the relevant period was current at the date when proceedings were commenced and it is necessary for determination of the action that the new party should be substituted[94]; or
(b) the relevant period arises under section 11 or 12 of the 1980 Act and the court directs that those provisions should not apply to the action by or against the new party."

Thus, in short, an action will not necessarily be defeated by virtue of misjoinder or nonjoinder of parties. The object of this rule was to give effect to one of the aims of the

89. *Ibid* at 718.
90. [1959] 1 Ch 298.
91. *Ibid* at 304.
92. See fn 89, *supra*.
93. The term "relevant period of limitation" is defined as meaning any time limit which applies to the action under the 1980 Act, or any foreign time limit which applies to the action by virtue of the Foreign Limitation Periods Act 1984.
94. See also, s 35(5)(b) and (6)(b) of the 1980 Act.

Judicature Acts of bringing all parties to a dispute relating to one subject-matter before the court at the same time so that actions can be determined without the consequent delay, inconvenience and expense of separate actions and trials.[95]

Rule 6(6) states that the addition or substitution of a new party shall be treated as necessary only where the court is satisfied that:

"(a) the new party is a necessary party to the action in that property is vested in him at law or in equity and the plaintiff's claim in respect of an equitable interest in that property is liable to be defeated unless the new party is joined, or

(b) the relevant cause of action is vested in the new party and the plaintiff jointly but not severally, or

(c) the new party is the Attorney General and the proceedings should have been brought by relator proceedings in his name,[96] or

(d) the new party is a company in which the plaintiff is a shareholder and on whose behalf the plaintiff is suing to enforce a right vested in the company,[97] or

(e) the new party is sued jointly with the defendant and is not also liable severally with him and failure to join the new party might render the claim unenforceable."

Where the court permits a new party to be joined either as plaintiff or defendant, it should be noted that the effect of sections 35(1)(b) and 35(2)(b) is that the claim is deemed to have been made at the date of commencement of the original action. Rule 6(6) is comprehensive and exhaustive of the circumstances in which the joinder or substitution of parties is permissible.[98]

Where there is a change in the identity of a party, RSC Order 15, rule 7 allows for the substitution of a new party. This should be distinguished from Order 15, rule 6 and Order 20, rule 5 which, as has been seen, regulate the situation where a new or an existing party seeks to introduce a new claim into the proceedings after the relevant time limit has expired. Order 15, rule 7 provides:

"(1) Where a party to an action dies or becomes bankrupt but the cause of action survives, the action shall not abate by reason of the death or bankruptcy.

(2) Where at any stage of the proceedings in any cause or matter the interest or liability of any party is assigned or transmitted to or devolves upon some other person, the Court may, if it thinks it necessary in order to ensure that all matters in dispute in the cause or matter may be effectually and completely determined and adjudicated upon, order that other person to be made a party to the cause or matter and the proceedings to be carried on as if he had been substituted for the first mentioned party."

95. *Byrne* v. *Brown* (1889) 22 QBD 657 at 666–67 *per* Lord Esher MR. See also, *Montgomery* v. *Foy* [1895] 2 QB 321; the Supreme Court Act 1981, s 49(2) and (3).

96. Where an action has been commenced by the plaintiff in his own name rather than being instituted by way of relator proceedings, the court can remedy the mistake. See *Att-Gen* v. *Pontypridd Waterworks* [1908] 1 Ch 388.

97. A derivative action brought on behalf of a company by a shareholder under the fraud on the minority exception to the rule in *Foss* v. *Harbottle* (1843) 2 Hare 461, requires the leave of the court (see further, Gower, *Principles of Modern Company Law*, 6th ed (London: Sweet & Maxwell, 1997) Ch 23). This provision is designed to ensure that where the proceedings are commenced in a timely manner i.e. before expiry of the limitation period, but leave is not granted until after the limitation period has expired, the plaintiff's action will not be defeated by the time bar.

98. It is exhaustive only in situations within Ord 15, r 6 in which the expiry of the limitation period is relevant. It does not operate to limit the scope of Ord 15, r 7 (*infra*): *Yorkshire Regional Health Authority* v. *Fairclough Building Ltd* [1996] 1 All ER 519, considered *infra*.

Although the identity of the party changes, the claim itself does not and so there is no question of a new cause of action being asserted. Accordingly, it is not open to the defendant to plead a limitation defence when the new plaintiff replaces the old. The interrelationship between section 35 of the Limitation Act 1980 and Order 15, rule 7 was considered by the Court of Appeal in *Yorkshire Regional Health Authority* v. *Fairclough Building Ltd.*[99] As a result of the reorganisation of the National Health Service, the YRHA successfully applied to the court to substitute a health trust as plaintiffs in an action for breach of contract and negligence after the relevant limitation period had expired. The defendants appealed on the basis that the substitution constituted a new claim under section 35(2) and (3) of the 1980 Act and therefore the court did not have jurisdiction to allow the substitution. It was held that the definition of "new claim" in section 35(2) did not include the substitution of a party who had succeeded to a claim in existing proceedings and which did not involve a new cause of action. The two limbs of section 35(2) were mutually exclusive. Section 35(2)(a) was restricted to claims involving a new cause of action but not the substitution or addition of a new party, while section 35(2)(b), which referred only to claims involving the addition or substitution of a new party, includes such claims which also involved a new cause of action. Thus, substitution within the ambit of Order 15, rule 7 did not fall within either of these statutory provisions, and therefore the substitution of the trust for the plaintiff was not a "new claim" within the meaning of section 35 of the Limitation Act 1980.

(d) Dismissal for want of prosecution and abuse of process

The law of limitations is concerned with the time which has elapsed between the accrual of a cause of action and the issue and service of the writ. Where the writ has been served but thereafter the plaintiff fails to proceed with reasonable diligence in following the procedural requirements of the Rules of the Supreme Court, the defendant may apply to the court to have the action dismissed for want of prosecution. Limitation rules are relevant since they affect the circumstances in which the court's jurisdiction to dismiss a claim will be exercised. More particularly, the approach of the courts depends upon whether an application for dismissal for want of prosecution is made before the relevant limitation period has expired or whether it is made after the plaintiff's action has become time barred.

The relationship between dismissal for want of prosecution and abuse of process was considered by the House of Lords in *Grovit* v. *Doctor*,[100] in which it was held that the commencement and continuation of litigation which a plaintiff had no intention of carrying to trial could amount to an abuse of process so that the defendant was entitled to have the action struck out and if justice so required, the court would dismiss the action. The

---

99. *Ibid.* See also, the judgment of Mance J in *Industrie Chimiche Italia Centrale* v. *Alexander Tsavliris & Sons Maritime Co, The Choko Star* [1966] 1 All ER 114.

100. [1997] 1 WLR 640, HL. See also, *Taylor* v. *Ribby Hall Leisure Ltd, The Times*, 6 August 1997, CA, in which Mummery LJ held that submissions on delay and prejudice in relation to the court's contempt and supervisory jurisdiction should generally be made at the substantive hearing rather than during an application to strike out.

plaintiff's inactivity could be relied on to establish abuse of process and the same evidence could support an application to dismiss for want of prosecution.

(e) Grounds for dismissal for want of prosecution

The grounds upon which an application may be made to the court to dismiss an action for want of prosecution were laid down by the Court of Appeal in *Allen* v. *Sir Alfred McAlpine & Sons Ltd*[101] in which it was held that the court may, in its discretion, dismiss an action for want of prosecution if one of the following conditions are fulfilled, namely:

    (i) that the plaintiff's default has been intentional and contumelious, or

    (ii) that there has been an inordinate and inexcusable delay which is such as to cause serious prejudice to the defendant, or

    (iii) that such delay gives rise to a substantial risk that a fair trial of the issues in the litigation will not be possible.[102]

The onus of proving that either of these conditions is satisfied is on the defendant. Diplock LJ recognised that such an order is draconian, and will not be made without giving the plaintiff an opportunity to remedy his default and, in any case, rarely before the expiry of the limitation period.[103] Salmon LJ thought that the same principles applied whether the defendant's application is made because of the plaintiff's failure to comply with the Rules of the Supreme Court, or under the court's inherent jurisdiction.[104] Both judges recognised that the exercise of this discretion involves striking a balance between the position of the plaintiff and the defendant.

The requirements for seeking the dismissal of an action for want of prosecution were reformulated by Lord Diplock in *Birkett* v. *James*,[105] in which he said:

"The power should be exercised only where the court is satisfied either (1) that the default has been intentional and contumelious, e.g. disobedience to a peremptory order of the court or conduct amounting to an abuse of process of the court; or (2)(a) that there has been inordinate and inexcusable delay on the part of the plaintiff or his lawyers, and (b) that such delay will give rise to a substantial risk that it is not possible to have a fair trial of the issues in the action or is such as is likely to cause or to have caused serious prejudice to the defendants either as between themselves and the plaintiff or between them and a third party."[106]

Lord Diplock's statement of the governing principles were subjected to critical scrutiny by the House of Lords in *Grovit* v. *Doctor*.[107] Lord Woolf, who delivered the principal speech, observed that although the first condition links abuse of process with delay which

---

101. [1968] 2 QB 229. See also *Industrie Chimiche Italia Centrale* v. *Alexander G. Tsavliris & Sons Maritime Co, The Choko Star* [1990] 1 Lloyd's Rep 516.

102. There must be a causal link between the delay and the prejudice suffered by the defendant: *Halls* v. *O'Dell* (1991) 35 SJ (LB) 204, CA; *Trill* v. *Sacher* [1993] 1 WLR 1379 at 1399; *Purcell Meats (Scotland) Ltd* v. *Intervention Board for Agricultural Produce, The Times*, 5 June 1997.

103. [1968] 2 QB 229 at 259.

104. *Ibid* at 268.

105. [1978] AC 297.

106. *Ibid* at 318.

107. [1997] 1 WLR 640, HL.

is intentional and contumelious, the prevention of abuse of process "has by itself long been a ground for the courts striking out or staying actions by virtue of their inherent jurisdiction irrespective of the question of delay"[108] and Lord Diplock's formulation does not affect this as a separate ground for striking out. He went on to note that the requirement laid down by the second principle that the delay has to cause "serious prejudice" to the defendants, has attracted much criticism,[109] the central point being that the rules of civil procedure are in need of reform to allow for the courts to adopt a proactive role in case management.[110] Not surprisingly, Lord Woolf endorsed the criticisms which *Birkett* v. *James* has generated, and stated that:

"[T]here was now on the horizon the introduction of the sort of process of reform to the rules of procedure which Lord Griffiths thought was required. In this situation it is at least open to question whether it is not preferable to await the outcome of the implementation of the new rules before making a substantial inroad on the principles indorsed by Lord Diplock in *Birkett* v. *James*. They should by case management prevent the delay happening. If delays did happen they could provide the court with wider powers to mitigate the consequences."[111]

However, notwithstanding the proposals for case management contained in the Woolf Report,[112] his Lordship stressed that under the present rules both the court and defendants had the means to achieve greater control over delay. He took the view that:

"The courts should more readily make 'unless orders', that is, orders that an action should be struck out unless certain steps are taken at certain times. The advantage of such an order is that it places the onus on the plaintiff to justify the action being allowed to continue whereas in the case of an

---

108. *Ibid* at 419. Generally, one of the parties to an action will apply for dismissal, however, in *Kerr* v. *National Carriers Ltd* [1974] 1 Lloyd's Rep 365, Edmund Davies LJ stated, at 367, that; "it cannot be too clearly appreciated in the profession that the Rules of the Supreme Court are there to be observed, and that parties cannot by mutual cordiality prolong the trial of actions by agreeing to adjournments in the interlocutory stage . . . there is a supervising duty vested in the Court of scrutinising cases . . . " Accordingly, since dismissal for want of prosecution lies within the inherent jurisdiction of the Court, the Court can, in exceptional cases, strike out an action on its own motion irrespective of the views of the parties.

109. See *Department of Transport* v. *Chris Smaller (Transport) Ltd* [1989] AC 1197 at 1204–05, in which Lord Griffiths referred to a statement of Kerr LJ in his judgment in *Westminster City Council* v. *Clifford Culpin & Partners* (1987) 137 NLJ 736 that the law needs to be changed both in substance and procedurally and that the principles laid down in *Birkett* v. *James* are unsatisfactory and inadequate. They are far too lenient to deal effectively with excessive delays and breed excessive further delays and costs in their application. See, also, *Kincardine Fisheries Ltd* v. *Sunderland Marine Mutual Insurance Ltd, The Times,* 12 February 1997, where the issue before the court was the approach to be adopted where co-defendants seek to strike out the plaintiff's claim for want of prosecution. Colman J observed that: "The sooner the whole structure of that jurisdiction was simplified the better. It was difficult to see why there should not be a general jurisdiction to strike out for want of prosecution any claim which for any reason whatever was simply too stale for a fair trial." It was held that each defendant was entitled to rely as inordinate delay, on any period of time during which, so far as that defendant was concerned, the plaintiff had failed to prosecute the proceedings with that degree of despatch which could normally be expected in relation to the particular claim. Further, in determining whether a particular period of inordinate delay was inexcusable in relation to that defendant, the court had to look at the proceedings as a whole, as distinct from isolating the claim against the defendant from the claims against the other defendants.

110. This issue has now been been addressed by Lord Woolf in his report, *Access to Justice, Final Report to the Lord Chancellor on the Civil Justice System in England and Wales* (July 1996). The Woolf Report proposes a system of automatic sanctions on both parties for failure to comply with any rule, order, direction or timetable. It would be for the plaintiff guilty of delay to apply for relief against the sanction which would include an order striking out the claim.

111. [1997] 1 WLR 640 at 644.

112. *Supra,* fn 110.

application to strike out the onus was on the defendant to show the action should be struck out."[113]

It will generally be the case that the fault giving rise to the delay will not lie with the plaintiff personally but rather his solicitor, and it would be clearly unjust to deprive the plaintiff of his chance to recover the damages to which he could otherwise be entitled. The Court of Appeal in *Allen* v. *Sir Alfred McAlpine & Sons Ltd*[114] took the view that where the solicitor is insured, the plaintiff will not generally be prejudiced by the dismissal of the action, since he will be able to recover against the solicitor in negligence.[115] But where the solicitor is "uninsured or impecunious"[116] the court, in exercising its discretion to dismiss the action, must balance the prejudice caused to both the defendant on the one hand, and the "innocent" plaintiff, on the other. However, the House of Lords in *Birkett* v. *James*[117] held that the existence of such an action against a solicitor should be disregarded entirely.

What constitutes "inordinate delay" must depend on the facts of each particular case, for it is "highly undesirable and indeed impossible to attempt to lay down a tariff".[118] However, it is clear that the longer the delay, the more likely that this will be seen to have caused serious prejudice to the defendant. In *Shtun* v. *Zaljejska*[119] the Court of Appeal held that in determining whether the defendant has suffered prejudice through the impairment of witnesses' recollections as a result of delay, the court had to examine all the evidence of the case. In appropriate circumstances the court could draw an inference of prejudice without the necessity of specific evidence that prejudice flowed from the loss of memory in a particular period.[120] This apparent easing of the burden borne by the defendant in such circumstances clearly reflects the current view of the judiciary towards the issue of delay particularly in the light of the proposals contained in the Woolf Report.

It is settled that except where the default has been intentional and contumelious, the power to dismiss an action should not normally be exercised prior to the expiry of the limitation period. The position was stated by Lord Diplock in *Birkett* v. *James*.[121] He said:

"I am of opinion that the fact that the limitation period has not yet expired must always be a matter of great weight in determining whether to exercise the discretion to dismiss an action for want of prosecution where no question of contumelious default on the part of the plaintiff is involved; and in cases where it is likely that if the action were dismissed the plaintiff would avail himself of his

113. *Supra*, fn 111.

114. [1968] 2 QB 229.

115. Salmon LJ said "when there is inordinate and inexcusable delay likely to cause the defendant serious prejudice, the action should normally be dismissed and the loss attributable to the dismissal borne by those whose negligence has caused it" (*ibid* at 270).

116. [1968] 2 QB 229 at 269.

117. [1978] AC 297, Lord Salmon dissenting.

118. *Per* Salmon LJ, *supra*, fn 114, at 268. See further, *Rath* v. *CS Lawrence & Co Partners* [1991] 1 WLR 399, CA; *Trill* v. *Sacher* [1993] 1 WLR 1379.

119. [1996] 1 WLR 1270, CA. See also, *Spooner* v. *Webb, The Times*, 24 April 1997.

120. Applying *Roebuck* v. *Mungovin* [1994] 2 AC 224, in which Lord Browne-Wilkinson (with whom all the other law lords agreed), rejected the view expressed in *Hornagold* v. *Fairclough Building Ltd* [1993] PIQR 400, that there had to be specific evidence of prejudice rather than a bald assertion that the delay had prejudiced the defendant. Lord Browne-Wilkinson stated that a judge could infer a further loss of memory from any substantial delay. See also, *Re Manlon Trading Co Ltd* [1995] 3 WLR 839 and *Blackburn* v. *Wadkin plc*, 12 December 1996, HHJ Fawcus, CC (Manchester). In *Al-Fayed* v. *Emanouel Antiques Ltd, The Times*, 22 August 1997, Roch LJ held that stress and business disruption could amount to prejudice sufficient to strike out an action.

121. [1978] AC 297.

legal right to issue a fresh writ the non-expiry of the limitation period is generally a conclusive reason for not dismissing the action that is already pending."[122]

Accordingly, the court will not normally exercise its power to dismiss an action for want of prosecution before it has become time barred since the plaintiff is entitled to issue a fresh writ within the limitation period for the same cause of action. The reason is clear and obvious. If an action was dismissed prior to the expiry of the limitation period, this could only result in aggravating the delay and increasing the costs of the claim, it having to be brought twice. The argument that the court should also have the power to prevent the plaintiff instituting a fresh action was robustly rejected by Lord Diplock, who said:

> "It assumes that the court has power to treat as amounting to inordinate and inexcusable delay in proceeding with an action a period shorter than that within which Parliament by a Limitation Act has manifested its intention that a plaintiff should have a legal right to commence proceeding with his action ... So in such a case, at any rate, time elapsed before issue of the writ which does not extend beyond the limitation period cannot be treated as inordinate delay; the statute itself permits it ... where all that the plaintiff has done has been to let the previous action go to sleep, the court in my opinion would have no power to prevent him starting a fresh action within the limitation period and proceeding with it with all proper diligence notwithstanding that his previous action had been dismissed for want of prosecution."[123]

There is authority which at first sight appears to support the view that an action may be dismissed prior to the expiry of the limitation period and a fresh writ struck out as an abuse of the process of the court, on the basis of the doctrine of estoppel. In *Spring Grove Services Ltd* v. *Deane*[124] the plaintiff's solicitor in the original action had informed the defendant that the action had been abandoned. Thereafter, the defendant lost touch with one of his intended witnesses who had gone overseas. Subsequently, the defendant successfully applied to the court to strike out the plaintiff's action for want of prosecution. Still within the limitation period, the plaintiff issued a second writ which in essence reflected the earlier claim. The Court of Appeal held that the second action was an abuse of the process of the court. In the course of delivering his speech in *Birkett* v. *James*, Lord Edmund Davies subjected the transcript of *Spring Grove Services Ltd* v. *Deane* to close scrutiny and doubted whether it could be regarded as "authority for the proposition that a second writ, asserting the same claim as that made in an earlier writ struck out for want of prosecution, can in its turn be struck out as being necessarily an abuse of process of the court even though issued within the limitation period".[125] His Lordship found that although there was a suggestion in the earlier proceedings that the plaintiffs had misled the defendant by representing that they had abandoned the action, "it seems clear that the first writ was struck out solely for want of prosecution".[126] Lord Edmund Davies left the question open as to whether or not a plaintiff who misleads a defendant into thinking that

---

122. *Ibid* at 322. In *Instrumatic Ltd* v. *Supabase Ltd* [1969] 1 WLR 519 at 522 Lord Denning MR stressed that: "The period of limitation is six years. It has not run. If this action were dismissed, the plaintiffs could start another action tomorrow. So what good is it to dismiss the claim for want of prosecution?" See also, *Department of Health and Social Security* v. *Ereira* [1973] 3 All ER 421, CA; *Department of Transport* v. *Chris Smaller (Transport) Ltd* [1989] AC 1197, HL.

123. [1978] AC 297 at 320–21.

124. (1972) 116 SJ 844.

125. [1978] AC 297 at 333.

126. *Ibid.*

an action against him has been abandoned, will be prevented from issuing a fresh writ.[127]

It may happen that the plaintiff is induced by the defendant's conduct to believe that the action will proceed to trial despite the plaintiff's earlier delay. The issue arising here is whether the defendant can then apply to have the action struck out for want of prosecution, or whether his conduct will amount to an equitable estoppel or waiver of rights? In *Roebuck* v. *Mungovin*[128] the House of Lords held that although the defendant's conduct is a relevant factor to be taken into account by the judge in exercising his discretion to dismiss an action, it will not of itself operate as an absolute bar to such an order, provided, of course, that the plaintiff has been guilty of inordinate and inexcusable delay which prejudiced the defendant. With respect to the weight to be accorded to the defendant's conduct, Lord Browne-Wilkinson said that the judge must take account of all the circumstances of the particular case. His Lordship went on to illustrate his proposition:

"At one extreme, there will be cases . . . where the defendant's actions are minor (as compared with the inordinate delay by the plaintiff) and cannot have lulled the plaintiff into any major additional expenditure; in such a case a judge exercising his discretion will be likely to attach only slight weight to the defendant's actions. At the other extreme one can conceive of a case where, the plaintiff having been guilty of inordinate delay, the defendant has for years thereafter continued with the action thereby leading the plaintiff to incur substantial legal costs; in such a case the judge may attach considerable weight to the defendant's activities."[129]

In *Allen* v. *Sir Alfred McAlpine & Sons Ltd*[130] Diplock LJ opined that a plaintiff's disobedience of a peremptory order would constitute sufficient grounds to justify the court striking out an action for want of prosecution on the basis that the plaintiff's delay was intentional and contumelious.[131] In this regard, the Court of Appeal in *Janov* v. *Morris*[132] had to consider the question of whether a second writ issued in these circumstances was an abuse of the process of the court. Briefly, the facts were that the plaintiff had issued a writ claiming damages for breach of contract. The defendant delivered particulars of defence and counterclaimed for non-delivery. Other steps were then taken, including the delivery of further and better particulars of the defence. This was then followed by a 10-month lull during which the plaintiff failed to take any further steps. The defendant then applied to have the action dismissed for want of prosecution. The master ordered that that the action would be struck out *unless* the plaintiff served his summons for directions by a specified date. The plaintiff failed to comply with the order and consequently, judgment was given for the defendant. While still within the primary limitation period, the plaintiff issued a second writ pleading the same cause of action. The defendant successfully applied to the master under RSC Order 18, rule 19 to strike out the action as an abuse of the process of the court. It was held by the Court of Appeal that the issue of whether

127. Lord Diplock took the view (at 320) that there may well be exceptional cases, of which *Spring Grove Services Ltd* v. *Deane* may be an example, where the court should exercise its inherent jurisdiction and stay the proceedings.
128. [1994] 2 AC 224. See also *Blaenau Gwent BC* v. *Robinson Jones Design Partnership Ltd* (1997) 53 Con LR 31.
129. *Ibid* at 576. In *Hunter* v. *Skingley, The Times*, 7 May 1997, the Court of Appeal held that where there was substantial initial delay on the part of the defendant followed by delays for which the plaintiff was responsible, it was appropriate to allocate prejudice.
130. [1968] 2 QB 229.
131. See also, the judgment of Diplock LJ in *Tolley* v. *Morris* [1979] 1 WLR 592 at 603.
132. [1981] 1 WLR 1389, CA.

or not an action should be struck out under Order 18, rule 19 was within the discretion of the court. Further, in the exercise of its discretion, the court should uphold the principle that peremptory orders should be obeyed, so that in the absence of any proper excuse by the plaintiff for his non-compliance, the court should strike out the action.

Dunn LJ distinguished *Birkett* v. *James*[133] on the basis that it was concerned with an application to strike out on the ground of inordinate and inexcusable delay.[134] Watkins LJ observed that once a prospective litigant embarks upon litigation, he thereby subjects himself to the rules and orders of the court, so that a failure to conform with any of these may cause him to be penalised. Watkins LJ reasoned that the plaintiff's failure to comply with the peremptory order was contumacious. He said:

"In the event of his action being ordered to be struck out for failure to obey a peremptory order, he may appeal against that order seeking, if necessary, an extension of time within which to do so . . . If a litigant neglects to avail himself of that procedure and brings a fresh but precisely similar action to that ordered to be struck out without any explanation then or at any later time for a failure to obey the peremptory order, he should not be surprised that the commencement of the second action is found to be an abuse of the process of the court and for that reason it, too, is struck. To behave in such a way is in my judgment to treat the court with intolerable contumely. This is a matter which can properly be taken into account in the exercise of the court's discretion."[135]

In *Re Jokai Tea Holdings Ltd*[136] the Court of Appeal stressed that the failure to comply with a peremptory order must be deliberate. Browne-Wilkinson V-C explained that the rationale underlying the court's power to strike out a plaintiff's action or, as was in issue, a defendant's defence, is that it is contumelious to disobey an order of the court but: "if a party can explain convincingly that outside circumstances account for the failure to obey the peremptory order and that there was no deliberate flouting of the court's order, his conduct is not contumelious and therefore the consequences of contumely do not flow."[137]

A defendant who enters a counterclaim is also under a duty to proceed expeditiously. In *Zimmer Orthopaedic Ltd* v. *Zimmer Manufacturing Co Ltd*,[138] the plaintiffs sued the defendants for infringement of a trademark. The defendants entered a defence and counterclaim but no further steps were taken for five years until the plaintiffs served notice of intention to proceed. The defendants applied to have the action dismissed for want of prosecution. The application was granted by the Court of Appeal, but on terms that the counterclaim should also be struck out. The court adopted the view that since the defendants had an active claim which they could have prosecuted had they chosen to do so, they could not now complain of the plaintiffs' delay.

---

133. [1978] AC 297.

134. The decision of the House of Lords in *Tolley* v. *Morris* [1979] 1 WLR 592 was similarly distinguished.

135. *Supra*, fn 132, at 1395.

136. [1992] 1 WLR 1196. In *Bailey* v. *Bailey* [1983] 1 WLR 1129, the Court of Appeal held that where the first action is struck out for want of prosecution and not for disobedience of a peremptory order of the court, the issue of a second writ within the limitation period was not, of itself, an abuse of process of the court.

137. *Ibid* at 1202 (*per* Browne-Wilkinson V-C).

138. [1968] 1 WLR 1349, CA. See also, *Akhtar* v. *RD Harbottle (Mercantile) Ltd* (1982) 126 SJ 643, CA; *Austin Securities Ltd* v. *Northgate and English Stores Ltd* [1969] 1 WLR 529, CA; *Trill* v. *Sacher* [1993] 1 WLR 1379.

(f) Dismissal for want of prosecution and section 33 of the Limitation Act

It has already been seen that section 33 of the 1980 Act gives the court discretion in personal injury cases to disapply the limitation periods imposed by sections 11 and 12 of the Act. Section 33(1)(a) directs the court to have regard to the degree to which the limitation periods prejudice the plaintiff. The operation of section 33 in cases where there has been delay was considered by the House of Lords in *Walkley* v. *Precision Forgings*.[139] Due to the negligence of his solicitor, the plaintiff had failed to prosecute his claim under a writ issued in 1971. In 1976 the plaintiff issued a fresh writ bringing the same cause of action which was served in February 1977. The defendants applied to have the action dismissed for want of prosecution on the basis that they would suffer prejudice if the second action were allowed to proceed because of the long delay since the cause of action accrued. It was held that the prejudice caused to the plaintiff was due to the negligence of his solicitors, it was not caused by the time limits imposed by sections 11 or 12. Consequently, section 33 had no application. Lord Diplock observed that:

"[O]nce a plaintiff has started an action (the first action) within the primary limitation period it is only in the most exceptional circumstances that he would be able to bring himself within [section 33] in respect of a second action brought to enforce the same cause of action. If the first action is still in existence, as it was in the present case when the matter was before the master and the judge, *cadit quaestio*; he has not been prevented from starting his action by [section 11 or section 12] at all, so the provisions of those sections cannot have caused him any prejudice. Does it make any difference that the first action is no longer in existence at the time of the application under [section 33] either because it has been struck out for want of prosecution or because it has been discontinued by the plaintiff of his own volition? In my view, it does not. These are self inflicted wounds."[140]

Where a plaintiff has issued a writ after the expiration of the limitation period having obtained leave under section 33, it has been held that the principles established in *Birkett* v. *James* are inapplicable.[141]

(g) Suspension of time bar where the plaintiff is under a disability

Section 28(1) of the 1980 Act provides that where a plaintiff is under a disability at the time when the cause of action accrued, "the action may be brought at any time before the expiration of six years from the date when he ceased to be under a disability or died (whichever first occurred) notwithstanding that the period of limitation has expired". A person is under a disability for the purposes of the Act if he is a minor i.e. under the age of 18[142]; or if he is of unsound mind.[143] In *Stubbings and Others* v. *United Kingdom*[144] three British citizens complained that they had been denied access to court as a result of

139. [1979] 1 WLR 606.
140. *Ibid* at 619.
141. *Biss* v. *Lambeth Health Authority* [1978] 1 WLR 382, CA; *Tolley* v. *Morris* [1979] 1 WLR 592. See also the speeches of Lord Diplock and Lord Edmund Davies in *Birkett* v. *James* [1978] AC 297.
142. Family Law Reform Act 1969, s 1. Therefore, a plaintiff whose cause of action arises during his or her minority must bring suit within the prescribed limitation period which will begin to run on the plaintiff's eighteenth birthday.
143. Section 38(2). A person is of unsound mind if he is a person who, by reason of mental disorder within the meaning of the Mental Health Act 1959, is incapable of managing and administering his property and affairs: Limitation Act 1980, s 38(3). See also, *Thomas* v. *Plaistow* [1997] 6 CL 88, CA, in which it was held, *inter alia*, that "disability" includes serious memory problems, forgetfulness, depression and inability to concentrate.
144. Case No 36–37/1995, *The Times*, 24 October 1996.

the prescribed statutory limitation period applicable to their civil claims for damages founded upon allegations of sexual abuse suffered in childhood. In essence, the applicants claimed that the psychological after-effects of the abuse prevented them from realising they had a cause of action against their abusers until after the applicable limitation period had expired,[145] i.e. upon attaining the age of 24. Consequently, they argued that Article 6.1 of the European Convention on Human Rights had been breached.[146] It was held by the ECHR that the applicants' right of access to a court had not been impaired. The Court agreed with the Government's submission that the time limit in question was not unduly short and in fact, was longer than the extinction periods for personal injury claims set by some international treaties.[147] Further, the Court found that the relevant time limit was proportionate to the legitimate aims of ensuring legal certainty and finality, particularly when viewed from the perspective that had the applicants commenced actions shortly before the expiry of the limitation period, the courts would have been required to adjudicate on events which had taken place approximately 20 years earlier.

It should be noted that where the disability occurs after the action has accrued, the running of time will not be suspended. However, in personal injury actions, a subsequent disability will entitle the plaintiff to apply to the court under section 33 to disapply the limitation period (see Ch 19, *infra*).

145. The House of Lords held that on its true construction, the three-year limitation period prescribed by s 11 of the Limitation Act 1980 was confined to personal injury actions founded upon negligent, as distinct from intentional, breaches of duty. Accordingly, the statutory concessions provided by ss 11(4) and 33(1) of the 1980 Act could never be available in cases of intentional injury. In such cases the relevant limitation period was six years as laid down in s 2 of the 1980 Act; see *Stubbings* v. *Webb* [1993] AC 498, HL.

146. Article 6.1 of the Convention states, so far as is relevant: "In the determination of his civil rights and obligations . . . everyone is entitled to a . . . hearing . . . by [a] . . . tribunal . . . ".

147. Such as the Warsaw Convention for the Unification of Certain Rules relating to International Carriage by Air 1929, (as amended by the Hague Protocol), and the Athens Convention relating to the Carriage of Passengers and their Luggage on Board Ships 1974, which allowed two years from the date of disembarkation in which to bring a claim for personal injury sustained during international carriage by air and sea respectively.

PART II

CONTRACT AND COMMERCIAL LAW

CHAPTER 8

RUNNING OF TIME IN SIMPLE CONTRACT ACTIONS

The Limitation Act 1980 distinguishes between simple contracts and specialties, stipulating that in the case of the former time runs for six years from the date of breach[1] and in the case of the latter time will run for a period of 12 years, also from the date of breach.[2] Accordingly, although the limitation period in each case differs, accrual of the cause of action is triggered by the same event, namely the breach of contract. Furthermore, although the 1980 Act stipulates limitation periods of six years and 12 years according to the type of contract concerned, it is also possible for the parties to agree upon a limitation period which is either shorter or longer than that provided for in the Act, subject to whether that agreement is permitted by law. For example, in consumer contracts and contracts under which one party contracts on the written standard terms of the other party, both of which are governed by the Unfair Contract Terms Act 1977, and contracts governed by the Unfair Terms in Consumer Contracts Regulations 1994[3] it is possible that an agreement to either shorten or lengthen a limitation period may be invalid on the ground that it unreasonably or unfairly makes enforcement of the contract subject to restrictive or onerous provisions.[4]

The Limitation Act 1980, s 5 provides that "An action founded on a simple contract shall not be brought after the expiration of six years from the date on which the cause of action accrued."

SIMPLE CONTRACTS

What constitutes a simple contract, as opposed to a specialty is difficult to define. It has been said that:

"Debts by simple contract are such, where the contract upon which the obligation arises is neither ascertained by matter of record, nor yet by deed or special instrument, but by mere oral evidence, the most simple of any: or by notes unsealed, which are capable of more easy proof and (therefore only) better than a verbal promise."[5]

---

1. Limitation Act 1980, s 5.
2. Limitation Act 1980, s 8. See further Ch 15.
3. SI 1994/3159.
4. See Unfair Contract Terms Act 1977, s 13(1)(a); Unfair Terms in Consumer Contracts Regulations 1994, reg 4(4) and Sch 3(1)(q).
5. 2 Blackstones Commentaries 465–66.

At one stage, the preferred epithet was that of the "parol" contract,[6] but this suggests one which is made orally. However, a simple contract also includes one which is in written form, but which does not amount to a specialty. Perhaps a better word to describe the type of contract under consideration is the "informal contract".[7]

Although the Blackstone definition above relates only to debts, it is clear that it can relate to other forms of simple contract, the essence of which is that they may be proved by oral or written evidence, not under seal and are supported by a valuable consideration.

CONCURRENT CONTRACTUAL AND TORTIOUS OBLIGATIONS

Given the advancement of the modern tort of negligence, it has become apparent that there are circumstances in which a plaintiff may be able to frame an action concurrently in contract and tort. This has important effects for the law of limitation of actions since actions in tort and contract are differently dealt with so far as accrual of the cause of action is concerned. It will be seen elsewhere that in a tort action, the cause of action accrues when the plaintiff suffers damage, whereas for the purposes of a contract action, the cause of action accrues on breach with the result that time may start to run in each case from a different date.

While it is clear that obligations arising from a contract and those imposed via the law of tort may coincide, there is the difficulty that these two branches of the law of obligations are conceptually different. A number of generalisations serve to distinguish between contractual and tortious duties, although it has to be admitted that these generalisations are subject to exceptions. In the first place, it is said that contractual obligations are voluntarily assumed by the parties to the contract, being an expression of their free will, whereas tortious obligations are imposed by law, representing minimum social standards of behaviour. However, there are contractual obligations which are imposed by law, such as the statutory implied terms in sale of goods contracts[8] and those terms implied by the courts in cases of necessity.[9] Similarly, there are tortious obligations which arise where a defendant has voluntarily entered into a relationship with the plaintiff from which a duty of care arises. In many of these instances it is also possible that there is a contractual relationship between the parties. Examples include the duty of care owed by an occupier to his lawful visitors under the Occupiers' Liability Act 1957, the duty owed by an employer to his employees to provide safe working conditions and the duty owed by the giver of advice under the rule in *Hedley Byrne & Co* v. *Heller & Partners Ltd.*[10] Moreover, many tortious duties can be varied by agreement between the parties, thus illustrating that voluntary choice can be relevant in the context of legally imposed duties.

A second ground for distinguishing between tortious and contractual liability is that where there has been a breach of duty, the remedy offered in each case differs. It is said

6. See *Rann* v. *Hughes* (1778) 7 Term Rep 350.

7. See Williston, *Contracts*, s 12; American Law Institute, *Restatement of the Law of Contracts*, s 11.

8. Sale of Goods Act 1979, ss 13 (implied term as to correspondence with a description), 14 (implied terms as to satisfactory quality and fitness for purpose) and 15 (implied terms in contracts for the sale of goods by sample). The extent to which liability for breach of these implied terms can be excluded or limited is severely restricted by the provisions of the Unfair Contract Terms Act 1977.

9. See *Liverpool City Council* v. *Irwin* [1977] AC 239.

10. [1964] AC 465.

that the purpose of an award of damages for breach of contract is to put the plaintiff into the position he would have been in had the contract been performed as agreed,[11] whereas the purpose of an award of tort damages is to restore the status quo by returning the plaintiff to the position he was in before the defendant committed the tort complained of.[12] The underlying rationale behind these rules is that if a contract is performed according to the expectations of the parties, the plaintiff's position will be made better, but that remedies for breach of a tortious obligation are concerned with compensating a plaintiff because his position has been made worse by the defendant. However, this distinction is also subject to doubt on both sides. For example, the general limitations on the recovery of damages for a breach of contract in the form of the rules on remoteness of loss and mitigation of loss appear to restrict the extent to which the plaintiff's full expectations of performance are protected with the result that, in most cases, the plaintiff is confined to his out-of-pocket loss. Moreover, contract damages may be awarded where the plaintiff's position has been worsened as a result of the defendant's breach, as is the case where the breach of contract results in death or personal injury or where damage to goods is caused by a bailee for reward. Furthermore, in limited circumstances, it appears that an award of tort damages can protect the plaintiff's expectation of interest, such as where there is an award of damages for personal injury which relates to lost future earnings and where negligent advice on the part of a solicitor results in the plaintiff being unable to benefit from a bequest which it was intended he should receive.[13]

The most common instance in which concurrent contractual and tortious obligations may arise is where there is a contract for the supply of a service under which there is likely to be an implied term to the effect that the service provider will exercise reasonable care and skill. But this contractual duty is often co-extensive with the common law duty of care also owed in the law of tort by the service provider to his neighbour.

Initially the common law approach to contract and tort was that the two branches of the law did not overlap at all. What seemed to stand in the way of the recognition of concurrent liability was a belief that a duty imposed by law could not be allowed to override a duty undertaken by the will of the parties to a contract. However, following the seminal decision in *Donoghue* v. *Stevenson*[14] it became apparent that a rigid division between contract and tort was no longer possible. In particular, the view that a legally imposed duty of care might interfere with voluntarily assumed contractual obligations was blown out of the water with the recognition that A could owe a duty of care to B despite the fact that this might affect the contractual relations existing between A and C. But despite the undoubted importance of the decision of the House of Lords in *Donoghue* v. *Stevenson*, it did not impinge on the problem of determining whether A could owe a duty of care in tort to B when there was an existing contractual relationship between A and B.

Despite the importance of the decision in *Donoghue* v. *Stevenson* for the relationship between actions framed in contract and those framed in tort, the courts were slow to depart from the old view that there was no overlap between these two branches of the common law.[15] Furthermore, in some instances where the logical approach would have been to

---

11. *Robinson* v. *Harman* (1848) 1 Exch 850 at 855 *per* Parke B.
12. *Livingstone* v. *Rawyards Coal Co* (1880) 5 App Cas 25 at 35 *per* Lord Blackburn.
13. See *Ross* v. *Caunters* [1980] Ch 297; *White* v. *Jones* [1995] 1 All ER 691.
14. [1932] AC 562.
15. See e.g. *Jarvis* v. *May, Davies, Smith, Vandervell & Co* [1936] KB 405.

recognise that a plaintiff might have concurrent rights, a compromise solution was adopted. For example, in *Ballett* v. *Mingay*[16] the defendant, a minor, had borrowed a microphone and amplifier from the plaintiff, but wrongfully failed to return the equipment as he had parted with possession of it. In the light of the defendant's minority, any contract between the parties would have been void. Accordingly, the plaintiff elected to sue the defendant for either detinue[17] or conversion, both of which were recognised to be actions framed in tort.[18] The defendant argued that the plaintiff should not be allowed to sue in tort when to do so would amount to an unacceptable means of avoiding the consequences of having entered a void contract. In dismissing the defendant's defence, the court held that the plaintiff was not raising an argument that the defendant was in breach of contract. Instead it was held that the defendant had gone outside the terms of the bailment altogether by parting with possession of the goods. It is difficult to see how this distinction can be justified since if there was a contract, the defendant was in breach of a term which required the borrowed goods to be returned. Accordingly, the plaintiff's election to sue for detinue and conversion had to be seen as a means of circumventing the voidness of the contract.

The area in which the problem of concurrent contractual and tortious liability has become most acute is where the issues of breach of contract and negligence coincide. Initially, the accepted judicial view was that if an action would have existed in law, whether or not the plaintiff and the defendant were parties to a contract, then the action was one which sounded in tort rather than in contract. Thus it was held that where the defendant had contracted to clean a chandelier and in the process of performing the contract negligently damaged the chandelier, the action was to be regarded as tortious in nature.[19] However, the position would have been different had the breach of contract fallen outside the scope of recovery in tort. For example, had the plaintiff suffered economic loss as a result of the defendant's breach, instead of the physical harm actually suffered, there would have been no action in tort at the time.

Later developments have demonstrated that in certain limited circumstances, negligently caused economic loss is now actionable in tort under the rule in *Hedley Byrne & Co Ltd* v. *Heller & Partners Ltd*.[20] In particular where a defendant with a special skill gives negligent advice, being aware that it is foreseeable that the plaintiff will rely and does, in fact, rely on the advice, a duty of care is owed, especially where the defendant has voluntarily assumed a relationship with the plaintiff which gives rise to the duty to take

16. [1943] KB 281.

17. Abolished as a tort and replaced by the statutory tort of unlawful interference with goods by the Torts (Interference with Goods) Act 1977. What had to be established for the purposes of the old tort of detinue was that the defendant had wrongfully withheld from the plaintiff chattels to which the plaintiff had a better title. Ordinarily, this would require a demand for the return of the goods to be made by the plaintiff which the defendant wrongly refused to comply with. One of the particular difficulties with the old action for detinue was that until there had been a demand and a wrongful refusal to return the chattel demanded, the plaintiff's action had not accrued. Accordingly, until the enactment of the Limitation Act 1939, s 3, it was quite likely that simply by failing to assert his title to goods, the true owner kept his action alive for an almost indefinite period of time: see *Clayton* v. *Le Roy* [1911] 2 KB 1031 at 1048 *per* Fletcher-Moulton LJ.

18. *Bryant* v. *Herbert* (1878) 3 CPD 389 held that detinue was a tort for the purposes of the County Courts Acts, although in the same case, Brett LJ considered that the origins of the action for detinue lay in a fictitious contract from which the defendant could not resile. Moreover, in historical terms, an action based upon the old form of declaration *detinue sur bailment* was, in essence, an action in contract.

19. *Jackson* v. *Mayfair Window Cleaning Co Ltd* [1952] 1 All ER 215.

20. [1964] AC 465.

reasonable care. Although in *Hedley Byrne* there was no contractual relationship between the plaintiff and the defendant, it was accepted later that advice given in the course of contractual negotiations could equally give rise to a duty situation.[21] The upshot of this development was that if a plaintiff can sue in tort for losses suffered as a result of the defendant's failure to take reasonable care, it should not be held that the plaintiff should be confined to an action in contract, especially if the effect of doing so would be to subject the plaintiff to the possibly more disadvantageous limitation period in contract actions which very often starts to run from an earlier date than that which applies to an action in tort.

Despite the logic of allowing the plaintiff to choose whether to frame his action in contract or in tort, the courts obdurately continued to maintain the traditional distinction, at least for the purposes of limitation of actions.[22]

In what has been regarded as a decision which flew in the face of much higher authority, Oliver J in *Midland Bank Trust Co Ltd* v. *Hett, Stubbs, Kemp & Co*[23] held that a solicitor could be sued by his client for a negligent failure to carry out his professional duties either in contract or in tort. Moreover, in what some might regard as an aberration, the House of Lords, by a majority, in *Junior Books Co Ltd* v. *Veitchi Co Ltd*[24] decided that an action for economic loss in the form of diminution in the value of part of a building, caused by a sub-contractor who had negligently performed his contractual obligations to the main contractor, could be framed in tort, despite the fact that a contractual claim against the main building contractor had been compromised by the plaintiff.[25]

What some of the more adventurous forays into the arena of concurrent liability failed to appreciate was that the terms of a contract generally represent the voluntarily assumed obligations of the parties to that contract which should not be overridden by a legally imposed duty sounding in tort. One logical consequence of *Junior Books* v. *Veitchi* was that it had become possible to regard all negligent breaches of contract as torts. However, development along these lines would have caused serious problems for the purposes of the law of limitation of actions so far as identifying the date on which the cause of action accrues.[26]

These specific limitation problems can be avoided if it is determined that the cause of action in contract and tort accrues at the same time, but this will not always be possible. In *Midland Bank Trust Co Ltd* v. *Hett, Stubbs, Kemp & Co*[27] the defendants were a firm of solicitors engaged to act on behalf of a farmer who had granted his son, the plaintiff, an option to purchase a farm which the plaintiff was working and for which he was paying rent. The defendants failed to register the option. Six years after granting the option, the farmer changed his mind and sought to defeat the plaintiff's option by conveying the farm to his wife for a nominal consideration. The plaintiff then sued the solicitors for both a breach of contract and for negligence under the rule in *Hedley Byrne* v. *Heller*. Oliver J concluded that the defendants did owe a duty of care to the plaintiff quite independently

21. *Esso Petroleum Co Ltd* v. *Mardon* [1976] 2 All ER 5.
22. See e.g. *Bagot* v. *Stevens Scanlan & Co* [1966] 1 QB 197—action for professional negligence brought by a client against his architect sounded in contract only.
23. [1979] Ch 384. See also *Batty* v. *Metropolitan Realisations Ltd* [1978] QB 554.
24. [1983] 1 AC 520. Politely referred to as "a decision on its own facts" based on the unique relationship of proximity between the parties.
25. See Atiyah, *An Introduction to the Law of Contract*, 5th ed, 1995, 383, n 40.
26. See Ch 18.
27. [1979] Ch 384.

of any contractual duty and that the cause of action arose when damage was caused. In the present case, it was considered that damage resulted to the plaintiff when the farm was sold in 1967 and that since a writ was issued in 1972, the plaintiff's action in tort was not time barred.

So far as the contractual action was concerned, Oliver J concluded that this was not a case of negligent advice which had been relied upon by the plaintiff to his detriment. Instead, the negligence of the defendant consisted of a failure to perform the obligation to register the option. This duty was considered to be continuing in nature and continued until the defendants were unable to perform the duty to register the option as a result of the sale of the farm. Accordingly, the cause of action in contract accrued at the same time as it did in tort, namely when the farm was sold. It followed from this that the plaintiff's contractual action was also within the six-year limitation period. The conclusion arrived at by Oliver J in *Hett* does not explicitly answer the important question whether the plaintiff could elect whether to sue in contract or in tort regardless of the consequences. For example, suppose the dates on which time began to run, in each case, were different, it would be necessary to decide whether the plaintiff could choose the more favourable tort date despite the fact that he might be out of time for the purposes of suing on his contract.

Older cases which admit to the existence of concurrent liability took the view that in such circumstances, the plaintiff was bound by the least favourable period of limitation,[28] which inevitably led to the later conclusion that if there were concurrent contractual and tortious duties, the plaintiff was confined to his cause of action in contract.[29] However, as *Hett* illustrates, the cause of action in contract cases does not always accrue at a later stage than that arising under a concurrent tortious claim. Other considerations relevant to the question whether concurrent tortious and contractual liability should be recognised include the detail with which contractual obligations have been worked out by the parties and whether the recognition of a concurrent right of action in tort would serve to undermine the agreement reached by the parties. For example, it has been held that a plaintiff will not be allowed to frame his action in tort, if to allow him to do so would create in favour of the plaintiff rights in excess of those permitted by the contract between the parties.[30] Thus it was observed by Lord Scarman, expressing the opinion of the Privy Council in *Tai Hing Cotton Mill Ltd* v. *Liu Chong Hing Bank Ltd*[31]:

"Their Lordships do not believe that there is anything to the advantage of the law's development in searching for a liability in tort where the parties are in a contractual relationship. Though it is possible as a matter of legal semantics to conduct an analysis of the rights and duties inherent in some contractual relationships, including that of banker and customer, either as a matter of contract law, when the question will be what, if any, terms are to be implied, or as a matter of tort law where the task would be to identify a duty arising from the proximity and character of the relation between the parties, their Lordships believe it to be correct in principle and necessary for the avoidance of confusion in the law to adhere to the contractual analysis: on principle because it is a relationship

---

28. *Howell* v. *Young* (1826) 5 B & C 259; *Smith* v. *Fox* (1848) 6 Hare 386; *Bean* v. *Wade* (1885) 2 TLR 157.

29. *Groom* v. *Crocker* [1939] 1 KB 194; *Bagot* v. *Stevens Scanlan & Co* [1966] 1 QB 197.

30. See *National Bank of Greece SA* v. *Pinios Shipping Co (No 1)* [1989] 1 All ER 213 at 223 *per* Lloyd LJ and at 232 *per* Nicholls LJ; *Bank of Nova Scotia* v. *Hellenic Mutual War Risks Association (Bermuda) Ltd, The Good Luck* [1989] 3 All ER 628 at 664 *per* May LJ; *Greater Nottingham Co-operative Society* v. *Cementation Piling & Foundations Ltd* [1988] 2 All ER 971 at 984 *per* Purchas LJ and at 991 *per* Mann LJ; *Pacific Associates Inc* v. *Baxter* [1989] 2 All ER 159 at 170 *per* Purchas LJ.

31. [1986] AC 80 at 107.

which the parties have, subject to a few exceptions, the right to determine their obligations to each other, and for the avoidance of confusion because different consequences follow according to whether liability arises from contract or tort, e.g. the limitation of actions . . .

Their Lordships do not, therefore, embark on an investigation as to whether, in the relationship between banker and customer, it is possible to identify tort as well as contract as a source of the obligations owed by one to the other. Their Lordships do not, however, accept that the parties' mutual obligations in tort can be any greater than those to be found expressly or by necessary implication in their contract . . . the banks cannot rely on the law of tort to provide them with greater protection than that for which they have contracted."

This view should not, however, be taken to mean that it is impossible for tortious duties to exist within a contractual relationship. All Lord Scarman was saying was that tortious duties cannot exist where they are at variance with what the parties to the contract have agreed regarding the matter of their obligations. Thus it will not be possible for the plaintiff to sue in tort where to allow him to do so would avoid the effect of an exemption clause agreed upon by the contracting parties.[32] Moreover, the manner in which the parties to a contract or a series of contracts have structured their relationship will often be relevant in determining whether a tortious duty may be superimposed on the obligations arising from those contracts. For example, where a building owner, main building contractor and sub-contractors have entered into a series of contractual relationships all of which are geared towards the satisfactory completion of the main building contract, it may be that all related parties have contracted with each other on the assumption that certain risks are to be borne by one of the parties. In these circumstances, to hold that a sub-contractor, for example, owes a duty of care to the building owner in respect of one of those risks, might serve to undermine a contractual undertaking entered into by the building owner or the main contractor on which all other parties have based their own contractual undertakings.[33]

However, there are circumstances in which a tortious duty of care may be owed even where the effect of holding that such a duty exists is to outflank the contractual structure expressly set up by the parties. For example, in *Henderson* v. *Merrett Syndicates Ltd*[34] it was held by the House of Lords that a sub-agent acting on behalf of indirect Lloyd's Names owed a tortious duty of care to those Names despite the fact that there was no contract between the parties. Thus, although there was a conscious decision not to create a contractual structure by ensuring that there was an intermediary placed between the plaintiff and the defendant, a tortious duty of care was still held to exist on the part of the defendant sub-agent. Lord Goff opined that the contractual structure argument was often a relevant consideration,[35] but not in this case, apparently because the facts of the case were unusual, with the result that there might be other cases based on the Lloyd's fiasco which might reveal relevant contractual provisions capable of preventing a tortious duty of care from being owed. Lord Goff also observes that in the case of building contracts, if a sub-contractor performs work which is not of the required standard, ordinarily, there will be no liability in tort to the building owner since the sub-contractor will not be taken

---

32. *William Hill Organisation Ltd* v. *Bernard Sunley & Sons Ltd* (1982) 22 BLR 1. See also *New Zealand Shipping Co Ltd* v. *AM Satterthwaite & Co Ltd, The Eurymedon* [1975] AC 154.
33. See e.g. *Norwich City Council* v. *Harvey* [1989] 1 All ER 1180.
34. [1994] 3 All ER 506.
35. *Ibid* at 534.

to have assumed responsibility to the owner since the structure of the contractual relationships between the various parties will be inconsistent with any such assumption of responsibility.[36]

What is not made clear in *Henderson* is how the facts of that case differ from other cases in which the contractual structure is such as not to give rise to tortious liability as between the defendant and the plaintiff. Even a distinction based on the difference between economic loss and physical harm is not now sustainable since following *Marc Rich & Co* v. *Bishop Rock Marine Ltd*[37] the contractual structure argument was relevant in a case in which cargo owners were owed no duty of care by a classification society in respect of physical harm to their property caused by the alleged negligence of the society. It was considered that to impose a duty of care upon a classification society in respect of their role as surveyors of ocean-going vessels would outflank the agreed allocation of risks arising under the contract made between the cargo owners and the ship owners. The principal reason for arriving at this conclusion was that to impose liability on the classification society would be unreasonable and unjust since the cost of insuring against claims in respect of ships surveyed by the classification society would ultimately be passed on to the ship owner.

At present, the law in this area is in a state of flux, and it is becoming increasingly apparent that the House of Lords needs to provide guidance on when the contractual structure argument must be taken into account and when it may be ignored. It is suggested that to take the contractual structure argument too far would have the effect of reintroducing the "privity of contract" fallacy supposedly disposed of in *Donoghue* v. *Stevenson*.[38] A more sensible approach would be to take account of only those contractual provisions which expressly militate against the imposition of a tortious duty of care in circumstances in which the plaintiff could not have been unaware of the consequences of those contractual terms, such as where there is an express exclusion or limitation of liability which would otherwise be covered by the introduction of a tortious duty. Such a position prevails in some other common law jurisdictions. Thus it was observed in *Central Trust Co* v. *Rafuse*[39] that:

"A concurrent or alternative liability in tort will not be admitted if its effect would be to permit the plaintiff to circumvent or escape a contractual exclusion or limitation of liability for the act or omission that would constitute the tort. Subject to this qualification, where concurrent liability in tort and contract exists, the plaintiff has the right to assert the cause of action that appears to be the most advantageous to him in respect of any particular legal consequence."

Although it was held in *Simaan General Contracting Co* v. *Pilkington Glass Ltd (No 2)*[40] that there was no room for tortious duties because the parties' contractual obligations

---

36. See also *Simaan General Contracting Co* v. *Pilkington Glass Ltd (No 2)* [1988] QB 758 at 781 *per* Bingham LJ.

37. [1995] 3 All ER 307.

38. [1932] AC 562.

39. (1986) 31 DLR (4th) 481 at 522 *per* Le Dain J. Concurrent liability also exists in Irish law: *Finlay* v. *Murtagh* [1979] IR 249. In New Zealand and Australia, there are doubts on the matter, although there seems to be a move in the direction of the acceptance of concurrent contractual and tortious duties. Contrast *McLaren Maycroft & Co* v. *Fletcher Development Co Ltd* [1973] 2 NZLR 100 (liability contractual) and *Rowlands* v. *Collow* [1992] 1 NZLR 178 (liability concurrent). See also *Aluminium Products (Qld) Pty Ltd* v. *Hill* [1981] Qd R 33 (concurrent liability) and *Hawkins* v. *Clayton* (1988) 154 CLR 539 (against concurrent liability, but preferring to allow the plaintiff to sue in tort rather than to imply a contractual duty to take reasonable care).

40. [1988] QB 758

had been *exhaustively* defined, it is implicit that where there is less exhaustive definition, tortious duties may survive. Furthermore in *Johnstone* v. *Bloomsbury Area Health Authority*[41] it was held that tortious duties of care may be owed in an employment relationship since these could be dovetailed with the duties owed under the contract. However, much will turn on how explicit is the contractual term. For example, in *Johnstone* a hospital doctor was required by his contract of employment to be available for work for up to 88 hours per week on average, but this could be overridden by the tortious duty owed by an employer to provide a reasonably safe place of work and safe working conditions, if there was a danger to the employee's health. However, if the contract had been worded in such a way as to impose an absolute contractual obligation to work 88 hours a week, to impose a tortious duty of care in respect of the employee's health might be regarded as being inconsistent with the express terms of the contract, especially in light of the view of Browne-Wilkinson VC that[42] "if there is a contractual relationship between the parties their respective rights and duties have to be analysed wholly in contractual terms and not as a mixture of duties in tort and contract".

The problem that this possibility of concurrent liability creates for limitation purposes is that the date on which the cause of action accrues may differ according to whether the action is framed in contract or in tort. Generally, where there is a contractual relationship, the easy answer is that " . . . if a contract is in existence this is the natural vehicle for recourse".[43] However, to insist on a purely contractual analysis, as did Browne-Wilkinson V-C in *Johnstone* does have its deficiencies. For example, for the purposes of limitation of actions, if the plaintiff must sue for breach of contract rather than for breach of a tortious duty of care, the provisions of the Latent Damage Act 1986 will have no application, since this Act has been construed to apply only to actions based on breach of a tortious obligation.[44] Moreover, if Browne-Wilkinson V-C's view is taken to its logical conclusion the whole of the law of employers' liability and the law relating to the supply of services pursuant to a contract should be regarded as matters of contract rather than tort, which surely could not have been intended.

CONTRACTUAL AND RESTITUTIONARY CLAIMS[45]

Given that the recognition of the law of restitution as a distinct branch of the law of civil obligations is only of comparatively recent origin, it is not surprising that the Limitation Act 1980 does not make specific reference to such actions, especially those for moneys had and received. In this regard, it has been observed that the Limitation Act 1980, s 5 must also " . . . be taken to cover actions for money had and received, formerly actions on the case . . . though the words used cannot be regarded as felicitous".[46] From this, it follows that a restitutionary claim will be barred six years after the cause of action accrues, but clearly, this cannot be the same date as that which applies to actions for breach of a

---

41. [1991] 2 All ER 293.
42. *Ibid* at 304.
43. *Société Commerciale de Réassurance* v. *ERAS (International) Ltd* [1992] 2 All ER 82 at 85 *per* Mustill LJ.
44. *Iron Trade Mutual Insurance Co Ltd* v. *JK Buckenham Ltd* [1990] 1 All ER 808; *Société Commerciale de Réassurance* v. *ERAS (International) Ltd* [1992] 2 All ER 82 and see also Ch 20.
45. See further Ch 17.
46. *Re Diplock* [1948] Ch 465 at 514 *per* Lord Greene MR.

simple contract, since there may not be a breach of contract from which time begins to run. Moreover, restitutionary claims may also arise out of the commission of a wrong by the defendant, in which case, the contractual limitation period is clearly inapplicable. What should also be noted is that, generally, contractual and tortious claims are for an unliquidated amount, the extent of recovery being based on the loss suffered by the plaintiff. In contrast, a restitutionary claim is based upon the unjustified enrichment of the defendant, and therefore turns on the recovery of a specific amount.

What is necessary is to identify the gist of the plaintiff's cause of action, since this sets the point from which time will run. For these purposes, the gist of a restitutionary claim appears to be the injustice of the defendant being allowed to retain a benefit gained at the expense of the plaintiff.[47] For these purposes, it is arguable that the plaintiff should only become time barred where the lapse of time has the effect of removing the injustice associated with the enrichment of the defendant at his expense. Generally, this will be the case where the lapse of time may be taken as an indication of the plaintiff's waiver of his rights, or where the effect of the passage of time is to prejudice the defendant's ability to satisfactorily establish a defence to the action brought by the plaintiff. Given these considerations, it is suggested that an appropriate policy basis for the setting of an appropriate limitation period for a restitutionary claim is that set out in *Lindsay Petroleum Co* v. *Hurd*[48] in which it was observed by Lord Selborne that it may be practically unjust to give a remedy either because the conduct of the plaintiff amounts to a waiver of his rights or has acted in such a way as to make it unreasonable to grant him a remedy, having regard to the length of the delay and what has been done during the period of delay.[49]

ACCRUAL OF THE CAUSE OF ACTION

The basic rule of contract law is that a breach of contract is actionable without proof of damage, although a plaintiff who has suffered no damage will receive only nominal damages, but for limitation purposes, his action is nonetheless maintained. Since damage is not a requirement in order for there to be a cause of action, it follows that the date on which time begins to run cannot be the same as that applicable to an action framed in tort, but starts, instead, at the time of the breach of contract.

The origins of the choice of the date of breach date back to the action on assumpsit, for which purposes it has been held that it is immaterial at what stage the promise is made as the relevant six-year limitation period runs from the date on which the promise was broken.[50] Furthermore, it is of no relevance that damage suffered by the plaintiff occurs after the breach of contract since it was said in *Gibbs* v. *Guild*[51] that:

" 'Action on the case', as used in the statute, was a general term including actions on assumpsit or contract, actions for negligence or for fraud, and for other causes of action; and it was well settled that in actions on assumpsit, the time ran from the breach of contract, for that was the gist of the

---

47. See McLean, "Limitation of Actions in Restitution" (1989) 48 CLJ 472.
48. (1874) LR 5 PC 221.
49. *Ibid* at 239–40 discussed in detail in Ch 3.
50. *Gould* v. *Johnson* (1702) 2 Salk 422.
51. (1881) 8 QBD 296.

action, and the subsequent damage, although happening within the six years next before the suit, did not prevent the application of the statute."[52]

A particular problem which this rule gives rise to is that, subject to rules on fraud, concealment and mistake,[53] if the damage suffered by the plaintiff as a result of the defendant's breach of contract takes years to manifest itself, the plaintiff may not be aware of the breach of contract in time to be able to bring his action within the limitation period. Thus in *Battley* v. *Faulkner*[54] in 1810, the defendant contracted to sell to the plaintiff a quantity of spring wheat, warranted to be suitable for planting. Since the plaintiff purchased for the purposes of resale rather than personal use, the wheat was sold on to a sub-purchaser under the description "spring wheat" later in the year. The sub-purchaser planted the wheat in the spring of 1810 but the crop failed because what had been supplied was winter wheat. The sub-purchaser issued his writ against the plaintiff in 1811, but did not obtain judgment until 1818, by which time the plaintiff was out of time so far as any action against the defendant was concerned. The cause of action arose on the defendant's breach of contract in 1810 when there was a delivery of wheat of a different kind to that contracted for.[55] In the circumstances, it would have been better for the plaintiff to have issued his writ before the outcome of the proceedings brought by the sub-purchaser was known, in order that the plaintiff's action against the defendant could be preserved.[56]

Similarly, in *Lynn* v. *Bamber*[57] in 1921 the plaintiff contracted to purchase 240 "Purple Pershore" plum trees from the defendant, but discovered in 1928 that what he had purchased were "Coe's Late Red" plum trees, which were of inferior quality. Since time ran from the date of the defendant's breach of warranty, which was given in December 1921, the plaintiff's action was time barred in the absence of proof of fraud or concealment of the breach.

Where the contract is one for the provision of a service, the problem of damage being caused at a late stage is equally applicable. For example in *Howell* v. *Young*[58] a client alleged negligence on the part of his lawyer, claiming that he had been induced to lend money to a third party in the belief that his loan would be adequately secured. In fact the property on which the loan was secured proved to be insufficient to secure the total amount of the loan. However, the insufficient security only became known after the six-year limitation period had expired. Since this was a contract for the provision of advice, it was held that the cause of action accrued when the advice was given and the mortgage was executed, it being irrelevant that damage was only suffered when the security was discovered to be inadequate. According to Bayley J[59]:

"In an action for words which are actionable in themselves, a special damage is frequently alleged in the declaration, although it is not the ground of the action, and the plaintiff may recover without proving the special damage. In such a case the allegation of special damage is a mere explanation of the manner in which the conduct of the defendant has become injurious to the plaintiff. So in this

---

52. *Ibid* at 302 *per* Field J. See also *Battley* v. *Faulkner* (1820) 3 B & Ald 288 at 292 *per* Abbott CJ and at 293 *per* Bayley J.
53. Limitation Act 1980, s 32 and see Ch 6.
54. (1820) 3 B & Ald 288.
55. *Ibid* at 295 *per* Best J.
56. *Ibid.*
57. [1930] 2 KB 72.
58. (1826) B & C 259. See also *Short* v. *McCarthy* (1832) 3 B & A 626; *Forster* v. *Outred & Co* [1982] 1 WLR 86.
59. *Ibid* at 265.

case, the purpose for which the allegation is introduced, is precisely similar. Where, indeed, words are not actionable of themselves, but become so by reason of the consequential damage, then it must be alleged and proved; because it constitutes the cause of action. In an action of assumpsit, the Statute of Limitations begins to run not from the time when the damage results, but the time when the breach of promise takes place."

Accordingly, the plaintiff's cause of action arose when he took the insufficient security, since if the plaintiff had sued at that stage, the jury would have had to give damages for the probable loss which the plaintiff was likely to suffer in consequence of the invalidity of the security.[60]

What has been said above in relation to concurrent contractual and tortious liability is also relevant in the context of contracts for the provision of services, since if the plaintiff's action sounds in both contract and tort, he may be able to select the cause of action most favourable to him. In most cases, for limitation purposes, this will be his action in tort, since time runs from the date on which damage is caused, ignoring the date of any breach of contract.

Since the gist of an action for breach of contract is that a promise has been made which has been broken, a new cause of action will arise each time there is a breach of contract. It follows that it is possible, in the context of a particular contract, for several limitation periods to run according to the date on which each breach of contract occurs. This is particularly the case where the contract contains obligations of a continuing nature such as a lease requiring the tenant to maintain the property in a reasonable state of repair or to pay rent on a regular basis. In these circumstances, a fresh cause of action will accrue on the occasion of each successive breach by the tenant of a covenant to repair[61] or on the occurrence of each failure to pay rent in accordance with the terms of the lease.[62] Similarly, in the case of a credit agreement, each successive failure by the debtor to pay instalments will create a new cause of action.[63]

(a) Anticipatory breach

A complicating factor which may affect the position of a plaintiff suing for a breach of contract is that, in some instances, the defendant's breach may be anticipatory in the sense that the defendant makes it clear that he will not be able to perform his contractual obligations before the date on which they are due to be performed.[64] In these circumstances, since the rule emerging from *Howell* v. *Young* is that time begins to run against the plaintiff as soon as he is in a position to be able to sue, it must follow that in the case of an anticipatory breach, time runs from the date on which the plaintiff becomes able to sue. Thus it has been observed in *Bell* v. *Peter Browne & Co*,[65] in a different context that:

"A remediable breach is just as much a breach of contract when it occurs as an irremediable breach, although the practical consequences are likely to be less serious if the breach comes to light in time to take remedial action. Were the law otherwise, in any of these instances, the effect would be to

---

60. *Ibid* at 268 *per* Holroyd J.
61. *Spoor* v. *Green* (1874) LR 9 Exch 99.
62. *Bowyer* v. *Woodman* (1867) LR 3 Eq 313.
63. *Arnott* v. *Holden* (1852) 18 QB 593.
64. See *Hochster* v. *De La Tour* (1853) 2 El & Bl 678.
65. [1990] 3 All ER 124.

frustrate the purpose of the statutes of limitation, for it would mean that breaches of contract would never become statute-barred unless the innocent party chose to accept the defaulting party's conduct as a repudiation or, perhaps, performance ceased to be possible."[66]

The problem with an anticipatory breach of contract is that the plaintiff has two choices. As the facts of *Hochster* v. *De La Tour*[67] illustrate, the plaintiff may accept the defendant's breach and sue immediately he becomes aware of the defendant's intention not to perform,[68] thereby bringing to an end his own performance obligations under the contract.[69] Accordingly, in *Hochster*, the plaintiff could cease to make himself available for employment as a courier when he sought his remedy for breach of contract in May 1852 despite the fact that the contract for the plaintiff's services was not due to be performed until June 1852. What underlies the decision seems to be that either the defendant has rendered it impossible for himself to perform the contract, or that there is an implied promise that neither party will do anything to the prejudice of the other which is inconsistent with what has been undertaken.[70] On the basis that the cause of action accrues when the plaintiff is first able to sue, it must follow from this that time will run from the defendant's breach of this implied undertaking not to do anything which might prejudice the plaintiff's expectation of employment. That breach can occur where there is an express repudiatory breach as in *Hochster* v. *De La Tour*, but a breach may also be found by implication from the conduct of the defendant. Thus if the defendant agrees to grant the plaintiff a lease on land he owns as from a specified date, but chooses instead to execute a lease in favour of someone else before the date agreed, the plaintiff may sue immediately, not having to wait until the date agreed for the commencement of the lease.[71] Similarly, a contract for the sale of specific goods to be delivered on a specified date is breached by the defendant if, before the agreed date, the goods are sold to someone else,[72] since if the contract is for the sale of specific goods, only those goods may be used in performance of the contract.

The second course of action available to the plaintiff in the event of an anticipatory breach is to wait until the date on which performance is due and sue at that later date. However, there are dangers associated with such a delay, since some other event may occur which discharges the parties from the duty to perform their obligations under the contract. Moreover, from a limitation perspective, while the plaintiff waits to see if the defendant will perform the contract on the due date, time has already started to run against him. This has the effect of making it a dangerous practice to wait for the agreed date of performance, especially in cases where the anticipatory breach occurs at a very early stage and there are a number of years to go before the agreed date of performance, such as might

66. *Ibid* at 127 *per* Nicholls LJ.
67. (1853) 2 El & Bl 678.
68. See also *Mersey Steel & Iron Co* v. *Naylor Benzon & Co* (1884) 9 App Cas 434 at 442–43 *per* Lord Blackburn.
69. *Denmark Productions Ltd* v. *Boscobel Productions Ltd* [1969] 1 QB 699.
70. (1853) 2 El & Bl 678 at 688–89 *per* Lord Campbell CJ.
71. *Ford* v. *Tiley* (1828) 6 B & C 325. See also *Synge* v. *Synge* [1894] 1 QB 466 (promise in a marriage settlement to leave a house and land to the plaintiff, broken by a disposition to a third party); *Lovelock* v. *Franklin* (1846) 8 QB 371 (promise to assign the defendant's interest in land to the plaintiff in seven years' time, broken by assignment of the same interest to another); *Short* v. *Stone* (1846) 8 QB 358 (breach of promise to marry found in the fact that the defendant married someone else).
72. *Bowdell* v. *Parsons* (1809) 10 East 359.

be the case with certain long-term contractual relationships associated with the construction or shipbuilding industries. For example in *Reeves* v. *Butcher*[73] the plaintiff lent £426
to the defendant for a period of five years, the contract providing that interest payments
of 7 per cent should be made on a quarterly basis and subject to a term which allowed the
plaintiff to call in the full amount of the loan if any interest payment remained unpaid for
a period of 21 days from the date on which it became due. In fact the defendant made no
payments of interest at all, with the result that the first remediable breach of contract
occurred within 21 days of the date on which the first quarterly interest payment became
due. The plaintiff's writ was issued within six years of the end of the five-year loan period,
but it was argued by the defendant that the action to recover the principal debt and interest
was time barred since, from the date of the first remediable failure to pay an interest
instalment, the plaintiff was contractually entitled to call in the full amount of the loan
immediately. Expressing the unanimous opinion of the Court of Appeal, Lindley LJ held
that:

"This expression 'cause of action' has been repeatedly the subject of decision, and it has been held,
particularly in *Hemp* v. *Garland*[74] . . . that the cause of action arises at the time when the debt could
first have been recovered by action. The right to bring an action may arise on various events; but
it has always been that the statute runs from the earliest time at which an action could be
brought."[75]

(b) The date of breach

Since the gist of an action on a simple contract is that there has been a breach of contract,
it is essential to ascertain when that breach occurs in order to be able to identify the date
on which time begins to run against the plaintiff. The answer to this important question
will lie in an interpretation of the terms of the contract, since it will be necessary to
identify what obligations have been undertaken (or are imposed by law, in the case of
some implied terms). What has to be asked is what has been promised and when did the
defendant fail to fulfil that promise with the result that the plaintiff's cause of action has
accrued.

Accordingly, when the breach of contract occurs is essentially a question of fact,
dependent upon a proper interpretation of the terms of the contract made between the
parties. For example, it is possible that before it can be said that A is in breach of contract
some condition or contingency must have been satisfied by the other party, B, with the
result that what might ordinarily be regarded as a breach of contract by A ceases to be a
breach because B has failed to fulfil the contingency upon which A's liability for breach
of contract depends. For example, in *Bentworth Finance Ltd* v. *Lubert*[76] a consumer debtor
defaulted in making instalment payments under a hire purchase agreement. Ordinarily this
could be regarded as a sufficiently serious breach of contract to allow the creditor to
commence default proceedings under the terms of the agreement. However, it transpired
that the creditor had failed to supply the debtor with copies of legal documents showing
a change of ownership in the goods subject to the credit agreement. In the event, it was
held that there was no breach of contract on the part of the debtor, since his liability under

73. [1891] 2 QB 509.
74. (1843) 4 QB 519.
75. [1891] 2 QB 509 at 511.
76. [1968] 1 QB 680.

the contract was dependent on the prior performance of the creditor's obligation to supply the relevant documentation. It may also be relevant to consider whether the contract requires simultaneous performance on the part of both parties to the contract. For example, in the absence of any provision in a contract for the sale of goods as to a period of credit, it is provided that the seller's obligation to deliver and the buyer's obligation to pay for the goods sold are simultaneous performance obligations.[77] It follows from this that the buyer cannot sue the seller in respect of an alleged breach of contract unless he has performed or is ready to perform his obligations under the contract. However, if there is provision for credit, the buyer's obligation to make payment is delayed until the expiry of the agreed period of credit, with the result that the seller's obligation to deliver is no longer to be performed simultaneously with the buyer's obligation to tender payment. Accordingly, for the purposes of the buyer's payment obligations, time will not begin to run against the seller until the agreed period of credit has expired. Thus in *Helps* v. *Winterbottom*[78] a contract for the sale of wool provided the buyer with a period of six months' credit, the price being payable by a bill of exchange covering a period of two or three months, at the buyer's option. A majority of the court held that this effectively provided the buyer with up to nine months' credit, with the result that there could be no breach of contract in respect of the buyer's payment obligations until the expiry of nine months from the date of entry into the contract. Although the contract was apparently construed as one giving the buyer up to nine months' credit, strictly this was not the case, since if there was evidence which showed that the buyer had not presented a bill of exchange at the end of the period of six months' credit, the seller would have an action for not delivering to the seller a good security for the amount owed under the contract. However, as two members of the court observed, this would not allow the seller to recover the whole amount of the debt, but merely the reasonably foreseeable loss flowing from the failure to deliver the bill on time.[79]

Generally, whether or not there has been a breach of contract will depend upon a consideration of all the circumstances surrounding the act or omission alleged to constitute the breach. Thus in *Transoceanic Petroleum Carriers* v. *Cook Industries Inc, The Mary Lou*[80] a voyage charterparty provided that the charterer should nominate a safe port for the loading of a cargo of grain or soyabeans. The port nominated by the charterers was New Orleans, which at the time of nomination was a safe port. However, due to known characteristics of the River Mississippi in certain weather conditions, part of the passage used by ships seeking to gain access to the port had become heavily silted. As a consequence of this, the ship was badly damaged and the question arose as to whether there was a breach of contract on the part of the charterers and, if so, at what stage the breach occurred. Two possibilities presented themselves, namely that the warranty was merely that the port nominated was safe at the time of nomination or, alternatively, that the port nominated would continue to be a safe port up to and including the time when the chartered vessel came to use the port. In the event, Mustill J concluded that the relevant date for determining when the plaintiff's cause of action will accrue in circumstances such as these is the date on which damage is caused,[81] which for the purposes of the present

77. Sale of Goods Act 1979, s 28.
78. (1831) 2 B & Ad 431.
79. *Ibid* at 433 *per* Lord Tenterden CJ and at 434–35 *per* Littledale J.
80. [1981] 2 Lloyd's Rep 272.
81. *Ibid* at 278. See also *The Hermine* [1978] 2 Lloyd's Rep 37; *The Pendrecht* [1980] 2 Lloyd's Rep 56.

case meant that the date of accrual of the cause of action did not arise until the time when the ship attempted to use the port of New Orleans at a time when it was not safe and there was available survey evidence to show that this was the case. However, this should not be taken to mean that the cause of action will always arise at the time of attempted use of the port, since there may be circumstances in which the port nominated is unsafe from the outset and the ship owner uses this as a justification for not permitting his ship to proceed to the nominated port. In these circumstances, it is more appropriate to regard the cause of action as arising at the time of nomination rather than at the time of intended use of the nominated port, since the important consideration is whether there is a condition precedent to the duty of the vessel to proceed to the nominated port that the port nominated should be a safe one to use.[82]

(c) Continuing breaches of contract

Although the general rule is that a specific date must be identified on which the breach of contract occurred, there may be circumstances in which such precise identification is not possible, especially in cases in which the breach of contract consists of an omission to do something which the contract requires. For example, it may be that the contract is unclear on the time at which a particular obligation is to be performed or alternatively there may be a breach of contract which can be remedied by the party in breach while there continues between the parties a relationship capable of giving rise to continuing obligations. For example in *Shaw* v. *Shaw*[83] the defendant promised to marry the plaintiff in 1937 and subsequently, in 1938, went through a form of bigamous marriage with her. The two cohabited and the plaintiff made substantial contributions to the defendant's farming business. In 1950 the defendant's lawful wife died and in 1952, the defendant also died intestate, whereupon the plaintiff, at the direction of the children[84] of her "marriage", discovered the true state of affairs because she had no claim in intestacy. The plaintiff's action against the defendant's estate alleged breach of promise to marry,[85] but it was met by a plea of limitation on the basis that the breach of contract had occurred many years before the writ was issued. However the Court of Appeal considered, *inter alia*, that there was an implied and continuing warranty on the part of the defendant that he was free to marry. This warranty was made at the time of his promise to marry the plaintiff in 1937 and was taken to continue during the defendant's lifetime. The bigamous marriage could not be taken to have satisfied the defendant's warranty as such marriages were regarded as being void and contrary to public policy,[86] therefore, it followed that the defendant continued to breach the warranty until 1950 when his lawful wife died. Accordingly, since the plaintiff's action was brought shortly after the defendant's death in 1952, it was well within the six-year limitation period, the last breach of the continuing warranty having

---

82. See *Reardon Smith Line Ltd* v. *Australian Wheat Board, The Houston City* [1954] 2 Lloyd's Rep 148.
83. [1954] 2 QB 429.
84. Who also happened to be the defendants, in the present case, as representatives of the deceased's estate.
85. The action for breach of promise to marry was abolished by the Law Reform (Miscellaneous Provisions) Act 1970, s 1. However, the principles of limitation of actions remain unaffected.
86. *Wilson* v. *Carnley* [1908] 1 KB 729; *Spiers* v. *Hunt* [1908] 1 KB 720. These cases both involved a promise by a man known by the promisee, at the time of the promise, to be married. *Shaw* v. *Shaw* differed in that the plaintiff was unaware of the defendant's married status at the time of the promise. It therefore followed that there was no obstacle to the enforcement of the warranty in these circumstances.

occurred in 1950. As was observed by Singleton LJ, the plaintiff was entitled to damages for breach of promise because she was "entitled to consider that if Shaw had fulfilled his promise . . . the plaintiff would have been his widow. If she had been she would have had the rights of a widow."[87] Moreover, there was also a further ground on which the plaintiff's cause of action was preserved since, because the defendant had deliberately hidden the fact of his earlier marriage, there had been a fraudulent concealment, which prevented time from running against the plaintiff.[88]

The concept of the continuing warranty also underlies the decision of Oliver J in *Midland Bank Trust Co* v. *Hett, Stubbs & Kemp*[89] in which the defendant solicitors were taken to owe a continuing contractual duty to the plaintiff, their client's son, in respect of their undertaking to register a ten-year option to purchase a farm granted in the plaintiff's favour. The solicitor argued that since their obligation was to register the option within a reasonable time of completion of the transaction under which it was acquired, the breach of contract occurred when the defendants failed to do what was required of them under the contract. Since more than six years had expired since the first occasion on which the option could have been registered, it was argued that the plaintiff's contractual action was out of time. However, applying the notion of the continuing warranty, Oliver J held that the duty of the solicitors was to effect a valid registration of the option and that this duty continued until such time as it became impossible to perform. Accordingly, it became impossible to register the option either when the land was sold by the plaintiff's father to a third party, so that registration of the option would not be effective, or when the agreed duration of the option itself expired, so that it could no longer be exercised. What is important to appreciate is that the defendants' breach of contract did not consist of the giving of negligent advice. Instead, what they were guilty of was nonfeasance in "failing to take such steps as were necessary and practicable to ensure that [the option] was binding on the land into whosesoever hands it might come before any third party acquired a legal estate".[90] As such, this was a continuing duty rather than one fixed to a specific date or one which had to be performed within a reasonable time of a specific date, in which case time would start to run after that reasonable time had expired.[91]

Subsequently, it has become apparent that the reasoning employed by Oliver J will only be applied sparingly, and that as a general rule, the courts will look for a once-and-for-all date on which the breach of contract occurred. Thus in *Bell* v. *Peter Browne & Co*[92] the plaintiff employed the defendant solicitors to act on his behalf in respect of a planned divorce settlement. In breach of contract, the defendants failed to cause the execution of a declaration of trust, in favour of the plaintiff, on the matrimonial home and also failed to register a caution with the Land Registry in respect of any dealings in the property. As a consequence of this breach, the plaintiff lost a one-sixth interest in the proceeds of sale when the property was subsequently sold by the plaintiff's former spouse. The settlement had been entered into in 1978, but no action was commenced until 1987, by which time it was held that the plaintiff's action was time barred since the breach of contract was

87. [1954] 2 QB 429 at 439.
88. See Ch 6.
89. [1979] Ch 384. See n 27 above and associated text.
90. *Ibid* at 435 *per* Oliver J.
91. Cf *Bean* v. *Wade* (1885) 2 TLR 157.
92. [1990] 3 All ER 124.

considered to have occurred in 1978. Nicholls LJ said of the Limitation Act 1980, s 5 that:

"That section precludes the bringing of an action founded on a simple contract after the expiration of six years from the date on which the cause of action accrued. Ascertaining that date involves identifying the relevant terms of the contract and also the date on which the breach relied on occured ... Mr Bell's solicitor was retained to take all those steps which a reasonably careful solicitor would take in respect of the agreed arrangements for the transfer of the house ... and the retention by him of a beneficial interest ... Mr Bell's solicitor was to ensure that on a sale of the house Mr Bell would receive his share of the proceeds.

Clearly, all those steps needed to be taken at the time of the transfer, or in the case of lodging a caution, as soon as reasonably practicable thereafter. When the solicitor failed to take those steps in 1978 he was, thereupon, in breach of contract. This was so even though the breach, so far as it related to lodging a caution, remained remediable for many years."[93]

So far as the failure to obtain a declaration of trust is concerned, this reasoning cannot be faulted, but there is greater difficulty in reconciling this decision with *Hett* so far as the alleged breach in failing to lodge a caution is concerned. The reasoning employed by Oliver J in *Hett* suggests that had the plaintiff in that case sued the solicitors for their failure to register the option some two months after the option had been granted, there might have been a technical action for breach of contract, but that it would have been struck out as an abuse of the process of the court.[94] However in *Bell*, Nicholls LJ dismissed as irrelevant the fact that if a remediable breach is discovered in time for it to be remedied there might be less serious consequences for the plaintiff.[95] However, Nicholls LJ did concede that there are circumstances in which a contractual obligation does "arise anew for performance day after day"[96] such as a landlord's or a tenant's covenant to keep the leased property in a good state of repair.[97] What seems to have been used by Nicholls LJ to set *Hett* and *Bell* apart is that in the former, there was a continuing relationship between the plaintiff and the defendants, whereas in the latter all dealings had ceased after the conclusion of the divorce proceedings.[98]

93. *Ibid* at 126.
94. *Midland Bank Trust Co* v. *Hett, Stubbs & Kemp* [1979] Ch 384 at 435.
95. *Bell* v. *Peter Browne & Co* [1990] 3 All ER 124 at 127.
96. *Ibid.*
97. *Spoor* v. *Green* (1874) LR 9 Exch 99 at 111 *per* Bramwell B.
98. *Bell* v. *Peter Browne & Co* [1990] 3 All ER 124 at 127.

CHAPTER 9

DEBTS AND RELATED PAYMENT OBLIGATIONS

NEGOTIABLE INSTRUMENTS, PAYMENT ON DEMAND, ACCOUNTS, SURETIES AND ASCERTAINMENT OF SUMS DUE

As will be seen,[1] where money is lent and the contract does not specify the date for its repayment and no security is given, the Limitation Act 1980, s 6, postpones the running of time until a written demand is made. However, promissory notes, cheques and bills of exchange are unaffected by this provision. The right of action on such instruments generally accrues when payment is due. It was held in *Savage* v. *Aldren*[2] that if the bill or note is payable on demand, no demand is necessary to enforce payment and time begins to run from the date of the bill or note, or from the date of its delivery, if later. This rule was succinctly stated in *Re Brown's Estate*[3] by Chitty J who said: "The law is quite settled that, with regard to a promissory note payable on demand, no demand is necessary before bringing the action . . . "[4] Where a bill is payable at sight, time begins to run from the date of its presentment provided the place of payment is specified.[5] If the bill becomes payable at a fixed time after date or a specified period after sight or demand, time begins to run upon the expiration of that period. Where a bill of exchange is dishonoured, time begins to run when notice of its dishonour is received,[6] and it is immaterial that the parties anticipated its dishonour at an earlier time.

With respect to the banker-customer relationship, it was held in *Lloyds Bank Ltd* v. *Margolis*,[7] that where the banker permits his customer to overdraw on the terms of entering a legal charge, which provides that the money then due or thereafter to become due is to be paid on demand, the cause of action did not accrue until that demand was made. Upjohn J said that: "As between the customer and banker, who are dealing on a running account, it seems to me impossible to assume that the bank were to be entitled to sue on the deed the very day after it was executed without making a demand and giving the customer a reasonable time to pay."[8]

Money advanced by a customer to a bank is a loan and is therefore a debt.[9] In the case of current and deposit accounts held with a bank or building society, the Court of Appeal

---

1. *Infra.*
2. (1817) 2 Stark 232. See also, *Norton* v. *Ellam* (1837) 2 M & W 461.
3. [1893] 2 Ch 300.
4. *Ibid* at 304.
5. *Holmes* v. *Kerrison* (1810) 2 Taunt 323.
6. *Eaglehill* v. *J Needham (Builders) Ltd* [1973] AC 992, HL.
7. [1954] 1 WLR 644, the facts are considered *infra*.
8. *Ibid* at 649.
9. *Foley* v. *Hill* (1844) 2 HL Cas 28.

has held that where a customer's account is in credit, then subject to any agreement to the contrary, a demand by the customer is a necessary ingredient in the cause of action against the banker for money lent.[10] However, time runs against the bank from the date of the last transaction entered against an overdrawn account, so that the action will be barred after six years in the absence of a demand or an acknowledgement.[11]

Where the obligation is to pay a collateral sum as distinct from a present debt,[12] the issue is whether time begins to run from the granting of the surety or from the making of the demand. In *Re Brown's Estate*[13] the mortgagee advanced the mortgagor £3,000 on the security of certain property. In the mortgage deed the mortgagor and his father covenanted jointly and severally that they would, on demand, repay the sum borrowed. Some 22 years later, in July 1889, a demand was made against the father's estate. It was argued that a demand was not necessary so that time ran from the execution of the mortgage. Nevertheless, Chitty J held that where there is a promise to pay a collateral sum on request, the request ought to be made before the action is brought. Accordingly, time began to run from the making of the demand. For co-sureties, the right of contribution accrues when liability is quantified by the first surety being called upon by the creditor to settle the debt.[14] It should be noted that if the surety's undertaking is given after the point in time when the principal debt was advanced, it follows that the principal debt will become time barred before the surety. The question which arises is whether or not the surety will become time barred with that debt? In *Carter* v. *White*[15] it was held that the surety survives the principal debt since it is, in substance, a distinct and separate agreement.

It is not uncommon, particularly in commercial transactions, for the contract to stipulate that a sum of money will become payable by one party to the other should certain specified events occur. Such contracts frequently go on to provide that a third party will fix the sum payable. Where this is the case, it becomes a question of construction of the contract as to whether this constitutes an arbitration clause,[16] or whether it is intended that the third party will act as an expert. Where the latter is the case, the decision of the expert will generally be a precondition before any action on the sum so fixed will accrue.[17]

CONTRACTS OF GUARANTEE AND CONTRACTS OF INDEMNITY

Whether or not a contract is one of guarantee or one of indemnity may have important consequences for the purposes of the running of time in the event of an alleged breach of

10. *Joachimson* v. *Swiss Bank Corporation* [1921] 3 KB 110. See also, *Atkinson* v. *Bradford Third Equitable Benefit Building Society* (1890) 25 QBD 377, (deposit accounts), in which Lopes LJ said at 383: "No cause of action arose until the notice of [the depositor's] intention to withdraw his money had been given and had expired, and he, or someone with his written authority, had produced the loan pass book." Where the claim is for wrongful debits, it follows that a demand is also a prerequisite to the accrual of the action: *National Bank of Commerce* v. *National Westminster Bank* [1990] 2 Lloyd's Rep 514, applying *Joachimson* v. *Swiss Bank Corporation*.
11. *Parr's Banking Co Ltd* v. *Yates* [1898] 2 QB 460.
12. *Birks* v. *Trippet* (1666) 1 Wms Saund 32.
13. *Supra*, fn 3.
14. *Wolmershausen* v. *Gullick* [1893] 2 Ch 514. The special two-year time limit for claiming contribution contained in the Limitation Act 1980, s 10 should be noted.
15. (1883) 25 Ch D 666.
16. See, for example, *Produce Brokers Co Ltd* v. *Olympia Oil and Coke Co Ltd* [1916] 1 AC 314, HL; *Cunliffe-Owen* v. *Teather and Greenwood* [1967] 1 WLR 1421, CA. See Ch 11.
17. *Royal Norwegian Government* v. *Constant & Constant* [1969] 2 Lloyd's Rep 431.

the contract. The distinction between the two types of contract is one which has evolved at common law largely because of the different requirements as to the form in which a contract of guarantee is required to be made.[18]

A contract of guarantee is one under which one person, the guarantor, promises the actual or potential creditor of the principal debtor that he will assume *secondary* liability to answer for the debt owed by the principal debtor to the creditor, should the principal debtor fail to fulfil his obligations to the creditor. Accordingly, a contract of guarantee is regarded as an accessory contract, which can only be valid as between the guarantor and the creditor if there is a valid principal obligation as between the creditor and the principal debtor. Since the guarantor's liability is only secondary, it follows that the primary debtor still remains liable for the debt. Moreover, since the guarantor's liability is considered to be co-extensive with the liability of the principal debtor, if the principal debt is discharged, so also will be the liability of the guarantor, unless there is an agreement to the contrary in the contract of guarantee.[19] Thus if the contract under which the debt arises is void on the grounds of a common mistake, it follows that an associated guarantee, being an accessory contract, will also be avoided.[20]

An additional complication so far as contracts of guarantee are concerned is that there appears to be more than one form which the contract may take.[21] In the first place, there are guarantees under which the guarantor undertakes to pay an instalment, if the principal debtor fails to pay. But there are also performance guarantees under which the guarantor undertakes that the principal will perform his contractual obligations. It will be seen below that, generally, in the case of a guarantee of the first variety, time runs from the date on which the guarantor fails pay the instalment when called upon to do so. In the case of performance guarantees, the relevant date for the purposes of the running of time is the date on which the principal fails to perform his contractual undertakings.

In a contract of indemnity, the indemnifier assumes a primary liability in respect of a loss suffered or a debt owed by the person indemnified. In other words, in a contract of indemnity, there is a primary obligation which exists quite independently of the means by which the indemnified loss comes about. This primary liability may be assumed by the indemnifier alone or jointly with the principal debtor, but the essence of the contract is that the indemnifier contracts, as principal, to pay in the event of a stipulated loss being suffered by the other party to the contract of indemnity. Accordingly, the difference between the two types of contract is that a guarantor promises to pay the creditor *if the debtor fails to pay*, whereas an indemnifier undertakes primary liability for the debt. In terms of accrual of the cause of action, this means that someone who provides an indemnity is in breach of contract when the debt becomes due for payment and payment is not forthcoming, but a guarantor is only liable for the debt if the principal debtor fails to pay the creditor and the terms of the contract of guarantee provide for liability on the part of the guarantor.

The distinction between contracts of indemnity and those of guarantee may become blurred at the edges, especially in cases where the contract entered into is of a hybrid

---

18. By virtue of the Statute of Frauds 1677, s 4, a contract of guarantee is required to be either in writing or evidenced by some written means. In contrast, no such requirement applies to a contract of indemnity.
19. *Moschi* v. *Lep Air Services Ltd* [1973] AC 331 at 349 *per* Lord Diplock.
20. *Associated Japanese Bank (International) Ltd* v. *Crédit du Nord SA* [1988] 3 All ER 903.
21. See *Moschi* v. *Lep Air Services Ltd* [1973] AC 331 at 344–45 *per* Lord Reid.

nature. For example, there may be cases in which both a guarantee and an indemnity may be combined in a single contractual document.

So far as the question of limitation of actions is concerned, the key issue is to determine when the guarantee is activated so that the guarantor becomes liable to pay. Generally, when this event occurs will turn upon a proper construction of the terms of the guarantee and the contract under which the principal debt arises. As a general rule, the important consideration in this regard will be to ask when the guarantor suffers damage as a result of entering into the contract of guarantee. This may be when the debtor defaults,[22] but it is equally possible for damage to be suffered by a guarantor at an earlier stage, such as where events cause the guarantor's liability to become more onerous. Accordingly, it is a question of fact in each case whether damage is caused to the guarantor before the date on which the debtor defaults under his contract with the creditor.[23]

(a) Contracts of guarantee or surety

(i) The liability of the guarantor under the guarantee

If there is no express provision in the contract, the general rule is that the liability of the guarantor will arise at the same time as that of the principal debtor with the result that time will begin to run simultaneously in favour of both the guarantor and the debtor.[24] Accordingly, it is unlikely that there will be any advantage in pursuing the guarantor as opposed to the debtor, if the limitation period has expired in respect of the latter. Although the liability of the guarantor is secondary to that of the principal debtor, it does not follow from this that the creditor has to notify the guarantor of any default on the part of the debtor, unless there is a requirement to this effect in the contract of guarantee.[25]

In some instances it is possible that the liability of either the guarantor or the debtor continues when time has expired in respect of a possible action against the other. In order to determine whether this is the case, it will be necessary to consider the terms of the contract of guarantee and the terms of the contract under which the debtor's initial liability came into existence, since these terms may have the effect of extending or restricting the liability of the principal debtor.

In some instances, it may be clear from the contract of guarantee that the amount guaranteed is payable on demand, in which case, the guarantor will become liable to pay as soon as the creditor makes his demand in accordance with the terms of the guarantee.[26] For these purposes, it seems that unless there is a limited guarantee, and the guarantee is regarded as payable on demand, if a demand for payment has been sent by the creditor, time will run from the date of that first demand, even if the debtor does not receive that demand and a second demand for payment is subsequently sent.[27]

If the contract of guarantee is subject to unusual terms relating to the matter of how the demand should be made, this could affect the liability of the guarantor, thereby delaying the date on which the cause of action accrues. For example in *Bradford Old Bank* v.

22. *Ibid* at 348 *per* Lord Diplock.
23. *Tabarrok* v. *EDC Lord & Co (a firm)* (1997) *The Times*, 14 February *per* Aldous LJ (CA).
24. *Parrs Banking Co Ltd* v. *Yates* [1898] 2 QB 460.
25. *Hitchcock* v. *Humfrey* (1843) 5 Man & G 559.
26. *Re Brown's Estate* [1893] 2 Ch 300; *Bradford Old Bank* v. *Sutcliffe* [1918] 2 KB 833.
27. *Bank of Baroda* v. *Patel* [1996] 1 Lloyd's Rep 391.

Sutcliffe[28] two company directors guaranteed a bank loan taken out by the company of which they were directors. As security for the loan, the company issued debentures in favour of the lending bank. The contract of guarantee stated that it was given in order to protect the bank from loss on realisation of the debentures and also stated that payments under the guarantee would be made on demand. Some 18 years later, the bank sold the debentures, but discovered that they were of inadequate value to cover the amount of the loan which remained unpaid. Accordingly, the bank sought to enforce the guarantee, but did so 21 years after it had first been given. In the event, it was held that the action was not time barred, since no liability on the guarantee could arise until the bank suffered a loss on the debentures and subsequently made a demand under the terms of the guarantee. It follows from this that the general rule for the purposes of a contract of guarantee is that if there is a contract under which a guarantor agrees to pay a collateral sum, the cause of action can only accrue when there is a future default under the terms of the principal contract. However, in some cases, it may be clear from the terms of the contract of guarantee that the guarantee relates to a present debt which is already payable. In these circumstances, the cause of action will accrue on the date on which the guarantee is given.[29] Accordingly, in *Colvin* v. *Buckle*[30] a guarantee that payments to be made under a loan agreement would be met by the debtor was conditional on certain future events. Until those events, on which the guarantee depended, occurred, it could not be held that the cause of action against the guarantor arose. It followed from this that the cause of action only came into existence once the specified circumstances came about, and until that stage, time did not begin to run against the plaintiff. It proved to be irrelevant that, for the purposes of the principal contract, liabilities between the parties were quantified at a much later stage.

It can be seen from these cases that a distinction is drawn between a promise to pay a collateral sum and a promise to pay a present debt. Generally, it will normally be the case that a contract of guarantee involves the payment of a collateral sum, especially where the terms of the contract can be construed in such a way to indicate that the guarantor's liability to pay is not intended to arise immediately. Thus if the contract requires the surety to pay certain sums of money "in the meantime", it is likely that the obligation of the surety will be regarded as one to pay a collateral sum.[31]

In other instances, it may be clear that the liability of the guarantor to pay under the terms of the guarantee is not related to the date on which the cause of action against the debtor accrues under the principal contract. For example, in *Sheers* v. *Thimbleby & Son*[32] a guarantee had been given as to the safety of certain investments. For these purposes, it was held that the cause of action in respect of the guarantee arose immediately the investment became unsafe, regardless of when the liability of the principal debtor arose under the investment contract.

Where the contract of guarantee relates to a loan of money by the creditor to the debtor which is due to be repaid by instalments which include an amount by way of interest on the loan, it is likely that there will be a series of possible actions in favour of the creditor, each one related to each instalment as it becomes due. The effect of such contracts to repay

28. [1918] 2 KB 833.
29. *Birks* v. *Trippet* (1666) 1 Wms Saund 28 at 32.
30. (1841) 8 M & W 680.
31. *Re Brown's Estate* [1893] 2 Ch 300.
32. (1897) 76 LT 709.

a sum of money by fixed instalments is that an action in respect of the sum of money lent may have become time barred, but actions in respect of later instalments may still be within time since the cause of action in respect of each separate instalment will not accrue until the date on which each instalment becomes due to be paid. For example, in *Parrs Banking Co Ltd* v. *Yates*[33] an action under a guarantee was considered to be time barred so far as the principal debt was concerned, but the guarantee also applied to interest, commission and other banking charges which became due after the principal debt had been incurred. Such of those amounts which had been guaranteed in the six years prior to the commencement of proceedings were considered to be recoverable.

The terms of the guarantee may also set out the period of time during which the guarantee is to remain valid, in which case, if the event in respect of which the guarantee has been given does not occur until after the guarantee has expired, the guarantor will not be liable to the creditor. Moreover, as a matter of construction, the court may conclude that a guarantee is only intended to remain in force for a reasonable time. In such a case, if the debtor defaults after a reasonable time has expired, the guarantee may be unenforceable against the guarantor even where it is not expressed to run for any particular length of time.[34] Conversely, it may have been agreed that the guarantee should create a continuing obligation on the part of the surety and that the guarantee should continue to apply to any outstanding balance and any future balance owed by the principal debtor as it becomes due. In these circumstances, it has been held that the guarantee relates to each debit balance, a cause of action accruing in favour of the creditor when each such debit balance is constituted rather than when advances are made to the principal debtor.[35]

(ii) The liability of the debtor to the guarantor

Since, where there is a contract of guarantee, the liability of the guarantor is secondary to that of the debtor, it is possible that arrangements may have been entered into between the guarantor and the debtor. These arrangements may also affect the matter of accrual of the cause of action under the contract of guarantee by defining when the liability of the guarantor will arise.

Even in the absence of agreement between the guarantor and the debtor, the latter is under an implied obligation to indemnify the guarantor. This implied obligation comes into existence when the guarantee is given, but remains dormant until the guarantor pays the debtor's debt. Accordingly, an action in respect of the implied undertaking to indemnify the guarantor does not accrue until the guarantor has paid in accordance with the terms of the guarantee.[36] However, the indemnity only extends to those debts which are enforceable, with the result that the guarantor will have no action against the debtor in respect of a principal debt which has become time barred.[37] Thus if, in error, the surety pays a debt which is already time barred, he will be unable to recover the amount he has paid from the principal debtor.

The guarantor also has other rights against the debtor. First, there is a right to bring proceedings against the debtor to compel him to pay the creditor, as soon as the guarantor

33. [1898] 2 QB 460.
34. See *Henton* v. *Paddison* (1893) 68 LT 405.
35. *Wright* v. *New Zealand Farmers' Co-operative Association* [1939] AC 439.
36. *Wolmershausen* v. *Gullick* [1893] 2 Ch 514; *Re A Debtor (No 627 of 1936)* [1937] Ch 156.
37. *Re Morris, Coneys* v. *Morris* [1922] 1 IR 81.

becomes liable to pay the creditor under the terms of the contract of guarantee. Moreover, as soon as any payment is made to the creditor, whether it be the full amount of the debt or not, the guarantor has an immediate right to be indemnified by the debtor in respect of that sum which has been paid under the terms of the contract of guarantee.

(iii) Co-guarantors

It is possible that a debt may be guaranteed by more than one person. In such a case, each co-guarantor makes himself individually liable for the full amount of the debt in the event of non-payment by the principal debtor. If one of two co-guarantors pays the debt, he will be entitled to recover from the other co-guarantor such proportion of the debt as the other is expected to pay. Accordingly, payment of a debt by one co-guarantor will result in the accrual of a cause of action in his favour as against the second co-guarantor. However, this cause of action will only accrue as from the time of the discharge of the debt.[38] Moreover, it is irrelevant that, at the time of the action for contribution as between the creditor and the co-guarantor, time has expired.

(iv) Delayed guarantees

In some instances, a guarantee may be given after the debt to which it relates was first incurred. In such a case, the principal debt will become statute barred at an earlier time than the date on which any action for enforcement of the guarantee becomes time barred. Despite the fact that any action by the creditor against the principal debtor will be treated as being out of time, the liability of the guarantor under a delayed guarantee will continue for the normal six-year period, running from the date on which the delayed guarantee was given.[39]

(b) Contracts of indemnity

It has been observed above that the principal distinction between a contract of guarantee and one of indemnity is that a guarantor incurs only a secondary liability to pay a debt, whereas under a contract of indemnity, the indemnifier is liable as principal in respect of a loss to which the other party to the contract has not contributed. It follows from this that but for the existence of the contract of indemnity, the indemnifier would not incur liability to the other party in respect of the loss suffered by him.

Whether or not there is an undertaking to indemnify a person may be the subject of express agreement, in which case, special regard must be had to the terms of the contract of indemnity.[40] But it is also possible for an indemnity undertaking to be implied, in which case it is unlikely that there will be any specific terms relating to the undertaking in question. For example if a ship's master fails to comply with the requirements of a charterparty, with the result that the ship owner is not immune from suit, an indemnity on the part of the charterers may be implied on the basis that there has been a breach of

38. *Davies* v. *Humphreys* (1840) 6 M & W 153; *Re Snowdon* (1881) 17 Ch D 44; *Wolmershausen* v. *Gullick* [1893] 2 Ch 514. The position may be different in relation to an action for contribution as between two co-trustees: *Robinson* v. *Harkin* [1896] 2 Ch 416.
39. See *Carter* v. *White* (1883) 25 Ch D 666.
40. The classic case of an express indemnity is the insurance contract. As to which see Ch 12.

contract by the charterers in tendering a bill of lading entirely different from the charterparty.[41]

The most important issue in indemnity contracts is to ascertain when the indemnifier becomes liable with the result that time begins to run against the plaintiff. The key question in this regard is whether the plaintiff's cause of action accrues when the loss occurs in respect of which the indemnity has been given or when the extent of the liability of the indemnifier is ascertained. In historical terms, common law rules and those developed in equity appear to have been in conflict. The position at common law seems to have been that a right to indemnity arose only when the plaintiff had made a payment to the third party,[42] the reason for this being that before time could run at common law, there had to be a complete, as opposed to a partial, cause of action. Accordingly, it was irrelevant to consider when the event which gave rise to liability actually occurred.[43] Similarly irrelevant, at common law, was the date on which the liability of the plaintiff was quantified.[44] In equity, the position appears to have been that a right in favour of the person to be indemnified arose when he became liable to suffer the loss in respect of which the indemnity was given,[45] subject to a right to preserve that action until the date on which the extent of liability was ascertained or established.[46]

The modern law on the subject is now somewhat confused in the light of a number of decisions, which, at face value, appear to conflict. In *Bosma* v. *Larsen*,[47] a decision based upon an express contract of indemnity, the owners of a vessel agreed to charter it under the terms of a time charter, subject to an express agreement that the charterers would indemnify the owners against all consequences of, or liabilities arising from, signature of a bill of lading on the part of the ship's master. Subsequently, agents acting on behalf of the master did sign a bill of lading with the result that the ship owners became liable to a third party under the terms of the bill of lading for damage which had been caused to the cargo. The owners then claimed against the charterers under the indemnity clause in respect of the liability they had incurred. The charterers argued that the claim under the indemnity clause was time barred on the ground that the cause of action in favour of the owners accrued when their liability to the third party was incurred, rather than on the date when that liability was discharged. Given that this was a case of express indemnity, it is not surprising that McNair J paid very close attention to the specific wording of the contract. In so doing, he concluded that it would not be proper to "apply a label to a particular obligation in a document and then to deduce from that label the legal consequences which may flow from other contracts to which the same label can be attached . . ."[48] Instead, it was considered necessary to construe the contract according to the intentions of the parties, in the light of the particular wording of the contract made

41. *Krüger & Co Ltd* v. *Moel Tryvan Ship Co Ltd* [1907] AC 272 at 276 *per* Lord Loreburn LC and at 281 *per* Lord James.
42. *McGillivray* v. *Hope* [1935] AC 1.
43. *Huntley* v. *Sanderson* (1833) 1 Cr & M 467.
44. *Collinge* v. *Heywood* (1839) 9 Ad & El 633; *Re Richardson, ex parte Governors of St Thomas's Hospital* [1911] 2 KB 705.
45. *Wolmershausen* v. *Gullick* [1893] 2 Ch 514; *Ascherson* v. *Tredegar Dry Dock & Wharf Co Ltd* [1909] 2 Ch 401.
46. *County & District Properties Ltd* v. *Jenner & Son Ltd* [1976] 2 Lloyd's Rep 728 at 734 *per* Swanwick J. See also *Robinson* v. *Harkin* [1896] 2 Ch 416 applying a similar caveat to the question of contribution as between two trustees in *pari delicto* when the claim of the *cestui que trust* had not been quantified by judgment.
47. [1966] 1 Lloyd's Rep 22.
48. *Ibid* at 27 *per* McNair J.

between them. It was held that the use of the word "liabilities" in the indemnity clause should be taken to indicate that there was an obligation to indemnify against "the incurring of liability", at which point the cause of action accrued. It was not necessary to wait for the liability to the third party to be discharged following payment by the indemnifier. Accordingly time was considered to have run from the earlier of the two dates considered and the ship owner's action was therefore time barred.

The problem thrown up by *Bosma* v. *Larsen* is that if the courts are going to place so much emphasis on the specific wording of the contractual document containing the indemnity clause, there is little room for the development of any sort of a coherent principle, since each case will turn upon its own peculiar facts and the skill of the contract drafter in defining when liability on the contract of indemnity will arise. Furthermore, there is an additional difficulty with McNair J's decision in *Bosma* v. *Larsen* in that, although it is clear that as a result of the way in which the indemnity was worded, time began to run when the liability of the indemnifier to pay first came into existence, there will be circumstances in which it is not known what that liability amounts to in monetary terms. Accordingly, on this analysis, time may be running, but it still remains impossible to enforce the terms of the indemnity clause until quantification has taken place. If this quantification is dependent upon the outcome of litigation or some other process involving a third party, it is quite possible that an action under the indemnity provision will become time barred before the monetary liability of the indemnifier is known.

In the light of some of these uncertainties, it is not surprising that there have been instances on which *Bosma* v. *Larsen* has not been followed. For example, in *Jenner* v. *County & District Properties*[49] Swanwick J, in the context of an express indemnity clause in a building contract, held that *Bosma* v. *Larsen* could be departed from in cases where equity so demanded. Accordingly, in *Jenner* it was considered that until ascertainment of the fact and extent of liability on the part of the person to be indemnified, equity prevented time from running. The view of Swanwick J was that the equitable approach to the question of time afforded a workable general principle which could be applied regardless of the specific wording of the contract of indemnity. Accordingly, Swanwick J opined that "an indemnity against a breach, or an act, or an omission, can only be an indemnity against the harmful consequences which flow from it, and I take the law to be that the indemnity does not give rise to a cause of action until those consequences are ascertained".[50]

Clearly, at face value, the decisions in *Bosma* and *Jenner* were in conflict, and there appeared to be little ground on which they could be reconciled. However, the task of reconciliation fell to Neill J in *Telfair Shipping Corporation* v. *Inersea Carriers SA, The Caroline P*[51] which, unlike the preceding two cases, was concerned with an implied as opposed to an express indemnity. In *Telfair* the master of a ship had signed bills of lading "as presented", as required by the terms of the charterparty entered into between the ship owners and the charterers. In fact the effect of these signed bills of lading was to impose on the owners certain liabilities in excess of those provided for in the contract of charter. The question then arose as to whether the charterers were under an implied obligation to

49. [1976] 2 Lloyd's Rep 728.

50. *Ibid* at 736. See also *Bradley* v. *Eagle Star Insurance Co Ltd* [1989] AC 957 and see also Ch 12 regarding indemnity insurance contracts.

51. [1985] 1 All ER 243. Approved by the Court of Appeal in *The Fanti and Padre Island* [1989] 1 Lloyd's Rep 239.

indemnify the owners in respect of losses arising from these liabilities. In response to an action brought by the owners, the charterers pleaded that any right to recover an indemnity was time barred on the ground that the liability to which the implied indemnity related was to the consignees and that the cause of action accrued as soon as there was any breach of a relevant term of the charterparty. In this case it was argued that the first such breach was when the cargo was badly stowed and the bills of lading were issued. In contrast, the owners contended that the relevant date, for the purposes of the running of time, was the date on which the amount in respect of which the indemnity was given became quantified, which could only be the date on which an award of damages against the owners became settled.

In attempting to produce order out of the chaos produced by the conflicting decisions in *Bosma* and *Jenner*, Neill J chose to draw a tripartite distinction between actions based on a breach of contract *simpliciter*, actions based on an express indemnity agreement and actions based upon an implied indemnity. The question arises whether A, the person who has become liable to B, may obtain redress from C.

In the case of an action for damages for breach of a contractual warranty, if A becomes liable to B as a consequence of a breach by C of a contract between A and C, ordinary principles of limitation of actions come into play. Accordingly, it becomes necessary to consider the date on which the breach of contract or the breach of warranty by C occurs, since it is from this date that time will begin to run in respect of the indemnity given by A to B. In these circumstances, the amount of the indemnity will be assessed on ordinary *Hadley* v. *Baxendale*[52] principles.

In the case of an express indemnity agreement, the specific wording of the contract becomes paramount and, as asserted in *Bosma* v. *Larsen*, it becomes necessary to have very close regard to the specific wording of the contract and to construe that wording according to the intentions of the parties. Thus, if the indemnity is one against liability as in *Bosma* the cause of action under the indemnity clause will accrue when A incurs liability to B, unless there is a contrary indication to be found in the contract. In this instance, it is possible that liability may be contingent on the occurrence of some other event,[53] in which case, application of the *Bosma* principle may give rise to difficulties. However, if the indemnity is classified as a general indemnity, time will not run until A's liability to B has been established and ascertained.[54] For example in *R & H Green & Silley Weir Ltd* v. *British Railways Board*[55] the third parties contracted to carry out tipping operations in a railway cutting owned by the Railways Board, the work being done in 1970 and 1971. Under the terms of that contract, it was agreed that the Board would be indemnified against all liability for personal injury, loss of or damage to property and any other loss, damage, costs and expenses which might arise in consequence of the agreement between the parties. In 1974 the plaintiffs, whose land adjoined the cutting, sued in respect of damage caused by the tipping operation. Eventually, the third party was joined in the action in 1979, but the third party pleaded the time bar. Preferring the principle set out by Swanwick J in *County & District Properties Ltd* v. *Jenner*, Dillon J held that time could only run under a general indemnity against liability when the liability of the Board had

---

52. (1854) 9 Exch 341.
53. *Forster* v. *Outred & Co (a firm)* [1982] 2 All ER 753.
54. In this respect, *Bosma* v. *Larsen* appears to have been confined to its own peculiar facts.
55. [1985] 1 All ER 237.

been established and ascertained, in which case, the Board was still able to enforce the indemnity clause against the third party.

The third type of indemnity identified in *Telfair* is one which can be implied from the nature of the dealings between the parties. Given the absence of any specific agreement on the matter of the indemnity, it follows that this will be a general indemnity, the extent of which is unlikely to be ascertainable until payment has been made. For example, in *Collinge* v. *Heywood* [56] there was a contract to indemnify the plaintiff against costs under which it was decided that the cause of action accrued only when he paid the costs rather than when the costs were incurred or when the attorney's bill was delivered to him.

It follows from the absence of specific contractual undertakings as to the matter of the implied indemnity that these will normally be regarded as indemnities against the discharge of liability rather than against incurring liability. As a result, it will normally be the case that time will not start to run until liability is established and quantified. However, it appears that there may have been exceptional circumstances in which equitable rules required the defendant to set up a fund for the purposes of meeting liability, should it be established subsequently. But those equitable principles would not result in payment having to be made until the precise extent of liability had been ascertained.

CONTRACTS OF LOAN

At common law, subject to a small number of exceptions, if there was no provision in a contract of loan specifying a date for repayment, time was taken to run as from the date on which the loan was made.[57] Similarly, if the loan was taken to be repayable on demand, the creditor was in a position to ask for repayment at his choice, with the result that the common law rule on accrual of the cause of action was that time should also run from the date of the advance[58] rather than from the date of the demand. However, subsequently the rule which has evolved is that in the case of a contract of loan expressed to be payable on demand, time will run as from the date of the demand if the contract can be construed so as to produce that result. In *Lloyds Bank Ltd* v. *Margolis*[59] a mortgage deed, executed in September 1936 in respect of a farm, provided for repayment on demand. The bank in whose favour the legal charge had been created demanded payment when they discovered that the owner intended to sell the farm in December 1938. Subsequently, the farm was vested in the purchaser in 1944 and in November 1950 the bank issued a summons to enforce its security by either foreclosure or sale. It was argued on behalf of the debtor that the bank was out of time since in the case of advances which preceded the mortgage, time should run from the date on which the mortgage was taken out, as opposed to subsequent advances in respect of which time should run from the date on which the advance was

---

56. (1839) 9 Ad & El 633.

57. *Garden* v. *Bruce* (1868) LR 3 CP 300.

58. *Collins* v. *Benning* (1701) 12 Mod 444. In contrast, if a bill was expressed to be payable after sight, the rule appeared to be that the cause of action did not accrue until the bill was presented for payment: *Holmes* v. *Kerrison* (1810) 2 Taunt 323. Cf the position in relation to guarantees, considered above, following the decision in *Bradford Old Bank* v. *Sutcliffe* [1918] 2 KB 833.

59. [1954] 1 All ER 734.

made. However, Upjohn J concluded that the making of a demand was a condition precedent to the recovery of the debt and that since the first demand was not made until December 1938, the 12-year limitation period applicable to actions to recover land had not expired.[60] On a proper construction of the mortgage deed, the bank would not be in a position to recover the money advanced until a demand was made. According to Upjohn J:

" . . . where there is the relationship of banker and customer and the banker permits his customer to overdraw on the terms of entering into a legal charge which provides that the money which is then due or is thereafter to become due is to be paid 'on demand', that means what it says. As between the customer and banker who are dealing on a running account, it seems to me impossible to assume that the bank were entitled to sue on the deed the very day after it was executed without making a demand and giving the customer a reasonable time to pay."[61]

At common law, if the contract could be construed in a way which allowed the court to conclude that there was a fixed or determinable date on which the loan became repayable, time would run from that date, rather than from the date of the loan. Thus in *Waters* v. *Earl of Thanet*[62] a contract of loan provided that the debtor would repay whenever his circumstances were such as to enable him to do so, in which case he could be called upon to repay. In the circumstances, it was held that no demand was necessary and that time began to run from the date on which the debtor became able to repay the loan, regardless of the fact that the creditor might not have been aware of the debtor's ability to repay.

The underlying reason for the common law rule appears to be that the running of time against the creditor must commence on the earliest date on which the debtor could be called upon to repay the loan. However, the effect of the common law rule that time could run from the date on which the advance was made was capable of prejudicing the creditor, since it was quite likely that a creditor without substantial commercial acumen could be considered to be out of time where his demand for repayment was made several years after he had advanced the loan to the debtor. Although this common law rule, if applied rigidly, was capable of producing hardship, it was mitigated to a certain extent by the rules on part payment and acknowledgment, considered below. Moreover, the courts were also prepared to adopt a fairly flexible approach to the question whether a demand was a prerequisite to the accrual of a cause of action and in many instances were able to conclude that, as a matter of construction, time only began to run when a demand was made.[63]

Many contracts of loan may be made by way of deed, in which case rules on specialties will apply.[64] Moreover, the common law rule was unlikely to adversely affect commercial lenders since it would be in their interests to specify a date by which payment in full should be made. However, in the case of informal loan arrangements, such as those between members of a family or between friends, it became apparent that loans were made without there being any agreement as to the date of repayment, in which case the common

---

60. Now covered by the Limitation Act 1980, s 15(1).
61. [1954] 1 All ER 734 at 738.
62. (1842) 2 QB 757.
63. See e.g. *Joachimson* v. *Swiss Bank Corporation* [1921] 3 KB 10.
64. See Ch 15.

law rule would apply and despite the absence of a demand for repayment, an action to recover the amount lent could be time barred.[65]

(a) Informal contracts of loan

In the case of informal contracts of loan, the Limitation Act 1980 departs from the normal principle contained in section 5 that time runs for six years from the date of accrual of the cause of action. Instead, section 6(2) of the 1980 Act provides that section 5 will not operate to bar a right of action on a contract of loan where the contract is one which—

(a) does not provide for repayment of the debt on or before a fixed or determinable date and

(b) does not effectively make the obligation to repay conditional on a demand for repayment made by or on behalf of the creditor or on any other matter.

Section 6(2) goes on further to provide that section 5 will apply, nonetheless, where in connection with taking the loan, the debtor has entered into a collateral obligation to pay the amount of the debt, or any part of it, on terms which would exclude the application of section 6 to the contract of loan if they applied directly to repayment of the debt. Moreover, by virtue of section 6(3), where the creditor makes a demand in writing for repayment of a debt, section 5 is deemed to apply as if the cause of action had accrued on the date on which the demand was made.

A moot point is whether the two elements of definition of those loans to which section 6 applies, contained in section 6(2), both have to be complied with in order for the loan to qualify for the section 6 exemption or whether those elements constitute alternative elements in the definition. A literal reading of section 6(2) would seem to suggest that in order for a loan to satisfy the exempting provisions of section 6, it should fall within both elements of the definition. Accordingly, the contract of loan should be one which specifies no date for repayment on or before a fixed or ascertainable date and which does not effectively make the obligation to repay conditional upon a demand by the creditor or someone acting on his behalf. However, there are policy reasons which could be taken to suggest that the two elements of section 6(2) should be regarded as alternative qualifying grounds.

When the issue of informal loans was considered by the Law Reform Committee, it was observed that the difficulties created by such contracts will arise both where there is no date specified for repayment and where the contract merely stipulates that the loan is repayable on demand.[66] In either event, if there is no date for repayment or if an inexperienced creditor makes his initial demand at a very late stage, there is the possibility that an

---

65. See Law Reform Committee, *Twenty-First Report on Limitation of Actions,* 1977, Cmnd 6923, para 3.22. Whether or not these are enforceable contracts at all seems to depend upon whether they are entered into "at arm's length", since there is a general presumption to the effect that contracts between family members are not entered into with an intention to create legal relations unless there is evidence to the contrary: *Balfour* v. *Balfour* [1919] 2 KB 571; *Jones* v. *Padavatton* [1969] 1 WLR 328. Likewise, "social arrangements" between friends are often so loose and informal that it is impossible to derive any intention to create legal relations: *Simpkins* v. *Pays* [1955] 2 KB 571. In either event, it is possible that there is no enforceable contract of loan in the first place, in which case no cause of action will accrue. However, there are also many instances of binding contractual relations between family members, for example, a husband can be his wife's tenant: *Pearce* v. *Merriman* [1904] 1 KB 80.
66. Law Reform Committee, *Twenty-First Report on Limitation of Actions,* 1977, Cmnd 6923, para 3.20.

action to recover the debt will be time barred. However, on the literal wording of section 6(2), in order to qualify for section 6 exemption, the contract of loan must both specify no date for repayment *and* fail to make the debt repayable on demand. Unfortunately, the drafting of section 6 is ambiguous and probably fails to give effect to the intentions of the Law Reform Committee,[67] but as it stands, it is suggested that the literal interpretation must be given to the words of section 6(2).

Where section 6(1) applies to a qualifying loan, the normal contractual limitation period is disapplied with the result that there is no limitation period in respect of such contracts. However, this position is modified in cases where there is a demand in writing by virtue of the provisions of section 6(3) and where the debtor has entered into a collateral undertaking by virtue of section 6(2).

An unfortunate effect of the combined provisions of section 6(2) is that of lack of clarity, and there is every likelihood that they may be misinterpreted, because within the single subsection there is to be found an exception, an exclusion and a deeming provision, all of which are capable of being confused.[68] When determining whether section 6(2) applies in a given case, the court of first instance has a two-fold duty. First, it is necessary to determine whether the loan under consideration qualifies under both section 6(2)(a) and (b). Then it becomes necessary to ask what is the effect of the collateral security provided by the debtor.

In *Boot* v. *Boot*[69] in 1983, the plaintiff had agreed to sell a house occupied by his son and daughter-in-law (the defendant) for £33,000, £8,000 of which constituted a loan by the plaintiff to the defendant and which was secured by a promissory note payable on demand. After the failure of the defendant's marriage in 1990, the plaintiff made a demand for repayment which was resisted by the defendant on the ground that the debt had become time barred.

The Court of Appeal concluded that the loan did qualify under section 6(2) since it did not provide for repayment on a fixed or determinable date and did not make payment conditional on a demand for repayment by the creditor. Accordingly, it then became necessary to consider the effect of the promissory note, in order to determine whether this collateral undertaking prevented the application of section 6 to the debt. In this last respect, it was concluded that the terms of the promissory note, if applied to the original contract under which the debt arose, would not prevent the application of section 6. Accordingly, it followed that for the purposes of this loan, time could only run from the date on which the debtor received a written demand for repayment, which meant that for the plaintiff's purposes, his action to recover the amount of the loan was not time barred under section 5 of the 1980 Act.

(b) Demand in writing

Although for the purposes of section 6(3) there must be a demand in writing, there is nothing in the general law which requires the demand to be addressed to the debtor. For example, it is possible for a demand for payment to be addressed directly to the debtor's bank. Thus in *Joachimson* v. *Swiss Bank Corporation*[70] it was considered that a demand

---

67. See Morgan, *Current Law Statutes Annotated*, 1980, part 11 c. 58/6.
68. See *Boot* v. *Boot* (1996) *The Times* 9 May, *per* Waite LJ.
69. *Ibid.*
70. [1921] 3 KB 110.

for payment of that part of a loan which remained outstanding had been made where a creditor served a garnishee order on his debtor's bank account. This would seem to suggest that it is immaterial that the debtor has not received the demand and that the only relevant date for the purposes of the running of time is the date on which the demand is made by the creditor, rather than the date on which the debtor receives the demand for payment.

(c) Collateral undertakings

The special rules which apply to informal contracts of loan which disapply the general contractual limitation period in the Limitation Act 1980, s 5 are, themselves, excluded in cases where the debtor has entered into a collateral undertaking, in connection with taking out the loan, that the amount of the debt, or any part of it, will be repaid. Accordingly, if the debtor delivers a promissory note as security for the debt, the normal limitation period in section 5 will then apply,[71] with the result that time will run against the creditor from the date on which a demand for payment is made. Thus if the original contract of loan makes no provision for repayment or if it provides for payment on demand, but the debtor gives the creditor a post-dated cheque or furnishes a promissory note payable on a fixed future date, there is no need for the creditor to make a written demand for payment and a cause of action in favour of the creditor will accrue on the date specified in the cheque or the promissory note. It would seem to follow from this that if a dated promissory note is issued and the creditor does not act upon it within a period of six years from the date on which it becomes enforceable, the effect of section 6 is that the creditor will then be time barred.

An important consideration is what is meant by the words, "in connection with taking the loan" to be found in section 6(2). Plainly, these words must be construed more broadly than simply "at the time of taking out the loan". It would appear reasonable to expect there to be some causal connection between the collateral undertaking and the original contract of loan, but there does not appear to be any reason to expect the collateral undertaking to be entered into simultaneously with the original contract under which the debt arises. However, for practical purposes, it is likely that the contract of loan and the collateral undertaking to repay will be entered into at approximately the same time, since, in order for there to be a connection between the two, the consideration for the collateral undertaking is, in all probability, likely to be the making of the advance by the creditor in the first place. If the contract of loan is entered into and then, two or three years later, a collateral undertaking to repay is given so as to calm fears held by the creditor as to whether the debt will be repaid, it is suggested that there will be insufficient connection between the collateral contract and the taking out of the loan.

TIME LIMIT FOR ACTIONS TO ENFORCE JUDGMENTS

Section 24(1) of the Limitation Act 1980 provides that an action shall not be brought on any judgment after the expiration of six years from the date on which it became enforceable. In practice, such actions are rare since they will be dismissed as an abuse of the

---

71. See Limitation Act 1980, s 6(2). For these purposes, s 6(4) provides that the words "promissory note" shall have the same meaning as that given in the Bills of Exchange Act 1882, s 83(1).

process of the court if the ordinary process of execution on the judgment in question was available.[72] Although section 24 applies only to a judgment obtained in England and Wales, the limitation period in respect of a foreign judgment is also six years on the basis that such an action is a simple contract debt. This point was settled by Alderson B in *Williams* v. *Jones*[73] where he said: "The true principle is, that where a Court of competent jurisdiction adjudges a sum of money is to be paid, an obligation to pay it is created thereby, and an action of debt may therefore be brought upon such judgment. This is the principle on which actions on foreign judgments are supported."[74]

While the term "action" is defined as including "any proceedings in a court of law",[75] it should be noted that it was held in *WT Lamb & Sons* v. *Rider*[76] (which was recently followed by the Court of Appeal in *National Westminster Bank* v. *Powney*[77] and in *Lowsley* v. *Forbes*[78]) that section 24 is not concerned with procedures to enforce judgments already obtained but only with substantive rights to bring an action on a judgment. Thus in *Re a debtor (No 50A/SD/95)*[79] the Chancery Division held that bankruptcy proceedings commenced by statutory demand based on a default judgment made more than six years previously were statute barred by section 24(1). The petitioning creditor argued that while the six-year limitation period laid down by section 24(1) applied to an action, the bankruptcy proceedings were not such an action but rather a process of execution following the default judgment. Judge Paul Baker QC, sitting as a judge of the High Court, rejected this contention, and held that bankruptcy proceedings are an "action" on a judgment and therefore came within the definition contained in section 38(1) of the Limitation Act 1980. He stated that: "It seems to me that bankruptcy proceedings are, first of all, a new proceeding so that it can be properly said that the proceedings are newly brought and are not in any way continuing some previous proceedings pursuant to the judgment or anything of that nature".[80]

Although there is no statutory time limit for enforcement proceedings, such proceedings are, in any case, governed by RSC Order 46, rule 2(1). This prohibits the issue of a writ of execution without the leave of the court in a number of cases, including: "(a) where six years or more have elapsed since the date of the judgment or order" which it is sought to enforce. The point has been made that the corollary of this is that the court has power to authorise execution proceedings after six years have passed.[81]

Section 24(2) of the 1980 Act provides that no arrears of interest in respect of any judgment debt shall be recovered after the expiration of six years from the date on which the interest became due. This provision appears to be an exception to the general rule that

---

72. *Pritchett* v. *English and Colonial Syndicate* [1899] 2 QB 428. However, where on the facts of the particular case execution will not suffice, enforcement by further action will be justified provided such action was within the limitation period prescribed by s 24 of the Limitation Act 1980: *ED & F Man (Sugar) Ltd* v. *Haryanto, The Times,* 9 August 1996, CA. Leggatt LJ stressed that it would be for the defendant to show that any second action constituted an abuse of process.

73. (1845) 13 M & W 628.

74. *Ibid.* See, also, *Dupleix* v. *De Roven* (1705) 2 Vern 540; *Grant* v. *Eastern* (1883) 13 QBD 302; *Shaw* v. *Allen* (1914) 30 TLR 631.

75. Limitation Act 1980, s 38(1).

76. [1948] 2 KB 331, CA. After six years leave is required to enforce a judgment: RSC Ord 46, r 2(1).

77. [1991] Ch 339, CA.

78. [1996] CLC 1370.

79. [1997] 2 All ER 789.

80. *Ibid* at 792.

81. *Lowsley* v. *Forbes* [1996] CLC 1370 at 1375, *per* Evans LJ.

once an action for the principal sum is barred, an action for arrears of interest will also be barred.[82] It is therefore possible that where an action to enforce a judgment became time barred in 1996, an action for arrears of interest for, say the period 1994–96, could be brought up to the year 2000. A further point which arises in relation to section 24(2) is that read literally, it would seem to apply to actions for enforcement since, unlike subsection (1), it is not prefaced by the term "an action". However, the Court of Appeal in *Lowsley* v. *Forbes*[83] held that the subsection does not apply to enforcement proceedings. Saville LJ subjected the wording of section 24 to extensive examination and concluded that:

"There is nothing to suggest that s 24 of the 1980 Act was intended to do more than reduce the 12-year period for an action on the judgment to six years. The division into two subsections seems to me to be simply an example of differences in drafting style and hardly likely to have been intended to produce a different effect from the section it replaced.[84] Thus it seems to me that (as under the 1939 Act) the limitation on the recovery of interest is only applicable to actions on a judgment . . . it is true that the two periods are now the same and [the defendant] submitted that it followed that unless subsection (2) was free standing it was surplusage, but to my mind this is not the case, since the six year period in subsection (1) could be extended by, for example, an acknowledgement or part payment."[85]

Although the Limitation Act 1980 is silent on applications to *set aside* a judgment, the Rules of the Supreme Court allow such applications where, for example, a judgment is entered in default of appearance,[86] or of the serving of a defence.[87] In this respect, RSC Order 12, rule 2 provides that an action by a defendant to set aside any judgment, order or other step must be brought promptly.[88]

BANKRUPTCY AND INSOLVENCY

As has been seen, the purpose of the Limitation Act 1980 is to specify time limits within which actions of various classes are to be brought. In insolvency proceedings, the class of action is generally founded on simple contract for which the limitation period is six years from the date on which the cause of action accrued.[89] In this context "action" must be taken to mean any form of initiating process and would include a creditors' petition.[90]

For bankruptcy proceedings, the rules governing proof of debts are laid down by the Insolvency Act 1986. Section 30(3) of the 1986 Act provides that provable debts includes "all debts and liabilities, present or future, certain or contingent, to which the debtor is

82. *Elder* v. *Northcott* [1930] 2 Ch 422.
83. *Supra*, fn 81.
84. Section 24 was based on the Limitation Act 1939, s 2(4) which provided: "An action shall not be brought on any judgment after the expiration of twelve years from the date on which the judgment became enforceable, and no arrears of interest in respect of any judgment debt shall be recovered after the expiration of six years from the date on which the interest became due".
85. [1996] CLC 1370 at 1375. See also, *Ezekial* v. *Orakpo*, *The Times*, 16 September 1996, CA.
86. RSC Ord 13.
87. RSC Ord 19.
88. See also, RSC Ord 13, r 7 and Ord 19, r 7.
89. Limitation Act 1980, s 5. The term "action" is defined in s 38(1) of the 1980 Act to include: "any proceeding in a court of law . . . ".
90. See, *Re Cases of Taffs Well Ltd* [1992] Ch 179 at 188 (Judge Paul Baker QC); *Re Karnos Property Co Ltd* (1989) 5 BCC 14; *Re a debtor (No 50A/SD/95)*, *supra*, fn 79. In *Re a bankruptcy notice* [1907] 1 KB 478, Fletcher Moulton LJ said, at 482, that an application for a bankruptcy notice "is not a method of enforcing a judgment. It is the commencement of proceedings of far wider effect".

subject at the date of the receiving order, or to which he may become subject before his discharge by reason of any obligation incurred before the date of the receiving order". In general, a provable debt arises out of the debtor's contractual and contingent liabilities as at the date of the receiving order.[91]

In the case of an insolvent company the liquidator will distribute the proceeds from the realisation of its assets in discharge of the company's liabilities and debts. To determine whether or not creditors qualify to have their debts discharged during the liquidation process, the debt must, as with bankruptcy proceedings, be provable. The procedure governing proof of debts in this context is now contained in the Insolvency Rules 1986,[92] the underlying principles of which are common to both bankruptcy and winding up.[93]

For provable debts in both personal and corporate insolvency, time will cease to run for limitation purposes on the making of the relevant order or, in the case of a voluntary liquidation, on the passing of the resolution to wind up.[94] For a petitioning creditor it was held in *Re Cases of Taffs Well Ltd*[95] that time ceased to run from the date of the presentation of his petition. Against this, however, the court stressed that a petitioning creditor did not act on behalf of all the other creditors so that time did not stop running against them until the making of the winding up order which converts their original contractual rights into proprietary rights under a trust.[96] Judge Paul Baker QC explained that:

"[T]he petitioning creditor does not bring an action on behalf of all the other creditors of a company known and unknown so as to stop time running against them. Indeed, some of them may be owed debts not then due and so could not bring actions at that point. Against them, time has not *started* to run. A petitioning creditor does not petition for the general good but rather in the hope of recovering his own debt or part of it . . . it would be strange if, by presenting a petition, a petitioner must be considered as saving creditors whose time was about to run out, and thus contrary to his own interest increase the number of claims to the fund."[97]

It has been argued that the approach adopted by the learned judge is wrong in so far as it offends one of the basic tenets of insolvency law, namely, that of "collectivity", the point being that the remedy sought by the petitioner implicates the entire body of creditors.[98] Accordingly, the prudent course of action for a creditor whose claim arises from a cause of action which is close to its time bar is to proceed by issuing a writ even though

---

91. The term "liabilities" is defined by the Insolvency Act 1986, s 30(8).
92. Insolvency Rules 1986, rr 4.73–4.99; 12.3.
93. See, Fletcher, *The Law of Insolvency*, 2nd ed (London: Sweet & Maxwell, 1996), Ch 23.
94. *Re Fleetwood & District Electric Light & Power Syndicate* [1915] 1 Ch 486.
95. [1992] Ch 179.
96. In *Ayerst* v. *C & K (Construction) Ltd* [1976] AC 167, the issue was whether the effect of a winding-up order was to divest the company of the beneficial ownership of its assets within the meaning of s 17(6)(a) of the Finance Act 1954. The House of Lords held that the making of a winding-up order brought into operation a statutory scheme dealing with the assets. All the powers of dealing with the company's assets are exercisable by the liquidator for the benefit of those persons only who are entitled to share in the proceeds of sale. The company itself, while remaining the legal owner, could not share beneficially in any part of the proceeds. Lord Diplock, at 180, stated that: "All that was intended to be conveyed by the use of the expression 'trust property' and 'trust' [by the authorities cited to the House] was that the effect of the statute was to give to the property of a company in liquidation that essential characteristic which distinguished trust property from other property, *viz.,* that it could not be used or disposed of by the legal owner for his own benefit, but must be used or disposed of for the benefit of other persons."
97. *Supra*, fn 90, at 189.
98. See, for example, the judgment of Brightman LJ in *Re Lines Bros Ltd* [1983] Ch 1 at 20, who observed that: "The liquidation of an insolvent company is a process of collective enforcement of debts for the benefit of the general body of creditors".

some other creditor has petitioned for a winding-up order, since the limitation period may well expire before the order is eventually granted. [99] However, if the limitation period has not expired at the date of the order, proof may nevertheless be lodged even though it will have expired by the time proof is effected.[100] It follows that where a debt has become time barred, the creditor will be precluded from lodging proof in the company's winding up even though the company may have voluntarily discharged the debt at a point in time before the onset of its insolvency. The expiration of the limitation period here does not extinguish the debt itself, only the creditor's remedy.[101]

RESTORING A DISSOLVED COMPANY TO THE REGISTER

Upon dissolution a company's existence ceases and it cannot thereafter be sued.[102] All proceedings by or against a company do not merely go into abeyance upon a company's dissolution but, in fact, are terminated.[103] Nevertheless, it is often the case that persons may wish to pursue a claim involving a dissolved company, or additional assets belonging to the former company subsequently come to light.[104] In this respect, the Companies Act 1985, ss 651 and 653 provide two means by which a company may be restored to the register so as to allow new proceedings to be brought against it.

(a) Power of court to declare dissolution of company void

Section 651(1) provides that where a company has been dissolved, the court may, on an application by the liquidator of the company or by any person appearing to the court to be interested, make an order, on such terms as it thinks fit, declaring the dissolution to be void. By section 651(4) such an application may not be made more than two years from the date of the dissolution of the company. Upon the company's reinstatement, such proceedings may be taken as might have been taken if the company had not been dissolved. In *Re Philip Powis Ltd*[105] it was argued that the words "on such terms as it thinks fit" found in section 651(1) empowered the court to undo the abatement of an action which had been commenced prior to the company's dissolution. In rejecting this submission, and holding that the court did not have jurisdiction to validate such proceedings, Sir John Knox said that: "Explicit legislative authority would be needed to allow the court subsequently to restore to life that which had come to a permanent end and to validate actions by and against the company notwithstanding the dissolution".[106]

99. Fletcher, *op cit*. In his judgment, Judge Baker QC expressly rejected *dicta* in *Re River Steamer Co* (1871) 6 Ch App 822 at 831 (Mellish LJ) and in *Re Overmark Smith Warden Ltd* [1982] 1 WLR 1195 at 1202 (Slade J) to the effect that the date of the presentation of the petition is the relevant date for determining when time ceases to run.

100. *Re General Rolling Stock Co, Joint Stock Discount Company's Claim* (1872) 7 Ch App 646, CA.

101. *Ibid*. See also, *Re River Steamer Co, Mitchell's Claim* (1871) 6 Ch App 822; *Re Art Reproduction Co Ltd* [1952] Ch 89. Cf s 17 of the Limitation Act 1980, considered in Ch 23, *infra*.

102. Dissolution occurs automatically three months after the registrar has been notified of the completion of the winding-up procedure: Insolvency Act 1986, ss 94, 106, 172(8), 201, 205.

103. *Re Philip Powis Ltd, The Times*, 30 April 1997 (Sir John Knox, sitting as a judge of the High Court).

104. *Re Forte's Manufacturing Ltd* [1994] BCC 84 at 87 *per* Hoffmann LJ.

105. *Supra*, fn 103.

106. The scope of the court's jurisdiction under section 651 was considered at length by Judge Paul Baker QC, sitting as a High Court judge, in *Re Townreach Ltd (No 2486190)* [1994] 3 WLR 983.

Section 651(5) goes on to provide that an application for the purpose of bringing an action against the company for damages for personal injuries or under the Fatal Accidents Act 1976 may be brought at any time, subject to the applicable limitation periods.[107] In *Re Workvale Ltd*[108] the Court of Appeal held that in exercising the discretionary powers conferred by section 651(5), the court was required to consider the discretionary powers granted by section 33 of the Limitation Act 1980 whereby the court may, in its discretion, extend the limitation period for actions in respect of personal injuries or death.[109] Briefly, the facts of the case were that in September 1983 the plaintiff, an employee of Workvale Ltd, suffered personal injuries by falling off a ladder while at work. In July 1986 the company was dissolved and in September 1986, some 24 days before the expiration of the primary limitation period, the plaintiff issued a writ naming the company as defendant. This was, of course, a nullity since the defendant did not exist. After much delay, during which the plaintiff died, his widow, as personal representative, brought an application to have the company restored to the register. This was heard in January 1991. At first instance, Harman J took the view that although the primary limitation period had long since expired, he should grant an order under section 651 unless satisfied to a high degree of certainty that the court, when trying the personal injuries action, would refuse a section 33 extension order. He accordingly restored the company to the register, on the basis that: "Having considered the matter as best I can I do not think I should prevent the widow *in limine* from seeking to test her luck before a Queen's Bench judge."[110]

However, the Court of Appeal, disapproving this approach, held that where the limitation period has expired, the court will have to consider whether there is an *arguable* case for a section 33 extension. Accordingly, on the application under section 651, the court's deliberations will, of necessity, encompass an initial consideration of the relative merits of the prospective section 33 application which will be made following the company's restoration to the register.

The problem of reconciling section 33 of the 1980 Act with section 651(5) of the Companies Act 1985 will not arise where the court is able to exercise the power conferred by section 651(6). This provision grants to the court the power to direct that the period between the dissolution of the company and the making of the order under section 651(1) shall not count for limitation purposes.[111] It is probable that this discretion will be exercised where it is considered that an application under section 33 has such a high probability of success as to render it unnecessary,[112] since the effect of section 651(6) is to bring the action back within the three year time limit imposed by section 11 of the Limitation Act 1980. In this respect the Court of Appeal in *Re Workvale Ltd*[113] went further than Harman J by adding that:

"As the case now stands, there will have to be an application in the Queen's Bench Division or in the county court, as the case may be, for a section 33 order. The material put before the court will

107. This provision was added by the Companies Act 1989, s 141(3). See *Bradley* v. *Eagle Star Insurance Co Ltd* [1989] AC 957, the issue of which is now directly addressed by the amendment introduced by the 1989 Act. The applicable time limits are laid down by ss 11 and 12 of the Limitation Act 1980.

108. [1992] 1 WLR 416, CA.

109. See Ch 19.

110. [1991] 1 WLR 294 at 302.

111. This gives statutory force to the decision of Roxburgh J in *Re Donald Kenyon Ltd* [1956] 1 WLR 1397, a case brought under what is now s 653 of the Companies Act 1985, *infra*.

112. As on the facts of *Re Workvale Ltd* [1992] 1 WLR 416, CA.

113. *Ibid*.

be the same material as is now before us. There is, as I understand it, nothing extra that either side will want to adduce for the purpose of the section 33 application. So there is no point in putting the parties to the extra expense and continued delay that the further application will inevitably entail. It was, in my opinion, open to Harman J., if satisfied that a section 33 application would succeed, to exercise the power conferred on the court by section 651(6) and to allow, [as asked in the motion] that 'the period between 22 July 1986 and the date of restoration of the company be excluded from the limitation period in respect of the applicant's claim for damages' ."[114]

(b) Objection to striking off by person aggrieved

Section 653 applies where the registrar has, by virtue of section 652, struck a defunct company off the register. It provides that if a company or any member or creditor of it feels aggrieved by the company having been struck off, he may apply before the expiration of 20 years from the publication in the *Gazette* of the notice under section 652, and the court may, if satisfied that the company was at the time of the striking off carrying on business or in operation, or otherwise that it is just that the company be restored to the register, order the company's name to be restored.[115]

In granting an order under section 653 in *Re Donald Kenyon Ltd*,[116] Roxburgh J was mindful that "common justice" required that there should be inserted in the order a proviso that in the case of creditors who were not time barred at the date of the company's dissolution, the period between that date and the company's restoration to the register should not be counted for limitation purposes.[117] This has now become a common-form provision inserted in such orders.[118] Whether or not such an order has the effect of ousting a limitation defence arose in *Re Advance Insulation Ltd*.[119] The plaintiff, a worker in the building industry, contracted pleural disease as a result of exposure to asbestos. One of the companies he had worked for in 1956 had been struck off the register in 1968, and in 1986 his solicitors sought to have it restored having found that the company had had an employers' liability policy with the Prudential Assurance Co Ltd. In July 1987, the registrar made an order, in common-form, restoring the company to the register. In August 1987 the plaintiff issued a writ which was served with a statement of claim in September. The insurers pleaded limitation and in his reply, the plaintiff stated that he would rely on the court's discretion under section 33 of the Limitation Act 1980 and also on the registrar's order. The trial was set down for November 1988 but in the previous September, the insurers applied to have the proviso in the registrar's order set aside. The Prudential argued that the special jurisdiction contained in section 33 of the 1980 Act made it wrong in principle for an order in common-form under section 653 of the Companies Act 1985 to be made, since such an application, made *ex parte,* deprived them of a defence under the Limitation Act. Hoffmann J rejected this contention on the basis that the appeal was made out of time, given that the insurers had known of the registrar's order since August 1987. Since that time, both parties had proceeded on the basis that the order had been validly made, at least until just a matter of weeks before the trial. It was therefore too late to overturn that assumption. Hoffmann J took the view that it would be

114. [1992] 1 WLR 416 at 424 *per* Scott LJ.
115. Companies Act 1985, s 653(1) and (2).
116. [1956] 1 WLR 1397. See fn 111, *supra*, and associated text.
117. *Ibid* at 1401.
118. A point made by Hoffmann J in *Re Advance Insulation Ltd* (1989) 5 BCC 55.
119. *Ibid.*

unfair to the plaintiff to delay the trial of his action given that no adequate explanation had been given for the lapse of time before the insurers had sought to have the order set aside.[120]

PART PAYMENT AND ACKNOWLEDGMENT

If a defendant acknowledges the plaintiff's rights or if a debtor makes a part payment of a debt owed by him to his creditor, the effect may be to revive a cause of action with the result that time begins to run, once more, against the defendant or the debtor. However, this should not be taken to mean that a new cause of action arises, but merely that time runs afresh from the date of the acknowledgment or part payment.[121]

(a) Acknowledgment of debts

The notion of acknowledgment of a debt is one which predates the Limitation Act 1939 and was based on a desire by the courts to prevent defendants from using the Statute of Limitations to avoid liability in circumstances in which it was clear that the defendant had indicated that he acknowledged a liability towards the plaintiff some time after the cause of action had initially accrued. Without the development of principles along these lines, it would be all too easy for a defendant or a debtor to give an acknowledgment or make a token payment of part of the debt in the hope that this would buy time and lull the plaintiff or the creditor into a false sense of security and, in the process, delay serving a writ on the defendant or the debtor.

Initially, the basis upon which this revival of the plaintiff's cause of action was justified was by way of an implied promise. This promise was said to be implied from the fact of the acknowledgment or the part payment.[122] However, because the theoretical under-pinning of the exception was the implied promise, it soon became apparent that if no such promise could be implied, time would continue to run, without interruption, against the plaintiff or the creditor from the date on which the debt was first incurred or the plaintiff's cause of action first accrued.[123] Inevitably, there were difficulties in ascertaining when the necessary promise could be implied and it has been observed judicially that the task became almost impossible since, "the decisions on the exact meaning and effect of the precise words employed by generations of shifty debtors, are ... irreconcilable".[124]

Given the inconsistencies inherent in the implied promise theory, which is known to be an inadequate basis for explaining many restitutionary principles, it is important that the

---

120. See also, *Re Regent Insulation Co Ltd, The Times*, 5 November 1981.

121. *Busch* v. *Stevens* [1963] 1 QB 1.

122. See *Spencer* v. *Hemmerde* [1922] 2 AC 507 at 519 *per* Lord Sumner and *Surrendra Overseas Ltd* v. *Government of Sri Lanka* [1977] 1 WLR 565 at 573 *per* Kerr J for two discussions of the historical development of rules on part payment and acknowledgment. The upshot of the implied promise theory was that almost anything short of an outright denial of liability was capable of giving rise to an implied promise on the part of the debtor that he acknowledged the existence of the debt, with the result that time could start to run afresh against him.

123. *Tanner* v. *Smart* (1827) 6 B & C 603.

124. *Spencer* v. *Hemmerde* [1922] 2 AC 507 at 534 *per* Lord Sumner.

Limitation Act 1939 and its successor the Limitation Act 1980 make no reference to implied promises at all.[125]

Under the Limitation Act 1980, ss 29 to 31, the doctrine of acknowledgment applies in two distinct sets of circumstances. First, the doctrine applies where any right of action to recover land, or an advowson, or any right of a mortgagee of real or personal property to bring a foreclosure action has accrued.[126] Secondly, the doctrine also applies where any right of action has accrued to recover any debt or any other liquidated pecuniary claim or any claim to the personal estate of a deceased person or to any share or interest in any such estate.[127]

The Limitation Act 1980, s 29(5) provides that:

"Subject to subsection (6) below, where any right of action has accrued to recover—

(a) any debt or other liquidated pecuniary claim; . . .

and the person liable or accountable for the claim acknowledges the claim or makes payment in respect of it the right shall be treated as having accrued on and not before the date of the acknowledgment or payment."

In qualification of this basic principle, section 29(6) provides further that:

"A payment of a part of the rent or interest due at any time shall not extend the period for reclaiming the remainder then due, but any payment of interest shall be treated as a payment in respect of the principal debt."

(i) Acknowledgment by whom?

For the purposes of section 29, it is a general requirement that an acknowledgment is in writing[128] and signed by the person liable on the debt, or an agent acting on his behalf.[129] However, the Act also allows for the possibility of an acknowledgment by an agent on behalf of his principal.[130] In this last event, it is important to establish the extent of the agent's authority, since it is clear that if the agent lacks express or implied authority to make an effective acknowledgment on his principal's behalf, then the precise requirements of section 30(1) will not have been complied with. So far as the issue of authority to acknowledge is concerned, it is important to consider the status of the agent who gives the acknowledgment, since it is possible that the agent is a person who would not normally be expected to be in a position to acknowledge the existence of a debt. Thus while it would be reasonable to assume that a company director does have authority to acknowledge a debt owed by the company, the same is not true of an auditor appointed by the same company, since the proper role of an auditor is to audit company accounts and to provide information for the guidance of the company itself. It follows from this that, as a general rule, a statement made by an auditor will be considered not to have been made to the

125. The same cannot be said of earlier statutory provisions which gave effect to the rule developed at common law. See e.g. Statute of Frauds Amendment Act 1828; Real Property Limitation Act 1833; Civil Procedure Act 1833; Mercantile Law Amendment Act 1856; Law of Property Amendment Act 1860; Real Property Limitation Act 1874.

126. See Ch 23 regarding actions to recover land, advowsons and mortgages of real property.

127. See Ch 23 regarding claims to personal estates of deceased persons.

128. For these purposes, the act of initialling a document will suffice: *Lord St John* v. *Boughton* (1838) 2 Sim 219.

129. Limitation Act 1980, s 30(1).

130. Limitation Act 1980, s 30(2)(a).

creditor. Accordingly, it was held in *Re Transplanters (Holding Company) Ltd*[131] that an auditor's signature on a company balance sheet was insufficient to amount to an acknowledgment of debts referred to in that document. The mere fact that the auditors were also referred to as chartered accountants was regarded by Wynn-Parry J as a purely descriptive matter. He observed further that,[132]

" . . . an auditor of a company (apart from any special contract, and there is none in this case) is not an agent of the company, at any rate for the purpose of being able to bind the company by merely signing the normal certificate at the foot of the balance sheet. To hold otherwise would be contrary to the Companies Act . . . But I cannot spell out of the certificate anything which would amount to an acknowledgment within . . . the Limitation Act . . . because I cannot spell out of his relations with the company . . . any authority to do anything in the nature of giving an acknowledgment . . . "

However, this should not be taken to mean that in all circumstances a signature on a balance sheet cannot be regarded as an acknowledgment. For example in *Jones* v. *Bellgrove Properties Ltd*[133] a balance sheet signed by accountants who were described as agents of the company and which identified the debt under consideration was taken to be a sufficient acknowledgment of the debt. It seems that this may be regarded as an unusual decision based upon a finding of fact that, in the particular circumstances, the auditors reported in their capacity as agents. Similarly, if an acknowledgment can be found in notes attached to company accounts, it will be possible to regard such a statement as one which satisfies the requirements of section 30, provided the accounts and the notes have been given to the creditor.[134]

It is also likely that a solicitor writing a letter on behalf of his client may be taken to act as an agent.[135] However, it still remains important to ascertain whether an agent is authorised to make an acknowledgment on behalf of the debtor. For example, where a solicitor ceases to act for his client, the agency will also be considered to have come to an end.[136] Similarly, it may be implicit in the nature of the express authority that certain actions are not allowed. For example, an agent appointed to make a full discharge of a debt will not have implied authority to make only a part payment.[137] Clearly, express authorisation will provide the clearest evidence of authority to act in this way, but it is also possible that appropriate inferences may be drawn from the conduct of the parties. Thus in *Wright* v. *Pepin*[138] a solicitor acting on behalf of the mortgagor of property wrote letters to solicitors acting for the mortgagee which initially demanded that there should be a proper statement of account. However, in later letters, the solicitor impliedly referred to her client's indebtedness to the mortgagee. Harman J considered that all that was necessary by way of acknowledgment was that the debtor or his agent should recognise the existence of the debt. So far as the matter of the agent's authority is concerned, it was considered

131. [1958] 2 All ER 711.
132. *Ibid* at 714.
133. [1949] 2 All ER 198.
134. *Ledingham* v. *Bermejo Estancia Co Ltd* [1949] 1 All ER 749. For these purposes, notes to the accounts may be regarded as part of the accounts: Companies Act 1985, Sch 4, para 35.
135. It appears that a receiver may also be regarded as an agent on behalf of the debtor whose estate he represents: *Chinnery* v. *Evans* (1864) 11 HL Cas 115; *Lilley* v. *Foad* [1899] 2 Ch 107; *Wandsworth Union* v. *Worthington* [1906] 1 KB 420.
136. *Newbould* v. *Smith* (1866) 33 Ch D 127.
137. *Lindsell* v. *Bonsor* (1835) 2 Bing (NC) 241.
138. [1954] 2 All ER 52.

sufficient that the agent was authorised to write the letter in which the acknowledgment was to be found. According to Harman J:

"It seems clear that it is not necessary that the agent should have authority to acknowledge, for instance ... the existence of the mortgage. It seems to be enough that the agent should have authority to write the letter which she does in fact write, and that what is said in the letter is within the scope of the agent's authority."[139]

Accordingly, in *Wright* v. *Pepin,* since the solicitor had express authority to put her client's affairs in order, it was possible to imply an authority to acknowledge the existence of the mortgage debt, in which case, the action by the mortgagee was not time barred.

What seems to emerge from *Wright* v. *Pepin* is that a solicitor can have a general authority in excess of that specifically conferred on him by the debtor. However, in *Re Beavan (No 2)*[140] a trustee had been appointed to manage the affairs of a man who had become of unsound mind. During the lifetime of that man, the trustee acknowledged a number of debts owed by him. However, strangely, these acknowledgments were considered not to have the effect of reviving a cause of action in favour of the creditors on the ground that the trustee was considered not to have authority to give an acknowledgment. If in *Wright* v. *Pepin* a solicitor with express authority to manage her client's affairs is also possessed of an implied authority to acknowledge the client's debt, it seems strange that the same could not also be said of the trustee in *Re Beavan*. However, it may be argued that there are important differences between agents and trustees, which may be taken to justify the decision. In particular, it is important that Neville J in *Re Beavan* was adamant that the trustee was not an agent at all. Since trustees do not act in a representational capacity as do agents, there may be some justification for the view that time should continue to run until the date of the beneficiary's death.

So far as corporate debtors are concerned, a complicating factor may be that the company owes a debt to one of its directors. This can give rise to difficulties in cases where the director who is also the creditor has appended his signature to a document which may be construed as an acknowledgment of the debt. In *Re Transplanters (Holding Company) Ltd*[141] the company balance sheet had been signed by auditors and two of the directors, one of whom was the applicant in the present case, having lent money to the company. In determining that the signed balance sheet could not be regarded as an effective acknowledgment, Wynn-Parry J observed that if the signature of the applicant could amount to an effective acknowledgment, it would mean that a creditor could acknowledge a debt owed to himself and thereby revive a cause of action in his own favour, which would clearly give rise to an unacceptable state of affairs. In reaching his conclusion, Wynn-Parry J applied the decision of Maugham J in *Re Coliseum (Barrow) Ltd*[142] in which it was observed that[143]:

"The difficulty in the present case is that the promise, if any, is a promise by the directors, as a board acting on behalf of the company, to pay to themselves the amount of the directors' fees, and it seems to me that this is not, in the circumstances, a promise to pay on behalf of the company. Having regard to the position which a director, as agent of the company, necessarily occupies in relation to

139. *Ibid* at 56.
140. [1912] 1 Ch 196.
141. [1958] 2 All ER 711.
142. [1930] 2 Ch 44.
143. *Ibid* at 47.

the company, it would not have been competent action for the board, acting as a board, to authorise the giving of a definite promise to pay themselves."

What lies behind this line of reasoning is that a creditor should not be seen to be able to promise to pay himself and so be able to revive his own cause of action. This is especially the case where company directors and personal representatives are concerned since they owe fiduciary duties, and if such persons were allowed to acknowledge a debt in favour of themselves, those fiduciary duties would be broken. However, if there is an independent ratification of an acknowledgment, it appears that this will make the acknowledgment effective. For example, in *Re Gee & Co (Woolwich) Ltd*[144] a balance sheet containing an acknowledgment of a debt owed to the plaintiff had been signed by the directors of the defendant company, who also happened to be the plaintiff's executors. On the face of it, therefore, the plaintiff's representatives had acknowledged the debt owed to the plaintiff. However, the acknowledgment was held by Brightman J to be effective on the basis that the decision of the directors had been ratified at a general meeting of the company attended by persons who represented all the shareholders in the company.[145] It seems to follow from this that the principle established in *Re Transplanters Ltd* may be side-stepped in the case of small companies with limited numbers of members. Subject to rules on agency, if an acknowledgment is to be effective, it must be given by the debtor or someone acting on his behalf to the creditor or someone acting on his behalf. Accordingly, the admission of a debt contained in an inland revenue affidavit submitted for the purposes of obtaining probate should not suffice, since such documents are not addressed to the debtor.[146] The proper interpretation of such a document is that it is to be regarded as a statement made to the court and cannot be construed as a promise to pay to the creditor any amount referred to in the document.[147]

(ii) Liquidated sums

It is important to emphasise from the outset that section 29(5)(a) is concerned only with liquidated sums, with the result that if there is a need to ascertain the amount due by reference to some other process, the debt will not fall within the scope of the subsection. Accordingly, it will be necessary for there to have been some sort of agreement between the parties to the effect that a stated sum is due to be paid by the debtor to the creditor. For this reason, it is unlikely that section 29(5)(a) will have any application outside of contractual actions for a specific sum, such as an action for the price under the Sale of Goods Act 1979, s 49 or some other contract, such as a tenancy agreement, under which a specific sum becomes due to be paid on an agreed date or on the occurrence of some event specified in the contract. Less clear examples of liquidated sums appear to include claims on a *quantum meruit*[148] since such claims are dubiously considered to be sufficiently certain in terms of their contractual description to allow the court to ascertain the

---

144. [1975] 1 Ch 52. See also *Parker & Cooper Ltd* v. *Reading* [1926] Ch 975; *Re Duomatic Ltd* [1969] 2 Ch 365.
145. In fact the meeting was attended by only the directors who had signed the balance sheet, but since some of the shares were held jointly by one of those directors and a third party who was absent from the meeting, all shareholders were represented.
146. *Bowring-Hanbury's Trustee* v. *Bowring-Hanbury* [1942] 1 All ER 516; affirmed [1943] 1 All ER 48. Cf *Tristram* v. *Harte* (1841) 3 Ir Eq Rep 386.
147. *Ibid* at 517 *per* Bennett J.
148. See also "actions to recover money" considered below.

amount due to be paid to the creditor. In *Amantilla* v. *Telefusion Ltd*[149] the question arose whether section 29(5)(a) could apply to a *quantum meruit* claim for the reasonable value of building works provided under a contract which failed on the ground that there had been no agreement as to price. It was held by John Davies QC that, "A *quantum meruit* for a 'reasonable sum' lies in debt because it is for money due under a contract. It is a liquidated pecuniary claim because a 'reasonable sum' . . . is a sufficiently certain contractual description for its amount to be reasonably ascertainable."[150]

What the trial judge did in these circumstances was to apply a rule similar to that used in contracts for the sale of goods where there is no agreement as to price,[151] but these all presuppose the existence of an otherwise valid contract. In *Amantilla*, fortunately, there was an acknowledgment by the defendants that there was a valid contract for building work, but whether the same approach could be taken to a case where work is commenced on the basis of a letter of intent and no subsequent agreement is reached may be doubtful.[152] In this last event, there is no contract and presumably an insufficiently clear contractual description for the amount due to be reasonably ascertainable. In these circumstances, if there are factual difficulties in ascertaining the precise sum due to be paid, it is still possible that a claim on a *quantum meruit* could be regarded as a claim for an unliquidated amount, thereby preventing an apparent acknowledgment of the amount due falling within the provisions of section 29(5)(a). A particular problem highlighted by *Amantilla* is that there is no provision in the Limitation Act for purely restitutionary claims, since the Act works on the basis that a particular claim may be characterised as one arising in contract or one arising in tort. Arguably, there is a case for treating all claims on a *quantum meruit* as falling within section 29(5)(a) whether they be contractual claims or not.[153]

(iii) Disapplication of the statutory provisions on acknowledgment

Although the provisions of sections 29 to 31 are stated to apply in general terms to any debt or claim to a liquidated sum, there are certain actions which are expressly stated to be unaffected by an alleged acknowledgment with the result that there can be no extension of time based on such an acknowledgment. Thus actions for damages under the Fatal Accidents Act 1976[154] and a claim for contribution between tortfeasors under the Civil Liability (Contribution) Act 1978[155] are matters in respect of which the provisions on acknowledgment and part payment are expressly disapplied. In any event, it is probably unlikely that an action for damages under the Fatal Accidents Act would be regarded as an action for anything other than an unliquidated sum, given that the court will have to assess the claimant's entitlement to damages.

---

149. (1987) 9 Con LR 139.
150. *Ibid* at 145.
151. Sale of Goods Act 1979, s 8(2). See also Supply of Goods and Services Act 1982, s 15(1). Similar considerations may also apply at common law where there is no agreement on the matter of an agent's entitlement to commission: *Way* v. *Latilla* [1937] 3 All ER 759.
152. As in *British Steel Corp* v. *Cleveland Bridge & Engineering Co Ltd* [1984] 1 All ER 504 and *Peter Lind & Co Ltd* v. *Mersey Docks & Harbour Board* [1972] 2 Lloyd's Rep 234.
153. See McLean, "Limitation of Actions in Restitution" (1989) 48 CLJ 472 at 478.
154. Limitation Act 1980, s 12(3).
155. Limitation Act 1980, s 10(5)

(iv) Repeated extensions

Provided a limitation period is still running, subject to the operation of section 29(6), it may be repeatedly extended by virtue of section 29(7). Accordingly, by virtue of section 29(5), the right to recover a debt will be treated as having accrued on and not before the date of the most recent acknowledgment. However, the operation of section 29(7) is subject to the overriding rule that once an action has become time barred, it cannot be revived even by way of an acknowledgment. It follows that if a debt becomes due for payment on 1 March 1990, in the absence of an acknowledgment before 1 March 1996 the creditor's action will be time barred and a written acknowledgment made on 10 March will have no effect. In contrast, if the written acknowledgment is made on 1 February 1996, time will run afresh in favour of the creditor and further acknowledgments in January 2002 and December 2007 will serve to keep the creditor's action alive.

(v) Effect of acknowledgment and part payment of debts on third parties

By virtue of the Limitation Act 1980, s 31(6) an acknowledgment of a debt or any other liquidated pecuniary claim will also bind the acknowledgor etc and his successors, but not any other person. In contrast, under section 31(7) where there is a part payment in respect of any debt or other liquidated pecuniary claim, that payment will bind all persons liable in respect of the debt or claim.

It should be observed that the effect of a payment in respect of a debt etc in section 31(7) is to bind all persons liable, whereas an acknowledgment under section 31(6) binds only the acknowledgor and his successors. Thus, part payment by one partner will bind all other partners,[156] since for the purposes of section 31(7) the other partners are persons liable in respect of the debt. Conversely, an acknowledgment would not have the same effect on a partner, since a fellow partner would not be regarded as a successor. Other effects of section 31(7) are that a part payment by the principal debtor will cause the re-accrual of the cause of action against a surety, since the latter is someone who is secondarily liable and therefore a person who falls within the meaning of the phrase, "person liable in respect of the debt".[157] In similar vein, if a guarantor makes a payment to the creditor in respect of interest owed by the principal debtor, the effect of such a part payment will be to cause time to run again in favour of the creditor and against the principal debtor.[158]

(vi) Sufficiency of the acknowledgment

A further difficulty presented by the 1980 Act is that it does not define the term "acknowledgment", but whether or not a particular action is to be classified as such will be regarded as a question of fact in each case.[159] The key problem in this regard is that a decision based upon the specific words used by one debtor cannot be regarded as a precedent when dealing with the language used by another debtor. Accordingly, there is probably little

---

156. *Goodwin* v. *Parton & Page* (1879) 41 LT (NS) 91; affirmed (1880) 42 LT (NS) 568.
157. *Re Powers, Lindsell* v. *Phillips* [1881–1885] All ER Rep 971.
158. *Re Seager's Estate, Seager* v. *Aston* (1857) 26 LJ Eq 809.
159. *Jones* v. *Bellgrove Properties Ltd* [1949] 2 KB 700.

value in drawing definite conclusions from case law which turns on a simple matter of construction of the words used in any particular case.[160]

Certainly, a document which expressly acknowledges that a specific sum is due to be paid will suffice for the purposes of section 29(5)(a), but it will also be sufficient if the document concerned makes it possible to ascertain the sum due by reference to extrinsic evidence. However, if the document in question amounts to a denial of liability, it will not suffice to cause time to run afresh against the debtor. For example in *Kamouh* v. *Associated Electrical Industries International Ltd*[161] the plaintiff's brother had performed services on behalf of the defendants, in respect of which the plaintiff sought to recover payment. In response to the brother's request for payment, a letter had been sent on the defendant's behalf in which it was stated that they recognised the brother was out of pocket to the extent of £100,000 but which also amounted to a denial that there was any agreement to remunerate him in respect of the work he had done. The letter also contained an admission that the brother had been paid sums on account of out-of-pocket expenses, but that until the defendants received an account in respect of those expenses, they would not make any further payments. Had this letter been regarded as an acknowledgment of the debt, its effect would have been to revive the cause of action in respect of the debt so that the plaintiff, who acted in a representative capacity, would not have been out of time. In concluding that the letter relied upon by the plaintiff admitted nothing and could not be regarded as an acknowledgment, Parker J observed,[162] "It is clear that an acknowledgment within the statute does not have to say in terms, 'I acknowledge that a certain sum is due,' but it does have to get as far as being an admission that something is due and that something must be ascertainable by extrinsic evidence."

It might be seen to follow from this that if there is an admission that a debt is due, but no stated means of ascertaining how much is due, the document containing the admission will not suffice as an acknowledgment. This will be especially the case where the document in question can be construed as amounting to a denial of liability on the ground that the amount of the debt is subject to a set-off or cross-claim.[163] What is necessary is that:

" . . . taking the debtor's statement as a whole, as it must be, he can only be held to have acknowledged the claim if he has, in effect, admitted his legal liability to pay that which the plaintiff seeks to recover. If he has denied liability, whether on the ground of what in pleader's language is called 'avoidance', or on the ground of an alleged set-off or cross-claim, then his statement does not amount to an acknowledgment of the creditor's claim. Alternatively, if he contends that some existing set-off or cross-claim reduces the creditor's claim in part, then the statement, taken as a whole, can only amount to an acknowledgment of indebtedness for the balance."[164]

What militates in favour of this approach is that it is in accordance with good sense and justice and that if a statement is to be regarded as an acknowledgment, it must be taken as a whole, so that the creditor cannot take from a document that which suits his purposes but ignore matters contained in the document which amount to a denial of liability.[165]

---

160. *Spencer* v. *Hemmerde* [1922] 2 AC 507 at 519 *per* Lord Sumner.
161. [1980] 1 QB 199.
162. *Ibid* at 209.
163. *Surrendra Overseas Ltd* v. *Government of Sri Lanka* [1977] 2 All ER 481 at 489 *per* Kerr J.
164. *Ibid* at 489–90 *per* Kerr J.
165. *Ibid* at 490 *per* Kerr J.

Similar reasoning also seems to apply to a failed defence pleaded in earlier judicial proceedings. In *Re Flynn (deceased) (No 2)*[166] an action was commenced against the deceased's estate in respect of a debt of $75,000 due under the terms of a promissory note given by the deceased. Although the promissory note was dated 13 June 1957 and the proceedings were commenced apparently out of time in 1964, it was argued that since there had been proceedings in a New York court in which a defence denying liability had been entered, but which had been expressly rejected, there was a sufficient acknowledgment of the debt. Buckley J in the Chancery Division held that the mere fact that the denial of liability had been rejected in the New York court could not amount to an acknowledgment of the debt, since it was based on an outright denial of liability on the part of the debtor. Since what is required is a recognition on the part of the debtor that the debt exists, a defence which amounts to a confession and avoidance cannot be relied upon, since the fact of the confession has to be read in the light of the purported avoidance of liability.[167] However, it does not necessarily follow from this that a statement contained in the pleadings cannot be regarded as an acknowledgment, provided it can be construed in such a way as to amount to an admission of the claim against the debtor.[168] For these purposes, it appears that the date on which the pleading is first entered will be the effective date for the revival of the cause of action, and time will not run afresh from day to day while the action continues.[169] Where an acknowledgment is derived from the pleadings, it is generally considered that the plaintiff should make his allegation in the form of his statement of claim rather than in the form of a reply to a plea on the part of the defendant that the debt is statute barred.[170]

Whether or not the acknowledgment must provide some clear means of ascertaining the precise amount of the debt is a moot point in the light of the decision in *Dungate* v. *Dungate*[171] which distinguishes the earlier decision in *Good* v. *Parry*.[172] In *Dungate*, a debtor borrowed money on various dates in 1956 and 1957. In 1959, the debtor undertook to repay one of these sums, then subsequently wrote to his creditor in 1962 inviting him to "keep a check on totals and amounts I owe you, and we will have account now and then". However, nowhere in the letter was there a statement of the precise amount owed by the debtor. In 1964 the plaintiff commenced proceedings, against the administratrix of the debtor's estate, for recovery of all debts. It was accepted that the undertaking to repay one loan of £500 was not time barred due to the 1959 acknowledgment and payments of interest, but in respect of all other debts it was claimed that the creditor was out of time, on the basis that the letter written in 1962 did not amount to a sufficient acknowledgment of those debts. Both Edmund Davies J at first instance and the Court of Appeal were prepared to regard the letter of 1962 as reviving the creditor's cause of action in respect of all of the alleged debts, on the basis that it constituted an unqualified admission of

---

166. [1969] 2 All ER 557.
167. *Ibid* at 562.
168. *Horner* v. *Cartwright*, 11 July 1989, unreported, CA.
169. *Ibid.*
170. *Busch* v. *Stevens* [1963] 1 QB 1. Here it was observed that the plaintiff will be penalised in terms of costs should the allegation come in the form of a reply.
171. [1965] 3 All ER 393; affirmed [1965] 3 All ER 818, albeit on a different ground. Edmund Davies J took the view that tax deduction certificates which referred to interest paid on a loan could amount to a sufficient acknowledgment. However, since these were not given to the creditor, the Limitation Act 1980, s 30 would not be complied with. See further (viii) below regarding the recipient of the acknowledgment.
172. [1963] 2 All ER 59.

indebtedness, it being immaterial that the precise amount of the debt was not stated in the letter. Instead, it was considered that oral evidence could be admitted to prove the amount of the debt, thereby allowing the creditor to proceed with his action. What convinced Edmund Davies J of the correctness of his decision was that in *Jones* v. *Bellgrove Properties Ltd*[173] there was found to be a sufficient acknowledgment in an entry in company accounts which referred to the total amount of debts owed to "sundry creditors" of whom the plaintiff was one, but who was owed less than the total amount of the debt referred to.

What seems to matter, following *Dungate*, is that there is at least some clear admission that a debt is owed in language which is unequivocal as to the existence of the debt. After that, it does not matter that the precise amount of the debt remains undisclosed, provided there is extrinsic evidence which can be admitted at a later stage which proves how much is owed.

In *Good* v. *Parry*, by way of contrast, the debtor had written to the creditor, stating that "the question of outstanding rent can be settled in a separate agreement as soon as you present your account". In the event, it was decided that there was no acknowledgment at all, since, employing the language of Davies LJ: "After a very careful review of the authorities . . . in my view the letter did not acknowledge the claim; it only acknowledged that *there might be a claim.*"[174]

Accordingly, the ratio of *Good* v. *Parry* was that there was no acknowledgment at all, since the language employed by the debtor was equivocal as to the question whether any amount at all was owed, but had there been a sufficient acknowledgment, it would not have mattered that the precise amount of the debt was identified in the letter. Similarly, a statement to the effect that a payment is made on an *ex gratia* basis cannot be construed as an admission of liability or an acknowledgment.[175] In contrast, the letter in *Dungate* admitted that something was owed, but did not state how much. The language of the judgments in *Good* v. *Parry* also seem to support that conclusion since it was observed by Lord Denning MR that:

"Nowadays . . . there is no necessity to look for a promise, express or implied. There need only be an acknowledgment of a debt or other liquidated amount. That means, I think, that there must be an admission that there is a debt or other liquidated amount outstanding and unpaid. . . . In order to be an acknowledgment, however, the debt must be quantified in figures or, at all events, it must be liquidated in this sense that it is capable of ascertainment by calculation, or by extrinsic evidence, without further agreement of the parties."[176]

Accordingly in *Good* v. *Parry* a statement to the effect "I admit I owe you the sum shown in this rent book" would suffice, provided there was evidence to show how much that debt amounted to. *Good* v. *Parry* would appear to be consistent with what was held in *Dungate* in the sense that if there is acceptable extrinsic evidence to identify the amount of the debt, then there is no need for the acknowledgment to make reference to the specific amount owed, provided that no further agreement between the parties is required in order to ascertain the amount of the debt, so that it may be regarded as a liquidated sum.

173. [1949] 2 All ER 198.
174. [1963] 2 All ER 59 at 62.
175. *Kamouh* v. *Associated Electrical Industries International Ltd* [1980] 1 QB 199.
176. [1963] 2 All ER 59 at 61.

Whether or not a particular statement can amount to a sufficient acknowledgment may depend upon other rules of procedure. For example, the normal assumption is that a statement made without prejudice by a solicitor acting on behalf of his client will not be admissible in evidence and therefore will not constitute an acknowledgment of a debt owed by the client.[177] However, to be a valid without prejudice communication, there must be an offer to negotiate a compromise or an offer to take part in negotiations. Accordingly, a letter which is marked "without prejudice" but which denies the claims made by the other party and which does not offer to negotiate or make a settlement will not be regarded as a genuine without prejudice communication. If the privilege does not attach to the document, it follows that the document could be regarded as an acknowledgment, although if all it does is to deny the creditor's claim, for reasons considered above, it will still fail to amount to a sufficient acknowledgment, since it does not admit liability.[178] Also, where a communication fails to satisfy the requirements for a valid "without prejudice" communication, should there be a subsequent compromise or settlement, each party will be estopped from raising issues which form part of that compromise or settlement.[179]

Where extrinsic evidence is admitted, it can relate to a number of different matters. For example, provided there is a sufficient acknowledgment of the fact that a debt is due, the additional evidence may be admitted in order to connect the acknowledgment with the debt,[180] or to ascertain the amount of the debt.[181] Likewise the evidence may identify the date of execution of the document containing the acknowledgment[182] or may serve to connect a series of documents which between them satisfy the requirement of sufficiency.[183] It is also possible to admit secondary evidence in order to show that a written acknowledgment which has subsequently been lost was, in fact, made.[184]

(vii) Timing of the acknowledgment

Where an acknowledgment is given prior to the date on which the limitation period applicable to that debt has expired, time will start to run once more from the date of the acknowledgment. However, if the acknowledgment is made after the expiry of the limitation period, the debt should remain time barred and the acknowledgment should not be capable of reviving the cause of action. This is confirmed, in particular, by the wording of the Limitation Act 1980, s 29(7), which in relation to repeated acknowledgments, states that "a right of action, once barred by this Act, shall not be revived by any subsequent acknowledgment or payment". Moreover, in *Consolidated Agencies Ltd* v. *Bertram Ltd*[185] a number of acknowledgments contained in company balance sheets were prepared at a time when the debt to which they related was still actionable, but by the time the balance

---

177. *Re Daintrey, ex parte Holt* [1893] 2 QB 116; *Buckinghamshire CC* v. *Moran* [1990] 1 Ch 623; *Rush & Tomkins Ltd* v. *Greater London Council* [1989] AC 1280.

178. *Buckinghamshire CC* v. *Moran* [1989] 2 All ER 225, [1990] 1 Ch 623.

179. *Colchester Borough Council* v. *Smith* [1992] 2 All ER 561 affirming Ferris J [1991] 2 All ER 29 and see also Ch 23.

180. *Read* v. *Price* [1909] 2 KB 724 at 737 *per* Farwell LJ; *Jones* v. *Bellgrove Properties Ltd* [1949] 2 All ER 198.

181. *Dungate* v. *Dungate* [1965] 3 All ER 393.

182. *Edmunds* v. *Downes* (1834) 1 Cromp & M 459.

183. *McGuffe* v. *Burleigh* (1898) 78 LT 264.

184. *Read* v. *Price* [1909] 2 KB 724.

185. [1965] AC 470.

sheets were signed by responsible directors, the debts to which those acknowledgments related had become time barred. Accordingly, since the acknowledgments related to a past liability, they were not sufficient under the relevant Indian legislation[186] which the Privy Council was called upon to interpret.

The conclusion reached for the purposes of the Indian legislation, however, did not take account of the decision of the Court of Appeal in *Jones* v. *Bellgrove Properties Ltd*[187] to the effect that an acknowledgment made in 1945 which related to debts incurred in 1936 and 1937 was sufficient for the purposes of the Limitation Act 1939 ss 23 and 24. Clearly, the problem created by this decision is that in 1945 any action in respect of the debts under consideration was apparently time barred, with the result that the recognition that the acknowledgment revived that action was apparently inconsistent with the conclusion arrived at by the Privy Council in *Consolidated Agencies Ltd* v. *Bertram Ltd.*

It would appear to be a requirement of the provisions of the Limitation Act 1980 that the acknowledgment should indicate that the debt is recognised and that a claim exists at the date on which the acknowledgment is given or that the debt existed on a date which falls within the currency of the limitation period.[188] But this is not a requirement that, in all cases, there must be an acknowledgment of an *existing* liability.[189] Instead, it may be sufficient acknowledgment if there is a debt in existence at the time the document containing the acknowledgment is prepared, even though it may not be signed until some later date. Accordingly in *Re Gee & Co (Woolwich) Ltd*[190] a balance sheet which contained an acknowledgment of the defendant company's debt to the plaintiff had been signed by the directors of the of the company some time after the debts to which the document referred had become time barred. However, Brightman J concluded that he was not bound to follow the decision in *Consolidated Agencies* and chose to regard the subsequent signatures as relating back to the time at which the document was prepared.

The conclusion arrived at by Brightman J in *Re Gee* does seem to be inconsistent with the principle that once an action has become time barred, it cannot be revived by a subsequent acknowledgment. Moreover, it is perhaps significant that the cases relied upon by Brightman J in *Re Gee* do not specifically reach any decision on the question of the timing of the acknowledgment, since in each case, they are concerned with somewhat different issues.

(viii) The recipient of the acknowledgment

For an acknowledgment to be effective, it must be made to the creditor, with the result that a document which in other circumstances might be regarded as a sufficient acknowledgment of a debt will not satisfy the requirements of section 29(5)(a) if it is addressed

---

186. Indian Limitation Act 1908, s 19(1), the provisions of which are identical to those contained in the Limitation Act 1980, s 29.
187. [1949] 2 All ER 198.
188. *Howcutt* v. *Bonser* (1849) 3 Exch 491.
189. See *Re Gee & Co (Woolwich) Ltd* [1975] 1 Ch 52 at 70 *per* Brightman J.
190. [1975] 1 Ch 52. See also *Re Overmark Smith Warden Ltd* [1982] 1 WLR 1195. But cf *Consolidated Agencies Ltd* v. *Bertram Ltd* [1965] AC 470 PC, in which an acknowledgment of past liability was considered to be ineffective, which appears to have turned upon the date on which the acknowledgment was signed rather than upon the date on which the document containing the acknowledgment was first prepared. It is a salient consideration that in *Re Gee & Co*, Brightman J regarded the Privy Council opinion to be inconsistent with English authority on the point in question.

to some other person. Thus in *Bowring-Hanbury's Trustee* v. *Bowring-Hanbury*[191] an admission that a debt was owed which was contained in an Inland Revenue affidavit submitted for the purpose of obtaining probate could not be regarded as a sufficient acknowledgment, since it was addressed to the court rather than to the creditor.

Furthermore, the acknowledgment must be given to the creditor at a time when he has a sufficient right to enforce the debt. Generally, in relation to title to land, the rule is that an acknowledgment given to a person whose title has not yet accrued will be insufficient.[192] However, this does not mean that the benefit of a valid acknowledgment given to the assignor of a debt cannot be passed on to the assignee. But since the assignee will take the benefit of the contract "subject to equities", if the assignor would have been out of time, so also will be the assignee of the debt, as he will be unable to recover from the debtor more than could have been recovered by the assignor.

(b) Part payment

A part payment is merely a species of acknowledgment, since by tendering the payment of part of a debt, the debtor is effectively admitting that the debt exists and that he remains liable upon the contract under which the debt came into existence.

(i) Payment "in respect of" a debt

What seems to be required of the payment is that it should be taken to be an admission that the balance of the debt remains due. Accordingly it was said in *Surrendra Overseas Ltd* v. *The Government of Sri Lanka*[193] that: "A part payment, like an acknowledgment, can only revive the cause of action and start time running afresh if it provides evidence in the form of an admission by the debtor that the debt remains due despite the passage of time."[194]

Accordingly, in that case, a payment was made by charterers "in respect of" the ship owner's claim, but on closer examination, it was clear that all the payment covered was the full amount of the much more limited liability which the charterers accepted they had to the ship owners. It followed that the full amount of the debt which the owners claimed was due to them was neither acknowledged nor could there be said to have been a "payment on account".

Similarly in *Kleinwort Benson Ltd* v. *South Tyneside Metropolitan Borough Council*[195] the plaintiff bankers entered into a series of rate swap contracts with the defendant local authority between 1983 and 1986. Subsequently, in unconnected proceedings, this variety of contract was declared to be *ultra vires* the powers of the local authority, with the result that all further payments under those contracts by the defendants were stopped. Moreover, the effect of the *ultra vires* decision was that the contracts were declared to be void *ab initio*. So far as the restitutionary liability was concerned in respect of some of the payments admitted by the defendants, it was claimed that the Limitation Act 1980, s 5

191. [1943] 1 All ER 48. Cf *Tristram* v. *Harte* (1841) 3 Ir Eq Rep 386.
192. *Holland* v. *Clark* (1842) 1 Y & C Ch Cas 151.
193. [1977] 1 WLR 565. See also *Re Footman Bower & Co Ltd* [1961] Ch 443 at 449 *per* Buckley J.
194. *Ibid* at 577 *per* Kerr J.
195. [1994] 4 All ER 972. Approved in *Kleinwort Benson Ltd* v. *Birmingham City Council* [1996] 4 All ER 733.

applied so as to render any action on the part of the plaintiffs to recover those amounts time barred. The plaintiffs contended in return that there had been four payments made by the defendants after those which were subject to the limitation question, which were alleged to be part payments falling within section 29(5). Since these were restitutionary claims for moneys had and received, it was necessary to determine when the cause of action arose for the purposes of section 5. For these purposes, it was concluded that the relevant date was the date on which the money was paid by the plaintiff to the defendant. Since proceedings were commenced on 27 March 1991, any payment made before 27 March 1985 was prima facie time barred. In the present case, payments were made by the defendants in December 1985 and June 1986, 1987 and 1989 and it was alleged by the plaintiffs that these constituted "payments in respect" of the right of the plaintiffs to recover in full the amount of the debt owed to them. However, at the time these payments were made, the defendants did not realise that they were doing so under a void contract and that there was therefore a restitutionary right in favour of the plaintiffs.

According to Hobhouse J, the correct question to be asked was:

" . . . whether for the purposes of answering the question posed by section 29(5) one has to have regard to the actual position as understood by the parties at the time of the part payment, or whether it suffices to have regard to an analysis which the law places on that payment although the parties were at the material time unaware of it."[196]

Applying the judgment of Kerr J in *Surrendra Overseas Ltd*[197] there must be "evidence of an admission of liability for the debt claimed". It followed that since there was no evidence that at the time the defendants made their payments they realised that there was any existing restitutionary liability, the payments made by them could not be regarded as part payments within the meaning of section 29(5).

The precise wording of section 29(5) is that the part payment must be made in respect of the debt owed to the creditor. It follows from this that it must be possible to identify something in the actions of the debtor or his agent which constitutes an appropriation of the payment to a particular debt. Accordingly, if it is the creditor who appropriates the payment to one of a number of debts owed by the debtor to the creditor, it will not be possible to regard the payment as one made in respect of any particular debt. Thus if a defendant makes a payment in respect of a debt which is subsequently void for illegality and the creditor then appropriates that payment to another valid debt, there is no payment by the debtor in respect of the valid debt.[198] However, where payments are in respect of a running account debt, it appears that the outstanding balance at any given time will be regarded as a single debt, in which case, regular payments into that account may be regarded as payments in respect of the amount then owed. Thus in *Re Footman Bower & Co Ltd*[199] the applicant, a timber merchant, supplied goods to a firm of cabinet makers and debited their running account as and when goods were supplied. The latter made a number of payments on account, none of which was made in respect of any particular debt. Subsequently, the firm of cabinet makers went into receivership in 1953, the last payments into the account having been made in July 1953 at a time when the firm's indebtedness extended to more than £595. The applicants lodged a proof in the winding-up proceedings

---

196. *Ibid* at 980.
197. [1977] 1 WLR 565 at 577.
198. See *Kleinwort Benson Ltd* v. *South Tyneside MBC* [1994] 4 All ER 972.
199. [1961] 2 All ER 161.

in April 1959 and the question arose whether the payments made by the firm could be regarded as payments in respect of the debt claimed by the applicants. Buckley J stated the general rule that:

"In my judgment . . . one must look at the act and intention of the debtor to see whether the payment is made in respect of the particular debt . . . Just as an acknowledgment can only acquire that character by the act of the debtor or his agent, so also . . . a payment . . . can only acquire the characteristic of being made 'in respect of' the debt by the act of the debtor or his agent. Consequently . . . appropriation by a creditor of a sum received from the debtor towards satisfaction of a particular debt, be it statute barred or not, cannot make such appropriation a 'payment in respect thereof' . . . "[200]

However, in *Re Footman, Bower* since the payments were all made into the same account, the true nature of the debtor's liability was a single and undivided debt for the amount of the balance owing at the time of each payment. On this basis, each time a payment into the account was made, it had the effect of causing time to run once more against the debtor, since a payment "on account" can be regarded as an admission of a greater liability.[201] This remains the case, despite the fact that, so far as current accounts are concerned, a payment in is presumed to be a payment in discharge of the earliest outstanding debt.[202]

In contrast with a debt owed under a running account, the position is different where there are a number of specific and distinct debts owed by the debtor to the creditor. In such a case, the intentions of the debtor become paramount, since the debtor has a choice as to which debt he chooses to make payment in respect of.[203] If the debtor makes no such choice, the creditor may choose which debt is to be repaid,[204] but this will fail to satisfy the requirements for the purposes of a part payment. Alternatively, if neither party makes an election, it will be assumed that claims which have not become statute barred are to be paid before those which have become time barred.[205]

(ii) Qualifying payments

What amounts to a part payment seems to have been given a broad interpretation by the courts. Clearly, cash payments and those by way of a negotiable instrument will suffice, but it is also the case that a payment in the form of money or money's worth will also satisfy the requirements of the Limitation Act. Accordingly, it has been held that an agreement to the effect that the creditor should be allowed to live rent free at property owned by the debtor and be provided with the produce of the debtor's labour can constitute money's worth, so long as there is a sufficient connection between the "free provision" and the debt.[206] Likewise, an agreement to maintain the creditor's child has been regarded as money's worth.[207] What is necessary, therefore, is some accommodation

---

200. *Ibid* at 164.
201. *Friend* v. *Young* [1897] 2 Ch 421 at 436 *per* Stirling J.
202. *Clayton's case* (1816) 1 Mer 572.
203. *Re Footman, Bower & Co Ltd* [1961] 2 All ER 161 at 164 *per* Buckley J.
204. *Mills* v. *Fowkes* (1839) 5 Bing (NC) 455.
205. *Nash* v. *Hodgson* (1855) 6 De GM & G 474.
206. *Re Wilson & Wilson* [1937] Ch 675. See also *Beamish* v. *Whitney* [1909] 1 IR 360 (supply of potatoes on account of mortgage interest dues).
207. *Bodger* v. *Arch* (1854) 10 Exch 333.

by the debtor which the parties agree is to be regarded as "equivalent to a payment in money".[208]

A more difficult issue will arise where the "payment" involves neither money nor money's worth, but there is nonetheless something of value in its widest sense which passes to the creditor. In *Maber* v. *Maber* [209] the plaintiff lent his son £80, subject to interest charges and supported by a promissory note. For some time, no payment was made in respect of either capital or interest, due to the fact that the son and his wife, the defendant, resided abroad. While the limitation period in respect of this debt was still running, the plaintiff's son and the defendant returned to England, whereupon the son offered to pay the outstanding interest, putting his hand into his pocket as if to reach for the money required to satisfy the debt. However, the plaintiff declined the offer, in the presence of the defendant, and indicated to her that he would forego payment in respect of interest due on the loan, passing to her a receipt for the interest due on the loan. Subsequently, the son's promissory note was indorsed to the effect that the interest due on the loan had been paid. Later there were further disputes as to repayment of the debt and the question arose whether the debt had become time barred.

Clearly, there was no sufficient acknowledgment of the debt, since there was nothing in writing signed by the son, with the result that the question arose whether a payment had been made as a result of the son putting his hand in his pocket. A majority of the court[210] held that a deemed payment had been made on the basis that the assignment of the interest due on the loan to the defendant could be regarded as something of value. In effect, what had happened was that such interest as was owed by the son was treated as if it had been paid to his father and then impliedly assigned to the plaintiff.[211] However, this decision was not unanimous and in a persuasive dissenting judgment, Bramwell B argued that there had been no change of legal position and that, in effect, these facts did not differ from a situation in which a creditor tells a debtor to keep the interest for himself.[212] In these circumstances, there would be no more than a gift by the creditor to the debtor, so why should matters differ because a relative, in fact, derives the benefit? In *Maber* there was documentary evidence of the debt, in the form of the indorsement on the promissory note, but this was signed by the creditor and, as such, would not satisfy the requirements of the Limitation Act in relation to acknowledgments, since the signature on the document was that of the creditor rather than the debtor, and it is established law that the creditor cannot acknowledge a debt owed to himself. The reasoning employed by the majority may be supported if the actions of the son could be construed as the tendering of payment, as opposed to making payment itself, but it is clear from the language used by Martin B that this line of argument was not relied upon. Martin B observed that his "decision steers clear of the cases about an agreement or promise to pay".[213] Accordingly it must be assumed that there was no tender of payment in the view of the court.

---

208. *Ibid* at 340 *per* Parke B.
209. (1867) LR 2 Exch 153, Court of Exchequer Chamber.
210. Martin, Channell and Piggott BB.
211. But the modern law of assignment no longer requires payment, with the result that the fiction that there was a payment to the father is no longer an available argument.
212. (1867) LR 2 Exch 153 at 157.
213. *Ibid* at 156.

However, for the purposes of the law of limitation, it appears to have been held in *Amos v. Smith*[214] that the tender of payment is to be regarded as the equivalent of payment. In *Amos v. Smith* the defendant and her husband were parties to a marriage settlement of which the plaintiffs were trustees. Settlement money was lent by the plaintiffs to the husband at interest, the defendant and her husband agreeing to repay the interest. Subsequently, the defendant gave receipts in respect of interest due, although no money in fact changed hands. The unanimous opinion of the court[215] was that there had been a "part satisfaction" of the debt, which was to be regarded as the equivalent of part payment. As was observed by Martin B:

"In my opinion whatever would prove a plea of payment is sufficient . . . The husband ought to have paid the trustees the interest as it became due, and the trustees ought to have handed it to the wife; and if that had been done, beyond all doubt it would have taken the case out of the Statute of Limitations."

This may be taken as an indication that the mere tender of payment will suffice for the purposes of the Statute of Limitations, although in a passing reference to *Amos v. Smith* in *Maber v. Maber* Martin B uses language which may also be taken to indicate that *Amos v. Smith* is also a case in which payment was taken to have been made.[216]

SOLICITORS' COSTS

(a) General issues

It was seen in Chapter 5 that time begins to run from the date of the accrual of the cause of action. In *Read v. Brown*[217] Lord Esher MR defined "cause of action" as "every fact which it would be necessary for the plaintiff to prove, if traversed, in order to support his right to the judgment of the Court. It does not comprise every piece of evidence which is necessary to prove each fact, but every fact which is necessary to be proved".[218] However, the accrual of the cause of action will not necessarily coincide with the date on which the plaintiff first had the right to commence legal proceedings against the defendant. In this regard, the Solicitors Act 1974, s 69 prohibits the bringing of an action by a solicitor on a bill of costs until the expiry of one month after delivery of the bill to the client.

In *Coburn v. Colledge*[219] the issue was whether the cause of action accrued to the plaintiff when the bill of costs was delivered to the defendant or on the later date, i.e. at the expiration of one month from the date of delivery. On 30 May 1889 the plaintiff completed certain work for the defendant as his solicitor. On 12 June the plaintiff posted his bill of costs to the defendant. In the meantime the defendant had left for Australia and did not receive the bill until sometime in 1891. When the defendant returned to England, the plaintiff commenced his action on 12 June 1896. By way of defence, the defendant argued that the action was time barred. The Court of Appeal held that the cause of action accrued when the work was completed, and the statutory provision requiring the expiry of

214. (1862) 1 H & C 238.
215. Martin and Bramwell BB, Channell B concurring.
216. (1867) LR 2 Exch 153 at 155.
217. (1888) 22 QBD 128, CA.
218. *Ibid* at 131, citing *Cooke v. Gill* LR 8 CP 107.
219. [1897] 1 QB 702, CA.

one month before commencing an action was merely a procedural point which did not affect the cause of action. Further, a solicitor who has client money in his hands is not prevented from retaining the amount due out of that money. Lord Esher MR, in construing the Solicitors Act 1843,[220] stated that:

"It takes away, no doubt, the right of the solicitor to bring an action directly the work is done, but it does not take away his right to payment for it, which is the cause of action. The Statute of Limitations itself does not affect the right to payment, but only affects the procedure for enforcing it in the event of dispute or refusal to pay. Similarly, . . . the Solicitors Act 1843, deals, not with the right of the solicitor, but with the procedure to enforce that right . . . It assumes that he has a right to be paid the fees, charges, and disbursements, but provides that he shall not bring an action to enforce that right until certain preliminary requirements have been satisfied."

The effect of the decision in *Coburn* v. *Colledge* is that a solicitor has five years and eleven months to bring an action for the amount of his bill of costs. Chitty LJ explained that this restriction is imposed for the protection of clients, for otherwise a solicitor might postpone for any time the delivery of his bill of costs, and so prevent the limitation period from beginning to run.[221]

(b) Taxing a bill of costs

Section 70 of the Solicitors Act 1974 provides that a client's right to apply for taxation must be exercised not later than one year after the date on which the bill is paid. In *Harrington* v. *Tew*[222] the House of Lords held that the court has no jurisdiction in any circumstances, either under the Act or by virtue of its inherent jurisdiction, to order taxation where a client fails to comply with this requirement. Where, however, a client alleges serious professional misconduct on the part of his solicitor, the Law Society may refer the bill to a taxing master for consideration.

---

220. See now the Solicitors Act 1974.
221. *Supra,* fn 219 at 710.
222. [1990] 2 AC 523, HL.

CHAPTER 10

CONTRACTS FOR THE SUPPLY OF GOODS AND SERVICES

CONTRACTS FOR THE SUPPLY OF GOODS

Where there is a contract for the supply of goods, the limitation issues which may arise can depend on the type of contract which the parties have entered into. For present purposes, the three main types of contract to be considered include contracts of sale within the meaning of the Sale of Goods Act 1979, credit transactions not falling within the meaning of a contract of sale[1] and other contracts which involve an element of supply of goods, but which do not fall within the definition of a contract for the sale of goods.[2] Under a contract for the sale of goods, a number of possible breaches of contract may be identified, each of which can give rise to different problems of limitation of actions.

(a) The seller's action for the price

The seller may have an action for the price where the buyer wrongfully neglects or refuses to pay for the goods in accordance with the terms of the contract at a time when property in those goods has passed to the buyer.[3] This is an action for a liquidated sum in the sense that the price has been agreed between the parties and since the primary objective of a contract for the sale of goods is the absolute transfer of ownership in those goods, in accordance with the terms of the contract, the seller does not need to sue for unliquidated damages, but may, instead, seek what amounts to compulsory performance of the buyer's primary obligation under the contract, namely, payment of the price.

Under the Sale of Goods Act 1979, s 28 the obligation of the seller to deliver and the obligation of the buyer to pay for the goods are regarded as concurrent conditions of the contract. It follows from this that the buyer will not be bound to pay and the seller will not be bound to deliver the goods until the other party is ready to perform his primary contractual obligation.

For the purposes of limitation of actions, it becomes necessary to determine at what point time will begin to run against the party in breach. So far as the seller's action for the price is concerned, much will depend upon the specific terms of the contract. For example,

---

1. Such as contracts of hire purchase, under which the debtor is under no obligation to purchase the goods, but has merely an option to purchase.

2. As defined in the Sale of Goods Act 1979, s 2(1). Such contracts are partially governed by the Supply of Goods and Services Act 1982, in relation to the statutory implied terms which apply to such contracts.

3. Sale of Goods Act 1979, s 49(1). If property in the goods has not passed, the seller will be confined to an action for damages for non-acceptance under the Sale of Goods Act 1979, s 50: *Colley* v. *Overseas Exporters Ltd* [1921] 3 KB 302.

if the contract provides for delivery on a specific date, then by virtue of section 28, the buyer's obligation to pay will crystallise on that date since payment and delivery are concurrent conditions of the contract. If the contract contains no date for delivery, then, as a result of the concurrency of the duties to pay and deliver, time ought to start running against the seller from the time he indicates that he is ready and willing to deliver the goods.[4]

It is also important to emphasise that, for the purposes of an action for the price, there must have been a wrongful neglect or refusal to pay the price. Accordingly, whether or not the seller's action under section 49 will be successful will depend upon whether the buyer has some justification for his refusal or neglect.

In certain circumstances, the seller may also maintain an action for the price where property in the goods has not passed to the buyer, since if the contract provides for payment of the price on a "day certain", the price is payable on that date, irrespective of the time at which property passes and whether or not the goods which are the subject of the contract have been appropriated to the contract.[5] Effectively the relationship of seller and buyer becomes one of creditor and debtor on the due date, and time will begin to run against the seller from the end of the day on which payment becomes due under the terms of their contract. For the purposes of this provision it is important, however, that the contract does specify in clear terms the date on which payment is to become due or provides some mechanism by which a day certain can be ascertained. Accordingly, the provisions of section 49(2) will have no application where the contract provides for "prompt payment, cash against invoice"[6] since contractual language of this nature does not state clearly the date on which the invoice is to be delivered and is therefore equivocal as to the date on which the price becomes payable. However, if there are terms which make it possible to ascertain when the price is payable, section 49(2) may still apply. Thus in *Workman Clark & Co Ltd* v. *Lloyd Brazileno*[7] a contract for the construction of a ship provided for payment of the price by instalments which became due when the process of construction reached certain stages of completion. The seller was held entitled to recover these sums, as they became due, under section 49(2) despite the fact that no specific dates for payment were contained in the contract. It was considered that once a certain stage of completion had been reached, the sum due in respect of that amount of work became due on the date of completion of the work.

The effect of section 49(2) is that the seller is in a position to be able to sue for the price before the date of delivery. Where this is the case, it leaves open the possibility that the seller may recover the price and then fail to deliver the goods as required by the contract. If this subsequent failure is due to a breach of contract on the part of the seller, the buyer, of course, will have his own remedy for non-delivery, but it is also possible that the seller

---

4. *Ibid*, s 28.

5. *Ibid*, s 49(2).

6. *Henderson & Keay Ltd* v. *AM Carmichael Ltd* 1956 SLT 58. See also *Stein Forbes & Co* v. *County Tailoring Co* (1916) 86 LJKB 448.

7. [1908] 1 KB 968. This decision should not be regarded as laying down a general rule to the effect that wherever the date for payment is ascertainable the seller may sue for the price, since damages may be a more appropriate remedy. However in *Workman Clark* the plaintiff was unable to recover damages, in which case, unless he could sue for the price, he would have been left without a remedy.

will treat the buyer's initial failure to pay on the due date as a reason for terminating the contract. In these circumstances, it seems, quite remarkably, that even though the buyer does not receive the goods he has contracted for he may remain liable to pay any sums due under the contract prior to the date on which the seller exercised his right to terminate the contract.[8] This decision was reached despite the fact that the Sale of Goods Act 1979, s 28 clearly states that the duty to deliver and the duty to accept and pay for goods are concurrent conditions of the contract. Assuming the decision in *Hyundai Heavy Industries Ltd* v. *Papadopoulos*[9] is correct, time will start to run against the seller from the date of non-payment of the outstanding instalment despite the fact that the buyer is left without a remedy in respect of the non-delivery.

Apart from the provisions of section 49, it appears that there may be a further instance in which the seller may sue for the price, namely where risk has passed prior to the date on which property is due to pass and the goods are lost or destroyed by an event which falls within the risk doctrine.[10] In such a case, the seller's action for the price will accrue on the date on which the damage complained of occurs, namely, the loss of or the damage to the goods contracted for.

The seller's action for the price will also be dependent upon any agreement between the parties as to any period of credit. Thus if the seller effects delivery, but allows the buyer a stated period of credit, time will not begin to run against the seller until the credit period has expired.[11] Thus in *Amos & Wood Ltd* v. *Kaprow*[12] the plaintiffs gave the defendants sole selling rights in respect of patented spring-action lipstick containers. The terms of the contract provided for an initial order of 1,000 gross (144,000) at a price of 108s per gross, subject to a premium payment of £300 and subject to a $2\frac{1}{2}$ per cent discount for prompt payment within seven days of delivery. The defendants took deliveries under the terms of this contract, but failed to make payments within seven days of delivery of five instalments. Subsequently, the plaintiffs wrote to the defendants stating that they would regard the agreement as having been broken unless all outstanding payments were received within two days. No payment was received, with the result that the plaintiff sued for £187 due in respect of deliveries made and also sought to terminate his obligations under the contract. Given that the contract provided for seven days' credit, it was clear that the plaintiff could not sue immediately upon delivery. Contrary to the view of the trial judge, the defendant did not have a reasonable time within which to pay any amount due under the contract, since in respect of each delivery there was a breach of contract at the commencement of the eighth day after receipt of each instalment.[13] What this also illustrates is that for the purposes of a severable contract, the seller's action for the price under section 49 applies to each instalment. Accordingly, the seller may sue for the price in respect of each instalment as it becomes due under the terms of the contract.[14]

---

8. *Hyundai Heavy Industries Ltd* v. *Papadopoulos* [1980] 1 WLR 1129.
9. *Ibid.*
10. *Manbré Saccharine Co Ltd* v. *Corn Products Ltd* [1919] 1 KB 198.
11. *Helps* v. *Winterbottom* (1831) 2 B & Ad 431; *Wayne's Merthyr Steam Coal & Iron Co* v. *Morewood & Co* (1877) 46 LJQB 746.
12. (1948) 64 TLR 110.
13. *Ibid* at 111 *per* Somervell LJ.
14. *Re Blyth Shipbuilding Co Ltd* [1926] Ch 494.

(b) Damages for non-acceptance and for non-delivery

Under the Sale of Goods Act 1979 the seller may maintain an action for damages against the buyer where the buyer wrongfully neglects or refuses to accept and pay for the goods[15] and the buyer, similarly, may maintain an action for damages against the seller where the latter wrongfully neglects or refuses to deliver the goods contracted for.[16] In these circumstances, normally time will run against the plaintiff from the time or times when the goods ought to have been delivered or accepted. Accordingly, close regard will have to be had to the specific terms of the contract. For the purposes of an action for damages for non-acceptance, it will be necessary to ask when the buyer ought to have accepted the goods and in the case of an alleged failure on the part of the seller to deliver, to ask when the seller ought to have delivered the goods.[17] This will be a simple task where the contract is explicit on the timing of performance. However there will be instances when the process of identifying the date on which performance should have taken place will be more difficult. If the contract provides that delivery may be effected within a stated period, then the seller must be given to the end of that period in which to complete performance, unless there is evidence of a prior anticipatory repudiation. Similarly, as observed above, if the buyer has a period of credit under which the date of payment is delayed, the buyer will not be obliged to pay until the period of credit has expired.

Where there is an anticipatory breach of contract on the part of either buyer or seller, the party not in breach of contract has a choice between accepting the breach and proceeding immediately to recover a remedy in respect of that breach or electing to wait until the contractual date for performance. If the latter course of action is adopted, the date on which the cause of action accrues will remain the date on which the party in breach should have performed his contractual obligation. If the plaintiff accepts the repudiatory breach, and treats himself as being discharged from further performance of the contract, the remedy in damages he receives will be quantified by reference to the difference between the contract price and the market price for similar goods at the time of intended performance, on the assumption that the contract contains a specified date for delivery and payment.[18] Where the contract contains no specified date for payment, it will be necessary for the court to ascertain a subsequent date by which it would be reasonable to expect performance on the part of the party guilty of the anticipatory breach of contract, in which case damages will be assessed on the basis of the difference between the contract price and the market price on the date on which performance could reasonably have been expected.[19] However, the position for the purposes of limitation of actions is somewhat different. Here it will be necessary to identify the earliest date on which the plaintiff could have issued his writ for the purposes of an action for damages. In these circumstances, it is clear that where there is an anticipatory breach on the part of either buyer or seller, time

---

15. Sale of Goods Act 1979, s 50(1).

16. *Ibid*, s 51(1).

17. This may be inferred from the fact that where there is an available market for goods, the plaintiff's quantum of damages will be based upon the difference between the contract price and the market price for similar goods at the time of proposed performance of the contract: Sale of Goods Act 1979, ss 50(3) and 51(3).

18. See *Tredegar Iron & Steel Co Ltd* v. *Hawthorne Bros Ltd* (1902) 18 TLR 716 (seller's damages for non-acceptance); *Melachrino* v. *Nickoll & Knight* [1920] 1 KB 693 (buyer's damages for non-delivery).

19. *Tai Hing Cotton Mill Ltd* v. *Kamsing Knitting Factory Ltd* [1979] AC 91.

will run from the date on which the repudiatory breach was accepted[20] since that must be regarded as the date on which the plaintiff was first able to sue in respect of the breach of the other party. Thus time will run against the buyer from the date on which the seller expressly or impliedly indicates that he is unable or unwilling to deliver the goods contracted for and time will run against the seller from the date on which the buyer makes it known that he will not pay for the goods if they are delivered.

(c) The right to sell, freedom from encumbrances and quiet enjoyment

The Sale of Goods Act 1979, s 12(1) implies a condition into the contract of sale to the effect that, in the case of a sale, the seller has a right to sell and that in the case of an agreement to sell, the seller will have a right to sell the goods at the time when property in the goods is to pass to the buyer. Failure to comply with this term will give rise to a right to reject in favour of the buyer, but he will also be able to recover damages in respect of any consequential loss suffered as a result of the seller's breach.

It follows from these provisions that in the case of a sale, if the seller has no right to sell at the time of contracting, time will begin to run against the buyer from the date of contracting even though the defect in the seller's title might not be discovered until some later date.[21] Thus in *Rowland* v. *Divall*[22] the seller had no right to sell a car since it had been stolen from its rightful owner. The first buyer, who purchased the car in May, then resold it in June and discovered the seller's defect in title in September and at the request of the second purchaser, refunded the purchase price. In an action to recover the purchase price paid in May, the first buyer was held to be entitled to succeed on the ground that there had been a total failure of consideration. In terms of limitation of actions, since this was a sale rather than an agreement to sell, time would have started to run against the first buyer from the date of the contract in May, since this was the date on which he was first able to sue, regardless of his lack of awareness of the defect in title.

Although section 12 is headed "Implied terms about title etc." it is more concerned with the question of the right to sell, the word title appearing only in section 12(3) concerned with the transfer of a limited title to goods. As such, it is possible that the seller may be able to pass to the buyer a right to sell despite the fact that he has no such right himself.[23] Accordingly, there is the possibility that a seller with a defective title may subsequently perfect that title, with the result that there is no breach of section 12(1), but the language of section 12(1) seems to suggest that this will only be possible in the case of an agreement to sell rather than a sale, which by virtue of the definition of a contract for the sale of goods in section 2(1) of the 1979 Act requires a transfer of the absolute legal interest in the goods which are the subject matter of the contract.[24] It follows that the important issue from a limitation of actions perspective is whether the seller has a right to sell the goods at the time when property in the goods is to pass to the buyer. If there is no

---

20. *Reeves* v. *Butcher* [1891] 2 QB 509. See also Ch 8.
21. Failure to comply with the requirements of s 12 may also give rise to the possibility of an action in tort for conversion, especially in cases where the goods have been stolen from their rightful owner, as to which see Ch 22.
22. [1923] 2 KB 500.
23. *Niblett Ltd* v. *Confectioners' Materials Ltd* [1921] 3 KB 387 at 401–402 *per* Atkin LJ.
24. See also Sale of Goods Act 1979, s 2(4) which envisages the transfer of property at the time of sale.

such right at that time, there is a breach of condition,[25] in which case, the buyer's cause of action accrues at that time.

A further consideration in cases which fall within section 12(1) is that the seller may have attempted to cover up his imperfect right to sell the goods contracted for. In these circumstances, it is possible that his actions may amount to fraud or a deliberate concealment of facts relevant to the buyer's cause of action. In these circumstances, the running of time against the buyer may be delayed until such time as the buyer becomes aware of the fraud or concealment or with reasonable diligence could have discovered the fraud or concealment.[26]

The remaining provisions of the Sale of Goods Act 1979, s 12 imply warranties on the part of the seller to the effect that the buyer will be able to take the goods sold free from any charge or encumbrance not disclosed or known to the buyer before the contract is made[27] and that the buyer will enjoy quiet possession of the goods.[28] Since these are warranties only, the buyer will be entitled to pursue no more than an action for damages in the event of breach, but it is clear from the nature of the warranty in section 12(2)(b) that breach may occur otherwise than at the time of the contracting and unlike section 12(1), regard need not be had to the date on which it was intended that property should pass to the buyer. The position under section 12(2)(a) appears to be somewhat different, since the warranty of freedom from encumbrances is stated to apply only up to the time at which property in the goods passes to the buyer, in which case the protection provided seems to differ in no material respect from that provided by section 12(1).

At one stage, it was thought that there was no substantial difference between the implied condition that the seller had a right to sell and the implied warranties relating to quiet possession and freedom from encumbrances, since the view appeared to be that if the seller had no right to sell, this would also amount to an encumbrance and an interruption of the buyer's quiet possession. Accordingly, in *Niblett Ltd* v. *Confectioners' Materials Ltd*[29] there was considered to be a breach of section 12(1) and section 12(2) where cans of milk bore labels which infringed a trademark owned by a third party. The seller was considered to have no right to sell under section 12(1), but by virtue of the fact that the buyer had to remove the offending labels before they could assume quiet possession, there was also a breach of section 12(2). While it is clear that the cause of action under section 12(1) arises at the time when property is to pass under the terms of the contract, it seems that for the purposes of section 12(2) the cause of action arises at a later stage, being based upon the date on which the buyer's quiet possession of the goods is disturbed. In *Niblett Ltd* v. *Confectioners' Materials Ltd*[30] Atkin LJ observed:

"I think there was also a breach of the implied warranty in sub-s. 2, that the buyer shall have and enjoy quiet possession of the goods. It may be that possession would not be disturbed if the only cause of complaint was that the buyer could not dispose of the goods, and that the warranty is confined to *disturbance of possession* of the goods delivered under the contract of sale. The warranty so interpreted was broken. The appellants were never allowed to have quiet possession."[31]

25. *Niblett Ltd* v. *Confectioners' Materials Ltd* [1921] 3 KB 387 at 403 *per* Atkin LJ.
26. Limitation Act 1980, s 32 and see Ch 6.
27. Sale of Goods Act 1979, s 12(2)(a).
28. *Ibid*, s 12(2)(b).
29. [1921] 3 KB 387.
30. *Ibid*.
31. *Ibid* at 403. Emphasis added.

Accordingly, the gist of the action under section 12(2)(b), at least, is disturbance of the buyer's right of quiet possession. In a case such as *Rowland* v. *Divall*[32] the fact that the car was stolen meant that there was a breach of section 12(1), but it is equally the case that the seller's breach of contract also resulted in a disturbance of the buyer's right of quiet possession for the purposes of section 12(2)(b). However, it is arguable that time would run against the buyer from a different date in respect of each separate breach. Under section 12(1), the relevant date would have been the date of contracting in May, since the contract was one of sale rather than an agreement to sell. However, in the case of the breach of section 12(2)(b), time would only run from the date on which the buyer's quiet possession of the car was disturbed, which was in September when it was discovered that some other person had a superior title. Accordingly, for limitation purposes, time may run against the buyer from different dates.

The implied warranty in section 12(2)(a) also raises a further difficulty in that it requires the goods to be free from and to remain free from undisclosed encumbrances, up to the date on which property is to pass. Accordingly, this warranty operates both at the time of contracting and on into the future in cases where the time of passing of property is delayed. While, at one stage, it was thought that section 12(1) and (2) covered similar ground where the defect in title was present at the time of contracting, it subsequently became apparent that section 12(2)(b), at least, extended beyond the date of contracting. In *Microbeads AG* v. *Vinhurst Road Markings Ltd*[33] a contract for the sale of certain roadmarking equipment had been entered into in January 1970, at a time when another company had applied for a patent in respect of the design on which the roadmarking equipment was based. The specification for the patent had been filed in 1967 and letters patent were granted in 1972. The buyers of the equipment were dissatisfied with its performance and withheld payment under their contract of sale with the plaintiffs, who subsequently sued for the balance of the price still owing to them. In their defence, the buyers argued, *inter alia,* that the defendants were in breach of section 12(1), in that they had no right to sell. The Court of Appeal concluded that the sellers did have a right to sell at the time when property passed to the buyer, but that there was also a breach of section 12(2)(b) because the buyers did not have quiet possession and enjoyment of the goods sold. This breach occurred on the date of publication of the letters patent in 1972 which was after conclusion of the contract of sale. Since the breach of warranty only occurred on this later date, time would not begin to run against the buyer in respect of his action for damages until the date on which his quiet enjoyment of the goods was disturbed.

(d) The buyer's action for breach of an express or implied condition or warranty relating to goods

The range of possible actions which may be brought by the buyer in respect of the goods purchased include an action for breach of the implied term that goods should correspond with any sample supplied[34] or description given,[35] that goods supplied should be of

---

32. [1923] 2 KB 500. See above fn 21 and associated text.
33. [1975] 1 WLR 218.
34. Sale of Goods Act 1979, s 15.
35. *Ibid*, s 13.

satisfactory quality[36] and be fit for the particular purpose intended by the buyer.[37] Moreover, there may also be express warranties or conditions dependent on the particular language used by the parties. Generally, these conditions and warranties will be taken to have been given at the time of contracting and if what is delivered fails to comply with the relevant term of the contract, the earliest time at which any breach giving rise to a cause of action will have occurred is the date on which the goods are delivered to the buyer.[38] This will remain the case regardless of the fact that damage might not be suffered or discovered by the buyer until a much later stage.[39]

One curiosity which arises out of the reworded statutory definition of satisfactory quality in section 14(2)[40] is that an aspect of satisfactory quality is that the goods supplied should be reasonably durable. Previously, the issue of durability had been treated as the subject-matter of a warranty associated with the implied condition of fitness for purpose, but the warranty of durability, although implied at the time of contracting, would continue for a reasonable period thereafter.[41]

Where there is a problem of lack of durability, the buyer will not become aware of it until some time after the conclusion of the contract, in which case the question may arise whether there should be a different starting date for the purposes of limitation of actions. The problem which arises in this context is whether the relevant date for the running of time in cases of lack of durability should be equated with the approach adopted in relation to latent defects. So far as latent defects are concerned, the position adopted is that, regardless of the date of discovery of the defect, time will run from the date on which the breach of contract occurs. In the case of a latent defect, the assumption is that while the defect remains hidden, it is nonetheless present at the time the contract is entered into, in which case time will run from the date on which goods subject to a latent defect are delivered to the buyer.[42] Whether the new requirement of durability is subject to a similar requirement is unclear from the amended wording of the Sale of Goods Act 1979, s 14(2), but it is possible that the relevant date for the purposes of the breach of contract might be regarded as the date on which the defect in the goods arose rather than the date of delivery, in which case time will run against the buyer from a later stage than in cases of latent defects which were present at the time the contract was entered into. In commercial contracts for the sale of goods, where the goods are to be shipped, much will depend on the contents of the bill of lading. Thus in *Mash & Murrell Ltd* v. *Joseph I Emmanuel Ltd*[43] the bill of lading stated that goods were "shipped in apparent good order and condition" but were discovered to have deteriorated by the time the ship arrived at its destination. It

---

36. *Ibid*, s 14(2).
37. *Ibid*, s 14(3).
38. See *Battley* v. *Faulkner* (1820) 3 B & Ald 288; *Walker* v. *Milner* (1866) 4 F & F 745 and see Ch 8.
39. The date of damage or the date on which the fact of damage could reasonably have been discovered will be relevant if the action is brought against the producer of the defective product under the Consumer Protection Act 1987, Part I or in tort on the basis of the "narrow" rule in *Donoghue* v. *Stevenson* [1932] AC 562. See generally Chs 18 and 21.
40. Effected by the Sale and Supply of Goods Act 1994.
41. *Lambert* v. *Lewis* [1982] AC 225.
42. See *Crowther* v. *Shannon Motor Co Ltd* [1975] 1 WLR 30 in which the buyer was assisted by an assertion by a previous owner of a second-hand car that when he supplied the vehicle to the defendant, it was "clapped out", thereby indicating that the defect was present at the time of sale: [1975] 1 WLR 30 at 33 *per* Lord Denning MR.
43. [1961] 1 All ER 485. Reversed on its facts in [1962] 1 All ER 77. See also *The Rio Sun* [1985] 1 Lloyd's Rep 350 and *Beer* v. *Walker* (1877) 46 LJQB 677.

is clear, for the purposes of the running of time, that the breach of contract occurred on the date of loading and that the contract required the goods to be loaded in such a state that they could endure a normal journey and be of the desired standard of quality on arrival.[44] In these circumstances, the buyer can be assumed to rely on what is stated in the bill of lading, but as a result of that reliance, the breach can be taken to have occurred at the time the goods were loaded on board the vessel. However, in a consumer contract for the sale of goods, there is no similar documentation on which the buyer of goods can rely, in which case it might be argued that the requirement of durability is continuing in nature and as such breach occurs from day to day while ever the goods are not sufficiently durable to satisfy the requirements of section 14(2). This will be particularly the case where a problem of durability arises and the consumer-buyer seeks rectification of the defect and continues to consult the supplier of the goods with a view to effecting a proper repair of the defective goods.[45]

So far as latent defects are concerned, Mustill J in *Transoceanic Petroleum Carriers* v. *Cook Industries Inc*[46] drew a distinction between patent and latent defects in determining whether a port could be regarded as safe. He opined that where a port is patently unsafe to berth at, a prudent shipmaster would recognise the danger and be able to circumvent it through the exercise of reasonable care and skill.[47] As such, where there is a patent defect, in a sense, the port cannot be said to be unsafe, although this will not always be the case, since if a patent danger cannot be averted even by the exercise of reasonable care, the port must then be regarded as unsafe.[48] However, as Mustill J observed, the position so far as latent defects are concerned is different. In the context of whether a port can be regarded as unsafe in the light of hidden dangers he opined that:

" . . . even a prudent master would not realize that there was any reason why he should not make use of the port at once. This being so, I can see no ground for holding that just because it is only a long-standing cause of inaccessibility which puts the charterer in breach of the warranty of safety, the same must necessarily be true where the master has reasonably proceeded in ignorance of a concealed danger and has thereby damaged his ship."

What this indicates is that the time at which the breach of warranty may occur may differ according to the circumstances of the case. Nonetheless, time will run against the person in whose favour the warranty is given from the date on which the breach of warranty occurs, which in the case of latent defects in goods supplied will normally be the date on which the goods are delivered to the buyer, since from that time onwards, the buyer has a cause of action against the seller, even though the defect may not be discoverable at that stage.

Since the implied terms in the Sale of Goods Act 1979 and other similar provisions in other contracts for the supply of goods are statutorily based, it might be thought that an action for rejection or for damages for breach of the implied terms is to be regarded as an action on a statute.[49] However, it is important to appreciate that despite the fact that the

44. *Ibid* at 488 *per* Diplock J.
45. See Ch 8 on the matter of continuing breaches of contract.
46. *Sub nom. The Mary Lou* [1981] 2 Lloyd's Rep 272 and see Ch 8.
47. *Ibid* at 279. See also *The Pendrecht* [1980] 2 Lloyd's Rep 56.
48. *Ibid.*
49. Thereby falling within the provisions of the Limitation Act 1980, s 8(1), in respect of which there is a 12-year limitation period, as opposed to the six-year period which applies to actions for breach of contract. See further Ch 15.

implied terms are in statutory form, the gist of the action still remains one for breach of contract, in which case the normal limitation period for the purposes of a contract action will continue to apply.

CONTRACTS FOR THE SUPPLY OF SERVICES

In the case of contracts for the supply of services, a number of terms are implied into the contract by virtue of the provisions of the Supply of Goods and Services Act 1982. These consist of terms to the effect that the supplier of the service will perform the contract, exercising reasonable care and skill,[50] that, in the absence of any express term of the contract as to the time of performance, the work contracted for will be carried out within a reasonable time of the making of the contract[51] and that the recipient of the service, in the absence of any other term of the contract as to the charge payable, will pay no more than a reasonable amount for the service provided.[52] So far as the duty to exercise reasonable care and skill is concerned, it is clear that there will be a concurrent action in both tort and contract in favour of the person for whom the service is provided, since a failure to exercise reasonable care and skill on the part of the service provider will also reveal an action in the tort of negligence. However, for limitation purposes, the action in tort accrues on the date on which damage is caused, unless some other more favourable limitation period is applied, being based on the date on which the plaintiff could reasonably have discovered that he had suffered damage.[53] In contrast, if the action is one for breach of contract, time will start to run against the plaintiff from the date on which a breach of contract occurred,[54] in which case, a plaintiff suing for a breach of contract may be out of time before the date on which the period of limitation for the purposes of a negligence action expires.

The date on which damage is caused for the purposes of the paradigm variety of damage, for tort purposes, namely physical harm to the person or property, generally, does not cause too many difficulties, except in the case of latent damage which is now catered for in special provisions considered elsewhere.[55] However, later developments in the tort of negligence have demonstrated that, in limited circumstances, a plaintiff may be able to bring an action in respect of pure economic loss where this has resulted from the failure of the defendant to exercise reasonable care in relation to the provision of advice under the rule in *Hedley Byrne & Co Ltd* v. *Heller & Partners Ltd.*[56] However, under this rule, it is clear from the requirement of proximity of relationship that the parties to the action will be in all but a contractual relationship, but nonetheless the action will sound in tort. The difficulty this has raised for the purposes of limitation of actions is that it may not be immediately obvious when that damage first occurred, thereby rendering it difficult to ascertain the date on which the plaintiff's cause of action accrued. But since the action is

50. Supply of Goods and Services Act 1982, s 13.
51. *Ibid*, s 14.
52. *Ibid*, s 15.
53. See Chs 18 and 20.
54. *Bagot* v. *Stevens Scanlan & Co* [1966] 1 QB 197.
55. See Ch 19 regarding personal injuries and Ch 20 regarding latent damage other than personal injury.
56. [1964] AC 465, considered in Ch 18.

one which sounds in tort, if the damage suffered is regarded as latent damage, a "discoverability" test may be applied, if the wording of the Limitation Act 1980, s 14A[57] is considered to apply to *Hedley Byrne* liability. Oddly, this places the non-contractual plaintiff in a better position than a person who has a direct contractual relationship with a service provider who has caused damage as a result of his failure to exercise care in relation to the provision of the service, since it has been accepted that the new rules on latent damage have no application to contractual actions.[58]

Since, in a contract for the supply of a service, such as a construction contract, the damage caused by a failure to exercise reasonable care may remain hidden for a number of years, the plight of the building owner, in such cases, is extreme, since it is quite possible that the owner will be time barred before he realises that any substantial damage has been suffered as a result of a breach of contract on the part of the main contractor or some other professional service provider with whom he has a direct contractual relationship, such as an architect or a structural engineer. In these circumstances, it is perhaps pertinent that the present editor of one of the leading works on construction contracts advises building owners that it is of the highest importance that they should ensure that their contracts should be under seal, so as to preserve the right to sue for a period of 12 years under the rules on specialties in the Limitation Act 1980, s 8.[59]

One way in which the building owner can avoid the problems associated with latent damage is to require the parties with whom he deals to provide indemnities in respect of certain varieties of foreseeable loss. The importance of a contractual indemnity is that, as a general rule, the cause of action on the indemnity will not arise in favour of a third party suing the person giving the indemnity until such time as the extent of the liability has been ascertained or established,[60] since an indemnity can only relate to the harmful consequences which flow from the act or omission in respect of which the indemnity is given.[61] Furthermore, the way in which some indemnity clauses may be worded can have the effect of substantially improving the position of the building owner under a construction contract if the indemnity relates to an entire group or series of obligations undertaken by the indemnor. Where this is the case, if the range of contractual obligations is sufficiently wide, the effect of the indemnity may be such that virtually all of the principal contractual obligations become subject to the indemnity clause, with the effect that the building owner has secured additional time within which to enforce the terms of the contract in the event that defects take time to reveal themselves. In these circumstances, it might still be argued that where the indemnity relates to a breach of a contractual obligation owed by the person giving the indemnity to the party indemnified, the cause of action should still accrue on the date on which the initial breach of contract occurred,[62] but this argument has been

---

57. Inserted by the Latent Damage Act 1986, s 1. See further Ch 20.
58. See *Iron Trade Mutual Insurance Co Ltd* v. *JK Buckenham Ltd* [1990] 1 All ER 808; *Société Commerciale de Réassurance* v. *ERAS (International) Ltd* [1992] 2 All ER 82, considered in Ch 20.
59. Duncan Wallace, *Hudson's Building Contracts*, para 4–288. For consideration of rules on specialties, see Ch 15.
60. *County & District Properties Ltd* v. *Jenner* [1976] 2 Lloyd's Rep 728 at 734 *per* Swanwick J; Cf *Bosma* v. *Larsen* [1966] 1 Lloyd's Rep 22 and see also Ch 9 for a wider discussion of the position in respect of contractual indemnities.
61. *Ibid* at 736 *per* Swanwick J.
62. See e.g. *Bosma* v. *Larsen* [1966] 1 Lloyd's Rep 22.

rejected in other cases.[63] Thus if the cases rejecting this proposition are correct, it will be possible for a party sued for breach of contract to join as additional parties to the action someone who has given an indemnity in respect of his own breach of contract so that proceedings may continue within six years of the date on which damage was caused, despite the fact that the proceedings are brought more than six years from the date on which the initial breach of contract first occurred.

In the case of construction contracts, it is possible that some of the contractual obligations undertaken are regarded as continuing in nature, in which case the defendant may be under a duty to reconsider the work he has contracted to carry out during the currency of the period of performance. For example, it is common for an architect or engineer to be under a duty to have regard to the design of a building during the period of construction.[64] Accordingly, if an architect has produced a design which proves to be defective in some material respect while the process of construction is under way, he will come under a duty to reconsider the design and correct any defects which have come to light.[65] Since this duty is continuing in nature, it will continue until the date of completion of the building. In other cases, the relationship between the parties may continue after the process of construction is complete. For example, it is possible that the builder remains the owner of the building and becomes a landlord pursuant to a lease entered into with the tenant of the building concerned. In these circumstances, if the tenant is injured as a result of the defective state of the property he has leased, the builder/owner may come under a continuing duty to take such steps as are reasonable to avoid the possibility of physical injury.[66] Whether this notion of the continuing duty should also extend to architects and engineers is subject to some doubt. In *Eckersley* v. *Binnie & Partners Ltd*[67] at first instance, civil engineers responsible for the design of the Abbeystead water pumping station, which was the scene of an explosion at which a number of visitors were injured, were considered to have been negligent in failing to have regard to contemporary knowledge regarding underground methane accumulation. Relevant knowledge in this respect could have been acquired both before and after the completion of the construction of the pumping station, but no distinction appeared to have been drawn between knowledge which could have been acquired before and after completion. However, in the Court of Appeal, it was considered that the imposition of duties of the kind suggested would be "novel and burdensome". On the other hand there is nothing in the decision which rules out such a possibility, although as Bingham LJ observed, "the nature, scope and limits of such a duty require to be very carefully and cautiously defined".[68]

63. *County & District Properties Ltd* v. *Jenner* [1976] 2 Lloyd's Rep 728; *Green & Silley Weir Ltd* v. *British Railways Board* [1985] 1 All ER 237.

64. See *Brickfield Properties Ltd* v. *Newton* [1971] 1 WLR 862; *Merton LBC* v. *Lowe* (1981) 18 BLR 130. On the matter of continuing contractual duties see also Ch 8.

65. *Brickfield Properties Ltd* v. *Newton* [1971] 1 WLR 862 at 873 *per* Sachs LJ.

66. *Rimmer* v. *Liverpool City Council* [1985] QB 1.

67. (1988) 18 Con LR 1.

68. *Ibid* at 146–47.

CHAPTER 11

ARBITRATION[1]

STATUTORY PERIOD FOR COMMENCING AN ARBITRATION

(a) General application of the Limitation Act 1980

The Arbitration Act 1996, s 13(1) provides that the Limitation Acts are to apply to arbitration proceedings as they apply to legal proceedings. In most cases this will mean that the Limitation Act 1980 will be applicable. Arbitration proceedings falling within the Arbitration Act 1996 do not therefore, derive their limitation rules from arbitration, but rather from the classification of proceedings in the Limitation Act 1980 itself, so that arbitration proceedings must be commenced within the period specified by the Limitation Act 1980 which is appropriate to the cause of action.

Where a limitation period is set out in some other piece of legislation to which the Limitation Act 1980 is subject, that period is the relevant period for arbitration proceedings: this point is made clear by the Arbitration Act 1996, s 13(4)(a), which defines the Limitation Acts as the 1980 Act and any other enactment (whenever passed) relating to the limitation of actions. An arbitration relating to product liability will, therefore, be subject to the limitation periods in the Consumer Protection Act 1987. Legislation which operates to implement into English law an international convention containing a limitation period is some other enactment for this purpose. This is the effect of *Denny, Mott & Dickinson Ltd* v. *Lynn Shipping Co Ltd*,[2] in which it was held that the Carriage of Goods by Sea Act 1971, which ratified the Hague-Visby Rules, operated to give effect to the one-year limitation period running from the date of the discharge of the cargo contained in the Hague-Visby Rules for the commencement of proceedings in cargo cases, and that the consignee could not rely upon the usual six-year period in contract cases in his action against the shipowner.[3] This was so despite the fact that the Hague-Visby Rules, where they are adopted by the parties, operate as a contract.

---

1. This chapter is based upon the provisions of the Arbitration Act 1996, which came into force on 31 January 1997 and which applies to all arbitration proceedings commenced after that date. Earlier legislation, the Arbitration Acts 1950, 1975 and 1979, and the Limitation Act 1980, s 34, was repealed with effect from that date.

2. [1963] 1 Lloyd's Rep 339.

3. The Hague-Visby Rules provide in general terms that they are to apply in the event of repugnancy, so that, unless there is an express agreement to exclude the repugnancy rule, the one-year period is to prevail over any period agreed by the parties: *Unicoopjapan and Marubeni-Iida Co Ltd* v. *Ion Shipping Co, The Ion* [1971] 1 Lloyd's Rep 541. Even where the repugnancy clause is excluded by the parties, there is authority for the proposition that the one-year period overrides any agreed period: *Sabah Flour and Feedmills* v. *Comfez Ltd* [1987] 2 Lloyd's Rep 647.

Not all arbitrations come within the Arbitration Act 1996, and in particular oral arbitration agreements are excluded[4] although the common law validity of oral arbitration agreements is preserved.[5] There is no statutory provision which sets out limitation periods for oral arbitration agreements, although it has been assumed that the Limitation Acts apply in the usual way.[6] Statutory arbitrations are also outside the Arbitration Act 1996, as they are non-consensual, although the 1996 Act has in general been extended to such arbitrations, and the limitation provisions in particular remain applicable.[7]

(b) The commencement of arbitration proceedings

(i) Methods of commencement

The Limitation Act 1980 requires proceedings to have *commenced* within the limitation period. The parties are free to agree on the events which must occur before the arbitration proceedings are to be taken to have commenced.[8] If they have failed to reach any express agreement, the Arbitration Act 1996 provides default provisions which set out the matters which must be satisfied for arbitration proceedings to be deemed to have commenced.[9] The default rules reflect the various ways in which arbitrations are in practice to be held.

(1) Where the arbitrator is named or designated in the arbitration agreement, arbitral proceedings are commenced in respect of a matter when one party serves on the other a notice in writing requiring him to submit that matter to the person so named or designated.[10] The key word here is "require": a notice which demands appointment is within the section,[11] whereas one which merely requests an appointment or which indicates that a demand will be made at a later date does not suffice.[12] The status of the often used phrase "We hereby require this dispute to be referred to arbitration" is uncertain.[13] Communication is also required: a unilateral uncommunicated act, e.g. the appointment by one party of his own arbitrator, does not of itself commence the proceedings.[14]

(2) Where the arbitrator or arbitrators are to be appointed by the parties, arbitral proceedings are commenced in respect of a matter when one party serves on the other party a notice in writing requiring him or them to appoint an arbitrator or

---

4. Arbitration Act 1996, s 5.

5. Arbitration Act 1996, s 81(1)(b).

6. *Ramdutt Ramkissen Das* v. *ED Sassoon & Co* (1929) 140 LT 542; *Chandris* v. *Isbrandtsen-Moller Co Inc* [1951] 1 KB 240.

7. Arbitration Act 1996, s 94.

8. Arbitration Act 1996, s 14(1).

9. Arbitration Act 1996, s 14(2).

10. Arbitration Act 1996, s 14(3).

11. *Nea Agrex SA* v. *Baltic Shipping Co Ltd, The Aghios Lazaros* [1976] 2 Lloyd's Rep 47 ("please advise your proposals to settle this matter or name your arbitrators"); *The Sargasso* [1994] 1 Lloyd's Rep 162; *Frota Oceanica Brasiliera SA* v. *Steamship Mutual Underwriting Association (Bermuda) Ltd, The Frotanorte* [1995] 2 Lloyd's Rep 254; *Cruden Construction Ltd* v. *Commission for New Towns* [1995] 2 Lloyd's Rep 387.

12. *Surrendra Overseas Ltd* v. *Government of Sri Lanka* [1977] 1 Lloyd's Rep 653 ("Owners will be putting this matter to arbitration. We will be advising you . . . in due course"); *Vosnoc Ltd* v. *Transglobal Projects Ltd, The Times*, 27 August 1997.

13. In *The Aghios Lazaros* [1976] 2 Lloyd's Rep 47 Lord Denning MR thought that this formulation would be adequate, although the point was left open by the rest of the court in that case and also in *Surrendra Overseas Ltd* v. *Government of Sri Lanka* [1977] 1 Lloyd's Rep 653.

14. *Interbulk Ltd* v. *Ponte dei Sospiri Shipping Co, The Standard Ardour* [1988] 2 Lloyd's Rep 159.

to agree to the appointment of an arbitrator in respect of that matter.[15] It does not appear to be necessary for valid service for the party serving the notice to have appointed his own arbitrator when service is effected.

(3) Where the arbitrator or arbitrators are to be appointed by a person other than a party to the proceedings, arbitral proceedings are commenced in respect of a matter when one party gives notice in writing to that person requesting him to make the appointment in respect of that matter.[16] It will be noted that a request for action suffices where a third party has the duty to make the relevant appointment, in contrast to the demand required of the other party under (1) and (2) above.

These provisions are not exhaustive or mandatory, and it is possible for arbitration proceedings to be commenced in some other way, although it must be presumed that the courts would not recognise any method which left the respondent in any doubt that proceedings had been commenced.[17] Where judicial proceedings have been brought in respect of a matter falling within a binding arbitration clause, an application for a stay of those proceedings[18] does not amount to the commencement of arbitration proceedings, as under English law the grant of a stay of judicial proceedings does not amount to a reference to arbitration.[19]

(ii) Service of the notice

It will be noted that in situations (1) and (2) notice must be "served" on the other party, whereas in situation (3) notice must be "given" to the other party. This drafting anomaly, while curious, appears not to be of any significance.[20] "Service" is to be effected in accordance with section 76 of the Arbitration Act 1996. The parties are free to agree on how service is to be effected,[21] but in the absence of agreement a number of default rules are provided.[22]

(1) A notice or other document[23] may be served by a person on any effective means.[24]

(2) If a notice or other document is addressed, pre-paid, and delivered by post—

---

15. Arbitration Act 1996, s 14(4).

16. Arbitration Act 1996, s 14(5).

17. E.g., service of a notice on a third party who is not an authorised recipient of notice even though he may be acting for the party in question: *Blackpool BC* v. *Parkinson*, 58 Build LR 85.

18. Under s 9 of the Arbitration Act 1996. A stay must be granted unless the arbitration agreement is null and void, inoperative or incapable of being performed.

19. *Channel Tunnel Group Ltd* v. *Balfour Beatty Construction Ltd* [1993] 1 All ER 664; *Star Shipping AS* v. *China National Foreign Trade Corporation, The Star Texas* [1993] 2 Lloyd's Rep 445. English law has in this respect failed to implement Art II.3 of the New York Convention, which provides that the court on staying its proceedings is to "refer the parties to arbitration".

20. The Departmental Advisory Committee, chaired by Saville LJ, produced a commentary on the Bill in February 1996, and noted the distinction but thought that it did not give rise to any problem: para 359.

21. Arbitration Act 1996, s 76(1).

22. Arbitration Act 1996, s 76(2).

23. Defined as including any form of communication in writing: Arbitration Act 1996, s 76(5). A fax has been held to suffice: *The Sargasso* [1994] 1 Lloyd's Rep 162.

24. Arbitration Act 1996, s 76(3). This is a relaxation of the previous law, the Limitation Act 1980, s 34(4), which set out specific service requirements, although the courts nevertheless held that any suitable method would suffice.

(a) to the addressee's last known principal residence or, if he has been carrying on a trade, profession or business, his last known principal business address,[25] or

(b) where the addressee is a body corporate, to the body's registered or principal office.[26]

(iii) Judicial assistance with service

If it is not reasonably practicable for service to be effected as agreed or in any of the above ways, and there is no agreed arbitral procedure for resolving the problem,[27] a party may apply to the court for assistance. On application, the court may specify how service is to be effected, or it may dispense with the need for service.[28] The purpose of this provision is to overcome the obstacles raised by a party who deliberately seeks to avoid being served. There are nevertheless two difficulties with the fallback judicial procedure. The first is that the parties can contract out of it, so that if it has been agreed that there is to be no application to the court in the event that service cannot be effected, the arbitration would seem to be doomed to collapse. The second is that it is not clear when service is deemed to have been effected following a successful application to court: the possibilities are the date of application to the court, the date of the court's order, or the date on which the court's order is executed by the applicant. Whichever is correct, a party who has waited until near the end of the limitation period before attempting to effect service may find himself time barred if it becomes necessary to seek the court's assistance, as the court has no power to suspend statutory time limits pending its consideration of the matter.

(c) Suspension of limitation period where award is challenged

An arbitration award may be set aside or declared to be of no effect under the Arbitration Act 1996 on application to the court on one of three grounds: the arbitrators had no jurisdiction to hear the matter (Arbitration Act 1996, s 67); there was a serious irregularity in the proceedings which has led to substantial injustice to one or more of the parties (Arbitration Act 1996, s 68); and there was an error of law in the proceedings which has substantially affected the rights of one or more of the parties (Arbitration Act 1996, s 69). Where the award is set aside or declared null and void, it may be necessary for fresh proceedings—either judicial or arbitral—to be commenced. If time runs from the accrual of the original cause of action, there is a strong possibility that the limitation period may have expired. For this reason, the Arbitration Act 1996, s 13(2) provides that where the court sets aside or nullifies an award, it may declare—as regards the subject-matter of the arbitration—that the period between the commencement of the arbitration and the date of the court's order is to be disregarded. The claimant is thus restored to his original position, and is free to commence fresh proceedings.

---

25. In *NV Stoom Maats de Maas* v. *Nippon Yusen Kaisha, The Pendrecht* [1980] 2 Lloyd's Rep 56 it was held that service at business premises outside business hours would be effective.

26. Arbitration Act 1996, s 76(4).

27. Arbitration Act 1996, s 77(3) assumes that there might be some such process in place.

28. Arbitration Act 1996, s 77(1)–(2). Any appeal from the court's decision requires the leave of the court itself: Arbitration Act 1996, s 77(4).

(d) Scott v. Avery clauses

In *Scott* v. *Avery*[29] the House of Lords upheld the validity of an arbitration clause which rendered arbitration a condition precedent to the right of either party to bring an action against the other, the effect being that recourse could be had to the courts only to enforce any arbitration award. Although it was argued that the clause was void on public policy grounds by effectively ousting the jurisdiction of the courts, the House of Lords saw no public policy objection to it. Given that the cause of action is the award rather than the wrongful conduct which has led to the award, in the absence of statutory intervention the position would be that there is no limitation period relating to the commencement of the arbitration proceedings but merely a six-year limitation period running from the making of the award. This possibility is removed by the Arbitration Act 1996, s 13(3), which provides that, "in determining for the purposes of the Limitation Acts when a cause of action accrued, any provision that an award is a condition precedent to the bringing of legal proceedings in respect of a matter to which an arbitration agreement applies shall be disregarded". For limitation purposes, therefore, time runs from the usual point at which the action would have accrued had the proceedings been judicial proceedings.

(e) Applicable law

Where the law applicable to the dispute between the parties is a law other than English law, the Foreign Limitation Periods Act 1984, s 1 provides that the limitation period is to be that of the relevant applicable law rather than the period indicated by the Limitation Act 1980, thereby reversing the common law principle that limitation is a matter for the procedural law of the forum, although section 2 of the 1984 Act goes on to state that the court has the power to apply English limitation periods if the application of that of the applicable law would produce "undue hardship":[30] this power presumably extends also to arbitrators. Determination of the applicable law in an arbitration is, in the absence of express choice by the parties, a matter for the arbitrators,[31] and if they decide that some other law governs the substantive agreement between the parties but they misapply the limitation period of that law, recourse cannot be had to the English courts even if the arbitration has its seat in England, Wales or Northern Ireland,[32] as the power of judicial review of errors of law is confined to errors of English law.[33]

(f) Addition of new claims to the proceedings

The Limitation Act 1980, s 35 permits a party to add a new claim or an additional party to proceedings; for limitation purposes, the fresh action is deemed to have been made at

---

29. (1856) 5 HL Cas 811.

30. See: *Jones* v. *Trollope & Colls Overseas Ltd* (1990) *The Times*, 26 January; *Hellenic Steel Co* v. *Svolamar Shipping Co Ltd, The Komninos S* [1990] 1 Lloyd's Rep 541. It is unclear whether the power to disapply the limitation period in the applicable law applies to contract cases, as the Rome Convention 1980, implemented in the UK by the Contracts (Applicable Law) Act 1990, provides in Art 10.1(d) that the applicable law is to supply the limitation period.

31. Arbitration Act 1996, s 46.

32. Seat is the basis of the jurisdiction of the English courts over an arbitration, with limited exceptions: Arbitration Act 1996, ss 2–3.

33. Arbitration Act 1996, s 82(1). Where, however, the limitation period is regarded as going to the jurisdiction of the arbitrators, it may be possible to challenge any decision of the arbitrators as to limitation on the basis of error of jurisdiction, as this seemingly does not exclude consideration of foreign law. For jurisdictional issues, see the Arbitration Act 1996, ss 30–32 and 67.

the time of the commencement of the original action. The result may be the inclusion of a time-barred new claim to proceedings commenced in time. This section apparently has no application to arbitration proceedings. In *Kenya Railways* v. *Antares Pte Ltd*[34] the claimants in arbitration proceedings commenced the action in time, and following the expiry of the limitation period sought to add an additional party to the proceedings, having discovered that the party originally proceeded against was not the person responsible for the claimants' loss. The Court of Appeal held that, as the original proceedings had not been validly commenced, there were no proceedings in existence to which a fresh party could be joined. The Court of Appeal further noted that the Limitation Act 1980, s 35 could rarely if ever apply to arbitrations: it would be contrary to the consensual basis of an arbitration for a fresh party to be added; and the addition of a new cause of action is inconsistent with the principle that the jurisdiction of the arbitrator rests upon the agreement of the parties to submit particular disputes to him and cannot extend to matters falling outside the arbitration agreement.

(g) Expiry of limitation period

Most limitation periods merely provide the respondent with a defence to the proceedings against him and do not operate to extinguish the cause of action. The limitation defence must, therefore, be taken in the arbitration itself, and it is up to the arbitrators to determine its validity[35] unless the parties have agreed that the matter is to be resolved by the courts. As limitation is simply a defence like any other and does not go to the arbitrators' jurisdiction,[36] the respondent will not be taken to have waived the defence by appearing in the proceedings and submitting substantive defences as well as the limitation defence,[37] although if the limitation defence is not taken in the arbitration it will not be possible for the losing party to ground an appeal to the court on it.[38]

The position is arguably different where the limitation clause operates to extinguish the cause of action, as the validity or otherwise of the limitation argument goes to the very jurisdiction of the arbitrators. The arbitrators are competent to make a ruling on the point if the arbitration agreement is appropriately worded,[39] but if they do so their ruling can be challenged under the various mechanisms provided by the Arbitration Act 1996 for resolving questions of jurisdiction.[40]

34. [1987] 1 Lloyd's Rep 424.

35. If the arbitrators err, their error is one of law, and if the parties have agreed to exclude any right of appeal for error of law, the court has no jurisdiction to consider the matter on appeal: Arbitration Act 1996, s 69.

36. See: *Leif Hoegh & Co A/S* v. *Petrolsea Inc, The World Era* [1992] 1 Lloyd's Rep 45; *Triad Shipping Co* v. *Stellar Chartering & Brokerage Inc, The Island Archon* [1993] 2 Lloyd's Rep 388.

37. *Re Astley and Tyldesley Coal & Salt Co and Tyldesley Coal Co* (1899) 80 LT 116; *Board of Trade* v. *Cayzer, Irvine & Co* [1927] AC 610.

38. Arbitration Act 1996, s 73, which sets out the general waiver principle.

39. Under the Arbitration Act 1996, s 30, following on from the principle of the severability of the arbitration agreement and the subject-matter of the dispute under s 7 of the 1996 Act.

40. In outline, this may be done by: an award by the arbitrators which may be challenged, including in proceedings to enforce the award, provided that the party pleading limitation has not submitted to the arbitrators' jurisdiction or has appeared under protest (Arbitration Act 1996, ss 31, 69, 72 and 73); an application to the court at any stage for declaratory relief, provided again that the party making the application has not submitted to the arbitrators' jurisdiction or has appeared under protest (Arbitration Act 1996, ss 72 and 73); and a request by the arbitrators or the parties to the court for a preliminary ruling on jurisdiction (Arbitration Act 1996, s 32).

THE COMMENCEMENT OF PROCEEDINGS BY AN ASSIGNEE

Rights under an agreement which is subject to an arbitration clause are not rendered unassignable merely because of the presence of the arbitration clause.[41] The effect of an assignment is to transfer any obligation on the assignor to go to arbitration to the assignee. Provided that the assignment has taken place, and the assignee has commenced the arbitration, within the limitation period, no further limitation problem arises. Any assignment after the expiry of the limitation period is clearly fatal to the assignee. The most complex situation is the intermediate possibility that the assignor has commenced arbitration proceedings within the limitation period and has then effected the assignment after the limitation period has expired: if the assignee is free to take over the arbitration proceedings, limitation issues will not arise, whereas if the assignee is not entitled to take over the arbitration proceedings, he must commence a fresh arbitration and will find himself time barred.

The point first arose in *The Felicie*.[42] Here, an arbitration had been commenced within the limitation period by an assured against its liability insurers for indemnification in respect of a claim brought by a third party. During the course of the arbitration, and after the expiry of the limitation period, the assured became insolvent and its rights against the insurers vested in the third party claimant under the Third Parties (Rights against Insurers) Act 1930. The third party sought to take over the arbitration proceedings. Phillips J held that the 1930 Act did not transfer outstanding proceedings to the third party, but only contractual rights, and accordingly it was necessary for fresh proceedings to be commenced by the third party.[43] Independently of the provisions of the 1930 Act itself, Phillips J ruled that an assignee of an agreement containing an arbitration clause could not be regarded as having taken over the proceedings by reason of the assignment to him: such a result might produce unfairness to the other party, who might face an award for the costs of both the assignor and the assignee; and if the assignment related to only some of the assignor's claims, the other party could find himself arbitrating simultaneously against the assignor and the assignee.

These objections were waved aside by Hobhouse J in *The Jordan Nicolov*.[44] This was a more typical case in which an arbitration had been commenced, and rights were assigned by the claimant to the assignee during the course of the arbitration and after the limitation period had expired. Hobhouse J ruled that a contract containing an arbitration clause was assignable after the arbitration had commenced, and that there was no need for

41. This is the result of the Court of Appeal's ruling in *Shayler* v. *Woolf* [1946] Ch 320, disapproving contrary *dicta* of Wright J in *Cottage Club Estates Ltd* v. *Woodside Estates Co Ltd* [1928] 2 KB 463. In *Montedipe SpA* v. *JTP-RO Jugotanker, The Jordan Nicolov* [1990] 2 Lloyd's Rep 11 the reasoning in *Shayler* v. *Woolf* was accepted as correct by Hobhouse J, whereas in *London Steamship Owners Mutual Insurance Association Ltd* v. *Bombay Trading Co Ltd, The Felicie* [1990] 2 Lloyd's Rep 21n Phillips J expressed the view that Wright J had been correct in principle.

42. [1990] 2 Lloyd's Rep 21n.

43. Phillips J was of the view that this would not create any limitation problems, as the third party's cause of action against the insurers was not based on the assured's action but rather on the Third Parties (Rights against Insurers) Act 1930, and that independent action did not accrue until the date of the assured's insolvency. However, in *Lefevre* v. *White* [1990] 1 Lloyd's Rep 569 Popplewell J ruled—without reference to *The Felicie*, which was at that point unreported—that the rights of an assignee under the 1930 Act are identical to those of the assured, and that the third party's action against the insurers accrues at the same point as the assured's action against the insurers. On this reasoning, the third parties in *The Felicie* would have been without remedy.

44. [1990] 2 Lloyd's Rep 11.

the assignee to commence fresh arbitration proceedings. The assignee's right to take over the existing proceedings was held to be subject to two procedural requirements: notice of the change of claimant has to be given to the arbitrator within a reasonable time; and the assignment must be a legal assignment complying with the requirements of the Law of Property Act 1925, s 136, in order to entitle the assignee to proceed in his own name, the assignee being able to produce evidence to the arbitrators of the assignment.[45]

The position under the 1930 Act remains uncertain. However, it would seem that ordinary assignments are governed by the ruling in *The Jordan Nicolov*, as the reasoning in that case was approved by the Court of Appeal in *Baytur SA* v. *Finagro Holdings SA*.[46] In *Baytur* the assignment had been equitable only, as notice had not been given to the other party as debtor, with the result that the assignee was required to proceed in the assignor's name rather than his own; however, as the assignor had been removed from the register of companies and had ceased to exist, the action had necessarily lapsed.

CONTRACTUAL LIMITATION PERIODS FOR COMMENCING AN ARBITRATION

(a) Contractual provisions and the judicial power of extension

Independently of statutory limitation periods, many agreements contain provisions which require proceedings to be commenced within a given period from a particular event (e.g., the discharge of cargo) or from the accrual of the cause of action. The potential for such clauses to operate in an oppressive manner, particularly where they were included in standard form contracts, led, in the Arbitration Act 1934, to the introduction of a judicial power to extend the agreed time limits. That power was re-enacted as the Arbitration Act 1950, s 27. The experience of s 27 of the 1950 Act was that time could be extended on the flimsiest grounds, and accordingly the Arbitration Act 1996, s 12, which replaced s 27 of the 1950 Act, is more tightly drawn. Many of the authorities on the 1950 Act are thus no longer of good authority on the new Act. The Arbitration Act 1996, s 12 is mandatory, and cannot be ousted by contrary agreement,[47] and it is to be emphasised that the power to extend applies only to contractual time limits and not to statutory time limits.[48]

Where time is extended, all rights which would otherwise have been lost because of the claimant's delay are restored to him. Thus, under a construction contract, if the contract provides that, unless arbitration is commenced within a given period, the claimant is bound by the figures set out in the final certificate, extension of time permits the claimant to challenge the figures.[49]

---

45. This proviso was fatal to the assignee in *The Jordan Nicolov*, as the assignee had not produced evidence of the assignment.

46. [1991] 4 All ER 129.

47. As was the case with the earlier provision: *Pittalis* v. *Sherefettin* [1986] 2 All ER 227.

48. Arbitration Act 1996, s 12(5). Some difficulty here surrounds the Carriage of Goods by Sea Act 1971, which ratifies the Hague-Visby Rules. The one-year time limit is statutory, so that it is not possible for the court to extend time: *Kenya Railways* v. *Antares Co Pte Ltd, The Antares* [1987] 1 Lloyd's Rep 424. However, if the parties have voluntarily adopted the Hague-Visby Rules when the Rules would not otherwise have applied, the one-year time limit is contractual rather than statutory and time can be extended: *Nea Agrex SA* v. *Baltic Shipping Co Ltd, The Aghios Lazaros* [1976] QB 933, overruling *Rolimpex Ltd* v. *Avra Shipping Co Ltd, The Angeliki* [1973] 2 Lloyd's Rep 226; *The Stena Pacifica* [1990] 2 Lloyd's Rep 234; *Vosnoc Ltd* v. *Transglobal Projects Ltd, The Times*, 27 August 1997.

49. *McLaughlin and Harvey* v. *P & O Developments*, 55 Build LR 101.

(b) Procedural aspects

The application can be made by any party to the arbitration proceedings, provided that three conditions are met.[50]

- (a) Notice has been given to the other parties.
- (b) The claim to which the proceedings relate has arisen. Provided that this is the case, the application can be made at any time, whether before or after the time limit has expired.[51]
- (c) Any arbitral procedure for extending time has been exhausted. It had been held by the House of Lords in *Comdel Commodities Ltd* v. *Siporex Trade SA*[52] that the existence of another procedure for the extension of time, in particular a discretion conferred upon the arbitrators to that effect, did not preclude the operation of the judicial power to extend time under earlier legislation, and it is clear that, by necessary implication, this decision has been given statutory effect by the 1996 Act. However, if arbitrators have been requested to extend time but have refused to do so, the non-interventionist ethos of the 1996 Act will doubtless operate to make the court reluctant in the extreme to override the arbitrators' decision on the matter.[53]

More than one application can be made: the fact that the court has previously extended time is no barrier to a further application.[54] An appeal from a ruling of the court may be made only with the leave of the court itself.[55]

(c) Elements of the power to extend

(i) The statutory provisions

Section 12(1) of the 1996 Act is as follows:

"Where an arbitration agreement to refer future disputes to arbitration provides that a claim shall be barred, or the claimant's right extinguished, unless the claimant takes within a time fixed by the agreement some step—

(a) to begin arbitral proceedings, or

---

50. Arbitration Act 1996, s 12(2).
51. Arbitration Act 1996, s 12(4).
52. [1990] 2 All ER 552, confirming *The Cunard Carrier* [1977] 2 Lloyd's Rep 261, *Ets Soules et Cie* v. *International Trade Development Co Ltd* [1979] 2 Lloyd's Rep 122 and *European Grain and Shipping Ltd* v. *Dansk Landsbrugs Grovvareselskab* [1986] 1 Lloyd's Rep 163, and overruling *Timmerman's Graan-en Maalhandel en Maalderij BV* v. *Sachs* [1980] 1 Lloyd's Rep 194.
53. The Departmental Advisory Committee, February 1996, para 74, stated that it would be "difficult if not impossible" to persuade the court to intervene where the arbitrators had refused to do so. The position under the earlier legislation was different, in that the courts did not regard themselves as restrained by the arbitrators' own refusal to extend time when they were empowered to do so: *Ets Soules et Cie* v. *International Trade Development Co Ltd* [1979] 2 Lloyd's Rep 122; *European Grain and Shipping Ltd* v. *Dansk Landbrugs Grovvareselskab* [1986] 1 Lloyd's Rep 163; *Comdel Commodities Ltd* v. *Siporex Trade SA* [1990] 2 All ER 552.
54. Arbitration Act 1996, s 12(4).
55. Arbitration Act 1996, s 12(6). Under the earlier legislation, such leave was not required. In the event of an appeal, the Court of Appeal had been reluctant to interfere with the judge's exercise of his discretion unless he had plainly applied the wrong test: *Cast Shipping Ltd* v. *Tradax Export SA, The Hellas in Eternity* [1979] 2 Lloyd's Rep 280; *Graham H Davies (UK)* v. *Marc Rich & Co Ltd* [1985] 2 Lloyd's Rep 423; *Irish Agricultural Wholesale Society Ltd* v. *Partenreederei MS, The Eurotrader* [1987] 1 Lloyd's Rep 418.

(b) to begin other dispute resolution procedures which must be exhausted before arbitral proceedings can be begun, the Court may by order extend the time for taking that step."

(ii) Agreement to refer future disputes

The power to extend time in the Arbitration Act, s 12(1) is restricted to agreements to refer future disputes to arbitration, i.e., arbitration clauses: an agreement to submit an existing dispute to arbitration is assumed to be one made at arms' length and thus not one which demands the protection of the claimant.

(iii) "Claim shall be barred, or the claimant's right extinguished"

The Arbitration Act 1996, s 12(1) permits the court to extend time for the making of a "claim". That word is not defined by the Act, but authorities on the previous provision —which in this regard was worded identically—had made it clear that a claim is any matter in issue between the parties in the arbitration even though it is not a claim as that word would normally be understood. Thus in *Sioux Inc* v. *China Salvage Co, The American Sioux*,[56] the Court of Appeal held that the right of a shipowner to contest the sum claimed by salvors by commencing arbitration was a claim, and the time permitted for the commencement of the arbitration could be extended.[57]

The section is stated to be applicable to two types of clause: a clause which bars the claim, and a clause which extinguishes the claimant's right. The distinction is that the former merely requires arbitration to be commenced within a given period, failing which the matter cannot be arbitrated and must be resolved if at all by a court, whereas the latter operates to remove the claimant's action entirely if he fails to commence arbitration proceedings within the agreed period. The Arbitration Act 1950, s 27 by its terms applied only to clauses which barred claims, but the courts established that it extended also to clauses which extinguished the claim, as, were it otherwise, the court's power to extend time could be indirectly excluded by a simple drafting device.[58] The 1996 Act, therefore, simply codifies the previous position.

(iv) "To begin arbitration proceedings or other dispute resolution procedures"

The Arbitration Act 1950, s 27 provided that time could be extended to allow the claimant to give notice to appoint an arbitrator (the usual method of commencing an arbitration) or to take any other step to commence the proceedings. The new provision is wider, permitting time to be extended for the claimant to begin arbitration proceedings or "to begin other dispute resolution procedures which must be exhausted before arbitral proceedings can begin". The apparent purpose of the additional words is to make a minor change only, in recognition of the fact that arbitration agreements increasingly make provision for an initial attempt to settle by mediation or some other form of alternative dispute resolution

56. [1980] 3 All ER 154.
57. See also *Fordgate (Bingley) Ltd* v. *National Westminster Bank plc* [1995] EGCS 97.
58. *Consolidated Investment Contracting Co* v. *Saponaria Shipping Co Ltd, The Virgo* [1978] 3 All ER 988.

procedure.[59] The result is that if a claim has to be made within a given period, but there is a preliminary dispute resolution procedure to be attempted, time may be extended for the commencement of that procedure.

If the new words are to be interpreted narrowly, the fine distinction drawn by the courts under the earlier law between the commencement of the arbitration and the commencement of a preliminary procedure which is too remote from the arbitration to attract the judicial power to extend, has been preserved. The point may be illustrated by reference to shipping and rent review arbitrations. In *Jadranska Slobodna Plovidba* v. *Oleagine SA, The Luka Botic*[60] the Centrocon arbitration clause, which provides that "any claim must be made in writing and the claimant's arbitrator appointed within 12 months of final discharge" was held to impose an indivisible obligation upon the claimant, so that time for the making of a claim in writing could be extended, this being causally connected to the arbitration. By contrast, in *Babanaft International Co SA* v. *Avant Petroleum Inc, The Oltenia*,[61] any claim by cargo owners was to be extinguished unless it had been "presented to charterers in writing with all available supporting documents within 90 days from completion of discharge of the cargo concerned". The Court of Appeal's view of this obligation was that it had no necessary connection with arbitration, even though arbitration would normally follow after the presentation of the claim, and that time for the presentation of the claim could not be extended.

The rent review cases are to the same effect. It is common for a clause to provide that the landlord is to give the tenant six months' notice of an intended rent increase, time running backwards from the rent review date in the lease. The tenant may then serve a counter-notice within three months of receipt, the effect of which is to amount to a reference of the rent to arbitration. In *Richurst Ltd* v. *Pimenta*[62] it was held that the landlord's notice is not a step in arbitration proceedings as it is too remote from them, so that time cannot be extended for his giving notice. By contrast, it was held in *Pittalis* v. *Sherefettin*[63] that the tenant's counter-notice is a step in arbitration proceedings, as at that stage a potential dispute had arisen, so that time could be extended in favour of the tenant.

(v) Seat of the arbitration

As noted previously, the Arbitration Act 1996 applies only to arbitrations which have their juridical seat in England, Wales or Northern Ireland. Accordingly, if the seat of the arbitration is outside the jurisdiction, the English courts have no power to extend time in respect of the arbitration even if English law is the law chosen by the parties as governing the arbitration agreement and the arbitration procedure. This is an important change in the law, as under the Arbitration Act 1950, s 27, the court had the power to extend time where

59. Departmental Advisory Committee, February 1996 Report, para 74.
60. [1983] 3 All ER 602. Cf *Tradax Export SA* v. *Italcarbo Societa di Navigazione SpA, The Sandalion* [1983] 1 Lloyd's Rep 514.
61. [1982] 3 All ER 244, overruling *Nestlé Co Ltd* v. *Biggins* [1958] 1 Lloyd's Rep 398. Cf *Mariana Islands Steamship Corporation* v. *Marimpex Mineraloel-Handelsgesellschaft mbH & Co KG, The Medusa* [1986] 2 Lloyd's Rep 328.
62. [1993] 2 All ER 559.
63. [1986] 2 All ER 227.

the arbitration agreement was governed by English law irrespective of the location of the seat of the arbitration.[64]

(d) Judicial discretion

(i) Exercise of the discretion

The court may extend the time for such period and on such terms as it thinks fit.[65] The basis for the exercise of the court's discretion is set out in the Arbitration Act 1996, s 12(3):

"The court shall make an order only if satisfied—

    (a) that the circumstances are such as were outside the reasonable contemplation of the parties when they agreed the provision in question, and that it would be just to extend the time, or

    (b) that the conduct of one party makes it unjust to hold the other party to the strict terms of the provision in question."

The Arbitration Act 1950, s 27 was far more generous to the applicant, and permitted the court to extend time if failure to do so would result in "undue hardship". The drafting of the 1996 Act was a deliberate attempt to cut back on the previous broad approach. The authorities under the earlier provision[66] were to the effect that the provision was to be construed broadly, that relevant factors included the length of the delay,[67] the amount at stake (a particularly important consideration),[68] the role of the respondent in bringing about the delay,[69] the strength of the claimant's case[70] and prejudice to the respondent

64. *International Tank and Pipe SAK* v. *Kuwait Aviation Fuelling Co KSC* [1975] QB 224; *Mitsubishi Corporation* v. *Castletown Navigation Ltd, The Castle Alpha* [1989] 2 Lloyd's Rep 383.

65. Arbitration Act 1996, s 12(4).

66. For statements of general principle, see: *Liberian Shipping Corporation* v. *King & Sons Ltd, The Pegasus* [1967] 2 QB 86 and *Moscow V/O Exportkhleb* v. *Helmville Ltd, The Jocelyne* [1977] 2 Lloyd's Rep 121; *Libra Shipping and Trading Corporation Ltd* v. *Northern Sales Ltd, The Aspen Trader* [1981] 1 Lloyd's Rep 273; *Comdel Commodities Ltd* v. *Siporex Trade SA* [1990] 2 All ER 552.

67. The general trend was to treat delays which were short, in comparison to the time allowed to commence proceedings, leniently (*Intermare Transport GmbH* v. *Naves Transoceanicas Armadora SA, The Aristokratis* [1976] 1 Lloyd's Rep 552; *Navigazione Alta Italia SpA* v. *Concordia Maritime Chartering AB, The Stena Pacifica* [1990] 2 Lloyd's Rep 234; *Wenden Engineering Services Co Ltd* v. *Wing Hong Contractors Ltd* [1993] ADRLJ 53), and to extend time in the case of long delays where there was no prejudice to the respondent (*The Aspen Trader* [1981] 1 Lloyd's Rep 273), although even an excessive delay by reference to the time allowed was generally treated unsympathetically (*European Grain and Shipping Ltd* v. *Dansk Landbrugs Grovvareselskab* [1986] 1 Lloyd's Rep 163; *Pittalis* v. *Sherefettin* [1986] 2 All ER 227; *Emson Contractors Ltd* v. *Protea Estates Ltd* (1988) 4 Const LJ 119).

68. *Kruidenier (London) Ltd* v. *Egyptian Navigation Co, The El Amria* [1980] 1 Lloyd's Rep 166; *Transpetrol Ltd* v. *Ekali Shipping Co Ltd, The Aghia Marina* [1989] 1 Lloyd's Rep 62; *Sparta Navigation Co* v. *Transocean-America Inc, The Stephanos* [1989] 1 Lloyd's Rep 506; *Garrick Shipping Co* v. *Euro-Frachtkontor GmbH, The World Agamemnon* [1989] 2 Lloyd's Rep 316; *The Stena Pacifica* [1990] 2 Lloyd's Rep 234; *Comdel Commodities Ltd* v. *Siporex Trade SA* [1990] 2 All ER 552; *Patel* v. *Peel Investments (South)* [1992] 30 EG 88; *Fordgate (Bingley) Ltd* v. *National Westminster Bank* [1995] EGCS 97.

69. E.g., in failing to respond to correspondence or in indicating that he will not rely upon a time bar: *Steamship Co of 1912* v. *Anglo-American Grain Co Ltd, The Leise Maersk* [1958] 2 Lloyd's Rep 341; *The Pegasus* [1967] 2 QB 86; *SI Pension Trustees Ltd* v. *William Hudson Ltd* (1977) 242 EG 689; *The Al Fahia* [1981] 2 Lloyd's Rep 99; *The Ever Splendor* [1988] 1 Lloyd's Rep 245; *Transpetrol Ltd* v. *Ekali Shipping Co, The Aghia Marina* [1989] 1 Lloyd's Rep 62; *The Stena Pacifica* [1990] 2 Lloyd's Rep 234.

70. *Sanko Steamship Co Ltd* v. *Tradax Export SA* [1979] 2 Lloyd's Rep 273; *The Al Fahia* [1981] 2 Lloyd's Rep 99; *Tradax International SA* v. *Cerrahogulari TAS, The M Eregli* [1981] 2 Lloyd's Rep 169; *National Mineral Development Corporation* v. *Obestain Inc, The Sanix Ace* [1985] 1 Lloyd's Rep 246; *The Aghia Marina* [1989] 1 Lloyd's Rep 62.

flowing from the delay.[71] The absence of fault on the claimant's part was generally an important factor in his favour,[72] but the fact that the claimant[73] or his legal advisers[74] had been at fault in not commencing proceedings in time was not necessarily fatal to his application and indeed was no more than one of the factors to be considered. A tactical delay which had caused the applicant's problems was not, however, treated sympathetically,[75] and the court would lean against exercising its discretion in favour of extending time where the applicant could not give a satisfactory reason for his failure to meet the contractual period.[76] There was not, however, any single conclusive point. The court in essence undertook a balancing approach, under which the question often became whether the severe consequences of refusing to extend time were deserved by reference to the way the claimant had actually behaved.[77]

The 1996 Act has restored the position which was originally believed to prevail under the 1950 Act, namely, that time is to be extended in exceptional circumstances only.[78] The two grounds upon which time can be extended are extremely restrictive. The first—circumstances not contemplated by the parties when the clause was agreed—on its face excludes cases in which the claimant has himself been at fault, and renders irrelevant the size of the sum involved, previously a crucial matter. In the only decision on the subsection to date, *Vosnoc Ltd* v. *Transglobal Projects Ltd*,[79] a generous interpretation appears to have been adopted: in that case the court extended time where the applicant's notice to commence the arbitration had failed to meet the statutory requirements for validity, and it was emphasised that the term "circumstances" was to include all circumstances. It might be thought that this approach is not fully in accord with what was intended by the legislation. The second—the respondent's conduct—reflects a number of authorities under

---

71. *The Al Fahia* [1981] 2 Lloyd's Rep 99; *Emson Contractors Ltd* v. *Protea Estates Ltd* (1988) 4 Const LJ 119; *Sparta Navigation Co* v. *Transocean America Inc, The Stephanos* [1989] 1 Lloyd's Rep 506; *The World Agamemnon* [1989] 2 Lloyd's Rep 316; *Patel* v. *Peel Investments (South)* [1992] 30 EG 88; *Fordgate (Bingley) Ltd* v. *National Westminster Bank plc* [1995] EGCS 97.

72. *Nestlé Co Ltd* v. *Biggins & Co Ltd* [1958] 1 Lloyd's Rep 398; *Eastern Counties Farmers Ltd* v. *J & J Cunningham Ltd* [1962] 1 Lloyd's Rep 261; *Atlantic Shipping Co SA* v. *Tradax Internacional SA, The Bratislava* [1977] 2 Lloyd's Rep 269.

73. In both *Pittalis* v. *Sherefettin* [1986] 2 All ER 227 and *European Grain and Shipping Co* v. *Dansk Landbrugs Grovvareselskab* [1986] 1 Lloyd's Rep 163 failure by the claimant to seek legal advice counted against him. By contrast, if the claimant's error was not culpable the court would largely disregard it: *The Simonburn (No 2)* [1973] 2 Lloyd's Rep 145; *Libra Shipping and Trading Corporation* v. *Northern Sales Ltd, The Aspen Trader* [1981] 1 Lloyd's Rep 273; *The World Agamemnon* [1989] 2 Lloyd's Rep 316.

74. *The Eurotrader* [1987] 1 Lloyd's Rep 418;*Unitramp SA* v. *Jenson & Nicholson (S) Pte Ltd, The Baonia* [1991] 2 Lloyd's Rep 121; *Mitsubishi Corporation of Tokyo* v. *Guinomar Conakry* (1994) Lloyd's List, 13 August.

75. *The Simonburn (No 2)* [1973] 2 Lloyd's Rep 145; *Mediterranea Raffineria Siciliana Petroli SpA* v. *Kuwait Oil Tanker Co SAK, The Al Fahia* [1981] 2 Lloyd's Rep 99; *First Steamship Co Ltd* v. *CTS Commodity Transport Shipping, The Ever Splendor* [1988] 1 Lloyd's Rep 245.

76. *Alma Shipping Corporation* v. *Union of India, The Astrea* [1971] 2 Lloyd's Rep 494; *Aaby's Rederei A/S* v. *Union of India, The Evje* [1972] 1 Lloyd's Rep 129; *Moscow V/O Exportkhleb* v. *Helmsville Ltd, The Jocelyne* [1977] 2 Lloyd's Rep 121; *Sanko Steamship Co Ltd* v. *Tradax Export SA* [1979] 2 Lloyd's Rep 273.

77. *Consolidated Investment & Contracting Co* v. *Saponaria Shipping Co Ltd, The Virgo* [1978] 3 All ER 988, 994, *per* Geoffrey Lane LJ.

78. *Hookway & Co* v. *WH Hooper & Co* (1950) 84 Ll LR 443; *Raymond & Reid* v. *Granger* [1952] 2 All ER 152; *Jajasan Urusan Bahan Makanan* v. *Compania de Navegacion Geamar Sociedade de Responsabilidade Limitada* [1953] 1 Lloyd's Rep 511; *Watney, Combe, Reid & Co* v. *EM Dower & Co Ltd* [1956] 1 Lloyd's Rep 325; *Nestlé Co Ltd* v. *Biggins & Co Ltd* [1958] 1 Lloyd's Rep 398; *Sigalas & Sons* v. *Man Mohan Singh* [1958] 2 Lloyd's Rep 298; *Det Danske-Franske Dampskibsselskab A/S* v. *Compagnie Financière d'Investissements Transatlantiques, The Himmerland* [1965] 2 Lloyd's Rep 353.

79. *The Times*, 27 August 1997.

section 27 of the 1950 Act.[80] It is suggested that the word "conduct" in section 12(3)(b) of the 1996 Act should not refer purely to deliberate conduct, i.e., where the other party has sought to string out negotiations in the hope that proceedings will not be commenced, and should not carry any element of blameworthiness or lack of integrity. Thus, the fact that the respondent has participated in bona fide settlement negotiations and the claimant has failed to commence protective proceedings for fear of threatening those negotiations should not preclude the extension of time should those negotiations subsequently prove to be abortive.[81]

Even where one or other of the criteria for the making of an order extending time is satisfied, the court retains a residual discretion to refuse to make an order. It may act in this way, for example, where the application for extension out of time has not itself been made within a reasonable time.[82]

(ii) Imposition of terms

Under the 1950 Act the court often imposed terms upon the extension of time, including an order requiring the applicant to give security for the respondent's costs in the arbitration, those costs including the cost of the application for the extension of time.[83] The Arbitration Act 1996 has removed the power of the court to order security for costs in respect of the arbitration,[84] and this is now a matter for the arbitrators alone provided that the parties have not agreed that the arbitrators are not to order security for costs.[85] Accordingly, it would seem that the court cannot, as a condition of extending time, order security for costs, and it must also be doubtful whether the court can take into consideration in exercising its discretion whether the arbitrators themselves have the power to order security for costs.

TIME LIMITS WITHIN ARBITRATION PROCEEDINGS

(a) Nature of the time limits

Once the arbitration has commenced, there are various time limits which must be met by the parties and the arbitrators during the course of the proceedings. Some of these may be imposed by the agreement or by the arbitrators while others arise under the Arbitration Act 1996 itself. In most cases the time limits set out in the 1996 Act are default provisions, it being open to the parties to agree different periods. The court has a discretion, on application to it under section 79 of the Arbitration Act 1996, to extend any contractual or statutory time limit before or after its expiry. It may do so only if the arbitrators themselves have no power to extend time, and where a substantial injustice would otherwise

---

80. See the authorities cited in fn 69, *supra*.

81. But see *Irish Agricultural Wholesale Society Ltd* v. *Partenreederei MS, The Eurotrader* [1987] 1 Lloyd's Rep 418, where the fact that negotiations were ongoing between lawyers and insurers was held not to justify the claimant failing to take protective action.

82. *Richmond Shipping Ltd* v. *Agro Co of Canada Ltd, The Simonburn (No 2)* [1973] 2 Lloyd's Rep 145.

83. *The Al Fahia* [1981] 2 Lloyd's Rep 99; *Flender Werft AG* v. *Aegean Maritime Ltd* [1990] 2 Lloyd's Rep 27.

84. The court can order security for costs only in respect of proceedings before it in which an award is challenged: Arbitration Act 1996, s 70(6).

85. Arbitration Act 1996, s 38(3).

be done by failure to extend. Time limits imposed by the arbitrators themselves cannot be extended by the court, although once an award has been made it is open to a party to challenge the award on the basis that the procedure adopted by the arbitrators was so defective as to amount to serious irregularity resulting in substantial injustice.[86]

(b) Statutory time limits

The following are the most important time limits provided for by the 1996 Act. All are multiples of seven, so that time limits do not expire at weekends. All are extendible by the court:

(1) Appointment of arbitrators. Subject to contrary agreement, a sole arbitrator is to be appointed within 28 days and in all other cases an appointment is to be made within 14 days (Arbitration Act 1996, s 16).

(2) The time for the making of the award. There is no statutory period, and all will depend upon what the parties have agreed or what is reasonable in the circumstances. If the appropriate time is not complied with, the court may extend time (Arbitration Act 1996, s 50) or, alternatively, it may remove the arbitrators for failing to proceed with reasonable despatch (Arbitration Act 1996, s 24).

(3) An award may be challenged on the grounds of want of jurisdiction, serious procedural irregularity or error of law within 28 days of the date of the award (Arbitration Act 1996, s 70(3)). The date on which an award is made is the date agreed by the arbitrators or, failing any agreement, the date on which the award is signed by the last of the arbitrators (Arbitration Act 1996, s 54).

(c) Time limits imposed by arbitrators

The following are the most important time limits which may be imposed by arbitrators under the 1996 Act. The court has no jurisdiction to extend the time limits, other than indirectly in proceedings challenging the award on the ground of serious procedural irregularity.

(1) The arbitrators may extend the time within which an objection on jurisdictional grounds to the proceedings may be made: the general rule is that it must be made before any step in the proceedings has been taken (Arbitration Act 1996, s 31).

(2) The arbitrators may make such orders as they think fit for the conduct of the proceedings. In the event of non-compliance they may proceed *ex parte* (Arbitration Act 1996, s 41(4)) or make a peremptory order (Arbitration Act 1996, ss 41(5), 42).

(3) If the arbitrators are satisfied that there has been inordinate and inexcusable delay on the part of the claimant, and that the delay: (a) gives rise or is likely to give rise to a substantial risk that it is not possible to have a fair resolution of the issues in the claim; or (b) has caused or is likely to cause serious prejudice to the respondent, they may make an award dismissing the claim (Arbitration

---

86. Arbitration Act 1996, s 68.

Act 1996, s 41(2)).[87] The grounds on which this power may be exercised are identical to those which apply to the striking out of judicial proceedings for want of prosecution,[88] so that, other than in wholly exceptional circumstances, arbitrators should not strike out an action within the limitation period.[89] It should be noted that the arbitrators' decision is to be expressed as an award, which means that the claim is deemed to have been dismissed and cannot be resurrected in fresh proceedings by reason of the principle of *res judicata*.[90] It is nevertheless open to the claimant to challenge the award on the ground that it was obtained by serious procedural irregularity.

TIME LIMITS FOR ENFORCING ARBITRATION AWARDS

An arbitration award, irrespective of the seat of the arbitration, can be enforced in the same manner as a court judgment.[91] There is no legislative provision which sets out the limitation period for the enforcement of an award. The point was first considered by Otton J in *Agromet Motoimport Ltd* v. *Maulden Engineering Co (Beds) Ltd*.[92] Here, the cause of action accrued in 1976, and arbitration proceedings were held in February 1980, resulting in an award in the plaintiff's favour in March 1980. Enforcement proceedings were commenced in June 1983, and the defendants argued that the enforcement action was time barred, as the limitation period in respect of the proceedings had commenced in 1976. Otton J sensibly rejected the argument that time for the enforcement of an award begins to run from the date of the accrual of the original cause of action, as this would have the consequence of rendering many awards time barred (often before they had actually been made), and held that there is a separate limitation period in respect of the award. This is founded upon an implied obligation on the losing party to honour the award,[93] so that if the award is not honoured when it ought to have been honoured, the losing party is in breach of contract and that breach gives rise to a separate cause of action which has its own six-year limitation period.

87. This section re-enacts the Arbitration Act 1950, s 13A, added by the Courts and Legal Services Act 1990, s 102. The 1990 amendment was prompted by a series of House of Lords decisions, *The Hannah Blumenthal* [1983] 1 All ER 34, *The Antclizo* [1988] 2 All ER 513 and *The Bremer Vulkan* [1989] 1 All ER 897, which made it clear that arbitrators have no power to strike out for want of prosecution. It was held by the House of Lords in *L'Office Chérifien des Phosphates and Unitramp SA* v. *Yamashita-Shinnihon Steamship Co Ltd, The Boucraa* [1994] 1 All ER 20 that the Arbitration Act 1950, s 13A was retrospective in that it permitted arbitrators to take into account delay incurred prior to the commencement of the section in order to effect a striking out after the commencement of the section. It is to be assumed that s 41(2) of the 1996 Act is to be construed in the same way.

88. See Ch 7.

89. *James Lazenby & Co* v. *McNicholas Construction Co Ltd* [1995] 2 Lloyd's Rep 30.

90. It was thus argued in *James Lazenby, supra*, that striking out should be permitted within the limitation period, as the basis for the rule in judicial proceedings was that the plaintiff could simply issue a fresh writ within the limitation period, whereas an award dismissing the claim was final. Rix J held that the possibility of a fresh writ was only one basis for the rule, and that it was based equally on the proposition that delay could not be inordinate if the limitation period had not expired: on that basis, the rule ought to be extended to arbitration proceedings.

91. Arbitration Act 1996, s 66(1).

92. [1985] 2 All ER 436.

93. There is no express obligation on a party to honour an award, although the Arbitration Act 1996, s 40, does impose a duty upon the parties to an arbitration to do all things necessary for its proper and expeditious conduct.

It will be seen that Otton J held that implied obligation to honour the award arises when the award ought to have been honoured, which is not necessarily the date on which the award was made. It is open to the parties to agree on a period following the making of the award within which it must be honoured, and the expiry of that period will trigger the limitation period as that is the point at which the losing party is in breach of his obligation. If the parties have not laid down any period, it would seem that time does not run until a reasonable period has elapsed from the making of the award. In *International Bulk Shipping & Services Ltd* v. *Minerals & Metals Trading Corporation of India*[94] the parties had agreed that the awards, obtained at the end of 1984, were to be honoured "forthwith". Proceedings to enforce the awards were commenced in 1993, following a protracted period of negotiation during which the losing parties had been dissolved. The Court of Appeal held that this agreement conferred upon the losing party a reasonable time to pay, which should be regarded as no more than three months from the date of the award, and it followed that the enforcement proceedings were time barred. The Court of Appeal held that events during the six-year period following the three-months period of grace were not to be taken into consideration, and in particular the running of the limitation period was not deferred until the date on which the successful parties had made a formal demand for payment.

94. [1996] ADRLN 38.

CHAPTER 12

INSURANCE LAW

CLAIMS UNDER INSURANCE POLICIES

(a) The general position

(i) The assured's cause of action

There are no specific rules for limitation in insurance cases in the Limitation Act 1980, and insurance contracts come within the general rule that proceedings must be commenced within six years of the date on which the action accrued, or within 12 years from that date where the contract is in the form of a specialty. The real problem in insurance cases is ascertaining the date on which the assured's action against the insurer can be said to accrue. A number of possibilities present themselves: the date on which the event insured against has taken place; the date on which the event insured against has caused loss to the assured; the date on which the claim is made against the insurers; the date on which the assured has satisfied the terms of the contract necessary to establish the insurers' liability; the date on which the insurers have denied liability, and the date on which the insurers ought reasonably to have made payment.

There is a consistent line of authority for the proposition that the relevant date is the very first of these possibilities, the date on which the event insured against has taken place, the principle being that the insurer has agreed to hold the assured harmless against the occurrence of an insured event, and that when the event takes place the insurer is at that point in immediate and automatic breach of contract. This proposition, which appears to flow from the nature of insurance as a contract of indemnity, has been restated as follows[1]:

"I accept that, at common law, a contract of indemnity gives rise to an action for unliquidated damages, arising from the failure of the indemnifier to prevent the indemnified person from suffering damage, for example by having to pay a third party. I also accept that, at common law, the cause of action does not (unless the contract provides otherwise) arise until the indemnified person can show actual loss . . . This is, as I understand it, because a promise of indemnity is simply a promise to hold the indemnified harmless against a specified loss or expense."

This statement at first sight is authority for the proposition that it is the date at which the assured feels the loss, rather than the date at which the event insured against has occurred, which triggers the limitation period. However, it is suggested that the statement

---

1. *Firma C-Trade SA* v. *Newcastle Protection and Indemnity Association, The Fanti; Socony Mobil Oil Co Inc* v. *West of England Ship Owners Mutual Insurance Association (London) Ltd, The Padre Island* [1990] 2 All ER 705, *per* Lord Goff at p 717.

should not be read in that way, for it is established that—in the absence of wording to the contrary—a claim arises under an insurance policy as soon as the event which directly results in the loss has occurred, and not when the loss is manifested,[2] and the position would seem to be that it is the occurrence of the event which is the key factor.

The established position as traditionally stated is far from logical[3] and not always easy to apply, but now seems too entrenched to be denied. Perhaps a more satisfactory method of explaining the rule was suggested by Sir Peter Webster in *Callaghan* v. *Dominion Insurance Co*,[4] where the learned judge pointed out that an indemnity insurance policy is:

"an agreement by the insurer to confer upon the insured a contractual right which, *prima facie*, comes into existence immediately when the loss is suffered by the happening of an event insured against, to be put by the insurer into the same position in which the insured would have been had the event not occurred, but in no better position."

As will be seen, the general rule works rather differently in each of the various branches of insurance to which it applies, and is in any event only a presumption, in that the parties may by their contract stipulate that the assured's action is to accrue at some other point.

(ii) A secondary cause of action?

While it is undoubtedly the case that the assured's cause of action against the insurers accrues when the loss occurs, particular difficulty is occasioned by the fact that the insurer may deny liability under the contract or seek to avoid the contract for breach of duty, or simply fail to make payment within a reasonable time, and the question then arises as to whether the insurer's conduct in any of these regards is a separate breach of contract which gives rise to a fresh action for damages and also to a fresh limitation period. In principle there is a distinction between avoidance of a policy for a breach of duty which is unconnected to the claim and a bare refusal to make payment. In the former case, if the insurer's conduct is wrongful, there is a breach of contract which will attract its own limitation period. This may be of little use to the assured, for if the insurer has purported to avoid the policy after the loss has occurred, the avoidance may well be a breach of contract but it will avail the assured little if the limitation period for the claim has expired, for the assured may then be unable to prove any loss flowing from the insurer's wrongful avoidance. However, in the latter situation, the question is whether mere refusal to pay is breach of contract: as will be seen below, this possibility has been considered and rejected in marine insurance, but has been accepted in both property and liability insurance.

(b) Marine policies

(i) Loss of insured subject-matter

Marine insurance recognises three forms of loss: actual total loss (destruction of the insured subject-matter)[5]; constructive total loss (loss which does not amount to total

2. *Kelly* v. *Norwich Union Fire & Life Insurance Ltd* [1989] 2 All ER 888.
3. See the comments of Judge Kershaw QC in *Transthene Packaging Co Ltd* v. *Royal Insurance (UK) Ltd* [1996] LRLR 32.
4. *The Times*, 14 July 1997.
5. Marine Insurance Act 1906, s 57.

physical destruction but which for economic purposes is a total loss)[6]; and partial loss. The assured may, at his option, treat a constructive total loss as an actual total loss, by serving on the insurer a notice of abandonment, which entitles the assured to recover an indemnity based on total rather than partial loss.[7] The position in all cases is that the limitation period commences at the date of the casualty. This was confirmed by Hirst J in *Bank of America National Trust and Savings Association* v. *Chrismas, The Kyriaki*.[8] In this case the insured vessel was, in July 1985, disabled by a mechanical breakdown. The owners took the view that the loss was a constructive total loss, as the cost of repairs would exceed the insured value of the vessel, and accordingly a notice of abandonment was served on the insurers, but was subsequently rejected, both events occurring in September 1985. The question was whether proceedings commenced in July 1991—after six years from the loss but within six years from the date on which the notice of abandonment had been served and rejected. The insurers pleaded that the action was time barred, on the basis that the cause of action accrued on the date of the casualty. The plaintiffs—the assignees of the owners —argued that in a constructive total loss case the nature of the loss was not fixed until the service of the notice of abandonment. Hirst J, ruling for the insurers, held that the election by the assured did not affect the nature of the loss, but only the amount which could be recovered, so that the service of a notice of abandonment did not constitute an ingredient of the assured's cause of action. Accordingly, the action was time barred. Although this case does not deal with cases of actual total loss or partial loss, the underlying assumption in the ruling is the basic principle that the date of the casualty is the date at which the action accrues, and that that principle is not altered in the case of a constructive total loss even though there was an additional procedural requirement to the recovery of an indemnity based on total loss in that situation.

The limitation principle espoused in *The Kyriaki* is consistent with the related principle that an insurer's liability to the assured arises at the date of the casualty, the insurer being in breach of contract at that date, so that any subsequent failure to pay by the insurer cannot of itself give rise to a separate action for breach of contract, as damages cannot be awarded for a failure to pay damages.[9] In such a case, the assured's remedy for late payment is interest on the sum originally due. In *Ventouris* v. *Mountain, The Italia Express (No 2)*[10] the assured claimed from his insurers additional damages by way of distress and hardship flowing from the failure of the insurers to make prompt payment. Hirst J rejected the claim, and held that the insurers' failure to make payment was immaterial as the insurer was in breach of contract and liable for unliquidated damages as from the date of the casualty, and that damages had to be assessed as at that date. Although the case did not involve limitation, it lends conclusive support to the limitation position as expressed in *The Kyriaki*. *The Italia Express (No 2)* sets out the position under the Marine Insurance Act 1906 on the basis of the insurer's liability,[11] and although it is possible to contract out

6. Marine Insurance Act 1906, s 60.

7. Marine Insurance Act 1906, s 61. The notice must comply with the formal requirements of the Marine Insurance Act 1906, s 62.

8. [1993] 1 Lloyd's Rep 137. See also *Hong Kong Borneo Services Co Ltd* v. *Pilcher* [1992] 2 Lloyd's Rep 593.

9. *President of India* v. *Lips Maritime Corporation, The Lips* [1988] AC 395.

10. [1992] 2 Lloyd's Rep 281. See also: *Luckie* v. *Bushby* (1853) 13 CB 864; *Edmunds* v. *Lloyd Italico* [1986] 2 All ER 281; *Transthene Packaging Co Ltd* v. *Royal Insurance (UK) Ltd* [1996] LRLR 32; *Sprung* v. *Royal Insurance Co (UK) Ltd*, 1996, unreported.

11. Marine Insurance Act 1906, ss 67–74.

of much of the 1906 Act it may be that marine policies are assumed to operate consistently with the Act on this particular matter. No such presumption applies to non-marine property policies, and it may be that the wording of property policies is capable of being construed as setting a different point for the triggering of the insurer's liability and the assured's cause of action. It might also be noted that there is subsequent Court of Appeal authority for the proposition that there may be an additional implied obligation on the insurer to make payment within a reasonable time, although it may be that this cannot apply to marine insurance as it is not contemplated by the 1906 Act: these points as they apply to property policies are considered in that context, below.

(ii) General average losses

General average arises where a marine peril has occurred and one party has incurred expenditure, or sacrificed his own property, in the interests of other parties interested in the voyage. Where there has been expenditure or sacrifice by one party, he is entitled to a rateable contribution from the other interests (a general average contribution). A marine policy will cover the costs of expenditure or sacrifice by the assured, and also the amount of any general average contribution payable by the assured to another person. In practice, therefore, the allocation of losses is arranged between marine insurers by the exercise of subrogation rights, based on an adjustment effected by a professional average adjuster.

The limitation issue as regards general average is whether the claim arises at the date of the casualty or the date at which the adjustment is published. In *Chandris* v. *Argo Insurance Co Ltd*,[12] Megaw J opted for the former, and denied recovery to shipowners who issued proceedings within six years of the publication of the adjustment but after six years from the date on which the casualty giving rise to the general average losses had occurred. Megaw J further ruled that the practice of underwriters in the London market not relying upon limitation provisions in general average cases did not amount to any form of implied term or waiver preventing the pleading of a limitation defence in any particular proceedings.

(c) Property policies

The general rule here prevails: the occurrence of the peril is the event which triggers the insurer's liability, as that event puts the insurer in breach of contract and liable for unliquidated damages.[13] This was reaffirmed by Sir Peter Webster in *Callaghan* v. *Dominion Insurance Co*, in which the assured was held to be time-barred when making a claim in respect of a fire more than six years after the occurrence of the fire. While the proposition remains good law, its logic was doubted by Judge Kershaw QC in *Transthene Packaging Co Ltd* v. *Royal Insurance (UK) Ltd*.[14] In that case the assured submitted a

---

12. [1963] 2 Lloyd's Rep 64, relying on *dicta* in *Tate & Lyle Ltd* v. *Hain Steamship Co Ltd* (1934) 151 LT 249 and *Morrison Steamship Co Ltd* v. *Greystoke Castle* [1947] AC 265. The decision was followed by the Privy Council in *Castle Insurance Co Ltd* v. *Hong Kong Shipping Co Ltd, The Potoi Chau* [1983] 2 Lloyd's Rep 376, although distinguished on the facts as the insurers had issued bonds and guarantees which were themselves held to form the basis of the claim by shipowners.

13. *Jabbour* v. *Custodian of Israeli Absentee Property* [1954] 1 WLR 139. See also the authorities cited in fn 10, *supra*.

14. [1996] LRLR 32.

claim which the insurers regarded as excessive and fraudulent, and the insurers accordingly repudiated liability under the policy. The assured brought proceedings against the insurers for wrongful repudiation, and one question was whether the insurers had broken the contract by virtue of their repudiation. It was argued that there had not been a breach, as the mere occurrence of the loss automatically put the insurer in breach of contract, so that the assured's action was based not on the insurers' action but rather on the fact that there had been a loss. Judge Kershaw QC found it surprising that insurers are "collectively, in breach of contract hundreds or thousands of time every day, whenever a fire, a flood, a road accident or other such event occurs", and held that while that might be the general rule, it could be ousted by express wording. In the present case the policy provided that "in the event of the property . . . sustaining damage . . . the insurers will indemnify the insured by at their option repairing, replacing or paying the amount of the damage", and Judge Kershaw ruled that, as a matter of contract, it was this obligation which triggered the insurers' liability and not the occurrence of the event. Judge Kershaw refused to comment on the limitation situation, but it must follow from his judgment that such wording operates to oust the general rule and that, necessarily, the limitation period runs not from the date of the insured event but from the date on which the insurers have repudiated their obligation to make payment.

The question then becomes whether the wording of the policy is sufficient to replace the date at which the insurer's obligation arises and thus at which the assured's action accrues. *Transthene* decides that standard wording does have this very effect, although Judge Kershaw's express reservations on the limitation issue demonstrate the conceptual difficulties which surround the issue. As will be seen below, it would seem, in the light of *Callaghan* v. *Dominion Insurance Co*, Judge Kershaw's view of the case with which the common law rule may be displaced by express wording is itself no longer supportable.

An additional possibility is that it is an implied term of a property policy that the insurer makes payment within a reasonable time, and that where the insurer's primary obligation under the policy arises at the date of the occurrence of the insured event, there is a further implied obligation which may give rise to a fresh cause of action at a later date. In *Sprung* v. *Royal Insurance (UK) Ltd*[15] the assured's business premises were damaged by vandals. The insurers denied liability. Subsequently the assured's business collapsed, and he commenced proceedings against the insurers claiming the insurance moneys plus further damages representing the loss of his business brought about by the insurers' failure to pay within a reasonable time. The Court of Appeal held that the latter claim was arguable, but that it had not been made out on the facts, as the proximate cause of the assured's loss of his business was not the conduct of the insurer but rather the assured's own impecuniosity.

(d) Life policies

The position under a life policy is as for other policies, i.e., that the date at which the limitation period begins to run is the date of the death of the life assured under the policy.[16] It does not appear to have been suggested in any life case that there is an implied term on

---

15. 1996, unreported.
16. *Re Haycock's Policy* (1876) 1 Ch D 611; *London & Midland Bank* v. *Mitchell* [1899] 2 Ch 161. Both cases involved mortgagees.

the insurer requiring payment to be made within a reasonable time, giving rise to a separate cause of action and a separate limitation period.

(e) Liability policies

Under a liability policy, the assured's loss is, subject to contrary wording,[17] taken to have occurred when the assured's liability has been established and quantified, and not at the earlier date on which the wrongful act which ultimately gives rise to the assured's liability to the third party has taken place even though the occurrence of that act may trigger an obligation on the assured to notify the insurer that an event likely to give rise to a claim has occurred.[18] Liability is established and quantified for this purpose on the date of any judgment, arbitration award or binding settlement in favour of the third party against the assured.[19] A reinsurance contract, which resembles a liability policy in some respects even though it is not as a matter of strict law a liability policy for all purposes,[20] operates on the same principle: the reinsured's action against the reinsurer accrues when the reinsured's liability is established and quantified by a judgment, arbitration award or binding settlement.[21]

The conceptual difficulty of the possible secondary action against the insurers for wrongful repudiation or failure to pay in due time arises in a particularly acute fashion in liability insurance. In a property case, there will generally be a loss suffered by the assured which sets the limitation period running, and there may be a subsequent breach by the insurer which triggers a distinct limitation period: as long as the assured treats his original loss as constituting his action, and does not wait for the insurer to deny liability or to fail to pay, the limitation period should not operate as a trap. The problem in liability insurance is that the event which gives rise to the claim against the assured will be notified to the insurer under the terms of the policy, but may not amount to a loss under the policy for some years, until the date on which the third party victim obtains a judgment, award or settlement against the assured: in that interim period, it may be that the insurer denies liability under the policy for the loss as and when it becomes ascertained and quantified. The question here is whether the assured is entitled to wait for the judgment, award or settlement against him before commencing proceedings against the insurer, or whether the insurer's pre-loss repudiation constitutes the relevant cause of action in respect of which proceedings have to be commenced; if the latter is the case, it may be necessary for the assured to seek declaratory relief within six years of the insurer's repudiation even though there is no certainty at that point that there will be a finding of liability against him.

The only authority on this point is the judgment of Popplewell J in *Lefevre* v. *White*.[22] Here, the assured was involved in a motor vehicle accident in July 1972 in which a third party suffered serious personal injuries. The insurers, in March 1973, wrote to the assured

---

17. In particular, "pay to be paid" wording: see *infra*.
18. As in *Walker* v. *Pennine Insurance Co* [1980] 2 Lloyd's Rep 156.
19. *London Steamship Owners Mutual Insurance Society Ltd* v. *Bombay Trading Co Ltd, The Felicie* [1990] 2 Lloyd's Rep 20; *Cox* v. *Bankside Members Agency Ltd* [1995] 2 Lloyd's Rep 437.
20. This complex matter is discussed at length in Butler and Merkin, *Reinsurance Law*, Ch A.3.2.
21. *Halvanon Insurance Co Ltd* v. *Companhia de Seguros do Estado de Sao Paulo* [1995] LRLR 303.
22. [1990] 1 Lloyd's Rep 569.

denying liability on the basis of the unroadworthy condition of the assured's vehicle.[23] The assured did not respond to this communication, and on 16 December 1981, judgment was given against him in favour of the third party. On 8 December 1987 the assured commenced proceedings against the insurer. If the assured's action had accrued on the insurers' repudiation, he was time barred. By contrast, if the assured's action accrued when his liability was established and quantified, he was in time, albeit only by a matter of days. Popplewell J ruled that on the facts before him the limitation period in principle commenced on the insurers' repudiation of liability in 1973. However, as the repudiation was anticipatory in nature, in that the insurers had stated that they would not perform their obligations as and when those obligations accrued, the assured was given an option whether to accept the repudiation and commence proceedings, or to disregard the repudiation and await the due date for performance by the insurers of their obligation, i.e., the date on which the assured's liability had been established and quantified. On the facts, by not responding to the insurers' repudiatory conduct, the assured had elected to maintain the contract in force, and thus did not have a cause of action as of the date of repudiation. On this reasoning, the assured's action accrued only when his liability had been established and quantified, and accordingly the action was not time barred.

This reasoning has much to commend it, but it nevertheless contains a trap in that if the assured chooses to respond to the insurers' denial of liability, and in some way intimates that he regards the insurers as in breach of contract and that he has accepted the repudiation, time will begin to run against him as from the date of the repudiation. It may be, however, that the assured would fall into this trap only by some unequivocal statement to the effect that he is electing to treat the contract as at an immediate end. Nevertheless, if the assured does respond to the insurers, care must be taken to ensure that an election of this type cannot be inferred.

(f) Contractual variations

(i) Contract terms varying the limitation period

It is permissible in insurance, as in other forms of contract, for the parties to agree that there is to be a shorter or longer limitation period. In *Walker* v. *Pennine Insurance Co*[24] the assured's motor liability policy provided that if the insurers disclaimed liability in respect of a claim the assured was required to commence legal proceedings against them within 12 months, failing which his claim was deemed to have been waived. The assured was involved in an accident in August 1970, details of which were notified to the insurers, who denied liability in February 1971. Judgment was given against the assured in favour of the injured party in 1976, at which point the assured sought a declaration as to the insurers' liability to him. The Court of Appeal held that the assured's claim had arisen in 1970, even there was no accrued liability at that point, and as he had not commenced protective declaratory proceedings within a year of the insurers' denial of liability, he was time barred. It is uncertain whether this case remains good law, as the Unfair Terms in Consumer Contracts Regulations 1994 might well operate to strike down a provision

---

23. This would no longer be a defence to the third party's claim, as the Road Traffic Act 1988, s 149, prevents a motor insurer from denying liability to a victim of the assured in almost all circumstances. The facts in *Lefevre* occurred shortly before the law was altered, originally by the Road Traffic Act 1972.

24. [1980] 2 Lloyd's Rep 156.

which in effect requires an assured to issue legal proceedings against his insurers before it is clear that he has incurred any liability in respect of which insurance cover is required.

(ii) Contract terms varying the accrual of the action

The general principle that the assured's action accrues when the casualty insured against takes place depends for its operation on what is to be regarded as the casualty insured against. Some policies may treat the insured loss not as the occurrence of a peril but rather some subsequent action by the assured, e.g., reinstating damaged premises or making payment to a third party to whom the assured has incurred liability. A distinction must be drawn, however, between contract terms which merely impose conditions on the manner in which the assured must prove his loss which operate as defences or which relate to valuation, and contract terms which actually vary the event which triggers the insurer's liability.

Ordinary terms which require the assured to give notice or proofs of his loss as a condition of the policy or as a condition precedent to the insurer's liability do not postpone the running of the limitation period, but are concerned only to regulate the procedure whereby the assured can make a claim against the insurers. This would seem to follow from *Coburn* v. *Colledge*,[25] in which it was held that the limitation period for a solicitor's bill for his costs ran from the date on which the work was completed rather than from the date of the issue of the bill, on the basis that the former gives rise to the cause of action and the latter is merely concerned with its proof. A supporting analogy is *The Kyriaki*,[26] in which Hirst J held that the right of an assured under a marine policy to serve a notice of abandonment in respect of a constructive total loss and thereby to recover on the basis of an actual total loss rather than a partial loss, was not an essential ingredient of the assured's cause of action; although that case turned on the proper construction of the Marine Insurance Act 1906, it might be thought that a notice clause is not an essential ingredient of the assured's cause of action, but merely a step which must be taken by him to allow his claim to proceed.

Equally, an obligation to go to arbitration does not of itself restrict the assured's cause of action, as it is well established that an arbitration clause does not remove the right of the assured to go to court,[27] but merely requires the court to stay its proceedings.[28] The exception to this principle is an arbitration clause in *Scott* v. *Avery*[29] form, which prevents any cause of action from arising until an arbitration award has been obtained, although even this principle is subject to the statutory exception that if judicial proceedings are brought in respect of a contract containing a *Scott* v. *Avery* arbitration clause, and the court is of the view that the arbitration agreement is null and void, inoperative or incapable of being performed, the court may set aside the arbitration clause and hear the action on its merits.[30]

---

25. [1897] 1 QB 702.
26. [1993] 1 Lloyd's Rep 137.
27. See, of the many authorities, *Doleman & Sons* v. *Osset Corporation* [1912] 3 KB 257.
28. Under the Arbitration Act 1996, s 9.
29. (1856) 5 HL Cas 811.
30. Arbitration Act 1996, s 9(5).

The classification of terms was given extended consideration by Sir Peter Webster in *Callaghan* v. *Dominion Insurance Co*. In the earlier *Transthene* case Judge Kershaw QC had ruled that a clause which conferred upon the insurer the right either to make payment or to reinstate damaged property operated to postpone the running of time until the insurer's election had been made. That decision, while not referred to by Sir Peter Webster in *Callaghan*, is inconsistent with the result in *Callaghan*. Sir Peter Webster held that a clause which entitled the insurer to reinstate rather than to pay was concerned purely with the calculation of the assured's loss and not with the determination of the date on which it arose. It was further held that a variety of other terms were either defences or went to calculation of loss. Such terms included: the measure of indemnity by reference to reinstatement value; the postponement of payment until reinstatement had been effected; conditions precedent as to the making of claims, including notice and arbitration provisions; the insurer's right of salvage; and the existence of rateable proportion provisions which removed or reduced liability where some other insurance was in place. In the light of *Callaghan* it is clear that only the plainest express wording will operate to extend the ordinary trigger date for the running of the limitation period.

A clause more difficult to classify is the "pay to be paid" provision which is found in mutual marine insurance issued by P & I clubs, and also in many reinsurance agreements, particularly excess of loss contracts. Under such wording, the insurer is not obliged to make payment until the assured (or reinsured) has made payment to the third party to whom he is liable. The effect of such wording is, apparently, to convert the contract from one under which the loss is defined as the establishment of the assured or reinsured's liability, into one under which the loss is defined as actual payment by the assured or reinsured. A pay to be paid clause will be effective only where it is clear from the contract as a whole that the insurer or reinsurer's obligation is to provide an indemnity for actual payment, so that express pay to be paid wording may well bow to the other terms of the contract,[31] but where such a clause does operate to postpone the insurer or reinsurer's liability its impact on limitation is unclear. It might be thought that a pay to be paid clause defines the insurer's or reinsurer's obligation rather than creates the machinery whereby a claim can be pressed, but the point awaits determination. In principle, equal difficulty arises with a property policy which provides that the assured is to be indemnified only on providing proof that the damaged property has been reinstated: there is a strong presumption against a property policy being so construed,[32] as in the event of unambiguous wording it becomes arguable that the event insured against is expenditure on reinstatement rather than the initial damage. However, as has been seen above, in *Callaghan* v. *Dominion Insurance Co* Sir Peter Webster held that even wording of this type was not sufficient for the common law date of peril principle.

It is strongly arguable in the case of a consumer contract governed by the Unfair Terms in Consumer Contracts Regulations 1994 that any term which postpones the insurer's

---

31. In *The Fanti and The Padre Island* [1990] 2 All ER 705 the House of Lords gave full effect to a pay to be paid clause in a P & I liability cover. By contrast, in *Charter Reinsurance Co Ltd* v. *Fagan* [1996] 2 All ER 46 the House of Lords held that an excess of loss reinsurance contract was by its general terms expressed to be against liability and not actual payment, and that the pay to be paid clause was quantitative rather than temporal in nature.

32. Cf *Maclean Enterprises Ltd* v. *Ecclesiastical Insurance Office plc* [1986] 2 Lloyd's Rep 416. But contrast *Anderson* v. *Commercial Union*, 1997, unreported (Ct. of Sess.).

liability until actual payment (in the case of liability insurance) by the insured or reinstatement (in the case of property insurance) by the assured would be struck down by the Regulations, whether the term was expressed as procedural machinery or as an element of the assured's cause of action.

THIRD PARTIES (RIGHTS AGAINST INSURERS) ACT 1930

(a) Effects of the Act

The Third Parties (Rights against Insurers) Act 1930 is concerned to ensure that where the victim of a wrongdoer successfully brings proceedings against the wrongdoer, the proceeds of any liability insurance which the wrongdoer possesses are paid to the victim in the event of the wrongdoer's insolvency. Without the Act, on the wrongdoer's insolvency the insurance moneys would pass into the general fund available for distribution to all creditors, and the victim whose claim has triggered the payment of those moneys would be confined to a dividend.[33]

The 1930 Act accordingly provides that, where the assured has become bankrupt or, in the case of a company, has been wound up or subjected to receivership or administration, any rights which the assured has against his liability insurers are transferred to the third party victim. The victim, having established the assured's liability by obtaining a judgment, arbitration award or binding settlement, may then commence proceedings against the insurer on the same basis as if he were himself the assured party. The victim cannot use the Act before he has established and quantified the assured's liability to him,[34] and is subject to the same defences which the insurer possessed as against the assured himself, e.g., breach of the duty of utmost good faith[35] or of a notification condition,[36] failure to pay the premium,[37] the obligation to go to arbitration,[38] and the obligation to make payment to the victim before any claim may be made.[39]

(b) Resurrecting dissolved companies: limitation issues

In *Bradley* v. *Eagle Star Insurance Co*[40] the House of Lords ruled that the establishment and quantification of the assured's liability was a necessary precondition to the operation of the 1930 Act, and that, where the assured was a company which had been dissolved before proceedings had been brought against it to establish its liability, it was not possible to invoke the 1930 Act against the assured's liability insurers even though the insurers had

---

33. *Re Harrington Motor Co* [1928] Ch 105.
34. *Post Office* v. *Norwich Union Fire Insurance Society* [1967] 1 All ER 577; *Bradley* v. *Eagle Star Insurance Co* [1989] 2 WLR 568. This has also been held to mean that the victim cannot seek information as to the wrongdoer's insurance position before he has established and quantified the wrongdoer's liability: *Upchurch Associates* v. *Aldridge Estates Investment Co Ltd* [1993] 1 Lloyd's Rep 535; (1994) *The Times*, 17 May.
35. For example, *Cleland* v. *London General Insurance Co Ltd* (1935) 51 Ll LR 156.
36. For example, *Pioneer Concrete (UK) Ltd* v. *National Employers Mutual General Insurance Association Ltd* [1985] 2 All ER 395; *Cox* v. *Bankside Members Agency Ltd* [1995] 2 Lloyd's Rep 437.
37. *Murray* v. *Legal and General Assurance Society Ltd* [1970] 2 QB 495.
38. For example, *Freshwater* v. *Western Australia Assurance Co Ltd* [1933] 1 KB 515.
39. *The Fanti and The Padre Island* [1990] 2 All ER 705, a decision which effectively removed the protection of the 1930 Act where the contract is in pay to be paid form.
40. [1989] 2 WLR 568.

been identified. The only possible relief was where the company had been dissolved less than two years previously, as section 651 of the Companies Act 1985 permitted a company to be restored to the register within two years of its dissolution, although this provision was necessarily of limited use. The *Bradley* decision had a potentially devastating effect in long-tail liability cases, particularly employers' liability cases, where the harmful effects of the assured's negligent act had not become apparent for some years after the act had taken place, for if the assured had been removed from the register of companies before the victim was even aware that he had a cause of action, it would not be possible to commence proceedings against the assured in order to invoke the 1930 Act against the assured's liability insurers.

This decision was regarded as unduly harsh, and Parliament accordingly modified the law in the victim's favour, by introducing an amendment to the Companies Act 1985, s 651.[41] Under the amended version of the section, which operates with retrospective effect, there is no time limit for the resurrection of a company where its resurrection is sought in order to establish its liability for death or personal injury[42]; in all other cases, the two-year time limit remains.[43] Accordingly, where a victim suffers personal injuries, and discovers some years later that a dissolved company was responsible for those injuries, the company can be resurrected at any time and if its liability is then established an action can be brought against its liability insurers.

It will be appreciated that in many of the cases in which the Companies Act 1985, s 651 is of assistance, there may be a separate limitation problem facing the victim, in that the victim's action against the dissolved company is time barred. Parliament recognised that there is little point in resurrecting a company by restoring it to the register, if the purpose of resurrection is to bring an action against it to which it has a complete defence. For this reason section 651(5) provides that the court is to refuse an order restoring the company to the register "if it appears to the court that the proceedings would fail by virtue of any enactment as to the time within which proceedings must be brought". This provision works without difficulty where there is a fixed time limit for the bringing of proceedings,[44] but its meaning is rather more elusive in the vast majority of personal injury cases, as section 33 of the Limitation Act 1980 gives the court a wide discretion to extend time limits: the position is, therefore, that there is a limitation period which *might* defeat the claim, but not one which *would* automatically do so. This renders uncertain whether the possible effect of a limitation provision is to be taken into account at the resurrection stage.

The application of section 651 of the Companies Act 1985 to cases involving the possible use of section 33 of the Limitation Act 1980 was considered by the Court of Appeal in *Re Workvale (No. 2)*.[45] On 27 September 1983 the victim was injured at work. The employing company was dissolved on 22 April 1986, within the three-year limitation period allowed for the action. A writ was issued on 3 September 1983, just within the limitation period, but unfortunately the writ named the employing company as the defendant; as the company had ceased to exist, the writ was invalid and was struck out in January 1990. At that point an application was made by the victim for the restoration of

41. By the Companies Act 1989, s 141.
42. Companies Act 1985 s 651(5).
43. Companies Act 1985 s 651(4).
44. For example, under the Consumer Protection Act 1987, in respect of product liability.
45. [1992] 2 All ER 627.

the employing company to the register, to pave the way for a fresh action in which its liability could be established. The employing company's insurers opposed the application, arguing that the limitation period for the personal injury action had expired and that it was necessary for the victim to show in restoration proceedings that the court would exercise its discretion under section 33 of the Limitation Act 1980 in his favour before restoration could be ordered. The Court of Appeal rejected this approach, and held that it was enough for the victim to show in the restoration proceedings that he had an arguable case for the exercise of that discretion in his favour at trial; the appropriate place to deal with the question was at trial and not at the preliminary stage: the order for restoration was, on this basis, made.[46]

The Companies Act 1985, s 651(6) confers a discretion on the court, when making an order restoring a company to the register, to order that the period between the dissolution of the company and the making of the order is to be discounted for limitation purposes. Where, therefore, a company has been dissolved within the limitation period, and it is subsequently restored to the register, the court can at the same time preserve for the benefit of the applicant that part of the limitation period which had not expired at the date of the company's dissolution, thereby avoiding the need for an application under section 33 of the Limitation Act 1980 to be made for the purposes of later proceedings.[47] In *Re Workvale* the Court of Appeal held that if the victim has demonstrated an arguable case that he would receive an extension under section 33, and the insurers are parties to the restoration proceedings and have had an opportunity to rebut the argument, then if the court determines to restore the company to the register an order under section 651(6) of the Companies Act 1985 should be made as a matter of course, to spare the parties the expense of arguing section 33 issues at a later date.

(c) The victim's action against the insurer: limitation issues

(i) Judicial proceedings

An action cannot be brought under the 1930 Act until the assured has become insolvent and the victim has established and quantified the assured's liability. It would appear to follow that, as the victim's action against the insurer is complete when the last of these two events occurs, the limitation period for that action ought to run from that point. This analysis was presumed to be correct by Phillips J in *The Felicie*,[48] although the issue was apparently not argued. In that case the insurer and assured were in arbitration when the assured became insolvent. The victim sought to take over the arbitration proceedings. Phillips J held that a third party could not by statutory assignment take over the right to participate in an arbitration, so that it would be necessary for him to initiate new proceedings, but that this did not cause him any hardship as the limitation period under the 1930 Act did not arise until the assured had become insolvent.

46. The Court of Appeal rejected the rather stricter test laid down by Harman J at first instance, [1991] 2 WLR 294, that the victim would have to show a high degree of probability that the s 33 discretion would be exercised in his favour, although the learned judge found that even that test was satisfied on the facts.
47. Assuming, of course, that the proceedings are commenced within the unexpired part of the limitation period.
48. [1990] 1 Lloyd's Rep 21n.

The above analysis was rejected by Popplewell J in *Lefevre* v. *White*[49] (without reference to *The Felicie*) where the matter was considered at length. It will be recalled that in *Lefevre* the assured injured the victim in a road traffic accident in 1972, but his insurers denied liability in 1973. Judgment was given against the assured at the end of 1981, and the assured commenced proceedings against his insurer within days of the expiry of the limitation period at the end of 1987. After the proceedings had been commenced, and soon after the limitation period had expired, the assured became insolvent. The victim sought to rely upon the 1930 Act against the assured's insurers. Popplewell J held that the effect of the statutory transfer of "rights under the contract" effected by the 1930 Act was to put the victim in precisely the same position as the assured, and that the limitation period which applied to the assured's action governed also the victim's action against the insurers. Popplewell J further ruled that the benefit of the writ which had been issued by the assured against the insurer within the limitation period was not transferred to the victim by virtue of the assured's insolvency, as the Act transferred only rights created by the contract of insurance and not steps taken to enforce those rights.

The result of *Lefevre* v. *White* is, therefore, that once the victim has established the assured's liability, time begins to run against the victim under the 1930 Act immediately.[50] The victim cannot sit back and await the assured's successful prosecution of a claim against his insurers, as the assured may not commence the action within the limitation period or, if he does, he may become insolvent after the limitation period has expired and the victim will not be able to mount fresh proceedings. He must, therefore, seek to enforce any judgment, award or settlement as soon as possible, so that if the assured is unable to meet it and is forced into insolvency there is plenty of time to pursue the insurers. It is nevertheless submitted that Popplewell J's reasoning is open to doubt on a number of fronts: it gives rise to the possibility that the victim may become time barred before he has the right to bring an action at all (where the assured becomes insolvent outside the limitation period); it is contradictory in that if the victim does not have a fresh action against the insurer for limitation purposes, it would seem logical that he can take over the existing action where a writ has been issued by the assured within the limitation period; and it has been said that any decision which defeats the rights of the third party under the 1930 Act on limitation grounds beyond his control would be "diametrically opposed to the purposes of the Act" and "suspect".[51]

(ii) Arbitration proceedings[52]

Similar issues arise where there is an arbitration clause in the insurance agreement. In *The Felicie*[53] the assured's liability towards the victim for a cargo claim was established and quantified by a judgment on 21 July 1981. The assured was put into provisional liquidation on 24 June 1987, and arbitration proceedings were commenced against the insurer on 17 July 1987. On 29 July 1987, after the expiry of the limitation period, the assured was

---

49. [1990] 1 Lloyd's Rep 569.

50. Indeed, it might conceivably run from an earlier date, if the assured has accepted the insurer's repudiation of liability under the policy if this has occurred prior to the victim establishing the assured's liability: see *supra*.

51. *The Felicie* [1990] 2 Lloyd's Rep 21n, *per* Phillips J.

52. See also the discussion in Ch 11.

53. [1990] 2 Lloyd's Rep 21n.

wound up. The victim sought to participate in the arbitration in his own name. Phillips J held that the 1930 Act did not assign to the victim the right to take over arbitration proceedings: different issues other than those in the arbitration agreement might arise; the insurer might be prejudiced if the victim is not good for the costs of the arbitration should the claim fail; there was no machinery whereby the victim could be joined as existed in judicial proceedings; and if there was more than one victim, the arbitration might be converted from bilateral into multilateral. Phillips J held instead that the correct approach was to regard the insolvency of the assured as constituting the final event necessary to bring about the accrual of the victim's action against the insurer, so that the victim would have a further six years to commence his action against the insurer. Phillips J went on to say that, if he was wrong on the running of time for the victim's action against the insurer, he would have held that the victim did have the right to participate in the arbitration by way of assignment, as it would not be right to have the victim's claim defeated in a fashion diametrically opposed to the purposes of the 1930 Act.

As commented above, it would seem from *Lefevre* v. *White* that Phillips J was indeed wrong on the time bar applicable to the victim's claim against the insurer, and that the assured and the victim are in an identical position in this respect. Assuming that *Lefevre* v. *White* is correct—although for the reasons given earlier, this must be open to doubt—it follows that Phillips J would have regarded his own judgment in *The Felicie* as incorrect, and that the 1930 Act did indeed permit the victim to take over the arbitration. Support for that very proposition is to be found in the subsequent judgments of Hobhouse J in *The Jordan Nicolov*[54] and of the Court of Appeal in *Baytur SA* v. *Finagro Holding SA*,[55] in each of which it was held that a voluntary legal assignment of a contract containing an arbitration clause was effective to transfer to the assignee the right to take over existing arbitration proceedings in his own name provided that notice was given to the arbitrators and to the other party. Although those decisions do not automatically undermine the authority of *The Felicie*, the objections to automatic assignment under the 1930 Act raised by Phillips J do not appear to have troubled later courts in the case of a voluntary assignment.

54. [1990] 2 Lloyd's Rep 11.
55. [1991] 4 All ER 129.

CHAPTER 13

PATENTS AND COPYRIGHT

The owner of intellectual property rights who wishes to bring an action for infringement under the Patents Act 1977 must normally issue the writ within six years of the wrongful act.[1] The tortious nature of such proceedings was recognised by the House of Lords in *Sevcon Ltd* v. *Lucas CAV Ltd*.[2] It seems, paradoxically, that the result is that time will begin to run against the plaintiff before the cause of action becomes vested in him. This arises because infringement can occur after the application for a patent has been filed yet, by virtue of section 69(2) of the Patents Act 1977, proceedings can only be brought after the grant of the patent, although such proceedings can encompass infringements between application and grant. The defendant's act must infringe not only the claims finally included but also those in the published application.[3]

As has been seen,[4] where an action is commenced within the limitation period but the plaintiff fails to proceed with reasonable diligence, the defendant may apply to the court to have the action dismissed for want of prosecution. The defendant must establish that there has been an inordinate and inexcusable delay which is such as to cause serious prejudice to him; the classic example of such prejudice being where the memory of witnesses is impaired as a result of the delay.[5]

The doctrines of acquiescence and laches are also important in this context.[6] The defendant may raise the defences if he can prove that the plaintiff, by failing to bring proceedings expeditiously, either acquiesced in the defendant's infringement so that he can be deemed to have sanctioned it (estoppel),[7] or knowing that the defendant has infringed his right, fails to bring suit (negligent inactivity).[8] The rationale of this rule was explained by Oliver J in *Taylor Fashions Ltd* v. *Liverpool Victoria Friendly Society*[9] who

---

1. Limitation Act 1980, s 2(1). There are exceptions for cases of fraud and mistake. More generally, see Ch 3.

2. [1986] 1 WLR 462.

3. Patents Act 1977, s 69(2).

4. See Ch 7 (Pleading and Procedure).

5. *Allen* v. *Sir Alfred McAlpine & Sons Ltd* [1968] 2 QB 229; *Birkett* v. *James* [1978] AC 297; *Compagnie Française de Télévision* v. *Thorn* [1978] RPC 735; *Bestworth* v. *Wearwell* [1986] RPC 527; *Dept of Transport* v. *Smaller* [1989] AC 1197; *Halls* v. *O'Dell* (1991) 35 SJ (LB) 204; *Horstman Gear* v. *Smiths Industries* [1979] FSR 461; *Shtun* v. *Zaljejska, The Times*, 18 April 1996.

6. See Ch 3.

7. *Duke of Leeds* v. *Earl of Amherst* (1846) 2 Ph 117 at 123. See also, Cotton LJ, *Proctor* v. *Bennis* (1886) 36 Ch D 740 at 758–61.

8. See *Glasson* v. *Fuller* [1922] SASR 148; *Willmott* v. *Barber* (1880) 15 Ch D 96.

9. [1982] 1 QB 133. Applied in *Film Investors Overseas Services SA* v. *Home Video Channel Ltd, The Times*, 2 December 1996 (acquiescence destroying a claim for infringement of copyright).

said "it would be unconscionable for a party to be permitted to deny that which, knowingly or unknowingly, he has allowed or encouraged another to assume to his detriment".[10] Further, where the plaintiff seeks equitable relief, he may be refused the remedy on the ground of laches or acquiescence.[11] In *Bulmer* v. *Bollinger,*[12] Goff LJ stated that injunctive relief may be refused where there has been delay together with "something . . . to encourage the wrongdoer to believe that he does not intend to rely upon his strict legal rights, and the wrongdoer must have acted to his prejudice in that belief".[13]

The Copyright Designs and Patents Act 1988 lays down the limitation periods governing copyright on the one hand, and rights in performances on the other. Where the plaintiff brings civil proceedings requiring the delivery up of material which infringes either right, section 113(1) of the 1988 Act provides that such action must be brought within six years of the date when the infringing copy or apparatus etc was made, although this period can be extended on the grounds of fraud or disability.[14] In criminal proceedings the limitation period is also six years, but it should be noted that extensions are not granted.[15]

10. *Ibid* at 151.

11. *Re Sharpe* [1892] 1 Ch 154. See also, *International Scientific Communications* v. *Pattison* [1979] FSR 429 (acquiescence as a bar to an account of profits).

12. [1978] RPC 79.

13. *Ibid* at 134–36.

14. Copyright Designs and Patent Act 1988, s 99 (copyright), s 195 (performance rights). The Limitation Act 1980, s 38(2) provides that a person shall be treated as under a disability while he is an infant, or of unsound mind.

15. Section 108 (copyright), s 109 (performance rights).

CHAPTER 14

BAILMENT

"A bailment, traditionally defined, is a delivery of personal chattels on trust, usually on a contract, express or implied, that the trust shall be duly executed, and the chattels redelivered in either their original or an altered form, as soon as the time or use for, or condition on, which they were bailed shall have elapsed or been performed."[1]

Where the bailee misuses or damages the goods which are subject to the bailment he will, of course, be liable. The issue that may arise in the context of bailment is the need to identify the precise nature of the bailee's liability. Although most bailments arise by virtue of contract, nevertheless[2] it is possible for the relationship of bailor–bailee to exist independently of any contractual undertaking, for example, where goods are gratuitously loaned. Here the relationship is consensual, and so the question which has arisen is whether liability can be tortious or otherwise? In *Building and Civil Engineering Holidays Scheme Management Ltd* v. *Post Office*[3] Lord Denning MR stated:

"At common law, bailment is often associated with a contract, but this is not always the case . . . An action against a bailee can often be put, not as an action in contract, nor in tort, but as an action on its own, *sui generis*, arising out of the possession had by the bailee of the goods."

Yet, if the bailor's claim against the defendant-bailee is founded upon the defendant's common law duties it seems that the plaintiff's action lies in tort.[4] The issue assumes greater complexity where the defendant's wrongdoing gives rise to a restitutionary response. Where the plaintiff's cause of action in tort for compensatory damages is time barred, will he still be able to maintain a claim for restitutionary damages? In *Chesworth* v. *Farrar*[5] the court attempted to address these issues. The bailment in this case arose because the defendant took possession of the plaintiff's goods under a court order. The defendant then wrongfully disposed of the goods by selling them. The plaintiff's action in tort was time barred, but the claim for money had and received was held not to be caught by the time bar because an action in "quasi-contract or restitution" was distinct from an action in tort. It is perhaps unfortunate, however, that the court did not go on to consider the implications of its decision from a limitations' perspective.[6]

---

1. *Halsbury's Laws* (4th ed, reissue) Vol 2, at para 1801.
2. See, for example, *Turner* v. *Stallibrass* [1898] 1 QB 58.
3. [1966] 1 QB 247.
4. See the judgment of Edmund Davies J in *Chesworth* v. *Farrar* [1967] 1 QB 407.
5. *Ibid*. For a fuller analysis of this decision, see Birks, *An Introduction to the Law of Restitution* (Oxford: Clarendon Press, 1989) at p 349. See, also, Palmer and McKendrick (eds), *Interests in Goods* (London: Lloyd's of London Press Ltd, 1993), Ch 23.
6. In this regard, see Chs 8 and 17.

CHAPTER 15

ACTIONS ON A SPECIALTY

The Limitation Act 1980, s 8 provides:

"(1) An action on a specialty shall not be brought after the expiration of 12 years from the date on which the cause of action accrued.

(2) Subsection (1) above shall not affect any action for which a shorter period of limitation is prescribed by any other provision of this Act."

There is no specific definition of a specialty in the 1980 Act, but it has been said that, "The most obvious and most common case of an action upon a specialty is an action based on a contract under seal".[1] Specialties need to be considered from an historical perspective. In relation to debts, the Limitation Act 1623 only applied to debts arising out of a simple contract rather than those based on a signed, sealed deed or other instrument. Despite the different form, an action on a specialty is regarded, nonetheless, as a variety of contract action, with the result that time will start to run against the plaintiff from the date of breach, but the fact that there are markedly different limitation periods under the Limitation Act 1980, ss 5 and 8 means that it is important to be able to distinguish an action for breach of a simple contract from one which is based upon a specialty.

On occasions, the task of distinguishing the one from the other is simplified by the fact that there is a statutory declaration to the effect that a particular variety of obligation is to be regarded as a specialty. For example, the Companies Act 1985, s 14 provides that the obligations of the members of a company, under the Memorandum and Articles of Association of the company, to pay money to the company in respect of their shareholding, is to be regarded as an action upon a specialty. Accordingly, the company may avail itself of the longer 12-year limitation period, rather than the six-year period which applies to an action founded on breach of a simple contract. Other similar declarations also apply to other company law obligations, such as the obligation of a contributory in winding-up proceedings.[2]

While the obligation of a shareholder to his company is expressly covered by the Companies Act 1985, s 14, what is less clear is whether any of the obligations owed by a company to its membership take the form of an action on a specialty or whether they are subject to the limitation period applicable to simple contract actions in the Limitation Act 1980, s 5. Generally, the position seems to be that an action by a shareholder against the company is to be regarded as a simple contract action, since there is not always clear

---

1. *Collin* v. *Duke of Westminster* [1985] QB 581 at 601 *per* Oliver LJ.
2. Companies Act 1985, s 508.

211

evidence to the effect that the company has sealed the contract which binds it with its members.[3] This matter is discussed in further detail elsewhere.[4]

Historically, a statute, bearing the Royal seal, is regarded as "the highest form of specialty".[5] Thus it has been stated that the word specialty is "an archaic word of somewhat imprecise meaning; it includes contracts and other obligations in documents under seal, and also, traditionally, obligations arising under statutes".[6]

However it will be seen below that this view is capable of causing conflict as between the operation of section 8 to which a 12-year limitation period applies and section 9, in relation to suing on a statute, to which a six-year limitation period applies.[7] So great is the conflict that it has been suggested that since the enactment of the Limitation Act 1939, which was the first Limitation Act to contain specific provisions to deal with actions on a statute, an action on a specialty should be confined to actions based on deeds and contracts under seal.[8]

While, historically, the origins of the special rules on specialties were confined to debts, it has later come to be established that any contract under deed or seal is to be regarded as a specialty, in respect of which very strict requirements were applied. However, these strict requirements seem to have been relaxed in recent years. Thus it was observed in *Stromdale & Ball Ltd* v. *Burden*[9]:

"Meticulous persons executing a deed may still place their finger on the wax seal or wafer on the document, but it appears to be that, at the present day, if a party signs a document bearing a wax or wafer or other indication of a seal, with the intention of executing the document as a deed, that is sufficient adoption or recognition of the seal to amount to due execution as a deed."

What is clear, however, is that making a contract under seal is regarded as a serious process and it does serve some useful purpose, especially in cases where money is tied up and no demand is likely to be made for it for some considerable time. It is for this reason that a different limitation period is applied to specialties as opposed to simple contracts, in respect of which the plaintiff can be expected to bring his action at an earlier stage. In *Aiken* v. *Stewart Wrightson Members' Agency Ltd*[10] the plaintiffs were members of five Lloyd's syndicates for the 1985 underwriting year of account. They brought actions against members' agents for breach of contract and for negligence in respect of run-off reinsurance which resulted in other reinsurance provision being avoided. Fortunately for a number of the plaintiffs, their agreement with the members' agents were under seal, and the question arose whether they could avail themselves of the longer 12-year limitation period provided under section 8(1). One of the arguments raised on behalf of the defendants was that the rule on specialties applied only to actions for specific performance of an obligation. However, Potter J opined that there was no foundation for such a submission and that, in any case, if that submission were correct, it would mean that successive

---

3. *Re Compania de Electricidad de la Provincia de Buenos Aires Ltd* [1980] Ch 146. See also *Re Art Production Ltd* [1952] Ch 89 and *Re Artisans Land & Mortgage Corporation* [1904] 1 Ch 796.

4. See Ch 24.

5. *Central Electricity Generating Board* v. *Halifax Corporation* [1962] 3 All ER 915 at 919 *per* Lord Reid.

6. Franks, *Limitation of Actions*, 1959, p 188. See also *Holdsworth's History of English Law*, 5th ed, Vol 3, p 103.

7. See further Ch 25.

8. *Lievers* v. *Barber, Walker & Co* [1943] 1 KB 385 at 398 *per* Goddard LJ.

9. [1952] Ch 223. See also *First National Securities Ltd* v. *Jones* [1978] Ch 109.

10. [1995] 3 All ER 449.

law reform bodies had consistently misunderstood the law. For example, the Law Revision Committee[11] observed:

"In the case of specialty actions . . . we consider that the present period of twenty years is too long, but that there should be a longer period for these actions than for actions of simple contract. There ought, we think, to be a method by which rights can be protected from the operation of statutes of limitation for a considerable period. Money is frequently advanced on bonds or debentures or similar instruments, which is not expected or intended to be repaid for a long period and on which payment of interest is waived or suspended. It would be an inconvenience to insist that the lender should call in his loan within six years or lose his rights. Again there are occasional cases where the nature of the transaction is such that claims arising from it will not be known for many years . . . It should at least be possible for a prudent man to secure his position by executing an instrument under seal. See *Lynn* v. *Bamber* ([1930] 2 KB 72). Accordingly we recommend that the period of limitation for actions upon instruments under seal should be twelve years."[12]

It will be recalled that *Lynn* v. *Bamber* was an action on a simple contract to which a six-year limitation period applied, so that the plaintiff was out of time before he was even aware that a cause of action had accrued in his favour.[13] However, it seems reasonably clear from the thinking of the Law Reform Committee that he could have been a "prudent man" in protecting his position by making a contract under seal, thus suggesting that the rule on specialties can apply to any contractual obligation made under seal. This is frequently the case where major building works are concerned, so that in such cases, the parties have agreed that the limitation period will be one of 12 years rather than six.[14]

---

11. *Fifth Interim Report (Statutes of Limitation)*, Cmd 5334, 1936. See also *Twenty First Report, Final Report on Limitation of Actions*, Cmnd 6923, 1977.
12. *Ibid* at para 5.
13. See Ch 8.
14. See *Aiken* v. *Stewart Wrightson Members' Agency Ltd* [1995] 3 All ER 449 at 460 *per* Potter J.

CHAPTER 16

EQUITABLE RELIEF IN CONTRACTUAL AND COMMERCIAL LAW MATTERS

The issue of limitations in the context of equitable remedies is coloured by the very nature of the relief itself—the dominant feature being its discretionary character.[1] It is therefore valuable to briefly review the approach adopted by the courts towards the granting of equitable relief, and particular reference will be made to the decree of specific performance.

Where the common law remedy of damages, to which the successful litigant is entitled as of right, proves to be inadequate, the lacuna may be plugged by the court granting equitable relief. The approach of the courts was explained by the Master of the Rolls in *Flint* v. *Brandon*[2] who said:

"This court does not profess to decree a specific performance of contracts of every description. It is only where the legal remedy is inadequate or defective that it becomes necessary for courts of equity to interfere ... In the present case complete justice can be done at law. The matter in controversy is nothing more than the sum it will cost to put the ground in the condition in which by the covenant it ought to be."[3]

The range of equitable remedies which have evolved to supplement the limited relief available at law has been described as equity's greatest contribution to the development of English law,[4] and may be granted to enforce both equitable and legal rights. The hallmark of the court's equitable jurisdiction is its discretionary nature. However, this does not translate into some arbitrary and unpredictable mechanism for the granting of relief but rather, it is exercised in accordance with a settled corpus of rules.[5] Although the remedies of specific performance and injunctions are generally regarded as the most significant creation of equity, it should be noted that the range of equitable remedies is far reaching and includes, for example, rescission and rectification of contracts, Mareva injunctions, Anton Piller Orders, orders for delivery up and cancellation of documents, account and receivers.[6]

The basic premise underlying the award of equitable relief is that *equity acts in personam*. This imbues the jurisdiction of equity with the ability to act in relation to property located outside the court's jurisdiction for if the defendant is within the jurisdiction, he or

---

1. For the doctrines of laches and acquiescence see Ch 3, *supra*.
2. (1803) 8 Ves 159.
3. *Ibid.*
4. See Hanbury and Martin, *Modern Equity* (London: Stevens & Sons, 1997) p 30 *et seq.* See generally, Pettit, *Equity and the Law of Trusts* (London: Butterworths, 1997); Spry, *Equitable Remedies* (London: Sweet & Maxwell, 1990); Meagher, Gummow, Lehane, *Equity: Doctrines and Remedies* (Sydney: Butterworths, 1992).
5. *Haywood* v. *Cope* (1858) 25 Beav 140 at 151 (*per* Romilly MR).
6. See generally, Snell, *Principles of Equity* (Sweet and Maxwell, 1990); Spry, *op cit.*

she can be compelled personally to perform the contractual obligation. For example, in *Penn* v. *Lord Baltimore*[7] the court enforced an agreement relating to the boundaries of Pennsylvania and Maryland on the basis that "the conscience of the party was bound by this agreement, and being under the jurisdiction of this Court, which acts *in personam*, the Court may properly decree it as an agreement".[8] This approach was explained by Lord Selborne LC in *Ewing* v. *Orr Ewing*[9] in the following terms:

"The Courts of Equity in England, are, and always have been, courts of conscience, operating *in personam*, and not *in rem*; and in the exercise of this personal jurisdiction they have always been accustomed to compel the performance of contracts and trusts as to subjects which were not either locally or *ratione domicilii* within their jurisdiction. They have done so as to land, in Scotland, in Ireland, in the Colonies, in foreign countries."[10]

Further, it would appear that the principle is not restricted in scope to land but may apply to all types of property. For example, in *Potter* v. *Broken Hill Co Pty Ltd*[11] the principle was applied to a foreign patent.

GENERAL PRINCIPLES GOVERNING THE AWARD OF SPECIFIC PERFORMANCE IN ACTIONS FOR BREACH OF CONTRACT[12]

Equitable relief in the form of specific performance is only available where the contract in question is valid and binding upon the parties. It is not available where the contract is not supported by consideration even if the contract is under seal. In this situation the plaintiff's remedy is restricted to damages at law.[13]

In accordance with the principle that "equity does not act in vain",[14] the court will not award equitable relief unless it is certain that the defendant is in a position to comply with the decree.[15] Accordingly, specific performance will not be granted where the contract is for a personal service or where performance cannot be guaranteed without the constant supervision of the court.[16] Thus, the court will not generally specifically enforce a contract to construct or repair buildings. However, equitable relief is flexible in operation so that, for example, the notion of corporate personality will not necessarily preclude an order of specific performance being made against the particular company's controlling share-holder. In *Jones* v. *Lipman*[17] the defendant contracted to sell his house to the plaintiff. He

7. (1750) 1 Ves Sen 444.
8. *Ibid.* See Hanbury and Martin, *op cit,* at 695, which cautions that this jurisdiction is not as wide as may first appear. The land in question was subject to the Crown. Cf *Re Hawthorne* (1883) 23 Ch D 743, in which the land in question was located in Saxony, and was therefore not subject to the Crown. The court refused jurisdiction. See further, *Deschamps* v. *Miller* [1908] 1 Ch 856. See also, the Civil Jurisdiction and Judgments Act, 1982, s 30.
9. (1883) 9 App Cas 34.
10. *Ibid* at 40. More recently, the House of Lords emphasised in *Westdeutsche Landesbank Girozentrale* v. *Islington London Borough Council* [1996] 2 All ER 961 at 988 that the linchpin of equity is conscience (Lord Browne-Wilkinson).
11. (1905) 3 CLR 479.
12. For a full analysis see Spry, *op cit.*
13. *Jeffery's* v. *Jeffery's* (1841) Cr & Ph 138.
14. *Tito* v. *Waddell (No 2)* [1977] Ch 106 at 326.
15. *Elliot* v. *Pierson* [1948] Ch 452.
16. *Rigby* v. *Connol* (1880) 14 Ch D 482; *Chinnock* v. *Sainsbury* (1860) 30 LJ Ch 409; *Scott* v. *Rayment* (1868) LR 7 Eq 112.
17. [1962] 1 WLR 832.

then transferred the house to a company over which he had complete control. The plaintiff brought an action for breach of contract and sought specific performance of the agreement. Russell J, in holding that the veil of incorporation should in the circumstances be pierced so that specific performance could be ordered against both the company and the vendor, observed that: "The defendant company is the creature of the first defendant [the vendor], a device and a sham, a mask which he holds before his face in an attempt to avoid recognition by the eye of equity."[18]

The classic formulation of a decree of specific performance was given in *Wolverhampton and Walsall Railway Co* v. *London and North Western Railway Co*[19] by Lord Selborne LC who said it:

" . . . presupposes an executory as distinct from an executed agreement, something remaining to be done, such as the execution of a deed or a conveyance, in order to put the parties in the position relative to each other in which by the preliminary agreement they were intended to be placed."[20]

The essential question is whether an award of damages would leave the plaintiff in a position which, in all material respects, he or she would have been in had the contract been specifically performed.[21] The position was stated by Lord Selborne in *Wilson* v. *Northampton and Banbury Junction Rly*[22] who said: "The Court gives specific performance instead of damages only when it can by that means do more perfect and complete justice."[23] If damages are inadequate because, for example, the obligation under the contract is continuing in nature, so that a series of actions for damages would be required, or because only nominal damages are available at law, the court may order the contract to be performed in specie. The issue was cogently summarised by Lord Redesdale in *Harnett* v. *Yielding*[24]:

"Unquestionably the original foundation of these decrees was simply this, that damages at law would not give the party the compensation to which he was entitled: that is, would not put him in a situation as beneficial to him as if the agreement were specifically performed. On this ground, the court in a variety of cases, has refused to interfere, where from the nature of the case, the damages must necessarily be commensurate to the injury sustained."[25]

The adequacy of damages or other remedies available at law is determined according to settled principles irrespective of whether the subject-matter of the contract is real or personal property.[26] In relation to real property however, the received wisdom is that each parcel of land is unique and therefore has a special value, so that damages are regarded as an inadequate remedy to compensate for the right to acquire or dispose of an interest

---

18. *Ibid* at 836.
19. (1873) LR 16 Eq 433.
20. *Ibid* at 439. See *Tito* v. *Waddell (No 2)*, *supra*, fn 14, at 322.
21. *Beswick* v. *Beswick* [1968] AC 58. Damages may be considered an inadequate remedy where the defendant is insolvent or of doubtful solvency so that an award of damages is likely to be ineffective, see *Evans Marshall & Co Ltd* v. *Bertola SA* [1973] 1 WLR 349 at 380–81; *The Oakworth* [1975] 1 Lloyd's Rep 581; *Neale* v. *Mackenzie* (1837) 1 Ke 474.
22. (1874) 9 Ch App 279.
23. *Ibid* at 284.
24. (1805) 2 Sch & Lef 549.
25. *Ibid* at 553.
26. *Lamare* v. *Dixon* (1873) LR 6 HL 414.

in it.[27] The fact that a vendor of an interest in land has an equal right to specific perform-ance accords with the doctrine of affirmative mutuality.[28]

With respect to personal property, the traditional view was that:

"A court of equity will not, generally, decree performance of a contract for the sale of stock or goods, not because of their personal nature, but because damages at law, calculated upon the market price of the stock or goods, are as complete a remedy to the purchaser as the delivery of the stock or goods contracted for; inasmuch as, with the damages, he may purchase the same quantity of the like stock or goods."[29]

Nevertheless, where damages are not adequate in restoring the plaintiff to the position the plaintiff would have been in had the contract for personalty been performed, the court may, in its discretion, order specific performance. The critical question seems to be whether the chattels are readily available in the market place so that the plaintiff can acquire them from an alternative source.[30] Thus, it can be said that most commercial contracts for the purchase of goods will not warrant a decree of specific performance.[31] However, specific performance has been ordered of a valuable work of art,[32] an ancient altar embellishment,[33] and a licensed taxi-cab.[34] If company securities, stock or shares are readily obtainable in the market the contract will not be specifically enforceable,[35] and should the purchaser have to pay more than the contract price, the award of damages will reflect this.[36] Conversely, if the securities are not available in the market, the contract will be specifically enforceable.[37]

Certain statutory provisions provide for specific performance. For example, the Sale of Goods Act 1979, s 52(1) confers on the court the discretion to order a contract for specific or ascertained goods to be specifically performed "without giving the defendant the option of retaining the goods on payment of damages". General principles as to the inadequacy

---

27. *Adderley* v. *Dixon* (1824) 1 Sim & St 607; *Turner* v. *Bladin* (1951) 82 CLR 463. Specific performance will be ordered even where the purchaser acquires land as part of his stock in trade, for example, in order to subdivide and resell: *Pianta* v. *National Finance & Trustees Ltd* (1964) 38 ALJR 232 at 233 *per* Barwick CJ. Cf *Loan Investment Corporation* v. *Bonner* [1970] NZLR 724 at 735.

28. *Cogent* v. *Gibson* (1864) 33 Beav 557; *Nives* v. *Nives* (1880) 15 Ch D 649. In *Turner* v. *Bladin* (1951) 82 CLR 463 at 473 the High Court of Australia (Williams, Fullagar and Kitto JJ) observed: "We are of the opinion that where the contract is of such a kind that the purchaser can sue for specific performance, the vendor can also sue for specific performance, although the claim is merely to recover a sum of money, and that he can do so although at the date of the writ the contract has been fully performed except for the payment of the purchase money or some part thereof."

29. *Adderley* v. *Dixon, supra,* fn 27 at 610, *per* Sir John Leach.

30. If the chattels in question are "articles of unusual beauty rarity and distinction" such as antique porcelain jars they will not be readily available in the market place: *Falcke* v. *Gray* (1859) 4 Drew 651.

31. *Dominion Coal Co Ltd* v. *Dominion Iron and Steel Co Ltd* [1909] AC 293.

32. *Lowther* v. *Lowther* (1806) 13 Ves 95.

33. *Duke of Somerset* v. *Cookson* (1735) 3 P Wms 390.

34. *Dougan* v. *Ley* (1946) 71 CLR 142, in which the High Court of Australia concluded that the taxi in question was not readily available from an alternative source given that it was already licensed and the number of licences issued by the relevant authority was strictly limited.

35. *Re Schwabacher* (1907) 98 LT 127.

36. *Cud* v. *Rutter* (1720) 1 P Wms 570; *Dorison* v. *Westbrook* (1722) 2 Eq Cas Abr 161; *Nutbrown* v. *Thornton* (1804) 10 Ves 159.

37. *Duncuft* v. *Albrecht* (1841) 12 Sim 189. In *ANZ Executors and Trustees Ltd* v. *Humes Ltd* [1990] VR 615, the holder of convertible notes issued by a company was awarded specific performance against the company of its contract to allot the shares. Brooking J found that the fact that the plaintiff did not wish to retain the shares but intended to resell them at a profit, did not defeat the claim.

of damages apply.[38] Thus in *Behnke* v. *Bede Shipping Co*[39] the court ordered the specific performance of a contract for the sale of a ship on the basis that the vessel was of "peculiar and practically unique value to the plaintiff".[40] The Companies Act 1985, s 195 provides that a contract to take up debentures, like one to take up shares, may be enforced by an order for specific performance.

Contracts to lend money are not generally specifically enforceable.[41] However, where a borrower agrees to pledge security, specific performance will be granted if the loan has in fact been made by the lender.[42] Further, an agreement to pay an annuity or some other periodical payment will be specifically enforced by the court for, otherwise, a separate action at law would be required in respect of each payment. The position was succinctly stated by Lord Upjohn in *Beswick* v. *Beswick*[43]:

"But when the money payment is not made once and for all but in the nature of an annuity there is even greater need for equity to come to the assistance of the common law. Equity is to do true justice to enforce the true contract that the parties have made and to prevent the trouble and expense of a multiplicity of actions . . . It is in such common sense and practical ways that equity comes to the aid of the common law and it is sufficiently flexible to meet and satisfy the justice of the case in the many different circumstances that arise from time to time. To sum up this matter: had C repudiated the contract in the lifetime of A the latter would have had a cast iron case for specific performance. Can it make any difference that by the terms of the agreement C is obliged to pay the annuity after A's death to B? Of course not. On the principle I have just stated it is clear that there can be nothing to prevent equity in A's specific performance action making an appropriate decree for specific performance directing payment of the annuity to A but during his life and thereafter to B for her life."[44]

A contract of indemnity requiring the indemnifier to satisfy the debt owed to the creditor will be enforced unless the agreement is to reimburse the debtor after he or she has settled the debt, in which case damages will be an adequate remedy.[45]

The effect of specific performance on the contract

Once the court has awarded specific performance, the terms of the contract, for example as to time of delivery or date of completion, are subject to the directions contained in the order.[46]

---

38. *Cohen* v. *Roche* [1927] 1 KB 169; *Sky Petroleum Ltd* v. *VIP Petroleum Ltd* [1974] 1 WLR 576; *CN Marine Inc* v. *Stena Line A/B, The Times*, 12 June 1982.

39. [1927] 1 KB 649.

40. *Ibid* at 661 (*per* Wright J).

41. *Locabail International Finance Ltd* v. *Agroexport* [1986] 1 WLR 657; *Loan Investment Corporation of Australasia Pty Ltd* v. *Bonner* [1970] NZLR 724.

42. *Rogers* v. *Challis* (1859) 27 Beav 175; *Western Wagon & Property Co* v. *West* [1892] 1 Ch 271.

43. [1968] AC 58. See also, *Keenan* v. *Handley* (1864) 2 De GJ & Sm 283.

44. *Ibid* at 97–98. In *Swift* v. *Swift* (1841) 3 Ir Eq R 267 the court ordered specific performance of an annuity of £40.00 pa. Lord Plunket LC said at 276–77: " . . . leaving the plaintiff to proceed at law and to get damages at once for all the breaches that might occur during the joint lives of her and the defendant, would, in effect, be altering the entire nature of the contract that she entered into: it would be compelling her to accept a certain sum, a sum to be ascertained by conjecture of a jury as to what was the value of the annuity. This would be most unreasonable and unjust . . . " See also, *Adderley* v. *Dixon* (1824) 1 Sim & St 607 at 611.

45. *McIntosh* v. *Dalwood (No 4)* (1930) 30 SR (NSW) 415 at 418.

46. *Singh* v. *Nazeer* [1979] Ch 474; see also [1980] 96 LQR 403.

INJUNCTIONS

An alternative means for enforcing a contract *in specie* is by the court granting an injunction and to this extent there is an overlap with specific performance. Moreover, in proceedings for specific performance, interlocutory and interim injunctions may be granted to restrain the disposal of the subject-matter of the contract before the final hearing. Similarly, such relief may be granted to prevent the removal of property from the court's jurisdiction.[47] The scope of the court's equitable jurisdiction was described by Jessel MR in *Smith* v. *Peters*[48] in the following terms: "I have no hesitation in saying that there is no limit to the practice of the court with regard to interlocutory injunctions so far as they are necessary and reasonable applications ancillary to the due performance of its functions, namely, the administration of justice at the hearing of the cause."[49]

Whereas only positive contractual obligations will be specifically enforced, the appropriate relief for preventing the breach of a *negative* contractual obligation is a prohibitory injunction ordering the defendant to refrain from doing what he has expressly agreed not to do.[50] On the other hand, a mandatory injunction, which is restorative in effect, will require the defendant to take action to remedy what he or she has done in breach of contract. Such relief may be granted even though the contract is one for which specific performance would be refused. Whether or not injunctive relief will be awarded depends upon the fairness of the result as between the parties. In *Charrington* v. *Simons & Co Ltd*[51] the defendant was compelled to remove a road wrongfully constructed by him. Buckley J, considering the basis upon which injunctive relief of this nature would be granted, emphasised that:

"A plaintiff should not, of course, be deprived of relief to which he is justly entitled merely because it will be disadvantageous to the defendant. On the other hand he should not be permitted to insist on a form of relief which will confer no appreciable benefit on himself and will be materially detrimental to the defendant."[52]

Given that mandatory injunctions are, by and large, concerned with restoring the status quo to the extent that the parties are restored to the position that existed before the unlawful act occurred,[53] difficulties surrounding supervision by the court do not generally arise to the same degree as with specific performance. The requirements governing the award of a mandatory injunction received extensive consideration by Lord Upjohn in *Redland Bricks Ltd* v. *Morris*.[54] His Lordship laid down four principles:

"(a) A mandatory injunction can only be granted when the plaintiff shows a very strong probability upon the facts that grave damage will occur to him in the future;
(b) damages must be an insufficient remedy;

47. *Preston* v. *Luck* (1884) 27 Ch D 497.
48. (1875) LR 20 Eq 511.
49. *Ibid* at 513. See also, *Hart* v. *Herwig* (1873) LR 8 Ch 860.
50. *Martin* v. *Nutkin* (1724) 2 P Wms 266; *Clegg* v. *Hands* (1890) 44 Ch D 503. A typical example is where the plaintiff seeks to enforce a restrictive covenant, see, for example, *Manners* v. *Johnson* (1875) 1 Ch D 673; *Achilli* v. *Tovell* [1927] 2 Ch 243.
51. [1970] 1 WLR 725. See also, *Lord Manners* v. *Johnson* (1875) 1 Ch D 673; *Jackson* v. *Normandy Brick Co* [1899] 1 Ch 438; *Shire of Hornby* v. *Dangdale* (1929) 29 SR (NSW) 118; *Kelsen* v. *Imperial Tobacco Co (of Great Britain and Milan) Ltd* [1957] 2 QB 334.
52. *Ibid* at 730.
53. *Kennard* v. *Cory Brothers & Co Ltd* [1922] 1 Ch 265; [1922] 2 Ch 1.
54. [1970] AC 652.

(c) unlike negative injunctions, regard must be paid to (i) whether the defendant behaved wantonly or unreasonably, and (ii) the hardship which would be caused by the grant of an injunction to a defendant who had behaved reasonably but wrongfully; and

(d) if an injunction be granted, it must be worded as to bring the defendant's attention to exactly what it is he is expected to do."[55]

The approach adopted by Lord Upjohn has been criticised as overly "conservative" and timid.[56] The first requirement relating to "grave damage" is patently inaccurate. An obvious example is trespass, such as the wrongful erection of an advertising hoarding, which is actionable *per se* without proof of special damage.[57] Further, in *Hooper* v. *Rogers*[58] Russell LJ stressed that "the degree of probability of future injury is not an absolute standard; what is to be aimed at is justice between the parties, having regard to all the relevant circumstances".[59] The third requirement relating to hardship is a ground for refusing the award of a prohibitory injunction.

THE EFFECT OF THE PLAINTIFF'S DELAY: VIGILANTIBUS, NON DORMIENTIBUS, AEQUITAS SUBVENIT

The Limitation Act 1980, s 36(1) provides that the time periods under ss 2, 4A, 5, 7, 8, 9 and 24 "shall not apply to any claim for specific performance of a contract or for an injunction or for other equitable relief ... " While actions at law are in general governed by the statutory limitation periods, equity developed its own doctrines of acquiescence and laches which are expressly preserved by s 36(2) as grounds for refusing relief.[60] Thus, "equity comes to the aid of the vigilant, not the sleepy". Accordingly, a party seeking equitable relief must act with due diligence and promptitude since delay in instituting proceedings "may furnish a defence in equity to an equitable claim".[61] The different meanings attributed to the term "acquiescence" have been discussed in Chapter 3, and were considered by Sir Samuel Griffith in *Cashman* v. *7 North Golden Gate Gold Mining Co*[62] where he stated:

"The term acquiescence is not a term of art. It was used in courts of equity as a term to characterize a defence which may be set up by a person against whom another makes a claim for equitable relief. It is a well known doctrine of equity that when a person claiming equitable relief has lain by for a long time and so conducted himself that it would be inequitable to permit him to complain of the defendant's actions, the court will refuse to grant the relief. The term also bears another meaning. It may be fairly applied to a man who, seeing an act about to be done to his prejudice, stands by and does not object to it. He may be very properly said to be acquiescing in that act being done. But the difference in point of law in the legal consequences of the two kinds of acquiescence is quite clear. A man who stands by and sees an act about to be done which will be injurious to himself, and makes no objection, cannot complain of that act as a wrong at all. He never has any right of action, because he stands by and allows the act to be done. Acquiescence in the other sense is a defence to an action

55. *Ibid* at 652.

56. Meagher, Gummow, Lehane, *op cit* at para 2196. Cf the approach of the Court of Appeal in *Acrow (Automation) Ltd* v. *Rex Chainbelt Inc* [1971] 1 WLR 1676.

57. *Kelsen* v. *Imperial Tobacco Co (of Great Britain and Ireland) Ltd, supra,* fn 51.

58. [1975] Ch 43.

59. *Ibid* at 50.

60. Discussed in Ch 3, *supra*. See, for example, *Lamshed* v. *Lamshed* (1963) 109 CLR 440.

61. *Re Sharpe* [1892] 1 Ch 154 at 168; *Ketley* v. *Gooden* (1977) 73 P & CR 305, CA. See also, the speech of Lord Selborne LC in *Lindsay Petroleum Co* v. *Hurd* (1874) LR 5 PC 221 at 239–40 and the judgment of Laddie J in *Nelson* v. *Rye* [1996] 2 All ER 186 *supra*, Ch 3.

62. (1897) 7 QLJ 152. See also, *Glasson* v. *Fuller* [1922] SASR 148.

for specific relief, on the ground that the plaintiff cannot be reinstated in his original position without doing injustice to the defendant, but it is not an answer to a cause of action already accrued."[63]

As has been seen, typically laches is available as a defence whenever it would be unjust to grant equitable relief to the plaintiff.[64] This arises where, for example, the defendant is prejudiced by the plaintiff's delay because of the effects of time upon the evidence which the defendant would wish to adduce[65]; or where the defendant incurs liability to a third party.[66] The prejudice suffered by the defendant must amount to more than mere inconvenience. Thus in *Lindsay Petroleum Co* v. *Hurd*[67] Lord Selborne observed that: "The situation of the parties having, therefore, in no substantial way been altered, either by the delay or by anything done during the interval, there is in these circumstances nothing to give special importance to the defence founded on time."[68]

Section 36(1) of the Act expressly recognises and preserves the notion of equity applying the statutory limitation period to equitable remedies "by analogy" as was the practice of the courts before the Limitation Act 1939: "the Statute does not absolutely bind Courts of Equity, but they adopt it as a rule to assist their discretion."[69] The doctrine was developed to prevent plaintiffs disguising their claims under the cloak of equity in order to bypass a statutory limitation period. To this end, it is underpinned by the maxim that "equity follows the law". Thus a plaintiff whose claim at law has been time barred will not generally be able to obtain specific performance.[70] However, as has been seen, the doctrine of analogy is not applied in cases involving fraud.[71] The nature of the doctrine was examined by Lord Camden in *Smith* v. *Clay*,[72] who observed:

"A Court of equity which is ever active in relief against conscience . . . has always refused its aid to stale demands, where the party has slept upon his right and acquiesced for a great length of time . . . *Expedit reipublicae ut sit finis litium,* is a maxim that has prevailed in this court in all times, without the help of an act of parliament. But, as the court has no legislative authority, it could not properly define the time bar, by a positive rule, to an hour, a minute, or a year; it was governed by circumstances. But as often as parliament had limited the time of actions and remedies, to a certain period, in legal proceedings, the Court of Chancery adopted that rule, and applied it to similar cases in equity. For when the legislature had fixed a time at law, it would have been preposterous for equity (which, by its own proper authority, always maintained a limitation) to countenance laches beyond the period, that law had been confined to by parliament."[73]

In essence then, the courts strive to harmonise equitable rules and legal rules through the vehicle of analogy subject to the proviso that the doctrine will not be enforced where it would be inequitable to do so, as in the case of a charity.[74]

---

63. *Ibid* at 153–54.
64. *Lindsay Petroleum Co* v. *Hurd* (1874) LR 5 PC 221.
65. For example, witnesses may perish, *per* Lord Halsbury LC in *Watt* v. *Assets Co* [1905] AC 317 at 329.
66. *Lamshed* v. *Lamshed, supra,* fn 60.
67. (1874) LR 5 PC 221.
68. *Ibid* at 240.
69. *Brooksbank* v. *Smith* (1836) 2 Y & C Ex 58 at 60, *per* Alderson B. See also, *Knox* v. *Gye* (1872) LR 5 HL 656, *supra*, Ch 3; *Metropolitan Bank* v. *Heiron* (1880) 5 Ex D 319 and *Re Robinson* [1911] 1 Ch 502. The significance of 1939 is that it was the year of the first major consolidation of limitations since the Statute of Limitations, 1623. See Spry, *op cit* at 409–10.
70. In *Crown* v. *McNeil* (1922) 31 CLR 76 at 100, Isaacs J observed that where a legal right is barred by statute, a court of equity " . . . has no more power to remove or lower that bar than has a court of law".
71. See Ch 3, *supra.*
72. (1767) 3 Bro CC 646n.
73. *Ibid.*
74. See *Magdalen College, Oxford* v. *Attorney-General* (1857) 6 HLC 189.

CHAPTER 17

RESTITUTIONARY CLAIMS FOR BENEFITS RECEIVED[1]

COMMON LAW OR EQUITY AS THE BASIS FOR RULES ON LIMITATION OF ACTIONS?

It is noticeable from the outset that the Limitation Act 1980 makes specific provision for limitation periods in contract actions and those which sound in tort, but that there is no specific provision for restitutionary claims. Instead, claims based on the reversal of an unjust enrichment have to be slotted in where they will fit. Accordingly, section 5 in respect of actions on a simple contract,[2] section 9 in respect of sums due by virtue of an enactment,[3] section 10 in respect of claims for contribution,[4] section 29 in respect of acknowledgment and part payment of a debt[5] and section 32(1)(c) in respect of mistakes[6] have all been called into play where appropriate in dealing with the limitation issues raised by restitutionary claims. Moreover, many aspects of a restitutionary claim raise the issue of proprietary remedies, with the result that the provisions of section 15 regarding actions for the recovery of land[7] and section 21 in respect of actions concerning trust property[8] may also provide guidance on the appropriate limitation period.

The major difficulty raised by the failure of Parliament to make express reference to the matter of limitation of actions in the case of restitutionary claims is that it is not entirely clear which direction should be taken. It is necessary to point out that the law of restitution consists of an amalgam of common law and equitable rules and as a result, it is possible that the applicable rules on limitation could have either a common law or an equitable flavour. It has been seen already that the Limitation Act 1980 section 36 specifies that the majority of limitation periods listed in the Act have no application to claims for equitable relief[9] and that, as a general rule, equitable principles of limitation of actions based on the doctrine of laches tend to be rather more flexible, but provide less certainty. Arguably, so far as the matter of limitation of actions is concerned, it could be said that the common law approach, based upon fixed time limits which run from the date on which the cause

---

1. See McLean, "Limitation of Actions in Restitution" [1989] 48 CLJ 472.
2. See Ch 8.
3. See Ch 25.
4. See Ch 25.
5. See Ch 9.
6. See Ch 6.
7. See Ch 23.
8. See Ch 23.
9. See Ch 3.

of action accrues, is preferable, since rules which limit the time within which an action may be brought ought to set out clearly when an action is in time and when it is not. In contrast, the equitable approach does have the value of being able to cope with the problem of injustice resulting from the strict application of a rigid time limit.

In historical terms, perhaps the most serious difficulty associated with restitutionary claims is the translation of the language of the old forms of action used in the Statute of Limitation 1623[10] to that of contract and tort in the Limitation Act 1939. Unfortunately what appears to have been ignored is that actions in assumpsit encompassed not just claims in contract, but also those which are restitutionary in nature such as an action for money had and received, an action for money paid, actions on a *quantum meruit* and actions on a *quantum valebat*.[11]

Although, generally, there is no specific provision for restitutionary claims, there are sections in the 1980 Act which will apply to certain types of action for a restitutionary remedy. For example, since the provision of a remedy in the event of frustration of a contract is expressly created by the Law Reform (Frustrated Contracts) Act 1943[12] and that remedy involves the payment of a sum of money which would not otherwise have been payable but for the provisions of the 1943 Act, it seems to follow that the remedy in question is one to which the six-year limitation period in the 1980 Act, s 9, will apply.[13]

Further, restitution is possible by way of legal compulsion in cases which fall within the provisions of the Civil Liability (Contribution) Act 1978, where one tortfeasor seeks to recover in respect of some of the liability he has incurred to the plaintiff by virtue of his wrongdoing from another tortfeasor who is also responsible for the same loss or damage. In these circumstances, the action for contribution must be brought within two years of the date on which the person seeking contribution first incurred liability to the plaintiff.[14]

ACCRUAL OF THE CAUSE OF ACTION

It is clear from the scheme of the 1980 Act that the running of time is to be based on the date on which the plaintiff's cause of action accrues. The difficulty in restitutionary claims is to determine when that date should be fixed. In actions in assumpsit the view was that the cause of action accrued at the date of breach of contract, since that was the gist of the action.[15] But this statement overlooks the fact that in a restitutionary claim there may not be a contract in respect of which there can be a breach. Moreover, the real gist of a

10. Under s 3 of that Act, there was a six-year limitation period in respect of all actions on assumpsit which included non-contractual claims such as those now found in the law of restitution.

11. Between these varieties of claim the following types of action would be covered: money paid under a mistake of fact or under duress or in pursuance of a void contract; money paid in consequence of a total failure of consideration; recovery of the reasonable value of goods or services under a contract which fails for want of authority or of certainty or due to a mistake or illegality; goods supplied or services supplied under an unenforceable contract and in certain cases of necessity e.g. salvage cases.

12. Section 1(2) and 1(3). For the purposes of s 1(3) it has been held that the cause of action accrues on the date of frustration of the contract, representing the date of failure of consideration: See *BP (Exploration) Ltd* v. *Hunt (No 2)* [1983] 2 AC 352.

13. See Ch 25.

14. See Ch 25.

15. *Gibbs* v. *Guild* (1881) 8 QBD 296 at 302 *per* Field J, and see Ch 8.

restitutionary claim differs from that in both contract and tort. It should be emphasised that in contract cases the gist of the action is that the defendant has not done that which he promised to do, from which it logically follows that time should run from the date of breach of contract. In most modern tort actions, the gist of the action is damage suffered by the plaintiff for which compensation is sought, with the result that time should run from the date on which damage is caused. Furthermore in the case of actions founded in contract and in tort, the purpose of a judicial remedy is to compensate the plaintiff for the loss or damage suffered as a result of the defendant's breach. However, the focus of a restitutionary claim is somewhat different, in that it is not the loss suffered by the plaintiff which matters, but the unjust enrichment of the defendant at the plaintiff's expense which is the primary focus of the court.

Fortunately, so far as restitutionary claims are concerned, there is no statutory definition of "accrual of the cause of action" and accordingly everything will turn on common law principles. It follows from this that there should be no difficulty in establishing the common law position in relation to accrual, since there are no awkward statutory provisions, based on a failure to appreciate the existence of restitutionary claims, into which claims based on unjust enrichment must be fitted.

Since the key factor in a restitutionary claim is the unjust enrichment of the defendant, it seems sensible that the appropriate date for the running of time should be the date on which the defendant receives the benefit from the plaintiff. For example in *Maskell* v. *Horner*[16] the plaintiff, a trader at Spitalfields Market, had paid tolls under duress of goods for a period of 12 years before he commenced his action. On the basis that the six-year rule applicable to contract actions also applied to this case, it was considered that no claim could be entertained in respect of those amounts paid more than six years from the date of issue of the writ. In terms of restitutionary theory, the decision seems to be justified, since the payments in respect of which the plaintiff could recover were all within six years of the last relevant receipt of a benefit by the defendant. Moreover, until the defendant has derived a benefit at the plaintiff's expense, it cannot be said that his claim differs from one for unliquidated damages awardable for a breach of contract.

What *Maskell* v. *Horner* does not cast light upon is what the position would have been if the plaintiff had been completely unaware for the first six years that he had been paying a sum of money he was under no duty to pay. In these circumstances, the rules of equity considered elsewhere[17] might take account of the reasons for the plaintiff's delay in bringing proceedings.

What this last problem reveals is that in a restitutionary claim there are two important factors. On the one hand, there must be receipt of a benefit by the defendant, but this merely indicates that there has been an enrichment. The second important factor is that the enrichment must be unjust. It is therefore arguable that for the purposes of a restitutionary claim, time should not start to run against the plaintiff until such time as the unjust factor is known to the plaintiff.

Generally, then, the cause of action in respect of a restitutionary claim for a sum of money will accrue when the benefit is received by the defendant. Thus in the case of a frustrated contract, the benefit is received by the defendant at the date of frustration of the

16. [1915] 3 KB 106.
17. See Ch 3.

contract,[18] and where there is an unpromised future event which fails to materialise, the plaintiff's cause of action will accrue when there is a total failure of consideration.[19]

Complications may arise if the court hearing the action manages to confuse a restitutionary claim with one based on a contractual debt. It has been seen already that a key feature in relation to contractual debts is whether or not there has been a demand for payment.[20] However, if the gist of the action in respect of a restitutionary claim is that there has been an unjust enrichment, then it should follow that the date of unjust receipt of the benefit should mark the beginning of the limitation period.

Unfortunately, there are cases which appear to have made the mistake of regarding the date of the demand for payment as a relevant consideration.[21] Such decisions should be regarded as incorrect in point of principle if restitutionary claims are to be given a proper place in the common law system. In contrast, there are other decisions which have correctly stated that there is no need for a demand,[22] which would seem to be in accordance with a proper understanding of the rules of the law of restitution. Thus it was observed in *Baker* v. *Courage & Co Ltd*[23] that:

"It was said that the cause of action is in the nature of a breach by the payee of a duty to hand over money which *ex aequo et bono* does not belong to him, but belongs to the payor, and that there can be no breach of that duty where the facts which give rise to the duty have not been brought to the payee's attention. It is clear that if that is right the payor might postpone the notification of his discovery and the making of his demand for an unlimited time and yet not have [time] run against him. But I think that the contention is fallacious. It seems to me that the cause of action in this case was complete independently of any notification of the discovery."[24]

THE EFFECT OF ACKNOWLEDGMENT AND PART PAYMENT

It has been seen already that in the case of contractual debts, an acknowledgment of a debt or a part payment of the debt by the defendant may cause time to run again in favour of the plaintiff, by virtue of the provisions of the 1980 Act, s 29(5).[25] However, the principal problem associated with this provision is that it may not apply to non-contractual claims based on a *quantum meruit*. In *Amantilla Ltd* v. *Telefusion Ltd*[26] there was a fortunate concession by counsel to the effect that there was a valid contract, in circumstances in which others might not have made the same concession. As a result of this, it was possible for Judge John Davies QC to express the view that, "A *quantum meruit* claim for 'a reasonable sum' lies in debt *because it is money due under a contract*. It is a liquidated pecuniary claim because 'a reasonable sum' . . . is a sufficiently certain contractual description for its amount to be reasonably ascertainable."[27]

---

18. *BP (Exploration) Ltd* v. *Hunt (No 2)* [1983] 2 AC 352.
19. *Guardian Ocean Cargoes Ltd* v. *Banco de Brasil (No 2)* (1992) *The Times*, 19 March.
20. See Ch 9.
21. See *Freeman* v. *Jeffries* (1869) LR 4 Exch 189.
22. See *Baker* v. *Courage & Co* [1910] 1 KB 56.
23. *Ibid*.
24. *Ibid* at 65 *per* Hamilton J.
25. See Ch 9.
26. (1987) Con LR 139.
27. *Ibid* at 145. Emphasis added.

Since there was a concession that there was a valid contract, the conclusion arrived at does no harm at all,[28] but the problem still remains whether the action can really be regarded as "contractual" in cases where there is no valid contract at all. For example in a number of cases there is no contract because of a failure to agree on some essential term or where a letter of intent is issued on the understanding that there will be a future mutual agreement which does not later materialise.[29] In these cases, it seems doubtful whether it would be proper to apply section 5 of the 1980 Act, since from the start, there is no contract between the parties, but there is, nonetheless, a restitutionary claim based on a *quantum meruit*.

In an action for restitution, the key issue is that of unjust enrichment, rather than whether there is or is not a valid contract. Given that this is the case, it seems perfectly proper that section 29(5) should apply so as to start time running afresh in favour of the creditor, since if the debtor has acknowledged the debt either in words or by his actions in paying part of the debt, then this constitutes an admission that there would be an unjust enrichment if he were to seek to claim that the creditor's right to recover the debt was time barred. However, the principal stumbling block in this respect is the use of the phrase "liquidated pecuniary sum" in section 29(5)(a) which may not necessarily cover all restitutionary money claims.

FRAUD AND MISTAKE

Once again, restitutionary claims pose a limitation problem where it is alleged that the cause of action involves an allegation of fraud or that a payment has been made under an operative mistake. It has been seen already that in such circumstances, the running of time is postponed until such time as the plaintiff becomes aware (or should reasonably have become aware) of the fraud on the part of the defendant[30] or becomes aware (or reasonably should have become aware) of the mistake.[31]

In the case of an operative common law mistake, it is clear from the provisions of section 32(1)(c) that time will not start to run against the plaintiff until such time as he is aware, or could with reasonable diligence have become aware of the mistake. However, the position in equity is less clear, since in an action for equitable relief, it is provided that nothing in the Limitation Act 1980 will affect the right of a court to refuse relief on the ground of acquiescence or otherwise.[32] Moreover, the provisions of section 32 are incomplete so far as the whole range of restitutionary claims is concerned. For example, there is a strong argument, based on restitutionary principles, that factors such as economic duress and undue influence should also be taken into account as well as fraud and mistake, so that time should not start to run against the plaintiff until such time as he is in a position to realise that there has been an unjust enrichment at his expense.

---

28. The conclusion is consistent with the provisions of the Sale of Goods Act 1979, s 8(2) which allows a court to set a reasonable price where there is no agreement between the parties on this matter. Similarly, common law rules also allow a similar result, provided there is a valid contract: *Way* v. *Latilla* [1937] 3 All ER 759.

29. See *William Lacey (Hounslow) Ltd* v. *Davis* [1954] 1 QB 428; *British Steel Corporation* v. *Cleveland Bridge & Engineering Co Ltd* [1984] 1 All ER 504.

30. Limitation Act 1980, s 32(1)(a) and see Ch 6.

31. Limitation Act 1980, s 32(1)(c) and see Ch 6.

32. Limitation Act 1980, s 36(2).

PART III

TORT

CHAPTER 18

LIMITATION PERIODS IN TORT ACTIONS: GENERAL PRINCIPLES

The Limitation Act 1980, s 2 provides that:

"An action founded on tort shall not be brought after the expiration of six years from the date on which the cause of action accrued."

The six-year limitation period[1] in tort actions therefore runs from the date of accrual of the cause of action, which requires identification of the gist of the action. When this date arises will depend on the nature of the tort committed by the defendant. Generally a distinction is drawn between torts actionable *per se*, those which require proof of damage and continuing torts.

In the case of torts actionable *per se*, the gist of the action is the commission of the wrong, with the result that there is no need for the plaintiff to show that any damage has been suffered. However, the most important modern torts, namely nuisance and negligence, both require proof of damage, in which case the limitation period will not start to run against the plaintiff until damage has been suffered.

CONTINUING TORTS

Some torts are continuing in nature, in which case a fresh cause of action will accrue from day to day while ever the tort continues to be committed. For example, in *Darley Main Colliery Co* v. *Mitchell*[2] the defendants operated a coal mine in such a way that damage was caused to the plaintiffs' land. In 1868 the plaintiffs sued in respect of damage caused to their land by slippage and received compensation. Subsequently, in 1882, the defendants ceased work on the mine, but there was further subsidence which adversely affected the plaintiffs' land and which was shown to have been caused by the failure of the defendants to leave adequate support in the abandoned mine.

Distinguishing the principle that only one action may be brought in respect of a single cause of action, the House of Lords held that a fresh cause of action accrued from day to day while the tort continued to be committed. Accordingly, while the mine remained in a dangerous condition, further torts continued to be committed with the result that there was a fresh cause of action on the event of the 1882 subsidence due to the continuing failure to provide adequate support after ceasing mining operations.

---

1. A shorter limitation period of three years applies to cases of defamation (Limitation Act 1980, s 4A and see Ch 22) and special rules also apply to cases of latent damage (Limitation Act 1980, s 14A and see Ch 20) and to cases of personal injury (Limitation Act 1980, s 11A and see Ch 19).
2. (1886) 11 App Cas 127.

Where there is a continuing tort, the cause of action accrues on each day the tort is committed, but it remains the case that the plaintiff's action is confined to that part of the wrong committed in the six years prior to the date on which the writ was issued. Thus it has been held that where a person was wrongfully imprisoned for a period of one month and was released on December 14, he could still sue in respect of the imprisonment on the last day of the period of imprisonment where the writ was issued on June 14.[3]

Although nuisance generally requires proof of damage, it is also a continuing tort, since it is based on the fact that the defendant has brought about a state of affairs which unreasonably interferes with the plaintiff's use or enjoyment of his property. Thus it may be possible for the plaintiff to bring successive actions in respect of a single state of affairs while it continues.[4] Given the possibility of a further action being brought in respect of a continuing state of affairs, the practical consequence of this is that a court will not give prospective damages,[5] except where damages are given in lieu of an injunction.[6]

A particular difficulty which may arise in relation to continuing torts is that, as a general rule, the plaintiff's cause of action must exist at the time when proceedings are commenced, otherwise, the plaintiff's action is liable to be struck out under RSC Order 18, rule 19 if it has been commenced prematurely. But it is clear that in the case of continuing torts, damage may continue to be caused during the currency of the proceedings and thereafter, in which case it becomes necessary to distinguish between instances in which the cause of action has not accrued at the time proceedings are commenced and instances in which the cause of action has already accrued but the loss suffered by the plaintiff is of a continuing nature.

In tort actions, this phenomenon of continuing loss is likely to arise in a number of situations. Clearly, the possibility of such loss exists in nuisance cases where the state of affairs alleged to constitute a nuisance is continuing. Similarly, where there is a trespass to land or it is alleged that the plaintiff has been falsely imprisoned, it is possible that the loss suffered by the plaintiff may be regarded as continuing in nature. Likewise, the same problem may arise in relation to a personal injury action based on the defendant's negligence where, at the date of trial and into the future, the plaintiff is unable to work due to his injuries and continues to endure pain and suffering. In each of these cases, the answer to the problem lies in the fact that all these varieties of loss suffered by the plaintiff arise out of the same cause of action, namely the original breach of duty on the part of the defendant.

TORTS ACTIONABLE PER SE

In the case of torts actionable *per se*, the gist of the action is the commission of the wrong which constitutes tortious conduct. Examples of such torts include libel and some varieties of slander, trespass to the person, including the tort of false imprisonment, trespass to land and a wrongful refusal by an innkeeper to provide accommodation to a traveller.[7]

3. *Hardy* v. *Ryle* (1829) 9 B & C 603, based on the provisions of the now repealed Constables Protection Act 1750, s 8, the relevant limitation period for which was a period of six months.
4. *Whitehouse* v. *Fellowes* (1861) 10 CB (NS) 765.
5. *Battishill* v. *Reed* (1856) 18 CB 696.
6. Chancery Procedure Amendment Act 1858 (Lord Cairns's Act), s 2. See now Supreme Court Act 1981, s 50.
7. *Constantine* v. *Imperial Hotels Ltd* [1944] KB 693.

Thus in cases of libel, a new tort is committed on each occasion defamatory material is published. It follows from this that if an action is commenced within three years[8] of the date on which there was a publication, the action will not be time barred, and this remains the case even where the first occasion on which the same defamatory material was published was more than six years before the date on which the writ was issued. Thus the defence of limitation will be defeated if there is evidence that there has been a single publication of the libel within the limitation period.[9] As such, it might appear that libel is also a continuing tort. However, this view is not strictly correct, since between each publication, the tort does not continue to be committed, although it is clear from the rule on repeated publication that a libel can be committed on more than one occasion, since there will be a fresh cause of action on the occurrence of each new publication of the defamatory statement.

Where the defendant is guilty of slander, the commencement of the limitation period will depend on whether the slanderous statement is actionable *per se* or whether it is actionable only on proof of damage. In the case of the majority of slanderous remarks, damage will have to be proved and time will only run from the date on which damage was caused to the plaintiff, but there are a limited number of instances in which slander is actionable *per se*, in which case time will start to run against the plaintiff from the date of publication. These limited number of cases include untrue allegations to the effect that the plaintiff has committed a criminal offence punishable by imprisonment in the first instance, untrue allegations of unchastity on the part of a woman,[10] untrue allegations that the plaintiff suffers from a communicable disease and untrue allegations that a person is unfit to pursue a profession.

False imprisonment is also a tort actionable *per se*[11] with the result that the cause of action will accrue on the date on which the plaintiff is intentionally, and without lawful excuse, deprived of his freedom of movement. In *Violett* v. *Symson*[12] the defendant maliciously opposed the plaintiff's discharge from custody, with the result that the plaintiff's period of imprisonment was prolonged. For the purposes of limitation of actions, it was considered that time should run against the plaintiff as from the date of the defendant's malicious intervention, rather than from the date on which the plaintiff was released from custody, since the reason for the detention of the plaintiff was the act of the court rather than the act of the defendant. However, it is clear that false imprisonment can also be a continuing tort while ever the imprisonment is the direct consequence of the defendant's act with the result that there is a fresh cause of action in respect of each day the false imprisonment continues.

As with other forms of trespass, a trespass to land is also actionable *per se* with the result that regard must be had to the date on which the wrong was committed by the defendant. For these purposes, the tort is one which is committed against the person in possession of the land.[13] It follows from this that a person who has an interest in the land but who is not in possession, such as a reversioner, will be required to prove that damage

---

8. Limitation Act 1980, s 4A (inserted by the Administration of Justice Act 1985, s 57). This comparatively short limitation period is subject to discretionary extension under the Limitation Act 1980, s 32A.

9. *Duke of Brunswick* v. *Harmer* (1849) 14 QB 185.

10. Slander of Women Act 1891.

11. *Coventry* v. *Aspley* (1691) 2 Salk 420; *Bailey* v. *Warden* (1815) 4 M & S 400.

12. (1857) 8 El & Bl 344.

13. *Wordsworth* v. *Harley* (1830) 1 B & Ad 391.

has been suffered, since the trespass will not be actionable, given the absence of a possessory interest. Thus in *Wordsworth* v. *Harley*[14] a surveyor of highways removed a fence, dug soil and erected a wall on land in respect of which the plaintiff was the reversioner. Since the reversioner was not in possession of the land, his action was held to have been time barred since the writ was issued outside the three-month period of limitation which ran from the date on which the wall was erected. However, for the purposes of the party in possession of the land, the trespass would have continued from day to day while ever the wall remained on the land, in which case, the action for trespass would have been successful while the wall remained in place. The reason for this appears to be that the person who commits trespass is under a continuing obligation to remove the offending object and is in breach of that obligation until removal takes place.[15] Thus in *Holmes* v. *Wilson*[16] the defendants, who were trustees of a turnpike road, built buttresses to support the road which resulted in a trespass to the plaintiff's land. The plaintiff accepted money paid into court by the defendants, but subsequently sued once more since the buttresses had not been removed. It was held that the fact of acceptance of the money paid into court could not be regarded as full and final settlement of the plaintiff's claim, since a new cause of action arose on each day the trespass continued.

It is important to distinguish between a continuing trespass and the consequences of a trespass, since the latter must be compensated on a once-and-for-all basis. For example, if the defendant digs a hole in the plaintiff's land, there is a trespass but no continuing presence of some unwanted article on the plaintiff's land, in which case the trespass will not be regarded as continuing from day to day.[17]

SINGLE-ACT TORTS DEPENDENT ON PROOF OF DAMAGE

It has been seen above that the general rule for the purposes of a tort action is that it must be commenced within six years of the date on which the cause of action accrued. For these purposes, it has been said that before a cause of action can be said to have accrued there must be available "every fact which it would be necessary for the plaintiff to prove, if traversed, in order to support his right to the judgment of the Court".[18] More specifically, this means that:

"the plaintiff in order to make out a course of action must assert certain facts, which if traversed, he would be put to prove. It is well known, of course, that any of those facts which is not traversed is taken to be admitted. The words 'if traversed' were inserted to make it clear that the facts spoken of were those which the plaintiff must allege in his statement of claim . . ."[19]

In other cases, a test, apparently more favourable to plaintiffs, has been suggested. For example, in *Board of Trade* v. *Cayzer, Irvine & Co Ltd*[20] Lord Dunedin spoke of a cause

---

14. *Ibid.* The action of trespass *quare clausum fregit* was not available with the result that the action had to be brought in case.
15. *Thompson* v. *Gibson* (1841) 7 M & W 456; *Konskier* v. *Goodman* [1928] 1 KB 421.
16. (1839) 10 A & E 503. See also *Toronto General Trust Corp* v. *Roman* (1962) 37 DLR (2d) 16.
17. *Spoor* v. *Green* (1874) LR 9 Ex 99.
18. *Read* v. *Brown* (1888) 22 QBD 128 at 131 *per* Lord Esher MR, cited with approval in *Coburn* v. *Colledge* [1897] 1 QB 702 at 706 *per* Lord Esher MR.
19. *Ibid* at 707 *per* Lord Esher MR.
20. [1927] AC 610.

of action consisting of that which makes action possible.[21] Taken in isolation, this might support an argument to the effect that if the grounds for action are unknown to the plaintiff, the cause of action is incomplete. However, the more conventional view appears to be to the contrary. Thus it was observed in *Williams* v. *Milotin*[22] that:

"When you speak of a cause of action you mean the essential ingredients in the title to the right which it is proposed to enforce. The essential ingredients in an action of negligence for personal injuries include the special or particular damage—it is the gist of the action—and the want of due care."[23]

It follows from this that where it is alleged by the plaintiff that the defendant has committed a single-act tort which is dependent on proof of damage, it becomes necessary to ascertain the precise date on which the earliest damage has been suffered by the plaintiff. This may not be easy given the wide variety of different types of damage which may flow from a single act. For example, where the defendant is guilty of slander actionable on proof of damage, there is harm to the plaintiff's reputation which may also, coincidentally, cause economic loss. In the case of alleged negligence on the part of the defendant, the result may be that the plaintiff suffers personal injury, property damage or pure economic loss. Similarly, the range of possible damage suffered by the plaintiff in a nuisance action may include harm to property, occasionally personal injury and sometimes economic loss.

Determining when damage has actually been suffered in each of these cases may be difficult, especially in cases where the harm suffered by the plaintiff initially remains hidden. In these circumstances time may have started to run against the plaintiff before he realises that he has suffered actionable damage.

The most problematic issue has been to determine when damage occurs for the purposes of the tort of negligence. This tort requires proof that a duty of care is owed by the defendant to the plaintiff; that there has been a breach of that duty and that the breach has resulted in the plaintiff suffering reasonably foreseeable damage. In determining when time should start to run against the plaintiff, two main tests have been applied. In the first instance, there is a test based upon the date on which the plaintiff suffers more than minimal damage as a result of the defendant's breach of duty[24] which does not have regard for the fact that the plaintiff may be unaware of the fact of damage. Secondly, there is an alternative test based upon the date when the plaintiff discovered, or with the exercise of reasonable diligence could have discovered that actionable damage has been suffered.[25] The first of these tests is clearly more favourable to defendants and has the advantage of certainty, but can also produce the apparently unfair result that a plaintiff is time barred before he is aware that any harm has been suffered. The second of these tests, while disposing of the element of unfairness to the plaintiff, raises a number of policy issues concerning the desirability of open-ended liability on the part of defendants and their insurers in cases where harm suffered by the plaintiff remains hidden and undiscovered for a number of years.

21. *Ibid* at 617.
22. (1957) 97 CLR 465.
23. *Ibid* at 474.
24. *Cartledge* v. *E Jopling & Sons Ltd* [1963] AC 758.
25. *Dutton* v. *Bognor Regis UDC* [1972] 1 QB 373; *Sparham-Souter* v. *Town & Country Developments Ltd* [1976] QB 858.

It was noted by the Law Reform Committee[26] that the ideal *terminus ad quo* would be an event which satisfied three conditions, namely:

"(a) it would be sufficiently near in time to the incidents giving rise to the claim to ensure that proceedings were instituted before the relevant evidence became either unobtainable or too stale to be reliable;

(b) it would be unmistakable and readily ascertainable;

(c) its occurrence would necessarily become known forthwith to the plaintiff."[27]

However, it was admitted by the Law Reform Committee that no one event could fulfil all three criteria at the same time. For example, where there is alleged negligence on the part of a builder who erects a structure on defective foundations which move some years later and after a period of delay result in cracking to the walls of the building, it has been suggested that there are eight possible dates or events which could be said to trigger the running of time.[28] In order, these are:

(1) the date on which the owner relied on a representation by the builder that the works would be properly erected;

(2) the date on which the first or last act of negligence in relation to the building was committed;

(3) the date on which the building was completed;

(4) the date on which any significant damage occurred;

(5) the date on which the owner, acting with reasonable diligence, could have discovered that damage had been suffered;

(6) the date on which the damage was actually discovered;

(7) the date on which the owner, acting with reasonable diligence, ought to have realised that damage was serious and that the fault lay with the builder and

(8) the date on which the owner actually realised that the damage was serious and that it was the fault of the builder.

Although negligent builder cases are capable of producing the largest number of possible variants for the purposes of the choice of an appropriate date for the running of time, similar problems may be identified in other areas. For example where the alleged negligence consists of the giving of negligent advice, time could run from the date on which the advice is given, or the date on which the advice was relied upon or acted upon, the date on which damage resulted or the date on which the recipient of the advice realised that damage had been suffered.

NEGLIGENCE AND THE COMPETING TESTS
FOR THE RUNNING OF TIME

It has been observed above that two competing tests were developed which indicated the time from which the limitation period would start to run in negligence actions. In *Cartledge* v. *E Jopling & Sons Ltd*[29] the plaintiff suffered personal injuries as a result of

26. *Final Report on Limitation of Actions,* Cmnd 6923, 1977.
27. *Ibid,* para. 2.1.
28. See Merkin, *Richards Butler on Latent Damage,* Lloyd's of London Press, 1987, pp 13–14.
29. [1963] AC 758.

the negligence of his employer, the defendant, in allowing the plaintiff and other steel dressers to work in dusty conditions which led them to suffer from pneumoconiosis, a lung disease which progressed very slowly, causing substantial injury before it would have been possible for the plaintiff to have discovered the extent of damage. Writs were issued in October 1956, but the House of Lords decided that damage suffered by the plaintiff must have occurred before October 1950, with the result that the action was out of time. The relevant test adopted for these purposes was based on the date on which damage was caused and that it was not relevant to consider on what date the plaintiff could reasonably have discovered the fact of damage. There was considered to be nothing in the then applicable Statute of Limitation to prevent a cause of action from accruing at a time when the plaintiff remained unaware of the facts which gave rise to that cause of action.[30] That this was the conclusion the House of Lords was forced to arrive at was a matter of some regret and some distaste. As Lord Reid observed:

"It appears to me to be unreasonable and unjustifiable in principle that a cause of action should be held to accrue before it is possible to discover any injury and, therefore, before it is possible to raise any action. If this were a matter governed by the common law, I would hold that a cause of action cannot accrue until either the injured person has discovered the injury or it would be possible for him to discover it if he took such steps as were reasonable in the circumstances. The common law ought never to produce a wholly unreasonable result."[31]

Subsequently, the effect of the decision in *Cartledge* v. *Jopling* was reversed for the purposes of actions in respect of personal injuries when the provisions of the Limitation Act 1963 (as amended)[32] eventually introduced a test based on reasonable discoverability and a shortened limitation period of three years. What remained unclear was whether different rules applied also to types of damage other than personal injury, since there were cases which continued to apply a discoverability test to latent damage suffered by a building owner in the event of negligent construction on the part of the builder in the absence of any express statutory provision sanctioning the use of such a test.[33]

The matter came for consideration later in the House of Lords in *Pirelli General Cable Works* v. *Oscar Faber & Partners*[34] in which the assumed facts were that the defendants, a firm of consulting engineers, had negligently prepared a building design which recommended the use of a material called Lytag to line the chimneys of the building. This material proved to be unfit for the purpose which the building owner had in mind, thereby occasioning what was, in truth, pure economic loss in the form of diminution in the value of the building. The building work had been completed in 1969 and no later than April 1970 cracks appeared in the chimneys, but these cracks did not become reasonably discoverable until October 1972 and were not, in fact, discovered by the owners until November 1977, a writ being issued in October 1978. In the House of Lords, it became necessary to determine on what date the plaintiffs' cause of action accrued, which, for present purposes, was considered to be the date on which the cracks in the chimneys first

30. *Ibid* at 784 *per* Lord Pearce.
31. *Ibid* at 772.
32. The original provisions of the 1963 Act required the plaintiff to commence his action within 12 months of discovering the injury. This 12-month period was subsequently extended to one of three years by the Law Reform (Miscellaneous Provisions) Act 1971, s 1(1).
33. See *Dutton* v. *Bognor Regis UDC* [1972] 1 QB 373; *Sparham-Souter* v. *Town & Country Developments* [1976] QB 858 (overruled by the decision in *Pirelli*).
34. [1983] 2 AC 1.

appeared. As in *Cartledge* v. *E Jopling & Sons Ltd*, the date on which the damage could have been discovered with the exercise of reasonable diligence was ignored. Accordingly, the cause of action in favour of the plaintiffs had accrued well before the earliest date on which they could have been aware of that damage, with the result that their action was commenced out of time. What seemed to underlie the reasoning of Lord Fraser[35] was that the date of discovery of significant damage could not affect the question of accrual of the cause of action, since discovery of the damage might depend on matters which are unconnected with the nature and extent of any damage suffered by the plaintiff. Moreover, other possible dates for the commencement of the limitation period were also rejected. In particular, Lord Fraser opined that the date of reliance on the defendants' advice and the date of completion of the building works, since on each of these occasions it was quite possible that the plaintiffs would not have suffered any damage at all.

Just as *Cartledge* v. *E Jopling & Sons Ltd* prompted swift legislative action in relation to personal injury cases, so also did the decision of the House of Lords in *Pirelli General Cable Works* v. *Oscar Faber & Partners*. By 1986, the matter had been referred to the Law Reform Committee[36] who recommended that latent damage cases, other than those involving personal injuries, should be subject to a reasonable discoverability test and a shortened limitation period of three years, effected by the Latent Damage Act 1986.[37]

The difficulty presented by the date of damage test adopted in both *Cartledge* and *Pirelli* is that it may be criticised on the grounds of both illogicality and uncertainty. The test may be said to be illogical since it can result in there being several different dates on which time may begin to run against a plaintiff arising out of the same set of facts. For example, where a builder negligently erects a structure under the terms of a contract made with the future building owner, time will run for the purposes of a common law negligence action from the date on which damage is suffered by the owner, which in the case of latent damage is likely to occur some time after the negligent act. But on the same facts, there is also a possible action for breach of contract which will run from the date of the breach of contract, namely the date of the builder's negligent act. At the same time, the owner will also have an action for breach of the statutory duty created by the Defective Premises Act 1972, in respect of which time runs from the date of completion of the dwelling.[38] A possible answer to this problem of multiplicity of starting dates for the purposes of the running of time would be to have a single starting date for all causes of action arising out of the same set of events.

The second criticism of the date of damage test is that it is capable of creating uncertainty—a criticism also levelled at the discoverability test. So far as the date of damage test is concerned, it will be seen below that it is often difficult to determine with any degree of certainty when damage has actually been suffered by the plaintiff. Very often, to determine when damage has been suffered, detailed reliance on the views of experts will be necessary, and it will not always be the case that the experts called by each of the parties will have a common view of the matter under consideration. Although the discoverability test may also be said to introduce the uncertainty that litigation may be commenced many years after the events to which it relates, the starting date for the purposes

---

35. With whom Lords Bridge, Brandon and Templeman concurred without passing comment.
36. *24th Report,* Cmnd 9390, 1986.
37. Now consolidated in the Limitation Act 1980, ss 14A and 14B.
38. Defective Premises Act 1972, s 1(5) and see also Ch 24.

of the running of time occurs on a date which can be ascertained with a greater degree of certainty than that which applies where the date of damage test is employed.

THE MEANING OF DAMAGE

The principal difficulties associated with the concept of damage for the purposes of the tort of negligence, in particular, are twofold. In the first place, past cases have been less than clear in distinguishing between damage to property and merely defective property. Secondly, there have been problems concerning the types of damage properly recoverable in an action for negligence.

The first of these questions also impinges on the second in that where property is merely defective, the kind of harm suffered by, for example, a building owner in a negligent construction case is more accurately categorised as economic loss, since the owner's complaint is that the building constructed for him is less valuable than the building he expected to be constructed for him since the defects in the property have to be remedied in order for his expectations of value to be realised. Viewed in this way, the problem of merely defective property raises an important policy issue as to the proper functioning of the law of tort and the law of contract, since economic loss in the form of a decrease in value of a thing contracted for is a type of loss which might be said to fall better into the province of contract law since it is a loss associated with absence of value for money.

(a) Burden of proof

Where the defendant pleads limitation and in so doing asserts that damage was suffered by the plaintiff outside the relevant period of limitation, the onus of proof falls on the plaintiff to show, on a balance of probability, that relevant damage did occur within the limitation period and that the writ has been served in time.

Where the date of damage test is applied and it is not immediately obvious when damage did occur, the incidence of the burden of proof will be a particularly important matter, since if the person required to plead and aver a particular issue is unable to call the proof necessary in support, he is destined to fail.

Where experts are called on either side and there is sufficient professional doubt as to what is the correct position, the party who bears the burden of proof is in a comparatively weak position, since all the other party has to do is to raise sufficient doubts in the mind of the court as to when damage did occur that it cannot be said one way or the other whether damage occurred on the particular date alleged by the plaintiff or not. In *Cartledge* v. *E Jopling & Sons Ltd*[39] Lord Pearce, approving the view expressed in the Court of Appeal in the same case, stated:

"When the defendant raises the Statute of Limitations the initial onus is on the plaintiff to prove that his cause of action accrued within the statutory period. When, however, a plaintiff has proved an accrual of damage within the six years . . . the burden passes to the defendants to show that the

39. [1963] AC 758.

apparent accrual of a cause of action is misleading and that in reality the cause of action accrued at an earlier date."[40]

In subsequent cases,[41] this view has been interpreted, in favour of plaintiffs, to mean that the plaintiff must demonstrate that he has suffered damage at any time within the six-year period prior to the issue of the writ and that, once this burden has been satisfied, it then falls upon the defendant to show that the damage complained of occurred at some time before the six years immediately preceding the date on which the writ was issued. On this basis, it is for the defendant to make out his limitation defence rather than for the plaintiff to refute it. This position was justified in *London Congregational Union Incorporated* v. *Harriss & Harriss (a firm)*[42] on the basis that the common law does not recognise limitation periods. According to Judge John Newey QC:

"It is for the plaintiffs to prove their case, but at common law there was no such thing as a limitation period and, therefore, initially the plaintiffs do not have to prove that their cause of action accrued after any particular date. The Limitation Acts have, perfectly properly, been raised by the defendants. They are putting forward a positive case that the plaintiff's action is statute-barred and, although I know of no authority . . . I think it must follow that the burden of proof is on them. When I am left . . . in the situation where I am uncertain whether the damp could have reached the plaster before the crucial date for limitation purposes, or whether it was afterwards, I think it must follow that the defendants have not discharged the legal burden."[43]

However, convincing as Judge John Newey QC's reasoning was, the Court of Appeal chose to reverse the earlier decision, expressly on the ground of a misdirection as to the incidence of the burden of proof. What appeared to support the view taken by the Court of Appeal was that the plaintiffs had not called any evidence to show that damage occurred on a specific date which fell within the limitation period, applying the tacit acceptance by Lord Pearce of the correctness of the view expressed in the Court of Appeal in *Cartledge* v. *E Jopling & Sons* that it is for the plaintiff to prove that their cause of action accrued within the limitation period.

According to Ralph Gibson LJ:

"Counsel for the plaintiffs argued that he had proved 'an accrual of damage' within the six year period . . . by proving the existence of damage within that period and that, on tendering that proof, the burden passed to the defendants 'to show that the apparent accrual of a cause of action is misleading and that in reality the cause of action accrued at an earlier date'. I cannot accept this contention. It confuses the existence, or continued existence, of damage or its consequences with accrual of damage, which is the coming into existence of damage. In my judgment, the burden on a plaintiff is to show that, on a balance of probabilities, his cause of action accrued, i.e. came into existence, on a day within the period of limitation. If he shows that, then the evidential burden would, as stated by Lord Pearce, pass to the defendant to show, if they can, that the apparent accrual of the plaintiff's cause of action was misleading etc."[44]

Accordingly, it cannot be assumed that because damage is proved to have existed at a certain date within the limitation period, it also follows that it accrued within the limitation

---

40. *Ibid* at 784.

41. *London Congregational Union Incorporated* v. *Harriss & Harriss* [1985] 1 All ER 335; *EDAC* v. *William Moss Group* (1985) 2 Con LR 1; *Perry* v. *Tendring DC* (1985) 3 Con LR 74.

42. *Ibid*.

43. *Ibid* at 343.

44. *London Congregational Union Incorporated* v. *Harriss & Harriss* [1988] 1 All ER 15 at 30. See also Sir Denys Buckley at 34 and O'Connor LJ at 37.

period and the onus falls on the plaintiff to call evidence in support of his contention that his action is not time barred.

(b) Diminished value and damaged property distinguished

The basic proposition in *Pirelli General Cable Works* v. *Oscar Faber & Partners* is that a cause of action, for the purposes of the law of tort, accrues when damage is suffered by the plaintiff. However, the mere fact that property proves to be defective does not mean that there has been damage to property in the traditional sense. Generally, in the context of a product liability claim[45] there is a distinction drawn between a defective product which damages other property owned by the plaintiff and damage to the defective product itself. For example, suppose that X purchases a television manufactured by Y from retailer Z and subsequently, due to defective design, the television explodes, causing damage to the consumer's lounge windows. Such damage may be properly regarded as "property damage" in the traditional sense, in that it is damage to property which was fundamentally sound prior to the accident, and subject to defences, X may proceed against Y under the Consumer Protection Act 1987, Part I or, in the event of proof of fault, under the rule in *Donoghue* v. *Stevenson*.[46] Alternatively, there will also be an action in favour of X (assuming he is the purchaser) against Z under the Sale of Goods Act 1979.[47] But there is the further question whether the defectiveness of the television itself may give rise to a valid claim, in tort, in favour of the purchaser. Such damage is generally regarded as not being the province of the law of tort since what the consumer has complained of is that the television is not worth the amount paid for it and that there is no "physical damage" within the normal understanding of the law of tort. Such damage is readily actionable under the Sale of Goods Act 1979, or other applicable legislation, on the basis that there has been a breach of the implied terms as to satisfactory quality or fitness for purpose, but problems may arise where a contractual claim has been compromised, where there is an enforceable exemption clause which protects the contractual supplier or where the contractual supplier has become insolvent.

The law in this area has become somewhat blurred in relation to defective buildings, despite the fact that a building is little more than a large (and expensive) product. Two particular problems have arisen in the past. In the first place, it is possible that defects due to negligent design, construction or surveying may result in damage to a building. The particular difficulty in this type of case is that if the negligent engineer, architect, builder or surveyor is considered to be in the same position as the manufacturer of the television in the example above, the damage to the building may be regarded as the result of mere defectiveness, in which case no actionable damage, for the purposes of the law of tort, has been suffered. The second problem thrown up by the building cases is that the loss suffered by the building owner may be regarded as no more than pure economic loss, in which case no duty of care may be owed by the defendant.

45. See further Ch 21.
46. [1932] AC 562.
47. See further Ch 10.

(i) Dutton v. *Bognor Regis UDC, Anns* v. *Merton LBC and the concept of property damage*

Despite the fact that the traditional language of tort law regarded the mere defectiveness of a product or a building as something which was not actionable damage, developments in the 1970s appeared to take tort law into previously uncharted waters. In *Dutton* v. *Bognor Regis UDC*[48] the primary question was whether a local authority could be liable for a negligent inspection of building foundations, but the case is also significant for a subsidiary issue concerning the date of damage. In that case, the local authority had questioned whether public policy would allow an action to be brought against the local authority when the primary limitation period in respect of negligent construction would run from the date on which damage was caused. The authority's argument was that to allow such an action to proceed would expose the authority to the possibility of stale actions based on its original negligent inspection. In response to this argument, the Court of Appeal held that time would run from the date of the negligent act, with the result that the local authority would not face large numbers of stale claims. Moreover, in relation to the kind of damage suffered by the plaintiff, the Court of Appeal was prepared to extend an action for negligence to cover what was no more than mere defectiveness. According to Lord Denning MR:

"[Counsel for the council] submitted that the liability of the council would . . . be limited to those who suffered bodily harm; and did not extend to those who suffered only economic loss . . .

I cannot accept this submission. The damage done here was not solely economic loss. It was physical damage to the house. If Counsel's submission were right, it would mean that, if the inspector negligently passes the house as properly built and it collapses and injures a person, the council are liable; but, if the owner discovers the defect in time to repair it—and he does repair it—the council are not liable. That is an impossible distinction. I would say the same about the manufacturer of an article. If he makes it negligently, with a latent defect (so that it breaks to pieces and injures someone), he is undoubtedly liable. Suppose that the defect is discovered in time to prevent injury. Surely he is liable for the cost of repair . . . "[49]

Subsequently, the reasoning employed by Lord Denning in *Dutton* was approved by the House of Lords in *Anns* v. *Merton LBC*.[50] In *Anns* the plaintiff was the occupant of a flat in a block of flats built on foundations which did not comply with building regulations. The defendant local authority, as in *Dutton*, had failed to carry out their inspection powers with the required degree of care and skill, with the result that the plaintiff's flat suffered damage. In holding that the defendants were liable for the cost of repairing those defects, Lord Wilberforce was careful to qualify the date on which the cause of action accrued in favour of the plaintiff. Unlike *Dutton* where Lord Denning regarded the date of the negligent act as the date from which time would run against the plaintiff, Lord Wilberforce equated the economic loss suffered in *Anns* with physical harm to the plaintiff's property. In his view, the cause of action could only arise when "the state of the building is such that there is a present or imminent danger to the health or safety of persons occupying it".[51]

This gloss on the matter of the running of time could not be said to be without its difficulties, since under Lord Wilberforce's test it would be necessary to identify the

48. [1972] 1 QB 373.
49. *Ibid* at 396.
50. [1978] AC 728.
51. *Ibid* at 760.

precise moment when a present or imminent danger to health or safety first came into existence.[52] The particular problem with this test is that when that present or imminent danger first presents itself, there will not necessarily be any physical damage, as such. Thus in the case of a building, there may be a present or imminent danger, but there may not be any cracking to the walls, at that stage, especially where the building suffers from a serious design fault.[53]

The next apparently significant development was the House of Lords' decision in *Junior Books Ltd* v. *Veitchi Co Ltd*[54] where a tortious duty of care, exceptionally, was held to exist in relation to the negligent performance of a building sub-contract for the installation of a factory floor. Although, as a result of later decisions of the House of Lords, the decision in *Junior Books* has been confined to what are regarded as the unusual facts of the case, it does have the effect of allowing an action in tort for what amounts to no more than a defective product. What this appeared to give rise to was the possibility of an action in the tort of negligence to allow recovery of loss of profit based solely on the defectiveness of the work carried out by the defendant. This contrasted with the traditional approach to tortious actions which required damage to property other than the defective product or building and was distinct from the *Anns* test which required a present or imminent danger to health or safety. What *Junior Books* did not decide was when the limitation period in respect of such an action should commence. The restrictions subsequently placed on the extent to which mere defectiveness is actionable in tort, mean that, for limitation purposes, where the plaintiff complains that the negligence of a builder or manufacturer has resulted in a merely defective product, there is no tortious damage. As a result of this, until there is some actionable physical damage in consequence of the defendant's breach of duty, time will not start to run against the plaintiff.

(ii) The retreat from Anns

Perhaps because of worry as to the possible far-reaching consequences of the decision in *Junior Books*, the late 1980s and early 1990s saw a rapid retreat from the principle in *Anns* and its implications for the running of time in negligence actions. In particular, there were two further visits to the House of Lords, which although not directly concerned with limitation of actions, do have important connotations for the determination of the date on which damage is caused in negligent builder cases.

In *D & F Estates Ltd* v. *Church Commissioners for England*[55] the House of Lords held that where a defect in a building or a product is discovered before it has caused either personal injury or physical damage, the cost of repairing that defect is not recoverable in the tort of negligence against the builder. Instead, such loss is the appropriate province of the law of contract or the province of the statutory tort created by the Defective Premises Act 1972, where it applies.[56] What underlay the decision was that the cost of repairing a defect which has not yet caused personal or physical harm can be regarded as no more than economic loss represented by the diminution in value of the defective building or

---

52. *Murphy* v. *Brentwood DC* [1990] 2 All ER 269 at 296 *per* Nicholls LJ.
53. *Ibid*. See also *Jones* v. *Stroud DC* [1988] 1 All ER 5.
54. [1983] AC 520.
55. [1988] 2 All ER 992.
56. As to which see further Ch 24.

product itself. Neither *Anns* v. *Merton LBC* nor *Junior Books Ltd* v. *Veitchi Co Ltd* was overruled, but neither case was followed.

It followed from the decision in *D & F Estates Ltd* v. *Church Commissioners for England* that, in the absence of a contractual relationship, a builder would owe no duty of care to the building owner in respect of simple diminution in value until such time as physical or personal harm could be shown to have occurred, but there still remained the vexed question of the position of other professionals engaged in the construction process. The decision in *Pirelli General Cable Works* v. *Oscar Faber & Partners*[57] had avoided the central issue in relation to the position of consultant engineers and architects by regarding what was patently economic loss as a variety of physical harm to property. Moreover, the decisions in *Pirelli* and *D & F Estates* did not address the position of local authorities acting under their statutory powers of inspection of building works, which remained covered by the broader principle advanced in *Anns* v. *Merton LBC*.

Subsequently, the decisions in *Anns* and *Dutton* v. *Bognor Regis UDC* were formally overruled by the seven-man decision of the House of Lords in *Murphy* v. *Brentwood DC*.[58] In *Murphy*, the question arose whether a building owner was owed a tortious duty of care by a local authority in respect of dangerous defects which had not been uncovered by the authority exercising its statutory powers of inspection, where those defects had not caused either personal injury or damage to property. The conclusion arrived at by the House of Lords was directly at variance with the decision of the House of Lords in *Anns*, on the issue of common law negligence, with the result that *Anns* was overruled. According to Lord Bridge:

"If a manufacturer negligently puts into circulation a chattel containing a latent defect which renders it dangerous to persons or property, the manufacturer, on the well known principles established by *Donoghue* v. *Stevenson* [1932] AC 562, will be liable in tort for injury to persons or damage to property which the chattel causes. But if a manufacturer produces and sells a chattel which is merely defective in quality, even to the extent that it is valueless for the purpose for which it is intended, the manufacturer's liability at common law arises only under and by reference to the terms of any contract to which he is a party in relation to the chattel; the common law does not impose on him any liability in tort to persons to whom he owes no duty in contract but who, having acquired the chattel, suffer economic loss because the chattel is defective in quality. If a dangerous defect in a chattel is discovered before it causes any personal injury or damage to property, because the danger is now known and the chattel cannot be safely used unless the defect is repaired, the defect becomes merely a defect in quality. The chattel is either capable of repair at economic cost or it is worthless and must be scrapped. In either case the loss sustained by the owner or hirer of the chattel is purely economic. It is recoverable against any party who owes the loser a relevant contractual duty. But it is not recoverable in tort in the absence of a special relationship of proximity imposing on the tortfeasor a duty of care to safeguard the plaintiff from economic loss. There is no such special relationship between the manufacturer of a chattel and a remote owner or hirer.

I believe these principles are equally applicable to buildings. If a builder erects a structure containing a latent defect which renders it dangerous to persons or property, he will be liable in tort for injury to persons or damage to property resulting from that dangerous defect. But, if the defect becomes apparent before any injury or damage has been caused, the loss sustained by the building owner is purely economic. If the defect can be repaired at economic cost, that is the measure of his loss. If the building cannot be repaired, it may have to be abandoned as unfit for occupation and therefore valueless. These economic losses are recoverable if they flow from breach of a relevant contractual duty, but, here again, in the absence of a special relationship of proximity they are not recoverable in tort. The only qualification I would make to this is that, if a building stands so close

57. [1983] 2 AC 1.
58. [1990] 2 All ER 908.

to the boundary of the building owner's land that after discovery of the dangerous defect it remains a potential source of injury to persons or property on neighbouring land or on the highway, the building owner ought, in principle, to be entitled to recover in tort from the negligent builder the cost of obviating the danger, whether by repair or by demolition, so far as that cost is necessarily incurred in order to protect himself from potential liability to third parties.

The fallacy which, in my opinion, vitiates the judgments of Lord Denning MR and Sachs LJ in *Dutton* [1972] 1 QB 373 at 474, 480–481 is that they brush these distinctions aside as of no consequence. Stamp LJ, on the other hand, fully understood and appreciated them and his statement of the applicable principles as between the building owner and the builder seems to me unexceptionable (see [1972] 1 QB 373 at 414). He rested his decision in favour of the plaintiff against the local authority on a wholly distinct principle which will require separate examination."[59]

The importance of these principles for the purposes of limitation of actions is that while *Murphy* is not concerned directly with the limitation issue, the decision does restrict the plaintiff's remedies in a significant way. One response to the decision in *Pirelli General Cable Works* v. *Oscar Faber & Partners* was the referral of the issue of latent damage to the Law Reform Committee whose *Twenty-Fourth Report*[60] resulted in the provisions of the Latent Damage Act 1986, which, in addition to the normal limitation period based upon the date of damage, introduced an alternative period based upon reasonable discoverability.[61] However, the effect of *Murphy* is to place much of what can be regarded as latent damage outside of the field of recovery, thereby imposing an important limitation on the extent to which latent damage is actionable at all under the tort of negligence. Following the principles established in *Murphy* economic loss is actionable in negligence only where there is a sufficiently close relationship of proximity between the parties, with the result that the majority of such cases will probably fall within the principles established in *Hedley Byrne & Co Ltd* v. *Heller & Partners Ltd*[62] which relate, predominantly, to negligent advice and misstatements rather than to negligent acts. Since *Junior Books Ltd* v. *Veitchi Co Ltd*[63] and *Pirelli General Cable Works* v. *Oscar Faber & Partners*[64] were not expressly overruled in *Murphy*, it would appear that they must now be explained in terms of close proximity, since in each case, the loss actually suffered fell squarely within the principles expounded in *Murphy* and must be regarded as cases of actionable economic loss. This is somewhat difficult, particularly so far as *Pirelli* is concerned, since in that case, there is an express *dictum* of Lord Fraser's to the effect that the fault of the consultant engineer was not to be equated with the fault of a solicitor who gives negligent advice.[65]

A further difficulty also thrown up by the decision in *Murphy* is the problem of ascertaining when the cause of action accrues if negligence actions in respect of economic loss are reclassified as actions for a negligent misstatement. As will be seen below, the normal approach to cases of negligent misstatement is that the cause of action accrues when the misstatement is relied upon, but where the advice relates to defective buildings, it is also possible that the cause of action will accrue when defects, such as the

---

59. *Ibid* at 925–26.
60. Cmnd 9390, 1986.
61. See Ch 20.
62. [1964] AC 465.
63. [1983] 1 AC 520.
64. [1983] 2 AC 1.
65. *Ibid* at 18.

cracking in *Pirelli*, first occurred or it might accrue when the owners first take over the building.

(iii) English law a backwater in the common law world?

The combined effect of the decisions in *D & F Estates* and *Murphy* is that English law has turned its back on the possibility of an action against builders and others associated with the construction of buildings in respect of the mere defectiveness of the construction. In order to succeed, the building owner must have a contractual basis for his claim, sue under the Defective Premises Act 1972, where it applies, or sue in respect of a negligent misstatement. This limited protection in the law of tort is not the same in other parts of the common law world in which *Anns* is regularly relied upon and there is no guarantee that the line of reasoning adopted in *D & F Estates* and *Murphy* will be followed.

In New Zealand, the law in respect of the tortious liability of builders, local authorities and other professionals engaged in the construction process has developed along different lines. Initially, case law was broadly consistent with the approach adopted in *Dutton* v. *Bognor Regis UDC* in regarding defective building claims as ones which involve physical damage to the premises,[66] pure economic loss being regarded as loss which is unassociated with any physical harm to the structure itself. However, subsequently, there was tacit recognition that claims in tort of this kind were concerned with the economic loss issue. For example, in *Mount Albert BC* v. *Johnson*[67] it was accepted that a building purchaser can recover in tort for economic loss caused by negligence, at least when the loss is associated with physical damage. The justification for this approach, in relation to local authorities, was based on the concept of reliance, in the sense that the purchaser of premises can be taken to rely on the authority to take reasonable care in performing its statutory functions.[68] Thus in *Williams* v. *Mount Eden BC*[69] Casey J observed:

" . . . the reasonable local authority would no doubt have accepted that . . . [their inspection powers] were intended to be exercised for the protection of those members of the public concerned with those buildings, whether as owners, occupiers or users. No doubt it would also have appeared to such an authority that many of them would have no opportunity or expectation of checking or controlling hidden details in its construction to ensure that appropriate standards have been complied with . . . "[70]

Furthermore, the type of reliance necessary for these purposes does not need to be specific reliance established on the facts of a particular case, but may be general reliance. For example it was observed in *Hope* v. *Manukau City Council*[71] that:

"There is no direct evidence that the plaintiff relied on the flat having been built in accordance with the byelaws and regulations. She did not say that she did. But she did say that she saw plans and specifications before she agreed to purchase the flat . . . I would be prepared to draw the inference

---

66. *Bowen* v. *Paramount Builders (Hamilton) Ltd* [1977] 1 NZLR 394.

67. [1979] 2 NZLR 234.

68. *Mount Albert City Council* v. *New Zealand Municipalities Co-operative Insurance Co Ltd* [1983] NZLR 190 at 196 *per* Cooke P.

69. [1986] 1 NZBLC 102,544.

70. *Ibid* at 102,550.

71. 2 August 1976, unreported, *per* Chilwell J. Cited in *Invercargill City Council* v. *Hamlin* [1996] 1 All ER 756 at 763–64 *per* Lord Lloyd of Berwick.

as a matter of common sense that the average prudent purchaser of a new residential flat expects that the byelaws and regulations will have been complied with . . . "

Subsequently, the principle of recovery of diminution in value loss was extended to apply to property defects other than those in building foundations, in which case there was no certainty that any physical damage would be caused to the building.[72] Accordingly, the principle was extended to what might appear to be cases of pure economic loss, although in each such case the loss, in the form of diminution in value of the building, had been suffered as a result of a defect in a physical object.[73]

Similar developments have also occurred in other common law jurisdictions. For example in Canada, a negligent building inspector and the municipality employing him is liable for economic losses suffered by a building owner.[74] Likewise in Australia, *Sutherland Shire Council* v. *Heyman*,[75] the authority on which the reasoning in *Murphy* is so heavily based, has been departed from in *Bryan* v. *Maloney*[76] where a negligent builder was liable for economic loss suffered by a subsequent purchaser of the defective building. In *Bryan* the reasoning in both *D & F Estates* and *Murphy* was rejected as being too narrow in approach. It was said that: "Their Lordships' view . . . seems to us, however, to have rested upon a narrower view of the scope of the modern law of negligence and a more rigid compartmentalisation of contract and tort than is acceptable under the law of this country."[77] Instead, liability in *Bryan* was based on the twin grounds of assumption of responsibility and purchaser-reliance.

As a result of these developments both in New Zealand and in other parts of the common law world, the Privy Council in *Invercargill City Council* v. *Hamlin*[78] was able to reach the conclusion that the law set out in *D & F Estates* and *Murphy* is not the law of New Zealand and that other common law jurisdictions may develop along different lines if conditions prevalent in that jurisdiction make this desirable.

In reaching this conclusion, the correctness of *Murphy* was not doubted, but it was noted that different policy considerations may prevail in different parts of the common law world which may justify the law moving in a different direction. In particular, the fact that there is no equivalent of the Defective Premises Act 1972 in New Zealand was regarded as a sufficient point of distinction allowing New Zealand common law principles to advance in a different direction to those applicable in England.[79] The consequences of these developments in New Zealand and other parts of the common law world for the purposes of limitation of actions are considered in more detail below.

72. *Brown* v. *Heathcote City Council* [1986] 1 NZLR 76 (failure by drainage board to warn of a danger of flooding); *Steiller* v. *Porirua City Council* [1986] 1 NZLR 84.
73. *Invercargill City Council* v. *Hamlin* [1996] 1 All ER 756 at 761 *per* Lord Lloyd of Berwick.
74. *City of Kamloops* v. *Nielsen* (1984) 10 DLR (4th) 641. Although decided before *Murphy* v. *Brentwood DC*, the reasoning in *Kamloops* was adopted in *Canadian National Railway Co* v. *Norsk Pacific Steamship Co* (1992) 91 DLR (4th) 289 and *Murphy* was rejected on the ground that it allowed "injustice merely for the sake of doctrinal tidiness" (1992) 91 DLR (4th) 289 at 365 *per* McLachlin J. See also *Winnipeg Condominium Corp No 36* v. *Bird Construction Co* (1995) 121 DLR (4th) 193.
75. (1985) 60 ALR 1.
76. (1995) 128 ALR 163.
77. *Ibid* at 173 *per* Mason CJ.
78. [1996] 1 All ER 756.
79. *Ibid* at 767 *per* Lord Lloyd of Berwick.

(iv) The position of local authorities

In overruling *Anns* v. *Merton LBC*[80] the House of Lords in *Murphy* held that a local authority owes no common law duty of care to owners or prospective purchasers of property to ensure that building plans are accurate or that building works have been properly carried out in accordance with those plans. The reason for this decision is that any loss suffered by the owner or the prospective purchaser is no more than pure economic loss represented by the diminished value of the property or the cost of repair resulting from the local authority's negligent act or omission. Since, in the majority of cases, there will be no duty of care, the question of limitation of actions becomes academic, until such time as English law takes the direction in *Invercargill City Council* v. *Hamlin*, discussed above. In the event that the negligence of the local authority does result in physical damage to property, ordinary principles of limitation of actions will come into play.

(v) No damage or no actionable duty—what is the difference?

The cases so far considered all raise issues which can be confused. The central focus of cases like *D & F Estates* and *Murphy* is whether the plaintiff is owed a duty of care in respect of a certain type of harm, namely, the defectiveness of a building acquired by the plaintiff. In contrast, in limitation of actions cases, the central focus is whether the plaintiff has suffered damage and on what date that damage was caused.

In *Junior Books Ltd* v. *Veitchi Co Ltd*[81] both the questions of damage and recoverable loss were under consideration since the House of Lords decided, exceptionally, that a duty of care could be owed in respect of the negligent performance of a contractual obligation which resulted in diminution in the value of a building, thereby causing a plaintiff to suffer economic loss. The damage issue is represented by the fact that it was decided that recovery was allowed in respect of a merely defective building or product. But the House of Lords also decided that the plaintiff was allowed to recover damages for loss of profit in an action which sounds in tort, thereby raising the issue of recoverable loss.[82]

Given the present state of the law following *D & F Estates* and *Murphy* it would appear that the cost of repairing a defective product or building before it has caused personal injury or property damage is not an actionable loss for the purposes of the tort of negligence. Accordingly, it follows from this that until such time as personal injury or property damage is caused by the defective product, the plaintiff will have suffered no damage for limitation purposes.

80. [1978] AC 728.

81. [1983] 1 AC 520.

82. Given the restrictions placed on the development of the *Junior Books* exception, it would appear to be confined to the unique circumstances which prevailed in that case. Accordingly, unless the plaintiff has a possessory or proprietary interest in damaged property, he will be owed no duty of care in respect of consequential loss of profit: *Leigh & Sillivan Ltd* v. *Aliakmon Ltd* [1986] AC 785. Moreover, if there is no evidence of a voluntary assumption of responsibility by the defendant in the plaintiff's favour, no duty will be owed in respect of loss of profit resulting from negligent product damage (*Simaan General Contracting Co* v. *Pilkington Glass Ltd (No 2)* [1988] QB 758) and special regard must be had to the terms of any contract between the parties (*Greater Nottinghamshire Co-operative Society* v. *Cementation Piling and Foundation Ltd* [1988] 3 WLR 396) and the terms of any contract between others forming part of a network of contracts, the terms of which the plaintiff should have known about (*Norwich City Council* v. *Harvey* [1989] 1 All ER 1180) since in each of these last two cases, the terms of the contract may be assumed to define the parties' obligations and the imposition of a tortious duty of care might be regarded as inconsistent with those contractual obligations.

In *Nitrigin Eireann Teoranta* v. *Inco Alloys Ltd*[83] the plaintiff owned a chemical plant at which a mixture of methane gas and steam was processed at very high temperatures and under considerable pressure. It was necessary to consider whether the plaintiff's action for damages for negligent construction was time barred where the defendants had supplied them with a defective pipe, the intended purpose of which was to carry the methane and steam mixture. The pipe suffered from cracking which became noticeable in July 1983, but despite reasonable investigations the cause of the cracking was not discovered at that time. In June 1984, further cracking occurred, followed by an explosion which damaged other property and caused the closure of the plaintiff's factory.

May J held that since the cause of the defect was not discoverable in 1983, no cause of action accrued at that time. All the plaintiff had to complain of at that stage was that there was a defective product, which did not disclose a cause of action in tort in favour of the plaintiff. Instead the cause of action accrued when the explosion occurred in June 1984, with the result that an action commenced in June 1990 was not out of time. As May J observed: "The loss sustained by the owner of a defective chattel which does not cause personal injury or damage to something other than itself is the cost of repairing or replacing the chattel. This is pure economic loss and ordinarily irrecoverable in negligence."[84]

Moreover, May J also held, *obiter*, that there would have been no difference if the defect could have been discovered in 1983, but was not so discovered because of an unreasonable failure to diagnose the fault in the pipe. This would not affect the accrual of the cause of action at the date on which the physical harm was caused, but the partial defence of contributory negligence would be relevant.[85]

(vi) Structures "doomed from the start"

In *Pirelli General Cable Works* v. *Oscar Faber & Partners*[86] the defendants sought to establish a starting point for the running of time which was so early that the plaintiffs' action had to be regarded as time barred. Amongst their arguments was one based on *Junior Books Ltd* v. *Veitchi* that the loss suffered being economic loss meant that the plaintiffs' cause of action accrued as soon as the building was complete. In response to this, Lord Fraser replied:

"The plaintiff's cause of action will not accrue until *damage* occurs, which will commonly consist of cracks coming into existence as a result of the defect even though the cracks or defect may be undiscovered and undiscoverable. There may perhaps be cases where the defect is so gross that the building is 'doomed from the start', and where the owner's cause of action will accrue as soon as it is built, but it seems unlikely that such a defect would not be discovered within the limitation period, Such cases, if they exist, would be exceptional."[87]

83. [1992] 1 All ER 854.
84. *Ibid* at 858.
85. *Ibid* at 862.
86. [1983] 2 AC 1.
87. *Ibid* at 16. The actual origins of the exception can be traced back to Megaw LJ's judgment in *Batty* v. *Metropolitan Property Realizations Ltd* [1978] 2 All ER 445 which did not raise any question of limitation of actions, but in which a house had been constructed at the top of a plateau which fell away at the back to a valley in which a stream ran. As a result of this, the plaintiff's back garden began to subside. According to Megaw LJ the plaintiff's house "by its instability . . . was, from the outset doomed". (*Ibid* at 450).

Precisely what this exception covers is not entirely clear since, as Lord Fraser admitted, any cases falling within the exception would be unusual. However, later in his judgment, Lord Fraser goes on to say "It seems to me that except perhaps where the advice of an architect or consulting engineer leads to the erection of a building which is so defective as to be 'doomed from the start', the cause of action accrues only when physical damage occurs to the building."[88]

This might be taken as an example of a case in which the "doomed from the start" exception might apply, but there is a particular difficulty in accepting this as a workable example. Since the exception was uttered in the context of an action for negligence, it must be the defendant's fault which is the cause of the property defect which renders the building or product "doomed from the start". It follows that where the defect in goods or a building is introduced before the date on which the plaintiff acquires an interest in the goods or the building, it should follow that the exception will have no application since it is the conveyance or transfer of ownership which results in the plaintiff's loss and without title or possession, the plaintiff cannot sue for negligence.[89] If in Lord Fraser's example of the advice given by an architect, the plaintiff initially has no interest but subsequently acquires already damaged property, his action will be complete when he takes his interest on conveyance, in which case his cause of action is complete at the time of transfer and there is no need to apply the "doomed from the start" exception. Accordingly, the "doomed from the start" exception must come into play at some stage after the plaintiff has acquired an interest in the building or product. The exception also seems to contemplate a defect so severe and the occurrence of damage so inevitable that time will run from the date on which the plaintiff acquired an interest in the property so as to be able to bring an action for negligence.

The principal reason for wishing to raise an argument to the effect that a building is "doomed from the start" will be to secure a decision to the effect that time starts to run from an earlier stage than the date on which damage is caused. As such, an argument that a building is "doomed from the start" is likely to be raised by a defendant who wishes to raise the time bar in order to avoid liability for damage caused by his negligence. Given these circumstances, it is understandable that the courts have approached this exception to the general rule of the running of time in negligence cases with a considerable degree of caution.

It has been noted above that the phrase "doomed from the start" is difficult to define and it may be that the reason Lord Fraser uttered these words was the time-honoured judicial tradition of not closing the door permanently on a truly exceptional situation that might arise at some future stage.[90] Moreover, on the only occasion the "doomed from the start" exception has been considered in the House of Lords, the two members of the court were less than kind in their treatment of it. Lord Brandon was of the opinion that what Lord Fraser said was "no more than *obiter dicta*".[91] Lord Keith emphasised that what was said in this regard was strictly unnecessary for the decision in *Pirelli* and that whatever the exception might mean, it could not be applied to a mere latent defect which was bound to result in damage at some stage, since that was precisely the problem with which *Pirelli*

---

88. *Pirelli General Cable Works* v. *Oscar Faber & Partners* [1983] 2 AC 1 at 18.
89. *Leigh & Sillivan Ltd* v. *Aliakmon Shipping Co Ltd* [1986] 2 All ER 145.
90. See *Ketteman* v. *Hansel Properties Ltd* [1985] 1 All ER 352 at 363 *per* Lawton LJ.
91. *Ketteman* v. *Hansel Properties Ltd* [1988] 1 All ER 38 at 52.

itself was concerned.[92] Furthermore, other restrictions have also been placed on the extent to which the exception, if it exists, can be relied upon. In particular, it seems that it will not apply to serious defects if they are unlikely to lead to a danger to health or safety for many years.[93] But in contrast, extreme cases where the defects were likely to be disclosed almost immediately might fall within the exception, for example if, through some oversight, a house is built without any drainage pipes at all below ground level.[94]

Despite the fact that the "doomed from the start" exception has received a lukewarm reception, there are still a small number of cases apparently based on it. In *Chelmsford DC v. TJ Evers Ltd*[95] in 1982 the plaintiffs commenced an action against the builders, architects and engineers responsible for the construction of houses with seriously defective roofs which had been completed in 1978. Given these dates, it would not have mattered what set of rules on limitation of actions were applied, since the plaintiffs' action would have been commenced within the limitation period. On the application of the defendants, Judge Smout QC considered whether the buildings were "doomed from the start", holding that they were, with the result that the plaintiffs' cause of action accrued when they took possession of the properties. Whether or not this was a proper application of the exception must be considered in the light of certain remarks made by Judge Smout QC in reaching his conclusion. At one point, he opined that the property was handed over in a damaged state, which for the reasons considered above means that the "doomed from the start" exception should not have applied.

Similar doubts also apply to the decision in *Tozer Kemsley & Millbourn (Holdings) Ltd v. J Jarvis & Sons Ltd*[96] in which Judge Stabb QC mistakenly confused two separate concepts, namely (1) where a building is handed over in a physically defective state, it is the conveyance which constitutes the cause of action and (2) where a building is handed over in a physically defective state, but where the defect is still to manifest itself, tortious rules on limitation will apply. It is only in the latter of these two cases that the "doomed from the start" exception will apply and then only if the defect is sufficiently serious to back-date the accrual of the cause of action.

In *Kaliszewska v. John Clague & Partners*[97] a bungalow was completed in 1970 and cracks began to appear in its walls in 1974. Cosmetic repairs were effected, but by 1976 it had become clear that the property was suffering from subsidence caused by seriously defective foundations. A writ was issued in 1982 with the result that if the property were "doomed from the start" the action would have been time barred, but if time were to run from 1976 the action would have commenced within the limitation period. While much of the judgment was concerned with the possibility of postponement,[98] based on the cosmetic repairs effected in 1974, Judge White also considered that the building was "doomed from the start", but also stated that the plaintiff had suffered actual damage at the date of transfer of the bungalow, in the form of economic loss representing the cost of repair. But if the loss was economic in nature this must mean that there was no actual physical

---

92. *Ibid* at 51. Lords Templeman, Griffiths and Goff agreed with Lord Keith on this matter.
93. *Jones v. Stroud DC* [1988] 1 All ER 5 at 13 *per* Neill LJ.
94. *Ibid.*
95. (1983) 25 BLR 99.
96. (1983) 1 Const LJ 79.
97. (1984) 5 Con LR 62.
98. See Ch 6.

damage at the date of transfer, in which case the "doomed from the start" exception was inapplicable.

There has been an attempt to explain these early cases in *London Congregational Union Incorporated* v. *Harriss & Harriss (a firm)*,[99] in which a defectively designed drainage system resulted in inevitable damage by flooding due to the positioning of surface water gullies. In effect the building, for all practical purposes, had become a relief tank for the storage of escaped sewage, which occurred on 11 occasions between 1971 and 1975! In the event, it was decided that the property was defective, but not damaged at the date of hand-over in 1970, with the result that the case was indistinguishable from *Pirelli*. Time, therefore, ran from the date of the first damage, namely the flooding in 1971. As a result, the action was commenced within the limitation period.

So far as the "doomed from the start exception" was concerned, Ralph Gibson LJ stated:

"The court was told that since the decision of the House of Lords in . . . *Pirelli* . . . the concept of 'doomed from the start' has been very frequently invoked in cases of this nature, but very rarely applied. Judge Newey referred in his judgment in this case to the decision of Judge Stabb in . . . *Tozer Kemsley* . . . as an example of a case within the meaning of Lord Fraser's dictum in . . . *Pirelli* and he so described his own decision in *Chelmsford DC* v. *TJ Evers Ltd* . . . a case in which roofs were liable to blow off at any moment. It would not be wise or useful to attempt to define the sorts of cases which will qualify for inclusion within the exceptional cases provided for by Lord Fraser's cautionary dictum . . . I would say that, in my view, the *Tozer Kemsley* case, on the assumption that actionable negligence had caused the defective plant to be incorporated in the building, could be regarded either as a case in which the defect resulting from negligent design constituted itself the physical damage . . . or as an example of a 'gross' defect within Lord Fraser's dictum: I do not think that there is any real difference. As to the insecure roofs in *Chelmsford DC* v. *TJ Evers Ltd*, I would again agree that such a defect might well also properly be regarded as giving rise to an immediate duty or clear need on the part of the building owner, in protection of himself or of others or of the building, to carry out repairs to remove the defect so as to avoid physical damage shown to be likely to occur in the immediate future, and thus a case . . . in which the law would accept that damage had occurred and the cause of action had accrued. In such circumstances also the defect is 'gross' and, I think, within the class of cases contemplated by Lord Fraser in his dictum."[100]

But in a strong dissenting judgment, Sir Denys Buckley properly distinguished between *defects* and *damage* as emphasised in *Pirelli*. He said:

"For my part, I think it is a misuse of language to describe a building which is constructed to a defective design as a 'damaged building'. It may be accurately described as a defective building, but the fact that it incorporates a defect of design does not import that it has suffered any physical damage. But the tort of negligence will not be actionable unless and until the plaintiff has suffered damage. The plaintiff may suffer damage by reason of physical damage to the building or in consequence of actionable loss arising in some other way."[101]

Accordingly, Sir Denys Buckley treats the case as one of economic loss, rather than as a case of a structure "doomed from the start" and, in fact, denies the existence of the exception as having any independent existence.

What emerges from the case law is that if a building or a product is useable, but defective, it cannot be regarded as "doomed from the start". It follows that if the exception is to apply, some test must be devised which identifies the particular circumstances

---

99. [1988] 1 All ER 15.
100. *Ibid* at 28.
101. *Ibid* at 33 *per* Sir Denys Buckley.

of its operation. In the *London Congregational Union* case, at first instance, Judge Newey proposed a test based upon whether the defect is such that "there was nothing practicable that could be done to save it".[102] But this test was rejected by Ralph Gibson LJ in the Court of Appeal where he said:

"it seems to me that the explanation of the limits of Lord Fraser's dictum which Judge Newey proposed . . . cannot be supported. In particular, I cannot accept that a case is to be treated as within an exception to the general rule if it can be shown that 'nothing practicable could be done' to save the building or that part of the building which is the subject of the action; nor can I accept that a case must be treated as outside any exception on the ground only that the repair or correction of the defect is practicable."[103]

But Ralph Gibson LJ does not suggest any alternative test himself. Clearly, in the light of Lord Keith's views in *Ketteman* v. *Hansel Properties Ltd*[104] the mere fact of inevitability of damage is not enough, since there must be some gross and obvious defect such as the example suggested by Neill LJ in *Jones* v. *Stroud DC*[105] of a building with no drainage pipes below ground level. But a defect of this kind may be gross, but not necessarily obvious from the start, which must cast doubt on the reasoning employed in *Kaliszewska* v. *John Clague & Partners*[106] which appears to be based on this ground.

Two factors may be relevant in determining whether a building or a product is "doomed from the start". In the first place, it may be considered whether it is inevitable that, in time, a gross and obvious defect will manifest itself. As a caveat, it should be observed that in the light of *Ketteman* v. *Hansel Properties Ltd*, the mere inevitability of damage is not a sufficient ingredient for the operation of the "doomed from the start" exception, but it is surely an essential and minimum requirement. Secondly, it may be that damage is inevitable in the light of the plaintiff's intended use of the property or the product.

So far as inevitability in time, *simpliciter*, is concerned, the case law suggests that this, alone, will not suffice to render a defect which is sufficiently gross to render the product or the property doomed from the start. For example, bricks which have been improperly fired so that, inevitably, they will absorb water do not render a building "doomed from the start".[107] Similarly, stone cladding which has been improperly fixed has failed to satisfy the test,[108] since what is required is "an impending inevitability".[109] In contrast, roofing material which is liable to blow off at any time[110] and a malfunctioning heating system[111] have questionably sufficed.

An equally questionable basis for determining whether a building is "doomed from the start" is to inject a subjective element by considering the plaintiff's intended use and to ask if it is inevitable that the building or product will be useless in the light of the plaintiff's requirements. For example, in *Pirelli* the chimney suffered no defect until it was actually used. However, this did not trigger the "doomed from the start" exception, even

---

102. [1985] 1 All ER 335 at 343.
103. [1988] 1 All ER 15 at 27.
104. [1988] 1 All ER 38 at 51, considered above.
105. [1988] 1 All ER 5 at 13.
106. (1984) 5 Con LR 62, considered above.
107. *Greater London Council* v. *Thomas McInerney & Sons* (1983), unreported.
108. *Kensington and Chelsea and Westminster Health Authority* v. *Wettern Composites Ltd* [1985] 1 All ER 346.
109. *Ibid* at 351 *per* Judge Smout QC.
110. *Chelmsford DC* v. *TJ Evers Ltd* (1983) 25 BLR 99.
111. *Tozer Kemsley and Millbourn (Holdings) Ltd* v. *J Jarvis & Sons Ltd* (1983) 1 Const LJ 79.

though the structure was intended to be used as a chimney, but could not be used as such. Likewise in *Dove* v. *Banhams Patent Locks*[112] in 1967 the defendant security firm fitted a security gate to the basement door of a house which the plaintiff subsequently purchased in 1976. A burglary occurred in 1979 and it was determined as a matter of fact that the installation of the gate had been carried out negligently. The defendants argued that time started to run against the plaintiff from 1967 since the installation was "doomed from the start". This argument was rejected by Hodgson J on the ground that it was impossible to say that the "doomed from the start" exception could come into play when, if there had been no burglary, the gate could not be said to be doomed at all. Similar reasoning also seems to apply to the *London Congregational Union* case where it was accepted that the drainage system only proved to be defective following the occurrence of heavy rain.

(c) Economic loss caused by negligent acts

Since the decision in *Murphy* v. *Brentwood DC*[113] it is clear that the extent to which economic losses are actionable in tort is severely limited, but there do remain cases in which a tortious action for economic loss will be successful. In the light of what has been said already, although *Pirelli General Cable Works* v. *Oscar Faber & Partners*[114] and *Junior Books Ltd* v. *Veitchi Co Ltd*[115] have not been overruled, the effect of *Murphy* is substantial: the reasoning of the House of Lords in *Pirelli* must be re-read and the likelihood of further application of the principle in *Junior Books* is minimal. What is now left is the possibility of recovery of economic loss in tort where there has been a negligent misstatement or negligent advice.

(i) Pirelli and economic loss

The landmark decision in the House of Lords in *Donoghue* v. *Stevenson*[116] is premised upon the plaintiff suffering physical harm to the person or to property, accordingly, there has been a general reluctance to allow tortious claims for financial losses which are unaccompanied by or not consequent on some form of physical harm. This reluctance was disposed of in *Hedley Byrne & Co* v. *Heller & Partners Ltd*[117] where the House of Lords recognised that an action in tort might lie in respect of pure economic loss resulting from negligent advice and negligent misstatements even in the absence of any form of physical harm. This development was taken a stage further in *Junior Books Ltd* v. *Veitchi Co Ltd*[118] in which the House of Lords extended the principle allowing the recovery of pure economic loss to negligent acts, such as negligent production, resulting in pure economic loss such as diminution in the value of the defective product itself or the cost of repairing the defective product, provided there existed between the plaintiff and the defendant a unique relationship of proximity. Although *Junior Books* says nothing about limitation of actions in economic loss cases, it nonetheless creates serious difficulties for the application of the

112. [1983] 2 All ER 833.
113. [1990] 2 All ER 908.
114. [1983] 2 AC 1.
115. [1983] 1 AC 520.
116. [1932] AC 562.
117. [1964] AC 465.
118. [1983] 1 AC 520.

test subsequently applied in *Pirelli General Cable Works* v. *Oscar Faber & Partners*[119] since the latter states that the plaintiff's cause of action accrues in the tort of negligence only when physical damage is caused. In *Junior Books* the plaintiff will have a cause of action for a defective product when he acquires an interest in it, represented by the financial cost to him of making good the defect. As a result, on one view, his cause of action may be regarded as complete on that date and the occurrence of subsequent physical damage arising from the defect must be immaterial in fixing the date on which the cause of action accrues. However, since the loss suffered by the plaintiff is financial loss, another view is that the cause of action accrues in favour of the plaintiff when it becomes obvious to a reasonable person that the product has decreased in value, which at least in the case of defective buildings will usually occur when it would be obvious to a reasonable property buyer that the property is not worth its unharmed market value.[120] But this alternative approach to the limitation question is equally at odds with the requirement in *Pirelli* that there must be physical damage before the plaintiff's cause of action can accrue.

Where the problem of the conflict between *Pirelli* and *Junior Books* has arisen in the past, it has generally been side-stepped. For example in the Court of Appeal in *Ketteman* v. *Hansel Properties Ltd*[121] Lawton LJ got round the apparent conflict in the following way:

"There are a number of answers to this submission; a short one will suffice. The *Junior Books* case was cited in *Pirelli*. It was not a limitation case at all. Their Lordships did not have to consider when a cause of action accrued. Both Lord Fraser and Lord Brandon (who agreed with Lord Fraser's speech in *Pirelli*) had been members of the Appellate Committee when the *Junior Books* case was decided. In *Pirelli* Lord Fraser rejected the notion that a person could recover for diminution in the value of a building by reason of defective foundations which had not yet led to physical damage to it, unless possibly the work could be said to have been doomed from the start . . . I am satisfied that *Pirelli* governs this case."[122]

Despite not being particularly short, this also fails to provide an answer to the problem in hand, since all it seems to suggest is that Lords Fraser and Brandon could not have been unaware of the possible problems associated with the conflict. Also, it would have been helpful if some of the other answers which Lawton LJ refers to could have been explained.

When courts have been faced with a submission that the cause of action accrues when the plaintiff takes initial possession of a defective product or building the general response has been to reject the submission, but not always to give reasons for doing so.[123] But in *London Congregational Union Incorporated* v. *Harriss & Harriss (a firm)*[124] Ralph Gibson LJ was prepared to give reasons for his decision, expressing the opinion that in *Junior Books*,

" . . . it was the defect resulting from the negligent work which was seen as being the cause of the need to spend money on putting right physical defects in the floor; it was not the mere existence of

---

119. [1983] 2 AC 1.
120. See *Invercargill City Council* v. *Hamlin* [1996] 1 All ER 756.
121. [1985] 1 All ER 352.
122. *Ibid* at 363.
123. For example, *Tozer Kemsley & Millbourn (Holdings) Ltd* v. *J Jarvis & Sons Ltd* (1983) 1 Const LJ 79 (Judge Stabb QC).
124. [1988] 1 All ER 15.

the faulty elements in design or construction which would lead to the coming into existence of physical defects."[125]

The difficulty is to ascertain precisely what Ralph Gibson LJ meant by this. What he might have been saying was that there was a point of distinction between *Junior Books* and *London Congregational Union* in that in the former the defendant was a sub-contractor responsible for the provision of a service whereas in the latter, the defendant was an architect, who could be regarded as the provider of the end product and that the two could be treated differently for the purposes of tortious liability. Certainly, it is true that architects are treated in the same way as the main building contractor and consultant engineers for the purposes of liability in that they all take primary responsibility for the quality of the end product, and to use the words of Ralph Gibson LJ architects are liable for "the mere existence of the faulty elements in design . . . which would lead to the coming into existence of physical defects". However, it is questionable whether the nature of the breach of duty on the part of a sub-contractor and an architect can make any difference so far as economic loss is concerned. In both *London Congregational Union* and *Junior Books* it cannot be denied that the result of the defendant's negligence was that there was a defective building and that, accordingly, economic loss had been suffered.

(ii) Defective buildings, defective products and economic loss

It has been seen already that, for the purposes of English law, if a building or a product damages itself, the effect of the decisions in *Murphy* v. *Brentwood DC*[126] and *D & F Estates Ltd* v. *Church Commissioners for England*[127] is that such damage, being pure economic loss, is generally not recoverable. However, the position is not the same in other parts of the common law world, as is clear from the decision of the Privy Council in *Invercargill City Council* v. *Hamlin*.[128] The consequences of the developments in *Invercargill* for the purposes of limitation of actions are considerable, since, in that case, it became necessary to ascertain the date from which time should run in cases involving pure economic loss. In *Invercargill City Council* v. *Hamlin* in 1972 a building inspector negligently approved building works despite the fact that the foundations had not been dug to a sufficient depth, with the result that over a period of years a number of cracks and minor defects appeared. In 1989 another builder suggested the problem might lie in the foundations, with the result that in 1990 proceedings commenced against the council, the original builder having gone out of business. Clearly, if the "date of first damage" rule applied in *Pirelli General Cable Works* v. *Oscar Faber & Partners*[129] the plaintiff's action would have been out of time since damage would have occurred in the early 1970s.

In determining when time started to run, there were earlier New Zealand authorities which suggested that it was more reasonable to select the date on which the defect in the property becomes apparent or manifest, rather than to allow time to run from the date on

125. *Ibid* at 25.
126. [1990] 2 All ER 908.
127. [1988] 2 All ER 992.
128. [1996] 1 All ER 756.
129. [1983] 2 AC 1.

which the damage first occurred.[130] The problem that such a starting date creates is the possibility that a defect might not be discovered until a very late stage, by which time the builder, architect or engineer might have retired. However, the way this can be dealt with is by means of the introduction of a statutory long-stop which prevents a civil action being brought more than a certain number of years after the date of the act or omission on which the proceedings are based.[131] Without such a rule, as the development of English law has shown, it is possible for a plaintiff to be out of time before he even becomes aware that he has suffered material, actionable damage.

In *Invercargill City Council* v. *Hamlin* Lord Lloyd noted that English law on this matter seems to have developed on the basis of a *non sequitur* in Lord Reid's reasoning in *Cartledge* v. *E Jopling & Sons Ltd*[132] to the effect that, because the Limitation Act expressly provides for postponement of the limitation period in cases of fraud, mistake and concealment, there can be no other instances in which the running of time is postponed. But there is no reason why this should be regarded as being the case, and in other jurisdictions the occurrence of damage test has been rejected in appropriate cases.[133] Moreover, Lord Lloyd in *Invercargill*[134] reasserted the distinction between defective building cases and cases of latent personal injury drawn by Geoffrey Lane LJ in *Sparham-Souter* v. *Town & Country Developments (Essex) Ltd*[135] that in the case of clinically unobservable bodily injury there is damage to the body, which cannot be disposed of, but undetectable damage to a building is remediable since the plaintiff "can get rid of his house before any damage is suffered".[136]

In *Invercargill City Council* v. *Hamlin* it was accepted that once it is recognised that these defective building cases all involve economic loss, the problems associated with the *Pirelli* date of damage test disappear, since the loss suffered by the plaintiff is diminution in value of the building he has purchased, and that diminution in value cannot occur until such time as a reasonable person could have become aware that his property is adversely affected by the defendant's negligence, subject to a caveat that a person cannot close his eyes to the truth where it is obvious that the property is defective. Lord Lloyd of Berwick opined that:

"Once it is appreciated that the loss in respect of which the plaintiff in the present case is suing is loss to his pocket, and not for physical damage to the house or foundations, then most, if not all of the difficulties surrounding the limitation question fall away. The plaintiff's loss occurs when the market value of the house is depreciated by reason of the defective foundations, and not before. If he resells the house at full value before the defect is discovered, he has suffered no loss. Thus in the common case the occurrence of the loss and the discovery of the loss will coincide.

---

130. *Mount Albert BC* v. *Johnson* [1979] 2 NZLR 234 at 239 *per* Cooke J; *Askin* v. *Knox* [1989] 1 NZLR 248 at 255 *per* Cooke P.

131. See Building Act 1991 (New Zealand), s 91(2) (10 years); Limitation Act 1980, s 14B(1) (15 years regarding latent damage other than personal injury); Limitation Act 1980, s 11A(3) (10 years regarding product liability claims).

132. [1963] AC 758 at 772.

133. See *Mount Albert BC* v. *Johnson* [1979] 2 NZLR 234; *Askin* v. *Knox* [1989] 1 NZLR 248; *City of Kamloops* v. *Nielsen* (1984) 10 DLR (4th) 641.

134. Expressing his regret that the decision in *Sparham-Souter* had been overruled in *Pirelli*: See [1996] 1 All ER 756 at 770.

135. [1976] QB 858.

136. *Ibid* at 880.

But the plaintiff cannot postpone the start of the limitation period by shutting his eyes to the obvious . . .

In other words, the cause of action accrues when the cracks become so bad, or the defects so obvious, that any reasonable homeowner would call in an expert. Since the defects would then be obvious to a potential buyer, or his expert, that marks the moment when the market value of the building is depreciated, and therefore the moment when the economic loss occurs."[137]

All of this, of course, is purely academic for the purposes of English law while the decisions in *D & F Estates* and *Murphy* remain in place, but it should also be noted that the test was considered to be applicable only to the problem of latent defects in buildings and was not to be regarded as having a more general application in the law of tort.[138]

What Lord Lloyd, in *Invercargill,* has done is to provide a credible alternative starting date for the purposes of the running of time which exposes the deficiencies of the decision in *Pirelli,* by recognising that physical damage is an irrelevance in diminution in value claims. Instead, what has to be appreciated is that diminution in value is something which does not occur immediately, so that the date of transfer need not be the date on which the cause of action is taken to accrue. However, it is also clear that what was said in *Invercargill* is applicable only to defective buildings, and that what was said may not be applicable to other varieties of economic loss.

The most directly comparable variety of economic loss caused by negligence arises in cases of negligent manufacture under the narrow rule in *Donoghue* v. *Stevenson*[139] where the manufactured product is merely defective and does not pose a danger to body or other property. While it is clear, at present, that there is no likelihood that English law will allow such an action to succeed outside of the narrow circumstances covered by *Junior Books Ltd* v. *Veitchi Co Ltd,*[140] it is also clear that should there be a change of direction, it will be necessary to address the problem of limitation of actions and to ask when the cause of action, if any, accrues.

It is important to emphasise that there are differences between defective products and defective buildings. In *Invercargill* Lord Lloyd makes the important point that the reasonable buyer of a defective building will become aware of the defectiveness of the property because his expert, namely his surveyor, will be able to identify the defect and will advise the potential purchaser accordingly.[141] It follows from this that the market price of the property will drop in order to reflect the cost of repairing the discoverable defect. In the case of defective products, however, the same professional structure is not in place. Generally, it is unlikely that cars, washing machines etc, will be surveyed or tested before purchase, in which case the date of diminution in value will not be so precisely ascertainable as in the case of defective buildings. Moreover, at present, the Consumer Protection Act 1987 does not cover diminution in value claims,[142] although there are European

---

137. *Invercargill City Council* v. *Hamlin* [1996] 1 All ER 758 at 772.

138. *Ibid* at 773 *per* Lord Lloyd of Berwick.

139. [1932] AC 562.

140. [1983] 1 AC 520.

141. Even in the case of defective buildings, it does not follow that the purchaser will always have his own "expert" as is illustrated in *Smith* v. *Eric S Bush (a firm)* [1990] 1 AC 831, since many purchasers, especially those at the lower end of the housing market, do not engage their own surveyor, but they will still have a building society valuation report to rely upon.

142. See Ch 21.

Community plans to introduce a producers' guarantee of quality,[143] which, if implemented, will require attention as to the matter of limitation periods.

(iii) Structures doomed from the start and economic loss

It has been seen above that there has been a general reluctance on the part of the judiciary to admit that economic loss claims pose a problem for the purposes of ascertaining when the cause of action accrues. However, in two judgments, the problem has been recognised and in both cases, the plaintiff's cause of action was taken to have accrued at the date of taking possession of the defective property, although in one of those cases the result was explained on the ground that the building was, dubiously, "doomed from the start".[144] The only other decision to directly impinge on this issue is to be found in the dissenting judgment of Sir Denys Buckley in *London Congregational Union Incorporated* v. *Harriss & Harris (a firm)*[145] where he pointed out that the building was defective when acquired by the plaintiffs. He goes on to point out that:

"If before any flooding occurred the plaintiffs had become aware of the defect they could, in my judgment, have thereupon sued in negligence without awaiting the occurrence of physical damage. It would have become demonstrable that the plaintiffs had suffered economic damage in consequence of the defendants' negligence in the form of the expense to which they would necessarily be put to remedy the defect, or in the form of the reduction of the realisable value of the property."[146]

(d) Economic loss caused by negligent words or advice

(i) Architects and engineers

The combined effects of the decisions of the House of Lords in *Hedley Byrne & Co* v. *Heller & Partners Ltd*[147] and its progeny and *Murphy* v. *Brentwood DC*[148] is that there has grown up, for the purposes of the recovery in tort of economic loss, a distinction between negligent acts and negligent words. Sadly, the distinction is very difficult to maintain, so much so that cases once treated as involving a negligent act have become reinterpreted as being based on negligent advice. One such case is *Pirelli General Cable Works* v. *Oscar Faber & Partners*[149] where a negligent design supplied by the defendant consultant engineers was regarded as the cause of cracking in a chimney subsequently built according to the defendant's design. At the time *Pirelli* was decided, consultant engineers were treated in the same manner as architects and main contractors, namely as the producer of a qualitatively defective product. However, since *Murphy*, economic loss of this type is no longer actionable in the tort of negligence, but *Pirelli* was not overruled by *Murphy*, but was re-explained as a case based on *Hedley Byrne* principles since the engineers were

---

143. See *Green Paper on Consumer Guarantees and After Sales Service* (COM(93) 509); *Proposal for a Council Directive on the Sale of Consumer Goods and Associated Guarantees* (COM (95) 520 final, 3 September 1996).
144. See *Kaliszewska* v. *John Clague & Partners* (1984) 5 Con LR 62, considered above.
145. [1988] 1 All ER 15.
146. *Ibid* at 33.
147. [1964] AC 465.
148. [1990] 2 All ER 908.
149. [1983] 2 AC 1. See also McKendrick, "Pirelli re-examined" (1991) 11 LS 326.

responsible for advising negligently on the design of the building. According to Lord Keith in *Murphy* v. *Brentwood DC*[150]:

"In a case such as *Pirelli* where the tortious liability arose out of a contractual relationship with professional people, the duty extended to take reasonable care not to cause economic loss to the client by the advice given. The plaintiffs built the chimney and they did so in reliance on that advice. The case could accordingly fall within the principles of *Hedley Byrne*."[151]

If this is a correct interpretation of *Pirelli* one consequence is that the question when does the cause of action, in such cases, accrue receives a different answer to that actually given in *Pirelli*. It will be recalled that the test applied in *Pirelli* was based on the date on which physical damage is caused, but if *Pirelli* is recast as a case of negligent advice, for reasons considered below, there is no physical damage and the cause of action accrues when the advice is relied upon. Presumably, the same reasoning may also apply to other professionals engaged in the construction process such as surveyors and maybe even architects, but probably not the main building contractor since it seems difficult to conceive of a situation in which he could be regarded as an advice giver. The problem to which this distinction between acts and words[152] gives rise is that words of advice such as those given by architects and engineers lead to the performance of the act of building and may be inseparable. Moreover, the interpretation given of *Pirelli* in *Murphy* ignores an express *dictum* of Lord Fraser to the effect that the engineers in *Pirelli* were not liable for negligent advice. This question arose since the engineers were seeking to establish that the plaintiff's cause of action arose at the earliest possible date by arguing that their design was similar to negligent advice given by a solicitor on a matter of law. In response to this Lord Fraser considered it unnecessary to rule on the point, but went on to say, "as at present advised, I do not think it is".

If the action against an engineer or an architect is reclassified as one concerned with negligent advice, the difficulty is to determine when the cause of action accrues in favour of the building owner or prospective purchaser. A number of possibilities arise. For example, it could be the date on which a physical defect in the property occurs or the date on which the owner acquired the defective property or the date on which the advice is relied upon, which is presumably the date on which instructions are given for the building process to commence. Furthermore, in the light of the developments in other parts of the common law world in building cases, a fourth possibility is added, namely that following the Privy Council decision in *Invercargill City Council* v. *Hamlin*[153] the cause of action may accrue when diminution in the value of the building is reasonably discoverable.

The last possible date on which the cause of action may accrue, in the absence of a test based on reasonable discoverability, is the date on which damage is caused, in accordance with the basic principles set out in *Pirelli*. But the test in *Pirelli* is based on the fact of physical damage to property, which is difficult to apply to cases in which the only loss suffered by the plaintiff is diminution in value based on the cost of repairing a defect which has come to light but which has not yet caused physical damage. The fact is that physical defects such as the cracking of the chimney in *Pirelli* are merely a manifestation

---

150. [1990] 2 All ER 908.
151. *Ibid* at 919.
152. See Stapleton (1991) 107 LQR 249.
153. [1996] 1 All ER 756.

of the economic loss caused by the diminution in value of the building which has occurred at a much earlier stage.

If *Pirelli* is correctly reassigned as a negligent advice case, the cause of action will accrue at the much earlier stage of reliance on the advice given with the result that there will be a financial detriment only after the date of reliance.

In a case such as *Pirelli* the date of reliance will be the date on which the plaintiffs accepted the plans submitted by the engineers and instructed the main contractors to commence construction work. From this time onwards, it becomes inevitable that, in the absence of substantial revision of the initial design, the result of instructing the main contractor to commence work will result in a defective building. However, there is an inevitable difficulty associated with applying this test to architects and engineers, since at the time of giving instructions for the commencement of the building work, the plaintiff, at that stage, will not have a possessory interest in the property, even though, at the same time, there is a diminution in the value of the property concerned due to the defendant's negligent advice. This serves as an important point of distinction between negligent advice on the part of architects and engineers, compared with that on the part of, for example, solicitors, who are likely to advise their clients on matters related to property owned or possessed by the client.[154] As noted above, if the plaintiff has no possessory or proprietary interest at the time damage is caused, no action will lie in respect of any economic loss consequent on that damage.[155]

Since neither the date of physical harm nor the date of reliance on the negligent advice seems to be an appropriate date from which to allow time to run against the plaintiff, this leaves the remaining possibility of accrual of the cause of action on the date of taking possession of the defective building. In these circumstances, the requirements of damage and possession are present and since the property is defective, there is the inevitability that money will have to be spent in order to rectify the defects. But there still remains the problem, identified in *Invercargill City Council* v. *Hamlin*, that until a reasonable prospective purchaser could be aware of the defect in the property, there is no likelihood that the market value of the property has been reduced. This is a compelling argument in support of a limitation period which starts not from the date of taking possession of the defective property, but rather from the date on which it could reasonably have been discovered that the value of the property has diminished as a result of the defendant's negligence.

(ii) Solicitors' negligence

For a number of years, it was believed that the liability of a professional adviser, such as a solicitor, was based upon contract, with the result that there would be no action in tort in respect of negligent performance of the adviser's contractual duties.[156] The problem this view gave rise to for the purposes of limitation of actions was that time would run from the date of breach of duty,[157] even though, as has been seen above, the normal starting point for the running of time in a negligence action is the date on which damage

---

154. See *Forster* v. *Outred & Co* [1982] 1 WLR 86; *Bell* v. *Peter Browne & Co* [1990] 3 All ER 124; *Moore (DW) & Co* v. *Ferrier* [1988] 1 All ER 400, discussed below.
155. *Leigh & Sillivan Ltd* v. *Aliakmon Shipping Co Ltd, The Aliakmon* [1986] AC 785.
156. See *Clark* v. *Kirby-Smith* [1964] Ch 506.
157. See *Howell* v. *Young* (1826) 5 B & C 259 and see Ch 8.

is caused. However in *Midland Bank Trust Co Ltd* v. *Hett, Stubbs & Kemp*[158] Oliver J took a different view, holding that a professional adviser owes a parallel tortious duty of care to his client. Moreover, in *Ross* v. *Caunters*[159] the tortious duty of care owed by a professional adviser was extended to third parties, albeit in limited circumstances, where the loss suffered by that third party was foreseeable. Although these cases are directly concerned with the position of solicitors, there is no reason why other professional advisers should not be in the same position where they owe both contractual and tortious duties of care and it is likely that limitation issues similar to those considered below will be relevant to the likes of accountants, stockbrokers, bankers and financial advisers.

The problem with cases of negligent advice is to ascertain the most appropriate date from which time should run. Just as in the case of defective buildings, there are a number of possibilities, and it is for the courts to select the most appropriate, having regard to the position of both plaintiff and defendant and the desire to produce a clear and workable rule which provides a starting date which is sufficiently understandable by all concerned. The various alternatives are, first the date on which the advice is given; secondly the date on which the plaintiff acts on the advice; thirdly the date on which loss as a result of acting on the advice becomes inevitable (the "no turning back" date) and finally the date on which financial loss is caused as a result of reliance upon the advice given. If the decision in *Pirelli General Cable Works* v. *Oscar Faber & Partners*[160] is applied the appropriate starting date in negligent advice cases would be the last of the four possibilities set out above. However, there is a problem with advice cases in that although it may take time for financial loss to result from the defendant's negligence, there are circumstances in which the plaintiff's earlier reliance on the defendant's advice means that it is inevitable that loss will be suffered, in which case, at that earlier stage, the plaintiff's action is complete.

Prior to the decision in *Pirelli* the position so far as limitation of actions was concerned still seemed to turn upon the date of the occurrence of breach, despite the fact that there was also a possible action in tort. Thus in *Forster* v. *Outred & Co*[161] the plaintiff took out a mortgage on her house in order to secure her son's debts, the mortgage deed being executed in February 1973 at the defendant's offices. At the time, the plaintiff was under the impression that the arrangement she had entered into was purely temporary, relating only to a bridging loan taken out by her son but this was not the case, as the mortgage covered all present and future liabilities of her son. The solicitor allegedly failed to explain to her the dangerous implications of signing the mortgage. In 1975, the plaintiff discovered what had actually happened when she received a demand from the mortgagee and in August 1975, she paid £69,281 to the mortgagee. Subsequently, in January 1977, the plaintiff issued a writ against the defendants, but did nothing more at the time. A further writ, alleging negligence on the part of the defendants, was issued in March 1980, but the defendants argued that the plaintiff's action was time barred. The question arose whether the plaintiff's cause of action accrued in February 1973, on the occurrence of the defendant's breach of contract or whether time should run against the plaintiff only from the date on which she was required to honour the mortgage deed in August 1975.

---

158. [1979] Ch 384.
159. [1980] Ch 297. See also *White* v. *Jones* [1995] 1 All ER 691.
160. [1983] 2 AC 1.
161. [1982] 1 WLR 86. See also *Melton & Walker* v. *Stanger* (1981) 125 SJ 861.

The Court of Appeal, relying on *Howell* v. *Young*[162] held that for the purposes of a negligence action, time should run from the date of the defendant's breach in 1973, but the reasoning in the judgment is in terms of damage suffered by the plaintiff, thereby foreshadowing the subsequent House of Lords decision in *Pirelli*. On the facts, it was held that the plaintiff had suffered actual loss in 1973, since her property had become subject to an encumbrance which reduced the value of her property, with the result that had she wished to do so she could have sued from then onwards. Accordingly, the test for accrual of the cause of action was one based upon reliance on the advice given by the defendants. Similarly, in *Baker* v. *Ollard & Bentley*[163] the plaintiff and two of her acquaintances agreed to purchase a house, the plaintiff contributing 49 per cent of the purchase price, the intention being that the plaintiff and her friends should occupy different parts of the house. The defendant solicitors were instructed to procure the grant of a freehold interest in the property, but succeeded only in obtaining a leasehold interest based on trust for sale, with the result that none of the parties could dispose of their interest without the assistance of the others. Subsequently, it became apparent that the mistake on the part of the defendants had adversely affected the saleability of the property concerned. In line with *Forster* v. *Outred & Co*, it was held that the plaintiff's cause of action accrued when the interest was granted rather than when she sought to sell the property.

The difficulty which faced the plaintiffs in these cases was that in *Forster*, had the plaintiff sued in 1973, quantification of her loss would have been very difficult and there is every likelihood that she would have been under-compensated, since any assessment of her likely loss would have to take account of the prospects of the plaintiff's son's business being successful. On this basis, any loss which had been suffered by the plaintiff was clouded in a contingency which might increase or decrease her overall loss resulting from the defendant's negligence, but it still remains the case that these doubts seem to relate merely to quantum of damages rather than liability for damages. Instead of suing in 1973, the plaintiff, in fact, waited until the mortgagee foreclosed, in which case the plaintiff lost her right to sue altogether, although this was because the writ issued in 1977 was not continued with. In *Baker*, the writ was served in April 1981, but the relevant interest was granted in April 1973; the damage suffered did not become apparent until the plaintiff's acquaintances sought to sell their interest in the property with vacant possession in December 1973, whereupon the plaintiff had to take steps to achieve the security of possession which the defendants had undertaken to secure for her.

In *Forster* v. *Outred & Co*, the defendant's negligence resulted in the plaintiff's present interest in her property becoming encumbered, but negligence on the part of a solicitor can also have the effect of failing to fulfil the client's expectations of acquisition of an interest in land. In each case, the general principle in *Forster* v. *Outred & Co* seems to apply. Thus in *Sullivan* v. *Layton Lougher & Co*[164] a solicitor was engaged to purchase the unexpired term of a lease, but failed to inform the plaintiff that the lease had already been extended under the Leasehold Reform Act 1967, so that no further extension was possible. For the purposes of the running of time, it was held that the plaintiff's cause of action accrued when the property was purchased, since from that time damage had been suffered because an interest had been acquired which was worth less to the plaintiff than it would have been

162. (1826) 5 B & C 259.
163. (1982) 126 SJ 593.
164. (1995) 49 EG 127, CA.

had the lease not already been extended. This remained the case despite the fact that the plaintiff's loss was not readily quantifiable until the date on which the plaintiff became entitled to receive the freehold in the property.

It should be observed that *Forster* v. *Outred & Co* does not lay down a rule of general application, in which every case of negligent advice will be dealt with on the basis of the date of the plaintiff's reliance on the advice given by the defendant. In *Forster* v. *Outred & Co* it is clear that the plaintiff did suffer financial loss before being called upon to honour her security. But in other cases it is less obvious that the same result should obtain where there is no immediate loss. Similarly, it can be said that the plaintiff in *Baker* v. *Ollard & Bentley* also suffered damage at the time of granting of the interest, since from that time the resale value of the property concerned was adversely affected, even though quantification of the amount of the plaintiff's loss might have been difficult.

With the arrival of the decision in *Pirelli* there were some initial suggestions that *Forster* v. *Outred & Co* might not survive.[165] However, in later cases, its correctness has been confirmed. For example in *DW Moore & Co Ltd* v. *Ferrier*[166] the plaintiff employed a third party under a contract of service which had been drafted by the defendants. The problem which subsequently arose was that the third party, after leaving the plaintiff's employment, set up in competition and there was no provision in the contract of service to prevent such competition, as had been asked for. There had been an attempt to draft such a clause, but it proved to be inadequately worded, as it purported to apply only if the third party ceased to be a member of the plaintiff company. In this case, the third party set up in competition at a time when he still held shares in the plaintiff company. The Court of Appeal held that the plaintiff's cause of action was complete when the badly drafted contract was drawn up by the defendants, since from that date onwards damage had been caused. There was no need to wait until the date on which the third party set up in competition.

Although the date of execution of a document will often be the date on which the plaintiff's cause of action accrues, this does not necessarily follow, as a matter of course, in each case. For example, in *DW Moore & Co* v. *Ferrier*[167] Neill LJ opined that:

"In the present case, the judge rightly rejected the notion that where a solicitor gives negligent advice, damage is presumed to occur at the time when the advice is acted on. I am satisfied that there is no such presumption. *It is a question of fact in each case whether actual damage has been established.* In the present case, to use the language of Templeman LJ in *Baker* v. *Ollard & Bentley* the plaintiffs suffered damage 'because [they] did not get what [they] should have got'. The plaintiffs' rights under the two agreements were demonstrably less valuable than they would have been had adequate restrictive covenants been included."[168]

The observation that, on the facts of a given case, damage may be said to have been caused at a date other than the date of execution of the negligently prepared document means that it becomes necessary to ascertain in what circumstances the date of execution

---

165. See e.g. *Dove* v. *Banhams Patent Locks Ltd* [1983] 2 All ER 833, 840 *per* Hodgson J. But cf *DW Moore & Co* v. *Ferrier* [1988] 1 All ER 400 at 409 *per* Neill LJ. See also *Aikman* v. *Hallett & Co*, 23 March 1987, unreported in which Steyn J dismisses the argument that *Pirelli* and *Forster* are inconsistent on the ground that *Forster* is concerned with economic loss whereas *Pirelli* is concerned with property damage. But for reasons considered above *Pirelli* may now be regarded as an economic loss case and what was said in that case regarding limitation of actions may not apply to the re-interpreted version of *Pirelli*.
166. [1988] 1 All ER 400.
167. *Ibid.*
168. *Ibid* at 409–10. Emphasis added.

ceases to be relevant. Moreover, in all of the cases considered so far, a document has been executed, but has failed to achieve the result required by the plaintiff, but if no document is executed at all, it is also necessary to consider when the plaintiff's cause of action accrues.

In the majority of cases where a document is executed, it seems likely that the date of execution will normally be the relevant date for the purposes of the running of time, but there may be instances in which there is some other trigger event which is the true date of accrual, despite the fact that the occurrence of this later event has been facilitated by the defendant's initial act. For example, in *UBAF Ltd* v. *European American Banking Corporation*[169] the defendant bank had organised a syndicated loan to two Panamanian shipping companies and was responsible for inducing the plaintiff bank to join the syndicate on the strength of statements made in 1974 which related to the financial security of the borrowers. The plaintiffs advanced loans of $500,000 to each of the companies in 1974, but the companies did not default until 1976, by which time some $880,000 remained outstanding. A writ issued in 1981 alleged negligent misrepresentation, against which the defendants pleaded that the plaintiffs' action was time barred, the inducement to make the loan having been relied on in 1974. The Court of Appeal held that the cause of action did not necessarily accrue when the plaintiffs were induced to advance the loan, but might have arisen at the later date when the worsening financial position of the borrowers caused the loans to be worth less than their face value.

According to Ackner LJ, "The mere fact that the innocent but negligent misrepresentations caused the plaintiff to enter into a contract which it otherwise would not have entered does not inevitably mean that it had suffered damage by merely entering into the contract."[170] For the purposes of the present case, Ackner LJ was prepared to accept that evidence would need to be led so as to allow the court to determine whether, at the date on which the money was advanced by the plaintiff, the value of the chose in action which it then acquired was, in fact, less than the sum lent by the plaintiff. This evidence might well show that no loss had been suffered simply through reliance on the defendants' statements. For example, given market conditions at the time, the financial difficulties faced by the Panamanian companies might have been caused by the collapse of the shipping market in the period between 1975 and 1976.

The other problem associated with the preparation of documents is that a solicitor may have been asked to prepare a particular document, but because of the advice received from the defendants, no document is, in fact, prepared. For example, suppose in *DW Moore & Co* v. *Ferrier* the defendant's negligence had consisted in giving advice to the effect that there was no need for the inclusion of a restraint of trade clause or that the desired outcome could not be achieved by the inclusion of a clause of the kind requested. In some instances, a document will be produced, in which case the date of execution will still remain relevant, as that will be the date on which a document should have come into existence containing a provision which would adequately protect the plaintiff. However, the position must be different if, for example, the defendant advises the plaintiff that there is nothing, legally, which can be done to achieve the plaintiff's desired goal. Here the effect of the defendant's advice is that the plaintiff may cease to employ the defendant

---

169. [1984] 2 All ER 226. See also *First National Bank plc* v. *Humberts (a firm)* [1995] 2 All ER 673 considered below in relation to the liability of valuers.
170. *Ibid* at 234–35.

with the result that no document is ever produced. Accordingly, the date on which a document should have come into existence may not be the date on which the cause of action accrues and it may be necessary to consider the date on which actual damage is caused, through, for example, the setting up of a rival business, to be the date on which the plaintiff's cause of action accrues.

A further problem which may arise in the case of an omission to act on the part of a solicitor is that regard must be given to the last date on which the effects of the omission could have been mitigated, especially in cases where the wrong committed by the defendant is of a continuing nature. For example in *Midland Bank Trust Co Ltd* v. *Hett, Stubbs & Kemp (firm)*[171] the defendants' wrong consisted of a failure to register an option to purchase land and the cause of action, in favour of the plaintiff, was considered to have accrued only when it became too late to register the option, since up to that date the defendants had the opportunity to remedy their omission, but had not done so. The cause of action was considered to arise on a day-to-day basis on each occasion the defendants failed to remedy the consequences of their negligence. In contrast, in *Bell* v. *Peter Browne & Co*[172] the defendants' negligence consisted of either a failure to arrange for the execution of a declaration of trust in respect of the matrimonial home, following the plaintiff's divorce, or a failure to register a caution at the Land Registry so as to warn others dealing in the property that the plaintiff had an interest. In consequence of the defendants' failure to take reasonable care, the plaintiff lost an interest in the proceeds of sale of the matrimonial home in accordance with the terms of a divorce settlement. Although the settlement occurred in 1978, the plaintiff did not issue his writ until 1987 and, for the purposes of his tort action, was considered to be time barred, since damage had occurred when the defendants failed to lodge a caution. Although this was regarded as a remediable breach, damage was still taken to have been caused by the initial failure to take care. Accordingly, time ran against the plaintiff from a different date according to whether his action was framed in contract or in tort. For the purposes of the tort action, Nicholls LJ said:

"One might have expected that parallel professional negligence claims based on contract and the tort of negligence would have a common starting date for the running of the six-year limitation periods applicable in most cases under the 1980 Act. But this is not so, because a cause of action based on negligence does not accrue until damage is suffered . . .

So when did Mr Bell first sustain damage by reason of his solicitor's negligence? On this it is necessary to distinguish between (a) the solicitor's failure to see that the parties' agreement was recorded formally in a suitable declaration of trust . . . and (b) their failure to protect Mr Bell's interest in the house or the proceeds of sale by lodging a caution. As to failure (a) clearly the damage, such as it may have been, was sustained when the transfer was executed and handed over. At that point Mr Bell parted with title to the house . . .

Mr Bell in the case of failure (b), as much as in the case of failure (a), did not receive the protection he ought to have received when he executed the transfer and parted with his title to the house. He was at risk from the outset. His interest was vulnerable. On the other hand, so long as Mr Bell's wife did not deal with the property, failure (b) could easily be put right and at little expense

I am unable to accept that remediability puts failure (b) on the other side of the line from failure (a)."[173]

171. [1979] 1 Ch 384. See also *Singer* v. *Harrison Clark*, 15 April 1987, unreported, and Ch 8.
172. [1990] 3 All ER 124. For the relevant issues arising from this case concerning limitation of actions in contract cases, see the discussion in Ch 8.
173. *Ibid* at 127–28.

It follows from this that in *Bell*, so far as the defendant's failure to execute a suitable declaration of trust was concerned, precisely the same reasoning is adopted as in *Forster* v. *Outred* and *DW Moore & Co* v. *Ferrier*, to the extent that the uncertainty of the plaintiff's estranged spouse's future actions was regarded as a matter relevant only to the quantum of loss rather than having any relevance to the accrual of the cause of action. But the same reasoning was also applied to the failure to lodge a caution, on the basis that damage had been suffered from the outset and that despite the fact that this breach was remediable, this had no effect on the date of accrual of the cause of action for negligence purposes, since Bell was unlikely to have been in a position to remedy the defendant's negligence once they "closed their file". What seems to distinguish this case and *Midland Bank Trust Co Ltd* v. *Hett, Stubbs & Kemp* is that in the latter, the file was never closed, since there was continuing correspondence between the plaintiff and the defendants, which would have allowed the latter to realise that a mistake had been made and take steps to rectify it.[174]

Thus far, the position of solicitors has been considered on the basis that their duty is one owed to the client, but it has been observed above that a solicitor may also owe a duty of care to a third party, albeit in limited circumstances. The circumstances must be necessarily limited since the solicitor's duty is primarily to his client and that duty will often require the solicitor to act in a hostile manner towards third parties.

Moreover, following the decision of the House of Lords in *White* v. *Jones*[175] there are certain conceptual difficulties associated with holding that a solicitor owes a tortious duty of care to a third party, not the least of which is that the third party may be seeking damages for the solicitor's breach of contract with his client; that the action is one for pure economic loss, which is generally not recoverable except under the principle in *Hedley Byrne & Co* v. *Heller & Partners Ltd*; that often, the alleged negligence of the solicitor will consist of no more than an omission to act rather than an act which may be characterised as negligent.[176] The problem with these cases is that no consideration appears to have been given to the question of limitation of actions, even though they necessarily are tort actions. Since the primary consideration for limitation purposes is the identification of a date on which the plaintiff's cause of action is complete, it is necessary to identify the earliest date on which the plaintiff could have sued. This may depend on the circumstances of the case. For example, in those cases in which a duty of care has been held to exist, the majority have involved negligence on the part of a solicitor in failing to properly advise his client on how to draw up an effective will.[177] However, in other cases, the solicitor's negligence has consisted of a failure to take action to ensure that his client does not cause foreseeable harm to a third party. Thus in *Al-Kandari* v. *Brown*[178] the alleged negligence consisted of a failure to ensure that a client could not leave the country, thereby enabling him to kidnap the plaintiff's children.

---

174. *Ibid* at 128 *per* Nicholls LJ. The same reasoning may also apply to cases of delay on the part of a solicitor which results in the plaintiff's medical negligence action being struck out, since there is a continuing relationship between the parties. Here the cause of action accrues on the date of striking out regardless of when the original loss occurred: *Hopkins* v. *McKenzie* [1995] 6 Med LR 26.

175. [1995] 1 All ER 691. See also *Ross* v. *Caunters* [1980] Ch 297; *Clarke* v. *Bruce Lance & Co* [1988] 1 WLR 881; *Al-Kandari* v. *Brown* [1988] QB 655.

176. *Ibid* at 698–701 *per* Lord Goff.

177. *White* v. *Jones* [1995] 1 All ER 691; *Ross* v. *Caunters* [1980] Ch 297; *Clarke* v. *Bruce Lance & Co* [1988] 1 WLR 881.

178. [1988] QB 655.

In the cases involving negligent advice given to a client preparing a will, it would be difficult to say that the plaintiff's cause of action is complete at the time the will is executed, since the testator may change his mind and change his will at a later stage.[179] In these circumstances, there is no duty of care owed to the third party, in which case it would be impossible to say that all the facts necessary in order to allow the plaintiff to sue are present. These cases are, therefore, distinguishable from *Forster* v. *Outred & Co* in which all the ingredients of liability, including damage, were present and that only the quantum of loss was uncertain due to the possible future actions of a third party. As was observed by Sir Donald Nicholls V-C in *White* v. *Jones*, when it was heard in the Court of Appeal:

"If an intended beneficiary has a cause of action against a negligent solicitor, time would run either from the date on which the will was made or ought to have been made or from the date of death. The first of these possibilities would be unsatisfactory: a beneficiary intended to take under a will can hardly be said to suffer loss during the testator's lifetime. The second would be unsatisfactory, because it would mean that time might not begin to run indefinitely, subject only to the 15-year longstop under s. 14B of the Limitation Act 1980."[180]

If the date of execution of the will cannot be said to be the date on which the third party plaintiff's action accrues, an alternative date for the running of time will be the date on which the testator dies or otherwise becomes unable to change his mind,[181] but as Sir Donald Nicholls V-C observed in the Court of Appeal in *White* v. *Jones*, this date could raise the spectre of uncertainty over the date on which the cause of action accrues. However, assuming the damage caused by the defendant's negligence is regarded as latent damage, there will be a 15-year long-stop on the liability of the defendant under the Limitation Act 1980, s 14B. However, this may be the only possible date for the purposes of the running of time, given that no duty of care is owed until such time as the testator has died. The difficulty with an assertion that the cause of action cannot accrue until there is a duty of care and a breach of that duty, is that there are cases which seem to suggest that a cause of action can accrue at a time when the plaintiff is still unable to commence proceedings.[182] But it is still suggested that if the ingredients of the tort of negligence are not all in place, the plaintiff should not be left in a position whereby time starts to run against him in circumstances in which he has no ability to commence proceedings against the defendant. Statutes of Limitation may well be regarded as Acts of Peace, but this would be to give the defendant peace at the price of injustice to the plaintiff.

179. See e.g. *Clarke* v. *Bruce Lance & Co* [1988] 1 WLR 881; *Hemmens* v. *Wilson Browne* [1994] 2 WLR 323.

180. *White* v. *Jones* [1993] 3 All ER 481 at 492. When this decision reached the House of Lords, members of the court did not address the issue of limitation of actions, but were concerned simply with the justice of imposing a duty of care.

181. For example, suppose the negligent solicitor has a power of attorney in respect of his client's affairs, the client now being of unsound mind: if the testator cannot change his mind, the ingredients of duty, breach and damage may now be in place.

182. See *Sevcon* v. *Lucas CAV Ltd* [1986] 2 All ER 104 decided under the Patents Act 1949, s 13(4). But this may be explicable on the basis that what was said in that case is specific to the statutory language used. In the alternative, it was asserted in *O'Connor* v. *Isaacs* [1956] 2 QB 288 that if a restriction on the ability of the plaintiff to sue prevents the cause of action from arising, this will also prevent the limitation period from running against the plaintiff. See further "The cause of action and the right to sue" considered below.

(iii) Other professional advisers

Where an insurance broker negligently fails to disclose material facts, it is likely that the insurer issuing the policy will seek to avoid it on the grounds of non-disclosure. In these circumstances, the insured has an action for negligence against the broker, but the question arises at what time does the plaintiff's cause of action accrue? In *Iron Trade Mutual Insurance Co Ltd* v. *JK Buckenham Ltd*[183] the defendant broker failed to procure effective reinsurance policies for the plaintiff, having failed to make full disclosure regarding the plaintiff's retention of risk, with the result that the reinsurer sought to avoid the policy. For the purposes of the plaintiff's cause of action in tort against the broker, it was held that since the insurer suffers damage when the voidable reinsurance contract is executed, this is also the date on which the tort action against the broker is complete. Similarly in *Islander Trucking Co Ltd* v. *Hogg Robinson & Gardener Mountain (Marine) Ltd*[184] in 1980, the plaintiff asked the defendant to obtain liability insurance. Subsequently the plaintiff claimed on the insurer who avoided the policy in 1985 on the grounds of non-disclosure. An action was commenced against the defendant broker in 1986, within the limitation period, but he pleaded that he had acted as an agent for others, who were joined as parties to the action in 1989. These other brokers asked to be released on the ground that the limitation period had expired. In line with *Iron Trade Mutual*, above, it was held that the cause of action against the negligent broker accrued when the voidable insurance policy was taken out, so that the action against these other brokers was out of time.

The general position adopted in relation to negligent execution of documents by solicitors was applied to the position of the negligent insurance broker. Just as a solicitor's client suffers damage when a document is negligently executed, the same is true of an insured whose policy of insurance is voidable due to the non-disclosure of the broker acting on his behalf. The most directly analogous decision was considered to have been that of Steyn J in *Aikman* v. *Hallett & Co.*[185] Here the plaintiff claimed he had been advised to surrender a valid head tenancy of a farm in return for a sub-tenancy which was much less secure and resulted in the plaintiff being served with a notice to quit. The plaintiff's cause of action was considered to be complete at the date of surrender since that was the date on which he received something less secure than he previously had. Applying the same reasoning to a voidable insurance policy, the insured, at the time of the acquisition of a voidable policy, has something less secure than he desires.

Apart from solicitors and insurance brokers, other professional advisers such as accountants and surveyors or valuers also give advice which may be reasonably relied upon by either a contractual client or, in the case of surveyors[186] and to a lesser extent accountants,[187] by third parties who have no contractual relationship with the adviser. So far as surveyors are concerned, the leading authority on matters of limitation of actions is to be found in *Secretary of State for the Environment* v. *Essex, Goodman & Suggitt (a firm)*[188] in which the Department of the Environment engaged the defendants to prepare a survey report on an office block. The surveyors negligently failed to notice a number of

---

183. [1990] 1 All ER 808.
184. [1990] 1 All ER 826.
185. 23 March 1987, unreported.
186. See e.g. *Smith* v. *Eric S Bush (a firm)* [1990] 1 AC 831.
187. See e.g. *Morgan Crucible Co plc* v. *Hill Samuel Bank Ltd* [1991] 1 All ER 148. But cf *Caparo Industries plc* v. *Dickman* [1990] 2 AC 605.
188. [1986] 2 All ER 69.

defects and, in reliance on the favourable report, the Department took a lease of the building. Judge Hawser QC held that the date on which the cause of action accrued was the date on which the plaintiffs relied upon the defendants' advice which was considered to be the date on which they were irrevocably committed to the lease. Until the date of irrevocable committal, the plaintiff was in a position to avoid the expense of repairing the building, thereby adopting the same test applied to the negligence of solicitors.

The action could not be equated with one against an engineer or an architect, since although the duty of all professionals concerned with buildings is to provide a proper product, the proper product in the case of an architect etc is the building itself, whereas the proper product for the purposes of a surveyor is an accurate report. According to Judge Hawser QC:

"The surveyor was employed to find out whether any damage existed, and if they failed to use reasonable care and skill to do so and to report it to the plaintiffs, they would have been liable as at the date when the plaintiffs acted on the report. If the defects in design, which the third defendants ought to have discovered, existed at all, it seems to me that they must have existed at the time of the survey for liability to arise."[189]

A further function performed by surveyors is that of valuation of premises. If a valuation is negligently effected, one possibility is that the plaintiff may claim that he has sustained loss through an inability to employ funds on other transactions because the negligence of the valuer has caused him to commit those funds to the transaction in respect of which the valuation was given. In *First National Commercial Bank plc* v. *Humberts (a firm)*[190] the defendants had valued the future worth of a lease of a commercial development, as a result of which the plaintiffs lent £2.6 million, secured on the lease, and in the belief that the lease was worth £4.4 million. Subsequently the borrower became insolvent and the security taken proved to be insufficient to allow the amount owed to be recouped. The valuers argued that the plaintiff's action was out of time, the writ having been issued 6 years and 10 months after the date of the valuation. The plaintiffs counterargued that since the negligent valuation did not cause them any loss until the date on which the security proved to be insufficient, their action was not time barred.

On the issue of limitation of actions, it was held that the date on which damage is caused is a question of fact in each case and there is no hard-and-fast rule to the effect that the reasoning in defective document cases will always be the proper test to apply. According to the Australian High Court decision in *Warley Australia Ltd* v. *State of Western Australia*[191] economic loss may take a variety of forms and the answer to when the cause of action accrues will require consideration of the precise interest which has been infringed and the nature of that infringement.

In *Swingcastle Ltd* v. *Alastair Gibson (a firm)*[192] Neill LJ opined that in order to be able to recover in respect of loss sustained through an inability to employ funds on other transactions, the claimant had to establish that he would have used the money in the manner claimed. The plaintiffs in *First National Commercial Bank plc* v. *Humberts* had asserted that they would have used the money advanced for other purposes, and there was no evidence to show that any other transactions which could have been entered into in the

189. *Ibid* at 74.
190. [1995] 2 All ER 673.
191. (1992) 109 ALR 247.
192. [1990] 3 All ER 433, CA, affirmed [1991] 2 AC 223, HL.

relevant period would have been of any greater value than the transaction which was made. Accordingly, the losses claimed to have been suffered by the plaintiffs came into existence within the six-year limitation period and the action was not time barred.

The position of accountants is a matter not widely considered in the case law, which may be a consequence of the general tendency not to hold accountants responsible for a failure to take care outside of a contractual relationship with their clients. However, in *Moon* v. *Franklin*[193] an accountant wrongly advised his client to allow a partnership to cease trading, which resulted in substantial tax liability by bringing into operation the provisions of the Income and Corporation Taxes Act 1988, s 118, on the cessation of the partnership. The cause of action was held to accrue on cessation of trading, since it was only on that date that the increased tax liability became inevitable, with the result that the later date, on which the accounts for the relevant period were signed, could be ignored.

THE CAUSE OF ACTION AND THE RIGHT TO SUE

It has been seen above that a cause of action in tort is complete only when damage has been suffered by the plaintiff. However, there may be circumstances in which a plaintiff who has a cause of action, for other reasons, is unable to commence proceedings. In *Sevcon Ltd* v. *Lucas CAV Ltd*[194] an action concerning patent infringement was considered by the House of Lords to be an action in tort, but there were statutory provisions[195] which prevented proceedings for patent infringement being brought until such time as the patent had been granted. However, those provisions also stated that once a patent had been granted, the plaintiff would be allowed to sue in respect of infringements which occurred between the date of application for a patent and the date on which the patent was granted. In *Sevcon*, the first infringement occurred between the dates of application and grant. Despite what seems to be the unjust consequences of the decision, it was held that the plaintiffs' cause of action accrued when there was an infringement, even though, at that time, no action could be brought. Accordingly, by the time the statute allowed the plaintiff to sue, the action was time barred.[196]

In *O'Connor* v. *Isaacs*[197] in 1942, magistrates, acting in excess of their powers, had ordered the plaintiff that he should pay maintenance. As a result of non-compliance with the order, the plaintiff was imprisoned on a number of occasions between 1942 and 1945. Eventually, in 1954, the lack of jurisdiction was identified, the maintenance order was quashed, and the plaintiff sued both the magistrates and those responsible for his incarceration. The question arose whether the plaintiff's cause of action accrued in 1945, when he was last imprisoned or whether the cause of action accrued in 1954 when the maintenance order was quashed, since prior to that last date there would have been lawful grounds for the restraint of his freedom.

Diplock J[198] considered whether the quashing of the maintenance order could be regarded as merely the removal of a procedural bar to the bringing of an action which had

193. 19 December 1991, unreported.
194. [1986] 2 All ER 104.
195. Patents Act 1949, s 13(4).
196. This may be explained on the basis that the decision is peculiar to the particular facts of this case, being based on an interpretation of the express words of a statutory provision.
197. [1956] 2 QB 288. See also *Musurus Bey* v. *Gadban* [1894] 2 QB 352.
198. With whose judgment the Court of Appeal agreed.

accrued at an earlier date or whether the quashing of the order was an essential requirement before a cause of action in favour of the plaintiff could accrue at all. In the event, Diplock J considered the quashing of the order to be no more than the removal of a procedural bar, in which case, the plaintiff's cause of action had arisen in 1945 with the result that an action commenced in 1954 was out of time. However, what this case also recognises is that if a particular restriction on the ability of the plaintiff to sue can be regarded as something which prevents the plaintiff's cause of action from maturing, this will have the effect of preserving the plaintiff's right to sue by moving forward the date on which the cause of action accrues.

CHAPTER 19

PERSONAL INJURIES

Under the Limitation Act 1939, no distinction was drawn between personal injury caused by negligence and other types of damage, with the result that in cases of latent personal injury, it was possible for a plaintiff to be time barred before he even realised that damage had been suffered, since the general limitation period in tort and contract actions was one of six years which ran from the date of accrual of the cause of action. Subsequently, a distinction between personal injury claims and other types of claim was made when the six-year limitation period was reduced to one of three years by the Law Reform (Limitation of Actions etc) Act 1954, on the basis that, in most instances, a writ would have been served well before the end of the six-year period.

However, no provision was made for latent personal injury until the Limitation Act 1963, which allowed a plaintiff to apply to the court for leave to bring a time-barred action in cases in which the plaintiff could show that he was ignorant of certain facts relating to his cause of action. The problem with the 1963 Act was that it was generally regarded as so badly drafted that few could understand when its provisions came into play. Indeed it was once stated that the 1963 Act had "a strong claim to the distinction of being the worst drafted Act on the statute book".[1]

The Limitation Act 1963 was replaced by the Limitation Act 1975 which followed closely the recommendations of the Orr Committee[2] and introduced what is the present structure to be found in the Limitation Act 1980, ss 11 to 14 and s 33. The effect of these rules is to retain the basic three-year limitation period running from the date of accrual of the cause of action, but to this is added an alternative three-year period which runs from the date on which the plaintiff became aware of his injuries and of his right of action. Moreover, the court is given a discretion, under section 33 of the 1980 Act, to override the three year limitation periods in cases where justice so demands, so as to allow an action to proceed out of time.

The Limitation Act 1980, s 11 provides:

"(1) This section applies to any action for damages for negligence, nuisance or breach of duty (whether the duty exists by virtue of a contract or of provision made by or under a statute or independently of any contract or any such provision) where the damages claimed by the plaintiff for the negligence, nuisance or breach of duty consist of or include damages in respect of personal injuries to the plaintiff or any other person.

(1A) This section does not apply to any action brought for damages under section 3 of the Protection from Harassment Act 1997.[3]

---

1. *Central Asbestos Co* v. *Dodd* [1973] AC 518 at 529 *per* Lord Reid.
2. *Interim Report on Limitation of Actions in Personal Injury Claims,* Cmnd 5630, 1974.
3. Inserted by the Protection from Harassment Act 1997, s 6.

(2) None of the limits given in the preceding provisions of this Act shall apply to an action to which this section applies.

(3) An action to which this section applies shall not be brought after the expiration of the period applicable in accordance with subsection (4) or (5) below.

(4) Except where subsection (5) below applies, the period applicable is three years from—

(a) the date on which the cause of action accrued; or
(b) the date of knowledge (if later) of the person injured.

(5) If the person injured dies before the expiration of the period mentioned in subsection (4) above, the period applicable as respects the cause of action surviving for the benefit of his estate by virtue of section 1 of the Law Reform (Miscellaneous Provisions) Act 1934 shall be three years from—

(a) the date of death; and
(b) the date of the personal representative's knowledge.

(6) For the purposes of this section 'personal representative' includes any person who is or has been a personal representative of the deceased, including an executor who has not yet proved the will (whether or not he has renounced probate) but not anyone appointed only as a special personal representative in relation to settled land; and regard shall be had to any knowledge acquired by any such person while a personal representative or previously.

(7) If there is more than one personal representative and their dates of knowledge are different, subsection 5(b) above shall be read as referring to the earliest of those dates."

THE MEANING OF PERSONAL INJURY CLAIMS

It is important to emphasise that the wording of section 11 is such that it will not be confined simply to actions for damages for personal injuries, since it is concerned with "any action for damages for negligence, nuisance or breach of duty . . . where the damages claimed by the plaintiff . . . *consist of or include damages in respect of* personal injury to the plaintiff or any other person". For these purposes, personal injury includes any disease or impairment of a person's physical or mental condition.[4] It is generally accepted that in addition to physical injury and illness, the term personal injury will also be interpreted to include psychiatric damage suffered as a consequence of a relevant breach of duty and mental distress resulting from the commission of a tort or other breach of duty.[5]

Also included in the meaning of "impairment" will be injury suffered on a cumulative basis over a period of time, such as progressive deafness resulting from an employer's failure to provide protective equipment such as ear muffs, where an employee is required to work in noisy conditions.[6]

4. Limitation Act 1980, s 38(1).
5. See *Archer* v. *Brown* [1985] QB 401 (deceit); *Perry* v. *Sidney Phillips & Son (A firm)* [1982] 1 WLR 1297 (negligent performance of a contract requiring the exercise of reasonable care and skill); *Harris* v. *Lombard (New Zealand) Ltd* [1974] 2 NZLR 161 (wrongful repossession of goods subject to a hire purchase agreement); *Ichard* v. *Frangoulis* [1977] 1 WLR 556 (loss of a holiday due to a road traffic accident); *Jarvis* v. *Swan's Tours Ltd* [1973] QB 233 (mental distress caused by a failed holiday). But mental distress is not ordinarily recoverable in most actions for breach of contract unless the contract is one to provide freedom from distress or if the contract is for the provision of enjoyment: *Hayes* v. *James & Charles Dodd (a firm)* [1990] 2 All ER 815.
6. *Berry* v. *Stone Manganese Marine Ltd* [1972] 1 Lloyd's Rep 182.

(a) Professional negligence and personal injury

There are some actions which are not covered by section 11 despite the fact that they emanate from an accident which has involved injury. For example, where a person is injured in an accident, but he loses the chance to obtain recompense due to, for example, the negligence of a solicitor, the defendant's breach of duty does not cause personal injury, although it does prevent the plaintiff from recovering damages. In these circumstances, the three-year rule in section 11 will not apply to the action against the solicitor, and the normal six-year rule in either section 2 or section 5 will apply. For example in *Ackbar* v. *Green & Co*[7] insurance brokers failed to obtain insurance against the risk of personal injury to the plaintiff. When the plaintiff was injured, he discovered that he was uninsured. The writ was issued more than three years from the date of the accident, but within the six-year period. The defendants argued that the three-year rule in what is now section 11 applied, since the damages claimed were "in respect of" personal injuries. However, it was held that the normal six-year rule applicable to general tort actions should apply, as the essence of the plaintiff's claim was the broker's breach of duty.

It should be noted, however, that the words "in respect of" are capable of a different interpretation. Thus in *Patterson* v. *Chadwick*[8] the plaintiff sued his former solicitors for allowing the limitation period to expire before issuing a writ for medical negligence. It was held by Boreham J that this was an action in respect of personal injury, for the purposes of what is now the Supreme Court Act 1981, s 34, since there was some connection with personal injury, to the extent that the nature and extent of the personal injuries suffered by the plaintiff were an essential element in the proof of the claim.

(b) Wrongful conception and personal injury

Other actions which may fall outside the scope of section 11 appear to include those in respect of "wrongful birth" or "wrongful conception" (as is now the preferred phrase)[9] since the gist of the action is that, at the point of conception, the injury claimed by the parents originates.[10] As a consequence of that conception, a child is born which must be maintained, against the expectations of its parents.[11] As such, these claims might appear to be for expenditure incurred and the mother's loss of income resulting from an unwanted pregnancy. Accordingly it was said in *Naylor* v. *Preston Area Health Authority*[12] that:

" . . . [I]t was pointed out, quite correctly, that in the context of the proposal to treat medical negligence as personal injury actions, while an action for personal injuries is defined in Ord. 1, r. 4 in wide terms as meaning 'an action in which there is a claim for damages in respect of a person's death', and 'personal injuries' includes 'any disease and any impairment of a person's physical or mental condition' and would thus often include actions for medical negligence, some would not be included, e.g. a claim for damages for *failing* to impair a person's physical condition, where the allegation was that a vasectomy failed to achieve its object."[13]

---

7. [1975] 1 QB 582.
8. [1974] 1 WLR 890.
9. It is the conception of the child rather than the birth which is the gist of the action: *Walkin* v. *South Manchester Health Authority* [1995] 4 All ER 132 at 140 *per* Auld LJ and at 144 *per* Neill LJ.
10. *Ibid* at 140 *per* Auld LJ.
11. See *Pattison* v. *Hobbs*, *The Times*, 11 November 1985.
12. [1987] 2 All ER 353. The action turned on an interpretation of RSC Ord 1, r 4.
13. *Ibid* at 363 *per* Lord Donaldson MR.

There may be circumstances in which an action can be framed in such a way as to turn it into one for personal injury damages only. For example, in the case of a failed sterilisation, it might be pleaded that a second sterilisation will involve pain and suffering and that delivery of the unwanted child subjected the mother to additional pain. Thus it was observed in *Allen* v. *Bloomsbury Health Authority*[14] that:

"It is hard to see how s. 11 of the Limitation Act 1980 would apply to a *claim limited to the financial costs* associated with the upbringing of the unwanted child since this would be ... a straightforward *Hedley Byrne* v. *Heller* type of claim for foreseeable economic loss caused by negligent advice or misstatement."[15]

But if the claim is not *limited to the financial losses* suffered, the implication is that section 11 might be applicable. However, a different view is that all claims for wrongful conception are to be regarded as personal injury action which fall within the scope of section 11. In *Walkin* v. *South Manchester Health Authority*[16] the plaintiff underwent a sterilisation operation which failed because uterine tubes which had been subject to heat treatment remained functional. The plaintiff's writ did not include a claim for damages for personal injury, being confined to the financial consequences of the failed operation. Despite this, the action was still treated as one for personal injuries because the plaintiff would have been able to claim for both pain and suffering and the economic loss associated with the unwanted conception and both claims arose out of the one cause of action, namely the unwanted pregnancy. Moreover, although a failed sterilisation cannot be regarded as personal injury, as the plaintiff is left as she was before, there is "impairment" within the meaning of the Limitation Act 1980, s 38(1) in the form of the unwanted conception. Since the claim for economic loss stemmed from that "impairment" it too had to be regarded as a claim for damages in respect of personal injuries. According to Auld LJ, "The question whether an action is for damages in respect of personal injuries is one of substance, not a matter of pleading. As [counsel for the defendants] submitted, the claim for damages, or the head of loss, must be considered in the context of the cause of action to which it relates."[17]

Thus what matters is "the underlying reality, rather than the pleader's pen".[18] It seems to follow from *Walkin* that it will not be possible for counsel for the plaintiff, in cases of this kind, to sub-divide the loss suffered by the plaintiff so as to render section 11 inapplicable. While this will mean that the six-year rule under section 2 will be inapplicable, the application of section 11 means that the court still has a discretion to allow an action to proceed out of time under section 33.

(c) Breach of contract and personal injury

Section 11(1) expressly includes in its definition of "breach of duty" a breach of contractual duty. Thus the sale of a defective product which causes personal injury and also amounts to a breach of one of the implied terms in the Sale of Goods Act 1979, s 14, or

---

14. [1993] 1 All ER 651.
15. *Ibid* at 658 *per* Brooke J. Emphasis added.
16. [1995] 4 All ER 132.
17. *Ibid* at 141.
18. *Ibid* at 140, citing Potter J at first instance.

a breach of a contractual obligation to exercise reasonable care in private medical treatment will both fall within section 11. In each such case, the three-year rule in respect of limitation of actions will apply to the personal injury aspect of the plaintiff's claim for damages.

It should be noted that there is no need for the claim to be one which is based on the notion of concurrent contractual and tortious liability, with the result that section 11 can apply to the breach of a strict contractual duty which does not raise any issue of a failure to exercise reasonable care on the part of the defendant. In *Howe* v. *David Brown Tractors (Retail) Ltd*[19] in 1982 the plaintiffs, a father and son who between them ran a horticultural business, purchased a tractor fitted with a recotiller, which malfunctioned, causing serious injury to the son's leg in an accident which occurred in January 1985. Accordingly, the primary limitation period expired in January 1988, but the writ was not issued until July 1988, which meant that the question of the operation of the section 33 discretion also came into play.[20] Subsequently, in December 1988, a consent order was granted allowing section 11 to be disapplied under section 33 and the plaintiff amended his claim to cover loss of profit suffered in consequence of the personal injury. The defendant then claimed that section 11 applied and that, since the writ was not issued within the three-year limitation period, the claim was barred and that no additional parties could be added after the expiry of the limitation period.[21] The Court of Appeal agreed that the action was covered by section 11, since the consequence of the supply of the defective tool was that the plaintiff suffered personal injury.[22] Moreover, since section 11 covers not just the plaintiff, but also "any other person", personal injury suffered by an employee of the company (the plaintiff) was also covered. Accordingly, this was a claim for personal injury damages which fell within section 11.

(d) Election between actions for different types of loss

A particular problem raised by cases such as those in respect of wrongful conception and breach of contract is that they may involve claims for damages for personal injury and for economic loss. A matter which has been considered is whether the plaintiff can elect to forego his claim for personal injury damages in order to be able to use the normal six-year period applicable to other actions for breach of contract or breach of a tortious obligation. It has been seen above that on one view such an election is acceptable, at least by implication.[23] However, in *Brunsden* v. *Humphrey*[24] the view expressed was that different causes of action arose in respect of personal injury and property damage. Conversely, in other cases, where different kinds of loss have been suffered but they are sufficiently closely related, they have been treated as forming part of the same claim. Thus in *Howe* v. *David Brown Tractors (Retail) Ltd*[25] Nicholls LJ said, "The claim for financial loss is as much a claim for 'damages in respect of personal injury' as is the claim in respect of

---

19. [1991] 4 All ER 30.
20. See below.
21. RSC Ord 15, r 6(5)(b) and see Ch 7.
22. *Howe* v. *David Brown Tractors (Retail) Ltd* [1991] 4 All ER 30 at 41 *per* Nicholls LJ.
23. See *Pattison* v. *Hobbs*, *The Times*, 11 November 1985.
24. (1884) 14 QBD 141.
25. [1991] 4 All ER 30.

the physical injury itself".[26] What matters is the underlying reality rather than the pleader's pen, with the result that the court has to determine what is the substance of the claim. Thus in *Walkin* v. *South Manchester Health Authority*[27] it was held that, in a case of wrongful conception, the economic loss associated with bringing up the unwanted child and the personal injury in the form of pain and suffering emanate from the same cause of action, the action as a whole is to be treated as one for personal injury, even where no damages are claimed for the personal injury suffered. From this it follows that the implication in *Pattison* v. *Hobbs* that severance of different heads of loss is possible must be regarded as incorrect.

Problems could arise as between male and female sterilisation operations which go wrong, since in the case of a failed vasectomy, at first sight, there is no pain and suffering on the part of the male patient, since he does not become pregnant and might be considered to suffer no personal injury. If such a distinction is made, the problem is that male and female sterilisation operations might be subject to different rules on limitation of actions, since the action by the male will be in respect of nothing other than financial loss. However, in *Walkin* v. *South Manchester Health Authority,* Auld LJ took a different view to the effect that:

"In each case, the personal injury is the mother's unwanted pregnancy; consequences such as physical pain and suffering of the mother, and nervous anxiety and distress and financial costs suffered by either [parent] are caught by the words of section 11(1), 'damages in respect of personal injuries to the plaintiff or any other person'."[28]

However, there may be cases which are not caught by Auld LJ's view of the physical harm suffered by the male parent. For example, if a man becomes the father of a child due to a failed vasectomy but is no longer in any form of relationship with the child's mother and the mother looks to the man for maintenance, any loss suffered by the man will be purely financial.[29]

(e) Trespass to the person and personal injury

In *Letang* v. *Cooper*[30] the plaintiff was injured when the defendant ran over her legs in his car. For reasons which did not surface in the law reports, the plaintiff failed to bring an action for negligently caused personal injury within the time limit allowed for such actions. In order to get round the problems caused by the delay, the plaintiff's action was couched in terms of the intentional tort of trespass to the person, which, if successful, would have been within the limitation period for torts not involving personal injury. The Court of Appeal held that an action for *unintentional* trespass which caused physical injury had to be regarded as an action based upon negligence, in which case, if that negligence results in personal injury, it is an action to which section 11 applies. But what this decision left open was the position where the defendant is guilty of *intentional* trespass which results in personal injury.

---

26. *Ibid* at 41.
27. [1995] 4 All ER 132.
28. *Ibid* at 142.
29. *Ibid*, per Roch LJ.
30. [1965] 1 QB 232.

On a broad view, the wording of section 11 is sufficiently wide to cover cases of intentional trespass which result in personal injury, since the phrase "breach of duty" could be construed so as to cover intentional wrongs. However, in *Stubbings* v. *Webb*[31] the House of Lords has come to a contrary view. In that case, the plaintiff alleged that she had been the victim of sexual abuse during her childhood, for which her stepfather and stepbrother were responsible. The trauma of these events had caused her to try to forget what had happened with the result that she did not issue her writ until August 1987, many years after reaching the age of majority in January 1975. It was argued for the plaintiff that this was an action in respect of personal injuries, in which case the three-year knowledge-based limitation period could apply, as if this were akin to a case of latent personal injury. If it had been necessary to decide whether the plaintiff could or could not have been aware that she had suffered serious personal injury, the tenor of the House of Lords' judgments indicated that the plaintiff would not have been successful,[32] but the outcome of the appeal turned on other grounds.

On the issue whether section 11 could apply to cases of intentional trespass, it was determined that it was not the intention of Parliament that the provisions contained in that section should apply to such cases, because that was the conclusion arrived at by the Tucker Committee in 1949, on whose recommendations the limitation period in personal injury cases was first reduced to three years.[33] This might have been an acceptable position to take in 1949, because at that stage, there was no discretion to extend the limitation period in favour of a plaintiff in personal injury actions generally. Moreover, the House of Lords also declined to follow an earlier decision to the effect that an assault occasioning actual bodily harm could be regarded as a case involving personal injuries.[34] It is also arguable that the Tucker Committee did not regard their recommendations as having nothing to do with cases of trespass to the person, since they did include in the range of actions intended to be covered by the Report, "such actions as claims for negligence against doctors".[35] If by this they meant no more than medical negligence the words used would have meant nothing since such actions would be covered by the words, "negligence, nuisance or breach of duty" in what is now section 11. Accordingly, it is arguable that what was referred to are cases of "medical battery" such as the performance of an invasive procedure without consent, in which case some instances of trespass to the person were intended to be covered by the provisions on personal injuries.

In *Stubbings* v. *Webb* Lord Griffiths emphasised the fact that there was a deliberate breach of duty which took the case outside of the area covered by section 11 which is concerned with accidental harm. However, in cases of battery, it does not follow that the defendant intends to cause *personal injury,* if this is what Lord Griffiths is concerned about. It is clear that, for the purposes of the tort of battery, the intention must relate to the act rather than the consequence of that act, so that school-yard pranks, if regarded as unacceptable in the ordinary conduct of daily life, could be regarded as a battery, even

---

31. [1993] 2 WLR 120.

32. *Ibid* at 126 *per* Lord Griffiths, where it is observed that it would be difficult to accept that "a woman who admits she has been raped does not realise that she has suffered a significant injury".

33. Considerable reliance was placed on the report of the Tucker Committee (*Report of the Committee on the Limitation of Actions,* Cmd 7740, 1949) para 23 which regarded actions for trespass to the person, false imprisonment, malicious prosecution or defamation as falling outside of their recommendations on actions for personal injuries.

34. *Long* v. *Hepworth* [1968] 1 WLR 1299.

35. Cmd 7740, 1949, para 23.

though the consequence of the act (injury) is not intended.[36] Another problem associated with Lord Griffiths' concern with deliberate acts is that occasionally an employer may be tempted to deliberately ignore safety regulations put in place for the protection of employees. If what Lord Griffiths is saying is that section 11 does not apply to any form of deliberate conduct, the effect might be to take some industrial injury cases out of the rules on limitation of actions provided for in section 11, which must surely be unacceptable.

Unfortunately, the effect of the decision of the House of Lords is to put the victim of a deliberate assault in a weaker position than the person who suffers accidental harm. The decision in *Stubbings* v. *Webb* also produces some strange anomalies that make the position of the victim of a deliberate assault even more untenable. In the light of the provisions of section 14A, which apply to latent damage caused as a result of the defendant's negligence, other than that covered by section 11,[37] it might be argued that the plaintiff suffered latent damage. However, the House of Lords in *Stubbings* v. *Webb* seem to have treated the action as one for intentional trespass, in which case this probably cannot be regarded as a negligence action for the purposes of section 14A.[38] Conversely, if the victim of a deliberate assault is killed, his dependants will have a claim under the Fatal Accidents Act 1976, subject to certain qualifications, but there is no doubt that a person killed as a result of a deliberate assault is covered by the provisions of the Limitation Act 1980, s 12, to which the three-year discoverability test for limitation purposes does apply together with a discretion to disapply the limitation period. In the light of this, perpetrators of a deliberate assault are advised to fall short of killing their victim!

Strangely, if the victim dies, the position of the estate is the same as if the victim had lived, since the operation of the Law Reform (Miscellaneous Provisions) Act 1934 is subject to the Limitation Act 1980, s 11(5), which is subject to the decision in *Stubbings* v. *Webb*.

It is also important to emphasise that before *Stubbings* v. *Webb* applies and section 11 is considered not to be relevant, the precise nature of the plaintiff's claim has to be considered. Once this has been done, it may emerge that what the plaintiff has complained of is not the deliberate trespass, but the failure of others to take reasonable care to provide protection from personal injury. For example in *Seymour* v. *Williams*[39] the plaintiff complained that she had been physically and sexually abused by her father when she was a child and that her mother was aware of this. The father pleaded guilty to incest and was sentenced to eight years' imprisonment. Eight years after reaching the age of majority, the plaintiff sued both her mother and her father, but both actions were struck out by the trial judge on the basis that they related to the tort of trespass and that the six-year limitation period had expired. However, the plaintiff successfully appealed against the decision in respect of her mother on the basis that this was an action for negligence in the form of her failure to prevent the plaintiff from being exposed to the unnecessary risk of injury or

36. See e.g. *Wilson* v. *Pringle* [1986] 2 All ER 440. On the facts, schoolboy pranks were not regarded as unacceptable in the ordinary conduct of daily life, but the same conduct on the part of a teacher might have satisfied that test.

37. See Ch 20.

38. In *Société Commerciale de Réassurance* v. *ERAS International Ltd* [1992] 2 All ER 82 at 85, it was observed by Mustill LJ that the words "any action for damages in negligence" must denote that the defendant has committed the tort of negligence, with the result that even an action for "contractual negligence" is not covered by s 14A. It seems logical to conclude that an intentional assault also fails to amount to negligence.

39. [1995] PIQR 470, CA.

further injury. Such an action was governed by section 11, which allowed the court to exercise its discretion to allow the action to proceed outside the limitation period.

Whatever may be said of the decision in *Stubbings* v. *Webb*, later events have revealed that Parliament still regards intentional wrongdoing which results in physical or mental impairment to be a matter which falls outside the provisions of section 11. In particular, the Protection from Harassment Act 1997 creates a new criminal offence of harassment, based on the defendant's knowledge that his actions amount to harassment or in circumstances in which the defendant ought to know that his course of conduct amounts to harassment.[40] Although the 1997 Act creates a number of criminal offences, it also provides for the availability of a civil action for damages, in the event of a contravention of the prohibition of harassment under section 1 of the Act,[41] which action may cover the anxiety caused by the harassment and any financial loss occasioned by the act of harassment.[42] While the anxiety caused by a person guilty of harassment might be regarded as a form of personal injury, similar to the distress caused to the purchaser of defective property resulting from the negligence of a building surveyor in conducting a building society survey[43] or the distress caused by a deliberate statement or action falling within the rule in *Wilkinson* v. *Downton*,[44] it is clear from the provisions of the 1997 Act that harassment is not to be regarded as a tort which is subject to the special provisions in the Limitation Act 1980, s 11 in respect of personal injuries.[45]

ACCRUAL OF THE CAUSE OF ACTION

The general limitation period in personal injury cases runs for three years from the date on which the cause of action accrued. For these purposes, it is necessary to ignore the date on which the plaintiff suffered injury, with the result that the three years will be measured from the beginning of the day following the date of damage.[46]

It has been noted already that the Limitation Act 1980 does not define the term "accrual", which means that its definition has to be found in the relevant case law. It has been seen already that for the purposes of an action in tort, the combined effect of *Cartledge* v. *E Jopling & Sons Ltd*[47] and *Pirelli General Cable Works* v. *Oscar Faber & Partners*[48] is that the plaintiff's cause of action accrues when damage is caused which is more than minimal. Thus a *de minimis* principle seems to apply which will allow insignificant personal injury to be ignored, so that no cause of action will accrue. Given that

---

40. Protection from Harassment Act 1997, s 1(1). Whether a person ought to know that his conduct amounts to harassment is judged from the position of a reasonable person in possession of the same information as the defendant: Protection from Harassment Act 1997, s 1(2).

41. *Ibid* s 3(1).

42. *Ibid* s 3(2).

43. As in *Perry* v. *Sidney Phillips & Son* [1982] 1 WLR 1297.

44. [1897] 2 QB 57.

45. Limitation Act 1980, s 11(1A), inserted by the Protection from Harassment Act 1997, s 6.

46. *Marren* v. *Dawson Bentley & Co Ltd* [1961] 2 QB 135. Moreover, the three-year period will also take account of the feasibility of gaining access to the court office in order to be able to issue the writ. Thus if the end of the three-year period falls at a weekend or on a public holiday when the court office is closed, the limitation period will be extended to take account of the fact that a court holiday has prevented the writ from being issued on time.

47. [1963] AC 758.

48. [1983] 2 AC 1, and see Ch. 18.

personal injuries are viewed seriously, it seems likely that the majority of personal injuries will be regarded as sufficiently serious to avoid being caught by the *de minimis* principle. Thus it has been held that physiological damage without symptoms is sufficient to give rise to a cause of action, if there is a possibility that the condition might worsen in the future, thereby leading to possible worry.[49]

However, if more than minimal damage is suffered, then by virtue of section 11(4)(a), the limitation period, for the purposes of the plaintiff's tort action for personal injury, will start to run, regardless of the plaintiff's knowledge of the fact that a cause of action has accrued in his favour.

It has also been seen that a plaintiff may suffer personal injury as a result of the defendant's breach of contract. For the purposes of an action for breach of contract, the date of damage is irrelevant, with the result that, for the purposes of section 11(4)(a), the plaintiff's cause of action will accrue on the date of the breach of contract.[50] This primary limitation period also fails to take account of the plaintiff's lack of knowledge that any harm has been suffered as a result of the defendant's breach of contract.

However, the plaintiff's lack of knowledge of the accrual of his cause of action is a factor which may trigger the court's discretion, under the Limitation Act 1980, s 33, to disapply normal rules on limitation of actions where justice so requires. Moreover, the plaintiff's knowledge is also the basis for the alternative limitation period in section 11(4)(b), which for the purposes of personal injury actions employs a discoverability test, considered in more detail below.

THE DATE OF KNOWLEDGE TEST

For the purposes of personal injury actions, either the limitation period runs from the date of accrual of the cause of action,[51] the date of which may differ according to whether the personal injury is caused by the commission of a tort or as a result of a breach of contract, or alternatively, time will run from the date of knowledge of the person injured, if the relevant knowledge is acquired at a later date than the date on which the cause of action accrued in favour of the plaintiff.[52]

The date of knowledge is defined in the Limitation Act 1980, s 14, which provides:

"(1) Subject to subsection 1A below,[53] in sections 11 and 12 of this Act references to a person's date of knowledge are references to the date on which he first had knowledge of the following facts—

(a) that the injury in question was significant; and
(b) that the injury was attributable in whole or in part to the act or omission which is alleged to constitute negligence, nuisance or breach of duty; and
(c) the identity of the defendant; and
(d) if it is alleged that the act or omission was that of a person other than the defendant, the identity of that person and the additional facts supporting the bringing of an action against the defendant;

49. *Patterson* v. *Ministry of Defence* [1987] CLY 1194.
50. See *Gibbs* v. *Guild* (1881) 8 QBD 296; *Battley* v. *Faulkner* (1820) 3 B & Ald 288 and see Ch 8.
51. Limitation Act 1980, s 11(4)(a).
52. *Ibid*, s 11(4)(b).
53. See Ch 21.

and knowledge that any acts or omissions did or did not, as a matter of law, involve negligence, nuisance or breach of duty is irrelevant.

(2) For the purposes of this section an injury is significant if the person whose date of knowledge is in question would reasonably have considered it sufficiently serious to justify his instituting proceedings for damages against any defendant who did not dispute liability and was able to satisfy a judgment.

(3) For the purposes of this section a person's knowledge includes knowledge which he might reasonably have been expected to acquire—

    (a) from facts observable or ascertainable by him; or

    (b) from facts ascertainable by him with the help of medical or other appropriate expert advice which it is reasonable for him to seek;

but a person shall not be fixed under this subsection with knowledge of a fact ascertainable only with the help of expert advice so long as he has taken all reasonable steps to obtain (and where appropriate, to act on) that advice."

For practical reasons the date of knowledge is far more important than the date on which the cause of action accrued, since it is inconceivable that a person will have gathered the required knowledge enabling him to commence proceedings before the date on which the cause of action accrued, although it is possible for the date of accrual and the date of knowledge to fall on the same day.

Although the language used in section 14 is couched in terms of the knowledge of the injured person, for practical purposes the relevant knowledge may be that of someone else. For example, in *O'Driscoll* v. *Dudley Health Authority*[54] the plaintiff commenced proceedings against the defendants in respect of injuries suffered at birth resulting from their failure to deliver her by caesarean section with the result that she suffered hypoxia, leading to severe brain damage. The plaintiff's condition was such that she had handed over effective management of her affairs to her parents. Accordingly, in determining whether the plaintiff had the required knowledge of the facts relevant to her cause of action, it was considered relevant to ascertain not just the knowledge of the plaintiff, but also that of her parents, in their capacity as the plaintiff's agents. In this respect, it was held that the knowledge of the parents could be imputed to the plaintiff for the purposes of section 14.

(a) The meaning of actual knowledge

The difficulty which the word "knowledge" throws up is that the required state of mind is difficult to define. At one extreme it could be said that a person does not have knowledge of a particular fact until it can be said with certainty that a certain state of affairs exists. On the other hand there may be circumstances in which "suspicion" or "belief" could be argued to satisfy the requirement of knowledge.

The problem of the distinction between belief and knowledge has arisen in cases in which the plaintiff initially believes that a certain defendant is responsible for his injuries, but on consultation with an expert those fears are allayed. For example in *Stephen* v. *Riverside Health Authority*[55] the plaintiff strongly believed that her symptoms were the result of an X-ray photograph which had been taken without proper precautions. However, she was assured that the dose of radiation she had received was not sufficient to cause her

---

54. [1996] 7 Med LR 408. See also *Atkinson* v. *Oxfordshire Health Authority* [1993] 4 Med LR 18.
55. [1990] 1 Med LR 261. See also *Davis* v. *Ministry of Defence*, *The Times* 7 August 1985.

any harm. Despite the strength of her initial belief, it was considered that the subsequent reassurance she had received was sufficient to prevent her from having acquired the necessary knowledge of her condition until a much later date.

Accordingly, knowledge has to be distinguished from mere suspicion or simple belief that a certain state of affairs exists. In *Davis* v. *Ministry of Defence*[56] May LJ said, " 'Knowledge' is an ordinary English word with a clear meaning to which one must give full effect: reasonable belief or suspicion is not enough. The relevant question merits repetition: when did the appellant first know that his [condition] was capable of being attributed to his conditions at work?"

Likewise, in *Nash* v. *Eli Lilly & Co*[57] Purchas LJ voiced similar views on the differences between a belief in a certain state of affairs and knowledge of that same state of affairs. Commenting on the view of May LJ in *Davis*, he said:

"Suspicion, particularly if it is vague and unsupported, will clearly not be enough, and neither would, in the view of May LJ, reasonable belief . . . We do not, of course intend to lay down a definition of the word 'knowledge' for the purposes of a statute in which Parliament left the word to speak for itself. In applying the section . . . we shall proceed on the basis that knowledge is a condition of mind which imports a degree of certainty and that the degree of certainty which is appropriate for this purpose is that which, for the particular plaintiff, may reasonably be regarded as sufficient to justify embarking upon the preliminaries to the making of a claim for compensation, such as the taking of legal or other advice."[58]

It follows from this that the issue of whether the plaintiff has acquired the necessary degree of knowledge is a question of fact in each case. In some instances, the required degree of knowledge will not be in place until the plaintiff has consulted an expert who has expressed a view which confirms the plaintiff's suspicions that more than trivial harm has been suffered. Thus in *Bentley* v. *Bristol & Western Health Authority*[59] the plaintiff's sciatic nerve was damaged during the course of a hip-replacement operation, a fact which was known to the plaintiff within a period of two months after the completion of the operation. However, she was not aware at that time that the reason for her impairment was a failure to carry out the operation safely. Since the plaintiff was considered to have received "universally negative information and advice, both medical and legal", it could not be said that she knew that her injuries were attributable to the defendant's negligence until she received confirmation of this suspicion by way of an expert's report.[60]

A factor of particular relevance to the definition of the word "knowledge" is that regard must be had to the particular purpose which section 14 serves, namely, to identify the period within which the plaintiff can be expected to commence proceedings against the defendant. In *Halford* v. *Brookes*,[61] Lord Donaldson MR observed that:

---

56. *Ibid.* CA Transcript 413.
57. [1993] 4 All ER 383. See also *Guidera* v. *NEI Projects (India) Ltd* [1990] CA Transcript 60.
58. *Ibid* at 391–92.
59. [1991] 2 Med LR 359. See also *Scuriaga* v. *Powell* (1979) 123 SJ 406 in which the defendant was "economical with the truth". Whether such cases of misinformation will trigger the discretion under s 33 to allow an action to proceed outside the limitation period is considered later in this chapter. The same misinformation might equally amount to deliberate concealment under s 32, as to which see Ch 6.
60. However, this seems to suggest that the plaintiff's unawareness of the matters of law relevant to a negligence action are relevant in the definition of knowledge, but such considerations are expressly stated to be matters which should be ignored in the proviso to s 14(1).
61. [1991] 3 All ER 559.

" . . . 'Knowledge' clearly does not mean 'know for certain and beyond possibility of contradiction'. It does, however, mean 'know with sufficient confidence to justify embarking on the preliminaries to the issue of the writ, such as submitting a claim to the proposed defendant, taking legal and other advice and collecting evidence'. Suspicion, particularly if it is vague and unsupported, will indeed not be enough, but reasonable belief will normally suffice. It is probably only in an exceptional case such as *Davis* v. *Ministry of Defence* that it will not, because there is some countervailing factor."[62]

The difficulty which this analysis presents is that if a person had the degree of knowledge required, but that is undermined from another source, there appears to be a conflict with the general rule on the running of time that once time has started to run, it runs continuously and without interruption.[63] Subsequently, this problem was addressed in *Nash* v. *Eli Lilly & Co*[64] in which it was made clear that subjective factors relevant to the individual plaintiff will have to be taken into account, such as the nature of the information received by the plaintiff, the extent to which the plaintiff paid attention to that information, his capacity to understand the information and an evaluation of the information received, especially if, in the circumstances of the case, it can be regarded as unbelievable, unreliable or uncertain.[65]

This does not mean that objective considerations are irrelevant under section 14, since it was emphasised by Purchas LJ in *Nash* v. *Eli Lilly & Co* that:

"The section . . . attaches consequences to the having of knowledge which depends upon information and understanding. It does not depend upon the character of a plaintiff with reference, for example, to how vindictive or forgiving he may be with reference to any injury done, nor whether he is acquisitive or self-denying, or long-suffering or self-pitying. Such attributes, when demonstrated, may be of assistance in judging the probability of conduct or the reliability of assertions but they do not determine whether a plaintiff has knowledge."[66]

It follows from this that firm belief and knowledge cannot be equated with each other in every case. There may be circumstances in which a person with a very strong belief that he is the victim of the defendant's negligence still requires confirmation from an expert source that his belief is well founded and until that confirmation is given, it cannot be said that the plaintiff has knowledge of all the facts necessary for him to confidently commence proceedings in respect of the injuries he has suffered. Moreover, if all the plaintiff has is a vague suspicion as opposed to a strong belief that the defendant's negligence is the cause of the harm suffered, and the case is complex, it is likely that the plaintiff will not be considered to have the required degree of knowledge until such time as the suspicion is confirmed by expert evidence.[67]

Conversely, if a person has a strong belief that he has sufficient grounds for seeking legal advice despite the negative nature of the expert opinion previously supplied, he may still be regarded as being possessed of the knowledge required for the purposes of section 14 with the result that time could start to run from the date on which that strong belief is established.[68] It would seem that for these purposes, if a person is prepared to take his case

62. *Ibid* at 573–74. The "countervailing factor" in *Davis* v. *Ministry of Defence* was, seemingly, that the expert advice contradicted the strongly held belief of the plaintiff, thereby negating the knowledge previously held.
63. See Ch 5.
64. [1993] 4 All ER 383.
65. *Ibid* at 392 *per* Purchas LJ.
66. *Ibid*.
67. *O'Driscoll* v. *Dudley Health Authority* [1996] 7 Med LR 18.
68. *Nash* v. *Eli Lilly & Co* [1993] 4 All ER 383 at 396 *per* Purchas LJ.

to a lawyer, he must be regarded as sufficiently confident of some degree of success, whereas merely consulting a doctor or some other expert may not be taken to display the same degree of confidence in one's understanding of the relevant facts. The problem this raises is that if seeking legal advice, in these circumstances, is tantamount to the admission of knowledge of all relevant facts, it seems to follow from this that seeking legal advice should always be regarded as an irrelevance in determining whether the plaintiff has the knowledge required for section 14 or any other provision of the Limitation Act 1980 which is concerned with the plaintiff's knowledge of relevant facts. But it would be difficult to assert that every person who consults a solicitor knows precisely why he does so. Very often the reason for doing so is that there is simply a suspicion that a wrong has been done and that the law may be able to provide a remedy. This is far from saying that the client is aware of all relevant facts for the purposes of prosecuting his or her claim for compensation.

(b) Significant injury (Limitation Act 1980, s 14(1)(a))

Section 14(1)(a) must be read in the light of section 14(2) which states that an injury is significant if the person whose state of knowledge is under consideration is such that he would reasonably have considered it sufficiently serious to justify the institution of proceedings for damages against a defendant who did not dispute liability and was able to satisfy a judgment.

The wording of section 14(1)(a) makes it clear that it is concerned with the person injured, but it also covers the personal representatives of a person who subsequently dies.[69] The test applied under section 14(1)(a) contains both objective and subjective elements so far as the person injured (or the personal representatives of the deceased) is concerned.

The effect of section 14(1)(a) is to require the person injured to have reasonable grounds, amounting to more than a mere suspicion or belief, that the injury suffered is sufficiently serious to justify setting in motion legal proceedings for the recovery of damages. To be able to reach this conclusion, the injured person may need to obtain expert advice, but by virtue of section 14(3), the knowledge of an expert, whom it is reasonable to consult, is deemed to be the knowledge of the person injured.

As has been observed above, a problem created by the test in section 14(1)(a) combined with section 14(3) is that there are serious difficulties associated with the determination of when it is reasonable for the injured person to appreciate the seriousness of what he has been told. This is especially so when members of the medical profession, faced with the possibility of a writ for medical negligence, may be tempted to be economical with the truth.

The difficulty of interpreting section 14(1) is added to by section 14(2) which indicates that injury is significant if the person injured "would reasonably have considered" it to justify the commencement of proceedings. It has been observed above that there are both subjective and objective elements in a test of this nature, which means that for the purposes of the objective element, something approaching a universal test can be applied, but in relation to the subjective elements, each case will turn on its own peculiar facts.

---

69. Limitation Act 1980, s 14(5) and see also the discussion of s 12, below.

In *McCafferty* v. *Metropolitan Police District Receiver*[70] Geoffrey Lane LJ observed that the use of the word "would" in section 14(2) is difficult to understand and that a better choice of words might have been "if he had considered the matter". Geoffrey Lane LJ then continued:

"Whatever the answer to this problem may be, it is clear that the test is partly a subjective test, namely: 'would this plaintiff have considered the injury sufficiently serious?' And partly an objective test, namely: 'would he have been reasonable if he did *not* regard it as sufficiently serious?' It seems to me that [subsection 14(2)] is directed at the nature of the injury as known to the plaintiff at that time. Taking *that* plaintiff's intelligence, would he have been reasonable in considering the injury not sufficiently serious to justify instituting proceedings for damages?"[71]

The problem with Geoffrey Lane LJ's approach is that it asks a negative question, whereas section 14(2) is couched in positive terms, asking whether it would have been reasonable to decide to sue.[72] Instead, the question might be posed in the following terms: "Would a decision to sue by this man have been a reasonable one?" If the answer is yes, the injury may be regarded as significant.[73]

The subjective element in the test applied under section 14(2) requires the court to consider the injured person's individual circumstances. Thus factors such as age, background, intelligence and disabilities will have to be considered in order to determine what reasonably could have been known. Accordingly, a person of "modest intellectual capacity" may be judged differently from a person of higher intellect.[74] However, some subjective considerations will be discounted. For example, if the plaintiff's injury is serious in objective terms, but is trivialised by the plaintiff, it is irrelevant that the plaintiff later realises that he has suffered serious injury.[75] Accordingly, if a hearing defect is regarded by the plaintiff as an "irritating nuisance" because he wants to avoid conflict where his job is insecure[76] or where the plaintiff does not want to be seen as "sponging" off his employers[77] it seems unlikely that the injury will be regarded, objectively, as serious. However, it should be noted that subjective considerations will be important in the context of the exercise of the discretion given under the Limitation Act 1980, s 33, discussed below.

The objective nature of the test under section 14(2) requires the court to look at the seriousness of the injury and the value which can be placed on it. Thus if a person, as advised, can expect to recover no more than nominal damages, he might not regard the injury as serious.[78] However, it should be noted that most considerations relating to insignificant damage are rendered irrelevant by the wording of section 14(2) which stipulates that the nominal defendant is one who admits liability and is solvent, which means that the central emphasis must be on the severity of the injury and its value in terms of possible compensation.[79]

70. [1977] 1 WLR 1073.
71. *Ibid* at 1081. The emphasis is that of Geoffrey Lane LJ.
72. See *Platt* v. *Quaker Oats Ltd* (1991) unreported, QBD.
73. *Ibid*, per Rougier J.
74. *Davis* v. *City and Hackney Health Authority* [1991] 2 Med LR 366.
75. See *Miller* v. *London Electrical Manufacturing Co Ltd* [1976] 2 Lloyd's Rep 284 at 287 *per* Lord Denning MR; *Harding* v. *People's Dispensary for Sick Animals* [1994] PIQR 270 at 273 *per* Butler-Sloss LJ. Note that the two cases relate to, respectively, the Limitation Act 1963 and the Limitation Act 1980.
76. *McCafferty* v. *Metropolitan Police District Receiver* [1977] 1 WLR 1073.
77. *Buck* v. *English Electric Co Ltd* [1978] 1 All ER 271. See also Davies (1982) 98 LQR 249.
78. *Patterson* v. *Ministry of Defence* [1987] CLY 1194.
79. See *Platt* v. *Quaker Oats Ltd* (1991) unreported, *per* Rougier J.

In *Dobbie* v. *Medway Health Authority*[80] emphasis was placed on the quantum of the injury rather than on the plaintiff's subjective valuation. Accordingly, time will not run against the plaintiff if he could reasonably have accepted the injury as a fact of life which is not worth bothering about.[81]

Particular problems may arise where the harm suffered as a result of the defendant's act or omission is in addition to harm already suffered by the plaintiff as a result of an earlier act or omission on the part of the defendant. For example, in *Nash* v. *Eli Lilly & Co*[82] the plaintiffs alleged that they had suffered side-effects from the use of the drug Opren, but drugs are known to have such effects, even though they are beneficial in other respects.[83] The court accepted that in the case of side-effects of which the plaintiff could have been aware, there was no significant injury for the purposes of the Limitation Act 1980. However, a distinction was drawn between such effects and unexpected or unacceptable consequences which could be regarded as significant injury. Accordingly, time will not begin to run against the plaintiff until there is an awareness of an injurious or unacceptable consequence and even then, this has to be judged against the severity of any symptoms. For example in *Nash* v. *Eli Lilly & Co* the plaintiffs suffered from adverse reaction to light for an unacceptable period of time even after cessation of treatment, which could be regarded as significant injury.

Where the plaintiff suffers what may be regarded as minor injury, but which is not covered by the *de minimis* principle, and this is followed by a discovery that more serious injury has been suffered, the plaintiff may face the prospect of time having started to run at the time the minor injury was suffered. For example in *Bristow* v. *Grout*[84] the plaintiff was involved in a road traffic accident in which he suffered leg and face injuries as a result of the defendant's negligence and for which the defendant's insurers accepted liability. Subsequently, the leg injuries developed into more serious damage to the hip and a writ was issued four years after the date of the accident. In the event, it was held that the original settlement by the insurers satisfied the whole claim with the result that the second claim was considered to be out of time. But it was observed that there is a difference between section 11 which refers to injuries (in the plural) whereas section 14(1)(a) refers to *the injury*, which means that under section 14(1)(a), the court must have regard to the particular injury in respect of which the claim is brought.[85]

In some instances, what is initially a minor injury may give rise to a risk that it may develop later into a much more serious injury. In these circumstances, the knowledge that more serious harm may develop ought to be sufficient to allow time to start running. If this is the case, the plaintiff ought to arrange for a protective writ to be issued in order to avoid discovering later that his action has become time barred. The problem with this course of action is that if the plaintiff sues through to judgment at this early stage, he may well receive reduced damages, based on discounts in respect of future possible loss.[86]

---

80. [1994] 4 All ER 450.
81. *Ibid* at 457 *per* Sir Thomas Bingham MR.
82. [1993] 4 All ER 383.
83. For example, drugs used in the treatment of cancerous growths can cause nausea and alopecia.
84. *The Times*, 3 November 1986.
85. See also *Horbury* v. *Craig Hall & Rutley* (1991) 7 PN 206, QBD.
86. Although it may be possible to ask for an award of provisional damages under the Supreme Court Act 1981, s 32A if there is a "serious chance" that as a result of the defendant's tort, the plaintiff will develop a serious disease or other serious deterioration in his condition. See also *Willson* v. *Ministry of Defence* [1991] 1 All ER 638.

(c) Attributability of the injury to the defendant's breach (section 14(1)(b))

By virtue of the Limitation Act 1980, s 14(1)(b), the plaintiff must have knowledge that the injury was attributable in whole, or in part, to the act or omission which is alleged to constitute negligence, nuisance or breach of duty. For these purposes, it seems that to attribute is to "reckon as a consequence of".[87] Accordingly, the question raised is one of factual causation, normally associated with the "but for" test in tort actions. In any case, the fact that the plaintiff is ignorant, in law, of his right to sue is expressly stated to be a matter to be discounted in ascertaining whether the plaintiff had the required knowledge in order to be able to sue.[88]

For the purposes of section 14(1)(b) there appear to be two important issues. First, it has to be ascertained what constitutes the relevant act or omission on the part of the particular defendant in the case under consideration. Secondly, it must be determined whether the plaintiff knew or ought to have known that the harm he has suffered is caused by that act or omission.[89]

For the purposes of the acts or omissions aspects of this two-part test, it is arguable that the plaintiff's knowledge need not be specific. In *Wilkinson* v. *Ancliff (BLT) Ltd*[90] it was held to be sufficient for the plaintiff to have a broad knowledge that his injuries are attributable to the defendant's act or omission and that he need not be aware of the specific act or omission responsible. For example in *Wilkinson* the plaintiff was aware in broad terms that his working conditions had exposed him to danger and that his employers, the defendants, had not taken reasonable precautions to protect him. His employment as a road-tanker driver required him to carry dangerous chemicals, inhalation of which caused chest congestion which caused him to visit a hospital in April 1981, although this was not fully diagnosed as bronchial asthma until December 1984 when a detailed medical expert's report was produced. The plaintiff had consulted a solicitor in 1982 and a writ was issued in March 1984, but this was not acted upon during its 12-month period of currency. The plaintiff sought to renew the writ, but the defendants applied to have the writ set aside as it was no longer valid to be served under RSC Order 6, rule 8(1), having been served out of time. The plaintiff argued that time could not run against him until the date of the detailed report in December 1984. However the Court of Appeal regarded the date of the plaintiff's visit to hospital in November 1981 as the relevant date for limitation purposes, since on that date the plaintiff could be said to have a broad knowledge that the defendant's act or omission was responsible for his injury. In addition, that hospital visit also confirmed that there had been specific breaches of duty on the part of the defendants in exposing the plaintiff to noxious and harmful chemicals. This meant that the defendants had an arguable case for asking the judge not to renew the writ after it expired in March 1985, although had it been acted on during its currency, that writ would have been served in time.

From this, it may be asserted that if the plaintiff's injuries are capable of being attributed to the defendant's act or omission as a possibility, time may start to run against the plaintiff. In *Guidera* v. *NEI Projects (India) Ltd*[91] Sir David Croom-Johnson stated that if

---

87. *Halford* v. *Brookes* [1991] 3 All ER 559 at 573 *per* Lord Donaldson MR.
88. Limitation Act 1980, s 14(1) (proviso).
89. *Colegrove* v. *Smyth* [1994] 5 Med LR 111 at 113 *per* Buckley J.
90. [1986] 3 All ER 427.
91. (1990) unreported, CA Transcript 60. The judgment of Sir David Croom-Johnson is discussed in detail and regarded as correct in *Nash* v. *Eli Lilly & Co* [1993] 4 All ER 383 at 397–98 *per* Purchas LJ.

it is merely possible that the defendant's act or omission is a cause of the plaintiff's injury, time can start to run, since one is not concerned with proof of liability, but merely with the knowledge of the plaintiff. However, this possibility must be more than merely fanciful, although since section 14(1)(b) does not require the injury to be "*reasonably* attributable" to the defendant's act or omission, the degree of knowledge does not need to be substantial.

The meaning of the word "attributable" in section 14(1)(b) has given rise to a number of problems because the word attributable is related specifically to the words "act or omission which is alleged to constitute negligence, nuisance or breach of duty". Taken in combination, these words might suggest that, contrary to the "broad test" applied in *Wilkinson* v. *Ancliff (BLT) Ltd* to the first consideration under section 14(1)(b), a different test applies to the second consideration. Certainly, there was a view, at one stage, that the plaintiff had to be aware that the particular breach of duty on the part of the defendant is the cause of his injury. This was taken to mean that the plaintiff had to be aware of more than just that the defendant's conduct has caused the damage complained of. While such a test might not cause difficulties in relation to road traffic accidents, for example, where it ought to be immediately obvious whether the defendant's act or omission is the cause of the plaintiff's injury, more difficult problems may arise in cases of alleged medical negligence. Here it may not be immediately obvious that the defendant's conduct is the cause of the injury complained of by the plaintiff, since despite a deterioration in the patient's condition, there may be a number of possible events which could be regarded as the cause. These could range from the side effects of drugs given to treat the plaintiff's condition, negligence on the part of a surgeon or simple failure of a medical procedure for reasons unconnected with any fault on the part of the defendant. However, against this it should be emphasised that the effect of the proviso to section 14(1) is that it is irrelevant that the plaintiff did not realise, as a matter of law, that the defendant's act or omission amounted to a relevant breach of duty.

Recent case law seems to have taken a fairly hard line, so far as plaintiffs are concerned, compared with some of the slightly older cases. In *Nash* v. *Eli Lilly & Co*[92] the Court of Appeal required a strong degree of specificity before it could be said that the plaintiff knew that his injury was attributable to the defendant's act or omission. Thus, in that case it was observed that:

"It was not, in our judgment, the intention of Parliament to require for the purposes of section 11 and section 14 of the Act proof of knowledge of the terms in which it will be alleged that the act or omission of the defendants constituted negligence or breach of duty. What is required is knowledge of the essence of the act or omission to which the injury is attributable . . .

We would refer back at this point to section 14(1)(a) in order to comment that, where the definition of 'significant' in section 14(2) uses for the concept of sufficiency that which would justify the institution of proceedings, that is merely to indicate the gravity of the injury and the effect it would have on the mind of the plaintiff and no more. The question of attributability to one or more defendants in the context of legal proceedings is dealt with under section 14(1)(b) and (c) and the requirement for any knowledge of the law is specifically excluded by the closing passage of section 14(1)."[93]

Thus, the plaintiff must know that there is some specific fact in relation to a medical procedure which has caused his injury, namely, the fact which is the basis of the allegation

92. [1993] 4 All ER 383.
93. *Ibid* at 398–99 *per* Purchas LJ.

against the defendant. In *Nash* v. *Eli Lilly & Co* it was necessary for the plaintiffs to be aware that the defendant had exposed them to a drug which was unsafe, in the sense that it could cause permanent sensitivity to light, or that the defendants had failed to take sufficient steps to guard against this possibility.[94]

In contrast to this earlier approach, the more recent decision of the Court of Appeal in *Broadley* v. *Guy Clapham & Co*[95] has indicated that a harder line will be taken. In *Broadley* the Court of Appeal overruled *Bentley* v. *Bristol & Western Health Authority*[96] holding that the test used by Hirst J was inconsistent with the proviso to section 14(1) regarding "matters of law". It was considered that what Hirst J's test required was knowledge detailed enough to enable the plaintiff's advisers to draft a statement of claim, but that was thought to go too far in favour of the plaintiff.

In *Broadley* the plaintiff underwent an operation for the removal of a foreign body from her knee in 1980. After the operation her condition did not improve and later examinations revealed that she was suffering from nerve palsy and left foot drop. In June 1983, the plaintiff consulted a solicitor who arranged for her to be seen by an orthopaedic surgeon who advised that the 1980 operation might have been conducted negligently. No further steps were taken to obtain an expert's report, with the result that the plaintiff then consulted another firm of solicitors. In August 1990, a writ was served on the defendants, the firm of solicitors who had failed to act quickly enough with the result that the plaintiff's action for medical negligence had become time barred. The defendants argued that the plaintiff's cause of action for medical negligence was time barred at such an early stage that any action against them would also be time barred. For the purposes of dealing with the defendant's submissions, it became necessary to determine when time started to run against the plaintiff in respect of her medical negligence action. It was considered that since she required two sticks with which to walk for a period of seven months following the knee operation, it must have occurred to her that there was something significantly wrong which could be attributed to the operation she had undergone. Accordingly, the plaintiff was taken to have constructive knowledge of a potential cause of action since a reasonable patient would have made further enquiries. The plaintiff had argued that time could not start to run against her until she had received confirmation that she had a cause of action by way of some expert report. In response to this Leggatt LJ said:

"The use of the words 'unreasonable', 'reasonably' and 'properly' would only be justified if section 14(1)(b) required knowledge that the injury was attributable to negligence. It is plain from the concluding words of section 14(1) that 'knowledge that any acts or omissions did or did not, as a matter of law, involve negligence' is irrelevant. In my judgement the only function of the words 'which is alleged to constitute negligence' is to point to the relevant act or omission to which the injury was attributable."[97]

An alternative way of putting the point is that the words "which is alleged to constitute negligence, nuisance or breach of duty" do no more than to identify facts which the

---

94. See also *Bentley* v. *Bristol & Western Health Authority* [1991] 2 Med LR 359 where the date of knowledge was delayed until the date of receipt of an expert's report. In that case, Hirst J distinguished between an *act* of invasive surgery and some *conduct or failure* on the part of the surgeon which can affect the safety of the operation. In Hidden J's opinion, the plaintiff could not be aware of the latter, which was the fact of which knowledge was required, until he had received an expert report. This test was accepted as correct by Hidden J in *Nash* v. *Eli Lilly & Co*, whose decision was confirmed as correct by the Court of Appeal.

95. [1994] 4 All ER 439.

96. [1991] 2 Med LR 359.

97. *Ibid* at 447.

plaintiff must be aware of before time will be considered to start running, but this does not mean that the plaintiff must be aware that those facts point to the existence of a breach of a rule of law or accepted code of behaviour.[98] Thus what section 14(1)(b) requires is that "one should look at the way the plaintiff puts his case, distil what he is complaining about and ask whether he had, in broad[99] terms, knowledge of the facts on which that complaint is based".[100]

A similar approach has been adopted in a further Court of Appeal decision in which the degree of knowledge required for the purposes of section 14(1) has been regarded as less than was previously considered to be the case. In *Dobbie* v. *Medway Health Authority*[101] in 1973, the plaintiff underwent an operation for the removal of a lump in her breast, but because the surgeon considered the lump to be cancerous, he performed a mastectomy. Subsequently, it was discovered that the growth was benign and that there had been no need to perform the mastectomy. The plaintiff suffered psychological illness as a result of the devastating effect of the operation upon her. It was not until May 1988 that the plaintiff discovered that another person in a similar position to herself had successfully sued her surgeon. In May 1989 the plaintiff commenced proceedings against the defendants. Understandably, the defendants entered a plea of limitation, but the plaintiff contended that until 1988, she was unaware that it would have been possible for the lump to be excised and subjected to a microscopic analysis, with the result that she did not have knowledge of the crucial act or omission on the part of the surgeon.

In line with the approach adopted in *Broadley* v. *Guy Clapham & Co*, it was held that time would start to run against a plaintiff from the time that she knew the injury on which her claim was founded was attributable to the act or omission of the defendant. This remained the case, despite the fact that the plaintiff was unaware that that act was actionable or tortious. It was considered to be inconsistent with the wording of section 14(1) to introduce a requirement that the "act or omission" referred to in that section should be actionable or tortious.[102] According to Sir Thomas Bingham MR:

"In *Wilkinson* v. *Ancliff (BLT) Ltd* . . . reference was made to a submission of counsel based on the use of the words 'act or omission' rather than 'conduct' in section 14(1)(b). I do not understand the court to have accepted that submission. But it is customary in discussing tortious liability to refer to acts and omissions, and I do not think the meaning of section 14(1)(b) would be any different had the reference been to conduct. Time starts to run against the claimant when he knows that the personal injury on which he founds his claim is capable of being attributed to something done or not done by the defendant whom he wishes to sue. This condition is not satisfied where a man knows that he has a disabling cough or shortness of breath but does not know that his injured condition has anything to do with his working conditions. It is satisfied when he knows that his injured condition is capable of being attributed to his working conditions even though he has no inkling that his employer may have been at fault."[103]

---

98. *Ibid* at 448 *per* Hoffmann LJ.

99. In *Broadley* v. *Guy Clapham & Co*, Balcombe LJ distinguishes between broad knowledge, specific knowledge, qualitative knowledge and detailed knowledge, concluding that qualitative and detailed knowledge are not requirements of section 14, since qualitative knowledge would require the plaintiff to be aware that the operation had been carried out in such a way as to unreasonably cause injury and detailed knowledge would be such as that required in order to draft a statement of claim. See [1994] 4 All ER 439 at 446–47.

100. *Ibid* at 448.

101. [1994] 4 All ER 450.

102. Such a decision would also ignore the recommendations of the Law Reform Committee, Twentieth Report, *Interim Report on Limitation of Actions in Personal Injury Claims*, Cmnd 5630, 1974.

103. [1994] 4 All ER 450 at 456.

This line of reasoning, although consistent with the approach adopted in *Broadley* v. *Guy Clapham & Co*, means that injury occurs as soon as the relevant operation is carried out. Counsel for the plaintiff in *Dobbie* v. *Medway Health Authority* then argued that, if this was the case, a person would be treated as being injured by an operation which was successful. This, it was argued, was not what the ordinary man in the street would regard as injury and that a distinction should be drawn between successful and unsuccessful medical procedures. However, this too, was rejected in the Court of Appeal, on the ground that to import such a distinction would be inconsistent with the definition of personal injuries in the Limitation Act 1980, s 38(1).[104] This rejection therefore seems to suggest that any person who undergoes surgery is injured at the date of the surgery, regardless of his lack of knowledge of any other facts relevant to his possible claim for damages, which may create a rule of a sufficient degree of certainty but is somewhat dubious in terms of justice.

The conclusion that, in the case of a surgical procedure, injury is suffered at the time of the relevant operation may well apply to negligent acts and negligent omissions not involving an element of delay[105] but it seems that a different approach may have to be adopted in relation to omissions which result in a crucial medical procedure being delayed. This remains the case despite the fact that it was observed by Steyn LJ in *Dobbie* v. *Medway Health Authority* that, "The word 'act' does not by itself describe something which ought not to have been done. And it would be impossible to attach a qualitative element to 'omission' but not to 'act'."[106]

In *Forbes* v. *Wandsworth Health Authority*[107] the Court of Appeal considered, unanimously for the purposes of section 14(1), that omissions may have to be treated differently from acts, since in the case of an omission it would be difficult to say that the patient is immediately aware that the defendant has been negligent and that even the wording of the proviso to section 14(1) does not mean that there can be no consideration of the date on which the plaintiff became aware that the defendant was guilty of negligence.

In *Forbes*, the plaintiff had a long history of circulatory problems and in October 1982, he was admitted to hospital for a bypass operation on his left leg. The operation proved not to be successful and a further unsuccessful operation was carried out the following day, during which it was decided to amputate the plaintiff's leg in order to prevent gangrene from setting in and in order to save the plaintiff's life. In June 1991, the plaintiff consulted a solicitor, who arranged for the advice of a vascular surgeon to be obtained. The expert advice indicated that amputation of the plaintiff's leg could have been avoided if there had been less delay on the defendants' part in restoring the blood supply to the plaintiff's leg, and that it was this delay rather than negligent treatment which had resulted in the amputation. The plaintiff issued a writ in December 1992 alleging negligence in the

---

104. *Ibid* at 461 *per* Beldam LJ.

105. Such a conclusion has recently been arrived at in *Jones* v. *Liverpool Health Authority* [1996] PIQR 251, CA, in which the reasoning in *Broadley* v. *Guy Clapham & Co* [1994] 4 All ER 439 was applied. In *Jones* there was an allegation that hospital treatment had been negligently carried out in 1974. In 1976 the plaintiff was advised by an expert that there was no evidence of negligence, but a different expert view emerged in 1987 which was confirmed in 1991. At a trial of the preliminary issues in 1993, it was considered that relevant knowledge of the negligent act must have existed in 1977, a view which was confirmed by Glidewell LJ (with whom Morritt LJ and Sir Thomas May agreed), stating that there was no need for the plaintiff to have knowledge of a possible cause of action.

106. [1994] 4 All ER 450 at 463.

107. [1996] 4 All ER 881.

form of failing to conduct the second operation sooner, but the defendants pleaded limitation of actions. The plaintiff contended that it was not possible for him to have known of
the defendants' negligence until he received the advice of his expert in October 1992 and
that, accordingly, his action was not time barred.

On the question whether the plaintiff had actual knowledge that his injury was attributable to the omission on the part of the defendants, it was held that the plaintiff's knowledge
that his injury was significant was established within a short time of the operation to
amputate his leg, but the plaintiff could not know that that injury was attributable to the
defendants' omission until a much later stage.

Cases concerning negligence in the performance of an operation[108] were distinguished
on the ground that where there is an operation, followed by a deterioration in condition,
that deterioration must be regarded as something other than a direct and inevitable consequence of the operation that was performed, but that such reasoning could not be applied
to cases of negligent advice which result in a person's leg being removed unnecessarily.[109]
Accordingly, the date of the medical procedure to remove the plaintiff's leg could not be
said to be the date on which the plaintiff knew of his injury, but he must have known that
his injury was significant within a very short time of the operation to amputate.[110]

On the issue of attributability, the Court of Appeal relied on two earlier cases which
supported the trial judge's opinion that the time of knowledge of the attributability of the
injury to the defendants' omission could be delayed. In *Smith* v. *West Lancashire Health
Authority*[111] the plaintiff had suffered hand injuries, and although an uncomplicated fracture of the ring finger was diagnosed, there had been a negligent failure to diagnose a
fracture of the little finger and a dislocation of the ring finger, with the result that
conservative treatment was prescribed. Later the plaintiff had to undergo an urgent operation which would have been unnecessary but for the delay and failure to diagnose. Russell
LJ concluded that the plaintiff could not have known that there had been an omission to
operate until such time as he was advised to this effect by an expert, since his knowledge
that there had been no operation could not amount to knowledge that there had been an
omission "which is alleged to constitute negligence" as it is necessary to know what has
been omitted.[112] Moreover in a latent damage case under section 14A(8)(a)[113] it has been
held that "the act or omission of which the plaintiff must have knowledge must be that
which is causally relevant for the purposes of an allegation of negligence".[114]

In *Forbes* v. *Wandsworth Health Authority*[115] it was observed by Stuart-Smith LJ
that:

108. Such as *Broadley* v. *Guy Clapham & Co* [1994] 4 All ER 439 and *Dobbie* v. *Medway Health Authority*
[1994] 4 All ER 450.
109. *Forbes* v. *Wandsworth Health Authority* [1996] 4 All ER 881 at 886 *per* Stuart-Smith LJ.
110. *Ibid.*
111. [1995] PIQR 514.
112. *Ibid* at 517.
113. As to which see Ch 20.
114. *Hallam-Eames* v. *Merrett* [1996] 7 Med LR 122; *The Times*, 25 January 1995 *per* Hoffmann LJ, with
whom Sir Thomas Bingham MR and Saville LJ agreed. This requirement was considered not to be a requirement
that the plaintiff must know he has a cause of action, but merely that "the plaintiff . . . must have known the facts
which can fairly be described as constituting the negligence of which he complains". To put this matter
differently, it has been held that in a complex case the act or omission alleged to constitute negligence must be
known by the plaintiff with some degree of specificity: *O'Driscoll* v. *Dudley Health Authority* [1996] 7 Med LR
18.
115. [1996] 4 All ER 881.

"In many medical negligence cases the plaintiff will not know that his injury is attributable to the omission of the defendant alleged to constitute negligence, in the sense that it is capable of being attributable to that omission, until he is also told that the defendant has been negligent. But that does not alter the fact that there is a distinction between causation and negligence; the first is relevant to section 14(1); the second is not. The fact that in such cases it may be necessary for the plaintiff also to know of the negligence before he can identify the omission alleged to have been negligent is nothing to the point. It does not mean that he falls foul of the closing words of section 14(1). For these reasons, I consider that the judge was correct in holding that there was no actual knowledge."[116]

This emphasis on the difference between causation and attributability has continued since the decision in *Forbes*. In particular in *Spargo* v. *North Essex District Health Authority*[117] it was asserted that the proper test to apply under section 14(1)(b) in respect of the issue of causation is a subjective test and the matter is not to be considered from the position of a reasonable laymen in the absence of expert confirmation. Accordingly, the proper question to ask is, "What did the plaintiff himself know?"

In *Spargo* the plaintiff complained that a misdiagnosis made 22 years ago had led to her being detained in a mental hospital between 1975 and 1981. What had led to these events was that in 1975 the plaintiff had been found wandering about in her nightdress, in an emaciated state. A consultant psychiatrist incorrectly diagnosed selective brain damage caused by excessive purging and dieting. The plaintiff's writ was issued 12 years after release from hospital, but it was argued for the plaintiff, and accepted by the trial judge, that she could not have had actual knowledge that her suffering was due to the misdiagnosis until she received an expert psychiatric report in 1991. In the Court of Appeal, it was held that the trial judge had confused the issues of causation and attributability by applying the much less rigorous attributability test to a question of causation, which carried with it an important subjective element. In the circumstances, the proper test was to ask what did the particular plaintiff know. In this case, it must have been obvious to the plaintiff, when she was released from hospital, that the cause of her suffering was the misdiagnosis and it did not require expert confirmation to confirm that fact.

(d) The identity of the defendant (section 14(1)(c))

There may be occasions on which the plaintiff is unaware of the identity of the defendant or defendants. Until this knowledge is acquired, time cannot run against the plaintiff. Thus if the plaintiff is injured by a hit-and-run driver, until the identity of the defendant is discovered, the plaintiff is not time barred in respect of any future action for damages for personal injuries. However, in this particular type of case, the plaintiff has the further option that he may seek compensation under the Motor Insurers' Bureau agreement with the Ministry of Transport in respect of third party injury under the Untraced Drivers' Agreement. For the purposes of this agreement, the identity of the driver is deemed to be known as soon as the accident happens.

A further problem of identification may arise where an employee is injured at work, but his immediate employer is part of a larger group of companies. In these circumstances, the "real" employer may not be immediately identifiable. For example in *Simpson* v. *Norwest*

116. *Ibid* at 889.
117. *The Times*, 21 March 1997, CA.

Holst Southern Ltd[118] the plaintiff was employed on a building site on which he suffered injury. His pay slips specified that his employer was "Norwest Holst Group" which was a group of associated companies, one of which was the defendant. The problem was that "Norwest Holst Group" had no legal identity, being a generic name for the group, but not being a company in its own right. Despite repeated requests from the plaintiff's solicitors, the insurers of Norwest Holst Group declined to identify the actual employer. It followed that until this information was supplied, time could not run against the plaintiff, with the result that an action started more than three years from the date of the accident was not time barred.

In contrast, in *Nash* v. *Eli Lilly & Co*[119] the Court of Appeal were of the opinion that a plaintiff in a similar position might be taken to have constructive knowledge of the identity of a corporate employer under the Limitation Act 1980, s 14(3)(a), since a reasonable person should be able to ascertain the identity of a corporate defendant by making enquiries of the appropriate regulatory agency responsible for taking deposit of public company documents such as the memorandum and articles of association. It was, however, admitted that there might be difficult cases in which precise identification might not be immediately possible.

Where the plaintiff's injuries are caused by one or other of two known defendants, but the plaintiff is not sure which of the two is responsible, section 14(1)(c) is of no assistance, since the appropriate course of action will be to sue both of them in the alternative.[120] Similarly, in medical negligence cases, where the plaintiff cannot identify which member of a health care team is responsible for his injuries, the plaintiff may still sue the health authority or National Health Service Trust vicariously, assuming the individual tortfeasor is an employee who was acting in the course of his employment.[121]

A further situation in which the identity of the true defendant may be obscured arises where the plaintiff sues his employer or some other defendant, but a third party is subsequently called as an additional defendant. For example, in *Walford* v. *Richards*[122] the plaintiff sued in respect of a road traffic accident. The defendant, the other driver, alleged that a garage responsible for defective repairs to his vehicle was the true defendant, but the plaintiff was not supplied with the name and address of the repairer, whose identity was first revealed in the course of evidence for the first defendant. Given the effect of section 14(1)(c), it was held that for the purposes of an action in respect of personal injuries brought against the repairers, time would not run against the plaintiff until he became aware of the identity of that person.

Where the sole problem is one of awareness that the act or omission of the defendant is the cause, in fact, of the plaintiff's injuries, the effect of the proviso to section 14(1) is that lack of awareness, as a matter of law, of who is the defendant, will not prevent time from running. Thus in *Broome* v. *Rotheray*[123] the plaintiff was injured at work when a steel angle fell from a lorry owned by another company. The plaintiff sued his employers, but did not discover until the date of the proceedings that a primary part of their defence was that the owners of the lorry had caused the accident. Since, from the facts known at the

118. [1980] 1 WLR 968.
119. [1993] 4 All ER 383. See also *Eidi* v. *Service Dowell Schlumberger SA* [1990] CLY 2961.
120. *Halford* v. *Brookes* [1991] 3 All ER 559 at 574 *per* Lord Donaldson MR.
121. *Cassidy* v. *Ministry of Health* [1951] 2 KB 343.
122. [1976] 1 Lloyd's Rep 526.
123. (1992) unreported, CA.

time of the accident, it was apparent that the lorry owners could have been responsible, any attempt to include the owners of the lorry as additional defendants would be contrary to RSC Order 15, rule 6(5), since the primary limitation period had expired. According to Balcombe LJ, all that was not known by the plaintiff was that, as a matter of law, the acts or omissions of the lorry driver involved a breach of a duty of care for which his employers were responsible.

(e) Liability for the acts of others (section 14(1)(d))

Section 14(1)(d) refers to allegations that the act or omission was that of a person other than the defendant and that until the plaintiff is aware of the identity of that person and any additional facts supporting the bringing of an action against the defendant, time will not run against the plaintiff.

Primarily, this subsection raises the issue of vicarious liability, where the plaintiff sues an employer for the tortious acts of one of his employees. In such a case, time will not run against the plaintiff until such time as he could reasonably have discovered the identity of the employer and the employee and the facts which entitle the plaintiff to bring an action. These facts will include knowledge that the employee was truly an employee and that he was acting in the course of his employment. Moreover, since the language of section 14(1)(d) is not couched specifically in terms of the employer-employee relationship, it is probably wide enough to cover the situation in which an independent contractor has carried out a non-delegable duty on the part of the person engaging his services.

Where section 14(1)(d) does apply, the plaintiff will have to be aware of the facts which would enable him to sue the employer. Thus it will be necessary for the plaintiff to be aware that the tortfeasor is an employee rather than an independent contractor performing a delegable duty. It will also be necessary for the plaintiff to be aware that the employee was acting in the course of his employment. On the other hand, there is no need for the plaintiff to be aware that, as a matter of law, the employer will be held vicariously liable for the acts of his employee. The difficulty this may give rise to is that it is not always easy to identify who is an employee since the answer to this question involves mixed questions of both law and fact.[124] Moreover, the answer to the question who is an employee may not be the same in every case. Many of the cases on the subject are concerned with tax or pension issues rather than with the question of tortious liability. Where the latter is the issue under consideration, the courts seem to be more lenient in the answer given, so far as the matter of plaintiff compensation is concerned.[125]

(f) Matters of law

It has been seen throughout the discussion of the specific elements of section 14(1) that the proviso to that section makes it clear that whether, as a matter of law, the defendant's act or omission amounts to negligence, nuisance or breach of duty is a matter which must be ignored in determining whether the plaintiff has the required degree of knowledge in

---

124. *Ready Mixed Concrete (South East) Ltd* v. *Minister of Pensions and National Insurance* [1968] 2 QB 497.

125. See e.g. *Rose* v. *Plenty* [1976] 1 WLR 141.

order to allow time to run against him. The reason for this is that section 14(1) is concerned with knowledge of relevant facts.

It follows from this that if the plaintiff has been badly advised by a solicitor on a matter of law, this will have no effect on his action for damages for personal injuries, although, in this instance, there may be an action for professional negligence on the part of the solicitor, so long as the action is not regarded as one "in respect of personal injuries" as may well be the case.[126] Similarly, incorrect legal advice given by a non-lawyer, such as a trades union official, will operate in a similar fashion.[127]

(g) Estoppel

In some instances, it is possible that the plaintiff is ignorant as to his legal rights because of something said to him by the defendant. In such a case, it is possible that the defendant may be estopped from relying on the limitation defence, despite the fact that, strictly construed, the proviso to section 14(1) prevents this eventuality.

In *Smith* v. *Central Asbestos Co Ltd*[128] the plaintiff was told by a works manager at his place of employment that it was not possible to claim both a disability pension and sue the employers for damages. The case was decided under the Limitation Act 1963, under which a misapprehension as to a material fact prevented time from running against the plaintiff. For the purposes of that Act, the Court of Appeal considered that the relevant exception applied until the misapprehension was corrected.

Whether the estoppel principle is valid has to be doubted in the majority of cases, since where the defendant misleads the plaintiff on a matter of law, it will often be the case that the words or actions of the defendant amount to a deliberate concealment of relevant facts under the Limitation Act 1980, s 32.[129] Thus if the defendant or his representative tells the plaintiff that "there is nothing to worry about" when the plaintiff raises a question about facts which might be taken to indicate negligence on the part of the defendant, there might be a case of deliberate concealment. But the same circumstances may also raise an estoppel, preventing the defendant from relying on the limitation defence.[130]

It should be observed that both section 14 and section 32 are concerned with facts rather than with matters of law, but this is often a distinction which is difficult to make. For example, a representation by the defendant concerning his legal rights may prevent time from running against the plaintiff, for example, where there has been an express admission of liability or an agreement not to rely upon the Limitation Act 1980.[131] Since estoppels are based on a combination of representation, reliance on that representation and alteration of position as a result of such reliance,[132] it ought to follow that if the plaintiff is tempted not to take action with the result that, apart from the operation of the doctrine of estoppel or the exercise of the court's discretion under the Limitation Act 1980, s 33, the plaintiff might otherwise have commenced proceedings, statements or conduct on the part of the

126. See *Broadley* v. *Guy Clapham & Co* [1994] 4 All ER 439.
127. See *Farmer* v. *National Coal Board, The Times*, 27 April 1985.
128. [1972] 1 QB 244. Affirmed on the facts in *Central Asbestos Co Ltd* v. *Dodds* [1973] AC 518 in which estoppel was not a matter under consideration.
129. See Ch 6.
130. *Westlake* v. *Bracknell District Council* (1987) 282 EG 868. But cf *Sheldon* v. *RHM Outhwaite (Underwriting Agencies) Ltd* [1994] 4 All ER 481, reversed on other grounds in [1995] 2 All ER 558.
131. See *Lubovsky* v. *Snelling* [1944] 1 KB 44.
132. *Rama Corporation* v. *Proved Tin & General Investments Ltd* [1952] 2 QB 147 at 149–50 *per* Slade J.

defendant or his representative should be regarded as sufficient to prevent time from running. Essentially an estoppel is an evidential device which may be taken to prevent a person from relying upon certain matters which might otherwise be called in evidence as part of a defence. Accordingly, it is suggested that the defendant's statements or conduct which serve to delay a plaintiff from pursuing legal rights which he might otherwise have pursued, but for those statements or conduct, should be regarded as sufficient to prevent time from running against the plaintiff, regardless of the precise language of the proviso to section 14(1).

Apart from questions of estoppel, the words or actions of the defendant are also factors which may allow the court to exercise its discretion to allow an action to proceed out of time.[133]

(h) Constructive knowledge (section 14(3))

It is clear from the language of the Limitation Act 1980, s 14(3) that the plaintiff's knowledge of relevant facts does not need to be actual knowledge, since it is provided that facts which could have been ascertained with the help of relevant expert advice, such as medical advice, will be deemed to be within the knowledge of the plaintiff if it was reasonable for the plaintiff to seek such advice. In addition to knowledge derived from the assistance of expert advice, section 14(3) also includes in the definition of "constructive knowledge" knowledge of facts which are observable or ascertainable by the plaintiff.

(i) Facts observable or ascertainable by the plaintiff

On one view, the test imposed by section 14(3) in this respect is partly objective and partly subjective. In the first place, the plaintiff is assumed to have knowledge which he, personally, might reasonably have been expected to acquire. Accordingly, the question to ask here is whether it is reasonable to expect the plaintiff in a particular case to have acquired the necessary knowledge, having regard to his own character, circumstances and limitations. In *Nash* v. *Eli Lilly & Co*[134] Purchas LJ observed that:

" . . . In our judgment, the proper approach is to determine what the plaintiff should have observed or ascertained, while asking no more of him than is reasonable. The standard of reasonableness in connection with the observations and/or the effort to ascertain are therefore finally objective but must be qualified to take into consideration the position, and circumstances and character of the plaintiff."[135]

However, the same view of section 14(3) was not shared by a majority of the Court of Appeal in *Forbes* v. *Wandsworth Health Authority*[136] in which the plaintiff, after an unsuccessful bypass operation, had his leg amputated in order to prevent the spread of gangrene. For some years after the operation nothing was done, but when the job of looking after the plaintiff became too onerous for the plaintiff's wife, the plaintiff decided

---

133. See Limitation Act 1980, s 33(3)(c), considered below.
134. [1993] 4 All ER 383. See also *O'Driscoll* v. *Dudley Health Authority* [1996] 7 Med LR 18, QBD, *per* Poole J, in which it seems that a relevant factor was the naivety of the plaintiff's parents in delaying the commencement of proceedings in respect of their daughter's injuries until she reached the age of majority at 21, despite the fact that the age of majority had been set at 18 for some time.
135. *Ibid* at 399.
136. [1996] 4 All ER 881. Stuart-Smith and Evans LJJ, Roch LJ dissenting on this issue.

to seek a further opinion in order to discover whether they could get financial help through suing the defendants.

In *Forbes*, both Stuart-Smith LJ and Evans LJ found it difficult to understand what was meant by Purchas LJ in *Nash* v. *Eli Lilly & Co* when he qualified his objective test with subjective considerations such as the intelligence of the plaintiff and other personal characteristics. According to Stuart-Smith LJ in *Forbes* v. *Wandsworth Health Authority*[137]:

"It does not seem to me that the fact that the plaintiff is more trusting, incurious, indolent, resigned or uncomplaining by nature can be a relevant characteristic, since this . . . undermines any objective approach.

I have come to the conclusion, therefore, that in the circumstances of this case, the deceased did have constructive knowledge. That knowledge could not be attributed to him immediately he came out of hospital; clearly he would have to have time to overcome the shock, take stock of his grave disability and its consequences and seek advice. That would take about 12 to 18 months."[138]

The view expressed by Stuart-Smith LJ, with whom Evans LJ agreed, is inconsistent with the views expressed by Purchas LJ in *Nash* v. *Eli Lilly & Co*, but the fact remains that both are decisions of the Court of Appeal. Accordingly, perhaps Stuart-Smith LJ ought to have regarded himself as bound by the earlier decision. This was certainly a matter which concerned Roch LJ in his dissenting judgment on the issue of constructive knowledge. Roch LJ regarded himself as bound by *Nash* v. *Eli Lilly & Co* despite the fact that he could not understand how subjective and objective elements in the test could be combined, as suggested by Purchas LJ. Roch LJ also opined that if Stuart-Smith and Evans LJJ were correct in regarding the relevant test to be purely objective, he too would have arrived at the same conclusion as they did.[139]

Clearly, there is a difference of opinion at Court of Appeal level and it would help if this matter could be considered by the House of Lords, but it is suggested that the majority view in *Forbes* is the correct view, especially since deserving cases may be dealt with by way of the court's discretion under section 33.

In cases like *Forbes*, the plaintiff may adopt one of two different courses of action. On the one hand, the plaintiff may simply accept the fact that the operation has gone wrong, but still keep faith with his surgeon and, as a result, do nothing. Alternatively, the patient may become immediately suspicious and seek a second opinion. Clearly, if the latter course of action is taken, the patient will know via his expert that he has suffered significant injury. But should the patient who waits be allowed to change his mind many years later, seek a second opinion, then claim that he did not know that he had suffered significant injury until the date on which he consulted the expert? The majority in *Forbes* thought that this should not be the case as it would lead to the defendant having to face a stale claim many years after the events to which it relates which would be difficult to contest.[140] Accordingly, there was an onus on the plaintiff to act promptly and if he did not do so, he could be fixed with constructive knowledge that he had suffered significant injury. The difficulty with this approach, which was identified by all members of the court in *Forbes*, is that it might not be desirable in policy terms if the effect of requiring the

137. *Ibid.*
138. *Ibid* at 891.
139. *Ibid* at 901.
140. *Ibid* at 890 *per* Stuart-Smith LJ.

patient to take prompt action is to encourage "ambulance chasing" on the part of lawyers and might serve to damage the doctor-patient relationship.[141]

To the general rule set out in *Forbes*, there may be an exception in cases where the plaintiff suffers initial injury of no great consequence which later develops into something much more serious. In these circumstances, the plaintiff can be forgiven for waiting until the gravity of the damage becomes so great that consulting a second opinion is justified without time having to run against him.[142]

The effect of section 14(3)(b) is to treat the plaintiff as if he or she had knowledge, even though the plaintiff is ignorant of the fact in question, or, at least, claims not to be aware of the fact in question. For example, in *Stubbings* v. *Webb*[143] Lord Griffiths considered *obiter* that a woman who admits she has been raped cannot realistically claim that she is not aware that she has suffered significant injury,[144] despite the fact that the rape by her stepfather was likely to have resulted in mental impairment which could have caused her to force the fact of her childhood abuse to the back of her mind.

The most common case in which a plaintiff will be fixed with constructive knowledge of relevant facts is where the plaintiff could reasonably have been expected to make enquiries, but fails to do so. For example, if a person is injured in a road traffic accident and does not make enquiries to discover the identity of the other driver, despite the fact that the plaintiff was aware that the other driver was prosecuted following the incident, the plaintiff cannot reasonably claim that he is unaware of the identity of the defendant.[145] Similarly, in *Farmer* v. *National Coal Board*[146] the plaintiff was unaware of how her father had died at work, but she could have found out from a close relative who attended the inquest relating to her father's death. Accordingly, to discover the relevant fact, it would have been simple enough to make enquiries of that relative. Likewise, past experiences at work may be regarded as a sufficient trigger to the memory to make appropriate enquiries. Thus in *Boynton* v. *British Steel plc*[147] the plaintiff had worked in noisy conditions from 1957 to 1980 and had been supplied with ear-plugs from 1977 onwards. Subsequently in 1980 he took on different work in less noisy conditions, in which he did not wear ear-plugs. In 1983, he noticed a distinct loss of hearing. He was advised to consult a specialist in 1984, but made no reference to his previous employment. On the advice of his brother, the plaintiff obtained a further expert opinion in 1992 when he was told he might have a claim for industrial deafness. No further action was taken by the plaintiff until 1993, when the defendant was first informed of the possible claim in September of that year. A writ was eventually issued in March 1995.

In determining whether the plaintiff could be said to have knowledge of the facts relevant to his cause of action, it was held that there was a difference between awareness of the possibility of a claim and the simple lack of a will to pursue a claim. There was no need for the plaintiff to seek expert advice in order to inform him that he had a hearing problem, accordingly a reasonable man in the same position as the plaintiff would have

141. *Ibid* at 890 *per* Stuart-Smith LJ and at 902 *per* Roch LJ.
142. *Ibid, per* Stuart-Smith LJ.
143. [1993] 2 WLR 120. The case actually decided that deliberate trespass did not fall within the language of section 11 and section 14, so that such cases are not personal injury actions.
144. *Ibid* at 126.
145. *Common* v. *Crofts* (1980) unreported, CA.
146. *The Times*, 27 April 1985, CA.
147. [1997] 7 CL 75, 8 October 1996, Recorder Rudland, Sheffield County Court.

been aware in 1984 that a noisy workplace could be damaging to one's hearing, especially in the light of the fact that he had been supplied with ear-plugs in his previous employment. Moreover, there was also no question of disapplying the normal limitation period under section 33,[148] since the prejudice to the defendant would be extreme by virtue of the facts that an important witness was dead, there would be difficulty in obtaining evidence, witnesses would be difficult to trace and the premises at which the injury was suffered had been destroyed.

A further difficulty may arise where the plaintiff, at one stage, was aware of a particular fact, but through the passage of time has forgotten the matter in question. Ordinarily, once a person has acquired knowledge, the courts are likely to take the view that he cannot lose that knowledge. In *Nash* v. *Eli Lilly & Co*[149] Purchas LJ opined that "references to a person's date of knowledge are references to the date on which he *first* had knowledge of . . . "[150] relevant facts.

It should follow from this that the plaintiff cannot, normally, claim to have forgotten something he once knew in order to allow time to run from a different date. However, there may be exceptional cases in which amnesia is forgivable. For example, where the plaintiff is under a disability, section 28 prevents time from running against the plaintiff while the disability lasts. If, during this period, the plaintiff acquires the necessary knowledge for the purposes of section 14, but later forgets, the question will arise whether time runs from the date on which the disability ends or the date on which the forgotten knowledge is re-acquired. In *Colegrove* v. *Smyth*[151] the plaintiff was a minor when her injuries were suffered, with the result that due to section 28, time would not run against her until she reached the age of majority. The plaintiff argued that her date of knowledge was later than the date of her eighteenth birthday, since she did not recall relevant facts she had once known until some time after she achieved majority.

Buckley J was of the opinion that if a person *genuinely* forgets a relevant fact in these circumstances, he cannot be fixed with constructive knowledge of that fact, if one is asked to consider the ordinary sense of the word knowledge.[152]

Of course this leaves open the question whether a person is to be fixed with knowledge of relevant facts where he has not genuinely forgotten but was still suffering from a disability at the time the knowledge was acquired. Clearly, this will be a question of fact and in *Colegrove* v. *Smyth* this was not a matter on which Buckley J had to reach a decision. On the facts, in *Colegrove* it was considered that it would be unreasonable to fix the plaintiff with knowledge of a relevant fact at the age of 18 or 19 merely because, when she was rigorously cross-examined by counsel, she was able to recall a fact of which she was aware at the age of 8 or 9.

(ii) Failure to seek expert advice

Under section 14(3)(b), the plaintiff is fixed with constructive knowledge of relevant facts where the advice he could have obtained by consulting a relevant expert would have made him aware that he had suffered significant injury.

148. See below.
149. [1993] 4 All ER 383.
150. *Ibid* at 395.
151. [1994] 5 Med LR 111, QBD.
152. *Ibid* at 116. Cf *Boynton* v. *British Steel plc* [1997] 7 CL 75, considered above at fn 147.

The test applied in this context is essentially objective[153] since it must be considered whether the plaintiff ought reasonably to have consulted an expert, in the light of the particular circumstances of the case. In these circumstances, it is suggested that the logical date on which time might start to run against the plaintiff is the date on which it might reasonably be expected that appropriate advice could have been given, as opposed to the date on which advice ought to have been sought. The date of the first consultation is unlikely to immediately produce evidence of significant injury, since time will usually be required in order to assess the results of the examination.[154] While the test in section 14(3)(b) is largely objective, it has been considered to contain subjective elements. For example, in *Driscoll-Varley* v. *Parkside Health Authority*[155] the court was prepared to take account of the plaintiff's state of intelligence, state of health and her fear of antagonising her doctor.[156] However, this may need to be reconsidered in the light of the criticism of a combined subjective and objective test under section 14(3)(a) in *Forbes* v. *Wandsworth Health Authority,* considered above. Although, both *Forbes* v. *Wandsworth Health Authority* and *Nash* v. *Eli Lilly & Co* are both specifically concerned with section 14(3)(a), it seems to be difficult to disentangle the two parts of section 14(3), since both are preceded by the words, "knowledge which [the plaintiff] might reasonably be expected to acquire . . . ".

This would seem to suggest that if the majority decision in *Forbes* v. *Wandsworth Health Authority* is correct then consideration of subjective factors is likely to result in intolerable confusion. Moreover, a subjective test might also be regarded as inconsistent with the precise language of section 14(3). In any case, if a consideration of subjective factors is thought to be necessary, this can be done if the court decides to exercise its discretion under section 33 to allow an action to proceed out of time, where justice so demands.[157]

Despite the fact that some decisions have espoused a subjective/objective test, there are some decisions based on section 14(3)(b) which have moved more towards a purely objective approach, even before the decision of the Court of Appeal in *Forbes*. For example, in *Murphy* v. *Milton Keynes Health Authority*[158] the plaintiff was taken to be aware that his broken ankle had not been properly aligned, since he was able to compare his two ankles following the operation. He delayed in consulting a solicitor in the hope that his condition might improve, but he was fixed with constructive knowledge of a significant injury as his suspicions could be regarded as sufficient to persuade a reasonable person to consult, at least, a general practitioner.

In some instances, it may be relevant to consider the plaintiff's resources, especially where it appears that he is only able to proceed if he is legally aided. For example, until Legal Aid Board approval is received, the plaintiff's solicitor may not be able to seek

153. Cf the test applied under the Limitation Act 1963 which was subjective, being based on the plaintiff's individual characteristics, which allowed Lord Reid in *Central Asbestos Co Ltd* v. *Dodd* [1973] AC 518 at 530 to say that "less is expected of a stupid or uneducated man than of a man of intelligence and experience".
154. Cf *Jones* v. *Bennett* [1976] 1 Lloyd's Rep 484 where the date on which it was considered reasonable to consult a lawyer was the date on which the plaintiff was fixed with constructive knowledge. However, lawyers may be able to give on-the-spot advice, but this may not be so with medical experts.
155. [1991] 2 Med LR 346.
156. *Ibid* at 357 *per* Hidden J. See also *O'Driscoll* v. *Dudley Health Authority* [1996] 7 Med LR 18 in which naivety appears to have been a consideration.
157. *Forbes* v. *Wandsworth Health Authority* [1996] 4 All ER 881 at 890 *per* Stuart-Smith LJ.
158. (1991) unreported, CA.

expert advice.[159] However, in the light of the analysis in *Forbes* v. *Wandsworth Health Authority*, this might now be a relevant factor only under section 33.

(iii) The proviso to section 14(3)

The proviso to section 14(3) states that a plaintiff will not be fixed with constructive knowledge of a fact which is ascertainable only with the help of expert advice, so long as he has taken all reasonable steps to obtain that advice, and where appropriate, act on it.

It is clear from the wording of the proviso that what matters is whether it is reasonable for the particular plaintiff to obtain advice, rather than to ask what a reasonable man would do in the same circumstances.[160] Accordingly, for the purposes of the proviso, subjective considerations are important, so that matters such as resources, intelligence, or state of health may serve to excuse the plaintiff from seeking advice, if that failure on the part of the plaintiff may be regarded as reasonable in the circumstances.

In some instances there may be an error on the part of the expert, such as a failure to disclose matters relevant to the plaintiff. In these circumstances, the plaintiff cannot be fixed with knowledge that he has not got when, due to the act or omission of the expert, appropriate advice has not been passed on. In *Marston* v. *British Railways Board*[161] a metallurgist was asked to report on the condition of a metal hammer. His advice merely related to whether the metal was too hard or too brittle. What his advice did not refer to was that the hammer was in a defective state from the start because of prior misuse—a fact which was readily discoverable. Since the failure to identify this fact was that of the expert, the plaintiff was not taken to have constructive knowledge of the readily discoverable fact, since it was only readily discoverable with the aid of expert advice.

A gloss on this problem may arise where the plaintiff initially has strong suspicions that he has suffered injury, but those suspicions are flatly contradicted by the advice given by an expert. In these circumstances, it would seem to be reasonable for the plaintiff to abandon the suspicions he once harboured and rely upon the expert advice, even if it proves to be erroneous. As a result, the plaintiff will not be fixed with constructive knowledge.[162]

Since the proviso applies to facts "ascertainable only with the help of expert advice", it might be argued that where a fact is capable of being discovered without the use of expert advice, the proviso is inapplicable.[163] Thus, it follows that a solicitor will not ordinarily be regarded as an expert for the purposes of section 14, since the plaintiff will normally be capable of being aware of the necessary facts which a solicitor is likely to tell him in order to ascertain whether it is possible to maintain an action against the defendant.[164] Thus enquiries such as asking the police or the fire brigade for their report on an accident and interviewing witnesses, although tasks often carried out by a solicitor, may

---

159. See *Khan* v. *Ainslie* [1993] 4 Med LR 319.

160. *Newton* v. *Cammell Laird & Co (Shipbuilders and Engineers) Ltd* [1969] 1 WLR 415.

161. [1976] ICR 124. See also *Newton* v. *Cammell Laird & Co (Shipbuilders and Engineers) Ltd* [1969] 1 WLR 415.

162. See *Davis* v. *Ministry of Defence* [1990] 1 Med LR 261 considered above.

163. See *Halford* v. *Brookes* [1991] 3 All ER 559 at 565 *per* Russell LJ.

164. *Fowell* v. *National Coal Board*, The Times, 28 May 1986. And see also *Leadbitter* v. *Hodge Finance* [1982] 2 All ER 167.

also be regarded as facts which the plaintiff can become aware of on his own initiative. It seems, therefore, that for the purposes of section 14, the word expert is taken to mean "expert in the sense in which it is used in relation to expert witnesses".[165]

However, although a solicitor may not be regarded as an expert, it does not follow that the plaintiff will not be fixed with the knowledge possessed on his behalf by his solicitor, since ordinary principles of agency will apply. Thus in *Simpson* v. *Norwest Holst Southern Ltd*[166] the court appears to have proceeded on the basis that the plaintiff was fixed with such knowledge as his solicitor ought reasonably to have acquired.[167]

DEATH OF THE PLAINTIFF

Special rules are applied under the Limitation Act 1980, s 11(5) to (7) where an accident results in the death of the plaintiff within three years of the date on which his cause of action in respect of personal injury first accrued.

It is provided that where an injured person dies before the expiry of the limitation period, a new cause of action will be substituted, which may be taken up by the personal representatives of the deceased as an action on behalf of the estate under the Law Reform (Miscellaneous Provisions) Act 1934, s 1.[168] The effect of section 11(5) is to make the cause of action survive for the benefit of the estate. It follows from this that an action in favour of the estate will become time barred either three years from the date of death of the injured person or three years from the date on which the personal representatives first had knowledge that significant injury had been caused to the deceased, whichever of these two dates is latest in time.

Personal representatives are defined in section 11(6)[169] as including any person who is or has been a personal representative of the deceased, including an executor who has not proved the will, but excluding a special personal representative in relation to settled land. The importance of section 11(6) is that the knowledge of the personal representative that the deceased suffered significant injury is a determining factor in identifying the date on which time should run in respect of an action brought on behalf of the estate. The same rules on knowledge are applied to the personal representatives as are applied to a plaintiff who lives and is able to sue on his own behalf.[170] Moreover, any knowledge acquired by a person before he was appointed to the position of personal representative may be taken into account in determining when time should start to run. In some instances, there may be more than one personal representative and each may be possessed of different knowledge. In these circumstances, the 1980 Act provides that the earliest date of knowledge of relevant facts will be decisive for the purposes of the running of time.[171]

---

165. *Ibid, per* Parker LJ.
166. [1980] 2 All ER 471. See also *Khan* v. *Ainslie* [1993] 4 Med LR 319 at 325 *per* Waterhouse J.
167. *Ibid* at 476.
168. Limitation Act 1980, s 11(5).
169. For an identical definition applicable to actions under the Consumer Protection Act 1987 see Limitation Act 1980, s 11A(6) discussed in Ch 21.
170. Limitation Act 1980, s 11(5).
171. *Ibid*, s 11(7).

ACTIONS UNDER THE FATAL ACCIDENTS ACT 1976

Although the position at common law was that when a person died, any action he might previously have had in respect of his injuries died with him, this position was altered by statute in 1934 as a result of the provisions of the Law Reform (Miscellaneous Provisions) Act 1934. The position now is that where a person dies as a result of his injuries, an action in favour of the deceased's estate is preserved under the 1934 Act. In addition to this, on death, a new cause of action accrues under the Fatal Accidents Act 1976 in favour of the dependants of the deceased in respect of the financial losses suffered by them in respect of their dependency.

For these purposes, the Limitation Act 1980, s 12 provides:

"(1) An action under the Fatal Accidents Act 1976 shall not be brought if the death occurred when the person injured could no longer maintain an action and recover damages in respect of the injury (whether because of a time limit in this Act or in any other Act, or for any other reason).

Where any such action by the injured person would have been barred by the time limit in section 11 of this Act, no account shall be taken of the possibility of that time limit being overridden under section 33 of this Act.

(2) None of the time limits given in the preceding provisions of this Act shall apply to an action under the Fatal Accidents Act 1976, but no such action shall be brought after the expiration of three years from—

(a) the date of death; or
(b) the date of knowledge of the person for whose benefit the action is brought;

whichever is the later.

(3) An action under the Fatal Accidents Act 1976 shall be one to which sections 28, 33 and 35 of this Act apply, and the application to any such action of the time limit under subsection (2) above shall be subject to section 39; but otherwise Parts II and III of this Act shall not apply to any such action."

The Limitation Act 1980, s 13 provides further that:

"(1) Where there is more than one person for whose benefit an action under the Fatal Accidents Act 1976 is brought, section 12(2)(b) of this Act shall be applied separately to each of them.

(2) Subject to subsection (3) below, if by virtue of subsection (1) above the action would be outside the time limit given by section 12(2) as regards one or more, but not all, of the persons for whose benefit it is brought, the court shall direct that any person as regards whom the action would be outside that limit shall be excluded from those for whom the action is brought.

(3) The court shall not give such a direction if it is shown that if the action were brought exclusively for the benefit of the person in question it would not be defeated by a defence of limitation (whether in consequence of section 28 of this Act or an agreement between the parties not to raise the defence, or otherwise)."

The general effect of section 12(1) is to bar an action brought by a dependant of the deceased if the death occurred at a time when the person injured could no longer maintain an action and recover damages in respect of that injury, for whatever reason, including a limitation defence. Moreover, for the purposes of determining whether any action on the part of the deceased would have been barred, the court may not take account of the possibility of discretionary extension under section 33.

In contrast, if the primary limitation period in favour of the deceased person had not expired at the time of death, the effect of section 12(2) is that a new three-year limitation period commences in favour of the dependants. This period will run from the date of death or the date of the dependants' knowledge,[172] whichever is later. In effect, what this means is that in favour of the dependants, the relevant limitation period may be extended to almost six years from the date of the accident which causes the initial injury, regardless of the question of knowledge of relevant facts on the part of the deceased or the dependants, provided death occurs marginally before the date on which the primary, accrual-based limitation period expires. Moreover, this period may be extended still further in cases where the dependants' date of knowledge is considered to be delayed, even if the deceased possessed the relevant knowledge prior to the date of death.

In the event that there is more than one dependant and the date on which one of them acquired relevant knowledge differs from the date on which the other or others become aware of relevant facts, time will run against each dependant from a different date.[173] Furthermore, since the rules on disability do apply to actions under the Fatal Accidents Act 1976, the running of time may be delayed still further in the case where a dependant is a minor.[174]

A difficulty created by the rule that time may run against different dependants from different dates is that the Fatal Accidents Act 1976 works on the basis that there will be a single action in respect of all dependency claims,[175] but the effect of the scheme under the Limitation Act 1980 is that time may run against one dependant from an earlier date than against another. This gives rise to the possibility that an action may be brought at a time when some dependants are time barred and others not. In these circumstances, the court has a power to direct that time-barred dependants may be excluded from the action.[176] Where the dependant or dependants are guilty of delay in commencing proceedings, with the result that the primary limitation period has expired, the court has a discretion under section 33 to allow the action to proceed out of time, where it is equitable to do so.[177] By virtue of section 33(5), the guidelines on the exercise of discretion in section 33(3)[178] will operate in relation to the exercise of the court's discretion as if references to "the plaintiff" were references to "any person whose date of knowledge is or was relevant in determining a time limit".

THE DISCRETION TO ALLOW AN ACTION TO PROCEED OUT OF TIME[179]

Provided the plaintiff brings his action within any limitation period provided for in the Limitation Act 1980, his right to bring that action cannot be defeated. However, where a limitation period has expired in relation to an action for personal injuries, it does not automatically follow that the plaintiff will be denied the right to proceed, since the court has a discretion to allow an action to be commenced out of time, if the circumstances of the case justify the exercise of the discretion.

172. For these purposes, knowledge has the same meaning as is applied to living plaintiffs, considered above. Rules on constructive knowledge also apply to dependants.
173. Limitation Act 1980, s 13(1).
174. *Ibid*, s 12(3).
175. Fatal Accidents Act 1976, s 2(3).
176. Limitation Act 1980, s 13(2).
177. *Ibid*, s 12(3).
178. Discussed in the following section.
179. For the operation of the discretion in relation to actions under the Consumer Protection Act 1987 see Limitation Act 1980, s 33(1A) and Ch 21.

The Limitation Act 1980, s 33 provides:

"(1) If it appears to the court that it would be equitable to allow an action to proceed having regard to the degree to which—

    (a) the provisions of section 11 or 12 of this Act prejudice the plaintiff or any person whom he represents; and

    (b) any decision of the court under this subsection would prejudice the defendant or any person whom he represents;

the court may direct that those provisions shall not apply to the action, or shall not apply to any specified cause of action to which the action relates . . .

(2) The court shall not under this section disapply section 12(1) except where the reason why the person injured could no longer maintain an action was because of the time limit in section 11.

If, for example, the person injured could at his death no longer maintain an action under the Fatal Accidents Act 1976 because of the time limit in Article 29 in Schedule 1 to the Carriage by Air Act 1961, the court has no power to direct that section 12(1) shall not apply.

(3) In acting under this section, the court shall have regard to all the circumstances of the case and in particular to—

    (a) the length of, and the reasons for, the delay on the part of the plaintiff;

    (b) the extent to which, having regard to the delay, the evidence adduced or likely to be adduced by the plaintiff or the defendant is or is likely to be less cogent than if the action had been brought within the time allowed by section 11 or (as the case may be) by section 12;

    (c) the conduct of the defendant after the cause of action arose, including the extent (if any) to which he responded to requests reasonably made by the plaintiff for information or inspection for the purpose of ascertaining facts which were or might be relevant to the plaintiff's cause of action against the defendant;

    (d) the duration of any disability of the plaintiff arising after the date of the accrual of the cause of action;

    (e) the extent to which the plaintiff acted promptly and reasonably once he knew whether or not the act or omission of the defendant, to which the injury was attributable, might be capable at that time of giving rise to an action for damages;

    (f) the steps, if any, taken by the plaintiff to obtain medical, legal or other expert advice and the nature of any such advice he may have received.

(4) In a case where the person injured died when, because of section 11, he could no longer maintain an action and recover damages in respect of the injury, the court shall have regard in particular to the length of, and reasons for, the delay on the part of the deceased.

(5) In a case under subsection (4) above, or any other case where the time limit, or one of the time limits, depends on the date of knowledge of a person other than the plaintiff, subsection (3) above shall have effect with appropriate modifications, and shall have effect in particular as if references to the plaintiff included references to any person whose date of knowledge is or was relevant in determining a time limit.

(6) A direction by the court disapplying the provisions of section 12(1) shall operate to disapply the provisions to the same effect in section 1(1) of the Fatal Accidents Act 1976.

(7) In this section 'the court' means the court in which the action has been brought.

(8) References in this section to section 11 include references to that section as extended by any of the preceding provisions of this Part of this Act or by any provisions of Part III of this Act."

It follows from these provisions that the court has a discretion to allow an action to be commenced outside the normal limitation period applicable to an action in respect of personal injuries, whether brought under section 11 or section 12, where the circumstances appear to justify this. However, it seems that this discretion will not apply to all forms of personal injury, since there are certain international conventions which cover passenger transport, such as the Convention relating to the Carriage of Passengers and their Luggage by Sea[180] which have their own rules on limitation of actions. In particular, regard has to be had to the general effect of specific rules on limitation of actions, since some rules, such as that contained in section 33, allow the court to exclude altogether a limitation period which has already run its course. However, the Carriage Convention contains rules in Article 16(3) which allow for suspension or interruption of a limitation period. Given the difference, it would appear that section 33 cannot be used to assist a plaintiff where the action is governed by the rules of the Convention.[181]

(a) Prejudice

It is important to emphasise the language used in section 33(1), since this specifies that the court should exercise the discretion only where the operation of section 11 or section 12 would operate to the prejudice of the plaintiff and that regard should also be had to the extent to which the exercise of the discretion would prejudice the defendant or any person whom he represents. It follows from this that the notion of prejudice is confined to the operation of sections 11 and 12 and that prejudice derived from some other source has to be ignored in determining whether the discretion may be exercised in favour of the plaintiff.

The particular requirement of section 33(1) is that the court must have regard to the prejudice to the plaintiff caused by the operation of the primary limitation period, set against the prejudice to the defendant caused by a decision to exercise the discretion. However, whichever way the court's decision goes, it remains the case that there will be prejudice to one or other of the parties. One relevant factor in determining the degree of prejudice suffered must be the strength or weakness of the plaintiff's case, since the stronger is his case the greater will be the prejudice suffered by the plaintiff if his action is not allowed to proceed out of time.

Although, as a general rule, the courts have stated that their discretion under section 33 is unfettered[182] it does appear to operate subject to the views expressed in *Walkley* v. *Precision Forgings Ltd.*[183] In *Walkley* a distinction was drawn between a plaintiff who had failed to issue a writ within the primary three-year period and one who had done so, but subsequently failed to proceed with his action and then sought to issue a second writ out of time. In this second case, the subsequent writ would be subject to normal rules on expiry of the limitation period and the court would not exercise discretion in the plaintiff's favour. The principal reasons why this was considered to be the case was that, otherwise than in wholly exceptional circumstances, the plaintiff could not be said to be prejudiced by the operation of section 11 or section 12, since the true cause of the prejudice to the plaintiff is his own delay in acting upon the writ which was issued within the limitation period and that there must always be some prejudice to the defendant in allowing an action to proceed out of time, since he will be put to trouble, expense and risk of liability.[184] In

180. Enacted by the Merchant Shipping Act 1979, Sch 3.
181. *Higham* v. *Stena Sealink Ltd* [1996] 3 All ER 660.
182. *Firman* v. *Ellis* [1978] QB 886; *Thompson* v. *Brown* [1981] 1 WLR 744; *Donovan* v. *Gwentoys Ltd* [1990] 1 All ER 1018.
183. [1979] 1 WLR 606. See Davies (1982) 98 LQR 249, 260–65; Morgan (1982) 1 CJQ 109; Jones (1985) 1 PN 159, 160.
184. *Ibid* at 618–19 *per* Lord Diplock.

Forward v. *Hendricks*[185] the plaintiff was injured in a road traffic accident. Within the three years following the date of the accident, a writ was issued and it was purportedly served on the defendant. However, it was later held that service was not effective since the proceedings were never brought to the defendant's attention. As a result of this finding, the plaintiff commenced a second action, which the defendant contested on the ground that the action was time barred. In response to an application to the court to exercise its discretion under section 33, it was held that where the first action is commenced within the primary limitation period, any prejudice suffered by the plaintiff must have been caused by his own delay and not by virtue of the operation of the primary limitation period set out in section 11. The one exception to this rule can be found in cases in which the defendant is estopped from relying on the limitation defence where the failure of the first action is due to improper conduct on the defendant's part. On the facts, there was no such conduct, with the result that the plaintiff's application to the court for the exercise of its discretion had to fail.

The rationale behind these cases was stated in *Chappell* v. *Cooper*[186] where it was observed that in such circumstances, " . . . the cause of . . . prejudice is not the provisions of section [11], that is to say the existence of the primary limitation period, but is the act or omission of himself or his solicitors in acting or failing to act as he or they have done in relation to that action . . . ".[187] To put it another way the reason why the plaintiff's application must fail is that either the first action will have been struck out for want of prosecution or will have been discontinued by the plaintiff of his own volition, but that in either event, the wounds are self-inflicted.[188] This restriction on the exercise of the discretion was considered to apply whatever was the reason for the plaintiff's failure to proceed, whether because solicitors had failed to issue the writ in time,[189] because the action was dismissed for want of prosecution or because the action was discontinued by the plaintiff for whatever reason. The paradox created by this rule is that, from the point of view of a possible action for professional negligence against a solicitor, the solicitor who has failed to issue a writ at all is in a marginally better position than the solicitor who does issue a writ in time, but subsequently fails to act upon it on his client's behalf, since in the latter case, the court will decline to exercise its discretion in favour of the solicitor's client.

Against the seemingly arbitrary distinction drawn in *Walkley* v. *Precision Forgings Ltd* it may be argued that the reasons which underlie the decision apply equally to some plaintiffs who fail to issue a writ within the primary limitation period, since it is their delay (or delay on the part of their legal adviser) which is the main cause of any prejudice which may be suffered, rather than the effect of section 11 or section 12.[190] Arbitrary though the rule may be, it is clear from Lord Diplock's judgment in *Walkley* that there may be exceptional circumstances in which the rule does not apply, in which case it may be possible for the court to exercise its discretion. These exceptional cases include instances of misrepresentation or improper conduct on the part of the defendant; cases where the

---

185. [1997] 2 All ER 395.
186. [1980] 2 All ER 463.
187. *Ibid* at 468 *per* Roskill LJ. See also *Walkley* v. *Precision Forgings Ltd* [1979] 1 WLR 606 at 609 *per* Lord Wilberforce and at 619 *per* Lord Diplock; *Deerness* v. *John Keeble & Son (Brantham) Ltd* [1983] 2 Lloyd's Rep 260 at 262–64 *per* Lord Diplock; *Forward* v. *Hendricks* [1997] 2 All ER 395 at 401 *per* McCowan LJ.
188. *Walkley* v. *Precision Forgings Ltd* [1979] 1 WLR 606 at 619 *per* Lord Diplock.
189. *Deerness* v. *John Keeble & Son (Brantham) Ltd* [1983] 2 Lloyd's Rep 260.
190. Including an action under the Law Reform (Miscellaneous Provisions) Act 1934.

first writ was invalid; cases in which the validity of the first writ is extended and cases in which it can be said that the plaintiff did not have the required knowledge of relevant facts for the purposes of section 14.

(i) Misrepresentation and improper conduct on the part of the defendant

If the plaintiff has been induced by the defendant to discontinue his action, it may be appropriate for the court to consider whether it should exercise its discretion in favour of the plaintiff. The rationale behind the exception seems to be that the defendant is estopped from relying on sections 11 and 12, in which case, as a matter of law, a rule of evidence prevents the defendant from arguing that the plaintiff's action is out of time.[191] Since this so-called exception is based on an estoppel, what will be required is clear evidence of a representation on which it is reasonable for the plaintiff to rely. For these purposes, it seems that the mere fact of acceptance of liability on the part of the defendant will not suffice to amount to a representation. What seems to be required is an unequivocal waiver of an intention to rely on the limitation defence,[192] so that the mere fact that the defendant has made an interim payment to the plaintiff under the terms of the original writ will not serve to give rise to the estoppel. In *Forward* v. *Hendricks*,[193] it was held that the mere fact that a defendant says he has not received service of the first writ will not suffice, since in such a case there is no conduct on which the plaintiff can be said to have relied. It was held by Waller LJ that[194]:

"The real question . . . is whether the plaintiff could sustain an argument that the failure of the first action was in any way due to improper conduct, or indeed any conduct of the defendant, which lulled the plaintiff into a circumstance where the first action was dismissed.
. . . in my view there is nothing that can be characterised as improper conduct by the defendant, indeed there is much for which the plaintiff or his advisers can be criticised."

(ii) First writ invalid

If for some technical reason the first writ, although issued in time, is invalid, the court may still exercise its discretion since the rule in *Walkley* v. *Precision Forgings Ltd* is inapplicable where no writ has been issued. Since the effect of invalidity is that the first writ is treated as a nullity, the practical effect of this is that, for the purposes of the rule in *Walkley,* it is as if no writ had been issued at all.[195] Thus if a writ is issued without leave as may be required by some statutory provisions,[196] the want of an application for leave to issue the writ will serve to render it a nullity. In this case, inability to serve a second writ may then give rise to the possibility of prejudice by virtue of the operation of section 11 or section 12.

In *Re Workvale Ltd (No 2)*[197] the plaintiff issued a writ against his employers at a time when he was unaware that the company had been dissolved. Subsequently, the plaintiff

---

191. *Deerness* v. *John Keeble & Son (Brantham)* [1983] 2 Lloyd's Rep 260 at 262 *per* Lord Diplock. See also *Forward* v. *Hendricks* [1997] 2 All ER 395.
192. *Ibid.*
193. [1997] 2 All ER 395.
194. *Ibid* at 403.
195. See *White* v. *Glass, The Times,* 18 February 1989, [1989] CA Transcript 148 ; *Rose* v. *Express Welding Ltd* (1986) unreported, CA.
196. Such as the Insolvency Act 1986, s 130(2).
197. [1992] 2 All ER 627.

died and his widow sought a declaration that the dissolution of the company was void under the Companies Act 1985, s 651(5) and that the company be restored to the register, with the result that the period between dissolution and restoration to the register could be ignored for limitation purposes. The defendant's insurers argued that, in these circumstances, the exercise of the court's discretion under section 33 ought to be ruled out on the ground that an action (albeit ineffective) had been commenced during the primary limitation period and that it was the plaintiff's solicitor's failure to notice that the company had been dissolved which caused any prejudice to the plaintiff. The Court of Appeal rejected this argument since the decision in *Walkley* v. *Precision Forgings Ltd* could be confined to cases in which an *effective* action is commenced within the primary limitation period. Accordingly, if what is commenced is an *ineffective* action by virtue of the fact that the defendant no longer existed as a legal person, the prejudice to the plaintiff was treated as having been caused by both the three-year limitation period and by the failure of the solicitors acting on behalf of the deceased to discover the fact of dissolution and take steps to remedy the position.[198]

In contrast, if the first writ remains valid, the sole cause of prejudice to the plaintiff will be the failure on the part of the solicitor to proceed with the action, which, under the rule in *Walkley*, is to be regarded as a failure on the part of the plaintiff which will prevent the discretion from being exercised.

(iii) Extension of the validity of the writ

Even where there has been a failure to serve the writ within the four-month period permitted under RSC Order 6, rule 8(1), the court has a discretion to renew the validity of that writ.[199] If a plaintiff has issued a writ within the primary limitation period but fails to proceed with it during the permitted period, any exercise of a discretion to extend the validity of the writ ought to operate on the same principles which apply to the exercise of discretion under section 33. In *Sanotra* v. *Surinder Kaur Sanotra*[200] two passengers on a bus driven by the defendant sued in respect of injuries resulting from a road traffic accident. One of these issued a writ within the primary limitation period, but failed to proceed with it in the time allowed and the other attempted to commence proceedings out of time. Accordingly, section 33 applied to the last case and Order 6, rule 8 to the former. The view expressed by Kerr LJ was that there was nothing to prevent the court from applying the same considerations to both plaintiffs, regardless of the fact that different discretions applied to each of them in cases which concerned the same defendant and arose out of the same facts. Moreover, he opined that it would be very strange if different considerations were to be applied simply because the source of the discretion, in each case, was different.

198. *Ibid* at 635 *per* Scott LJ.
199. Under RSC Ord 6, r 8(2) (amended by SI 1989/2427) extension is permitted for periods of up to four months at a time, and in exceptional cases for up to 12 months under RSC Ord 6, r 8(2A). Part of the difficulty with this discretion is that it may serve to deprive the defendant of a legitimate limitation defence, and given that the court also has a discretion under s 33 to allow an action to proceed out of time, it is normally the case that the court will decline to extend the validity of the first writ, except in exceptional circumstances, and require the plaintiff to issue a new writ instead, requiring the exercise of the court's discretion under s 33: *Chappell* v. *Cooper* [1980] 2 All ER 463.
200. (1987) unreported. See also *Waddon* v. *Whitecroft-Scovill Ltd* [1988] 1 All ER 996 at 1001 *per* Lord Brandon.

Despite the fact that the use of Order 6, rule 8, does appear to serve as a means of getting round the rule in *Walkley*, it is, nonetheless, a route with attendant difficulties. In the first place, the application to extend must come during the validity of the writ or in the four months following its expiry and, secondly, each application for extension will result in only an additional maximum of four months in which to act.[201]

(iv) Want of knowledge on the part of the plaintiff

Where a writ has been issued but not followed up, the reason for this failure may be that the plaintiff lacks the knowledge necessary for the purposes of the Limitation Act 1980, s 14.[202] Unusual circumstances such as these will render the rule in *Walkley* entirely irrelevant since the primary limitation period will not have expired, since want of relevant knowledge on the part of the plaintiff will mean that a second writ issued by the plaintiff is still in time. Thus in *Stephen v. Riverside Health Authority*[203] a first writ was issued within three years of the date of the operation which was alleged to have caused the plaintiff personal injury and a second writ was issued almost eight years later, in February 1988. However, since it was concluded that the plaintiff could not have acquired the necessary knowledge, for the purposes of section 14, until February 1985, the second writ was still issued within the primary limitation period.[204] The difficulty remains that if the plaintiff has gone to the trouble of issuing the first writ, there is, at least, an implication that he does possess the knowledge required by section 14, although that would appear not to be the case where the defendant is guilty of an omission, as opposed to an act, which causes personal injury.[205]

(b) Elements of the section 33 discretion

Subject to the operation of the rule on prejudice which may mean that the plaintiff is not entitled to ask the court to exercise its discretion in his favour, the court is then unfettered so far as concerns the exercise of that discretion.[206] In exercising the discretion, the court is assisted by a list of guidelines contained in section 33, but the existence of this list and the fact that there are earlier decisions which interpret the contents of that list might serve to interfere with the principle that the exercise of the discretion is to be regarded as unfettered. But given the view that the discretion is not fettered in any way, even if there is a line of cases which suggests that, in a particular set of circumstances, the discretion will not be exercised, it ought to follow that a court should not regard itself as bound by

---

201. *Singh v. Duport Harper Foundries Ltd* [1994] 1 WLR 769.

202. This is most likely to be the case where the plaintiff has a strong belief that his injuries are attributable to the act or omission of the defendant, but the belief has not yet been confirmed by evidence.

203. [1990] 1 Med LR 261. See also *Davis v. Ministry of Defence, The Times*, 7 August 1985.

204. This decision may have to be reconsidered on its special facts, since it has been made clear, subsequently, in *Nash v. Eli Lilly & Co* [1993] 4 All ER 383, that a person cannot acquire knowledge but then lose it because he has been advised by experts that the injury is not attributable to the act or omission of the defendant. It follows that the exception will operate only where the plaintiff has no knowledge, from the outset, that his injury is attributable to the act or omission of the defendant.

205. See the discussion of *Forbes v. Wandsworth Health Authority* [1996] 4 All ER 881 discussed above.

206. See *Donovan v. Gwentoys Ltd* [1990] 1 All ER 1018 at 1023 *per* Lord Griffiths. See also *Ramsden v. Lee* [1992] 2 All ER 204. Cf *Hartley v. Birmingham City District Council* [1992] 2 All ER 213 at 224 *per* Parker LJ who considered that guidelines might be laid down to indicate the circumstances in which the discretion might be exercised.

those decisions, if, exceptionally, it is thought right to exercise the discretion on that particular occasion.

The discretion lies in the hands of the court of first instance, with the result that it is unlikely that an appellate court will seek to interfere with the exercise of the discretion.[207] This will be especially the case where there is evidence which supports the decision taken at first instance.[208]

In deciding whether to exercise the discretion, section 33(1) indicates that this should only be done where "equitable". For these purposes, the word "equitable" has been interpreted to mean "fair and just",[209] which will require a court to balance the prejudice to the plaintiff of losing the right to bring an action against the prejudice to the defendant of having to face a late claim.[210] Whichever way the decision goes, it is apparent that prejudice will be faced by one or other of the parties, but the court must consider which of the two is likely to suffer the least prejudice as a result of the decision whether or not to exercise the discretion.

(i) Prejudice to the plaintiff and the defendant

Factors which may guide the exercise of the court's discretion will include the strength or weakness of the plaintiff's case. For example, it was observed by Lord Diplock in *Thompson* v. *Brown*[211] that:

"[Section 33] . . . appears to be drafted on the further assumption that the expiry of a limitation period before his action has been started must always prejudice the plaintiff in some degree . . . this too seems to me self-evident, unless the plaintiff's prospects of success in the action if it is allowed to proceed are so hopeless as to deprive it even of nuisance value . . . The degree to which the plaintiff would be prejudiced by being prevented from proceeding with his action will be affected by how good or bad would have been his prospects of success . . . "

However, the problem still remains that no matter how strong the plaintiff's case might be, there is still prejudice to the defendant if the plaintiff is allowed to commence his action out of time by virtue of the court having decided to exercise its discretion. Thus, in contrast to the position of the plaintiff in *Thompson* v. *Brown,* Lord Diplock observed of the position of the defendant that[212]:

"The effect of such a direction, and its only effect, is to deprive the defendant of what would otherwise be a complete defence to the action, viz. that the writ was issued too late. A direction under the section must therefore always be highly prejudicial to the defendant, for even if he also has a good defence on the merits, he is put to the expenditure of time and energy and money in establishing it, while if . . . he has no defence as to liability, he has everything to lose if a direction is given under the section. On the other hand if . . . the time elapsed after the expiration of the primary limitation period is very short, what the defendant loses in consequence of a direction might be regarded as being in the nature of a windfall."

The issue of the strength or weakness of the plaintiff's case is important, but it should also be noted that when it comes to weighing the prejudice to the plaintiff in declining to

207. *Conry* v. *Simpson* [1983] 3 All ER 369.
208. *Bradley* v. *Hanseatic Shipping* [1986] 2 Lloyd's Rep 34.
209. *Firman* v. *Ellis* [1978] QB 886; *Ward* v. *Foss, The Times,* 29 November 1993.
210. *Ward* v. *Foss, The Times,* 29 November 1993, *per* Hobhouse LJ.
211. [1981] 1 WLR 744 at 750. See also *Dale* v. *British Coal Corporation* [1992] PIQR 373 at 380 *per* Stuart-Smith LJ.
212. *Ibid.*

exercise the discretion under section 33 against that caused to the defendant if the action is allowed to proceed out of time, the strength/weakness argument has the effect of cancelling out the prejudice argument. This is so because if the plaintiff's case is strong there is substantial prejudice to the plaintiff in refusing to allow him to bring his action out of time. But, at the same time, if the discretion is exercised in the plaintiff's favour, there is equally substantial prejudice to the defendant in requiring him to face a very strong claim which, apart from the exercise of the discretion, would have been time barred. Conversely, where there is a very weak claim on the part of the plaintiff, he suffers less prejudice if the discretion is not exercised in his favour and the defendant suffers less prejudice if he is required to answer a weak claim outside the primary limitation period.[213]

While factors such as the strength or weakness of the plaintiff's case may have some influence on the way in which the discretion is exercised, it is nonetheless important to remember that whether or not it is exercised in the plaintiff's favour will depend on the specific circumstances of each case. Section 33 itself sets out certain considerations which are stated to be mandatory,[214] however, other matters will also affect the decision of the court. In particular, an appeal court will normally be very slow to interfere with the trial judge's decision on the facts, unless it can be shown that his decision was manifestly wrong.[215] It may also be relevant to consider the nature of the case in which the court is asked to exercise its discretion. What is clear from Lord Diplock's historical explanation of the development of the court's discretion to allow an action to proceed out of time in *Thompson* v. *Brown*[216] is that it was a response to the problem of "long maturing industrial diseases" resulting from the negligence or breach of statutory duty of an employer.[217] Accordingly, if the plaintiff requests that his action should be allowed to proceed out of time in some other type of case, it may be that his request will be viewed with less sympathy, since it must be appreciated that the exercise of the discretion under section 33 operates as "an exception to a general rule that has already catered for delay in starting proceedings that is due to excusable ignorance of material facts by the plaintiff as distinct from his lack of knowledge that the facts which he does not know may give him a good cause of action in law".[218]

Other considerations which may play a part in determining whether the discretion will be exercised in the plaintiff's favour seem to include the size of any possible award of damages should the plaintiff succeed, since the larger the likely award, the greater will be the prejudice to the plaintiff if the court decides not to allow his action to proceed out of time.[219] Moreover, if the plaintiff, in an action in respect of personal injury, is likely to receive a substantial payment if his action is allowed to proceed, it is very likely that he will have suffered very substantial injury, in which case the prejudice to the plaintiff will be all the more great if the court declines to exercise its discretion in his favour.

---

213. See *Hartley* v. *Birmingham City District Council* [1992] 2 All ER 213 at 224 *per* Parker LJ; *Ward* v. *Foss*, *The Times*, 29 November 1993, *per* Hobhouse LJ.

214. *Halford* v. *Brookes* [1991] 3 All ER 559 at 566 *per* Russell LJ, referring to the considerations set out in s 33(3).

215. *Ibid.*

216. [1981] 1 WLR 744 at 747.

217. See also *Halford* v. *Brookes* [1991] 3 All ER 559 at 570 *per* Nourse LJ.

218. *Thompson* v. *Brown* [1981] 1 WLR 744 at 752 *per* Lord Diplock.

219. *Pavan* v. *Holwill's (Oils) Ltd* (1989) unreported.

Where the court does decide to exercise its discretion in favour of the plaintiff, the problem is that this will cause the defendant prejudice, especially the defendant who has no other defence to the action other than the plea of limitation. Accordingly, if the court has to balance the prejudice to the plaintiff against that caused to the defendant, it might seem to follow from this that the most likely defendant to be able to resist a request that the court should exercise its discretion under section 33 is one who has no other defence to an action brought by the plaintiff. In *Hartley* v. *Birmingham City District Council*[220] the plaintiff was injured in an accident on school premises owned by the defendants. After having refused various offers of settlement from the defendants and their insurers, the plaintiff (through her solicitors) issued a writ one day outside the limitation period. The defendants admitted that they had no defence to the plaintiff's action other than that it was out of time and the plaintiff also admitted that she would have an unanswerable claim against her solicitors in respect of their delay in issuing the writ. Despite this, it was still considered appropriate to exercise the discretion in favour of the plaintiff. On the matter of the prejudice suffered by a defendant who has no defence to the action brought by the plaintiff other than the limitation defence which he will lose if the court exercises its discretion, Leggatt LJ opined that:

"The defendants' approach produces the bizarre, if logical, result that the prejudice to the defendants is greatest when they have no defence to the merits oɪ the claim, because not disapplying the limitation provision affords them a defence on liability which they would not otherwise have had. But a decision not to allow the action [*sic*][221] to proceed would cause the defendants to suffer no injustice whatever in being required to meet a claim of which they had prompt notice and which they had had every opportunity of preparing themselves to meet. Equity need not be concerned to afford adventitious protection to a tortfeasor who has not been deprived of any opportunity to defend himself."[222]

The important consideration when it comes to ask whether the defendant has suffered prejudice is that the purpose which underlies section 33 is that if the defendant has no defence to the plaintiff's claim, generally, there can be no good reason for not depriving the defendant of the shield otherwise provided by the limitation defence. Conversely, if the defendant has a good defence, other than that of limitation, then little prejudice will be suffered, other than that of having to pay for the costs of litigation.

What must have been important in *Hartley* was that the plaintiff's writ was issued only one day out of time. It must surely be that the prejudice to the defendant referred to in section 33 is that which results from his inability to conduct a defence in a fair and equitable manner and not merely that a limitation defence has been denied. Even the fact that the plaintiff might recover more in the way of damages should she sue her solicitor for negligent delay than she would have recovered from the original defendant has been regarded as an irrelevant consideration.[223] The fact remains that if the plaintiff has to go to the trouble of commencing new proceedings against a lawyer, especially one who is aware of the strengths or weaknesses of the plaintiff's case, immeasurable prejudice is suffered by the plaintiff.

Accordingly, it is suggested that the true root of any prejudice to the defendant must lie in the fact that the extent of the plaintiff's delay is so great that the lapse of time is such

220. [1992] 2 All ER 213.
221. This must surely read "a decision to allow the action . . . ".
222. *Hartley* v. *Birmingham City District Council* [1992] 2 All ER 213 at 226.
223. *Thompson* v. *Brown* [1981] 1 WLR 744 at 750 *per* Lord Diplock.

that the defendant's defence is prejudiced because of the inability of witnesses to recall relevant events or the inability of the defendant to obtain documents relevant to the proceedings. While a delay of one day in *Hartley* was not detrimental to the conduct of the defence, a delay of a longer period of some 16 months has been held to be sufficiently significant to prevent the discretion from being exercised in the plaintiff's favour,[224] even in the face of an unanswerable claim on the part of the plaintiff. Thus it would seem that the greatest prejudice likely to be suffered by the defendant is that of having to face a stale claim which he might have difficulty in defending due to a substantial lapse of time after the expiry of the primary limitation period. According to Hobhouse LJ in *Ward* v. *Foss*[225]:

"The prejudice to the plaintiff is indeed the prejudice which would result from being debarred from pursuing his action. But the prejudice to the defendant is not the prejudice of meeting a liability but of having to defend, or otherwise deal with, a stale claim. This prejudice to the defendant may well be no less, indeed it may be greater, where the claim is unmeritorious. I agree with Parker LJ and Leggatt LJ [in *Firman* v. *Ellis*] when they stressed the importance of the 'effect of the delay upon the defendant's ability to defend' and whether the defendant is still 'properly equipped to meet' the claim notwithstanding the delay that has occurred."

A further consideration in determining whether there is prejudice to the defendant is whether the plaintiff has an alternative defendant to sue, such as his own solicitor. However, even where the plaintiff has an alternative defendant against whom proceedings may be brought within the primary limitation period, and possibly, even, recover greater damages than might be recovered against the first defendant, the plaintiff is still placed in a position of uncertainty as to the outcome of these alternative proceedings and will be put to greater expense with the result that he or she will still suffer prejudice if the court decides not to exercise its discretion under section 33. To decide otherwise would create an almost immovable obstacle to the exercise of the discretion under section 33 on the basis that the simple removal of the limitation defence is so prejudicial to the defendant that the plaintiff must always sue the alternative defendant. This too would run against the view expressed by Lord Diplock in *Thompson* v. *Brown*[226] that:

" . . . even where, as in the instant case, . . . if the action were not allowed to proceed the plaintiff would have a cast-iron case against his solicitor in which the measure of damages will be no less than the amount he would be able to recover against the defendant if the action were allowed to proceed, some prejudice, although it may be only minor, will have been suffered by him. He will be obliged to find and to instruct new and strange solicitors; there is bound to be delay; he will incur a personal liability for costs of the action up to the date of the court's refusal to give a direction under section [33]; he may prefer to sue a stranger who is a tortfeasor with the possible consequences that may have on the tortfeasor's insurance premiums rather than to sue his former solicitors with corresponding consequences on their premiums. It was suggested that it might be more advantageous to a plaintiff to sue his own solicitor rather than the original tortfeasor since he could recover in an action against the solicitor interest on damages from the date on which the writ against the tortfeasor would have been issued if reasonable diligence had been shown, whereas against the tortfeasor he could only recover interest on damages from the later date, after the expiry of the primary limitation period, at which the writ was actually issued. This, however, is fallacious; he can recover the difference in the interest on damages between the earlier and the later date in a separate

224. *Mills* v. *Ritchie* (1984) unreported.
225. *The Times*, 29 November 1993, CA.
226. [1981] 1 WLR 744.

action against his solicitor for negligence even if the action against the first tortfeasor is allowed to proceed."[227]

Other considerations which may indicate prejudice to the defendant should the discretion be exercised seem to include the possibility of a change of position in the light of the delay on the part of the plaintiff in seeking to commence proceedings. For example in *Ward* v. *Foss*[228] Hobhouse LJ expressed the view that:

" ... if a defendant is to say that he is prejudiced, he must show something more than merely that he is going to be required to meet his legal liabilities. The prejudice must arise from some other additional element—some change of position which would not have occurred if the action had been brought within time—some belief by the defendant that he was not going to be troubled with the claim—some alteration in his financial position or some failure to make provision for the claim—the loss of real evidence—some difficulty in having a fair trial after the lapse of time. No list can be exhaustive and the statute requires the court to have regard to all the circumstances of the case. But it must be some factor over and on top of the legal liability of the defendant which creates the prejudice."

The important effect of section 33 is that the defendant does not have an immovable right to rely on the primary limitation period. As such, if the defendant suffers any prejudice, it must come from a source other than the removal of the limitation defence. This is clear from the view expressed in *Firman* v. *Ellis*[229] that it is the degree of delay which matters more than anything else. Ormrod LJ observed that the defendants (or more specifically, their insurers) were " ... attempting to take advantage of formal procedural mistakes by the plaintiff's solicitors (which have caused them no inconvenience, let alone any prejudice) to transfer liability for the plaintiffs' claims from the defendants' insurers to the plaintiffs' solicitors' insurers".[230]

The precise wording of section 33(1) also raises the question whether prejudice may be suffered by someone other than the plaintiff or the defendant. What section 33(1) requires the court to consider is the balance of prejudice between the plaintiff or any person whom he represents and the defendant or any person whom he represents. This might give rise to problems in cases in which the defendant is insured, since an insured defendant who loses a limitation defence could be said to suffer no prejudice at all if the plaintiff's action is allowed to proceed out of time and his insurer is required to pay under the terms of a relevant insurance policy. However, the prejudice suffered by the defendant's insurers is a matter which has been considered relevant in determining whether the discretion should be exercised. In *Firman* v. *Ellis*[231] Ormrod LJ considered that the insurance position of the defendant was a relevant factor in assessing the degree of prejudice suffered by the plaintiff and the defendant, although the decision on the facts in that case indicated that because the defendant was insured, he, personally, had suffered no prejudice as a result of the decision to allow the plaintiff's action to proceed despite the delay.[232] In the light of this, it seems likely that where a defendant is insured, the degree of prejudice to him in allowing the plaintiff's action to proceed will be small and that, therefore, the court's

227. *Ibid* at 750–51.

228. *The Times*, 29 November 1993, CA.

229. [1978] QB 886. Overruled, on the facts in *Walkley* v. *Precision Forgings Ltd* [1979] 1 WLR 606, but still regarded as persuasive authority on the effect of s 33: See *Hartley* v. *Birmingham City District Council* [1992] 2 All ER 213 at 223 *per* Parker LJ.

230. *Ibid* at 910.

231. [1978] QB 886.

232. *Ibid* at 912. See also Geoffrey Lane LJ at 916.

discretion is much more likely to be exercised in favour of the plaintiff. Accordingly, it was observed by Parker LJ in *Hartley* v. *Birmingham City District Council* that[233] " ... If the only benefit of a decision against the plaintiff is to benefit the defendant's insurer, this can in my view be no ground for saying that it is not 'fair and just' or 'equitable' that the action should proceed."

(ii) Public policy

A further important consideration is that of public policy. It must be asked how far it is right to allow the first defendant's insurers to attempt to shift responsibility for the initial accident, for which their client is undeniably responsible, to the insurers of the plaintiff's solicitors, especially when they have received the payment of premiums to cover the risk of the first defendant's negligence. In general, members of the judiciary with a keen eye for the policy implications of allowing the first defendant's insurers, on the first indication of a marginally late writ, to cry "snap", break off negotiations and plead the limitation defence,[234] are very likely to elect to exercise their discretion under section 33. As Ormrod LJ observed in *Firman* v. *Ellis*[235]:

"If insurance companies through their customers choose to take wholly unmeritorious technical points to avoid liability, they cannot complain if ultimately their ability to take them is severely restricted. To retain a highly formalistic procedure, the real effect of which is simply to transfer liability from the original tortfeasor's insurers to the plaintiff's solicitors' insurers, is not very impressive as a piece of public policy."

However, in terms of what is good policy, it should also be observed that if there are two insurers (namely those of the tortfeasor and the solicitor), two sets of premiums have been paid, in which case, some members of the judiciary may be less persuaded than was Ormrod LJ that it should be the first tortfeasor's insurers who must pay for the loss suffered by the plaintiff.[236]

A further policy consideration is that what has given rise to the chance to plead the limitation defence is the fact that the plaintiff's solicitors have been guilty of delay. This, too, may give rise to problems of public policy, in the sense that some members of the judiciary may be concerned that the process of litigation has not been effected in a proper and efficient manner. Accordingly, the view may be taken that it should be the solicitors and their insurers who should accept responsibility rather than the original tortfeasor.[237]

(iii) The "windfall" defence

In cases in which the defendant would otherwise have little chance of success against the plaintiff, but for the fact that the plaintiff's solicitors deliver the defendant with the unexpected benefit of issuing the writ out of time, the limitation defence which befalls the defendant is frequently referred to as a "windfall" defence. This will be especially so in cases in which the defendant has made interim payments to the plaintiff of the basis that

---

233. [1992] 2 All ER 213 at 224.
234. *Firman* v. *Ellis* [1978] QB 886 at 905 *per* Lord Denning MR.
235. *Ibid* at 911.
236. See *Deerness* v. *John Keeble & Son Ltd* [1983] 2 Lloyd's Rep 260 at 264 *per* Lord Diplock.
237. See e.g. *Ketteman* v. *Hansel Properties Ltd* [1988] 1 All ER 38 at 62 *per* Lord Griffiths, commenting on whether an amendment to pleadings should be allowed at a late stage.

there is no dispute as to liability. For example in *Ramsden* v. *Lee*[238] the defendant had been given notification of the plaintiff's claim in respect of injuries suffered in a road traffic accident within a month of the incident. The defendant did not dispute liability and, subsequently, the defendant made two interim payments. However, fortuitously for the defendant, the plaintiff's writ was issued six months out of time. Despite the plaintiff's delay in issuing the writ, the trial judge nonetheless exercised his discretion under section 33, but the defendant appealed on the ground that if there was no fault on his part, the primary limitation period should not be treated as a mere technicality which could be disapplied at will, especially in cases in which the plaintiff's delay was more than minimal. In the event, the Court of Appeal considered that the trial judge had properly exercised his discretion in favour of the plaintiff, despite the fact that the defendant had undoubtedly suffered prejudice in being deprived of what would otherwise be a valid limitation defence. However, given the circumstances of the case and the fact that the defendant had admitted liability from an early stage, all the defendant had lost was the so-called "windfall" defence, which was not sufficient to displace the considerable prejudice which would otherwise be suffered by the plaintiff if he were to be required to sue his solicitors for their delay in issuing the writ.

Even in the face of the delay of six months in *Ramsden* v. *Lee* between the date of expiry of the primary limitation period and the date on which the writ was issued, the Court of Appeal was not prepared to interfere with the trial judge's decision to exercise his discretion. In the light of this, it would seem to be likely that in the event of a much shorter delay, the courts will be even less likely to decide against the plaintiff where the defendant has admitted liability and the limitation defence comes by way of a windfall.

Thus in *Thompson* v. *Brown*[239] a delay of just 37 days in issuing the writ could be ignored in circumstances in which the initial claim had been made promptly and the defendants had admitted liability and their insurers had fully considered how much should be paid to the plaintiff in respect of the injuries suffered by him as a result of the defendant's admitted negligence. All the limitation defence served to provide the defendant and his insurers with was an unexpected "windfall" benefit. Accordingly, the prejudice suffered by the defendant, in such circumstances, could be regarded as no more than slight.[240]

Similarly, in *Hartley* v. *Birmingham City District Council*[241] the plaintiff gave the defendant prompt notification of his intention to sue in respect of injuries suffered while on the defendant's school premises, but issued a writ one day out of time. It was also accepted by the plaintiff that even if her application for a direction under section 33 were to be turned down she would have an unanswerable claim against her solicitors. The Court of Appeal considered that the trial judge's decision that to give a direction under section 33 would severely prejudice the defendants by depriving them of a "windfall" limitation defence could be ignored and that the discretion to disapply section 11 should have been exercised. It was held that the proper question to ask was whether it was equitable, i.e. fair and just, to allow the *plaintiff's* action to proceed rather than to concentrate on the question whether the exercise of the discretion under section 33 would deprive the *defendant* of a

---

238. [1992] 2 All ER 204.
239. [1981] 1 WLR 744.
240. See *Donovan* v. *Gwentoys Ltd* [1990] 1 All ER 1018 at 1024 *per* Lord Griffiths.
241. [1992] 2 All ER 213.

cast-iron, "windfall" limitation defence because of a short delay on the part of the plaintiff's solicitors.

What was considered to be important in determining whether it was fair and just to allow the plaintiff's action to proceed was the prejudice to both the plaintiff and the defendant if the action was or was not allowed to proceed in addition to the specific issues stated in section 33 and other relevant circumstances of the case under consideration. A particularly important consideration in relation to the question whether the defendant had suffered prejudice was that the delay did not affect the defendant's ability to defend the action on its merits.

In *Hartley*, Legatt LJ went so far as to imply that the loss of a cast-iron "windfall" defence could not amount to prejudice, since that loss amounted to "non-receipt of a benefit" rather than "loss" in its true sense.[242] However, it is arguable that this cannot be an accurate analysis of the true meaning of prejudice in the light of the view expressed in *Thompson* v. *Brown*[243] that any direction made under section 33 must always be regarded as highly prejudicial to the defendant, because even if he has a good defence on the merits, he is still required to expend time, energy and money in establishing his defence, while in contrast, if he has no defence on the matter of liability, he has everything to lose if the plaintiff's action is allowed to proceed out of time.[244]

(iv) The role of appellate courts

Since the exercise of a discretion will inevitably turn on the particular facts of each case, it is unlikely that an appellate court will overturn the decision of the trial judge in the majority of cases. The essential difficulty with a statutory discretion is that on the evidence, different minds might reach substantially different conclusions. What matters is whether the discretion has been exercised beyond the "generous ambit within which reasonable disagreement is possible".[245]

What is clear from the decision of the Court of Appeal in *Conry* v. *Simpson*[246] is that the discretion has been conferred by Parliament upon the trial judge and that it is not for an appellate court to reverse the exercise of the discretion unless it is clear that the trial judge has gone very wrong[247] or has erred in principle.[248]

These views would seem to suggest that it will only be in very rare circumstances that the decision of the trial judge as to whether the discretion should or should not be exercised will be interfered with. In particular, merely because an appellate court might have exercised the discretion differently had they been in a position to consider the matter from the start will not be a sufficient reason for interfering with the trial judge's decision. Something more, such as an error of principle, is required before an appellate court will

---

242. *Ibid* at 225.
243. [1981] 1 WLR 744.
244. *Ibid* at 750 *per* Lord Diplock.
245. *Yates* v. *Thakenham Tiles Ltd, The Times*, 19 May 1994; [1995] PIQR 135, *per* Wall J, CA.
246. [1983] 3 All ER 369.
247. *Ibid* at 374 *per* Stephenson LJ. See also *Halford* v. *Brookes* [1991] 3 All ER 559 at 566 *per* Russell LJ.
248. *Halford* v. *Brookes* [1991] 3 All ER 559 at 566 *per* Russell LJ.

intervene. Also where there is evidence which reasonably supports the decision taken by the trial judge, an appellate court will always decline to interfere with his decision.[249]

In order for an appellate court to overturn the decision of the trial judge, there must have been a failure to have properly applied principles relevant to the exercise of the discretion. Thus if the trial judge has misinterpreted the limits of his statutorily conferred discretion or has taken account of facts which, legally, should not have been considered, the appellate court may intervene. Factors which may sway an appellate court to reverse a decision taken at first instance have included the fact that one of the parties has changed position at a very late stage, such as where the defendant makes a late counterclaim.[250]

Ideally, the trial judge should state the reasons for exercising his discretion one way or the other, since this will demonstrate to the appellate court the principles on which the discretion has, or has not, been exercised in favour of the plaintiff. However, it would appear that where particular principles are not expressly referred to by the trial judge, it may still be assumed that they have been taken into account.[251] As was observed in *Nash* v. *Eli Lilly & Co*,[252] "a judge is not under a duty specifically to refer to each and every fact which he has found and upon which he has exercised his discretion".

(v) All the circumstances of the case

In addition to any specific matters referred to in section 33, section 33(1) requires the court to consider all the circumstances of the case in determining whether or not the discretion should be exercised in the plaintiff's favour. These circumstances include specifically the factors set out in section 33(3), considered below, but other factors may also be relevant, as appropriate. If there are relevant factors which fall outside the statutory check-list in section 33(3), but which have not been taken into account, it is possible that an appellate court may regard this failure as an error of law.[253] Thus it has been said that the list in section 33(3) is "exemplary, not definitive".[254]

It will be seen that on a strict interpretation of some of the guidelines in section 33(3) there are certain relevant factors which may not be covered in that list, but that should not matter since, if a factor not listed is relevant, it can be dealt with as one of the wider circumstances of the case.

One such consideration is the insurance position of both the plaintiff and the defendant.[255] For example, in *Liff* v. *Peasley*[256] the plaintiff was injured in a road traffic accident when he was a passenger in a car driven by the second defendant. Initially proceedings were brought against the first defendant, the driver of the other car in the collision. Subsequently, the first defendant's insurers denied liability under the policy they had issued and the claim then came to be dealt with by the Motor Insurers' Bureau (MIB). After the three-year limitation period had expired, the first defendant raised in defence an

---

249. *Conry* v. *Simpson* [1983] 3 All ER 369 at 374 *per* Stephenson LJ; *Bradley* v. *Hanseatic Shipping Co Ltd* [1986] 2 Lloyd's Rep 34.
250. *Feveyear* v. *Cole* [1992] PIQR 42.
251. *Eagil Trust Ltd* v. *Piggott-Brown* [1985] 3 All ER 119.
252. [1993] 1 WLR 782 at 803 *per* Purchas LJ.
253. See *Donovan* v. *Gwentoys Ltd* [1990] 1 All ER 1018; *Thompson* v. *Brown* [1981] 1 WLR 744.
254. *Nash* v. *Eli Lilly & Co* [1993] 1 WLR 782 at 802 *per* Purchas LJ.
255. See *Firman* v. *Ellis* [1978] QB 886 at 916 *per* Geoffrey Lane LJ.
256. [1980] 1 WLR 781.

allegation that the second defendant was to blame for the accident and there was then a late application by the plaintiff to join the second defendant as a party to the proceedings. The Court of Appeal held that there was insufficient evidence of prejudice to the plaintiff to warrant the exercise of discretion in his favour, since there was ample evidence of a cast-iron case against the first defendant and no reason to doubt that if judgment were given in the plaintiff's favour, the MIB would satisfy that judgment.

The fact that the defendant is insured is an important consideration in determining how much prejudice is suffered by him if he is deprived of a limitation defence. It has been seen already that a factor to consider is whether the plaintiff has an alternative action against his solicitors in respect of their delay in issuing a writ. If consideration of alternative actions is legitimate when considering the prejudice suffered by the plaintiff, it is equally legitimate to take into account that the defendant is insured and that someone else will pick up the bill should the defendant be liable.[257]

What is considered to be the correct approach to the issue of discretion under section 33 is that the defendant and his insurer should be regarded as a composite unit, even in cases where the plaintiff would have no claim against his legal adviser should the court's discretion not be exercised in his favour. Accordingly in *Kelly* v. *Bastible*[258] the view was expressed that if delay on the part of the plaintiff has the effect of severely prejudicing the defendant's chance of defending the action, it makes no difference whether the defendant is insured or not. It was considered that there is a difference between an insured defendant and a plaintiff who has an alternative action against his solicitor in respect of delay in issuing the writ, since the defendant has paid premiums in respect of his insurance cover. Moreover, an insurer is also entitled to expect, in fixing their premiums, that they will not be penalised by being made to fight a claim which the insured would not have been required to fight had he not been insured.[259] In addition to the insurance position, it may also be relevant to take account of the legal aid position in determining where the balance of prejudice lies, although on its own, it appears not to be a decisive factor. The key consideration is that where a defendant succeeds against a legally aided plaintiff, he stands very little chance of recovering his costs. Accordingly, where a legally aided plaintiff asks the court to allow his action to be heard out of time, there is an additional factor prejudicial to the defendant to weigh in the balance. Moreover, the fact that a plaintiff is legally aided is an indication that he is not well-off, which might lead to the view that similar considerations apply to an impecunious plaintiff who is not in receipt of Legal Aid Board support. In *Halford* v. *Brookes*[260] Lord Donaldson MR expressed the view that[261]:

" . . . just as in the case of an unassisted litigant the court would be entitled to take account of the fact that he was prepared to hazard his own assets in funding the litigation, so in the case of an assisted litigant the court is entitled to take account of the fact that the Legal Aid Board is backing this litigation in circumstances in which it is bound by statute to consider, and no doubt has considered, whether only a trivial advantage could be gained by the applicant from the proceedings to which the application relates."

---

257. See *Hartley* v. *Birmingham City District Council* [1992] 2 All ER 213 at 224 *per* Parker LJ.
258. *The Times*, 15 November 1996, CA.
259. *Ibid, per* Waller LJ.
260. [1991] 3 All ER 559.
261. *Ibid* at 577.

(c) The section 33(3) check-list

Apart from the broader requirement that the court should consider all the circumstances of the case, section 33(3) sets out a number of specific matters which the court must take account of, where relevant, in determining whether or not the discretion should be exercised in the plaintiff's favour. Although some aspects of section 33(3) relate directly to the issue of prejudice,[262] others are more concerned with the conduct of the parties to the action, thereby relating to the question whether it is equitable to exercise the discretion in favour of the plaintiff, at the expense of the defendant.[263] Moreover, regard must also be had to the position of the plaintiff's legal representative for the purposes of section 33(3)(d), although other provisions of section 33 clearly relate only to the position of the plaintiff or defendant *in personam*.

It should be emphasised that the contents of section 33(3) are merely guidelines and not rules of law. Accordingly, the trial judge is not under any obligation to consider the matters set out below. However, it has been observed that, although not essential, it would be a useful exercise for the trial judge to go through each element of section 33(3) to determine whether it is relevant to the issues under consideration at trial.[264]

(i) The length of, and the reasons for, the delay on the part of the plaintiff (section 33(3)(a))

The delay adverted to in this subsection is that which occurs between the date on which the primary limitation period expired and the date on which the plaintiff asks the court to exercise its discretion in his favour. The period of time which runs from the date on which the cause of action accrued is entirely irrelevant for present purposes, except to the extent that delay in this last respect may be regarded as one of the overall circumstances of the case and may be taken into account as an additional factor, if considered relevant.[265] Moreover, any question of the plaintiff's knowledge of relevant facts associated with the cause of action itself is also irrelevant for the purposes of the exercise of judicial discretion under section 33.

In *Donovan* v. *Gwentoys Ltd*[266] the House of Lords considered that it was relevant to take into account the whole period of delay between the date on which the cause of action accrued up to the date on which the plaintiff made an application to issue a writ out of time on the ground that any delay prior to the date on which the primary limitation period expired could be regarded as a relevant circumstance under the general provisions of section 33(3). Moreover, it would appear that no distinction should be drawn between the actual and the constructive knowledge of the plaintiff of relevant facts when it comes to determine whether the plaintiff's delay is excessive. In *Guidera* v. *NEI Projects (India)*[267] the Court of Appeal refused to regard delay following the plaintiff's actual and constructive awareness of the relevant facts for the purposes of section 14(3) as a relevant factor in determining whether they had a power to exercise discretion under section 33.

---

262. Section 33(3)(a) and (b).
263. Section 33(3)(c), (e) and (f).
264. *Barrand* v. *British Cellophane plc*, *The Times*, 16 February 1995, *per* Glidewell LJ.
265. *Donovan* v. *Gwentoys Ltd* [1990] 1 All ER 1018 at 1024 *per* Lord Griffiths.
266. *Ibid.*
267. (1990) unreported.

Accordingly, it would seem to follow from this that even delay following the plaintiff's actual knowledge of relevant facts is not to be considered in determining whether the discretion under section 33 should be exercised.

It has been seen already that there is no automatic right to ask the court to exercise its discretion where the delay is only for a short period of, say, one or two days, although it is likely in such cases that the court's decision will go in favour of the plaintiff in the absence of compelling evidence which supports a decision to the contrary in favour of the defendant. In the case of a delay of longer than one or two days, it is clear that the plaintiff will be required to give a satisfactory explanation as to why the delay has occurred, and if he fails to do so there may be strong reasons for not exercising the discretion in favour of the plaintiff. For example in *Buck* v. *English Electric Co Ltd*[268] Kilner-Brown J opined that extreme delay does not, of itself, preclude the exercise of the discretion under section 33, but a delay of several years (in *Buck*, one of five years) should create a rebuttable presumption that excessive delay should prevent the exercise of the discretion unless the plaintiff can give a plausible explanation for the length of the delay under consideration.

From this it is clear that there are two specific issues which must be considered in determining whether discretion should be exercised in favour of the plaintiff. The first of these is the length of the delay and the second is any reason or explanation for the delay on the part of the plaintiff.

The length of the delay, if excessive, would appear to give rise to a rebuttable presumption to the effect that the discretion under section 33 will not be exercised in the plaintiff's favour. However, it does not immediately follow that a long delay will automatically result in a refusal to exercise the discretion. This will be especially the case where there has been prompt notification of the plaintiff's claim, followed by delay in commencing proceedings, since in such circumstances, the defendant will still have had ample time to give the claim full consideration. Thus in *Ward* v. *Foss*[269] there had been prompt notification of the plaintiff's claim within two years of the date of the accident, followed by a delay on the part of the plaintiff's solicitors of four years beyond the date on which the primary limitation period had expired. Despite this delay, it was still considered appropriate to exercise the discretion in favour of the plaintiff. The rationale of the decision, in this regard, seems to be that a defendant who has had prompt notification of the plaintiff's claim can hardly be heard to say that he has not had the opportunity to investigate the claim and it would be wrong for him to assume that the claim has been dropped in the meantime.[270]

In contrast, in *Donovan* v. *Gwentoys Ltd*[271] the defendants were not informed of the nature of the plaintiff's claim until some five years after the date on which the accident occurred and were unable to commence any investigation of the claim until at least six years after the date of the accident. On these facts, it is not surprising that the House of Lords considered that the trial judge had wrongly exercised his discretion in favour of the plaintiff on the simple ground that there was only five and a half months' delay after the expiry of the primary limitation period.

---

268. [1978] 1 All ER 271.
269. *The Times*, 29 November 1993, CA.
270. See *Rothery* v. *Walker* (1993) unreported, *per* Stuart-Smith LJ.
271. [1990] 1 All ER 1018.

As Lord Griffiths observed[272]:

"The defendants opposed the application, submitting that they were gravely prejudiced in having to face a very stale claim, the existence of which they were unaware until five years after the accident, by which time it would be unrealistic to suppose that any meaningful enquiry could be conducted into the circumstances of the accident or the condition of the premises at the material time, and furthermore, that they were being sued in respect of an injury which they had had no opportunity to investigate until over six years after the accident."

Lord Griffiths went on later to opine that[273]:

"In weighing the degree of prejudice suffered by a defendant it must always be relevant to consider when the defendant first had notification of the claim and thus the opportunity he will have to meet the claim at the trial if he is not to be permitted to rely on his limitation defence . . . I have no doubt that the balance of prejudice, in this case, comes down heavily in favour of the defendants. It would not be equitable to require the defendants to meet a claim which they would have the utmost difficulty in defending when the plaintiff will suffer only the slightest prejudice if she is required to pursue her remedy against her solicitors."

Matters of notification apart, where there is only a short delay after the date on which the primary limitation period has expired, it seems likely that the prejudice suffered by the defendant will be minimal. Thus it has been held that, provided the defendant was notified of the plaintiff's intention to make a claim, a delay of one day after the expiry of the primary limitation period will cause the defendant no prejudice at all.[274] However, it has been noted above that a delay of a longer period will create a rebuttable presumption of prejudice to the defendant,[275] especially in cases in which the recollection of potential witnesses is likely to have faded somewhat.[276] Moreover, in cases of substantial delay, there may also be fears for the cogency of the evidence on which the defendant may seek to relay. However, the presumption is, nonetheless, rebuttable, since there may be circumstances in which the evidence remains reliable. For example, in *Buck* v. *English Electric Co Ltd*[277] an extensive delay of some nine years was not fatal to the plaintiff, since the defendants had dealt with a number of claims similar to that made by the plaintiff, with the result that investigations made by the defendant had relevant and readily usable evidence available to meet the claim if necessary. Accordingly, there was insufficient prejudice to the defendant to justify a refusal to exercise the discretion in favour of the plaintiff.

The second important consideration under section 33(3)(a) is the reason for the plaintiff's delay in commencing proceedings. Any number of reasons may be given for the plaintiff's delay, some of which may be based on subjective factors. It has been seen already that for the purposes of the primary limitation period, the plaintiff's subjective beliefs are irrelevant under section 14. However, these beliefs may well be relevant under section 33(3)(a).[278] That the relevant belief is a subjective one is clear from the contrast

272. *Ibid* at 1022.
273. *Ibid* at 1024–25. In the process of reaching this conclusion, Lord Griffiths regarded the decision of the Court of Appeal in *Eastman* v. *London Country Bus Services Ltd*, *The Times*, 23 November 1985, on this issue, to be unreliable and should not be followed.
274. *Hartley* v. *Birmingham City District Council* [1992] 2 All ER 213; *Hendy* v. *Milton Keynes Health Authority* [1992] 3 Med LR 114.
275. *Buck* v. *English Electric Co Ltd* [1978] 1 All ER 271 at 275 *per* Kilner-Brown J.
276. See *Boynton* v. *British Steel plc* [1997] 7 CL 75, 8 October 1996, Sheffield County Court.
277. [1978] 1 All ER 271.
278. *McCafferty* v. *Metropolitan Police District Receiver* [1977] 1 WLR 1073; *Coad* v. *Cornwall and Isles of Scilly Health Authority*, *The Times*, 30 June 1996, CA.

between paragraph (a) which contains no reference to the reasonableness of the plaintiff's conduct and paragraph (e), considered below, which does.[279]

Another possible reason for delay on the part of the plaintiff is that he may be, initially, unaware of his legal rights and only becomes so aware at a late stage, after the primary limitation period has expired. For example, there may be instances in which a novel type of claim arises, in respect of which, it seems, no one has previously sued, which might cause the plaintiff to delay before consulting a legal adviser until it is discovered that others have in fact successfully brought proceedings in respect of the type of injury concerned.[280] In such cases, excusable ignorance by the plaintiff of legal rights and the delay consequent on that ignorance may lead the trial judge to exercise his discretion in favour of the plaintiff. Similar considerations may also apply where the legal advice given to the plaintiff proves to have been erroneous, with the result that a writ is not issued until well after the date on which the primary limitation period expired, especially in cases in which no personal blame can be attached to the plaintiff.[281] Likewise, an error on the part of court officials may sometimes be the cause of the plaintiff's delay, such as where relevant paperwork is not completed in time despite a request on the part of the plaintiff to expedite matters.[282] However, it is unlikely that the court will regard a delay caused by a conscious choice on the part of the plaintiff as sufficient to allow the discretion to be exercised in his favour.[283]

The reasons for the plaintiff's delay must be balanced against the cogency of evidence argument with the result that a very long delay may so severely prejudice the defendant that even where there are good reasons for the extent of the delay, the balance of prejudice may weigh so heavily on the defendant's side that it would be wrong to exercise the discretion in favour of the plaintiff, especially where the defendant will find it difficult to defend the case in the light of the delay.[284]

Also relevant to section 33(3)(a) is the fact that the plaintiff might consider that the injury he has suffered is not sufficiently serious to warrant litigation. It has been seen already that the test applied under section 14 is objective, so that if a reasonable person ought to have realised that serious injury has been suffered, then time will start to run against the plaintiff regardless of his own subjective beliefs. However, under section 33 those subjective beliefs may be taken into account in determining whether the discretion should be exercised. Thus the discretion may be exercised in the plaintiff's favour if he regards the injury suffered as no more than an irritating nuisance not worth taking action over until it has become too late to do so. In these circumstances, a genuine belief on the part of the plaintiff that there is nothing seriously wrong may persuade the court to allow the action to proceed out of time. In *McCafferty* v. *Metropolitan Police District Receiver*,[285] it was observed by Lawton LJ that[286]:

" . . . the plaintiff revealed himself as a man who was not anxious to litigate over something he regarded as an 'irritating nuisance'. That is commendable. In my judgment the court should be

---

279. *Coad* v. *Cornwall and Isles of Scilly Health Authority, The Times,* 30 June 1996, *per* Ward LJ.
280. See *Brookes* v. *J & P Coates (UK) Ltd* [1984] 1 All ER 702.
281. *Halford* v. *Brookes* [1991] 3 All ER 559.
282. *Grenville* v. *Waltham Forest Health Authority* (1992) unreported, CA.
283. *Hodgson* v. *Stockton Casting Co Ltd* [1997] 8 CL 67, 15 January 1997, Teesside County Court, Judge Bryant (decision to spend available funds on a house).
284. See *Dobbie* v. *Medway Health Authority* [1994] 4 All ER 450.
285. [1977] 1 WLR 1073.
286. *Ibid* at 1081.

understanding of men who, after taking an overall view of their situation, come to the conclusion that they would rather go on working than become involved in litigation."

In other cases, the plaintiff might genuinely believe that his injury is one from which he might speedily recover, in which case delay is excusable. Alternatively, there are other plaintiffs who might regard a resort to litigation as a form of "sponging" from others. There may also be cases in which an employee injured at work might regard a resort to litigation as something which might damage his relationship with his employer.[287] For example in *Smith* v. *Central Asbestos Co Ltd*[288] it was observed by Lord Denning MR that[289] "it would not be wise for the plaintiff to bring an action against his employers, whilst he was still working for them, lest it embitter relations between them".

Similar considerations may also apply outside the workplace. For example, if the plaintiff is receiving medical treatment from a practitioner, who it is later alleged is guilty of negligence, regard might be had to the fact of a continuing relationship between doctor and patient. The fact that there is such a relationship might persuade the plaintiff not to commence proceedings until the relationship has come to an end so as to avoid the possibility that treatment might be discontinued.[290]

In some instances the distress caused by the accident in respect of which proceedings are eventually brought will be a matter deserving of consideration. This will be especially the case where the accident has resulted in death and a surviving partner or other close relative has difficulty in coming to terms with the fact of the death. For example, in *Jones* v. *City & Hackney Health Authority*,[291] the plaintiff witnessed the death of her son and, as a consequence, suffered severe depression which resulted in a delay in commencing proceedings. Because of her psychological state, the plaintiff did not want to become involved in litigation, a fact which was regarded as perfectly acceptable in the circumstances, thereby justifying the exercise of the discretion under section 33.

(ii) The extent to which, having regard to the delay, the evidence adduced or likely to be adduced by the plaintiff or the defendant is or is likely to be less cogent than if the action had been brought within [the primary limitation period] (section 33(3)(b))

It has been seen above that a relevant factor under section 33(3)(a) is the length of the delay on the part of the plaintiff and that one effect of a long delay is that the cogency of the evidence in respect of the plaintiff's action and the defendant's defence may be damaged by such a delay. It follows from this that there is the potential for substantial overlap between paragraphs (a) and (b). Probably the most common cogency problem will arise where the defendant or his insurers has disposed of the file relating to the plaintiff's possible claim in the light of the delay after expiry of the primary limitation period.[292]

The lack of cogency argument affects the plaintiff and the defendant in different ways. If there is a substantial delay which affects the cogency of the evidence in support of the

---

287. *Buck* v. *English Electric Co Ltd* [1978] 1 All ER 271.
288. [1971] 3 All ER 204.
289. *Ibid* at 210. A comment specific to the provisions of the Limitation Act 1963.
290. See *Driscoll-Varley* v. *Parkside Health Authority* [1991] 2 Med LR 346 at 357 *per* Hidden J. On the facts, the plaintiff's reason for not commencing proceedings was regarded as a relevant factor under s 14, thereby affecting the date on which the primary limitation period expired.
291. (1993) unreported, QBD.
292. See *Conry* v. *Simpson* [1983] 3 All ER 369.

defendant's defence, there is a substantial likelihood that the defendant will be prejudiced. In contrast, if the plaintiff's evidence in support of his cause of action is less cogent because of the plaintiff's delay in bringing procedings, the prejudice suffered as a result of a refusal to exercise the discretion under section 33 is actually diminished on the basis that the plaintiff's action is less likely to succeed if the action is allowed to proceed. In *Thompson* v. *Brown*[293] Lord Diplock said[294]:

"So far as the diminished cogency affects the defendant's evidence it increases the degree of prejudice he will suffer if the action is allowed to be brought despite the delay; but so far as diminished cogency affects the plaintiff's evidence and so reduces his chances of establishing his cause of action if the action is allowed to be brought it lessens the degree of prejudice the plaintiff will suffer if he is not allowed to bring the action at this late stage."

The two most likely bases upon which evidence may suffer from a lack of cogency are, first, that time has elapsed to such an extent that witnesses may have died or may have lost their recollection of relevant events or secondly, that relevant documentary evidence has been lost or destroyed. However, in certain circumstances, these arguments may lose their force, especially if the evidence in question may be obtained from another source. For example, it has been seen already, in relation to section 33(3)(a), that where there are a number of similar claims by, for example, a number of employees, it is likely that the defendant employer will have investigated his own system of work and, almost certainly, will have sufficient evidence on which to base his defence.[295] In these circumstances, it seems unlikely that the lack of cogency argument will carry very much weight at all. Similarly, there are certain types of accident which will routinely spawn a substantial quantity of paperwork relating to the accident, such as is the case with cases of alleged medical negligence. To argue that the passage of time will result in a lack of cogency in the defendant's evidence in such circumstances is hardly likely to hold water.

In other cases, it is possible that the accident will have resulted in some sort of public inquiry, as will normally be the case where there has been an accident involving most forms of public transport. Accordingly, even if the defendant claims to have mislaid his record of events, it is possible that there is other equally strong evidence on which the merits of the case can be judged. For example in *Ward* v. *Foss*[296] a coroner's inquest had been held following a road traffic accident in which three people had been killed. Moreover, there was also a detailed police report on the accident, which included plans and measurements of the scene of the accident. The plaintiff's action was brought well after the expiry of the primary limitation period, and the question arose whether the recollection of such witnesses as there were might have been affected by the passage of time. Both the trial judge and Simon Brown LJ in the Court of Appeal were of the opinion that there was little or no prejudice to the defendant in allowing the action to proceed out of time, since the mass of objective evidence available from sources other than the eye-witnesses was sufficient to allow the case to be properly decided on its merits.

Finally, there may also be circumstances in which inordinate delay actually allows the court to more easily reach a conclusion on the facts of the case. This will be particularly the case where there is no disagreement on liability and the key issue is that of quantifying

293. [1977] 1 WLR 744.
294. *Ibid* at 751.
295. See *Buck* v. *English Electric Co Ltd* [1978] 1 All ER 271.
296. *The Times*, 29 November 1993, CA.

the loss suffered by the plaintiff. In such circumstances, a delay in commencing proceedings may allow a more accurate assessment of, for example, the plaintiff's medical condition, so that assessment of the plaintiff's entitlement to damages is made easier. For example, in *Conry* v. *Simpson*[297] the defendant's insurers had destroyed their records and, in so doing, had lost a medical report on the plaintiff. However, since there had been an admission of liability, the only remaining question was that of quantum of damages, and since the plaintiff was alive and his injured knee could be examined, the results of a later examination would probably reveal more accurately the extent of loss than would have been the case had the lost medical report been used.

(iii) The conduct of the defendant after the cause of action arose (section 33(3)(c))

The conduct of the defendant after the cause of action arose is a further factor to be considered in determining whether or not the discretion under section 33 should be exercised in the plaintiff's favour. It is important to note that section 33(3)(c) is concerned with the defendant's conduct from the date of *accrual* of the cause of action rather than with his conduct as from the date on which time *begins to run* against the plaintiff. Since the date of accrual, in personal injury cases, will, more often than not, be much earlier than the date of the plaintiff's knowledge of relevant facts, which is usually the date on which time will begin to run, the court will be able to take account of conduct on the part of the defendant which prevents the plaintiff from gaining the knowledge required in order for time to begin to run. Such conduct may be taken into account under section 33 even if it does not amount to deliberate concealment for the purposes of section 32,[298] where that concealment relates to the plaintiff's right of action.

Relevant considerations for the purposes of section 33(3)(c) will be whether the defendant has responded reasonably and swiftly to requests made by the plaintiff for the supply of information. Accordingly, there would appear to be an onus on the plaintiff to ask the right questions, since there appears to be no general duty on the defendant to volunteer information. There is merely a duty not to obstruct the plaintiff in his quest for the truth.[299] Also relevant will be the ease with which access to premises etc has been given, so as to allow the plaintiff to ascertain facts pertinent to the plaintiff's cause of action.

It follows from the guideline set out in section 33(3)(c) that if the defendant has been obstructive or has caused negotiations towards a settlement to become protracted, the court will be more inclined to exercise the discretion in the plaintiff's favour. The importance of considerations of this kind is that, once time has started to run against the plaintiff, generally it will not stop running as a result of the way in which the defendant has conducted himself, with the result that delaying tactics are not, generally, regarded as relevant to the question whether the primary limitation period has expired.[300]

In cases of alleged medical negligence, examples of relevant conduct on the part of the defendant abound. For example, a failure to inform a patient or a relative of the patient what happened during the course of a medical procedure can be regarded as relevant conduct for the purposes of section 33(3)(c).[301] Similarly, a substantial delay in making

297. [1983] 3 All ER 369.
298. See Ch 6.
299. *Thompson* v. *Brown* [1981] 1 WLR 744 at 751 *per* Lord Diplock.
300. *Easy* v. *Universal Anchorage Co* [1974] 1 WLR 899.
301. *Atkinson* v. *Oxfordshire Health Authority* [1993] 4 Med LR 18.

medical records available until a court order is made in the plaintiff's favour is a sufficient reason for the court to exercise its discretion.[302]

Under section 33(3)(c) the conduct referred to is specifically that of the defendant, but it has also been held to include that of his legal advisers. Thus if the defendant's solicitors have failed to take witness statements so that, in the light of the plaintiff's delay, those witnesses' recollection of events is hazy, this too can be regarded as conduct which the trial judge may take into account.[303]

Problems of delaying tactics on the part of the defendant's solicitors are, of course, not confined to cases of medical negligence. In *Re Workvale Ltd (No 2)*[304] solicitors acting on behalf of an insurance company led the plaintiff's solicitors to believe that the defendant company was still in existence, when, in fact, it had been dissolved on insolvency. The effect of this was that the plaintiff took no alternative action in the belief that proceedings against the company were moving satisfactorily through the interlocutory stages.

The conduct which section 33(3)(c) is concerned with may be deliberate, but, apparently, does not have to be so in every case. Certainly a deliberate act on the defendant's part which has the effect of preventing the plaintiff from discovering the truth will almost certainly trigger the exercise of discretion under section 33. However, a genuine mistake on the defendant's part may also be taken into account if it has the effect of misleading the plaintiff. In *Marston* v. *British Railways Board*[305] the defendants supplied the plaintiff with a hammer which proved to be defective, thereby causing the plaintiff to suffer injury. Initially, and for some time thereafter, the defendants maintained, incorrectly, that the hammer was new. It was accepted that the defendants genuinely believed that they were telling the truth. Despite the fact that the defendants' position was maintained due to an honest mistake, Croom-Johnson J held that the simple act of giving misleading information is sufficient to allow the court to exercise discretion in favour of the plaintiff, since the defendants' act in giving misinformation was partly the cause of the plaintiff's delay in bringing proceedings. Whether or not *Marston* is correctly decided is not entirely clear since there have been comments in the House of Lords to the effect that it may have been incorrect on the facts.[306] Certainly there could be an argument to the effect that unintentionally misleading the plaintiff's advisers might not be regarded as conduct as such. But to the contrary, it may be argued that even if there is no conduct which misleads, section 33 requires the court to consider all the circumstances of the case. If the plaintiff's advisers have been misled, albeit without any sort of deliberation, this must still be regarded as a relevant circumstance.

Perhaps more controversially, it has also been held that the tender of an interim payment to the plaintiff can be regarded as relevant conduct for the purposes of section 33(3)(c). In *Marshall* v. *Martin*[307] the relevance of such a payment was considered to be that it amounts to an admission of the strength of the plaintiff's claim even if it does not constitute a complete admission of liability.

302. *Birnie* v. *Oxfordshire Health Authority* (1982) 2 *The Lancet* 281.

303. *Jones* v. *City & Hackney Health Authority* (1993) unreported, CA.

304. [1992] 2 All ER 627. See also *Simpson* v. *Norwest Holst Southern Ltd* [1980] 2 All ER 471 and *Hillier* v. *Hammersmith & Fulham London Borough Council* [1997] 6 CL 89, REG 96/7572, 14 March 1997, *per* Kennedy LJ, CA.

305. [1976] ICR 124.

306. See *Walkley* v. *Precision Forgings Ltd* [1979] 1 WLR 606 at 610 *per* Lord Wilberforce.

307. (1987) unreported, CA. See also *Rothery* v. *Walker* (1993) unreported, CA.

A further factor which may be relevant under section 33(3)(c) is that negotiations, supposedly intended to lead to a settlement, have been deliberately protracted by the defendant and his insurer and/or other advisers. Although it is true that even where such negotiations are in place, there is nothing to prevent the plaintiff from issuing a writ or from applying to renew a writ which has already been issued, the fact that such negotiations are in progress might easily persuade the plaintiff to delay in taking matters further. In *Halford* v. *Brookes*[308] Russell LJ opined that section 33(3)(c) is concerned with purely procedural matters in circumstances in which the forensic tactics of a defendant may lead to delay.[309]

(iv) The duration of the plaintiff's disability arising after the date of accrual of the cause of action (section 33(3)(d))

It is important that the disability referred to here is that which arises *after* accrual of the cause of action. If a disability, such as unsoundness of mind, is present prior to the date of accrual, it will postpone the running of time against the plaintiff until the disability no longer affects the plaintiff.[310] In contrast, section 33 is concerned only with *supervening* disability.

Although disability is defined so as to include minority and unsoundness of mind,[311] it is obvious that only unsoundness of mind can be relevant for the purposes of section 33, since minority can never supervene after the date of accrual of the cause of action. While the definition of disability in section 38(2) is quite clear, there have been cases in which the plaintiff's physical ability appears to have been taken into account.[312] However, such an approach would appear to directly contradict the express words of section 38(2) which may be taken to give a complete definition of the term disability for the purposes of the Limitation Act 1980, which should not be taken to include physical disability.[313]

It is suggested that a better basis on which the plaintiff's physical disability should be approached is to regard it as one of the "circumstances of the case", thereby falling into the residual category of factors which the court should take into account in deciding whether to exercise its discretion in favour of the plaintiff. This approach is supported in *Thomas* v. *Plaistow*[314]; in July 1984 the plaintiff suffered serious head injuries in a motor-cycle accident which caused loss of memory causing her to be unable to remember whether she or a person who claimed to be a pillion passenger was driving the vehicle. As a result of the plaintiff's inability to recall the salient facts, a writ was issued seven years and three months out of time. It was claimed on behalf of the plaintiff that the delay was due to her unawareness of the existence of the Motor Insurers' Bureau agreement in respect of uninsured drivers; that her physical ability, not amounting to mental disorder within the meaning of the Mental Health Act 1983, was such that it was difficult for her to seek legal advice; that she could not recall events until she experienced "flashback"

---

308. [1991] 3 All ER 559.
309. *Ibid* at 567.
310. Limitation Act 1980, s 28 and see Ch 6.
311. Limitation Act 1980, s 38(2).
312. *Pilmore* v. *Northern Trawlers Ltd* [1986] 1 Lloyd's Rep 552—attacks of dermatitis considered relevant.
313. See *Thompson* v. *Brown* [1981] 1 WLR 744 at 751 *per* Lord Diplock; *Rule* v. *Atlas Stone Ltd* [1987] CLY 2335 *per* Simon Brown J.
314. [1997] 6 CL 88, 23 April 1997, *per* Hirst LJ, CA.

memory recall in April 1994 and that her solicitors, for the purposes of her defence in a criminal action, had not advised her as to the possibility of a civil claim for damages. In the event, the Court of Appeal held that section 33(3)(d) was inapplicable on the ground that it was confined to disabilities amounting to a mental disorder under the Mental Health Act 1983, as defined in the Limitation Act 1980 section 38(2), and that lesser disorders should, properly, be dealt with under section 33(3)(a) since they are factors which fall within the reference to "all the circumstances of the case". However, the misconstruction of the language of section 33(3)(d) by the trial judge did not affect the overall correctness of the decision, with the result that the plaintiff was still allowed to commence her action out of time.

In support of those cases which have taken physical disability into account, it may be argued that the principal concern of section 33 is the reason for the plaintiff's delay after the primary limitation period has expired and it may be that the plaintiff's physical or mental condition, falling short of unsoundness of mind, may be a reason for the plaintiff's delay in commencing proceedings. For example, matters such as impairment of memory, forgetfulness, depression and inability to concentrate as a result of a physical condition could be relevant to the exercise of discretion under section 33.[315]

(v) The extent to which the plaintiff acted promptly and reasonably once he knew whether the act or omission of the defendant, to which the injury was attributable, might be capable at that time of giving rise to an action for damages (section 33(3)(e))

The knowledge referred to in section 33(3)(e) differs from the knowledge required for the purposes of section 14. It has been seen already that section 14, applying an objective test, is capable of attributing the knowledge of a reasonable person to the plaintiff, thereby introducing a test based on constructive knowledge. In contrast, section 33 is concerned only with the knowledge actually possessed by the plaintiff.

There is an overlap between paragraphs (a) and (e) to the extent that the length of and reasons for delay on the part of the plaintiff will also depend upon the plaintiff's state of knowledge of the facts which lead to that delay. However, there is a difference between the two paragraphs to the extent that paragraph (e) has as its central concern the conduct of the plaintiff after he has become aware of his legal right to sue for damages in respect of the injury he has suffered.

What matters for the purposes of section 33(3)(e) is whether any blame can be attached to the plaintiff in respect of his delay after becoming aware of his right to sue. Here a number of factors may be relevant. For example, it has been seen already that the plaintiff's emotional state following the death of a close relative or partner may be regarded as a sufficient reason for not immediately seeking to commence proceedings.[316] Similarly, the courts appear to be prepared to consider matters such as a desire not to prejudice an existing relationship with an employer[317] or medical adviser[318] or that some people might regard a resort to legal proceedings as a form of "sponging" off the

---

315. *Bater* v. *Newbold* (1991) unreported, CA *per* Ralph Gibson and Parker LJJ, disapproved in *Thomas* v. *Plaistow* [1997] 6 CL 88.

316. See *Rule* v. *Atlas Stone Ltd* [1987] CLY 2335.

317. See *Smith* v. *Central Asbestos Co Ltd* [1971] 3 All ER 204 at 210 *per* Lord Denning MR.

318. See *Driscoll-Varley* v. *Parkside Health Authority* [1991] 2 Med LR 346 at 357 *per* Hidden J.

defendant.[319] However, the case law in this area does not appear to be entirely consistent, since other equally sensitive matters have been regarded as irrelevant to the exercise of the discretion, such as a fear of losing one's job.[320]

It has been seen already that when considering the conduct of the defendant under section 33(3)(c), relevant conduct includes that of the defendant's legal advisers. So also under section 33(3)(e), delay attributable to the plaintiff's solicitor is to be treated as delay on the part of the plaintiff himself.[321] Moreover, where the delay is attributable to the plaintiff's lawyer, there is the possibility of an action for professional negligence, which, in turn, can reduce the prejudice suffered by the plaintiff as a result of the court's refusal to exercise its discretion in the plaintiff's favour. It does not follow from this that every case of delay on the part of the plaintiff's solicitors will automatically result in a refusal to exercise the discretion, since the court must have regard to the reasons for the delay. Thus if the solicitors have acted entirely properly, for example by seeking to obtain the necessary information in order to bring proceedings or to obtain legal aid, the plaintiff may still be regarded as having acted promptly and reasonably.[322]

(vi) The steps, if any, taken by the plaintiff to obtain medical, legal or other expert advice and the nature of any such advice he may have received (section 33(3)(f))

The final factor set out in the section 33 guidelines is the nature of any expert advice given to the plaintiff and the fact that the plaintiff has or has not sought such advice. Accordingly for the purposes of section 33(3)(f) there are two important questions, namely, has the plaintiff sought relevant expert advice and secondly, is the advice he has been given accurate or not?

Clearly, if the plaintiff has actual knowledge of his legal right to sue for damages, there will be few instances in which it will be excusable for him not to consult an appropriate expert. But if the plaintiff does consult a solicitor and is badly advised, this is a factor which may be considered in determining whether discretion should be exercised in his favour. For example in *Halford* v. *Brookes*[323] the plaintiff's 16-year-old daughter had been strangled and stabbed to death by a 15-year-old schoolboy who had subsequently confessed to attacking the girl with a knife. Subsequently, the boy made a statement which implicated his stepfather. At the criminal trial, the stepfather denied any responsibility and no prosecution was brought against him, but at the boy's trial, his version of events was accepted with the result that he was acquitted. The plaintiff then considered the possibility of civil proceedings, having been told, initially, that her only civil remedy consisted of a claim from the Criminal Injuries Compensation Board. On discovering that there was a possibility that she might sue for trespass to the person,[324] the plaintiff acted very promptly in commencing proceedings, with the result that it was considered appropriate to exercise the discretion in her favour. As Russell LJ observed[325]:

319. See *Buck* v. *English Electric Co Ltd* [1978] 1 All ER 271.
320. See *Miller* v. *London Electrical Manufacturing Co Ltd* [1976] 2 Lloyd's Rep 284.
321. See *Thompson* v. *Brown* [1981] 1 WLR 744 at 752 *per* Lord Diplock.
322. See *Yates* v. *Thakenham Tiles Ltd*, *The Times*, 19 May 1994; [1995] PIQR 135, CA.
323. [1991] 3 All ER 559.
324. Following the decision of the House of Lords in *Stubbings* v. *Webb* [1993] 2 WLR 120, the application of rules on personal injury cases to an action for trespass to the person must now be regarded as an error.
325. [1991] 3 All ER 559 at 567.

"The fact that she acted promptly once she knew of the existence of the right to sue for damages is expressly referred to in paragraph (e) as a circumstance to be taken into account when the court decides whether it would be equitable to allow the action to proceed. In my judgment the plaintiff has done all that could reasonably be expected of her and it would not be right to regard any part of the delay as being her responsibility. The reality of the case is that she did not know of the existence of her remedy and this I find to be entirely understandable in one . . . who is not versed in the law."

(d) The exercise of discretion and procedural matters

At one time the Limitation Act 1963 provided for a specific procedure requiring an application to the court to grant leave to bring an action out of time. However, this was abolished by the Limitation Act 1975. The abolition of this procedural requirement makes sense given that the Limitation Act does not prevent the commencement of an action out of time, but merely provides the defendant with a cast-iron defence should he choose to raise it.[326]

Under the Limitation Act 1980, there is no specific procedure under which the matter of the exercise of discretion under section 33 must be presented to the court. For these purposes, it is provided in section 33(7) that a reference to the court is a reference to the court in which the action is brought. However, it does not follow from this that an application for the exercise of discretion under section 33 can be heard only by the trial court. Case law indicates that the question of discretionary extension of the time bar can be heard as a preliminary issue as well as by any judge of the High Court or county court, including a judge in chambers.[327]

Generally, there are three ways in which the plaintiff may ask the court to exercise its discretion under section 33. First, there is the possibility of a preliminary, *ex parte* application before the writ is issued. Secondly, the plaintiff may issue his writ at the close of the pleadings and apply for leave to be granted as a preliminary point of law. Thirdly, it is possible to ask for the exercise of the discretion at the trial itself. Where the plaintiff makes a preliminary, *ex parte* application, the main problem is that where leave is given, it can only operate on a provisional basis, since before confirmation can be given, the other party must be given a chance to present his case.[328] Given this problem, there will be nothing to prevent the defendant from raising at the trial the question whether leave should have been granted at the preliminary hearing. Moreover in *Goodchild* v. *Greatness Timber Co Ltd*[329] it was observed that where there is an *ex parte* application, there is the risk that the costs of such a trial might be incurred in respect of a case which might fall apart at the full trial of the issues.

There may be good reasons for not allowing the discretion issue to be determined at a preliminary trial. In *Fletcher* v. *Sheffield Health Authority*[330] it was held by the trial judge that the defendant's application that the limitation issue should be tried as a preliminary issue should be rejected on three grounds. First, the case was complex, involving claims of alleged medical negligence, which if proved, would entitle the plaintiff to substantial damages. Secondly, there was no clear demarcation between the limitation and negligence

326. *Walkley* v. *Precision Forgings Ltd* [1979] 1 WLR 606 at 618 *per* Lord Diplock.
327. *Re Clark* v. *Forbes Stuart (Thames Street) Ltd* [1964] 1 WLR 836, CA.
328. *Ibid.*
329. [1968] 2 QB 372, CA.
330. [1994] 5 Med LR 156, CA.

issues. Thirdly, the same issues would have to be considered on the limitation point as would have to be considered when liability was decided upon. In the event, it was decided that the limitation issues were so inextricably connected with the issue of liability (especially causation) that it would be wrong to allow the limitation issues to be tried separately.

Where the plaintiff issues the writ and, at the close of the pleadings, asks for the issue of discretion under section 33 to be considered, there is the danger that such a course of action may result in substantial costs being incurred, greater than those which would be incurred should there be a preliminary application.

The final method, namely an application for the exercise of discretion at the trial itself, is the most expensive of all. As such it is the least common procedural ploy. However, such a situation may arise where the defendant seeks to set aside a decision at a preliminary trial to the effect that the discretion should be exercised in the plaintiff's favour.[331]

(e) Evidential matters

Since, in the majority of cases, it is for the plaintiff to establish the required facts relevant to his cause of action, it also follows that, on the issue of discretion under section 33, it is for the plaintiff to give evidence establishing the grounds on which the discretion should be exercised. Accordingly, for the purposes of the discretion under section 33, it is for the plaintiff to prove that there has been a delay in commencing proceedings and that he will suffer prejudice should the discretion not be exercised in his favour.[332]

It seems that not all normal rules of the law of evidence will apply to an application made under section 33. It has been seen above that one of the factors relevant to the exercise of the discretion is the nature of the advice received from an expert, including a legal adviser. Ordinarily, under evidential rules regarding legal professional privilege, communications between a client and his lawyer are regarded as privileged matters which do not have to be disclosed. However, since the nature of the legal advice received by the plaintiff is a key issue in determining whether the discretion may be exercised, the normal rule is dispensed with. In *Jones* v. *GD Searle Ltd*[333] the plaintiff alleged that she had received favourable advice on the likely success of her action at a very late stage. The defendant introduced interrogatories designed to discover the content of that legal advice, which would normally be protected by legal professional privilege. The Court of Appeal held that the Limitation Act 1980 may override normal evidential rules, so that the strict rules concerning legal professional privilege did not apply and, as a result, the plaintiff could be required to reveal the nature of the advice received. However, arguably, the decision goes too far since it does have the effect of revealing more information than is strictly necessary for the purposes of determining the salient issues for the purposes of section 33, although there does remain the danger that, if the plaintiff refuses to answer the interrogatories, the court might draw adverse inferences from the refusal to make a full disclosure.

---

331. See *Cozens* v. *North Devon Hospital Management Committee* [1966] 2 QB 318.
332. See *Barrand* v. *British Cellophane plc*, *The Times*, 16 February 1995, CA.
333. [1978] 3 All ER 654.

CHAPTER 20

LATENT DAMAGE

WHAT IS LATENT DAMAGE?

No serious difficulty arises in cases in which a plaintiff's cause of action accrues at the same time as the date on which the plaintiff became aware that he had a cause of action. For example in *D & F Estates* v. *Church Commissioners for England*[1] negligently applied plasterwork on a ceiling cracked and subsequently collapsed. For the purposes of the limitation issues, it was found by the trial judge that the date of collapse was also the date on which damage was caused for the purposes of the rule in *Pirelli General Cable Works Ltd* v. *Oscar Faber & Partners*.[2] Accordingly, the date of damage and the date of discoverability both coincided. Where difficulties may arise is in a case in which a plaintiff who is neither mistaken nor under a disability, and who is not adversely affected by fraud or deliberate concealment on the part of the defendant, is not reasonably able to discover the facts which allow him to commence proceedings after the date on which it is decided that significant damage has been caused as a result of the defendant's acts or omissions. In very extreme cases, it is even possible for the plaintiff not to become aware of the facts relevant to his cause of action until after the primary limitation period has expired.[3] This, in a nutshell, is the latent damage problem.

(a) Latent damage and latent defects

Although the Latent Damage Act 1986, considered below, uses the phrase "latent damage" to describe the problem, this disguises a problematical issue revealed in the case law, namely, the difference between "latent *damage*" and "latent *defects*". One illustration of the problem can be found in defective building cases, where a building has suffered physical damage before the date on which the plaintiff acquires an interest in the building. If the damage is undiscoverable at that date, but only becomes apparent at a much later stage, the problem is that time may have started to run against the plaintiff prior to the date on which he could reasonably have become aware that damage has been suffered. Such problems can arise where a building is constructed with inadequate foundations which subsequently results in cracking which reveals itself some years after the date of conveyance to the plaintiff.[4] Here the latent damage problem causes the greatest difficulties.

---

1. [1988] 2 All ER 992.
2. [1983] 2 AC 1 and see Ch 18.
3. See *National Graphical Association* v. *Thimbleby* (1983) 25 Build LR 91.
4. As in *Tozer Kemsley & Milbourn (Holdings) Ltd* v. *J Jarvis & Sons Ltd* (1983) 1 Const LJ 79.

The second type of case which may give rise to difficulty arises where a building or other product is defective at the date of receipt by the plaintiff, but does not suffer or cause damage until a much later date. Here it is the *defect* rather than the *damage* which is latent. For example where a burglar alarm or some other security system is defective at the time of installation, damage is not immediately suffered, but will be suffered once there is a break-in which is not detected.[5] Alternatively, the same problem can arise where a building with defective foundations suffers cracking following later movement of those foundations.[6] In these last two cases, there is no problem if the damage caused by the defect is apparent from the start, but greater problems will arise if this is not the case, since if the defect is latent and damage suffered as a result of that defect also remains hidden for some time, the plaintiff may be time barred before he is aware that any damage has been suffered.

(b) Latent personal injury[7]

Further problems can arise where the latent damage takes the form of personal injury. These problems were highlighted by the facts of *Cartledge* v. *E Jopling & Sons Ltd*[8] in which the widows of a number of steelworkers sued in respect of the death of their husbands from the disease pneumoconiosis. The workers had been fatally harmed as a result of having worked in a poorly ventilated working area which led them to inhale silica dust following sand-blasting operations. The House of Lords, with some reluctance, held that the claims were time barred because damage was suffered when the dust was inhaled, despite the fact that it was not for several years that the results of such inhalation became apparent. Accordingly, all of the plaintiffs were out of time.

Subsequently, Parliament reacted quickly by setting up the Edmund Davies Committee which reported in 1962[9]; this resulted in the passing of the Limitation Act 1963, subsequently to be followed by the Limitation Act 1975 which implemented the recommendations of the Orr Committee.[10] The important effect of the 1975 Act was to create a discoverability test, based on the date on which the plaintiff first, reasonably, became aware of the facts relevant to his cause of action, as an alternative to the normal starting date based on accrual of the cause of action. In addition to the primary limitation periods, legislation in respect of personal injury cases also gives the court a discretion to allow an action to proceed out of time where the prejudice suffered by the plaintiff as a result of the operation of the primary limitation period is greater than that which would be suffered by the defendant as a result of allowing the action to proceed out of time.

Superimposed on this structure are a set of rules flowing from the Consumer Protection Act 1987 in respect of personal injury, death and property damage caused by a defective product, which are based primarily on the date on which damage is caused by the defective product or on the date on which the plaintiff reasonably became aware of facts relevant to the cause of action, whichever is the later. However, both of these dates are

---

5. *Dove* v. *Banhams Patent Locks Ltd* [1983] 2 All ER 833.
6. *Thomas* v. *TA Phillips (Builders) Ltd* (1985) unreported.
7. See Ch 19.
8. [1963] AC 758.
9. Cmnd 1829, 1962.
10. *Interim Report on Limitation of Actions in Personal Injury Claims,* Cmnd 5630, 1974.

subject to a long-stop provision, which prevents any action from being brought later than 10 years from the date on which the defective product was first put into circulation.

(c) Latent damage claims not based on personal injury

The Limitation Acts 1963 and 1975 addressed only the problem of latent damage in personal injury claims and left untouched the problem as it affected other areas. Typical problems include damage caused by builders, engineers, providers of professional advice and other services, local authorities and manufacturers of defective goods. These activities are all potentially covered by the provisions of the Latent Damage Act 1986 which takes effect by inserting in the Limitation Act 1980 new sections 14A and 14B, which take on board a number of the features of other legislation which impinge on the issue of latent damage. For present purposes, the key features of the legislation are:

1. It applies only to actions for negligence where the damages do not relate to personal injury or death;
2. The rule that time starts to run at the date of accrual of the cause of action for a period of six years is retained;
3. There is an alternative limitation period based upon the plaintiff's knowledge of facts relevant to the cause of action which runs for a period of three years from the date of knowledge;
4. The limitation periods provided for are subject to a long-stop which bars an action 15 years after the date of the alleged negligent conduct of the defendant, regardless of the matter of accrual of the cause of action;
5. No discretion is given to the court to entertain the commencement of an action outside the limitation period;
6. Special provision is made for the application of rules in the Limitation Act 1980 regarding disability and deliberate concealment to the problem of latent damage;
7. Special provision is also made in property damage cases to allow for a fresh cause of action in favour of successive owners of damaged property, but no new limitation period is created.

Before the Latent Damage Act 1986, there was some dispute as to when the cause of action accrued in respect of latent property damage. In *Sparham-Souter* v. *Town & Country Developments,*[11] it was held that the period ran from the date damage was discovered. This created the possibility of almost indeterminate liability in the case of hidden defects. Other starting points for the limitation period also existed. For example, it has been seen already that in *Cartledge* v. *E Jopling & Sons Ltd*[12] the House of Lords had provided for the running of time from the date on which damage amounting to personal injury was caused. Various attempts were made to explain the differences between the rules on the commencement of the limitation period in latent damage cases. However, the general consensus was that the law was uncertain and confused.[13] In *Pirelli General Cable Works*

---

11. [1976] QB 858.
12. [1963] AC 758.
13. See Ch 18 for detailed discussion of this confusion.

v. *Oscar Faber & Partners*,[14] the House of Lords imposed a starting point for the running of time which was extremely unfavourable to a building owner, namely, the date on which damage was caused, irrespective of discovery, thereby bringing the law on latent property damage into line with that in respect of latent personal injury. The House of Lords in *Pirelli* admitted to an exception to the rule in the case of property which was "doomed from the start", in which case the limitation period would run from the date on which the plaintiff acquired a sufficient interest in the property to bring negligence proceedings. The extent of the exception and the meaning of "doomed from the start" are far from clear and are discussed elsewhere.[15]

THE SCHEME OF THE LATENT DAMAGE PROVISIONS IN THE LIMITATION ACT 1980

What is clear from the foregoing paragraphs is that there is fairly extensive provision for the problem of latent damage in personal injury cases, but until the enactment of the Latent Damage Act 1986 there was no provision for the problem outside of such cases. On the face of it, the Latent Damage Act 1986 made an important difference, but as will be seen below, developments at common law as to the types of damage actionable in the tort of negligence were to prove crucial. Moreover, the coverage provided for by the Latent Damage Act 1986 makes it clear that its provisions have no effect in relation to cases of death and personal injury, with the result that its provisions are confined to cases of property damage and economic loss, so far as the latter is actionable in tort.

The Limitation Act 1980 (as amended by the Latent Damage Act 1986), section 14A provides:

"(1) This section applies to any action for damages for negligence, other than one to which section 11 of this Act applies, where the starting date for reckoning the period of limitation under subsection (4)(b) below falls after the date on which the cause of action accrued.

(2) Section 2 of this Act shall not apply to an action to which this section applies.

(3) An action to which this section applies shall not be brought after the expiration of the period applicable in accordance with subsection (4) below.

(4) That period is either—

(a) six years from the date on which the cause of action accrued; or

(b) three years from the starting date as defined by subsection (5) below, if that period expires later than the period mentioned in paragraph (a) above.

(5) For the purposes of this section, the starting date for reckoning the period of limitation under subsection (4)(b) above is the earliest date on which the plaintiff or any person in whom the cause of action was vested before him first had both the knowledge required for bringing an action for damages in respect of the relevant damage and a right to bring such an action.

(6) In subsection (5) above 'the knowledge required for bringing an action for damages in respect of the relevant damage' means knowledge both—

(a) of the material facts about the damage in respect of which damages are claimed; and

(b) of the other facts relevant to the current action mentioned in subsection (8) below.

(7) For the purposes of subsection (6)(a) above, the material facts about the damage are such facts about the damage as would lead a reasonable person who had suffered such damage to consider it

14. [1983] 2 AC 1.
15. See Ch 18.

sufficiently serious to justify his instituting proceedings for damages against a defendant who did not dispute liability and was able to satisfy a judgment.

(8) The other facts referred to in subsection (6)(b) above are—

(a) that the damage was attributable in whole or in part to the act or omission which is alleged to constitute negligence; and
(b) the identity of the defendant; and
(c) if it is alleged that the act or omission was that of a person other than the defendant, the identity of that person and the additional facts supporting the bringing of an action against the defendant.

(9) Knowledge that any acts or omissions did or did not, as a matter of law, involve negligence is irrelevant for the purposes of subsection (5) above.

(10) For the purposes of this section a person's knowledge includes knowledge which he might reasonably have been expected to acquire—

(a) from facts observable or ascertainable by him; or
(b) from facts ascertainable by him with the help of appropriate expert advice which it is reasonable for him to seek;

but a person shall not be taken by virtue of this subsection to have knowledge of a fact ascertainable only with the help of expert advice so long as he has taken all reasonable steps to obtain (and, where appropriate, to act on) that advice."

So far as the matter of the long-stop or "overriding time limit", section 14B provides:

"(1) An action for damages for negligence, other than one to which section 11 of this Act applies, shall not be brought after the expiration of fifteen years from the date (or, if more than one, from the last of the dates) on which there occurred any act or omission—

(a) which is alleged to constitute negligence; and
(b) to which the damage in respect of which damages are claimed is alleged to be attributable (in whole or in part).

(2) This section bars the right of action in a case to which subsection (1) above applies notwithstanding that—

(a) the cause of action has not yet accrued; or
(b) where section 14A of this Act applies to the action, the date which is for the purposes of that section the starting date for the reckoning of the period mentioned in subsection (4)(b) of that section has not yet occurred;

before the end of the period of limitation prescribed by this section."

(a) Section 14A and personal injury actions

It is clear from the opening words of section 14A(1) that section 14A has no application to cases of personal injury covered by section 11 of the 1980 Act. However, this does not mean that all actions which remotely relate to the issue of personal injury are excluded from the operation of these provisions. It has been seen already that there are instances in which what appears to be an action for personal injury falls outside the provisions of section 11.[16] In particular, there are cases in which the real complaint is not that personal injury has been suffered, but that the plaintiff has incurred a financial loss as a consequence of the defendant's negligence. For example, there are instances in which the

16. See Ch 19.

plaintiff sues his solicitor for allowing his claim for personal injury damages to become time barred. Also, for reasons discussed elsewhere,[17] an action for damages in respect of the financial cost of rearing a child conceived following an unwanted pregnancy, following a failed sterilisation operation, is, in essence, a claim for economic loss rather than one for personal injury. Likewise, there may be cases in which, following an accident which results in personal injury, the plaintiff is wrongly advised by his doctor that he has only a limited capability in respect of work opportunities, with the result that he takes a job less well paid than that which he might otherwise have taken. These financial loss cases may be dealt with under the provisions of section 14A if they involve damage which may be regarded as latent damage.

As strictly worded, all section 14A excludes is actions in respect of personal injury under section 11. However, what this infelicitous wording fails to say is whether an action based on the Fatal Accidents Act 1976, to which section 12 of the 1980 Act applies, is also in the excluded group of cases. It would seem to be clear that Parliament intended section 14A not to apply to personal injury actions of any kind, but, on the face of it, cases covered by section 12 may also be covered by section 14A, although there seems to be no advantage to the plaintiff in selecting that route. The use of the words "action for damages for negligence" also has the effect that actions for trespass to the person which might appear to involve personal injury also fall outside the provisions of section 14A, since a trespass action has as its gist the commission of the wrongful act. In contrast the gist of a negligence action is the damage suffered by the plaintiff.

(b) Section 14A contract actions and tort actions other than for negligence

One difficulty raised by the wording of section 14A is that it only applies to "an action for damages for negligence". One question which has arisen in this regard is whether an action for breach of contract which entails an allegation that the defendant has failed to take reasonable care is capable of falling within these provisions. Following the decision in *Iron Trade Mutual Insurance Co Ltd* v. *JK Buckenham Ltd*[18] Kenneth Rokison QC had held that this provision was limited to actions for negligence framed in tort and did not cover "contractual negligence". This view has been confirmed as correct in *Société Commerciale de Réassurance* v. *ERAS (International) Ltd*,[19] in which Mustill LJ held (somewhat reluctantly)[20] that:

"The words 'any action for damages in negligence' denote to our minds an action asserting that the defendant has committed the tort of negligence, and are not wide enough to comprise what is often (albeit inaccurately) called 'contractual negligence'. This reading is reinforced by the express overriding of the ordinary provision for tort claims in section 2, coupled with the absence of any overriding of the provision for contractual claims in section 5."[21]

17. See Ch 19.
18. [1990] 1 All ER 808. See also *Islander Trucking Ltd* v. *Hogg Robinson & Gardner Mountain (Marine) Ltd* [1990] 1 All ER 826. It seems that the provisions of ss 14A and 14B do not apply to claims under the Defective Premises Act 1972: *Warner* v. *Basildon Development Corporation* (1991) 7 Const LJ 146.
19. [1992] 2 All ER 82 (note).
20. Mustill LJ (*ibid*, at 85) expressed the view that it defies common sense for actions framed in contract and tort based on the same facts to be subject to different rules on limitation and that it must now be accepted that there is concurrent liability and that separate rules on the accrual of actions in contract and tort pushes the evolution of the substantive law in the wrong direction.
21. [1992] 2 All ER 82 (note) at 85 *per* Mustill LJ.

In addition it was noted that when the provisions of section 11 and section 14A are compared, there is a stark difference since section 11 makes express reference to "contractual negligence" whereas section 14A merely refers to "negligence" *simpliciter*. On this basis, the draftsman must have meant to refer to actions in tort alone.[22] However, in terms of the mischief aimed at by section 14A, it may be argued that what Parliament intended was that a claim for damages should not be barred before the injured party is aware of the fact that he has a claim. However, Mustill LJ did not agree since the Law Reform Committee's 24th Report[23] which led to the Latent Damage Act 1986 was concerned almost exclusively with tort liability.[24] The oddity this produces is that a person who engages a professional adviser under the terms of a contract will not be able to make use of the provisions of section 14A unless he foregoes his contractual claim and chooses to sue in tort instead,[25] thereby placing him in the same position as a third party with no contractual relationship with the adviser. Where this problem is most likely to be real will be in cases of legal advice or advice given by architects, where it is not uncommon for a period of considerably more than six years to elapse before the consequences of their "contractual negligence" is discovered.

The reasoning applied in *Buckenham* and *ERAS* is logical, and if that logic is applied strictly, it should also follow that actions which have to be brought under the tort of nuisance, because no duty to take care can be established, will also be actions which cannot fall within the provisions of sections 14A and 14B. Similarly, any tortious duty which is categorised as strict[26] presumably fails to qualify as a wrong to which the latent damage provisions can apply on the same reasoning as has been applied to contract actions.

ACCRUAL OF THE CAUSE OF ACTION

It has been seen already that in a tort action, time starts to run from the date of accrual of the cause of action.[27] The date of accrual may differ from case to case, so that for example in a negligence action, time runs against a builder, in most cases, from the date on which damage occurs rather than from the date of discoverability. Frequently, the date of discoverability and the date of damage will be the same, but not always so. In the case of an action for breach of statutory duty against a local authority arising out of the Building Act 1984, s 37, time appears to run from the date on which the building becomes an imminent danger to public health or safety. However, section 38 of the same Act renders actionable as a breach of statutory duty any infringement of the Building Regulations when such infringement causes damage. This date may well be earlier than the date on which an imminent danger comes into existence. This problem still remains, following the decision of the House of Lords in *Murphy* v. *Brentwood District Council*[28] since the House of Lords chose not to comment on the statutory duty of a local authority other than to express some surprise that counsel had conceded that a local authority was under a statutory duty

22. *Ibid*, at 86.
23. *Final Report on Limitation of Actions*, Cmnd 6923, 1977.
24. [1992] 2 All ER 82 (note) at 86 *per* Mustill LJ.
25. *Bell* v. *Peter Browne & Co* [1990] 3 All ER 124.
26. Such as some varieties of trespass and some forms of liability under the Animals Act 1971.
27. Limitation Act 1980, s 2 and see Ch 18.
28. [1990] 2 All ER 908, discussed in Ch 18.

to protect an occupant of a building against dangers to health or safety. In an action under the Defective Premises Act 1972, a six-year limitation period runs from the date on which building work (or an attempt to rectify its defects) is complete. An important issue, which has been considered at length elsewhere,[29] is what is meant by damage for the purposes of the tort of negligence. It is clear that personal injury and damage to other property owned by the plaintiff will be regarded as actionable damage, but there is less clarity over the position of pure economic loss. The main difficulty is that following the House of Lords decision in *Murphy* v. *Brentwood District Council*[30] much of what used to be considered to be actionable economic loss is now no longer recoverable in a negligence action, since it is very likely that it will be held that no duty of care is owed by the defendant. In particular, it appears that damage caused by a defective building or other product to itself does not disclose a duty situation, with the result that much of the damage which may have been in mind when the Latent Damage Act 1986 was passed is no longer actionable damage for the purposes of the law of tort. Since qualitative defects in products or buildings do not generally give rise to a negligence action against the manufacturer or builder, no cause of action accrues to the consumer when the defect is merely present.

In the light of *Murphy*, there are effectively two situations in which economic loss will be actionable, despite the heavy criticism of the decision both at home and in other parts of the common law world.[31] The first of these is where the rule in *Hedley Byrne & Co Ltd* v. *Heller & Partners Ltd*,[32] as interpreted by later decisions of the House of Lords,[33] applies. The second is if there is a unique relationship of proximity as explained in *Junior Books Ltd* v. *Veitchi Co.*[34] As has been seen already, the likelihood of success on the second ground is very small, effectively leaving negligent advice cases as the only ones in which economic loss is actionable and which may give rise to the possibility of an action in respect of latent damage for the purposes of the present rules.

For the purposes of an action for damages for negligence which results in latent damage covered by the provisions of sections 14A and 14B, there are now two possible dates from which time may run against the plaintiff. The first of these, by virtue of section 14A(4)(a), is the date on which the cause of action accrued, thereby preserving the rule established in *Pirelli General Cable Works* v. *Oscar Faber & Partners*,[35] but for practical purposes this will rarely be the relevant starting date in cases of latent damage, for the reason that it is more likely than not that under this limitation period, the plaintiff will be out of time before he realises that relevant damage has been suffered. The second and alternative limitation period is likely to be the more important, being based on the plaintiff's knowledge of facts relevant to his cause of action, allowing the plaintiff to commence proceedings within three years of the date on which he acquired or should reasonably have acquired the necessary knowledge.[36]

An interesting question is whether section 14A(4) provides for two separate limitation periods or whether the combined contents of section 14A(4) may be regarded as providing

---

29. See Ch 18.
30. [1990] 2 All ER 908.
31. See especially the discussion of *Invercargill City Council* v. *Hamlin* [1996] 1 All ER 756 in Ch 18.
32. [1964] AC 465.
33. See *Henderson* v. *Merrett Syndicates Ltd* [1994] 3 All ER 506; *White* v. *Jones* [1995] 1 All ER 691; *Spring* v. *Guardian Assurance plc* [1994] 3 All ER 129.
34. [1983] 1 AC 520.
35. [1983] 2 AC 1.
36. Limitation Act 1980, s 14A(4)(b).

for a single period of limitation. The matter arose for consideration in *Busby* v. *Cooper*[37] in which the plaintiff sued in respect of the defendant's negligent advice in allowing her to purchase, on 14 April 1986, a property which proved to be suffering from a concrete deterioration defect. The main difficulty was that the plaintiff was not immediately aware of the defendant's possible liability and she only acquired the relevant knowledge after the primary, accrual-based, limitation period had expired. Once she did discover the relevant facts she acted promptly, seeking to join the defendant to proceedings already commenced against another party. Initially, the plaintiff's application was refused because the primary limitation period had expired before the date of her application. However the Court of Appeal considered that the effect of section 14A(4)(a) is to create one overall time limit of six years from the date of accrual of the cause of action, which is capable of extension for a period of three years under section 14A(4)(b). Accordingly, subsections (4)(a) and (b) do not create separate limitation periods, with the result that in *Busby* it was proper to allow the plaintiff to join the defendant as a party to the proceedings.[38] According to Hirst LJ:

"[I]t does no violence to the wording of section 14A(4) to construe it as laying down one overall time limit, since it is quite clear that subpara. (b) expressly identifies an extension of the primary period laid down in subpara. (a), seeing that the period referred to in subpara. (b) only comes into play if it expires later than the primary period. This is also consistent with the wording of section 14A(3) which refers to the 'applicable period' in the singular, and it also avoids what would be, to my mind, a very artificial and pedantic separation of the two periods into two compartments. It is also of interest . . . that this construction is in line with the Law Reform Committee's recommendation that the primary period should, in latent damage cases be 'subject to an extension' of three years."[39]

THE RELEVANCE OF THE PLAINTIFF'S KNOWLEDGE OF DAMAGE

In the case of both latent personal injury[40] and other forms of actionable latent damage, the Limitation Act 1980 provides for an alternative limitation period based on the plaintiff's knowledge or discovery of the harm or damage he has suffered. It has been seen already that in personal injury actions, the relevant provisions of the Limitation Act refer to the "date of knowledge" of the plaintiff as the date on which time may begin to run against the plaintiff. However, the phrase used in section 14A(1) is "the starting date for reckoning the period of limitation", although for practical purposes, in the case of cases of latent damage of all varieties, the catch-phrase, "date of discoverability", has come to be used to describe the date on which time may run against the plaintiff. Under the provisions of section 14A, the "starting date" is defined as the earliest date on which the plaintiff (or any person in whom the cause of action was vested) had both the knowledge required for bringing an action for damages in respect of the relevant damage and a right to bring such an action.[41]

---

37. [1996] CLC 1425.
38. See also Ch 7.
39. [1996] CLC 1425 at 1428–29.
40. See Ch 19.
41. Limitation Act 1980, s 14A(5).

The constituent elements of knowledge

It has been seen already that in the case of personal injury actions, there is a set of rules on the running of time based upon the plaintiff's knowledge of relevant facts relating to the cause of action.[42] A similar test is also applied to other forms of latent damage caused by the negligent conduct of the defendant under section 14A, although the wording of the relevant provision differs somewhat from that in respect of personal injury actions.

Under section 14A(6), the knowledge required to be possessed by the plaintiff before time may run against him is knowledge of two factors, namely, (a) of the material facts about the damage in respect of which damages are claimed and (b) of other facts relevant to the current action. Moreover for the purposes of the definition of knowledge, the plaintiff may be deemed to be aware of facts which a reasonable person suffering similar damage would have regarded as sufficiently serious to justify the institution of proceedings against a defendant who did not dispute liability and was in a position to be able to satisfy a judgment.[43]

For the purposes of determining what a reasonable person would do, it has been held that it is no excuse for a person to argue that his reason for delaying the commencement of proceedings is that he is fearful that he might be exposed as an illegal UK resident.[44] The reason for this is that a reasonable person is one who obeys the law and it would not be reasonable for a person to take a course of action which is calculated to enable him to disobey the law. For example in *Coban* v. *Allen*[45] the plaintiff came to the UK as a visitor, but continued to remain in the country as an overstayer. During the period of his residence, he set up in partnership with an associate, running a fish and chip shop. In 1986 the two partners quarrelled and the associate threatened to report the plaintiff to the immigration authorities unless he agreed to transfer his interest in the partnership to her for £5,000. In 1992, the plaintiff was informed by the immigration authorities that he would be allowed to stay in the UK, whereupon he commenced proceedings against the defendant solicitors alleging negligence in that his signature on the document transferring his interest in the partnership had been forged and that, in any case, he had not been paid the £5,000 agreed to be paid by the associate. The plaintiff alleged that his solicitors, the defendants, were negligent in not sufficiently safeguarding his interests. It was held that, once the plaintiff realised in 1986 that people other than himself and his associate were in occupation of the shop, any reasonable person would have consulted a solicitor, and that his failure to do so meant that he had constructive knowledge of the facts relevant to his cause of action by virtue of section 14A(10)(b). As to the plaintiff's fear that his illegal status might become known to the appropriate authorities, the Court of Appeal accepted a distinction drawn by counsel for the defendants, namely that while the plaintiff's conduct was understandable in the circumstances, that did not render it reasonable, since a reasonable man will obey the law.

The principal provisions on the matter of relevant knowledge are set out in sections 14A(6) to (8). It has been observed above that the effect of section 14A(6) is to require consideration of two separate matters. The first of these, covered by section 14A(6)(a), is that consideration should be given to the plaintiff's knowledge of material facts about the

---

42. See Ch 19.
43. Limitation Act 1980, s 14A(7).
44. See *Coban* v. *Allen*, *The Times*, 14 October 1996, CA.
45. *Ibid*.

damage in respect of which damages are claimed. For these purposes, section 14A(7) requires the court to consider the position of the plaintiff in the light of any expert advice he might have received. Secondly, for the purposes of the requirements set out in section 14A(6)(b) in relation to "other relevant facts", the court is guided by section 14A(8) to consider:

(a) that the damage was attributable in whole or in part to the act or omission which is alleged to constitute negligence;

(b) the identity of the defendant;

(c) if it is alleged that the act or omission was that of a person other than the defendant, the identity of that person and the additional facts supporting the bringing of an action against the defendant.

Although drafted somewhat differently from the provisions of section 14 in relation to personal injury actions, the provisions of section 14A(7) and (8) effectively require consideration of the same general issues considered elsewhere in this book.[46] Accordingly, the plaintiff must be aware of all facts material to his cause of action and the circumstances which would justify the institution of proceedings for negligence by a reasonable person.

The language of section 14A(7) requires the court to consider whether the damage suffered was "sufficiently serious" to justify the bringing of proceedings on the part of a reasonable person in the position of the plaintiff. Since the plaintiff will only have one opportunity to sue in respect of a single cause of action, it may be that a person does not sue immediately where there is only slight damage. However, suppose that damage later develops into something more serious: it would appear to be relevant under section 14A(7) to consider whether the plaintiff can be deemed to have been aware that he had a relevant cause of action in the light of the apparently minor damage in the early stages. For example in *Horbury* v. *Craig Hall & Rutley*[47] the plaintiff discovered that there was a defect in her chimney breast which, at the time, would have cost £132 to repair. The defect was one which had not been identified by the defendant surveyors when they surveyed the property prior to purchase by the plaintiff. Initially, no action was taken, but at a later stage the plaintiff discovered that the property in question also had a serious dry rot problem which would cost £56,000 to rectify. This last defect was also a matter which had not, but should have, been identified by the defendants. The plaintiff issued a writ, arguing that the earlier damage to the chimney breast was not sufficiently serious for her to have commenced proceedings, with the result that it was only when she was aware of the dry rot problem that she had the required knowledge for the purposes of running of time. However, Judge Bowsher QC said that despite the fact that some people might write off a claim for £132, there was nonetheless serious damage which warranted the bringing of proceedings. Accordingly, time ran against the plaintiff from the date on which she became aware of the defect in the chimney breast.

Judge Bowsher QC commented:

"Although personal injuries, even where not severe, can be more important than 'mere money', it is regarded as reasonable in this country at present to endure a modest amount of pain without bringing an action unless financial loss results (that may well change). On the other hand, when one

46. See Ch 19.
47. (1991) 7 PN 206, QBD. See also *Hamlin* v. *Edwin Evans (a firm)*, *The Times*, 15 July 1996.

is forced to pay out money which one has earned partly for the benefit of one's dependants, it is reasonable to be more ready to bring an action."[48]

Also relevant to the knowledge of the plaintiff is the identity of the defendant, by virtue of the provisions of section 14A(8)(b). From this provision, it follows that until the plaintiff is aware of the identity of the person against whom the writ is to be issued, time will not start to run, even if the plaintiff is aware that serious damage has been suffered.[49] The provisions in respect of knowledge of the defendant also extend to cases of vicarious liability, by virtue of section 14A(8)(c), since under that provision, time will not start to run against the plaintiff until he is aware of the "person other than the defendant" who it is alleged is responsible for the damage suffered by the plaintiff.

As is the case with the "discoverability test" in relation to personal injuries, the provisions of section 14A in relation to other forms of latent damage draw a distinction between knowledge of matters of fact and those of law. Under section 14A(9) knowledge that any act or omission did or did not, as a matter of law, involve negligence is to be regarded as irrelevant in determining the date on which time is to run against the plaintiff. Accordingly, if the plaintiff is possessed of knowledge which would justify a reasonable person in issuing a writ, time will start to run against the plaintiff, even though, at that time, the particular plaintiff did not appreciate that he was in a position to be able to institute proceedings because he did not appreciate that, as a matter of law, there was a relevant breach of duty on the part of the defendant.

Knowledge for the purposes of section 14A includes both actual and constructive knowledge by virtue of the provisions of section 14(A)(10) which specifies that knowledge includes both facts observable and ascertainable by the plaintiff and those ascertainable with the assistance of expert advice which it is reasonable to seek.[50] Accordingly, if a reasonable person would consult a lawyer or a surveyor or other appropriate expert adviser, but the particular plaintiff has done nothing, the latter will be assumed to have the knowledge which the reasonable person could have acquired.

LONG-STOP PROVISIONS

The Limitation Act recognises the potential of the three-year discoverability rule for creating indeterminate liability and in section 14B provides for a long-stop on all actions for latent damage of 15 years from the date of the relevant breach of duty which causes the damage. It is important to note that the long-stop provision operates from the date of breach of duty, rather than from the date on which the plaintiff acquired the relevant knowledge for the purposes of section 14A. It follows from this that there may be circumstances in which the plaintiff's cause of action has not accrued on the date when the long-stop provisions come into effect, but it is clear from the wording of section 14B that this is not a matter to be taken into consideration.[51] Similarly, where the alternative limitation period for the purposes of section 14A has not expired, the provisions of section 14B, which bar the cause of action, will take precedence.[52] The one exception to this over-

48. *Ibid.*
49. Thereby providing an exception to the rule in *RB Policies at Lloyd's* v. *Butler* [1950] 1 KB 76.
50. See *Coban* v. *Allen, The Times* 14 October 1996, considered above.
51. Limitation Act 1980, s 14B(2)(a).
52. Limitation Act 1980, s 14B(2)(b).

riding principle is that where there has been an act amounting to deliberate concealment for the purposes of section 32(1)(b) of the 1980 Act, the long-stop provisions will not apply.[53]

Since the long-stop provisions are based upon the fact of a relevant breach of duty of care, it is important to ascertain the date on which the relevant breach occurs. This date will differ from action to action. Thus, it has been seen already[54] that in cases of alleged negligent construction, for example negligence on the part of an engineer or a builder, the date of breach is normally regarded as the date on which construction is completed. In the case of negligent inspection by a local authority, the relevant date is the date of inspection, provided, of course, that a duty of care is owed at all. In the case of alleged negligent advice on the part of a professional such as a surveyor, the relevant date is the date on which the defectively prepared report is made available to the plaintiff so that he may rely upon its contents.

DISABILITY AND FRAUD

It has been seen already that the effect of fraud on the part of the defendant and disability on the part of the plaintiff will have the effect of postponing the running of time against the plaintiff. Special provision is made for the application of these rules to cases of latent damage, which are considered elsewhere in this book.[55]

TRANSFER OF DAMAGED PROPERTY

At common law, the purchaser of property damaged prior to the contract of sale had no action against the wrongdoer. His remedy, if any, is against the seller.[56] Thus, if D negligently damages V's property and V sells to P at market value, P cannot sue D once the damage becomes manifest. Moreover, V cannot assign the cause of action to P because, having received the market value from P, V has suffered no loss.

An attempt to resolve this problem is provided for in the Latent Damage Act 1986, s 3, which states that in these circumstances, a fresh cause of action is conferred on P against D. As far as the limitation issue is concerned, the action accrues when the damage occurred, but the limitation period is extended to three years from the date at which the cause of action became discoverable, subject to the usual long-stop.

The Latent Damage Act 1986, s 3 provides:

"(1) Subject to the following provisions of this section where—

(a) a cause of action ('the original cause of action') has accrued to any person in respect of any negligence to which damage to any property in which he has an interest is attributable (in whole or in part); and

(b) another person acquires an interest in that property after the date on which the original cause of action accrued but before the material facts about the damage have become known to any person who, at the time when he first has knowledge of those facts, has any interest in the property;

---

53. Limitation Act 1980, s 32(5), and see Ch 6.
54. See Ch 18.
55. See Limitation Act 1980, s 32(1)(a) (fraud) and s 28 (disability) and see Ch 6.
56. *Perry* v. *Tendring District Council* (1985) 3 Con LR 74.

a fresh cause of action in respect of that negligence shall accrue to that other person on the date on which he acquires his interest in the property.

(2) A cause of action accruing to any person by virtue of subsection (1) above—

(a) shall be treated as if based on breach of a duty of care at common law owed to the person to whom it accrues; and

(b) shall be treated for the purposes of section 14A of the 1980 Act . . . as having accrued on the date on which the original cause of action accrued.

(3) Section 28 of the 1980 Act . . . shall not apply in relation to any such cause of action.

(4) Subsection (1) above shall not apply in any case where the person acquiring an interest in the damaged property is either—

(a) a person in whom the original cause of action vests by operation of law; or

(b) a person in whom the interest in that property vests by virtue of any order made by a court under section 238 of the Companies Act 1985 . . .

(5) For the purposes of subsection (1)(b) above, the material facts about the damage are such facts about the damage as would lead a reasonable person who has an interest in the damaged property at the time when those facts become known to him to consider it sufficiently serious to justify his instituting proceedings for damages against a defendant who did not dispute liability and was able to satisfy a judgment.

(6) For the purposes of this section a person's knowledge includes knowledge which he might reasonably have been expected to acquire—

(a) from facts observable or ascertainable by him; or

(b) from facts ascertainable by him with the help of appropriate expert advice which it is reasonable for him to seek;

but a person shall not be taken by virtue of this subsection to have knowledge of a fact ascertainable by him only with the help of expert advice so long as he has taken all reasonable steps to obtain (and, where appropriate, to act on) that advice."

The interest referred to in the 1986 Act, s 3(1) is not specified to be an ownership interest. Accordingly, it would appear that these provisions will apply to the acquisition of any interest in property, be it legal or equitable. It follows therefore that the acquisition of a leasehold or reversionary interest will suffice for these purposes. Moreover, since the interest has to be one in property, as opposed to real property, it ought to follow that the acquisition of an interest in personal property ought also to suffice for the purposes of section 3.

The provisions of section 3(5) on the meaning of a material fact are similar, but not identical, to the provisions of section 14A. In particular, the required knowledge must be possessed by a person who has an interest in the property at that time. It follows from this that the requirements of section 3(5) are not complied with if a person first acquires the necessary knowledge after he has disposed of his interest in that property. However, a person who acquires the necessary knowledge before the date on which he acquires an interest in the property concerned would be covered by the provisions of the 1986 Act.

CHAPTER 21

THE CONSUMER PROTECTION ACT 1987

The Consumer Protection Act 1987, Part I[1] was enacted specifically for the purpose of giving effect to the European Community Directive on Product Liability[2] with a view to the introduction of a system of strict liability for dangerously defective products. It is to be seen as a complement[3] to the narrow rule in *Donoghue* v. *Stevenson*,[4] but not as a replacement for that rule. The main respect in which the common law rule and the statutory regime differ is that for the purposes of the former, the consumer of a negligently manufactured product bears the onus of proving all elements of the tort of negligence, including the existence of a duty of care, breach of that duty and that foreseeable damage has been suffered as a result of the breach. In contrast under the Consumer Protection Act 1987, the principal requirement is that a product should not be defective, with the result that the affected consumer does not have to prove fault on the part of the producer.

BASIC DEFINITIONS UNDER THE CONSUMER PROTECTION ACT 1987

The key concepts introduced by the Consumer Protection Act 1987 are that liability extends to the "producers" of "products" which prove to be "defective" in the sense that their "safety" is not what persons generally are entitled to expect, subject to certain limitations on liability, and that it imposes what appears to be a form of "strict liability".

(a) Producers

A producer is defined by the 1987 Act[5] as a manufacturer, a person who has won or abstracted a product and a person who has carried out an industrial or other process in relation to a product to which the essential characteristics of the product are attributable. Moreover, the definition of the word "producer" is further expanded through the inclusion in the definition of "own branders", namely those who hold themselves out as producers by affixing a trade mark to a product or puts his own name on a product which has been

---

1. Sections 1 to 9. For limitation purposes s 6(6) is of particular relevance in stipulating that the provisions of Sch 1 of the Act shall have effect for the purpose of amending the Limitation Act 1980.
2. Directive 85/374/EEC.
3. Consumer Protection Act 1987, s 2(6).
4. [1932] AC 562. For general principles of limitation of actions in tort cases see Ch 18.
5. Consumer Protection Act 1987, s 1(2).

produced by someone else.[6] Also included in the definition of the word producer is a person who imports a product into an EC Member State from a place outside the EC, provided this act of importation is done in the course of a business.[7]

(b) Product

Products are defined as including goods, whether or not incorporated into any other goods, or electricity.[8] Given the very broad definition of goods as including substances, the Act appears to cover virtually all moveable products, subject to specific exemptions. The major such exemption applies to primary agricultural produce and game which has not undergone an industrial process.[9] Thus fresh vegetables are probably excluded from the provisions of the Act, but frozen or otherwise processed vegetables will be regarded as products. Also excluded from the definition of a product is a building.

(c) Defectiveness

A product is defective if its safety "is not such as persons generally are entitled to expect".[10] This notion of what persons generally are entitled to expect is taken further in the Act which stipulates that matters such as the manner of marketing a product, its anticipated uses and the time of its supply must be taken into account.[11] Thus, what will be required is a cost-benefit analysis of the lack of safety of a product set against its target market, the utility of the product and other background circumstances at the time the product was put into circulation. In this sense, what the 1987 Act introduces may differ little from the fault-based principle in *Donoghue* v. *Stevenson*.

(d) Safety

The 1987 Act is tied to the notion of an unsafe product, and as such the Act is concerned with the capacity of a product to cause personal injury, death, and damage to property other than the defective product itself.[12] Accordingly, the 1987 Act will have no application, whatever, to qualitatively defective products, in respect of which the Sale of Goods Act 1979 will apply,[13] nor will the 1987 Act have any application to pure economic loss suffered otherwise than as a result of physical harm caused by the defective product. However, this will not prevent the recovery of damages for lost earnings etc, since these are economic losses consequent on physical injury.[14]

---

6. *Ibid*, s 2(2)(b).
7. *Ibid*, s 2(2)(c).
8. *Ibid*, s 1(2). For these purposes goods are further defined in s 45 as including substances, growing crops and things comprised in land by virtue of being attached to it and any ship, aircraft or vehicle.
9. *Ibid*, s 2(4).
10. *Ibid*, s 3(1).
11. *Ibid*, s 3(2).
12. *Ibid*, s 3(1) and s 5(1).
13. As to which see Ch 10.
14. See also Ch 19.

(e) Limitations on liability

As a result of specific provisions contained in the EC Directive on Product Liability, Member States were permitted to limit the liability of a producer in purely financial terms. As a result of this, a producer will not be liable for damage to property amounting in value to less than £275.[15] Furthermore, liability under the Act does not extend to damage to property which is not ordinarily intended for private use or consumption and which was intended by the user to be used for purposes other than private purposes.[16]

(f) Strict liability

Liability under the 1987 Act is said to be strict, in the sense that fault on the part of the producer does not have to be proved.[17] However, it has already been observed above that the definition of defectiveness imports a cost-benefit analysis, similar to that employed in determining whether there has been a breach of a tortious duty of care. Furthermore, certain defences are provided for in the Act which have the effect of introducing what looks like fault-based considerations. In particular, there is a "development risks" defence which requires consideration of the state of scientific and technical development at the time the product was put into circulation.[18] Other permitted defences are that the product was not defective when supplied, that the supplier was not acting in the course of a business and that the product was defective only because of compliance with other EC requirements.[19]

LIMITATION REQUIREMENTS OF THE CONSUMER PROTECTION ACT 1987

The limitation periods provided for in Schedule 1 of the 1987 Act are somewhat complex, consisting not just of a limitation on individual actions, but also providing for a 10-year long-stop after which all rights against the producer are extinguished, whether or not the general limitation periods contained in the Act have expired. Furthermore, the Act draws a distinction between personal injury claims and those relating to property damage. In the case of personal injury claims, the court is provided with a discretion to extend the limitation period,[20] provided the 10-year long-stop on the liability of the producer is not exceeded.

The Limitation Act 1980, s 11A[21] ("Actions in respect of defective products") provides:

"(1) This provision shall apply to an action for damages by virtue of any provision of Part I of the Consumer Protection Act 1987.

---

15. Consumer Protection Act 1987, s 5(4).
16. *Ibid*, s 5(3).
17. *Ibid*, s 2(1).
18. *Ibid*, s 4(1)(e).
19. *Ibid*, s 4 generally.
20. See also the general discussion of discretionary extension under the Limitation Act 1980, s 33, examined in Ch 19.
21. Inserted by the Consumer Protection Act 1987, Sch 1.

(2) None of the time limits given in the preceding provisions of this Act shall apply to an action to which this section applies.

(3) An action to which this section applies shall not be brought after the expiration of the period of ten years from the relevant time within the meaning of section 4 of the said Act of 1987; and this subsection shall operate to extinguish a right of action and shall do so whether or not that right of action had accrued, or time under the following provisions of this Act had begun to run, at the end of the said period of ten years.

(4) Subject to subsection (5) below, an action to which this section applies in which the damages claimed by the plaintiff consist of or include damages in respect of personal injuries to the plaintiff or any other person or loss of or damage to any property, shall not be brought after the expiration of the period of three years from whichever is the later of—

    (a) the date on which the cause of action accrued; and

    (b) the date of knowledge of the injured person or, in the case of loss of or damage to property, the date of knowledge of the plaintiff or (if earlier) of any person in whom his cause of action was previously vested.

(5) If in a case where the damages claimed by the plaintiff consist of or include damages in respect of personal injuries to the plaintiff or any other person the injured person died before the expiration of the period mentioned in subsection (4) above, that subsection shall have effect as respects the cause of action surviving for the benefit of his estate by virtue of section 1 of the Law Reform (Miscellaneous Provisions) Act 1934 as if for the reference to that period there were substituted a reference to the period of three years from whichever is the later of—

    (a) the date of death; and

    (b) the date of the personal representative's knowledge.

(6) For the purposes of this section 'personal representative' includes any person who is or has been a personal representative of the deceased, including an executor who has not yet proved the will (whether or not he has renounced probate) but not anyone appointed only as a special personal representative in relation to settled land; and regard shall be had to any knowledge acquired by any such person while a personal representative or previously.

(7) If there is more than one personal representative and their dates of knowledge are different, subsection 5(b) above shall be read as referring to the earliest of those dates.

(8) Expressions used in this section or section 14 of this Act and in Part I of the Consumer Protection Act 1987 have the same meanings in this section or that section as in that Part; and section 1(1) of that Act (Part I to be construed as enacted for the purpose of complying with the product liability Directive) shall apply for the purpose of construing this section and the following provisions of this Act so far as they relate to an action by virtue of any provision of that Part as it applies for the purpose of construing that part."

The Limitation Act 1980, s 14(1A)[22] provides:

"(1) In section 11A of this Act and in section 12 of this Act so far as that section applies to an action by virtue of section 6(1)(a) of the Consumer Protection Act 1987 (death caused by defective product) references to a person's date of knowledge are references to the date on which he first had knowledge of the following facts—

    (a) such facts about the damage caused by the defect as would lead a reasonable person who had suffered such damage to consider it sufficiently serious to justify his instituting proceedings for damages against a defendant who did not dispute liability and was able to satisfy a judgment; and

    (b) that the damage was wholly or partly attributable to the facts and circumstances alleged to constitute the defect; and

    (c) the identity of the defendant;

---

22. Inserted by the Consumer Protection Act 1987, Sch 1.

but, in determining the date on which a person first had such knowledge there shall be disregarded both the extent (if any) of that person's knowledge on any date of whether particular facts or circumstances would or would not, as a matter of law, constitute a defect and, in a case relating to loss of or damage to property, any knowledge which that person had on a date on which he had no right of action by virtue of Part I of that Act in respect of the loss or damage."

(a) The three-year rule

The basic rule in the Limitation Act 1980, s 11A, as a result of the changes brought about by the Consumer Protection Act 1987, is that the normal limitation period for tort actions contained in the Limitation Act 1980, s 2 is not to apply to actions in respect of defective products. Instead, there is a three-year limitation period, which by virtue of section 11A(4) runs from the later of the date of accrual of the cause of action or the date on which the plaintiff had the knowledge (or could with reasonable diligence have acquired the knowledge) required to be able to have discovered the existence of his cause of action.

Consistent with the approach adopted under the Limitation Act 1980, s 2, there is no definition of the time at which the plaintiff's cause of action accrues, but it would be consistent with the whole scheme of the 1980 Act if accepted principles on the meaning of "accrual of a cause of action" were to apply to these new provisions. It is clear from the provisions of sections 2(1), 3(1) and 5(1) of the Consumer Protection Act 1987 that the gist of the action is damage of a type defined in section 5(1), namely death, bodily injury or loss of or damage to property other than the defective product itself, in which case ordinary tort principles on the interpretation of when damage is caused will apply. Accordingly, it will be necessary for there to be more than just minimal damage[23] and, subject to other provisions of section 11A, it will be irrelevant that the plaintiff is unaware that damage has been suffered.

The provisions of section 11A are concerned only with cases in which a defective product has caused death, personal injury or damage to other property with the result that there is the potential for overlap with other provisions of the Limitation Act 1980 which also deal with the matter of personal injury and property damage.[24] From this it follows that if a plaintiff can bring his action at common law, he will be allowed to do so, thereby being able to avoid some of the more restrictive provisions to be found in section 11A.

(b) Personal injury resulting in death

Special provision is made for the situation in which a person is injured by a defective product with the result that he dies. Common examples might include cases of fatal food poisoning, provided the food has been the subject of an industrial process, and cases of fatal motor vehicle collisions caused by a design defect.

Where a person dies as a result of the commission of a tort, a cause of action survives in favour of the deceased person's estate under the Law Reform (Miscellaneous Provisions) Act 1934, s 1. For the purposes of an action brought under the Consumer Protection Act, the Limitation Act 1980, s 11A provides that where the damages claimed by the plaintiff include damages in respect of personal injuries suffered by the plaintiff or any other person and the injured person died before the expiry of the limitation period fixed

---

23. See *Pirelli General Cable Works* v. *Oscar Faber & Partners* [1983] 2 AC 1, discussed in Ch 18.
24. See Chs 18, 19 and 20.

by section 11A(4), the three-year limitation period runs from a different date in respect of the cause of action surviving under the 1934 Act. This new date is calculated by reference to the later of either the date of death or the date of the personal representative's[25] knowledge of the facts necessary in order to be able to commence proceedings.[26] In some instances, there may be more than one personal representative and each may be possessed of different knowledge. In these circumstances, the 1980 Act provides that the earliest date of knowledge of relevant facts will be decisive for the purposes of the running of time.[27]

(c) Knowledge

It is clear from the provisions of section 11A that an essential consideration is the state of knowledge of either the plaintiff bringing an action under the Consumer Protection Act 1987 or, in the case of defective products causing death, the state of knowledge of the deceased's personal representatives, since the date of first relevant knowledge will set the date for the purposes of the running of time when the primary date of damage period has expired.

The state of knowledge required in order for time to run against the plaintiff or the personal representative, as the case may be, is the same in each case.[28] An extensive definition of the relevant knowledge is now given in the Limitation Act 1980, s 14(1A), which applies to actions covered by section 11A and section 12 (Fatal Accidents Act 1976 cases). Broadly, three matters must be considered, namely knowledge about the nature of the damage caused, knowledge that the defect in the product has caused the damage and knowledge of the identity of the defendant.

The knowledge required of the nature of the damage suffered requires the court to consider when the plaintiff was first aware that the damage caused by the defect was such that a reasonable man who had suffered such damage would consider it sufficiently serious to justify his instituting proceedings for damages against a defendant who did not dispute liability and was able to satisfy a judgment.[29]

It should be noted that although the relevant knowledge is that of the particular plaintiff, the test to be applied uses the standard of a hypothetical reasonable plaintiff and a hypothetical defendant who admits liability and is shorn of shortcomings such as inability to pay damages.

Most likely to cause difficulty in this area is the problem of damage caused by defective pharmaceutical products, which may cause internal damage which takes many months or even years to manifest itself. Moreover, even where damage is caused and the early signs reveal themselves, ordinary consumers with little or no knowledge of medical matters may not immediately realise that there is a need to consult expert opinion. It is inevitable that the provisions of section 14(1A) will come into play in such circumstances, since the shortened three-year limitation period running from the date on which damage is caused

---

25. For these purposes a personal representative is taken to include a person who has been a personal representative and an executor who has not proved the will: Limitation Act 1980, s 11A(6).

26. Limitation Act 1980, s 11A(5).

27. *Ibid*, s 11A(7).

28. For the purposes of a personal representative, relevant knowledge includes that acquired while a personal representative or previously: Limitation Act 1980, s 11A(6).

29. Limitation Act 1980, s 14(1A)(a).

will almost certainly have expired in the majority of cases before the plaintiff realises that significant damage has been caused.

The second consideration is that the plaintiff must be aware that the damage suffered is wholly or partly attributable to the facts and circumstances alleged to constitute the defect. This seems to raise an issue of factual causation rather than legal causation or remoteness, since the proviso to section 14(1A) goes on to state that it is irrelevant whether the plaintiff was aware that particular facts would or would not "as a matter of law" constitute a defect.[30] Accordingly matters which raise an issue of factual causation in relation to defective products, such as warnings about use and whether a medical link may be made between the type of damage caused and the activity carried on by the defendant, will be important.

It should be noted that the language used in section 14(1A) is very similar to that used in both section 11, in relation to personal injuries and section 14A in relation to latent damage. These last two provisions have been in operation somewhat longer than section 14(1A) and have therefore attracted a certain amount of case law,[31] which cannot, as yet, be said of section 14(1A). However, it seems reasonable to assume that similarly worded provisions will receive similar treatment in the courts.

The third element of section 14(1A) requires the plaintiff to be aware of the identity of the defendant. Whilst this may not, at first sight, seem to raise any particular problems, experience of a similar requirement in the context of personal injury litigation has shown that there may be occasions on which the plaintiff can have difficulty in identifying a corporate defendant, where, for example, a company forms part of a larger group, that group having a generic title which carries with it no legal identity of its own.[32] Similar problems might also arise under the Consumer Protection Act, where, for example, a defendant seeks to establish that the producer of a component part he has used in his finished product is also responsible, jointly and severally, for the defectiveness of the end product.[33]

The proviso to section 14(1A) introduces two qualifications, one of which is considered above. The closing words of the proviso deal exclusively with the matter of property damage caused by defective products and has no comparator elsewhere in the Limitation Act. It provides that any knowledge had by a person on a date when he had no right of action by virtue of any provision of Part I of the 1987 Act is to be disregarded for the purposes of ascertaining when time should run. This provision is entirely logical in that any knowledge had by a person before any cause of action accrues by virtue of damage having been caused must be ignored, otherwise the plaintiff will be time barred before his cause of action has even accrued, which cannot be possible. In the second place, due to the passage of time, knowledge which has been acquired may be lost. If the plaintiff can prove this to be the case, he will not be deemed to have the necessary knowledge and time will not start to run against him until the relevant knowledge has been re-acquired. It should be emphasised that these concluding words of section 14(1A) only apply to cases

---

30. As has been noted in relation to personal injury cases, the reason why the comparable provision in s 14(1) was introduced was in order to reverse a line of cases which held that a plaintiff could not be fixed with the required degree of knowledge until he had taken legal advice: *Pickles* v. *National Coal Board* [1968] 1 WLR 997. But as worded this provision may go further.

31. As to which see Ch 20 and Ch 19.

32. See *Simpson* v. *Norwest Holst Southern Ltd* [1980] 1 WLR 968.

33. See Consumer Protection Act 1987, s 2(5).

of property damage caused by a defective product, with the result that pre-acquired knowledge relevant in a personal injury action will not be disregarded, which might produce the odd result that, where a plaintiff sues for both personal injury and property damage both caused by the same defective property, the court has to disregard certain information for the purposes of the property damage claim, but can take that matter into account in relation to the personal injury claim.

(d) The long-stop

Quite apart from the special rules on limitation of actions contained in sections 11A and 14(1A), section 11A(3) provides for a long-stop on all product liability claims 10 years after the "relevant time" specified in the Consumer Protection Act 1987, s 4. Section 4 of the 1987 Act provides for a number of defences to liability, one of which is that "the defect did not exist in the product at the relevant time"[34] and another of which is that the state of scientific and technical development "at the relevant time" was not such as to allow the defect to be discovered.[35] For the purposes of section 4, s 4(2) provides:

"In this section 'the relevant time', in relation to electricity, means the time at which it was generated, being a time before it was transmitted or distributed, and in relation to any other product means—

  (a) if the person proceeded against is a person to whom subsection (2) of section 2 above applies [producers, own-branders and importers] in relation to the product, the time when he supplied the product to another;
  (b) if that subsection does not apply to that person in relation to the product, the time when the product was last supplied by a person to whom that subsection does apply in relation to the product."

Accordingly, the long-stop is intended to run for a period of 10 years from the date when a producer, an own-brander or an importer into the EC last supplied the defective product to another. Accordingly, where the producer of an end product or the abstracter of raw materials first supplies a product to another person in the chain of distribution, thereby putting the product "on the market" there is a supply for the purposes of the Consumer Protection Act 1987, s 4(2) and the long-stop period starts to run, with the result that an action commenced more than 10 years from that date will be time barred, despite the fact that relevant knowledge for the purposes of the Limitation Act 1980, s 14(1A) could not have been acquired before that time.

So far as other "suppliers" are concerned, section 4(2)(b) of the 1987 Act stipulates that the relevant time is when the product was last supplied by a person who is a producer or deemed producer within the meaning of section 2(2). Thus, if a retailer is exceptionally regarded as a producer,[36] the relevant time for the purposes of the long-stop is the date on which the product was last put into circulation by a person who is a producer or a deemed producer.

The importance of the long-stop is that it provides for certainty in allowing producers to "close their ledger" after the long-stop period has expired. However, it should be noted that it does not apply to common law actions, with the result that if there is a parallel

34. *Ibid*, s 4(1)(d).
35. *Ibid*, s 4(1)(e).
36. As is possible due to the provisions of the Consumer Protection Act 1987, s 2(3).

common law action, there is nothing to prevent the consumer of a defective product using alternative means of seeking redress without being subject to section 11A(3).

Since more than one person can be a producer and since the relevant time may differ from one case to another, it is possible that there may be more than one long-stop period in relation to a single product. For example, suppose X produces generic pharmaceutical products in 1995 and in 1996 supplies them to Y who applies his own brand name to those products before supplying stocks to Z, a retailer, in 1997. Z subsequently supplies the product to a consumer who suffers internal injuries which do not manifest themselves for some time. In relation to X, the long-stop period will run from 1996, despite the fact that the product was manufactured the year before. In relation to Y, as an own-brander, the period will run from the time he supplied the product to another which will be in 1997. Although Z will not normally be regarded as a producer, since he is merely a supplier, he may become a "deemed producer" if he is unable to identify either X or Y as producers. In the case of Z, the relevant time is when the product was last supplied by a person who is a producer, which in the example above, is also 1997.

The practical effect of the long-stop provisions may also be seen as a departure from normal rules on limitation of actions. It has been seen already[37] that normally the effect of limitation periods is merely to bar the plaintiff's remedy, but not to extinguish his right of action. However, the way in which section 11A(3) is worded makes it clear that the consumer's right to sue in respect of a defective product is extinguished altogether, whether or not the cause of action has accrued. It has been seen already that in order to succeed in barring the plaintiff's remedy, the Statute of Limitations must be pleaded by the defendant. But since section 11A(3) extinguishes the plaintiff's right, this should mean that there is no need for the defendant to plead the long-stop. Moreover, some of the other methods of reviving a cause of action or otherwise getting round the time bar will be of no use in relation to the long-stop. For example, a plaintiff under a disability, in most cases, will not be time barred while the disability continues,[38] but this rule has no effect in relation to the long-stop provided for in section 11A(3).[39] Similarly, rules on fraud, concealment and mistake,[40] which normally extend the limitation period indefinitely, have no application to the long-stop under section 11A(3).[41] However, it is important to emphasise that it is only the long-stop which remains unaffected by rules on disability, fraud, concealment and mistake. Thus it would appear to be possible to extend the three-year knowledge-based limitation period on these grounds.

It has also been seen that in the case of actions in respect of personal injuries, it is possible for the court, at its discretion, to extend the period during which the writ can be served, if justice so demands.[42] However, once more, this discretion is not to be applied so as to defeat the long-stop in section 11A(3).[43] Moreover, since the discretion is confined, generally, to personal injury actions, it is also provided that it should not be used in relation to a claim for damages for loss of or damage to property under the Consumer

37. See Ch 18.
38. Limitation Act 1980, s 28(1) and see Ch 6.
39. *Ibid*, s 28(7).
40. *Ibid*, s 32(1).
41. *Ibid*, s 32(4A).
42. *Ibid*, s 33 and see Ch 19.
43. *Ibid*, s 33(1A)(a).

Protection Act.[44] What these provisions do not provide, however, is that the court's discretion can never be applied in relation to the 1987 Act. Thus, provided the long-stop cut-off date has not been reached, the court may, at its discretion, extend the limitation period in respect of a personal injuries claim, if it appears right to do so. Thus, the three-year knowledge-based period can be extended, subject to the operation of the long-stop.

(e) Special rules on the liability of retail suppliers

It has been noted above that it is possible for a retail supplier, exceptionally, to be regarded as a producer for the purposes of the 1987 Act.[45] The circumstances in which this may happen are that:

1. A person suffers damage as a result of a defective product and cannot practicably identify the producer;
2. That person, within a reasonable time of suffering damage, requests from the retailer information regarding the identity of the producer or producers (whether they are in existence or not);
3. The retailer fails to supply the required information or identify the person from whom he acquired the product, within a reasonable time of receiving the request.

Assuming all of these elements are complied with, the retailer will become a substitute producer for the purposes of the 1987 Act, so that the consumer is not left without some form of redress. Since this is also an action under Part I of the 1987 Act, it must follow that the rules on limitation of actions in sections 11A and 14(1A) must also apply to the retailer. As has been observed above, the rules on limitation, applied to a retailer, could cause difficulties in relation to the 10-year long-stop rules, since the long-stop cut-off date may arrive at different times according to who is the defendant in a given case. The most likely cause of unfairness, because of the operation of the rules on long-stops, will arise in the case of goods with a long shelf-life where there has been a substantial passage of time between the date on which a product was last supplied by a person regarded as a producer under the Consumer Protection Act 1987, s 2(2). For example, suppose A abstracts a raw material in 1990 and in that year supplies it to B who uses it to produce an end product in 1991. B then supplies the product to C, a wholesaler, in 1991 and C supplies the product to D, a distributor, in 1993 and D supplies it in 1995 to another distributor, E, who subsequently supplies the product to F, a retailer, in 1996. If G, the consumer, buys the product in 1998 and uses it for two years before it explodes, causing injury in 2001, he may ask F to identify the producer or producers. If F is unable or unwilling to comply with this request, he becomes a defendant under section 2(3) of the 1987 Act, but the long-stop period will run from 1991, since that is the date on which the product was last supplied by a person named in section 2(2), in which case G's action

---

44. *Ibid*, s 33(1A)(b).
45. Consumer Protection Act 1987, s 2(3).

against F is barred under the Consumer Protection Act. However, there may still be a contractual action under the Sale of Goods Act 1979, since the limitation period in that case will run for six years from the date on which the defective goods were delivered in 1988.[46]

46. See Ch 8 and Ch 10.

CHAPTER 22

SPECIFIC TORTS

The general rule on limitation of actions in tort cases is set out in Chapter 18. It has been seen there that a distinction needs to be drawn between torts based on a single act resulting in damage to the plaintiff, torts actionable *per se* and torts which are continuing in nature, since in each case, the date on which the cause of action accrues may differ according to the circumstances of the case. Moreover, some specific torts require special consideration due to special rules which apply in a given case.

DECEIT

The tort of deceit, which is also relevant for the purposes of a common law action in respect of a fraudulent misrepresentation and an action by a principal against either his agent or the third party where a bribe has been paid to the agent by the third party, is covered by special provisions of the Limitation Act 1980, s 32(1)(a). This matter is covered in more detail elsewhere,[1] but since the tort of deceit involves an allegation that the defendant is guilty of fraud and since fraud is the basis of the action, the effect of section 32(1)(a) is that time will not start to run against the plaintiff until he is aware or could with reasonable diligence have become aware of the fraud on the part of the defendant.

CONVERSION

Conversion is an act, or complex series of acts, of wilful interference, without lawful justification, with any chattel in a manner inconsistent with the right of another, whereby that other is deprived of the use and possession of it.[2] Conversion now encompasses every act which would previously have been detinue.[3] As a cause of action, conversion is a tort and as such is governed by the Limitation Act 1980, s 2, so that the relevant limitation period is six years from the date on which the cause of action accrues to the plaintiff. Time will therefore begin to run from the date of the wrongful interference with the plaintiff's

---

1. See Ch 6.
2. Salmond and Heuston, *Law of Torts*, 21st ed (London: Sweet and Maxwell, 1996), at p 98, cited with approval in *Lewis Trusts* v. *Barbers Stores* [1983] FSR 453 at 459. See also, *Douglas Valley Finance Co Ltd* v. *Hughes (Hirers) Ltd* [1969] 1 QB 738.
3. Torts (Interference with Goods) Act 1977, s 2; *Howard E Perry & Co* v. *British Railways Board* [1980] 1 WLR 1375. Section 14(1) of the 1977 Act defines "goods" as including all chattels personal other than things in action or money.

goods.[4] Where, however, the plaintiff's goods have been wrongfully detained, time will begin to run from the date when the defendant refuses to deliver up the goods.[5] The effect of the time limit expiring before the plaintiff brings an action to recover possession of the chattel is that the plaintiff's title will be extinguished.[6]

(a) Successive conversions

Section 3(1) of the 1980 Act provides that the period of limitation for all causes of action in respect of conversion is six years from the first or original conversion or wrongful detention unless, of course, the owner has recovered possession in the meantime. Accordingly, if after the original conversion a subsequent wrongful act takes place with respect to the chattel, for example, a third party wrongfully detains it, a new cause of action does *not* accrue. Any action for the return of the chattel, or for damages, must therefore be brought within six years of the first conversion.[7] The effect of this rule is that a subsequent "converter" has the benefit of the time which has run in favour of the first wrongdoer.

(b) Theft

Section 4 of the 1980 Act abrogates the rules contained in section 3 where the conversion amounts to theft.[8] Section 4 was passed to implement the view of the Law Reform Committee's *Twenty-First Report*[9] which concluded that it was undesirable that a thief could acquire title to stolen goods by virtue of the provisions in section 3. The drafting of this provision is overly complex and obscure. In essence, section 4 provides that time does not run in favour of a thief, or any person claiming through him, other than a purchaser for value in good faith. Thus, a purchaser for value of stolen property will acquire valid title six years after his purchase, but the original owner will still be able to bring an action against the original thief, or any subsequent thief, for its value, even if the limitation period has elapsed. Consequently, a thief cannot plead the limitation period by way of defence. Where, after the original theft, the chattel is converted by a purchaser for value in good faith, the six-year limitation period begins to run from the date of the purchase.[10] By section 4(4), where in an action for conversion it is proved that the chattel was stolen from the plaintiff or anyone through whom he claims, it shall be presumed that any subsequent conversion is related to the theft unless the contrary is shown.

---

4. *Granger* v. *George* (1826) 5 B & C 149.

5. *Philpott* v. *Kelley* (1835) 3 Ad & El 106; *Miller* v. *Dell* [1891] 1 QB 468.

6. Limitation Act 1980, s 3(2). See also, s 17 of the 1980 Act (extinction of title to land after expiration of the time limit). Until the Limitation Act 1939, the rule that expiry of the limitation period only barred the remedy but not the right applied to conversion as to other torts, see *Spackman* v. *Foster* (1883) 11 QBD 99.

7. "Chattel" is not defined in the Limitation Act 1980, it must therefore be taken as carrying its ordinary English meaning.

8. The term "theft" is defined by s 4(5) of the 1980 Act as including any conduct outside England and Wales which would be theft if committed in England and Wales, and any obtaining of property by deception within s 15(1) of the Theft Act 1968 and any obtaining by blackmail within s 21 of that Act. See, *Dobson* v. *General Accident Fire and Life Assurance Corp* [1990] 1 QB 274, CA.

9. The Report concluded: "It does not seem to us right that a thief or receiver should, whether or not he has been prosecuted, be able to establish by limitation a valid title to the stolen goods . . . Although the situation which troubles us may not often arise in practice, we think it is wrong for the law to extend the protection of limitation to the thief or receiver at the expense of the true owner" (at paras 3.1–3.18 and 3.4–3.5).

10. Limitation Act 1980, s 4(2).

It is necessary to consider section 4 in the context of section 32(1)(a) and (b) which postpones the running of time where the action is based upon the fraud of the defendant or where the defendant has deliberately concealed a material fact relevant to the plaintiff's right of action. In *Eddis* v. *Chichester Constable*[11] the Court of Appeal held that where the facts of the case triggered section 32, title to the goods will not be extinguished, and the limitation period will not begin to run until the fraud or relevant material facts are, or could reasonably have been, discovered. From a practical perspective, this may be of little importance since in the majority of conversion claims no material fact will have been concealed from the plaintiff.[12]

BREACH OF STATUTORY DUTY

The main difficulty which arises in the context of a breach of statutory duty is whether the breach amounts to the commission of a tort or not. Generally, it is accepted that most breaches of statutory duty will constitute the commission of a tort,[13] in which case normal rules applicable to tort actions by virtue of the Limitation Act 1980, s 2 will apply.[14] Accordingly, assuming the action requires proof of damage, the cause of action will accrue when damage is caused. However, some statutes which also create an action in tort, such as the Consumer Protection Act 1987, Part I[15] have their own special rules on limitation of actions which displace the normal rules applied under section 2 of the 1980 Act. If the statute creates a right which did not previously exist at common law and does not amount to an enactment which merely adds to existing common law rights, it is possible that it may be construed as an enactment to which section 9 of the 1980 Act applies.[16] At one stage this produced the anomaly that a rather longer limitation period applied in such a case. However, following the enactment of section 9, the relevant limitation period is one of six years running from the date on which the cause of action accrued.

NUISANCE

The main feature of the tort of nuisance which sets it apart from most other torts is that it is a tort of a continuing nature,[17] in the sense that a nuisance continues to be committed while ever the state of affairs which constitutes the nuisance continues to exist. However, nuisance is also a tort which is dependent upon proof of damage, in which case, until damage is caused to the plaintiff, the cause of action will not accrue.[18] Because of the continuing nature of the tort, however, a fresh cause of action arises on a day-to-day basis until the nuisance ceases to interfere with the plaintiff's interests.[19]

---

11. [1969] 2 Ch 345.
12. See, for example, *RB Policies at Lloyd's* v. *Butler* [1950] 1 KB 76.
13. *Clarkson* v. *Modern Foundries Ltd* [1957] 1 WLR 1210.
14. See Ch 18.
15. See Ch 21.
16. See Ch 25.
17. As to which see the discussion in Ch 18.
18. Such damage may be inferred: *Fay* v. *Prentice* (1845) 1 CB 828.
19. *Darley Main Colliery* v. *Mitchell* (1866) 11 App Cas 127.

TRESPASS

Those torts falling under the banner of trespass bear the significant characteristic of being actionable *per se*, that is, without the need to prove damage. It has been seen already that the gist of a negligence action is that damage has been suffered by the plaintiff; however, in contrast, the gist of an action for trespass to the person is the unlawful interference with the plaintiff's civil liberties. Accordingly, by its very nature an assault requires no contact and therefore is unlikely to cause damage. Similarly, it is accepted that there may be a battery despite the fact that the plaintiff's skin is not broken or damaged in any way and there may be an act of false imprisonment even where the plaintiff is totally unaware that his liberty has been restricted in any way at all.

In these circumstances, since damage is irrelevant, time will run from the date of the wrongful act.[20] Unfortunately, one effect of this rule is that the discretionary power of the court to disapply the ordinary limitation period in personal injury cases does not apply to torts actionable *per se*, but merely to an action for negligence.[21]

DEFAMATION

Defamation has attracted significant criticism for its substantive and procedural complexity and has been subjected to increasing scrutiny and legislative reform over the years.[22] As a tort it is unique in that liability is extinguished by the death of either party[23]; trial by jury is available at the instance of either party[24]; and legal aid is not available to either party (although a plaintiff will be entitled to legal aid where he brings an action based on an alternative cause of action, such as malicious falsehood, provided the facts will support such a claim[25]). Further, most forms of libel fall into the limited category of torts which are actionable *per se*, and certain classes of slander do not require proof of special damage in that the plaintiff can recover damages for the injury to his reputation without proving

20. See also Chs 18 and 19.
21. See Ch 19.
22. See the *Report of the Committee on the Law of Defamation* (Cmd 7536, 1948) under the chairmanship of Lord Porter which led to the Defamation Act 1952; see also, the *Reports of the Faulks Committee on Defamation* (Cmnd 5909, 1975), and the *Supreme Court of Judicature Procedure Committee Report on Practice and Procedure in Defamation* (the Neill Committee) (London: Lord Chancellor's Dept, 1991). The Defamation Act 1996 is based partly on the recommendations of the Neill Committee.
23. Actions for malicious falsehood are capable of surviving the death of a party. It should be noted that a company, as an artificial person, can sue in defamation to protect its commercial reputation. See, *Metropolitan Saloon Omnibus Co* v. *Hawkins* (1859) 4 H & N 87; *South Hetton Coal Co Ltd* v. *North Eastern News Association Ltd* [1894] 1 QB 133.
24. Although it should be noted that the Defamation Act 1996, ss 8–10 provides a "fast track" procedure which enables the court to dispose summarily of those cases that are inordinately weak, and provide "summary relief" in those that are inordinately strong.
25. *Joyce* v. *Sengupta* [1993] 1 All ER 897, CA. In contrast to defamation, a malicious or injurious falsehood is a false statement which in no way relates to the plaintiff's reputation. The plaintiff must prove that the words are untrue, that the defendant was motivated by malice and that he suffered actual damage. Proof of actual damage is not a necessary component where the Defamation Act 1952, s 3(1) applies. Section 3(1) provides: "In an action for . . . malicious falsehood, it shall not be necessary to allege or prove special damage—(a) if the words upon which the action is founded are calculated to cause pecuniary damage to the plaintiff and are published in writing or other permanent form . . . ".

that it has in fact been harmed.[26] The law presumes that some damage will arise in the ordinary course of things. More generally, however, slander requires proof of special damage,[27] and time will begin to run from the date of the publication when damage is suffered. The fact that the plaintiff is unaware of the slander will not prevent time running against him.[28]

Unlike so-called continuing torts—e.g., nuisance—a fresh cause of action accrues to the plaintiff on every occasion the defamatory statement is published. Thus, where defamatory material is contained in a book, magazine, journal or newspaper there will be a series of publications, each of which gives rise to a new cause of action. There will be publication by the author to the publisher, for which the author will be solely liable; there will be publication by the author *and* publisher to the printer for which both the author and publisher will be jointly liable; there will publication by the author, publisher and printer jointly to the distributor and the public, and so on.[29]

The time limit for bringing an action for defamation has been subject to change in recent years. Although it is an action in tort, defamation is not governed by section 2 of the Limitation Act 1980. The Administration of Justice Act 1985, s 57 inserted section 4A into the 1980 Act, which reduced the limitation period to three years from the date of accrual of the cause of action.[30] This period was further reduced by the Defamation Act 1996, s 5(2) which inserts a new section 4A into the Limitation Act 1980.[31] The new limitation period for actions for defamation or malicious falsehood is now one year from the date on which the cause of action accrued.

(a) Discretionary extension of the limitation period for actions for libel and slander

For causes of action for defamation accruing before 4 September 1996, the provisions in the "old" section 32A of the 1980 Act apply.[32] This provision confers on the High Court the discretion to grant an extension to the time limit where the limitation period has expired. The plaintiff must show that all or any of the facts relevant to the action did not become known to him until after the expiration of the limitation period. If granted, the extension will be for one year from the earliest date on which he knew all the facts

26. There are four classes of slander which are actionable without proof of special damage: (1) imputation of a criminal offence punishable with imprisonment; (2) imputation of a contagious or infectious disease likely to prevent other persons from associating with the plaintiff; (3) imputation of unchastity, a statutory exception created by the Slander of Women Act 1891, s 1; (4) imputation of unfitness, incompetence or dishonesty in any office, profession, calling, trade or business held or carried on by the plaintiff at the time when the slander was published. See further, Rogers, *Winfield & Jolowicz on Tort* (London: Sweet & Maxwell, 1994), Ch 12.
27. See the Defamation Act 1952, ss 2 and 3.
28. However, see the Limitation Act 1980, s 32A, (discussed *infra*).
29. *Duke of Brunswick* v. *Harmer* (1849) 14 QBD 185. Note the defence of innocent dissemination available to "mechanical distributors" such as booksellers, newspaper distributors and librarians, who play a subordinate part in the dissemination. See, *Bottomley* v. *Woolworth & Co* (1932) 48 TLR 521; *Sun Life Assurance Co of Canada* v. *WH Smith & Son Ltd* (1934) 150 LT 211.
30. The limitation period was reduced from six to three years following the report of the Faulks Committee, *supra*, fn 22, which recognised the need for speedy vindication of the plaintiff's character together with the desirability of relieving defendants from the anxiety, expense and inconvenience of a defamation action hanging over them for an unnecessarily long period.
31. The Defamation Act 1996 received Royal Assent on 4 July 1996. Section 5 of the Act came into force on 4 September 1996.
32. Inserted by the Administration of Justice Act 1985, s 57(4).

relevant to the cause of action. It should be noted that the extension is not available where the plaintiff discovers a fact relevant to the action just prior to the expiration of the time bar. Accordingly, to be eligible for relief, the plaintiff must prove that he discovered the fact after the limitation period has expired. With effect from 4 September 1996 the wording of section 32A of the 1980 Act was replaced by a new provision contained in the Defamation Act 1996.

(b) Discretionary exclusion of time limit for actions for defamation or malicious falsehood

The Defamation Act 1996, s 5(4) replaces section 32A of the Limitation Act 1980, and confers on the court a wide discretion to *exclude* the relevant limitation period. The "new" provision states, *inter alia*:

"32A(1) If it appears to the court that it would be equitable to allow an action to proceed having regard to the degree to which—

    (a) the operation of section 4A of this Act prejudices the plaintiff or any person whom he represents, and

    (b) any decision of the court under this subsection would prejudice the defendant or any person whom he represents,

the court may direct that that section shall not apply to the action or shall not apply to any specified cause of action to which the action relates.

(2) In acting under this section the court shall have regard to all the circumstances of the case and in particular to—

    (a) the length of, and the reasons for, the delay on the part of the plaintiff;

    (b) where the reason or one of the reasons for the delay was that all or any of the facts relevant to the cause of action did not become known to the plaintiff until after the end of the period mentioned in section 4A—

        (i) the date on which any such facts did become known to him, and

        (ii) the extent to which he acted promptly and reasonably once he knew whether or not the facts in question might be capable of giving rise to an action; and

    (c) the extent to which, having regard to the delay, relevant evidence is likely—

        (i) to be unavailable, or

        (ii) to be less cogent than if the action had been brought within the period mentioned in section 4A . . . "

On its face, the scope of this provision is wider than the previous law given that it does not restrict the grounds for the exercise of the court's discretion to the situation where relevant facts were not known to the plaintiff until after the action had become time barred.[33]

The term "facts relevant to the cause of action" in section 32A of the 1980 Act[34] was considered by the Court of Appeal in *C* v. *Mirror Group Newspapers*.[35] Following the parents' divorce the mother, C, was granted custody of the two children. With the consent

---

33. It should be noted, however, that in construing the previous s 32A Henry LJ stated in *Oyston* v. *Blaker* [1996] 2 All ER 106 at 115 that the provision confers on the judge the discretion "to do what was just in all the circumstances. It is subject only to the court's overriding duty to exercise any discretionary power vested in it by an enactment in a manner consistent with the legislative purpose of the enactment."

34. This term is retained in the new provision, see s 32A of the 1980 Act *supra*, as amended by the Defamation Act 1996, s 5(4).

35. [1997] 1 WLR 131, CA.

of the court, she took them on holiday to Tenerife but did not return to the United Kingdom. Instead, she disappeared with the children to Australia. The father, on learning that they were in Australia, applied for a court order for their return. At the conclusion of the hearing in March 1988, the judge lifted reporting restrictions in order to enlist the support of the media in locating the children. The father spoke to the press and made serious and untrue defamatory statements about C, including an allegation that she was involved with a drugs gang. These allegations were published by the respondents in March 1988 without making it clear, as did the other newspapers which carried the story, that the words were spoken outside court rather than in the course of the court proceedings. In 1990, C was deported from Australia and returned to the United Kingdom. In August 1993, C received a letter from the judge stating that to the best of his recollection the father had not made the allegations in court. In March 1994, C brought an action against the newspapers claiming damages for libel and malicious falsehood. At the trial, the respondents successfully applied to have the writs struck out as being time barred. C appealed, and sought to rely on section 32A of the Limitation Act 1980 on the basis that the facts relevant to her cause of action did not become known to her until after the expiration of the three-year limitation period.[36]

It was held that the "relevant facts" are those which the plaintiff has to prove to establish a prima facie case for defamation and did not include facts relevant to rebutting a possible defence. C's contention that it was only upon receipt of the judge's letter in August 1993 that she realised that the allegation that she was involved in drugs smuggling had not been made in court, so that the newspaper report was not covered by privilege, was not a relevant fact for the purpose of section 32A. In construing the provision, Neill LJ applied the so-called "statement of claim test, that is knowledge of the facts which should be pleaded in the statement of claim".[37]

(c) Extension of limitation period in case of disability

Section 5(3) of the Defamation Act 1996 amends section 28(4A) of the Limitation Act 1980 to the extent that for those actions to which section 4A of the 1980 Act applies, an action for libel or slander may be brought by the plaintiff under a disability "at any time before the expiration of one year from the date on which he ceased to be under a disability". A person is under a disability if he is an infant or of unsound mind.[38]

---

36. See now, the one year-limitation period introduced by the Defamation Act 1996, *supra*, fn 31 and associated text.

37. *Supra*, fn 35 at 138–139, applying *Johnson* v. *Chief Constable of Surrey*, *The Times*, 22 November 1992.

38. Limitation Act 1980, s 38(2). An infant is a person under the age of 18: Family Law Reform Act 1969, s 1. A person is of unsound mind if by reason of mental disorder within the meaning of the Mental Health Act 1959, as amended by the Mental Health Act 1983, he is incapable of managing and administering his property and affairs: Limitation Act 1980, s 38(3). See further, Ch 6.

PART IV

EQUITY, TRUSTS, PERSONAL REPRESENTATIVES AND REAL PROPERTY

EQUITY, TRUSTS, PERSONAL REPRESENTATIVES, RESTITUTIONARY CLAIMS AND REAL PROPERTY

EQUITY AND TRUST PROPERTY

It was seen in Chapter 16 that where a plaintiff seeks specific performance of a contract, an injunction or other equitable relief, e.g. an accounting of profits (see below), section 36 of the 1980 Act disapplies the normal time limits laid down in the relevant statutory provisions.[1] However, it will be recalled that the running of time may nevertheless be relevant in such actions because the court may refuse the equitable relief claimed on the basis of the plaintiff's acquiescence or laches. With respect to actions for breach of trust, the relevant limitation periods are contained in section 21 of the Act.

(a) Indefinite liability of fraudulent trustees—section 21(1) of the Limitation Act 1980

In two situations relating to actions in respect of trust property there is no applicable period of limitation, so that perpetual liability attaches to the trustee in question and to any recipients of the trust property (other than a bona fide purchaser for value).[2] First, it is provided by section 21(1)(a) of the 1980 Act that an action by a beneficiary under a trust in respect of any fraud or fraudulent breach of trust to which the trustee was a party or privy is not subject to a period of limitation.

The necessary conditions for section 21(1)(a) to apply warrant consideration. In determining the meaning of "fraud" for the purposes of this provision the decisions relevant to section 32 of the Act[3] are instructive. The general principle applicable is that fraud must be "a necessary allegation in order to constitute the cause of action".[4] The term "breach of trust", the meaning of which has long been a contentious issue, was considered *obiter* by Megarry V-C in his wide ranging judgment in *Tito* v. *Waddell (No 2).*[5] Although he declined to be drawn into the "perilous task"[6] of attempting any comprehensive definition, the learned judge went on to state: "I doubt whether defining a breach of trust in

---

1. Section 2 (tort), s 5 (simple contract), s 7 (actions to enforce awards where the submission is not by an instrument under seal), s 8 (specialties), s 9 (actions to recover a sum recoverable by virtue of any enactment), and s 24 (actions to enforce a judgment).

2. See generally, *Barnes* v. *Addy* (1874) LR 9 Ch 244 and the decision of Danckwerts J in *GL Baker Ltd* v. *Medway Building and Supplies Ltd* [1958] 1 WLR 1216 at 1222.

3. Postponement of the limitation period in case of fraud, concealment or mistake, see Ch 6.

4. *Beaman* v. *ARTS* [1949] 1 KB 550 at 558, *per* Lord Greene MR. See further, *Tito* v. *Waddell (No 2)* [1977] Ch 106 at 245.

5. *Ibid.*

6. *Ibid* at 248.

terms of a breach of duty, however widely cast or narrowly confined, carries the matter much further: for at once the further question arises of what is meant by a breach of duty by a trustee as such."[7]

Notwithstanding this judicial hesitancy, breach of trust has been defined as: "[a]ny act or neglect on the part of a trustee which is not authorised or excused by the terms of the trust instrument or by law . . . ".[8] Further, the point was made by Lindley LJ in *Re Chapman*[9] that: "The conduct of trustees ought to be regarded with reference to the facts and circumstances existing at the time when they had to act and which were known or ought to have been known by them at the time."[10]

The phrase "party or privy" in section 21(1)(a) was considered in *Thorne v. Heard*,[11] in which a trustee had negligently left funds from the sale of trust property with a solicitor (Searle) who embezzled them. It was held that the solicitor, in retaining the proceeds of sale, had not acted as the agent of the trustee or with his approval, the trustee being unaware of the fraud. Thus, mere negligence is not sufficient to render a trustee a "party or privy" to a fraudulent act. Kay LJ stated that:

"It has been argued that [the defendants] were party or privy to Searle's fraud. Even if it could be said that they were liable for his fraud, it is another thing to say that they were party or privy to it. I think that those words in the statute indicate moral complicity, which is not suggested in this case."[12]

Section 21(1)(b) of the 1980 Act provides that no limitation period is applicable to an action to recover from the trustee trust property or the proceeds of trust property in the possession of the trustee, or previously received by the trustee and converted to his use. The term "previously received by the trustee and converted to his use" was considered by the court in *Re Howlett*,[13] where the defendant trustee argued that it was restricted to the actual receipt of property, and since he had not received anything during his occupation of the land in question, the section did not apply. However, Danckwerts J held that it extended to a notional receipt, so that the defendant trustee who had in fact occupied the trust property for 20 years was deemed to have received rents and profits, and was therefore charged with an occupation rent. To fall within the scope of this provision a trustee's retention or conversion of trust property must be for his personal use; mere receipt of such property without more, is insufficient.[14]

Claims brought under section 21(1) may, of course, be defeated by acquiescence or laches.[15] Additionally, it should be noted that the Trustee Act 1925, s 61 confers discretion on the court to grant relief to a trustee where, in any action for breach of trust, the trustee has acted honestly and reasonably, and "ought fairly to be excused for the breach and for omitting to obtain directions from the court".[16] Further, by way of exception to section 21(1)(b), it is provided that where a trustee who is also a beneficiary under the trust

---

7. *Ibid.*

8. Underhill & Hayton, *The Law of Trusts and Trustees*, 15th ed (London: Butterworths, 1995) at p 1.

9. [1986] 2 Ch 763. See also, *Target Holdings Ltd* v. *Redferns* [1995] 3 WLR 352.

10. *Ibid* at 774.

11. [1894] 1 Ch 599, CA. See also, *Petre* v. *Petre* (1853) 1 Drew 371; *Re Fountaine* [1909] 2 Ch 382.

12. *Ibid* at 608.

13. [1949] Ch 767. See also, *Re Sharp* [1906] 1 Ch 793; *Wassell* v. *Leggatt* [1896] 1 Ch 554.

14. *Re Gurney* [1893] 1 Ch 590; *Re Page* [1893] 1 Ch 304; *How* v. *Earl Winterton* [1896] 2 Ch 626; *Re Fountaine, supra*, fn 11; *Re Tufnell* (1902) 18 TLR 705.

15. See Ch 3, *supra*.

16. See generally, *Re Windsor Steam Coal Co* [1929] 1 Ch 151.

honestly and reasonably distributes trust property amongst the beneficiaries he believes to be entitled, including himself, his liability in an action brought more than six years after the distribution is limited to the excess of the amount received by the trustee over his proper share.[17] For example, if a trustee of a fixed trust is aware of five beneficiaries, including himself, and, acting honestly and reasonably, distributes the fund to them, each will receive a one-fifth share. If another beneficiary then claims after the six-year limitation period laid down by section 21(3),[18] the trustee's liability is limited to the difference between one-fifth of the fund which was mistakenly received and one-sixth which should have been received i.e. one-thirtieth.

(b) Six-year time limit for other actions brought by a beneficiary

Section 21(3) of the Act prescribes a limitation period of six years in respect of other actions by a beneficiary to recover trust property, and in respect of fraud or fraudulent breach of trust, other than actions within section 21(1) or (2) or within any other provision of the Act. Thus, where a trustee has parted with trust property negligently or innocently, the limitation period will apply. However, the recipient of the trust property will be subject to indefinite liability unless he is a bona fide purchaser for value without notice.[19] Section 21(3) will apply where trust funds have been dissipated by a co-trustee,[20] but an action by the Attorney-General to enforce a charitable trust is outside the provision because there is no relevant beneficiary.[21] In *Tito v. Waddell (No 2)*[22] Megarry V-C expressed the view that an action by a beneficiary against a trustee (or other fiduciary) who purchases the beneficiary's interest is not an action "to recover trust property" nor is it a breach of trust.[23] Such actions fall within the general disability of fiduciaries to engage in self-dealing.

For actions falling within this provision the limitation period starts to run from the date on which the right of action accrued. It has been held that a beneficiary's cause of action accrues as soon as the breach of trust has been committed and not, necessarily, when the beneficiary suffers loss.[24]

(c) Reversionary interests

Section 21(3) goes on to provide that the right of action shall not be treated as having accrued to any beneficiary entitled to a future interest in the trust property until the interest falls into possession. In *Re Paulings Settlement Trusts; Younghusband v. Coutts & Co*[25] it was held that an invalid advance of capital did not cause the interest to fall into possession.

17. Limitation Act 1980, s 21(2). Cf a Benjamin order (*Re Benjamin* [1902] 1 Ch 723), giving the trustee liberty to distribute on the basis that a particular person is dead.
18. *Infra.*
19. See fn 2, *supra.*
20. *Re Tufnell, supra,* fn 14.
21. *Att-Gen* v. *Cocke* [1988] Ch 414.
22. [1977] Ch 106.
23. *Ibid* at 247. The point was made, however, that the issue would fall within the doctrine of laches. In this regard, the learned judge said, at 250, that: "I consider the matter to be one that falls within the equitable doctrine of laches, by which I mean pure laches and not any branch of laches which consists of applying a statute by analogy.".
24. *Thorne* v. *Heard* [1895] AC 495; *Re Swain* [1891] 3 Ch 233.
25. [1964] Ch 303.

Section 21(4) provides further protection to a trustee where one beneficiary's action is barred due to lapse of time but an action vested in another beneficiary is not. The section precludes the time-barred beneficiary from gaining any incidental benefit from the later action. Thus, as has been seen, section 21(3) will postpone the accrual of a right of action vested in a remainderman until his interest falls into possession. Consequently, if the life tenant's action is barred he cannot benefit from the remainderman's action. In this situation, the trustees will be entitled to the income of the property.[26]

(d) Who is a trustee for the purposes of section 21?

Section 38(1) of the 1980 Act provides that the term "trustee" carries the same meaning as provided in section 68(17) of the Trustee Act 1925 and therefore includes express trustees, personal representatives,[27] and trustees holding property on express, implied, resulting or constructive trusts. The term also extends to cases where the trustee has a beneficial interest in the trust property. Accordingly, a trustee may include certain fiduciary agents including a solicitor who receives money for investment or manages his client's affairs,[28] a mortgagee in respect of the proceeds of sale,[29] company directors,[30] and a company auditor entrusted with money by the company.[31] The term does not cover a trustee in bankruptcy,[32] nor a liquidator of a company in voluntary liquidation.[33]

Actions for breach of fiduciary duty *simpliciter* are not within the 1980 Act and therefore are not subject to a limitation period.[34] However, where a breach of fiduciary duty results in the imposition of a constructive trust, section 21 applies to determine the relevant limitation period.[35] Further, whether the case relates to a constructive or an express trust, the 1980 Act cannot be avoided by treating the claim as one of breach of fiduciary duty.[36] It has been said that:

"The fallacy . . . is to treat breach of fiduciary duty and breach of trust as different causes of action. In a case where, because of the existence of a fiduciary duty, a constructive trust comes into existence, breach of trust and breach of fiduciary duty are the same cause of action. Similarly, where an express trust has been created, breach of that trust and breach of fiduciary duty are also the same cause of action. It is therefore not possible to sidestep the limitation provisions of s.21(3) by referring to the action as one for breach of fiduciary duty."[37]

---

26. *Re Somerset* [1894] 1 Ch 231; *Mara* v. *Browne* [1895] 2 Ch 69. See also, the decision of Jacob J in *Armitage* v. *Nourse*, unreported, 17 July 1995 (discretionary trust), the basis of which is questioned by Professor Hayton in Hayton & Marshall, *Commentary and Cases on the Law of Trusts and Equitable Remedies*, 10th ed (London: Sweet & Maxwell, 1996) at p 817.

27. Subject to the 12-year limitation period applicable to actions claiming the personal estate of a deceased person laid down by s 22 of the Limitation Act 1980.

28. *Burdick* v. *Garrick* (1870) LR 5 Ch App 233; *Soar* v. *Ashwell* (1893) 2 QB 390.

29. *Thorne* v. *Heard*, supra, fn 24.

30. *Re Lands Allotment Co* [1894] 1 Ch 616; *Whitwam* v. *Watkin* (1898) 78 LT 188; *Tintin Exploration Syndicate Ltd* v. *Sandys* (1947) 177 LT 412; *Selangor United Rubber Estates* v. *Cradock (No 3)* [1968] 1 WLR 1555; *Belmont Finance Corporation* v. *Williams Furniture Ltd (No 2)* [1980] 1 All ER 393.

31. *GL Baker Ltd* v. *Medway Building & Supplies Ltd* [1958] 1 WLR 1216.

32. *Re Cornish* [1896] 1 QB 99.

33. *Re Windsor Steam Coal Co Ltd* [1928] Ch 609.

34. *Att-Gen* v. *Cocke*, supra, fn 21.

35. See *Nelson* v. *Rye* [1996] 2 All ER 186 at 198 (*per* Laddie J).

36. *Ibid.*

37. *Ibid.*

ACTIONS FOR AN ACCOUNT

Traditionally, an action for an account of profits could be brought either at law or in equity. However, the equitable remedy, which was more frequently used by litigants than its common law counterpart since it was procedurally less complex,[38] was not subject to a time limit *per se*.[39] By the late eighteenth century the received wisdom was that the equitable claim had superseded the common law action.[40] Thus, in *AG* v. *Dublin Corp*[41] Lord Redesdale stated that:

"The writ of account at common law did not exclude, but rather was superseded by the jurisdiction of the courts of equity on this subject; because the proceeding in equity was found to be the more convenient mode of calling parties to account—partly on account of the difficulty attending the process under the old count of account, but chiefly from the advantage of compelling the party to account upon oath, according to the practice of the courts of Equity."[42]

Further, the equitable action was wider in scope than the common law claim and was invoked where the action arose from a breach of fiduciary duty. Yet, prior to the Limitation Act 1980, an action at law for an account was subject to a six-year time period.[43] It therefore appeared that divergent rules applied to the two forms of action. This apparent dichotomy has not escaped judicial criticism. In *Tito* v. *Waddell (No 2)*,[44] Megarry V-C remarked that the "law of limitation in relation to actions for an account seems to be in a curious state".[45] Rationalisation has been achieved by section 23 of the 1980 Act which provides that an action for an account cannot be brought after the expiration of the time limit which is applicable to the claim which is the basis of the duty to account. In consequence, the time limit is made dependent upon the particular cause of action brought by the plaintiff. However, this solution has also attracted criticism. In *Att-Gen* v. *Cocke*[46] Harman J stressed that the duty to account arises out of a fiduciary relationship and not any particular breach of duty, so that the claim frequently has no applicable time limit. The symbiotic interrelationship between section 23 with a particular cause of action was explained by Laddie J in *Nelson* v. *Rye*.[47] He said:

"In my view s.23 of the 1980 Act simply confirms that the limitation period which applies to a particular cause of action applies equally to the relief by way of account which flows from it. For example, in this case certain claims for copyright infringement arise. Section 96(2) of the Copyright Designs and Patents Act 1988 entitles a copyright owner to seek relief by way of an account where

---

38. The common law action of account generally involved three stages: (i) a trial to determine whether the defendant was in fact an accounting party; (ii) an examination before court-appointed auditors to take an account and to determine the sum (if any) owing to the plaintiff; (iii) an action (in debt) by the plaintiff claiming the amount so determined. The procedure at each stage was cumbersome and technical, a *monstrum horrendum*; see Fifoot, *History and Sources of the Common Law* (London: Stevens & Sons, 1949), Ch 12.

39. Traditionally, equitable claims have not been caught by the limitation statutes. However, s 36(1) of the Limitation Act 1980 expressly recognises the power of the court to apply the common law limitation periods to equitable claims "by analogy", see Ch 3, *supra*.

40. *Ex parte Bax* (1751) 2 Ves Sen 388.

41. (1827) 4 ER 888.

42. *Ibid* at 898. See also, *Sturton* v. *Richardson* (1844) 13 M & W 17 at 20 in which Alderson B stated that the common law action was "so inconvenient, that it had been long discontinued, and parties have gone into a court of equity in preference".

43. See the Limitation Act 1939, s 2(2).

44. *Supra*, fn 4, at 250–52.

45. *Ibid* at 250.

46. *Supra*, fn 21, at 420.

47. *Supra*, fn 35. The facts are considered in Ch 3. The defence of laches succeeded.

infringement is proved. The effect of s.23 of the 1980 Act is that the limitation period for the account is the same as that for the claim for infringement. I do not accept that s.21 has the effect of circumventing and rendering nugatory the provisions of s.23. The former is concerned with whether or not there is a limitation period for actions for breach of trust, whereas the latter is only concerned with the limitation period to be applied to a form of relief which may be ordered in favour of a successful plaintiff."[48]

ACTIONS CLAIMING THE PERSONAL ESTATE OF A DECEASED PERSON

Section 22 of the 1980 Act lays down two different limitation periods in respect of actions by beneficiaries against the estates of deceased persons. First, section 22(a) imposes a 12-year limitation period for an action claiming the personal estate[49] of a deceased person or any share in such estate, whether under a will or intestacy. Time runs from the date on which the right to receive the share or interest accrued, which is generally the date of death.[50] Where the share or interest is to be paid out of a reversionary fund, time will not begin to run until the reversion falls in.[51] In *Re Diplock*[52] the Court of Appeal took the view that the wording of section 22 (formerly section 20 of the Limitation Act 1939) inevitably led to the conclusion that it "must apply to claims by an unpaid beneficiary against the executor or administrator—in other words to claims by a beneficiary 'to recover' his legacy or share".[53]

Secondly, section 22(b) lays down a six-year limitation period for actions to recover arrears of interest in respect of any legacy or damages in respect of such arrears. Time runs from the date on which the interest becomes due.

It should be noted that section 22 is expressly made subject to section 21(1) and (2). It is therefore critical to determine whether the action is brought against the personal representative *qua* personal representative or in his capacity as trustee,[54] for in the latter case the relevant provisions of section 21 will apply. Accordingly, time does not run against a personal representative in actions to recover trust property in his possession or previously converted to his use, or where the personal representative has acted fraudulently in relation to the estate. Whether sections 21(3) and 22 are mutually exclusive is unclear. A personal representative who assents to the vesting of assets in himself as trustee, which would, prima facie, have the effect of bringing any action against him subject to the six-

---

48. *Ibid* at 197.

49. Section 38(1) of the Act states that "personal estate" does not include chattels real. Where the action is for the recovery of land, s 15 applies which imposes a 12-year limitation period. In this case Sch 1, para 2 of the Act provides that for any claim to recover the land of a deceased person, the right of action shall be treated as having accrued on the date of his death. This is subject to two conditions namely: (a) that the deceased person was on the date of his death in possession of the land or, in the case of a rentcharge created by will or taking effect upon his death, in possession of the land charged; and (b) that the deceased was the last person entitled to the land to be in possession of it.

50. *Hornsey Local Board* v. *Monarch Investment Building Society* (1889) 24 QBD 1. The so-called "Executor's Year" (Administration of Estates Act 1925, s 44), during which the personal representative is not bound to distribute the deceased's estate, does not operate to postpone the running of time. Further, in *Prior* v. *Horniblow* (1836) 2 Y & C Ex 200, it was held that where there are no funds at the time of death, the running of time is postponed until the personal representative has the funds to meet the claim.

51. *Earle* v. *Bellingham (No 2)* (1857) 24 Beav 448; *Re Ludlum* (1891) 63 LT 330.

52. [1948] Ch 465.

53. *Ibid* at 512. See also, *Ministry of Health* v. *Simpson* [1951] AC 251 at 276–77, in which the House of Lords approved the approach taken by the Court of Appeal towards the construction of this provision.

54. *Re Oliver* [1927] 2 Ch 323. See also, fn 27, *supra*, and associated text.

year limitation period contained in section 21(3), will nevertheless be caught by perpetual liability if this was done as part of some fraudulent design. However, where a personal representative becomes a trustee by completing administration, it would appear that the 12-year limitation period in section 22 will continue to apply.

Actions by creditors of the deceased

Debts of a deceased do not die with the deceased.[55] Consequently, it is the duty of a personal representative to settle all debts of the estate with "due diligence having regard to the assets in their hands which are properly applicable for that purpose".[56] Where, in breach of duty, a personal representative distributes the estate to the beneficiaries without first satisfying the claims of creditors, the breach is termed *devastavit*. In this case, an unsatisfied creditor has a cause of action against the personal representative personally. The limitation period applicable to such an action is six years, and time starts to run from the date of the breach, i.e. the date of the wrongful distribution.[57] There has been some debate surrounding the nature of *devastavit*, the issue being whether the creditor's cause of action is founded in contract or in tort.[58] This question was considered by Chitty J in *Re Hyatt*,[59] who concluded that the claim is tortious:

"If it is necessary that the demand against the executor should be framed on the principle of *devastavit*, or if the creditor going out of his way chooses to sue him in that form, there is no question that he can plead the Statute of Limitations against the *devastavit* so charged . . . The creditor in such a case elects to treat the executor as his own debtor. If the plaintiff chooses to say, it is not the estate of the debtor that is liable, but it is you, the executor who are personally liable, the executor being then charged with his own personal wrongdoing or tort is entitled to avail himself of the benefit of the Statute of Limitations."[60]

If, however, the debtor charges his estate to secure payment of the debt, section 20 will govern the creditor's action to enforce the charge. Section 20(1) provides that no action shall be brought to recover: (a) any principal sum of money secured by a mortgage or other charge on property; or (b) any proceeds of the sale of land, after the expiration of 12 years from the date on which the right to receive the money accrued. Where the deceased debtor created a trust of funds from which debts were to be paid, section 21 (see above) will govern a creditor's action.[61] A general direction to pay debts is not sufficient to create a trust, although it may create a charge.[62]

LIMITATION PERIODS RELATING TO LAND

The subject of limitations with respect to real property is complicated by the various interests which a party may have in land. This section will therefore examine limitation

55. Law Reform (Miscellaneous Provisions) Act 1934, s 1; Proceedings Against Estates Act 1970, s 1.

56. *Re Tankard* [1942] Ch 69 at 72 (*per* Uthwatt J).

57. *Re Gale* (1883) 22 Ch D 820; *Lacons* v. *Warmoth* [1907] 2 KB 350. A creditor is not a beneficiary for the purposes of s 21 of the 1980 Act: *Re Blow* [1914] 1 Ch 233.

58. See Morgan, *Current Law Statutes Annotated*, 1980, Vol 2.

59. (1883) 38 Ch D 609.

60. *Ibid* at 616. This passage was cited with approval in *Lacons* v. *Warmoth*, *supra*, fn 57. See also, *Westminster Corp* v. *Haste* [1950] Ch 442.

61. *Re Oliver* [1927] 2 Ch 323.

62. *Re Balls Estate* [1909] 1 Ch 791; *Re Raggi* [1913] 2 Ch 206.

periods in actions to recover land, actions to redeem land and actions to recover money secured by a mortgage or charge. For present purposes, "land" includes freeholds, leases, tithes, rentcharges,[63] legal and equitable estates as well as an interest in the proceeds of sale of land held upon trust for sale.[64] A significant and distinguishing feature of limitations in this context is the rule contained in section 17 of the 1980 Act that expiration of the relevant limitation period results in the plaintiff's title to the land, as distinguished from the remedy sought, being extinguished.[65] The effect of this rule, therefore, is to bar the right that the person entitled to possession would otherwise enjoy.

(a) Time limit for actions to recover land

Section 15(1) of the 1980 Act provides that no action shall be brought by any person to recover any land after the expiration of 12 years from the date on which the right of action accrued to him. Section 15(7) refers to provisions contained in Part II of Schedule 1 which modify the limitation period in respect of actions brought by the Crown or any spiritual or eleemosynary corporation sole. The relevant limitation period for the Crown in actions to recover land is 30 years and in actions to recover foreshore,[66] it is 60 years.[67] References in the Limitation Act 1980 to a right of action to recover land include references to a right to enter into possession of the land or, in the case of rentcharges and tithes, to distrain for arrears of rent or tithe, and references to the bringing of such an action shall include references to the making of such an entry or distress.[68] Accordingly, in extinguishing the owner's title, any claim to recover rent arrears or to enter into possession is similarly extinguished.[69]

(b) Actions to recover future interests in land

Schedule 1 paragraph 4 of the 1980 Act[70] preserves the notion that in the case of an owner of a future interest in land, the limitation period does not start to run until the interest falls into possession by the determination of the preceding estate or interest. Further, although

---

63. "Rentcharge" means "any annuity or periodical sum of money charged upon or payable out of land, except a rent service or interest on a mortgage on land": Limitation Act 1980, s 38(1). Rentcharges are rare, and since the Rentcharges Act 1977 they can only be created in limited circumstances.

64. Section 38(1). This definition is now repealed by the Trusts of Land and Appointment of Trustees Act 1996, Sch 4, which came into force on 1 January 1997, see *infra*.

65. Discussed *infra*. See also, s 15(5) of the 1980 Act. Thus, the paper owner's title to the land is extinguished. See *Mulcahy* v. *Curramore Pty Ltd* [1974] 2 NSWLR 464. See further, *Mount Carmel Investments Ltd* v. *Peter Thurlow Ltd* [1988] 1 WLR 1078 at 1089: "When title to land is extinguished by the statute, the rights which that title carried must also be extinguished" (*per* Nicholls LJ). The policy underlying the Act would appear to be that "those who go to sleep upon their claims should not be assisted by the courts in recovering their property", *RB Policies at Lloyd's* v. *Butler* [1950] 1 KB 76 at 81.

66. See Ch 4.

67. Limitation Act, 1980, Sch 1, paras 10, 11.

68. Section 38(7).

69. See further, *Re Jolly* [1900] 2 Ch 616; *Mulcahy* v. *Curramore Pty Ltd*, *supra*, fn 65, at 476. In *Mount Carmel Investments Ltd* v. *Peter Thurlow Ltd supra*, fn 65, Nicholls LJ (delivering the judgment of the court), said at 1089: "If . . . extinguishment of title to land extinguishes also the right to claim rent which was payable in respect of land during the period of adverse possession, so also must it extinguish any claim to damages in respect of the land during that period . . . When title to land is extinguished by the statute, the rights which that title carried must also be extinguished."

70. This re-enacts the Limitation Act 1939, s 6.

life estates and estates in reversion or remainder are equitable interests,[71] they are nonetheless treated as legal estates for the purposes of the Act.[72] Section 15(2) provides for the limitation period in respect of future interests in land. In essence, it states that no action shall be brought by the person entitled to the succeeding estate or interest after the expiration of 12 years from the date on which the right of action accrued to the person entitled to the preceding estate or interest, or alternatively, six years from the date on which the right of action accrued to the person entitled to the succeeding estate or interest—whichever period last expires. Section 15(3) adds the following proviso namely, that section 15(2) does not apply to any estate or interest which falls into possession on the determination of an entailed interest, and which might have been barred by the person entitled to the entailed interest. Thus, a remainderman is treated as claiming through the tenant in tail in possession and both become time barred at the same time.[73] It should be noted that entailed interests are abolished by the Trusts of Land and Appointment of Trustees Act 1996, Sch 1, para 3, which provides that the creation of an entailed interest after the commencement of the Act (1 January 1997) now operates as a declaration of an absolute interest.

(c) Accrual of the right of action

Adverse possession

Before a right of action can be said to accrue, so that the period of limitation governing an action starts to run, it is provided that the particular land must be "in the possession of some person in whose favour the period of limitation can run".[74] The pertinent concept of "possession" in this context is "adverse possession". Therefore, the accrual of the right of action occurs on the date of the owner's *dispossession* by an adverse possessor,[75] or from the date on which a third party took adverse possession following *discontinuance* of possession by the owner.[76] Thus, in *Buckinghamshire County Council* v. *Moran*[77] Nourse LJ said that:

"In order that title to land may be acquired by limitation, (1) the true owner must either (a) have been dispossessed, or (b) have discontinued his possession, of the land; and (2) the squatter must have been in adverse possession of it for the statutory period before action brought . . . [dispossession is] where the squatter comes in and drives out the true owner from possession [while discontinuance occurs where] the true owner goes out of possession and is followed in by the squatter."[78]

71. Law of Property Act 1925, s 1.
72. Limitation Act 1980, s 18(1).
73. *Ibid*, s 15(1) and s 38(5).
74. Limitation Act 1980, Sch 1, para 8(1). To claim adverse possession, the possessor must be legally competent to hold title. See *Afton Band of Indians* v. *Att-Gen of Nova Scotia* (1978) 85 DLR (3d) 454.
75. Limitation Act 1980, Sch 1, para 1. In *Rains* v. *Buxton* (1880) 14 Ch D 537, Fry LJ held that in the absence of fraud, time begins to run from the date of the dispossession, not from the discovery of the dispossession. See also, *Wilson* v. *Martin* [1993] 24 EG 119.
76. Limitation Act 1980, Sch 1, para 1. See also, the Limitation Act 1980, Sch 1, para 8(1). It is irrelevant for the purposes of the Limitation Act, in the absence of fraud, that the paper owner is ignorant that he has been dispossessed, see *Wilson* v. *Martin's Executors* [1993] 1 EGLR 178.
77. [1990] 1 Ch 623.
78. *Ibid* at 644. See also, *Rains* v. *Buxton, supra*, fn 75; *Treloar* v. *Nute* [1976] 1 WLR 1295. In *McPhail* v. *Persons (Names Unknown)* [1973] Ch 447 at 456, Lord Denning MR defined a "squatter" as "one who, without any colour of right, enters on an unoccupied house or land, intending to stay there as long as he can".

He went on to add that the distinction between dispossession and discontinuance is a very fine one, "there being no practical distinction between what is necessary to exclude all the world in a case where the true owner has retained possession and in one where he has discontinued it".[79]

Dispossession can be seen in *Marshall* v. *Taylor*,[80] where the plaintiff and defendant were the owners of adjacent houses. The two houses were separated by a ditch, and on the plaintiff's side of the ditch, by a hedge. In 1868 the owner of the plaintiff's house laid drainpipes along the ditch into which he allowed the drainage of both his own and the defendant's house to run. At this time the plaintiff covered over the ditch, and the defendant incorporated it into his own garden by paving part of it and planting roses on another part. The plaintiff continued to cut his hedge from the defendant's side, and on two occasions opened up the ditch to clear the drainpipes. It was held that the acts of the defendant prevented the plaintiff using the land in any foreseeable way and were sufficient to dispossess him. In reaching his conclusion, Lord Halsbury stressed that the strip of land in question was enclosed, and the plaintiff could not gain access to it in any ordinary way. Lindley LJ, concurring, observed that taking all the circumstances into consideration, it was clear that the defendant had been in possession to the exclusion of the plaintiff, and all that the plaintiff had done was to clip the hedge.

Possession is a question of fact depending upon the circumstances of the particular case.[81] In *Lord Advocate* v. *Lord Lovat*[82] Lord O'Hagan said that possession

"must be considered in every case with reference to the peculiar circumstances. . . . The character and value of the property, the suitable and natural mode of using it, the course of conduct which the proprietor might reasonably be expected to follow with a due regard to his own interests—all these things, . . . are to be taken into account in determining the sufficiency of a possession."[83]

Subject to a number of statutory exceptions relating to certain tenancies, the general rule is that a person in possession of land with the permission of the owner, for example by virtue of a lease or licence, cannot be in adverse possession. In *Hughes* v. *Griffin*[84] the plaintiff brought an action against the defendant claiming possession of a bungalow. The defendant had married the plaintiff's uncle and lived with him in the bungalow of which he was the freehold owner. Although she had been told that the property would be hers on his death, her husband conveyed it to his nephew without informing her. After the conveyance, the plaintiff permitted his uncle to stay in the property. When the uncle died, the defendant refused to deliver up possession of the bungalow, claiming adverse possession through her late husband so that she was a person in whose favour the limitation period could run. In the alternative, she claimed a life tenancy by virtue of the will of her husband, on the basis of his possession. It was held that the continued occupation by her late husband was by mere licence of the nephew given from time to time and there was no intention on his part to create a tenancy at will. Since the husband's possession derived

79. [1990] 1 Ch 623 at 644–45. For a curious example of discontinuance, see *London Borough of Hounslow* v. *Minchinton* (1997) 74 P & CR 221, CA.

80. [1895] 1 Ch 641.

81. *Bligh* v. *Martin* [1968] 1 WLR 804 at 811 *per* Pennycuick J.

82. (1880) 5 App Cas 273. In *Wallis's Cayton Bay Holiday Camp Ltd* v. *Shell-Mex and BP Ltd* [1975] QB 94, Ormrod LJ remarked at 114 that "to the relatively untutored eye, it has all the appearances of a difficult question of law".

83. *Ibid* at 288. This passage was cited with approval by Lord Macnaghten in *Johnson* v. *O'Neill* [1911] AC 552 at 583 and by Lord Shaw of Dunfermline in *Kirby* v. *Cowderoy* [1912] AC 599 at 603.

84. [1969] 1 WLR 23.

from a lawful title (the licence), he was never in adverse possession of the property within the meaning of the Limitation Act. Harman LJ stated that:

"Nevertheless it does seem to me that 'adverse possession' means to some extent at least that which it says. Time cannot run, as I see it, in favour of a licensee and therefore he has no possession. It can run in favour of a tenant at will, because . . . a tenancy at will is put an end to at the end of the year and the tenant is deemed to be in adverse possession at the end of that time, so that in 13 years he acquires title to the land in question."[85]

In order to defeat a title by dispossessing the former owner, acts must be done which are inconsistent with his or her enjoyment of the soil for the purposes for which he or she intended to use it.[86] Mere non-user does not, in itself, amount to discontinuance of possession.[87] The point was made by Pennycuick J in *Bligh* v. *Martin*[88] that: "In very many cases possession cannot, in the nature of things, be continuous from day to day, and it is well established that possession may continue to subsist notwithstanding that there are intervals, and sometimes long intervals, between the acts of user."[89]

For example, in *Leigh* v. *Jack*[90] land which was lying unused and uncultivated was not adversely possessed by the defendant who had blocked the land to vehicles, it being the intention of the owner to devote it at some time in the future to public use as a road. Although the trespass was massive, it in no way prejudiced the purposes which the paper owner had in mind for the land.[91] In this respect it has been said that "the interests of justice are not served by encouraging litigation to restrain harmless activities, merely to preserve legal rights, the enjoyment of which is, for good reason, being deferred".[92] However, there is no rule of law that an owner with no present use for the land could not lose title to a squatter. Indeed, it is arguable that the approach of the courts has shifted in favour of the adverse possessor. The leading case is *Buckinghamshire County Council* v. *Moran*.[93] The plaintiff council acquired a plot of land on 20 October 1951 intending to develop it at some time in the future for a proposed road diversion. The council erected a fence, with a gate, along the boundary of the land which abutted a road, but nothing separated the plot from the defendant's property. The defendant's predecessors in title had treated it as part of their garden by mowing the grass, trimming the hedges and using it for their own purposes. The council stopped maintaining the plot, but occasionally sent an employee to carry out inspection visits which were generally conducted from a car window. In 1971 the defendant acquired the house knowing of the council's title to the

---

85. *Ibid* at 30. See also, *Moses* v. *Lovegrove* [1952] 2 QB 533, *per* Lord Evershed MR at 538 and Romer LJ at 544.

86. *Leigh* v. *Jack* (1879) 5 Ex D 264 at 273 *per* Bramwell LJ.

87. *Littledale* v. *Liverpool College* [1900] 1 Ch 19. Cf *London Borough of Hounslow* v. *Minchinton*, *supra*, fn 79.

88. *Supra*, fn 81.

89. *Ibid* at 811.

90. *Supra*, fn 86. See also, *Williams Brothers Direct Supply Ltd* v. *Raftery* [1958] 1 QB 159 in which the land in question was waiting to be developed at an opportune time in the future. Sellers LJ said, at 173: "The paper owners can, in the circumstances, make no immediate use of the land, and as the years go by I cannot accept that they would lose their rights as owners merely by reason of trivial acts of trespass or user which in no way would interfere with a contemplated subsequent user." Although the trespass in question amounted to a virtual occupation of the land, it in no way affected the owners' practical, as distinct from their legal, interests in the property. See further, *West Bank Estates Ltd* v. *Arthur* [1967] 1 AC 665.

91. As explained by Ormrod LJ in *Wallis's Holiday Camp* v. *Shell-Mex*, *supra*, fn 82, at 115.

92. *Ibid* at 116.

93. [1990] 1 Ch 623. See also *London Borough of Hounslow* v. *Minchinton*, *supra*, fn 79.

land and of their intention to build a road on it; he was also aware that his vendors were in the course of acquiring a possessory title to the plot. He placed a new lock and chain on the gate, for which he kept the key, and continued to cultivate the plot. The plaintiff council contended that the decision in *Leigh* v. *Jack* prevented a possessory title arising. However, the Court of Appeal held that dispossession may occur if two conditions are satisfied, namely: (a) that the defendant had the requisite intention to possess so as to amount to adverse possession (*animus possidendi*); and (b) that the defendant had factual possession of the land in so far as his acts in relation to the property must go beyond the merely trivial. Consequently, on the evidence, the defendant had demonstrated his intention to possess the plot. The reasoning adopted by Slade LJ is instructive:

"On any footing, it must, in my judgment, be too broad a proposition to suggest that an owner who retains a piece of land with a view to its utilisation for a specific purpose in the future can never be treated as dispossessed . . . In the present case, the defendant was well aware that the council had acquired the plot in order to construct a road on it at some time in the future and meantime had no present use for the land. This factor . . . should make the court the more cautious before holding that the defendant had had both a factual possession and *animus possidendi* sufficient to confer on him a possessory title. Nevertheless, every *Leigh* v. *Jack* type of case such as this must involve questions of fact and degree. I would, for my part, reject the submission that since the Act of 1980 there remains any 'special rule' which requires the words 'possessed' and 'dispossessed' or similar words to be given anything other than their natural and ordinary meaning in the *Leigh* v. *Jack* type of case . . . On the evidence in the present case [the trial judge] was, in my judgment, right in concluding that the defendant had acquired adverse possession of the plot by 28 October 1973 and had remained in adverse possession of it ever since. There is no evidence that any representative of the council has ever set foot on the plot since that date."[94]

We now turn to consider the requisite conditions for establishing dispossession.

(a) ANIMUS POSSIDENDI

The requisite intention to possess involves the intention by the squatter, acting in his own name, to exclude the world at large including the paper owner, so far as is reasonably practicable and so far as the process of the law will allow.[95] Although there are some *dicta* in the authorities which suggest that an intention to *own* is required,[96] nevertheless all that is required is an intention to *possess* for the time being. In *Buckinghamshire County Council* v. *Moran*[97] Slade LJ, adopting the formulation of the trial judge, said:

"What is required for this purpose is not an intention to own or even an intention to acquire ownership but an intention to possess—that is to say, an intention for the time being to possess the land to the exclusion of all other persons, including the owner with the paper title. No authorities cited to us establish the contrary proposition."[98]

The issue of intention is inferred from the acts of the adverse possessor. Enclosure of land by itself prima facie indicates the requisite *animus possidendi*. In *Seddon* v. *Smith*[99]

---

94. *Ibid* at 639–44.

95. *Powell* v. *McFarlane* (1979) 38 P & CR 452 at 471–72, *per* Slade J.

96. See, for example, *Littledale* v. *Liverpool College, supra*, fn 87, at 23, in which Lindley MR referred to "acts of ownership". In *George Wimpey & Co Ltd* v. *Sohn* [1967] Ch 487 at 510, Russell LJ said: "I am not satisfied that the actions of the predecessors in bricking up the doorway and maintaining a lock on the gate to the roadway were necessarily referable to an intention to occupy the [land] as their own absolute property."

97. *Supra*, fn 93.

98. *Ibid* at 643. See also, *Colchester BC* v. *Smith* [1992] Ch 421; *London Borough of Hounslow* v. *Minchinton, supra*, fn 79.

99. (1877) 36 LT 168 at 169.

Cockburn CJ took the view that "[e]nclosure is the strongest possible evidence of adverse possession", however he stressed that it was not conclusive in itself. Similarly, Russell LJ in *George Wimpey & Co Ltd* v. *Sohn*[100] said that: "Ordinarily, of course, enclosure is the most cogent evidence of adverse possession and of dispossession of the paper owner." The trespasser's acts must disclose an unequivocal intention:

"If his acts are open to more than one interpretation and he has not made it perfectly plain to the world at large by his actions or words that he has intended to exclude the owner as best he can, the courts will treat him as not having had the requisite *animus possidendi* and consequently as not having dispossessed the owner."[101]

It therefore follows that trivial acts by an adverse possessor will not generally amount to "possession". In *Tecbild Ltd* v. *Chamberlain*[102] the claimant's children had played on the disputed land as and when they wished and the family's horses had been tethered and exercised on it. The Court of Appeal held that the acts were equivocal and trivial and therefore did not constitute possession. By way of contrast, in *Buckinghamshire County Council* v. *Moran* the defendant's act of padlocking an existing gate thereby blocking the council's only access to the plot so that he had exclusive physical control was sufficient to show an unequivocal intention to possess. In *Newington* v. *Windeyer*[103] the Court of Appeal of New South Wales found that a number of neighbouring residents had adversely possessed an adjoining plot of open ground on the basis that for some 50 years they had cultivated the area as a garden; had employed a worker to mow the lawn; had used the area for parties, receptions and the display of sculpture; and had been assessed for rates on the land.

However, the construction of a new fence will not be enough to establish intention if outraged neighbours instantly remove it.[104] Further, the repair of an existing fence will also be insufficient. In *Wilson* v. *Martin's Executors*[105] the plaintiff had walked the boundary, cut chestnut, cleared firewood, cut trees for sale and repaired fences but the Court of Appeal held that these acts were not sufficiently unequivocal to establish adverse possession of the 2.5 acre estate. The squatter's own acts may operate to negate an intention to possess. In *Pavledes* v. *Ryesbridge Properties Ltd*[106] the squatter had complained to the paper owner that the fencing of the disputed plot had become dilapidated. It was held that "the squatter could not validly claim himself to be in adverse possession as against persons whom he actively requested to shoulder the responsibilities that possession has".[107]

The fact that the claimant's possession must be adverse does not mean that it must therefore be *hostile*. Both the paper owner and the "possessor" may be ignorant of the fact of adverse possession.[108] Both parties may mistakenly but genuinely believe that the claimant was the paper owner of the land and entered on it "as of right". Accordingly,

---

100. [1967] 1 Ch 487 at 511. See also, *Williams* v. *Usherwood* (1981) 45 P & CR 235.
101. Slade J in *Powell* v. *McFarlane*, *supra*, fn 95 at 472.
102. (1969) 20 P & CR 633.
103. (1985) 3 NSWLR 555.
104. *Marsden* v. *Miller, The Times*, 23 January 1992, CA.
105. [1993] 1 EGLR 178.
106. (1989) 58 P & CR 459. See also, *Morrice* v. *Evans, The Times*, 27 February 1989.
107. *Ibid* at 481.
108. *Rains* v. *Buxton*, *supra*, fn 75, at 539ff.

time will run against a true owner who is unaware that the title to the land was conveyed to him.[109]

(b) FACTUAL POSSESSION

In order for possession to start time running under the Limitation Act, it must be "open, not secret; peaceful, not by force; and adverse, not by consent of the paper owner".[110] The issue of factual possession depends upon the nature of the land in question and the manner in which land of that nature is commonly used. The fact that a particular act or course of conduct is held to amount to possession in one case, will not necessarily be followed in a later case where the nature or character of the land is different. Determining possession is therefore a question of fact, depending on all the circumstances. Thus, in *Redhouse Farms (Thorndon) Ltd* v. *Catchpole*[111] the only possible use of the land was for shooting, and it was held that the act of shooting pigeons over it was enough to constitute possession. In *Treloar* v. *Nute*[112] the disputed land had been used by the defendant to graze animals. He had also dumped spoil in a gully and stored stone and timber on it. When the defendant began building operations on the land, the plaintiff sought a declaration that she was the rightful owner. Of particular significance to the Court of Appeal in finding adverse possession was the defendant's act of dumping spoil. However, the court stressed that for the purposes of establishing adverse possession it is not necessary to show that the paper owner was inconvenienced.

It must be demonstrated that "the alleged possessor has been dealing with the land in question as an occupying owner might have been expected to deal with it and that no-one else has done so".[113] While acts which fall short of possession will not cause time to start running, nevertheless it is not necessary to show that the owner of the land has been dispossessed from the *whole* since adverse possession may be claimed in respect of a *part* only. For example, in *Rains* v. *Buxton*[114] the plaintiffs, together with their predecessors in title, had for some 60 years been in possession of a cellar beneath land belonging to the defendants. The plaintiffs sought to restrain the defendants carrying out certain works

109. *Palfrey* v. *Palfrey* (1974) 229 EG 1593 at 1595.

110. *Mulcahy* v. *Curramore Pty Ltd, supra,* at fn 65, at 475. Cf *Shaw* v. *Garbutt* (unreported, Supreme Court, NSW, 2 August 1996), in which the plaintiff claimed possessory title to a house which she occupied with a male companion. On several occasions when people came onto the land, including the paper owner and his family, the male companion had come out of the house brandishing a shotgun. The plaintiff was with her companion when some of these incidents occurred. Young J held that in the absence of evidence that the plaintiff had authorised her companion's conduct or that she exerted control over him, it did not disqualify her from acquiring possessory title. Importantly, the judge opined that even if she were responsible for her companion's actions this would not have prevented a title arising through adverse possession. He noted that in Canadian and United States cases, the tests applied for deciding whether possession is "adverse" do not require the absence of force or violence. Further, in two New South Wales decisions, the squatter's use of force had been regarded as a factor in establishing that the possession was "adverse": *Harnett* v. *Green (No 2)* (1883) 4 LR (NSW) (L) 292, where the squatter had warned people off the land and *Beever* v. *Spaceline Engineering Pty Ltd* (1993) 6 BPR 13,270, where the squatter brandished a shotgun to warn a surveyor off the land. Young J also stressed that a squatter's failure to pay the rates does not in itself preclude a claim to adverse possession. In the present case, the paper owner had continued to pay them despite the apparent willingness of the squatter to pay the rates. She had gone to the council with the intention of making payment only to be told that the paper owner had already done so. In this situation, non-payment was not a disqualifying factor. See also, *Shaw* v. *Garbutt (No 2)* (unreported, Supreme Court, NSW, 3 September 1996).

111. (1977) 244 EG 295 at 297 *et seq.*

112. [1977] 1 WLR 1295.

113. *Powell* v. *McFarlane, supra,* fn 95, at 471.

114. *Supra,* fn 75.

which would interfere with their use and enjoyment of the cellar. In granting the plaintiffs relief, Fry J said:

"I do not know at all whether the cellar was made with the permission of the predecessor in title of the defendants or not, and there is an entire absence of the proof of the fact of concealed fraud.

I therefore hold that the plaintiffs are by virtue of the Statute of Limitations entitled to the cellar, and the defendants, having intended to destroy something like half that cellar by their operations, were intending a wrong in respect of which the plaintiffs are entitled to an injunction."[115]

(d) Doctrine of implied licence

In the past the courts have used the device of an "implied licence" to deprive a squatter of his claim to adverse possession.[116] The approach adopted here was succinctly explained by Lord Denning MR in *Wallis's Cayton Bay Holiday Camp Ltd* v. *Shell-Mex and BP Ltd*,[117] who said:

"The line between acts of user and acts of possession is too fine for words. The reason behind the decisions is because it does not lie in that other person's mouth to assert that he used the land of his own wrong as a trespasser. Rather his user is to be ascribed to the licence or permission of the true owner . . . And it has been held many times in this court that acts done under licence or permitted by the owner do not give a licensee a title under the Limitation Act 1939."[118]

The practice of inferring a licence in this context, often from little evidence, clearly had a restrictive effect on the development of the law and it was finally disallowed by the Limitation Amendment Act 1980, s 4. This has now been incorporated into the Limitation Act 1980, Sch 1, para 8(4) which provides that for the purpose of determining whether a person occupying any land is in adverse possession it shall not be assumed by implication of law that his occupation is by permission of the person entitled to the land merely by virtue of the fact that his occupation is not inconsistent with the latter's present or future enjoyment of the land.[119] However, it should be noted that this provision goes on to expressly state that it is still open to the courts to infer a licence where such a finding is "justified on the actual facts of the case".[120]

(e) Adverse possession by a child

The phrase "some person in whose favour the period of limitation can run" contained in paragraph 8(1) of Schedule 1 of the 1980 Act does not preclude the running of time in favour of a child,[121] although it may prove difficult to establish that a minor had the requisite intent to possess the land to the exclusion of all others.

---

115. *Ibid* at 541.
116. *Leigh* v. *Jack, supra*, fn 86. See, for example, *Hughes* v. *Griffin, supra*, fn 84.
117. [1975] QB 94.
118. *Ibid* at 103.
119. See the Law Reform Committee's 21st Report, *Final Report on Limitation of Actions* (Cmnd 6923, 1977), para 3.47ff; *Buckinghamshire CC* v. *Moran*, [1990] 1 Ch 623 at 637. See also *London Borough of Hounslow* v. *Minchinton, supra*, fn 79, in which Millett LJ observed that *Leigh* v. *Jack* "no longer represents good law".
120. See *Buckinghamshire CC* v. *Moran, ibid* at 636–37 *per* Slade LJ.
121. *Willis* v. *Earl Howe* [1893] 2 Ch 545.

(f) Periodic tenancies

(i) Tenancies from year to year

The general rule is that a tenant is estopped from claiming adverse possession against his landlord during the currency of the tenancy because his possession is by consent.[122] In effect, therefore, a tenant's possession cannot be adverse until the period last covered by rent has expired.[123] Paragraph 5(1) of Schedule 1 to the Limitation Act 1980 provides that a tenancy from year to year or other period, without a lease in writing, shall be treated as being determined at the expiration of the first year or other period. By way of exception, it is provided that where any rent has subsequently been received in respect of the tenancy, the cause of action is treated as having accrued on the date of the last receipt of rent.[124]

The meaning of the phrase "tenancy from year to year or other period, without a lease in writing" was considered by the Court of Appeal in *Moses* v. *Lovegrove*,[125] in which one of the issues was whether a rent book was a "lease in writing". It was held that it was not, and the fact that it evidenced the terms of the tenancy was not enough. Lord Evershed MR said:

"The rent book is, I think, what it purports to be, and what it is called, a rent book, that is a book containing acknowledgments for payment of weekly sums of rent . . . I think that on the face of it, it was not intended to be, and is not a contract for granting a tenancy, still less a lease creating an estate."[126]

The construction of paragraph 5(1) of Schedule 1 was also considered in *Long* v. *Tower Hamlets LBC*.[127] On 4 September 1975 the landlord, a local authority, wrote to the appellant confirming its intention to grant him a quarterly tenancy of shop premises commencing on 29 September of that year. On 8 September the appellant indorsed a copy of the letter (the tenancy document), confirming his agreement to the specified terms. Three weeks later he took possession of the premises, but in 1977 he ceased to pay rent while continuing to remain in possession despite being served a notice to quit.

In 1995 the appellant brought an action against the local authority seeking a declaration that he was beneficially entitled to the premises. The basis of his claim was that since 1977 he had been in adverse possession of the premises within the meaning of the Limitation Act 1980, Sch 1, para 8(1) (above), with the result that by virtue of paragraph 5 the landlord's claim was statute barred. The deputy master granted the landlord's application to strike out his claim. On appeal, the local authority contended that the tenancy document was a lease in writing within paragraph 5(1), so that the limitation period began to run not when the appellant ceased to pay rent, but on 25 March 1984, when his tenancy was brought to an end by the expiration of the notice to quit.

It was held that the tenancy document was not a "lease in writing", and since it did not confer an immediate right to take possession, it was a reversionary lease not made by deed. Further, since it fell outside the Law of Property Act 1925, s 54(2), it was void for

---

122. *Shillabeer* v. *Diebel* (1980) 100 DLR (3d) 279 at 283.
123. *Hayward* v. *Chaloner* [1968] 1 QB 107 at 122 *per* Russell LJ.
124. Sch 1, para 5(2).
125. [1952] 2 QB 533.
126. *Ibid* at 536.
127. [1996] 2 All ER 683.

the purpose of creating a legal estate. Having reviewed the authorities, James Munby QC observed that:

"a written document, whatever its terms, however clearly referable to the existence of a lease, and however comprehensive it may be in setting out the terms of the lease, is not a 'lease in writing' for the purposes of para. 5(1) of Sch. 1 to the 1980 Act unless at law the document itself operates to 'pass an interest' . . . itself 'operates as a lease' . . . or itself 'creates an estate'."[128]

(ii) Tenancies at will

The same principles applicable to yearly tenancies (above) also apply to tenancies at will,[129] so that time does not run in favour of the tenant at will until his tenancy is actually determined.[130] Thus, if the tenant holds over without consent at the end of the lease, this will constitute adverse possession and time will begin to run against the reversioner.[131]

(g) Payment of rent to wrong landlord

Where there is a lease in writing at an annual rent of £10.00 or more, or £1.00 or more where the lease was granted before 1 August 1980,[132] and the tenant pays rent to the wrong landlord, this amounts to adverse possession of the land and time begins to run from the date the wrong landlord received the rent.[133]

(h) Forfeiture and breach of condition

Any right to forfeit or to terminate a lease for breach of condition is governed by the Limitation Act 1980, Sch 1, para 7. This provides that a right of action to recover land by virtue of a forfeiture or breach of condition shall be treated as having accrued on the date on which the forfeiture was incurred or the condition broken. By way of exception, paragraph 7(2) states that where the right to forfeit accrued to a person entitled to an estate in reversion or remainder, and the land was not recovered by virtue of that right, the right of action to recover the land shall not be treated as having accrued to that person until his estate or interest fell into possession, as if no such forfeiture or breach of condition had occurred. This makes it clear that the provision is designed to cover any right of forfeiture held by a remainderman or by a party to an agreement for a lease.

(i) Actions for rent arrears

Section 19 of the 1980 Act provides that no action shall be brought, or distress made, to recover arrears of rent, or damages in respect of arrears of rent, after the expiration of six years from the date on which the arrears became due. Section 38(1) of the Act defines "rent" as including a rentcharge and a rentservice. It goes on to define "rentservice" as meaning any annuity or periodical sum of money charged upon or payable out of land,

---

128. *Ibid* at 694.
129. See *Hughes* v. *Griffin* [1969] 1 WLR 23; see also fn 84, *supra*, and associated text.
130. Sch 1, para 4 to the 1980 Act.
131. See further, *Fairweather* v. *St Marylebone Property Co Ltd* [1963] AC 510.
132. Sch 1, para 8 to the 1980 Act.
133. Sch 1, para 6, *ibid*. This provision does not bind the Crown, see Ch 4, *supra*.

except a rent service or interest on a mortgage on land. Although the provision extends to actions by way of distress, such proceedings are rarely brought nowadays.[134]

The construction of section 19 was subjected to consideration by the Court of Appeal in *Romain* v. *Scuba TV Ltd*.[135] The principal issue in the case was whether the limitation period in a claim against a guarantor of a lessee's undertaking to pay rent is 12 years (as an action on a specialty[136]), or six years. Both the guarantee and the lease were under seal. Evans LJ stated that:

"I have come to the clear conclusion that s.19 applies the six-year time limit not only to actions against the lessee but also to actions against the guarantor of his undertaking to pay the rent reserved by the lease. In both cases, the action is brought to 'recover arrears of rent, or damages in respect of arrears of rent' and the absence of any express reference to the surety is not, in my judgment, significant. The legal nature of the cause of action against the surety is entirely apt to explain the reference to an action for damages, which otherwise would have no clear meaning at all."[137]

(j) Extinction of title

It was seen above[138] that section 17 provides that, subject to section 18 of the Act[139] and to section 75 of the Land Registration Act 1925, expiration of the relevant limitation period for a person bringing an action to recover land, including a redemption action, has the effect of extinguishing the title of that person. This accords with the general principle that title to land is relative.[140] Consequently a title is only secure to the extent that no other person can establish a better claim to it. Thus, where the title of a holder of a fee simple estate is extinguished, the squatter who successfully establishes adverse possession to the property acquires the title in fee simple. This cannot be challenged by the former holder since he is now statute barred from proceeding with any action for recovery of land. Further, upon expiry of the limitation period the owner loses his right to recover any outstanding rent for the period of the adverse possession; likewise his right to recover damages from the squatter.[141]

The Privy Council recently considered the position of an adverse possessor who had been in possession of leased land long enough to extinguish the rights of the tenant, but where the lease contained an option to renew which was exercised by the tenant. In *Chung Ping Kwan* v. *Lam Island Co Ltd*[142] the issue before the Board was whether the granting of a new leasehold interest resulted in a new title in the tenant entitling him to evict the squatter. It was held that it did not. The Privy Council adopted the view that since the renewal deprived the landlord of the right to possession, and therefore the right to evict the tenant during the term of the new lease, it followed that it also deprived the landlord of the right to oust the squatter. Since the tenant had "slept on his rights" by allowing the squatter to take possession during the term of the lease, it appeared to the Board that there was "no compelling reason why, as between [the tenant] and the trespasser, [the tenant's]

---

134. See *Abingdon Rural Council* v. *O'Gorman* [1968] 2 QB 811 at 819, in which Lord Denning MR commented that distress is an "archaic remedy which has largely fallen into disuse".
135. [1996] 2 All ER 377.
136. See the Limitation Act 1980, s 8.
137. *Ibid* at 381.
138. See fn 65 *supra*, and associated text.
139. The exceptions contained in s 18(2), (3) and (4) are considered *infra*.
140. See further, Gray, *Elements of Land Law*, 2nd ed (London: Butterworth's, 1993), at p 62 *et seq*.
141. *Re Jolly* [1990] 2 Ch 616; *Mount Carmel Investments Ltd* v. *Peter Thurlow Ltd* [1988] 1 WLR 1078.
142. [1996] 3 WLR 448.

rights under the renewal option in the lease should not be defeated, just as much as [the tenant's] other rights under the lease . . . ".[143] The new lease granted to the tenant under the option to renew did not result in a new limitation period running. The tenant's title had already been extinguished for once and for all.

(i) Unregistered land

Where the land in question is unregistered, a squatter's possession for 12 years does not of itself operate to transfer title from the paper owner. Put simply, the Limitation Act 1980 does not explicitly confer a "parliamentary conveyance" since the effect of section 17 is to extinguish the paper owner's title. In this respect, the governing principle was stated by Lord Radcliffe in *Fairweather* v. *St Marylebone Property Co Ltd*,[144] who said:

" . . . the decision of the Court of Appeal in 1892 in *Tichborne* v. *Weir*[145] . . . [held] that a squatter who dispossessed a lessee and 'extinguished' his title by the requisite period of occupation did not become liable in covenant to the lessee's landlord by virtue of any privity of estate. The point was fully considered by the members of the court and they unanimously rejected the idea that the effect of the limitation statute was to make a 'Parliamentary conveyance' of the dispossessed lessee's title or estate to the dispossessing squatter."

Accordingly, it is the indirect operation of the 1980 Act, taken together with the effects of adverse possession, which results in the squatter obtaining a new title.

It can be seen, therefore, that where the land in question is subject to a lease, the position of the squatter is a more complex issue than where a fee simple owner has had his title barred by adverse possession. The essential difficulty which arises is whether a dispossessed tenant can surrender to the landlord a lease which has become statute barred as against a squatter. This question was considered by the House of Lords in the *St Marylebone* case.[146] A tenant had been dispossessed by her sub-tenant. Time had expired and the tenant therefore surrendered her lease. The landlord claimed that his cause of action accrued on the surrender and sought possession from the squatter. By a majority, it was held that the landlord was entitled to recover possession from the squatter on the basis that the squatter's possession destroyed only the rights of the tenant and not the superior title of the landlord. Consequently, the tenant's surrender conferred upon the landlord an immediate right to possession. Lord Radcliffe stated that:

" . . . the effect of the 'extinguishment' sections of the Limitation Acts is not to destroy the lessee's estate as between himself and the lessor; . . . it would be incorrect to say that if he offers a surrender to the lessor he has nothing to surrender to him in respect of the land in the possession of the squatter. *Nemo dat quod non habet*, and I daresay that he does not, but, as Pearson L.J. indicated in the Court of Appeal,[147] the question here is not whether there are any exceptions from that general principle but whether, as a principle, it is relevant to the situation that we have here. In my opinion it is not."[148]

Notwithstanding the effect of section 17 of the Limitation Act 1980, the result is that the lease remains vested in the tenant, and that it is only as between the squatter and the

---

143. *Ibid* at 455. See also, *Bree* v. *Scott* (1904) 29 VLR 692.
144. [1963] AC 510.
145. (1892) 67 LT 735.
146. [1963] AC 510.
147. [1962] 1 QB 498 at 530.
148. *Supra*, fn 146, at 540.

tenant that the latter's interest is extinguished. The lease itself is not destroyed, so, as has been seen,[149] the tenant remains liable to the lessor on the covenants contained in the lease.[150] Further, a covenant which runs with the land, such as a covenant restricting user of the land, binds the land in equity and it can, therefore, be enforced against any subsequent owner of the land not being a bona fide purchaser for value of the legal estate without notice. Accordingly, such a covenant is binding upon land to which a squatter has subsequently acquired a statutory title by adverse possession.[151]

(ii) Registered land

The Limitation Act 1980 proceeds, in the main, on the basis of unregistered land; it is therefore necessary to reconcile its provisions with the Land Registration Acts 1925–1988. The effect of section 17 of the Limitation Act 1980 in extinguishing a title after 12 years of adverse possession does not apply to registered land. This is because quite simply, so long as the paper owner remains registered in the Land Register, his title cannot be said to have been extinguished. However, section 75 of the Land Registration Act 1925 provides that a person who acquires title to registered land by virtue of adverse possession is entitled to be registered as proprietor of that land for the appropriate interest thereby acquired. Until such registration is effected, section 75(1) provides that the registered proprietor holds the legal estate on trust for the squatter.[152] The effect of this provision is to grant the squatter the beneficial right to the land under trust. It is noteworthy that in *Fairweather* v. *St Marylebone Property Co Ltd*[153] Lord Radcliffe went on to consider what might have been the position had the land been registered, and was perturbed that the effect of the trust imposed by section 75(1), had it been applicable, would have conferred on the squatter the right to be registered as proprietor of the dispossessed owner's estate.[154] Further, by section 75(2) of the 1925 Act, the squatter may apply to be registered as proprietor of the land in question and, in the interim, his rights are regarded as an "overriding interest",[155] so that a transferee from the registered proprietor will be bound by the squatter's rights. Section 75(3) of the 1925 Act provides that the squatter shall be registered with absolute, qualified, possessory or good leasehold title, as may be appropriate. Initial registration with absolute title is rare as a previous proprietor may be able to avoid the Limitation Act 1980 by alleging fraud.[156] It is therefore common to register a possessory title only which may, of course, be subsequently changed to an absolute title.[157]

149. *Supra*, fn 145.
150. The decision in the *St Marylebone Property Co Ltd* case has not escaped criticism; see, for example, Professor Wade, in (1962) 78 LQR 541. See, further, the decision of the Supreme Court of Ireland in *Perry* v. *Woodfarm Homes Ltd* [1975] IR 104.
151. *Re Nisbet and Potts' Contract* [1906] 1 Ch 386, CA.
152. See *Bridges* v. *Mees* [1957] Ch 475, where the squatter claimed, as against a purchaser, a declaration and rectification of the register or alternatively a transfer of the land to him. An order was made for rectification.
153. [1963] AC 510.
154. *Ibid* at 542.
155. Land Registration Act 1925, s 70(1)(f).
156. Pain, *Adverse Possession: A Conveyancer's Guide* (Fourmat Publishing, 1992); Ruoff, *Land Registration Forms* (3rd ed, 1983).
157. See the Land Registration Act 1925, s 77, as amended by the Land Registration Act 1986, s 1(1).

With respect to registered leasehold land, the position is diametrically opposite to that laid down by the House of Lords in *Fairweather* v. *St Marylebone Property Co Ltd*[158] for unregistered leaseholds. This is because where the lease is registered, then if the squatter is registered as proprietor under the statutory trust contained in section 75(1) of the Land Registration Act 1925, a transfer of the lease results and only the squatter, as registered proprietor, can surrender the lease. This was the approach adopted by Browne-Wilkinson J in *Spectrum Investment Co* v. *Holmes*,[159] the facts of which are broadly analogous to those of *St Marylebone*, in so far as a leaseholder had been dispossessed by a sub-tenant. However, the sub-tenant's title was registered as first proprietor with possessory leasehold title. The leaseholder, on the basis of the decision in *St Marylebone*, decided to surrender her lease so that the landlord could recover his land. It was held that the Land Registration Act governed the manner in which a party's substantive rights are to be determined and transferred. Since the leaseholder was not registered as the leasehold owner at the time of her purported surrender, that surrender could not have the effect of transferring rights to the landlord. The effect of the registration of the squatter's title was to vest the term of the lease in him, so that only the squatter, as registered proprietor, could dispose of the lease. Browne-Wilkinson J stated that:

"Once the squatter is rightly registered as proprietor under section 75(3) the documentary lessee and the freeholder can no longer defeat the squatter's rights by a surrender . . . it must in my judgment follow that the squatter's rights (once registered) cannot be overridden. The difference between registered and unregistered land in this respect is an inevitable consequence of the fact that the Land Registration Act 1925 provides for registration of the squatter as proprietor and that registered proprietors have rights."[160]

An obvious question which arises from these decisions is whether the statutory trust imposed on the documentary lessee will operate to prevent a surrender. It appears that prior to the registration of the squatter's title, the lessee will be able to surrender a lease even after adverse possession has been completed. In the course of his judgment, Browne-Wilkinson J observed:

"But I am not deciding anything as to the position during the period between the date when the squatter obtains his title by adverse possession and the date on which he obtains registration of it. This is the period covered by section 75(1) . . . It may well be . . . that during the period preceding any registration of the squatter's rights, the documentary lessee (as registered proprietor of the lease) and the freeholder can deal with the legal estate without reference to a person whose rights are not recorded on the register."[161]

The fact that a tenant loses his title to a squatter will not release him from liability to the landlord on the covenants contained in the lease. Although the squatter is entitled to register his title, this does not give rise to privity of estate with the landlord and so he cannot be sued for rent or on other covenants between the lessee and the landlord.[162]

158. *Supra*, fn 153.
159. [1981] 1 WLR 221.
160. *Ibid* at 231. While Browne-Wilkinson J regretted the inconsistency, he noted, at 230, that the House of Lords in *Williams & Glynn's Bank Ltd* v. *Boland* [1980] 3 WLR 138, had stated that "if the words of the Land Registration Act 1925 are clear, they are to be given their natural meaning and not distorted so as to seek to produce uniformity in the substantive law as between registered and unregistered land".
161. *Ibid.*
162. *Tichborne* v. *Weir* (1892) 67 LT 735, CA.

However, if the lease contains a forfeiture clause the landlord can exercise his rights of re-entry against the squatter.[163]

POSTPONEMENT OF THE LIMITATION PERIOD

(a) Acknowledgment

To mitigate the effects of the Limitation Act 1623, the courts developed the principle that an acknowledgment of a right of action or a payment in respect of a debt, for example a mortgage,[164] had the effect of starting time running again. The rules are now contained in the Limitation Act 1980, ss 29–31. In actions to recover land, to foreclose or to redeem, an acknowledgment or part payment after the limitation period has run out has no effect since by virtue of section 17 of the 1980 Act the right is extinguished.[165]

(i) Formalities of acknowledgment

The Act does not define what amounts to an acknowledgment beyond laying down the formalities which must be satisfied for an acknowledgment to be effective. Section 30 provides that it must be in writing and signed by the person making it, or by his agent.[166] Section 30(2)(b) states that it must be made to the person, or to an agent of the person, whose title or claim is being acknowledged.[167] The point was made by Goddard CJ in *Jones* v. *Bellgrove Properties*[168] that whether or not a particular document is an acknowledgment "must depend on what the document states". Although the acknowledgment need not include an implied promise to pay, it must amount to a clear admission of the title or claim to which it relates.[169] Thus, a letter which admits part of the liability is not an acknowledgment of the disputed balance.[170] However, in *Edginton* v. *Clark*[171] a squatter wrote a letter to the owner's agent, not knowing the identity of the owner, offering to purchase the land. It was held that this was a sufficient acknowledgment of the owner's superior title.

(ii) The effect of acknowledgment on third parties

Section 31(1) of the 1980 Act provides that an acknowledgment of the title to any land by any person in possession will bind all other persons in possession during the ensuing period of limitation. Further, section 31(8) goes on to provide that an acknowledgment or

---

163. In *Tickner* v. *Buzzacott* [1965] Ch 426, Plowman J held that the squatter could not apply for relief against forfeiture.

164. Section 29(3) and (4).

165. *Sanders* v. *Sanders* (1881) 19 Ch D 373; *Nicholson* v. *England* [1926] 2 KB 93.

166. A company's auditors are not its agents for the purpose of acknowledging its debts: *Re Transplanters (Holding Company) Ltd* [1958] 1 WLR 822. However, a solicitor may have implied authority by a mortgagor to make an acknowledgment: *Wright* v. *Pepin* [1954] 1 WLR 635.

167. An Inland Revenue affidavit signed by the executor is not a sufficient acknowledgment of the testator's debt because it is not made to creditor: *Bowring-Hanbury's Trustee* v. *Bowring-Hanbury* [1943] Ch 104.

168. [1949] 2 KB 700 at 704.

169. *Kamouh* v. *Associated Electrical Industries International Ltd* [1980] QB 199.

170. *Surrendra Overseas Ltd* v. *Government of Sri Lanka* [1977] 1 WLR 565.

171. [1964] 1 QB 367.

payment by one of several personal representatives in respect of a claim against the estate of the deceased person will bind the estate.

(iii) Acknowledgment and mortgaged land

If the person in possession of the land acknowledges the title of the person to whom the right of action has accrued, time will begin running again.[172] By section 29(3), a payment of principal or interest by the person in possession of the mortgaged land has the same effect on a foreclosure action, namely time runs again from the date of the payment. Similarly, where a mortgagee is by virtue of the mortgage in possession of the mortgaged land and either receives any sum in respect of principal or interest of the mortgage debt, or acknowledges the title of the mortgagor or his equity of redemption, an action to redeem the land may be brought at any time before the expiration of 12 years from the date of the payment or acknowledgment.[173]

Section 31(2) of the 1980 Act provides that a payment in respect of a mortgage debt by the mortgagor or any other person liable for the debt, or by any person in possession of the mortgaged property, shall be binding on all other persons in possession of the mort-gaged property during the ensuing period of limitation. Where two or more mortgagees are, by virtue of the mortgage, in possession of the mortgaged land, an acknowledgment of the mortgagor's title or equity of redemption binds only him and his successors.[174] For the purposes of this provision, "successor" means personal representatives and any other person on whom the rights under the mortgage devolve.[175] Where the mortgagee giving the acknowledgment is entitled to only a part of the mortgaged land and not to any ascertained part of the mortgage debt, the mortgagor shall be entitled to redeem that part on payment of the corresponding proportion of the whole debt.[176] Where there are two or more mortgagors, an acknowledgment of the title or equity of redemption of one is treated as having been made to all the mortgagors.[177] Section 29(6) provides that a payment of a part of the rent or interest due at any time shall not extend the period for claiming the remainder then due, but any payment of interest shall be treated as a payment in respect of the principal debt. The effect of this provision is that time starts to run again in respect of the principal sum when rent or mortgage interest is paid.

(b) Formal entry

It has been seen that it is crucial for the paper owner who has been dispossessed of land to initiate proceedings for recovery, by issuing his writ, before the expiration of the limitation period. Should the paper owner fail to take such steps his title is extinguished. Merely sending a letter to the squatter demanding delivery up of possession of the land within the limitation period is not sufficient. It was held by the Court of Appeal in *Mount*

---

172. Limitation Act 1980, s 29(2). Unless such acknowledgment is made by the squatter, the paper owner must initiate possession proceedings within the prescribed time limit; see, *Mount Carmel Investments Ltd* v. *Peter Thurlow Ltd* [1988] 1 WLR 1078 at 1086, *per* Nicholls LJ, discussed *infra*.

173. *Ibid*, s 29(4). There is no requirement that the payment need be in money, and no money need actually pass: *Re Wilson* [1937] Ch 675, and *Maber* v. *Maber* (1867) LR 2 Ex 153.

174. Limitation Act 1980, s 31(3).

175. *Ibid*, s 31(9).

176. *Ibid*, s 34(4).

177. *Ibid*, s 35(5).

Carmel Investments Ltd v. *Peter Thurlow Ltd*[178] that the receipt of a communication from the paper owner demanding that the squatter quits the land will not terminate the squatter's possession. Nor does such receipt by the squatter operate to give the paper owner "constructive possession". Nicholls LJ said that "no one, either lawyer or non-lawyer, would think that a householder ceases to be in possession of his house simply by reason of receiving a demand that he should quit".[179] The judge went on to stress that: "Unless the squatter vacates or gives a written acknowledgment to the owner, the owner has to issue his writ within the prescribed time limit. Otherwise he is barred, because by section 15(1) he is barred from bringing any action to recover the land after the expiration of the 12 year period."[180]

LIMITATION PERIODS RELATING TO MORTGAGES

(a) Redemption actions

Section 16 of the Limitation Act 1980 provides that the right of a mortgagor,[181] (and any person claiming through him), to redeem becomes statute barred if the mortgagee remains in possession of any of the mortgaged land for 12 years. The mortgagor will therefore lose title to the land, or any part of it, of which the mortgagee has remained in possession.[182] The rights of a subsequent mortgagee may also be extinguished,[183] and he then ceases to be entitled to redeem the first mortgage. The position here was succinctly stated by Buckley J in *Cotterell* v. *Price*[184] who said:

"In my judgment, on the second mortgagee's right against the mortgagor becoming statute barred, the second mortgagee lost all estate and interest in the mortgaged property. He could no longer foreclose as against the mortgagor; he could no longer sue for possession, and as a result of the provisions of section 16 . . . his estate in the land had come to an end. It seems to me that, as a result, he lost his status as a mortgagee . . . no one who has no estate or interest recognised by law in the land can have an equity of redemption of that land, and when a second mortgagee loses his position *vis-à-vis* the mortgagor, as a mortgagee of the land, he ceases to be entitled to an equity of redemption of any prior mortgage."[185]

(b) Actions to recover money secured by a mortgage[186]

The mortgagee's right to bring an action to recover the principal money secured by a mortgage or other charge on property or to recover the proceeds of sale of the land is, by

178. [1988] 1 WLR 1078.
179. *Ibid* at 1085.
180. *Ibid* at 1086.
181. The term "mortgagor" is defined in the Law of Property Act 1925, s 205(1) (xvi) as including "any person from time to time deriving title under the original mortgagor or entitled to redeem a mortgage according to his estate or interest or right in the mortgaged property", and "mortgagee" is defined as including "a chargee by way of legal mortgage and any person from time to time deriving title under the original mortgage".
182. See the Limitation Act 1980, s 17, *supra*. In determining whether or not the mortgagee is in "possession", the court will take into account the particular character of the property in question, including its value and use: *Lord Advocate* v. *Lord Lovat* (1880) 5 App Cas 273; *Kirby* v. *Cowderoy* [1912] AC 599.
183. *Young* v. *Clarey* [1948] Ch 191.
184. [1960] 1 WLR 1097.
185. *Ibid* at 1102.
186. The Law of Property Act 1925, s 205(1) (xvi) provides that "mortgage" "includes any charge or lien on any property for securing money or money's worth . . . ".

section 20(1) of the 1980 Act, barred after 12 years from the date when repayment became due.[187] The accrual of the cause of action therefore triggers without having to wait for the occurrence of some future event.[188]

(c) Actions to foreclose

A mortgagee's rights to foreclose a mortgage and sue for possession are barred after 12 years from the date when he became entitled to possession.[189] A mortgagee's right to possession will be determined in accordance with the mortgage deed which may postpone possession until default occurs. Once the period for bringing an action for possession has expired, the mortgagee's title is extinguished.[190]

(d) Actions to recover arrears of interest

Section 20(5) of the 1980 Act lays down a six-year time limit for a mortgagor to sue for arrears of interest. A mortgagee who exercises his power of sale may keep all arrears of interest, and a mortgagor who wishes to redeem may do so only on the equitable terms of paying all arrears of interest. In *Edmunds* v. *Waugh*[191] the guiding principle was stated by Kindersley V-C, who said:

"The intention of the legislature, I think, was that if a man chose to let interest run into arrear for more than six years, and then come to a court of justice to recover the interest, he should only be entitled to recover six years' interest; but it does not follow that the legislature intended that the mortgagor who has lost his legal right, and comes to the court insisting on his equity to redeem, should be allowed—although he has failed to pay the interest which he ought to have paid for more than six years—to redeem on payment only of six years' interest. There would be no justice in such a construction of the statute."[192]

Where a first mortgagee sells the mortgaged property, the second mortgagee is entitled to all his arrears of interest out of any surplus proceeds unless, of course, the mortgage itself is barred.[193]

SETTLED LAND, TRUSTS OF LAND AND LAND HELD ON TRUST FOR SALE

As originally drafted, the Limitation Act 1980, s 18(1) provided that the provisions of the Act applied to equitable interests in land, "including interests in the proceeds of the sale of land held upon trust for sale", as they apply to legal estates. The effect of this provision is that a right to recover land shall be treated as accruing to a person in possession of an equitable interest as on the same date as if his interest were a legal estate in the land. Thus, although the interest is equitable it is deemed to be a legal estate for limitation purposes.

187. This provision also applies to mortgages of personal property.
188. *Farran* v. *Beresford* (1842) 10 Cl & F 319.
189. Limitation Act 1980, s 15(1) and s 20(4).
190. Limitation Act 1980, s 17, discussed *supra*, at fn 65 and associated text.
191. (1866) LR 1 Eq 418, applied by Stamp J in *Holmes* v. *Cowcher* [1970] 1 WLR 834. See, also, *Dingle* v. *Coppen* [1899] 1 Ch 726.
192. *Ibid* at 837.
193. *Young* v. *Clarey*, *supra*, fn 183; *Cotterell* v. *Price*, *supra*, fn 184.

However, it should be noted that the wording of section 18 has been amended by the Trusts of Land and Appointment of Trustees Act 1996.[194] In essence, the Act, which came into force on 1 January 1997, abolishes the dual system of trusts for sale and strict settlements created under the Settled Land Act 1925. Under the new simplified system, any trust of property which consists of or includes land,[195] including both trusts for sale and bare trusts,[196] is now a "trust of land".[197] The Act prohibits the creation of new Settled Land Act settlements. Existing settlements are unaffected by the new law and will continue to be governed by the Settled Land Act 1925 until no land or heirlooms remain in the settlement.[198] By way of exception, new settlements may continue to be created by resettlements and by the exercise of powers of appointment in such settlements.[199] Schedule 4 of the Trusts of Land and Appointment of Trustees Act 1996 specifies the extent to which the Limitation Act 1980 is repealed. The terminology used in section 18 of the 1980 Act is substantially affected by this provision in so far as section 18 is inconsistent with the provisions of the 1996 statute. Accordingly, the words "including interests in the proceeds of the sale of land held upon trust for sale" contained in section 18(1) are repealed. Further, Schedule 4 also amends the definition of "land" contained in section 38(1) of the 1980 Act to the extent that the words "including an interest in the proceeds of the sale of land held upon trust for sale" and the definition of "trust for sale" together with references in Schedule I, Part I to "proceeds of sale" are repealed.

Given that the 1996 Act saves existing Settled Land Act settlements, the dual system of trust will continue to exist for some considerable time. It follows that the original wording contained in the affected provisions of the Limitation Act 1980 is of continued relevance, and will remain so until those settlements created before 1 January 1997 come to an end. The following examination of section 18 therefore proceeds on the basis of its application to settled land and land held on trust for sale as created under the 1925 legislation.

(a) Settled land

Section 18(2) of the 1980 Act provides that the legal title of a tenant for life or a statutory owner is not extinguished so long as the right of action to recover the land of any person entitled to a beneficial interest in the land either has not accrued or has not been barred by the 1980 Act. Section 18(2)(b) goes on to elaborate by providing that the legal estate shall accordingly remain vested in the tenant for life or statutory owner and shall devolve in accordance with the Settled Land Act 1925. However, if and when every such right of action has been barred by this Act, his legal estate shall be extinguished.

---

194. The Act is based on the recommendations of the Law Commission in its 1989 Report, *Transfer of Land: Trusts of Land*, Law Com No 181. See, Oakley [1996] Conv 401; Hopkins [1996] Conv 411.

195. Trusts of Land and Appointment of Trustees Act 1996, s 1(1)(a).

196. *Ibid*, s 1(2)(a).

197. *Ibid*, s 1(1)(a). The conversion of trusts for sale into trusts for land is achieved by removing the duty to sell: ss 4(1), (2), 5(1) and Sch 2.

198. Although existing charitable, ecclesiastical and public trusts under the Settled Land Act 1925 were converted at the commencement of the 1996 Act into trusts of land.

199. Section 2(2) of the 1996 Act.

(b) Land held on trust for sale

Section 18(3) of the Limitation Act 1980 imports the provisions relating to tenants for life (above) to trustees of land. It provides that where any land is held upon trust, including a trust for sale,[200] and the limitation period for bringing an action to recover the land by trustees has expired, the interest of the trustees shall not be extinguished if and so long as the right of action to recover the land of any person entitled to a beneficial interest in the land or in the proceeds of sale[201] either has not accrued or has not been barred by the 1980 Act. However, section 18(3) goes on to provide that the trustees' interest is extinguished when the right of recovery of all those entitled to a beneficial interest in the land or in its proceeds of sale becomes time barred.

The above provisions relating to tenants for life and trustees of land should be read in conjunction with section 18(4) which provides that they may bring legal proceedings on behalf of beneficiaries who have not been time barred although the limitation period in respect of their own cause of action has expired. This may lead to lengthy limitation periods where land is subject to a life interest although, in any case, the true plaintiff in such actions is always the beneficiary whose action has not become barred.

By Schedule 1, paragraph 9 to the 1980 Act a beneficiary who is not solely and absolutely entitled in equity to the land or in the proceeds of sale[202] can never obtain title against the trustee or any other person entitled to a beneficial interest in the land or the proceeds of sale. The possession of the beneficiary is not adverse and therefore no right of action accrues to either the co-beneficiaries or the trustees. It should be noted that paragraph 9 has no application to bare trustees.[203]

LEASEHOLD REFORM ACT 1967

The object of the Leasehold Reform Act 1967 is to grant certain tenants holding long leases a right compulsorily to purchase either the freehold reversion or an extended term of years in the property which they occupy. The Act applies only to premises which consist of a "house".[204] Essentially, two substantive rights are conferred on a tenant who holds a "long tenancy", which is defined as a term certain which when granted was in excess of 21 years,[205] at a low rent.[206] First, a qualifying tenant has a right to require that his existing lease be replaced by a new tenancy for a term which expires 50 years after the expiry date of the existing tenancy.[207] Second, a qualifying tenant has the alternative right

---

200. The words "including a trust for sale" in s 18(3) and (4), *infra*, are repealed by the Trusts of Land and Appointment of Trustees Act 1996, Sch 4, see *supra*.

201. The words "or in the proceeds of sale" in s 18(3) and (4), *infra*, are also repealed, *ibid*.

202. The words "or in the proceeds of sale", "or in the proceeds", and "or the proceeds of sale" in Sch 1, para 9 to the 1980 Act are now repealed, see fn 200, *supra*.

203. *Bridges* v. *Mees* [1957] Ch 475.

204. Leasehold Reform Act 1967, s 2(1).

205. *Ibid*, s 3(1)(a).

206. *Ibid*, s 1(1)(a). See now the Leasehold Reform, Housing and Urban Development Act 1993, s 63. For the conditions relating to occupancy see the Leasehold Reform Act 1967, s 1(1)(b), as amended by the Housing Act 1980, s 141 and Sch 21, para 1(1). See, also, *Poland* v. *Earl Cadogan* [1980] 3 All ER 544; *Harris* v. *Plentex* (1980) 40 P & CR 483.

207. Leasehold Reform Act 1967, s 14(1).

to the enfranchisement of his lease, so that he is entitled compulsorily to purchase the freehold in the demised premises.[208]

The limitation issue in the context of the Leasehold Reform Act 1967 was considered in *Re Howell's Application*.[209] On 10 February 1953 the tenant took an assignment of the residue of a 99-year lease, which had originally been granted on 29 September 1907 at a yearly rent of £3.00. No rent had been paid since 29 July 1952, and the tenant had not received a demand for outstanding rent. The reversioner could not be traced, and in 1971 an order was made pursuant to section 27 of the Leasehold Reform Act 1967 that the tenant had a right to acquire the freehold. The issue was whether, in determining the amount of rent remaining unpaid for the purposes of section 27(5) of the Leasehold Reform Act 1967, rent which had become statute barred under the Limitation Act should be taken into account. Section 27(5) provides that when an application is made under this head, the tenant must pay into court "the amount remaining unpaid of any pecuniary rent payable for the house and premises up to the date of the conveyance". Pennycuick V-C held that the words "any pecuniary rent payable" should be construed as meaning rent the tenant was under an enforceable obligation to pay and excluded arrears which had become statute barred. Accordingly, the arrears of rent payable up to the date of the conveyance should be assessed as six years' rent at £3.00 a year, i.e., £18.00.

208. *Ibid*, s 8(1).
209. [1972] Ch 509.

PART V

MISCELLANEOUS LIMITATION PERIODS

CHAPTER 24

MISCELLANEOUS LIMITATION PERIODS

COMPANY LAW

(a) Effect of the memorandum and articles

The Companies Act 1985, s 14 provides:

"(1) Subject to the provisions of this Act, the memorandum and articles, when registered, bind the company and its members to the same extent as if they respectively had been signed and sealed by each member, and contained covenants on the part of each member to observe all the provisions of the memorandum and of the articles.

(2) Money payable by a member to the company under the memorandum or articles is a debt due from him to the company, and in England and Wales is of the nature of a specialty debt."

The statutory contract created by section 14 forms the basis of the legal relations between the company and its members, and the members *inter se*.[1] It therefore follows that the company can enforce the statutory contract against the members,[2] and the members can enforce it against each other. In general, the contract created by section 14 confers rights and imposes obligations on a member *qua* member, and not in any other capacity such as a solicitor or director of the company.[3]

Although section 14(2) declares that money payable by a member to the company is a specialty debt, the drafting of section 14, taken as a whole, is curious and has resulted in some anomalous results. In *Re Compania de Electricidad de la Provincia de Buenos Aires Ltd*[4] Slade J held, that as a matter of construction, the effect of section 14 is that while the company is treated as a party to the contract,[5] the contract was executed under seal only

---

1. Companies Act 1985, s 14. See, *Wood* v. *Odessa Waterworks Co* (1889) 42 Ch D 636; *Hickman* v. *Kent or Romney Marsh Sheep-Breeders' Association* [1915] 1 Ch 881. The company is also a party to the s 14 contract so that an action by a shareholder to enforce that contract for the company's benefit is a derivative action.

2. *Hickman* v. *Kent or Romney Marsh Sheep-Breeders' Association, ibid*.

3. *Rayfield* v. *Hands* [1960] Ch 1. See Hollington, *Minority Shareholders' Rights*, 2nd ed (London: Sweet & Maxwell, 1994) Ch 5. In *Hickman's case, ibid*, Astbury J stated, at 897, that "[a]n outsider to whom rights purport to be given by the articles in his capacity as such outsider, whether he is or subsequently becomes a member, cannot sue on those articles treating them as contracts between himself and the company to enforce those rights. Those rights are not part of the general regulations of the company applicable alike to all shareholders and can only exist by virtue of some contract between such person and the company... " This conclusion has generated significant criticism, see, for example, Wedderburn, "Shareholders' Rights and the Rule in Foss v. Harbottle" [1957] CLJ 194, at p 210; Sealy, *Cases and Materials in Company Law*, 6th ed (London: Butterworth's, 1996) at pp 115–16.

4. [1980] Ch 146. The court declined to follow *Re Artisans' Land & Mortgage Corporation* [1904] 1 Ch 796 which held that a shareholder's action in respect of a dividend was a claim on a specialty; note the reasoning of Slade J at 184–89. See also, *Re Northern Ontario Power Co Ltd* [1954] 1 DLR 627 and *Re Canada Tea Co Ltd* (1959) 21 DLR (2d) 90, in which the reasoning adopted by the court in *Re Artisans'* was doubted.

5. *Wood* v. *Odessa Waterworks Co, supra*, fn 1.

by the members. Accordingly, money owed by members to the company was a specialty contract for which the relevant limitation period is 12 years,[6] whereas money owed by the company by way of dividend or upon a return of capital was a simple contract debt, for which the limitation period is six years.[7]

(b) Unfairly prejudicial conduct

The Companies Act 1985, s 459 provides, *inter alia*, that a company member may petition the court for an order on the ground that:

"the company's affairs are being or have been conducted in a manner which is unfairly prejudicial to the interests *of its members generally*[8] or some part of the members (including at least himself) or that any actual or proposed act or omission of the company (including any act or omission on its behalf) is or would be so prejudicial."[9]

There is no limitation period for bringing proceedings under this provision, although in *Re DR Chemicals*[10] Peter Gibson J stressed that laches may bar relief on a section 459 petition,[11] providing such delay is inexcusable.[12]

(c) Pre-emption rights

A pre-emption right enables a shareholder to subscribe for any new shares that the company issues in proportion to his existing shareholding. Before the Companies Act 1980, a shareholder was only entitled to pre-emption rights if this was expressly conferred by the company's articles of association. The 1980 Act implemented the Second EC Directive by providing for statutory pre-emption rights in both private and public companies. This statutory right is restricted to equity shares. The relevant provisions are now contained in the Companies Act 1985, ss 89–92.

Section 92 of the 1985 Act provides a civil sanction for breach of the pre-emption rights against the company and every officer who knowingly authorised or permitted the contravention.[13] The company and the officers are jointly and severally liable to any person to whom an offer should have been made under the subsection or provision, for any loss,

---

6. Limitation Act 1980, s 8.

7. Limitation Act 1980, s 5. It should be noted that Table A of the Companies (Tables A–F) Regulations 1985, art 108 empowers the board of directors to forfeit dividends which have remained unclaimed for 12 years.

8. Italics supplied. This amendment, which was introduced by the Companies Act 1989, Sch 19, para 11, came into force in 1991.

9. See Hollington, *op cit*, fn 3.

10. [1989] BCLC 383.

11. *Ibid* at 397–98. See Ch 3 *supra*.

12. The Law Commission in its Consultation Paper No 142, *Shareholder Remedies* (London: Stationery Office, 1996), at para 20.11, recommends that there should be a limitation period for s 459 petitions. However, the Commission goes on to state that: "we make no provisional recommendation as to the length of limitation period, save where the conduct alleged to be unfairly prejudicial constitutes an invasion of the legal rights of, or some duty owed to, the applicant or the company. In that case, we provisionally consider that the limitation period ought to be no less than that (if any) which applies to that wrong. Accordingly, if the applicant complains that a director has taken assets belonging to the company for his own benefit, the limitation period should be no less than that applicable to that breach of duty." See the Limitation Act 1980, s 21(3), Ch 23, *supra*.

13. See the Companies Act 1985, ss 89 and 90.

damage, costs or expenses which the person has sustained by reason of the contravention.[14] Proceedings under this section must be commenced within two years of the delivery of the return of allotment in question.[15]

(d) Breach of directors' duties

After the lapse of six years, section 21 of the Limitation Act 1980 prohibits proceedings against a director for breach of duty. However, no limitation period applies to claims founded upon any fraud or fraudulent breach of trust, or to claims to recover trust property or the proceeds thereof which have been retained by the director or previously received by him and converted to his own use.[16]

(e) Wrongful trading

The Insolvency Act 1986, s 214 provides, *inter alia*, that if in the course of the winding up of a company which has gone into insolvent liquidation it appears that a director of the company, at some time before the commencement of the winding up, knew or ought to have concluded that there was no reasonable prospect that the company would avoid such an insolvent liquidation, the court may on the application of the liquidator of the company order that director to contribute such amount to the assets of the company as the court thinks fit. In *Moore* v. *Gadd*[17] the Court of Appeal held that proceedings brought under section 214 were within the ambit of section 9(1) of the Limitation Act 1980 as "an action to recover any sum recoverable by virtue of any enactment" so that the applicable limitation period was six years.[18] Peter Gibson LJ adopted the view that the words "in the course of the winding up of a company" in section 214 could not be construed as relating to a period of limitation as they "were in a form markedly dissimilar to periods of limitation found prescribed in the 1980 Act or in any other enactment prescribing periods of limitation". Further, the term "if in the course of the winding up of a company it appears" governed the period of jurisdiction of the court to make an order and did not govern the commencement of the proceedings.[19]

OTHER SPECIFIC LEGISLATION

The Limitation Act 1980, s 39 stipulates that the Act shall not apply where an alternative limitation period is prescribed under any other statute. By way of illustration, some such statutory provisions will now be examined.

---

14. Companies Act 1985, s 92(1).
15. Companies Act 1985, s 92(2).
16. See further, Ch 23.
17. *The Times*, 17 February 1997, CA.
18. Limitation Act 1980, s 9(1). The Insolvency Act 1986, s 214 does not lay down a limitation period for proceedings brought under it so as to satisfy the Limitation Act 1980, s 39.
19. The same phrase also appears in s 213 of the 1986 Act (misfeasance proceedings) and does not amount to the prescribing of a limitation period, see *Re Lands Allotment Co* [1894] 1 Ch 616, CA.

(a) Defective Premises Act 1972

The general principle at common law is that a plaintiff cannot recover damages in the tort of negligence for pure economic loss suffered as a result of a defect in a building.[20] However, the Defective Premises Act 1972, which applies to residential property only, imposes strict liability for financial losses resulting from breach of the statutory warranty that dwellings are to be constructed "in a workmanlike or, as the case may be, professional manner, with proper materials and so that as regards that work the dwelling will be fit for habitation when completed".[21] The duties are owed by "any person taking on work for or in connection with the provision of a dwelling" to "every person who acquires an interest" in it. As with the law of tort, the limitation period is six years, but under the Act time begins to run against the plaintiff on the date when the building is completed. The strictness of this requirement is clear given that damage resulting from faulty workmanship may not occur for some years after construction.

(b) Matrimonial Causes Act 1973

The Act provides for the dissolution of marriages by bringing proceedings for nullity. Section 13(2) specifies that petitions for nullity of marriage on the grounds contained in section 12[22] must be brought within *three years* from the date of the marriage.

(c) Family Law Act 1996

The underlying policy of the Family Law Act 1996 is that the parties should settle their arrangements for the future before the court will make a divorce order.[23] If the parties are not able to comply with the requirements of the Act[24] within a specified period—normally 21 months[25]—from filing the statement of marital breakdown which effectively triggers the proceedings, those proceedings lapse. In this event, if the parties still wish to divorce they will have to restart the divorce proceedings again which entails making a statement, waiting for the expiration of the period for reflection and consideration etc.

(d) Inheritance (Provision for Family and Dependants) Act 1975

The Act restricts the ability of testators to freely dispose of assets in so far as dependants can apply to the court for a share of the estate if reasonable financial provision has not been made for them by the deceased. Application for financial provision must be made within *six months* from the date on which representation with respect to the estate is first taken out, although the court is granted discretion to extend the time limit.[26] It has been held that the limitation period is a substantive provision and the discretion conferred by

---

20. *Murphy* v. *Brentwood DC* [1991] AC 398; *D & F Estates* v. *Church Commissioners for England* [1989] AC 177.

21. Defective Premises Act 1972, s 1(1).

22. There are six grounds laid down in the section on which a marriage is voidable.

23. Family Law Act 1996, s 3(1)(c).

24. Family Law Act 1996, s 9.

25. Which equates to one year after the end of the period for reflection and consideration, Family Law Act 1996, s 5(3)(b).

26. Inheritance (Provision for Family and Dependants) Act 1975, s 4.

the section is unfettered.[27] In deciding whether or not to exercise its discretion the court will take into consideration factors such as whether negotiations have taken place, whether the estate has already been distributed, and whether, in refusing the application for an extension, the court would remove the applicant's only source of redress.[28]

(e) Employment Protection (Consolidation) Act 1978

A complaint arising from an employee's right to redundancy payment must be brought to an industrial tribunal *six months* from the "relevant period".[29] A complaint of unfair dismissal to an industrial tribunal must be made within *three months* from the effective date of the termination of the employment.[30]

(f) Carriage of Goods by Sea Act 1971

In relation to bills of lading the Act, which gives effect to the Hague-Visby Rules, provides that an action for loss or damage to cargo must be brought within *one year* of their delivery or the date when they should have been delivered (Hague-Visby Rules, Art III, r 6). It is open to the parties to extend this period by agreement. The provision does not apply to an action for indemnity against a third party (Hague-Visby Rules, Art III, r 6 *bis*).

The 1971 Act does not apply to charterparties (Hague-Visby Rules, Art V). However, it is open to the parties to incorporate the Act or the Rules into a charterparty by inserting a Clause Paramount.

Where the Hamburg Rules apply, the limitation period is *two years* commencing from the day when the goods or part thereof have been delivered or the last day on which the goods should have been delivered (Hamburg Rules, Art 20). The parties may, by agreement, extend the limitation period.

(g) Maritime Conventions Act 1911

The Act states that an action in respect of collision for damages to property or cargo, personal injury, or loss to another vessel, or in respect of any salvage services, must be brought against the other vessel within *two years*. The limitation period starts to run from the date when the damage, loss or injury was caused or the salvage services were rendered. The Maritime Conventions Act 1911, s 8 grants the court discretion to extend the period if it is satisfied that there has not been any reasonable opportunity for the plaintiff to arrest the defendant vessel during the limitation period.

(h) Merchant Shipping Act 1979

Claims arising from the death of or personal injury to passengers and loss of or damage to baggage under a contract of carriage of passengers by sea are governed by the 1974

---

27. *Re Salmon, decd; Coard* v. *National Westminster Bank* [1980] 3 All ER 532.
28. *Ibid.*
29. Calculated in accordance with the formula specified in s 90(1), (2).
30. Section 67.

Athens Convention which was given the force of law by the Merchant Shipping Act 1979. The time bar is *two years*, commencing:

(a) in the case of personal injury, from the date of disembarkation of the passenger;

(b) in the case of death during carriage, from the date when the passenger should have disembarked;

(c) in the case of personal injury during the carriage which results in death after disembarkation, from the date of death, provided that it is within *three years* from the date of disembarkation;

(d) in the case of loss of or damage to luggage, from the date of disembarkation or from the date when disembarkation should have taken place, whichever is later (Athens Convention 1974, Art 16).

The 1974 Athens Convention is excluded from the Unfair Contract Terms Act 1977.

(i) Merchant Shipping (Oil Pollution) Act 1971

For claims for damage caused by oil pollution from merchant ships, section 9 of the Act provides that an action must be brought no later than *three years* after the claim arose, or later than *six years* after the occurrence or first of the occurrences resulting in the discharge or escape by reason of which the liability was incurred.

CHAPTER 25

ACTIONS TO RECOVER SUMS PAYABLE BY VIRTUE OF A STATUTORY PROVISION

It has been noted above that, in the past, problems were encountered in categorising certain types of action. One of these problems was that under the law prior to the Limitation Act 1939 there was no specific provision for actions to recover a sum of money due by virtue of the specific provisions of a statute. Accordingly, before 1939, statutory provisions which allowed for a right of action in favour of the plaintiff were treated as a form of specialty[1] to which a standard limitation period of 20 years applied.[2] Clearly, a limitation period of 20 years, now reduced to a period of 12 years by the Limitation Act 1980, s 8, applied to statutory provisions which create, for example, obligations similar to those found in the common law of tort or contract, would be anomalous. Accordingly, specific provision was made which reduced the relevant limitation period to one of six years, running from the date of accrual of the cause of action. The position is now covered by the Limitation Act 1980, s 9 which provides:

"(1) An action to recover any sum recoverable by virtue of any enactment shall not be brought after the expiration of six years from the date on which the cause of action accrued.
(2) Subsection (1) above shall not affect any action to which section 10 of this Act applies."

An initial complication created by the overlap between sections 9 and 8 is that an Act of Parliament has attached to it the Royal Seal. As such, a statute is also a specialty, in which case, it is capable of being subject to the much longer limitation period of 12 years, provided for in section 8 of the 1980 Act. One way of getting round this problem is to accept that section 8(2) specifically allows for the recognition of a shorter limitation period prescribed by the Limitation Act 1980. On this basis, it may be argued that although an Act of Parliament is a specialty, it is already provided for by section 9, in which case the 12-year period specified in section 8(1) is inapplicable. However, unfortunately, this argument will not work in every case.

The first problem is that section 9(1) is specifically concerned with an *action to recover money under a statute* and with no other variety of action. Accordingly, where the statutory remedy provided does not relate to the recovery of a sum of money, it will not fall within the provisions of section 9, in which case section 8 provides for a longer period of limitation of 12 years.

Two matters arise for consideration in this regard. First, what is meant by the phrase "any sum of money recoverable"? Secondly, what is meant by "an action . . . by virtue of any enactment"?

---

1. See Ch 15.
2. *Cork & Bandon Railway Co* v. *Goode* (1853) 13 CB 827; *Talory* v. *Jackson* (1638) Cro Car 513.

SUM OF MONEY RECOVERABLE

Central to the application of section 9 is that the statute must confer a right of payment of a sum of money. In determining what is meant by the phrase "sum of money", regard must be had to the effect of different types of statutory provision.

Clearly excluded from the ambit of section 9 will be any provision which confers on the plaintiff a benefit of a non-pecuniary nature. For example, the Leasehold Reform Act 1967, s 4 confers on a tenant the right to ask his landlord to sell the freehold interest in the demised property. Plainly, such a right cannot fall within the meaning of the phrase, sum of money.

Also falling outside the scope of section 9 are statutory provisions which imply obligations into a contract, thereby giving rise to an action for damages in respect of any breach. Such actions sound in contract and are covered by the Limitation Act 1980, s 5. Moreover, an action for damages, being an action for an unliquidated amount, is unlikely to be regarded as a sum recoverable by virtue of an enactment, since the amount payable is not ascertained or quantifiable according to a statutory formula.

A third group of statutory provisions raises the issue of breach of statutory duty. For example, a number of regulatory statutory provisions, such as the Factories Act 1961, s 29, make it a criminal offence to engage in a certain type of activity. The question will often arise whether there is any form of civil law redress in respect of a breach of such a statutory duty, the main problem being that the statute itself is silent on the matter. If a civil action for damages for breach of statutory duty does exist, that action will be regarded as an action in tort, to which the Limitation Act 1980, s 2, applies, since it is not an action in respect of a debt, but historically, an action on the case. To say otherwise would amount to overlooking the express words of the Limitation Act 1980, s 8(2) which preserves any shorter period of limitation specified in the 1980 Act.[3]

A fourth variety of statutory provision is one which clearly does confer a right to sue for unliquidated damages in the event of breach, without specifying the basis on which those damages will be awarded. Moreover, a statutory provision of this kind, such as the Misrepresentation Act 1967, s 2(1),[4] may also create rights which did not previously exist at common law under relevant rules of contract or tort. In all likelihood, these provisions will be treated by the courts as governed by either section 2 or section 5 of the 1980 Act, but there is also an argument to the effect that section 8 in respect of specialties will apply instead, but this would have the effect of imposing a limitation period of 12 years, not six.

Finally, there are statutory provisions which fall squarely within the ambit of section 9. These generally provide that the plaintiff is entitled to recover a specific amount or a sum ascertainable by reference to a statutorily defined formula. Examples include statutory provisions which allow a local authority to recover a specified sum following alteration of the boundary between two authorities.[5] Similarly, it has been held that a claim by a local authority against a landlord for reimbursement of expenses incurred as a result of having to put a leased property into a proper state of repair is capable of falling within section 9.[6]

---

3. *Aiken* v. *Stewart Wrightson Members' Agency Ltd* [1995] 3 All ER 449 at 459 *per* Potter J.
4. See also Defective Premises Act 1972, s 1, discussed in Ch 24.
5. *West Riding of Yorkshire County Council* v. *Huddersfield Corporation* [1957] 1 QB 540.
6. *Swansea City Council* v. *Glass* [1992] 2 All ER 680.

Likewise, it seems that an action in respect of compensation for compulsory purchase under the Compulsory Purchase Act 1965 is also governed by section 9.[7]

"AN ACTION... BY VIRTUE OF ANY ENACTMENT"

It is important to emphasise that there may be a degree of overlap between a statutory provision which allows for the recovery of a sum of money and an action which sounds at common law under rules relevant to the law of contract or the law of tort. For the purposes of previous rules which governed the recovery of sums by way of a statutory provision, the general position was that in order for rules on specialties to apply, the action had to be one which could only be based upon the statutory provision under consideration. Accordingly, if it was possible for the action to be framed under some common law rule, in the alternative, the action could not be said to be one covered by the exceptional rules which applied to specialties.[8] In seeking to decide whether an action is one based upon a statute, it has been said that the courts will take a broad and realistic view of all the circumstances.[9] In *Brueton* v. *Woodward*[10] there was an action for the recovery of a gaming debt, as provided for in the Gaming Acts 1835 and 1922. Apparently on the basis that no action in respect of gaming debts existed at common law and that the statutory provisions under consideration effectively created something akin to a contractual relationship between the parties, the action was considered to be one based upon a statute, with the result that a 12-year limitation period applied. Although it has been asserted that the effect of the Limitation Act 1939, s 2(1)(d) upon which the present section 9 is based, was to do away with the old case law on what was meant by an "action upon a statute",[11] unfortunately, this does not appear to be the case on the wording of both the 1939 and the 1980 Acts, since it will still be necessary to ascertain whether the action is one for a sum of money or not and statutory provisions which are not concerned with such matters may still continue to be regarded as actions upon a specialty and therefore governed by section 8.

The leading authority on the question whether an action is one by virtue of an enactment is now that of the House of Lords in *Central Electricity Generating Board* v. *Halifax Corporation*[12] in which the respondent corporation was in possession of a sum of money to which the CEGB claimed to be entitled. The background to the case arose out of statutory provisions which allowed for the nationalisation of the electricity supply and which, the respondents claimed, had the effect of making the CEGB the successor to the body which controlled the supply of electricity prior to the date on which the relevant statute came into force in 1948. If the CEGB was to be regarded as the successor of the

---

7. See *Hillingdon Borough Council* v. *ARC Ltd* [1997] 3 All ER 506.

8. See *Shepherd* v. *Hills* (1855) 11 Ex 55; *Gutsell* v. *Reeve* [1936] 1 KB 272; *Aylott* v. *West Ham Corporation* [1927] 1 Ch 30.

9. *West Riding of Yorkshire County Council* v. *Huddersfield Corporation* [1957] 1 QB 540 at 546–47 *per* Lord Goddard CJ.

10. [1941] 1 KB 680.

11. Newsom & Abel Smith, *Preston & Newsom's Limitation of Actions* (3rd ed, 1953) p 52.

12. [1963] AC 785. See also *Moore* v. *Gadd, The Times*, 17 February 1997 in which an action for a declaration under the Insolvency Act 1986, s 214, to the effect that a director knew or ought to have concluded that there was no reasonable prospect that a company would avoid going into liquidation and could therefore be called on to make a contribution to the assets of the company was covered by s 9.

earlier body, the effect of the statutory provision was to entitle the Board to the money held by the respondent corporation, dating back to the time before 1948 when some local authorities had electricity-generating powers. Furthermore, there was an express statutory provision to the effect that, in the event of a dispute as to entitlement, the matter was to be decided by the relevant Minister of State.[13]

The key issue, for present purposes, was whether the relevant limitation period ran for 6 or 12 years from the date of accrual. The House of Lords determined that the relevant period was one of six years on the basis that this was an action for a sum recoverable by virtue of an enactment, rather than one based upon a specialty. In arriving at this conclusion, the House of Lords was of the opinion that the Limitation Act 1939 had removed the distinction, previously drawn, between suing on a statute and suing in respect of a cause of action provided for by a statute. However, as has been observed above, this may not be an accurate reflection of the effect of the 1939 Act and some of the older distinctions may still be important in determining whether section 9 applies to an action or not. It will be seen below that many actions derived from the existence of a statutory provision, in fact, give rise to an action in tort—for example many actions for damages in tort for breach of statutory duty, and it would be difficult to say that these are, in truth, actions governed by section 9.[14] However, in terms of policy, the decision in *Central Electricity Generating Board* v. *Halifax Corporation* seems to suggest that whatever be the literal construction of the language of section 9, it will be treated as having disposed of the difficulties associated with the pre-1939 distinction between actions upon a statute and those in respect of a cause of action provided for by statute. While the view was expressed prior to 1939 that "a right to compensation . . . is a very different thing from a cause of action",[15] since the enactment of the Limitation Act 1939 a broader view has been taken to the effect that the provision which section 9 now replaces was capable of extending to cover "a cause of proceeding in a court of law."[16] For these purposes, it seems that every action is a proceeding, although not every proceeding will be regarded as an action.

On the analysis provided in *Central Electricity Generating Board* v. *Halifax Corporation*, if a statutory provision implies a term into a contract, such as is the case with the Sale of Goods Act 1979, s 12 to 15 and the Supply of Goods and Services Act 1982, ss 13 to 15, the action cannot be said to be based purely on the statute and will be governed instead by the limitation period applicable to an action for breach of contract under the Limitation Act 1980, s 5. However, even in this regard, there appears to be a distinction between those statutory provisions which add terms to an existing contract,[17] as is the case with the statutory provisions immediately referred to above, and those statutory provisions which create the contractual relationship between the parties.[18] The first type of case is properly to be regarded as an action founded in contract, as opposed to the latter type, which may be regarded as an action pursuant to a statutory provision, since but for the existence of

13. A matter which raises the issue of accrual of the cause of action, considered below.
14. In any event, actions for breach of statutory duty were regarded, historically, as actions on the case, not as actions for a debt, which were regarded as the only type of action to which rules on specialties could apply: *Pratt* v. *Cook & Son & Co (St Paul's) Ltd* [1940] AC 437; *Thomson* v. *Lord Clanmorris* [1900] 1 Ch 718; *Tees Conservancy Commissioners* v. *James* [1935] Ch 544.
15. *Turner* v. *Midland Railway Co* [1911] 1 KB 832 at 835 *per* Avory J.
16. *China* v. *Harrow UDC* [1954] 1 QB 178 at 187 *per* Sellers J.
17. *Aylott* v. *West Ham Corporation* [1927] 1 Ch 30; *Gutsell* v. *Reeve* [1936] 1 KB 272.
18. *Cork & Bandon Railway Co* v. *Goode* (1853) 13 CB 826; *Re Cornwall Minerals Railway Co* [1897] 2 Ch 74.

the statute, no action would sound in contract.[19] This may be regarded as a justification for the decision in *Brueton* v. *Woodward*[20] since the position at common law has always been that contracts of gaming and wagering are unenforceable in a court of law. However, it may also be noted that the effect of the common law rule is not to forbid the parties from entering into such contracts, but merely to render the contract unenforceable should a dispute ever arise. Accordingly, it may be argued that it was not the Gaming Acts 1835 and 1922 which *created* the contractual relationship, but the will of the parties to the contract.

If the proper view of the contract in *Brueton* v. *Woodward* is that the contract was created by the parties and that the statute merely created a remedial right which did not previously exist, the decision to apply the 12-year limitation period is tenuously justified. However, there are other cases which are more difficult still to justify. For example in *Pegler* v. *Railways Executive*[21] the House of Lords held that an action brought by a railway worker for compensation in respect of loss of security following a merger between two railway companies was one for a sum of money due under a statute, so that a six-year limitation period applied. Here the relevant statutory provision appears to have created the right to compensation, since there appears to have been no corresponding common law right, yet for some reason, the longer limitation period was not applied.

The view expressed in *Central Electricity Generating Board* v. *Halifax Corporation* is broadly consistent with the position adopted in *Pegler* on the basis that the CEGB's entitlement to the money held by the respondent corporation was entirely dependent on the provisions of the statute, in which case the appropriate limitation period is the six-year period now contained in section 9. Furthermore, although not expressly stated in the judgments in *CEGB* v. *Halifax Corporation*, there is support for the view that cases which fall within section 9 may be regarded as an express exception to the limitation rules relating to specialties set out in section 8(1), being covered by the language of section 8(2).

It must be admitted that there is potential confusion to be found in the wording of section 9; however, the way the courts have approached the issue of what is to be regarded as "an action . . . by virtue of any enactment" does appear to be consistent, but perhaps not in line with a literal reading of the words of the section. Recently, it has been asserted in *Hillingdon Borough Council* v. *ARC Ltd*[22] that:

"These authorities establish the following propositions.

   (1) The expression 'action' in s 9 is extremely wide, encompassing all proceedings in a court of law: *China* v. *Harrow UDC*.
   (2) The expression 'cause of action' in s 9 is correspondingly wide: *China* v. *Harrow UDC*.
   (3) What may not have been a cause of action under the Statute of Limitations 1623 may be a cause of action for the purposes of the Limitation Act 1980: *China* v. *Harrow UDC*.
   (4) The policy of the Limitation Acts, to prevent the litigation of stale claims, is equally applicable to claims against public authorities for sums payable by them pursuant to statute: *Central Electricity Board* case . . .
   (5) A cause of action may accrue for the purposes of s 9 although a constituent element of the cause of action, if disrupted, may have to be determined by someone other than a court of law: the *Central Electricity Board* case.

---

19. *Brueton* v. *Woodward* [1941] 1 KB 680.
20. *Ibid*, and see fn 10 above with accompanying text.
21. [1947] 1 All ER 355.
22. [1997] 3 All ER 506.

(6) An action may be for a sum recoverable by virtue of an enactment even though the liability in question is not and cannot be quantified when the action is commenced: *Moore* v. *Gadd*."[23]

Whatever may be said of the case law in respect of the recovery of a sum of money, there is no doubt at all that if the right conferred by the statute is one which does not involve the recovery of such a sum, then the action must be treated as one to which section 8(1), in respect of specialties, applies.

In *Collin* v. *Duke of Westminster*[24] the plaintiff, a tenant, sought an enfranchisement order under the Leasehold Reform Act 1967, s 4. Having disposed of the possibility that the plaintiff's rights might derive from the lease, it was held by the Court of Appeal that the statute conferred the right to enfranchisement of the leasehold title. On the issue of limitation, it was held that since the plaintiff was asking for the freehold title to the land to be transferred to him rather than a sum of money, section 9 could not apply. Accordingly, this brought the 12-year rule applicable to specialties into play, with the result that the action was commenced in time.

LIQUIDATED AND UNLIQUIDATED SUMS

An important consideration under section 9 is whether the sum payable must be a liquidated sum, a sum ascertainable by reference to a set formula or an unliquidated sum, based upon, for example, the loss suffered by the plaintiff. It makes sense to regard the right to receive a set amount or an amount based on a statutory formula as a right pursuant to a statutory provision[25] to which section 9 must apply. However, there is less clarity over the issue of unliquidated sums. For example, there are some statutory provisions which create rights which never previously existed at common law or in equity, but which provide for the payment of damages based upon the loss suffered by the plaintiff in consequence of the breach of the statutory provision. Prime examples include the Misrepresentation Act 1967, s 2(1) which allows for the recovery of damages in respect of a negligent misrepresentation which induces a party to enter into a contract he would not otherwise have made. Other examples include the Patents Act 1977, s 13(4) which allows for the recovery of damages by a patent owner against a person guilty of patent infringement. The problem with both these provisions is that, since they use the language of damages, there is no specified or ascertainable sum of money which may be said to be due under the provisions of a statute.

Some support can be found for the view that section 9 does not apply to these cases. In *Sevcon* v. *Lucas CAV Ltd*[26] it was assumed by the House of Lords that the Patents Act 1977, s 13(4) conferred an action in tort.[27] Although *Central Electricity Generating Board* v. *Halifax Corporation*[28] was referred to, on a separate issue, it is clear from the judgments that section 9 had no application to the action. This last conclusion is probably correct, in that the action was one for an unliquidated amount and therefore cannot be regarded as a

23. *Ibid* at 518–19 *per* Stanley Burnton QC.
24. [1985] QB 581.
25. See *Pegler* v. *Railway Executive* [1947] 1 All ER 355. Cf *Brueton* v. *Woodward* [1941] 1 KB 680.
26. [1986] 2 All ER 104.
27. *Ibid* at 106 *per* Lord MacKay.
28. [1963] AC 785.

sum "recoverable by virtue of an enactment". In the view taken in *Sevcon*, if the action is one founded in tort, a six-year limitation period is provided for, which is the same as the period provided for in section 9. However, it is questionable whether an action under section 13(4) of the Patents Act 1977 should be regarded as a tort action, since, but for section 13(4), no action would exist in favour of the grantee of a patent. If these views are correct the only remaining possibility is that since the action is based on a statute which has been referred to as "the highest form of specialty",[29] then it is an action to which the Limitation Act 1980, s 8(1), should apply, in the absence of any other limitation period which prevents the application of section 8(1). Accordingly, the plaintiff in an action under the Patents Act 1977, s 13(4) should have 12 years within which to commence his action.

Applying the same reasoning to the Misrepresentation Act 1967, s 2(1), the question arises whether an action for damages under that provision is an action which sounds in contract or in tort or whether it is an action for the recovery of a sum payable by virtue of an enactment or whether it is an action on a specialty. It is clear that an action under section 2(1) is not to be regarded as one which sounds in contract, since a misrepresentation, generally, is not a contractual term, and because tortious rules on the measure of damages are now applied to such actions.[30] But this does not necessarily mean that an action under section 2(1) is one which sounds in tort. In particular, there is a view to the effect that an action under section 2(1) is *sui generis* and is to be regarded as neither a contract action[31] nor a tort action, in that liability does not depend on the representor being under a duty of care.[32] If this view is correct, the seemingly bizarre consequence is that remedial rules relevant to a tort action are being applied to an action which does not sound in tort, but it is difficult to see what other rules might be applied in the circumstances.

As to the limitation issue, it would seem to follow that neither section 2 nor section 5 of the Limitation Act 1980 can be applied. Moreover, on the reasoning applied to the Patents Act 1977, s 13(4) in *Sevcon* v. *Lucas CAV Ltd* the limitation period provided for in the Limitation Act 1980, s 9 cannot apply either, since an action for damages is not an action for a liquidated sum or a sum ascertainable by a set formula. Accordingly, it is arguable that the applicable limitation period is that in respect of specialties in the Limitation Act 1980, s 8(1). This conclusion may be regarded as unpalatable and the view expressed, *obiter*, in *Sevcon* v. *Lucas CAV Ltd* that the Patents Act 1977, s 13(4) allows for an action in tort, taken in conjunction with the application of tort rules on damages to actions under the Misrepresentation Act 1967, s 2(1), may point in the direction of a possible judicial "fudge" on this issue.

ACTIONS IN CONTRACT, ACTIONS IN TORT AND ACTIONS COVERED BY SECTION 9

The need to distinguish between actions which fall within the provisions of section 9 and those governed by sections 2 and 5 is less important than it used to be, since the limitation

---

29. *Central Electricity Generating Board* v. *Halifax Corporation* [1962] 3 All ER 915 at 919 *per* Lord Reid.
30. *Royscot Trust Ltd* v. *Rogerson* [1991] 3 All ER 294.
31. *Howard Marine & Dredging Co Ltd* v. *Ogden* [1978] QB 574 at 595 *per* Bridge LJ.
32. *Ibid* at 596 *per* Bridge LJ.

period, in each case, is one of six years, running from the date on which the cause of action accrued. Nevertheless, it is clear from the discussion above that if a statutory provision creates a right in favour of the plaintiff which is simply in addition to rights which already exist at common law, the appropriate limitation period will be found in sections 2 or 5 rather than in section 9. It follows from this that, if a statutory provision confers on an employee a right to payment of salary lost through joining the armed forces in times of war, this may be regarded as a statutory variation of the contract of employment, which is to be regarded as subject to the contractual limitation period in section 5.[33]

In contrast, if the statutory provision creates a contractual relationship where none previously existed, the plaintiff's action may, properly, be regarded as one by virtue of an enactment. For example, in *Cork & Bandon Railway Co* v. *Goode*[34] a private Act allowed a company to sue shareholders for any outstanding sum due in respect of that person's shareholding. In the event, the court held that this was an action on a specialty to which, at the time, a 20-year limitation period applied. However, in the light of *Central Electricity Generating Board* v. *Halifax Corporation*, this may now be viewed differently and be treated as a case which falls within the provisions of section 9.

Whether an action is one which sounds in tort or is one covered by section 9 is a question which has received little attention in relation to the limitation issue. Since a tort action is primarily concerned with compensation, it would appear that if the remedy sought by the plaintiff is not a compensatory remedy, the action may be treated as one to which section 9 can apply. For example, in *Post Office* v. *Official Solicitor*[35] the Post Office brought an action against the defendant tortfeasor for reimbursement of the value of a disability pension they were required to pay one of their employees as a result of injuries suffered due to the defendant's negligence. It was held that this was not an action for compensatory damages, but was, instead, an action for an indemnity. As such, it could not be regarded as an action which sounded in tort.[36] Accordingly, the action was treated as one for a sum payable under the relevant provisions of the Workmens' Compensation Act 1925, which, in fact, provided their own rules on limitation of actions, with the result that rules contained in the relevant Limitation Act were disapplied.[37]

ACCRUAL OF THE CAUSE OF ACTION

On the basis that the action is one which falls within the provisions of section 9, it needs to be considered what event triggers the running of time. There is nothing in section 9 itself which helps to identify the date on which time begins to run, with the result that it has been left to case law to identify the date on which the cause of action will accrue. It will be recalled that a cause of action cannot accrue until such time as exists "every fact which is material to be proved to enable the plaintiff to succeed, every fact which the defendant would have a right to traverse".[38]

33. *Aylott* v. *West Ham Corporation* [1927] 1 Ch 30. See also *Gutsell* v. *Reeve* [1936] 1 KB 272.
34. (1853) 13 CB 826.
35. [1951] 1 All ER 522. Cf *Sevcon* v. *Lucas CAV Ltd* [1986] 2 All ER 104.
36. *Ibid* at 527 *per* Barry J.
37. See *Lievers* v. *Barber Walker & Co Ltd* [1943] 1 All ER 386.
38. *Cooke* v. *Gill* (1873) LR 8 CP 107 at 116 *per* Brett J, cited with approval in *Coburn* v. *Colledge* [1897] 1 QB 702.

It has been seen that the paradigm case falling within section 9 is one in which a liquidated sum is payable on the occurrence of an event specified in the statutory provision. On the assumption that the sum is payable immediately, it would seem to follow that the cause of action will accrue on the occurrence of the event which triggers the right to payment. Greater difficulties may arise in the second type of case which falls within section 9, namely, those in which the entitlement to a sum is based on a statutory formula. A particular problem is that the statutory formula may require a third party to reach some determination before the sum can be assessed. Alternatively, the statute may provide that a third party has the right to determine whether the specified sum is payable at all. In either event, it is possible that the date on which time starts to run might be delayed until such time as the third party has reached his decision. A problem of this nature arose in *Central Electricity Generating Board* v. *Halifax Corporation*[39] since the relevant statutory provision which vested moneys held by pre-nationalisation electricity-generating bodies in the Board also provided that in the event of a dispute as to entitlement, that dispute would be resolved by the decision of the Minister of State. The particular problem which arose in this case was that although nationalisation occurred on 1 April 1948, the dispute was not referred to the Minister until 3 January 1957 and the Minister did not give his decision until 18 September 1958. Despite the considerable delay, the House of Lords concluded that the cause of action accrued in 1948 on the basis that the Minister's decision was no more than evidence of facts which existed in 1948 when nationalisation occurred. What seemed to convince the House of Lords that this was the appropriate date for the running of time was that the decision of the Minister was not a precondition to the bringing of the action. Accordingly, in 1948 all the relevant facts were in place and the CEGB could have commenced its action at that stage.

It does not follow, as a matter of course, that the decision of a third party will always be irrelevant, since it is clear from the decision in *Central Electricity Generating Board* v. *Halifax Corporation* that there may be occasions on which the third party decision may be a precondition to the running of time.

A further consideration in cases arising under section 9 is the specific wording of the statutory provision, since this may indicate, expressly or impliedly, the date on which time is to run against the plaintiff. However, the provision must be relevant to the particular action brought by the plaintiff. For example, the Housing Act 1957, s 10 provides that a local authority has a power to charge to a landlord the cost of putting leased property into a proper state of repair. In *Swansea City Council* v. *Glass*[40] work was completed but the action was commenced more than six years from the date of completion, but within six years of the date on which the first demand for payment was made. Although section 10 of the 1957 Act makes specific provision for the limitation issue in respect of summary proceedings, stating that time will run from the date of the demand, it makes no reference to proceedings based on a writ or summons. The Court of Appeal was not prepared to assume that a provision in respect of summary proceedings would also operate in the same way for the writ issued in the present case. For these purposes, it was stated that "where

---

39. [1963] AC 785. See also *Hillingdon Borough Council* v. *ARC Ltd* [1997] 3 All ER 506, indicating that it is irrelevant that compensation under the Compulsory Purchase Act 1965, s 11, may still have to be quantified by the Lands Tribunal. The cause of action is complete on the date on which the purchasing authority enters the land.

40. [1992] 2 All ER 680, CA.

the cause of action arises from a statute, the question as to what is an inherent element in the cause of action is one of construction".[41]

Accordingly, applying the *Cooke* v. *Gill* formula,[42] all relevant facts were in place when the work was completed, in which case, the action was commenced out of time.

A particular difficulty may arise where a statutory provision allows for payment of "compensation" in the event of the plaintiff suffering a loss covered by the statute. It may be that, in such cases, time runs from the date of damage, consistent with the rule in tort actions, or from the date on which the plaintiff incurs the expense involved in having to repair the damage caused. In *Yorkshire Electricity Board* v. *British Telecommunications plc*[43] Robert Goff LJ emphasised the inclusion of the word "compensation" in the Public Utilities Street Works Act 1950, s 26(6) in deciding that time should run against the plaintiff from the date on which damage was caused, rather than from the later date on which loss was suffered as a result of that damage. This remained the case despite the fact that at the date of damage it was impossible to quantify the extent of the loss. Presumably, since the word "compensation" figured so highly in Robert Goff LJ's reasoning, the action was effectively equated with one based on tortious principles, the primary objective of which is compensation for loss suffered, in respect of which time runs from the date of damage, regardless of problems of quantification.[44] However, where a statutory provision refers to or implies the existence of a right of compensation, it may also indicate that interest is to be payable in respect of that compensation from a specified date. The specification of such a date will generally be a very strong indication that that date is the date on which the cause of action accrued. Thus in *Hillingdon Borough Council* v. *ARC Ltd*[45] the Compulsory Purchase Act 1965, s 11, specifies that interest is payable on an award of compensation from the date of entry until the date of payment, thereby indicating that the date of entry is the date of accrual of the cause of action in cases of compulsory purchase.[46] Furthermore, the fact that the amount of compensation has to be quantified by a reference to the Lands Tribunal may be regarded as a procedural matter under which an existing right to compensation is referred for decision.[47]

CLAIMS FOR CONTRIBUTION

The Limitation Act 1980, s 9 applies to all claims based on a statutory provision which are not otherwise covered by some other limitation period specified in the Act. One such alternative set of rules applies to claims for contribution, since it is specifically provided in section 9(2) that section 9(1) does not apply to an action covered by section 10. The Limitation Act 1980, s 10 provides:

"(1) Where under section 1 of the Civil Liability (Contribution) Act 1978 any person becomes entitled to a right to recover contribution in respect of any damage from any other person, no action

41. *Ibid* at 685 *per* Taylor LJ.
42. See fn 38 above.
43. 129 Sol J 468, CA. See also *West Riding of Yorkshire County Council* v. *Huddersfield Corporation* [1957] 1 QB 540.
44. See Ch 18.
45. [1997] 3 All ER 506.
46. *Ibid* at 519 *per* Stanley Burnton QC.
47. *Ibid*.

to recover contribution by virtue of that right shall be brought after the expiration of two years from the date on which that right accrued.

(2) For the purposes of this section the date on which a right to recover contribution in respect of any damage accrues to any person (referred to below in this section as 'the relevant date') shall be ascertained as provided in subsections (3) and (4) below.

(3) If the person in question is held liable in respect of that damage—

   (a) by a judgment given in any civil proceedings; or
   (b) by an award made on any arbitration;

the relevant date shall be the date on which the judgment is given, or the award (as the case may be).

For the purposes of this subsection no account shall be taken of any judgment or award given or made on appeal in so far as it varies the amount of damages awarded against the person in question.

(4) If, in any case not within subsection (3) above, the person in question makes or agrees to make any payment to one or more persons in compensation for that damage (whether he admits any liability in respect of the damage or not), the relevant date shall be the earliest date on which the amount to be paid by him is agreed between him (or his representative) and the person (or each of the persons, as the case may be) to whom the payment is to be made.

(5) An action to recover contribution shall be one to which sections 28, 32 and 35 of this Act apply, but otherwise Parts II and III of this Act (except sections 34, 37 and 38) shall not apply for the purposes of this section."

The relevant law in respect of claims for contribution by one wrongdoer against someone who has also contributed to the same damage suffered by the plaintiff is now governed by the Civil Liability (Contribution) Act 1978,[48] section 1 of which provides:

"(1) Subject to the following provisions of this section, any person liable in respect of any damage suffered by another person may recover contribution from any other person liable in respect of the same damage (whether jointly with him or otherwise).

(2) A person shall be entitled to recover contribution by virtue of subsection (1) above notwithstanding that he has ceased to be liable in respect of the damage in question since the time when the damage occurred, provided that he was so liable immediately before he made or was ordered or agreed to make the payment in respect of which the contribution is sought.

(3) A person shall be liable to make contribution by virtue of subsection (1) above notwithstanding that he has ceased to be liable in respect of the damage in question since the time when the damage occurred, unless he ceased to be liable by virtue of the expiry of a period of limitation or prescription which extinguished the right on which the claim against him in respect of the damage was based.

(4) A person who has made or agreed to make any payment in bona fide settlement or compromise of any claim made against him in respect of any damage (including a payment into court which has been accepted) shall be entitled to recover contribution in accordance with this section without regard to whether or not he himself is or ever was liable in respect of the damage, provided, however, that he would have been liable assuming that the factual basis of the claim against him could be established.

(5) A judgment given in any action brought in any part of the United Kingdom or by or on behalf of the person who suffered the damage in question against any person from whom contribution is sought under this section shall be conclusive in the proceedings for contribution as to any issue determined by that judgment in favour of the person from whom the contribution is sought.

(6) References in this section to a person's liability in respect of any damage are references to any such liability which has been or could be established in an action brought against him in England and Wales by or on behalf of the person who suffered the damage; but it is immaterial that whether

48. See generally Law Comm No 79, *Law of Contract, Report on Contribution* on which the 1978 Act is based.

any issue arising in any such action was or would be determined (in accordance with the rules of private international law) by reference to the law of a country outside England and Wales."

As to matters of interpretation of section 1, section 6 provides:

"(1) A person is liable in respect of any damage for the purposes of this Act if the person who suffered it (or anyone representing his estate or dependants) is entitled to recover compensation from him in respect of that damage (whatever the legal basis of his liability, whether tort, breach of contract, breach of trust or otherwise).

(2) References in this Act to an action brought by or on behalf of the person who suffered any damage include references to an action brought for the benefit of his estate or dependants.

(3) In this Act 'dependants' has the same meaning as in the Fatal Accidents Act 1976 . . . ."

(a) The importance of contribution

In many cases where damage is caused, the plaintiff's loss may result from the individual or cumulative wrongful actions of a number of persons. This is especially the case where latent building damage is suffered by a building owner because of the large number of people involved in the process of design and construction of buildings. For example, in the case of defective foundations to a building there could be individual or collective acts of negligence or other breach of duty on the part of an architect, a structural engineer, a builder and a local authority. Similarly large numbers of defendants may also be involved in claims in respect of a defective product since there may be relevant breaches of duty on the part of a designer, a manufacturer, an importer and the retailer.

Where a plaintiff has suffered a single, identifiable loss as a result of multiple breaches of duty on the part of a number of defendants, the common law allows that plaintiff to bring an action in respect of the full amount of that loss against any one of the potential defendants,[49] regardless of the comparative degree of the blameworthiness of each of those defendants. However, it might be regarded as an unfair rule which allows a single defendant to bear the full extent of that loss when others also bear some responsibility for the loss suffered by the plaintiff. The original common law rule in this respect was harsh in that it did not allow the defendant singled out by the plaintiff to seek any form of recompense or indemnity from other potential defendants, since his loss was treated as lying where it fell.[50] Subsequently, the harshness of the common law rule was mitigated by statutory intervention[51] culminating in the provisions of the Civil Liability (Contribution) Act 1978 set out above.

(b) Effects of the 1978 Act as between the plaintiff and the defendants

The 1978 Act does not affect the common law rule that the plaintiff may elect between multiple defendants as to which one he will sue, but is primarily concerned with the contribution position as between defendants. However, this is not to say that the 1978 Act has no effect on the position of the plaintiff. For example, the plaintiff, having made his initial choice, now has a right to bring later proceedings against another defendant.[52]

---

49. *Clark* v. *Newsam* (1847) 1 Ex 131.
50. *Merryweather* v. *Nixan* (1799) 8 TR 186.
51. An earlier attempt to dispose of the effects of the common law rule was to be found in the Law Reform (Married Women and Tortfeasors) Act 1935, s 6(1)(c).
52. Civil Liability (Contribution) Act 1978, s 3.

However, in respect of these later proceedings, the plaintiff will not be entitled to costs, in the absence of proof of a reasonable excuse for bringing those later proceedings.[53] Accordingly, the better approach for a plaintiff to adopt will be to sue all potential defendants in the same action.

By virtue of section 1(1) of the 1978 Act any person liable in respect of damage suffered by another may recover contribution from a second defendant liable in respect of the same damage, provided that the person suffering the damage, or a person representing his estate or dependants, is entitled to recover compensation. Moreover, it should be emphasised that section 6(1) of the 1978 Act specifies that it makes no difference what is the basis of the defendant's liability. Accordingly, it could be liability in tort or contract or some other form of liability for the damage suffered, including a breach of trust.[54]

The right of contribution is available in respect of both judgment debts and settlements out of court.[55] In order to qualify for a contribution from a third party (T), the defendant in the original proceedings (D) must satisfy two requirements. First D must show that he was liable to the plaintiff (P) immediately before the date of the judgment or compromise under which P was paid by D,[56] with the effect that it makes no difference to D's right of contribution that an action by P against D would have been time barred at the date of the contribution proceedings. Secondly, D must be able to show that T would have been liable for some or all of the loss suffered by P, had T been sued by P.[57] The burden of proof in this last respect is removed from D if T has, in fact, been sued by P in respect of part of his loss, since this is deemed to be conclusive evidence of T's liability to contribute.[58] Where T is held to be liable to contribute, the amount he will be required to pay will depend on the circumstances of the case. There is no fixed formula, but the court may order him to pay such sum as may be found by the court to be just and equitable, having regard to the extent of T's responsibility for the damage in question.[59]

(c) Limitation issues and contribution

(i) The position of the original defendant

The effect of section 1(2) of the 1978 Act is to entitle D, where he has been held liable to compensate P, to bring contribution proceedings against T even where, at the date of the contribution proceedings, an action by P against D would have been time barred.

As such, any primary limitation period as between P and D is regarded as an irrelevance. However, for these purposes, it is important to emphasise that D must be able to show that he was legally liable to P in order to be able to commence contribution proceedings against T. Thus if D made an *ex gratia* payment to P under which there was no admission of liability or there is a settlement between P and D with no indication of any acceptance of liability, D may not be able to seek a contribution from T.[60]

53. Civil Liability (Contribution) Act 1978, s 4.
54. Civil Liability (Contribution) Act 1978, s 6(1).
55. Civil Liability (Contribution) Act 1978, s 1(4).
56. Civil Liability (Contribution) Act 1978, s 1(2).
57. Civil Liability (Contribution) Act 1978, s 1(6). This may even apply to class actions: *Choudhury* v. *Hussain* (1989) 138 NLJ 1416.
58. Civil Liability (Contribution) Act 1978, s 1(5).
59. Civil Liability (Contribution) Act 1978, s 2(1). The amount awarded may range from zero to a full indemnity: Civil Liability (Contribution) Act 1978, s 2(2).
60. *Harper* v. *Gray & Walker* [1985] 1 WLR 1196.

(ii) The position of the third party

Relevant limitation periods for the purposes of contribution proceedings are set out in the Limitation Act 1980, s 10. For these purposes, D has a period of two years in which to commence contribution proceedings against T, time running from the date of accrual of D's right to bring those proceedings. The date of accrual is specified to differ according to the circumstances of the case. According to section 10(3), where D is liable to P by virtue of a judgment in civil proceedings or by virtue of an arbitration award, time will begin to run against D from the date of the judgment or award, this remaining the case where the quantum of damages is altered on appeal. Moreover, it appears that the judgment or award must also settle the amount of D's liability as well as its existence.[61]

Where D's liability is not based on a judgment or arbitral award, but on a settlement contract, section 10(4) provides that time will run against D from the date on which the contract is made rather than from the date on which the agreed sum is paid or payable. However, for these purposes, the agreement must relate to the amount of the settlement. Furthermore, by virtue of section 10(5) some provisions in Parts II and III of the 1980 Act do apply to contribution proceedings, with the result that rules on disability, fraud, deliberate concealment and mistake,[62] if appropriate, may serve to postpone the running of time or otherwise extend the limitation period. The general effect of the disapplication of Parts II and III of the 1980 Act means that rules on acknowledgment (sections 29–31) will not apply to contribution proceedings, so that the two-year limitation period provided for in such cases cannot be extended in a case where T acknowledges to D his responsibility for the harm suffered by P. Also excluded from consideration in contribution proceedings are the special rules on discretion applied to personal injury actions by virtue of section 33, but this seems to fit logically with the scheme in section 33 which is concerned with hardship to the plaintiff. Clearly, whether or not D is allowed to commence contribution proceedings against T will have no bearing on P, since he will have received compensation from D arising out of the earlier proceedings.

(iii) The operation of the Limitation Act 1980, s 10

A source of difficulty may arise due to the possibility of a conflict between two different limitation periods, namely that which applies to the contribution proceedings between D and T and that which applies to direct proceedings between P and T, had P decided to sue T directly.

If D sues T for contribution within the period provided for in section 10 and those proceedings are also brought at a time when a direct action by P against T would also have been within time, T can have no grounds for complaint since, regardless of the contribution proceedings, he could also have been sued by P for any loss caused by his breach of duty. The most likely set of circumstances in which events of this kind will come about is in a case where the running of time against P is dependent upon P's knowledge of relevant facts, regardless of the date on which damage is caused.[63]

---

61. *Ronex Properties Ltd* v. *John Laing Construction Ltd* [1982] 3 All ER 961.
62. Limitation Act 1980, ss 28 and 32, and see Ch 6.
63. As is provided for in personal injury actions by virtue of the Limitation Act 1980, s 11; defective products cases by virtue of the Limitation Act 1980, s 11A and latent damage cases as provided for by Limitation Act 1980, s 14A.

   Greater difficulty may be associated with cases in which a direct action by P against T would have been time barred at the time when the contribution proceedings are commenced within the time limit provided for in section 10. For example, suppose builder D negligently lays foundations to a building, which is sold to P in year 1, following a negligent inspection of those foundations by local authority T. If damage occurs in year 5 which becomes apparent in year 7 (at which point the house becomes unsafe) and P sues D in year 10, obtaining judgment in year 12, and D does not commence contribution proceedings until year 14, the problem which arises is that any action by P against T in year 14 would be commenced more than six years from the date on which P was aware of relevant facts. However, under section 10, D's action for contribution is commenced within the two-year period.

   A further difficulty which can arise in the context of latent damage claims and those in respect of defective products is that relevant rules on limitation of actions include a long-stop provision.[64] The problem this may give rise to is that an action by P against T may have become barred outright, not merely caught by an ordinary limitation period which bars the remedy but does not extinguish P's legal right. In these circumstances, the effect of the 1978 Act, s 1(3) is that there is a distinction between a bar on pursuing a remedy and a bar which extinguishes the cause of action. In the latter case, section 1(3) operates so as to prevent D from bringing contribution proceedings against T where a long-stop provision or some other rule of prescription extinguishes P's action against T.

   As a result of these rules, it becomes crucial to distinguish between long-stop provisions which extinguish the plaintiff's right of action and those limitation provisions which merely bar a remedy. In this respect, there is an important difference between the Limitation Act 1980, s 11A(3) in relation to defective products and section 14B(1) and (2) taken together which have the former effect and are therefore covered by section 1(3) of the 1978 Act, thereby preventing D from bringing contribution proceedings outside the long-stop period.

---

64. Limitation Act 1980, ss 11A(3) (10-year long-stop) and 14B(1) (15-year long-stop). See also Chs 20 and 21.

APPENDIX 1

LIMITATION ACT 1980

ARRANGEMENT OF SECTIONS

425

An Act to consolidate the Limitation Acts 1939 to 1980.

[13th November 1980]

PART I. ORDINARY TIME LIMITS FOR DIFFERENT CLASSES OF ACTION

Time limits under Part I subject to extension or exclusion under Part II

Time limits under Part I subject to extension or exclusion under Part II

1.—(1) This Part of this Act gives the ordinary time limits for bringing actions of the various classes mentioned in the following provisions of this Part.

(2) The ordinary time limits given in this Part of this Act are subject to extension or exclusion in accordance with the provisions of Part II of this Act.

Actions founded on tort

Time limit for actions founded on tort

2. An action founded on tort shall not be brought after the expiration of six years from the date on which the cause of actions accrued.

Time limit in case of successive conversions and extinction of title of owner of converted goods

3.—(1) Where any cause of action in respect of the conversion of a chattel has accrued to any person and, before he recovers possession of the chattel, a further conversion takes place, no action shall be brought in respect of the further conversion after the expiration of six years from the accrual of the cause of action in respect of the original conversion.

(2) Where any such cause of action has accrued to any person and the period prescribed for bringing that action has expired and he has not during that period recovered possession of the chattel, the title of that person to the chattel shall be extinguished.

Special time limit in case of theft

4.—(1) The right of any person from whom a chattel is stolen to bring an action in respect of the theft shall not be subject to the time limits under sections 2 and 3(1) of this Act, but if his title to the chattel is extinguished under section 3(2) of this Act he may not bring an action in respect of a theft preceding the loss of his title, unless the theft in question preceded the conversion from which time began to run for the purposes of section 3(2).

(2) Subsection (1) above shall apply to any conversion related to the theft of a chattel as it applies to the theft of a chattel; and, except as provided below, every conversion following the theft of a chattel before the person from whom it is stolen recovers possession of it shall be regarded for the purposes of this section as related to the theft.

If anyone purchases the stolen chattel in good faith neither the purchase nor any conversion following it shall be regarded as related to the theft.

(3) Any cause of action accruing in respect of the theft or any conversion related to the theft of a chattel to any person from whom the chattel is stolen shall be disregarded for the purpose of applying section 3(1) or (2) of this Act to his case.

(4) Where in any action brought in respect of the conversion of a chattel it is proved that the chattel was stolen from the plaintiff or anyone through whom he claims it shall be presumed that any conversion following the theft is related to the theft unless the contrary is shown.

(5) In this section "theft" includes —

(a) any conduct outside England and Wales which would be theft if committed in England and Wales; and

(b) obtaining any chattel (in England and Wales or elsewhere) in the circumstances described in section 15(1) of the Theft Act 1968 (obtaining by deception) or by blackmail within the meaning of section 21 of that Act;

and references in this section to a chattel being "stolen" shall be construed accordingly.

Time limit for actions for libel or slander

4A. The time limit under section 2 of this Act shall not apply to an action for libel or slander, but no such action shall be brought after the expiration of three years from the date on which the cause of action accrued.

Actions founded on simple contract

Time limit for actions founded on simple contract

5. An action founded on simple contract shall not be brought after the expiration of six years from the date on which the cause of action accrued.

Special time limit for actions in respect of certain loans

6.—(1) Subject to subsection (3) below, section 5 of this Act shall not bar the right of action on a contract of loan to which this section applies.

(2) This section applies to any contract of loan which —

    (a) does not provide for repayment of the debt on or before a fixed or determinable date; and

    (b) does not effectively (whether or not it purports to do so) make the obligation to repay the debt conditional on a demand for repayment made by or on behalf of the creditor or on any other matter;

except where in connection with taking the loan the debtor enters into any collateral obligation to pay the amount of the debt or any part of it (as, for example, by delivering a promissory note as security for the debt) on terms which would exclude the application of this section to the contract of loan if they applied directly to repayment of the debt.

(3) Where a demand in writing for repayment of the debt under a contract of loan to which this section applies is made by or on behalf of the creditor (or, where there are joint creditors, by or on behalf of any one of them) section 5 of this Act shall thereupon apply as if the cause of action to recover the debt had accrued on the date on which the demand was made.

(4) In this section "promissory note" has the same meaning as in the Bills of Exchange Act 1882.

Time limit for actions to enforce certain awards

7. An action to enforce an award, where the submission is not by an instrument under seal, shall not be brought after the expiration of six years from the date on which the cause of action accrued.

General rule for actions on a specialty

Time limit for actions on a specialty

8.—(1) An action upon a specialty shall not be brought after the expiration of twelve years from the date on which the cause of action accrued.

(2) Subsection (1) above shall not affect any action for which a shorter period of limitation is prescribed by any other provision of this Act.

Actions for sums recoverable by statute

Time limit for actions for sums recoverable by statute

9.—(1) An action to recover any sum recoverable by virtue of any enactment shall not be brought after the expiration of six years from the date on which the cause of action accrued.

(2) Subsection (1) above shall not affect any action to which section 10 of this Act applies.

Special time limit for claiming contribution

10.—(1) Where under section 1 of the Civil Liability (Contribution) Act 1978 any person becomes entitled to a right to recover contribution in respect of any damage from any other person, no action to recover contribution by virtue of that right shall be brought after the expiration of two years from the date on which that right accrued.

(2) For the purposes of this section the date on which a right to recover contribution in respect of any damage accrues to any person (referred to below in this section as "the relevant date") shall be ascertained as provided in subsections (3) and (4) below.

(3) If the person in question is held liable in respect of that damage —

    (a) by a judgment given in any civil proceedings; or
    (b) by an award made on any arbitration;

the relevant date shall be the date on which the judgment is given, or the date of the award (as the case may be).

For the purposes of this subsection no account shall be taken of any judgment or award given or made on appeal in so far as it varies the amount of damages awarded against the person in question.

(4) If, in any case not within subsection (3) above, the person in question makes or agrees to make any payment to one or more persons in compensation for that damage (whether he admits any liability in respect of the damage or not), the relevant date shall be the earliest date on which the amount to be paid by him is agreed between him (or his representative) and the person (or each of the persons, as the case may be) to whom the payment is to be made.

(5) An action to recover contribution shall be one to which sections 28, 32 and 35 of this Act apply, but otherwise Parts II and III of this Act (except sections 34, 37 and 38) shall not apply for the purposes of this section.

Actions in respect of wrongs causing personal injuries or death

Special time limit for actions in respect of personal injuries

11.—(1) This section applies to any action for damages for negligence, nuisance or breach of duty (whether the duty exists by virtue of a contract or of provision made by or under a statute or independently of any contract or any such provision) where the damages claimed by the plaintiff for the negligence, nuisance or breach of duty consist of or include damages in respect of personal injuries to the plaintiff or any other person.

(2) None of the time limits given in the preceding provisions of this Act shall apply to an action to which this section applies.

(3) An action to which this section applies shall not be brought after the expiration of the period applicable in accordance with subsection (4) or (5) below.

(4) Except where subsection (5) below applies. the period of applicable is three years from —

    (a) the date on which the cause of action accrued; or
    (b) the date of knowledge (if later) of the person injured.

(5) If the person injured dies before the expiration of the period mentioned in subsection (4) above, the period applicable as respects the cause of action surviving for the benefit of his estate by virtue of section 1 of the Law Reform (Miscellaneous Provisions) Act 1934 shall be three years from —

    (a) the date of death; or
    (b) the date of the personal representative's knowledge;

whichever is the later.

(6) For the purposes of this section "personal representative" includes any person who is or has been a personal representative of the deceased, including an executor who has not proved the will (whether or not he has renounced probate) but not anyone appointed only as a special personal representative in relation to settled land; and regard shall be had to any knowledge acquired by any such person while a personal representative or previously.

(7) If there is more than one personal representative, and their dates of knowledge are different, subsection (5)(b) above shall read as referring to the earliest of those dates.

Actions in respect of defective products

11A.—(1) This section shall apply to an action for damages by virtue of any provision of Part I of the Consumer Protection Act 1987.

(2) None of the time limits given in the preceding provisions of this Act shall apply to an action to which this section applies.

(3) An action to which this section applies shall not be brought after the expiration of the period of ten years from the relevant time, within the meaning of section 4 of the said Act of 1987; and this subsection shall operate to extinguish a right of action and shall do so whether or not that right of action had accrued, or time under the following provisions of this Act had begun to run, at the end of the said period of ten years.

(4) Subject to subsection (5) below, an action to which this section applies in which the damages claimed by the plaintiff consist of or include damages in respect of personal injuries to the plaintiff or any other person or loss of or damage to any property, shall not be brought after the expiration of the period of three years from whichever is the later of —

    (a) the date on which the cause of action accrued; and
    (b) the date of knowledge of the injured person or, in the case of loss of or damage to property, the date of knowledge of the plaintiff or (if earlier) of any person in whom his cause of action was previously vested.

(5) If in a case where the damages claimed by the plaintiff consist of or include damages in respect of personal injuries to the plaintiff or any other person the injured person died before the expiration of the period mentioned in subsection (4) above, that subsection shall have effect as respects the cause of action surviving for the benefit of his estate by virtue of section 1 of the Law Reform (Miscellaneous Provisions) Act 1934 as if for the reference to that period there were substituted a reference to the period of three years from whichever is the later of —

    (a) the date of death; and
    (b) the date of the personal representative's knowledge.

(6) For the purposes of this section "personal representative" includes any person who is or has been a personal representative of the deceased, including an executor who has not proved the will (whether or not he has renounced probate) but not anyone appointed only as a special personal representative in relation to settled land; and regard shall be had to any knowledge acquired by any such person while a personal representative or previously.

(7) If there is more than one personal representative and their dates of knowledge are different, subsection (5)(b) above shall be read as referring to the earliest of those dates.

(8) Expressions used in this section or section 14 of this Act and in Part I of the Consumer Protection Act 1987 have the same meanings in this section or that section as in that Part; and section 1(1) of that Act (Part I to be construed as enacted for the purpose of complying with the product liability Directive) shall apply for the purpose of construing this section and the following provisions of this Act so far as they relate to an action by virtue of any provision of that Part as it applies for the purpose of construing that Part.

Special time limit for actions under Fatal Accidents legislation

12.—(1) An action under the Fatal Accidents Act 1976 shall not be brought if the death occurred when the person injured could no longer maintain an action and recover damages in respect of the injury (whether because of a time limit in this Act or in any other Act, or for any other reason).

Where any such action by the injured person would have been barred by the time limit in section 11 or 11A of this Act, no account shall be taken of the possibility of that time limit being overridden under section 33 of this Act.

(2) None of the time limits given in the preceding provisions of this Act shall apply to an action under the Fatal Accidents Act 1976, but no such action shall be brought after the expiration of three years from —

(a) the date of death; or
(b) the date of knowledge of the person for whose benefit the action is brought;

whichever is the later.

(3) An action under the Fatal Accidents Act 1976 shall be one to which sections 28, 33 and 35 of this Act apply, and the application to any such action of the time limit under subsection (2) above shall be subject to section 39; but otherwise Parts II and III of this Act shall not apply to any such action.

Operation of time limit under section 12 in relation to different dependants

13.—(1) Where there is more than one person for whose benefit an action under the Fatal Accidents Act 1976 is brought, section 12(2)(b) of this Act shall be applied separately to each of them.

(2) Subject to subsection (3) below, if by virtue of subsection (1) above the action would be outside the time limit given by section 12(2) as regards one or more, but not all, of the persons for whose benefit it is brought, the court shall direct that any person as regards whom the action would be outside that limit shall be excluded from those for whom the action is brought.

(3) The court shall not give such a direction if it is shown that if the action were brought exclusively for the benefit of the person in question it would not be defeated by a defence of limitation (whether in consequence of section 28 of this Act or an agreement between the parties not to raise the defence, or otherwise).

Definition of date of knowledge for purposes of sections 11 and 12

14.—(1) Subject to subsection (1A) below, in sections 11 and 12 of this Act references to a person's date of knowledge are references to the date on which he first had knowledge of the following facts —

(a) that the injury in question was significant; and
(b) that the injury was attributable in whole or in part to the act or omission which is alleged to constitute negligence, nuisance or breach of duty; and
(c) the identity of the defendant; and
(d) if it is alleged that the act or omission was that of a person other than the defendant, the identity of that person and the additional facts supporting the bringing of an action against the defendant;

and knowledge that any acts or omissions did or did not, as a matter of law, involve negligence, nuisance or breach of duty is irrelevant.

(1A) In section 11A of this Act and in section 12 of this Act so far as that section applies to an action by virtue of section 6(1)(a) of the Consumer Protection Act 1987 (death caused by defective product) references to a person's date of knowledge are references to the date on which he first had knowledge of the following facts —

(a) such facts about the damage caused by the defect as would lead a reasonable person who had suffered such damage to consider it sufficiently serious to justify his instituting proceedings for damages against a defendant who did not dispute liability and was able to satisfy a judgment; and
(b) that the damage was wholly or partly attributable to the facts and circumstances alleged to constitute the defect; and
(c) the identity of the defendant;

but, in determining the date on which a person first had such knowledge there shall be disregarded both the extent (if any) of that person's knowledge on any date of whether particular facts or circumstances would or would not, as a matter of law, constitute a defect and, in a case relating to loss of or damage to property, any knowledge which that person had on a date on which he had no right of action by virtue of Part I of that Act in respect of the loss or damage.

(2) For the purposes of this section an injury is significant if the person whose date of knowledge is in question would reasonably have considered it sufficiently serious to justify his instituting

proceedings for damages against a defendant who did not dispute liability and was able to satisfy a judgment.

(3) For the purposes of this section a person's knowledge includes knowledge which he might reasonably have been expected to acquire —

(a) from facts observable or ascertainable by him; or
(b) from facts ascertainable by him with the help of medical or other appropriate expert advice which it is reasonable for him to seek;

but a person shall not be fixed under this subsection with knowledge of a fact ascertainable only with the help of expert advice so long as he has taken all reasonable steps to obtain (and, where appropriate, to act on) that advice.

Actions in respect of latent damage not involving personal injuries

Special time limit for negligence actions where facts relevant to cause of action are not known at date of accrual

14A.—(1) This section applies to any action for damages for negligence, other than one to which section 11 of this Act applies, where the starting date for reckoning the period of limitation under subsection (4)(b) below falls after the date on which the cause of action accrued.

(2) Section 2 of this Act shall not apply to an action to which this section applies.

(3) An action to which this section applies shall not be brought after the expiration of the period applicable in accordance with subsection (4) below.

(4) That period is either —

(a) six years from the date on which the cause of action accrued; or
(b) three years from the starting date as defined by subsection (5) below, if that period expires later than the period mentioned in paragraph (a) above.

(5) For the purposes of this section, the starting date for reckoning the period of limitation under subsection (4)(b) above is the earliest date on which the plaintiff or any person in whom the cause of action was vested before him first had both the knowledge required for bringing an action for damages in respect of the relevant damage and a right to bring such an action.

(6) In subsection (5) above "the knowledge required for bringing an action for damages in respect of the relevant damage" means knowledge both —

(a) of the material facts about the damage in respect of which damages are claimed; and
(b) of the other facts relevant to the current action mentioned in subsection (8) below.

(7) For the purposes of subsection (6)(a) above, the material facts about the damage are such facts about the damage as would lead a reasonable person who had suffered such damage to consider it sufficiently serious to justify his instituting proceedings for damages against a defendant who did not dispute liability and was able to satisfy a judgment.

(8) The other facts referred to in subsection (6)(b) above are —

(a) that the damage was attributable in whole or in part to the act or omission which is alleged to constitute negligence; and
(b) the identity of the defendant; and
(c) if it alleged that the act or omission was that of a person other than the defendant, the identity of that person and the additional facts supporting the bringing of an action against the defendant.

(9) Knowledge that any acts or omissions did or did not, as a matter of law, involve negligence is irrelevant for the purposes of subsection (5) above.

(10) For the purposes of this section a person's knowledge includes knowledge which he might reasonably have been expected to acquire —

(a) from facts observable or ascertainable by him; or
(b) from facts ascertainable by him with the help of appropriate expert advice which it is reasonable for him to seek;

but a person shall not be taken by virtue of this subsection to have knowledge of a fact ascertainable only with the help of expert advice so long as he has taken all reasonable steps to obtain (and, where appropriate, to act on) that advice.

Overriding time limit for negligence actions not involving personal injuries

14B.—(1) An action for damages for negligence, other than one to which section 11 of this Act applies, shall not be brought after the expiration of fifteen years from the date of (or, if more than one, from the last of the dates) on which there occurred any act or omission —

(a) which is alleged to constitute negligence; and

(b) to which the damage in respect of which damages are claimed is alleged to be attributable (in whole or in part).

(2) This section bars the right of action in a case to which subsection (1) above applies notwithstanding that —

(a) the cause of action has not yet accrued; or

(b) where section 14A of this Act applies to the action, the date which is for the purposes of that section the starting date for reckoning the period mentioned in subsection (4)(b) of that section has not yet occurred;

before the end of the period of limitation prescribed by this section.

Actions to recover land and rent

Time limit for actions to recover land

15.—(1) No action shall be brought by any person to recover any land after the expiration of twelve years from the date on which the right of action accrued to him or, if it first accrued to some person through whom he claims, to that person.

(2) Subject to the following provisions of this section, where —

(a) the estate or interest claimed was an estate or interest in reversion or remainder or any other future estate or interest and the right of action to recover the land accrued on the date on which the estate or interest fell into possession by the determination of the preceding estate or interest; and

(b) the person entitled to the preceding estate or interest (not being a term of years absolute) was not in possession of the land on that date;

no action shall be brought by the person entitled to the succeeding estate or interest after the expiration of twelve years from the date on which the right of action accrued to the person entitled to the preceding estate or interest or six years from the date on which the right of action accrued to the person entitled to the succeeding estate or interest, whichever period last expires.

(3) Subsection (2) above shall not apply to any estate or interest which falls into possession on the determination of an entailed interest and which might have been barred by the person entitled to the entailed interest.

(4) No person shall bring an action to recover any estate or interest in land under an assurance taking effect after the right of action to recover the land had accrued to the person by whom the assurance was made or some person through whom he claimed or some person entitled to a preceding estate or interest, unless the action is brought within the period during which the person by whom the assurance was made could have brought such an action.

(5) Where any person is entitled to any estate or interest in land in possession and, while so entitled, is also entitled to any future estate or interest in that land, and his right to recover the estate or interest in possession is barred under this Act, no action shall be brought by that person, or by any person claiming through him, in respect of the future estate or interest, unless in the meantime possession of the land has been recovered by a person entitled to an intermediate estate or interest.

(6) Part I of Schedule 1 to this Act contains provisions for determining the date of accrual of rights of action to recover land in the cases there mentioned.

(7) Part II of that Schedule contains provisions modifying the provisions of this section in their application to actions brought by, or by a person claiming through, the Crown or any spiritual or eleemosynary corporation sole.

Time limit for redemption actions

16. When a mortgagee of land has been in possession of any of the mortgaged land for a period of twelve years, no action to redeem the land of which the mortgagee has been so in possession shall be brought after the end of that period by the mortgagor or any person claiming through him.

Extinction of title to land after expiration of time limit

17. Subject to —

    (a) section 18 of this Act; and
    (b) section 75 of the Land Registration Act 1925;

at the expiration of the period prescribed by this Act for any person to bring an action to recover land (including a redemption action) the title of that person to the land shall be extinguished.

Settled land and land held on trust

18.—(1) Subject to section 21(1) and (2) of this Act, the provisions of this Act shall apply to equitable interests in land, including interests in the proceeds of the sale of land held upon trust for sale, as they apply to legal estates.

Accordingly a right of action to recover the land shall, for the purposes of this Act but not otherwise, be treated as accruing to a person entitled in possession to such an equitable interest in the like manner and circumstances, and on the same date, as it would accrue if his interest were a legal estate in the land (and any relevant provision of Part I of Schedule 1 to this Act shall apply in any such case accordingly).

(2) Where the period prescribed by this Act has expired for the bringing of an action to recover land by a tenant for life or a statutory owner of settled land —

    (a) his legal estate shall not be extinguished if and so long as the right of action to recover the land of any person entitled to a beneficial interest in the land either has not accrued or has not been barred by this Act; and
    (b) the legal estate shall accordingly remain vested in the tenant for life or statutory owner and shall devolve in accordance with the Settled Land Act 1925;

but if and when every such right of action has been barred by this Act, his legal estate shall be extinguished.

(3) Where any land is held upon trust (including a trust for sale) and the period prescribed by this Act has expired for the bringing of an action to recover the land by the trustees, the estate of the trustees shall not be extinguished if and so long as the right of action to recover the land of any person entitled to a beneficial interest in the land or in the proceeds of sale either has not accrued or has not been barred by this Act; but if and when every such right of action has been so barred the estate of the trustees shall be extinguished.

(4) Where —

    (a) any settled land is vested in a statutory owner; or
    (b) any land is held upon trust (including a trust for sale);

an action to recover the land may be brought by the statutory owner or trustees on behalf of any person entitled to a beneficial interest in possession in the land or in the proceeds of sale whose right of action has not been barred by this Act, notwithstanding that the right of action of the statutory owner or trustees would apart from this provision have been barred by this Act.

Time limit for actions to recover rent

19. No action shall be brought, or distress made, to recover arrears of rent, or damages in respect of arrears of rent, after the expiration of six years from the date on which the arrears became due.

Actions to recover money secured by a mortgage or charge or to recover proceeds
of the sale of land

Time limit for actions to recover money secured by a mortgage or charge or to recover proceeds of the sale of land

20.—(1) No action shall be brought to recover —

   (a) any principal sum of money secured by a mortgage or other charge on property (whether real or personal); or

   (b) proceeds of the sale of land;

after the expiration of twelve years from the date on which the right to receive the money accrued.

(2) No foreclosure action in respect of mortgaged personal property shall be brought after the expiration of twelve years from the date on which the right to foreclose accrued.

But if the mortgagee was in possession of the mortgaged property after that date, the right to foreclose on the property which was in his possession shall not be treated as having accrued for the purposes of this subsection until the date on which his possession discontinued.

(3) The right to receive any principal sum of money secured by a mortgage or other charge and the right to foreclose on the property subject to the mortgage or charge shall not be treated as accruing so long as that property comprises any future interest or any life insurance policy which has not matured or been determined.

(4) Nothing in this section shall apply to a foreclosure action in respect of mortgaged land, but the provisions of this Act relating to actions to recover land shall apply to such an action.

(5) Subject to subsections (6) and (7) below, no action to recover arrears of interest payable in respect of any sum of money secured by a mortgage or other charge or payable in respect of proceeds of the sale of land, or to recover damages in respect of such arrears shall be brought after the expiration of six years from the date on which the interest became due.

(6) Where —

   (a) a prior mortgagee or other incumbrancer has been in possession of the property charged; and

   (b) an action is brought within one year of the discontinuance of that possession by the subsequent incumbrancer;

the subsequent incumbrancer may recover by that action all the arrears of interest which fell due during the period of possession by the prior incumbrancer or damages in respect of those arrears, notwithstanding that the period exceeded six years.

(7) Where —

   (a) the property subject to the mortgage or charge comprises any future interest or life insurance policy; and

   (b) it is a term of the mortgage or charge that arrears of interest shall be treated as part of the principal sum of money secured by the mortgage or charge;

interest shall not be treated as becoming due before the right to recover the principal sum of money has accrued or is treated as having accrued.

Actions in respect of trust property or the personal estate of deceased persons

Time limit for actions in respect of trust property

21.—(1) No period of limitation prescribed by this Act shall apply to an action by a beneficiary under a trust, being an action —

(a) in respect of any fraud or fraudulent breach of trust to which the trustee was a party or privy; or

(b) to recover from the trustee trust property or the proceeds of trust property in the possession of the trustee, or previously received by the trustee and converted to his use.

(2) Where a trustee who is also a beneficiary under the trust receives or retains trust property or its proceeds as his share on a distribution of trust property under the trust, his liability in any action brought by virtue of subsection (1)(b) above to recover that property or its proceeds after the expiration of the period of limitation prescribed by this Act for bringing an action to recover trust property shall be limited to the excess over his proper share.

This subsection only applies if the trustee acted honestly and reasonably in making the distribution

(3) Subject to the preceding provisions of this section, an action by a beneficiary to recover trust property or in respect of any breach of trust, not being an action for which a period of limitation is prescribed by any other provision of this Act, shall not be brought after the expiration of six years from the date on which the right of action accrued.

For the purposes of this subsection, the right of action shall not be treated as having accrued to any beneficiary entitled to a future interest in the trust property until the interest fell into possession.

(4) No beneficiary as against whom there would be a good defence under this Act shall derive any greater or other benefit from a judgment or order obtained by any other beneficiary that he could have obtained if he had brought the action and this Act had been pleaded in defence.

Time limit for actions claiming personal estate of a deceased person

22. Subject to section 21(1) and (2) of this Act —

(a) no action in respect of any claim to the personal estate of a deceased person or to any share or interest in any such estate (whether under a will or on intestacy) shall be brought after the expiration of twelve years from the date on which the right to receive the share or interest accrued; and

(b) no action to recover arrears of interest in respect of any legacy, or damages in respect of such arrears, shall be brought after the expiration of six years from the date on which the interest became due.

Actions for an account

Time limit in respect of actions for an account

23. An action for an account shall not be brought after the expiration of any time limit under this Act which is applicable to the claim which is the basis of the duty to account.

Miscellaneous and supplemental

Time limit for actions to enforce judgments

24.—(1) An action shall not be brought upon any judgment after the expiration of six years from the date on which the judgment became enforceable.

(2) No arrears of interest in respect of any judgment debt shall be recovered after the expiration of six years from the date on which the interest became due.

Time limit for actions to enforce advowsons and extinction of title to advowsons

25.—(1) No person shall bring an action to enforce a right to present to or bestow any ecclesiastical benefice as patron of that benefice after the expiration of whichever of the following periods last expires, that is to say —

(a) a period during which three clerks in succession have held the benefice adversely to the right of presentation or gift of the person in question (or of some person through whom he claims); or

(b) a period of sixty years during which the benefice has been held adversely to that right;

and in no case after the expiration of a period of one hundred years during which the benefice has been held adversely to that right or to the right of some person entitled to a preceding estate or interest or an undivided share or alternate right of presentation or gift held or derived under the same title.

This subsection shall apply to the Crown or a bishop claiming a right to present to or bestow any ecclesiastical benefice as patron, but shall not affect the right of the Crown or a bishop to present or collate to any ecclesiastical benefice by reason of a lapse.

(2) Where any benefice becomes void after being held adversely to the right of presentation or gift of the patron of the benefice and a clerk is presented or collated to the benefice by Her Majesty or the ordinary —

(a) the possession of that clerk shall be treated as adverse; but
(b) where the benefice is avoided in consequence of the incumbent being made a bishop, the incumbency of the new clerk shall, for the purpose of subsection (1)(a) above, be treated as a continuation of the prior incumbency.

(3) Subject to section 75 of the Land Registration Act 1925, at the expiration of the period prescribed by this Act for any person to bring an action to enforce an advowson the title of that person to the advowson shall be extinguished.

Administration to date back to death

26. For the purposes of the provisions of this Act relating to actions for the recovery of land and advowsons an administrator of the estate of a deceased person shall be treated as claiming as if there had been no interval of time between the death of the deceased person and the grant of the letters of administration.

Cure of defective disentailing assurance

27.—(1) This section applies where —

(a) a person entitled in remainder to an entailed interest in any land makes an assurance of his interest which fails to bar the issue in tail or the estates and interests taking effect on the determination of the entailed interest, or fails to bar those estates and interests only; and
(b) any person takes possession of the land by virtue of the assurance.

(2) If the person taking possession of the land by virtue of the assurance, or any other person whatsoever (other than a person entitled to possession by virtue of the settlement) is in possession of the land for a period of twelve years from the commencement of the time when the assurance could have operated as an effective bar, the assurance shall thereupon operate, and be treated as having always operated, to bar the issue in tail and the estates and interests taking effect on the determination of the entailed interest.

(3) The reference in subsection (2) above to the time when the assurance could have operated as an effective bar is a reference to the time at which the assurance, as it had then been executed by the person entitled to the entailed interest, would have operated, without the consent of any other person, to bar the issue in tail and the estates and interests taking effect on the determination of the entailed interest.

PART II. EXTENSION OR EXCLUSION OF ORDINARY TIME LIMITS

Disability

Extension of limitation period in case of disability

28.—(1) Subject to the following provisions of this section, if on the date when any right of action accrued for which a period of limitation is prescribed by this Act, the person to whom it accrued was under a disability, the action may be brought at any time before the expiration of six years from the date when he ceased to be under a disability or died (whichever first occurred) notwithstanding that the period of limitation has expired.

(2) This section shall not affect any case where the right of action first accrued to some person (not under a disability) through whom the person under a disability claims.

(3) When a right of action which has accrued to a person under a disability accrues, on the death of that person while still under a disability, to another person under a disability, no further extension of time shall be allowed by reason of the disability of the second person.

(4) No action to recover land or money charged on land shall be brought by virtue of this section by any person after the expiration of thirty years from the date on which the right of action accrued to that person or some person through whom he claims.

(4A) If the action is one to which section 4A of this Act applies, subsection (1) above shall have effect as if for the words from "at any time" to "occurred)" there were substituted the words "by him at any time before the expiration of three years from the date when he ceased to be under a disability".

(5) If the action is one to which section 10 of this Act applies, subsection (1) above shall have effect as if for the words "six years" there were substituted the words "two years".

(6) If the action is one to which section 11 or 12(2) of this Act applies, subsection (1) above shall have effect as if for the words "six years" there were substituted the words "three years".

(7) If the action is one to which section 11A of this Act applies or one by virtue of section 6(1)(a) of the Consumer Protection Act 1987 (death caused by defective product), subsection (1) above —

    (a) shall not apply to the time limit prescribed by subsection (3) of the said section 11A or to that time limit as applied by virtue of section 12(1) of this Act; and

    (b) in relation to any other time limit prescribed by this Act shall have effect as if the words "six years" there were substituted the words "three years".

Extension for cases where the limitation period is the period under section 14A(4)(b)

28A.—(1) Subject to subsection (2) below, if in the case of any action for which a period of limitation is prescribed by section 14A of this Act —

    (a) the period applicable in accordance with subsection (4) of that section is the period mentioned in paragraph (b) of that subsection;

    (b) on the date which is for the purposes of that section the starting date for reckoning that period the person by reference to whose knowledge that date fell to be determined under subsection (5) of that section was under a disability; and

    (c) section 28 of this Act does not apply to the action;

the action may be brought at any time before the expiration of three years from the date when he ceased to be under a disability or died (whichever first occurred) notwithstanding that the period mentioned above has expired.

(2) An action may not be brought by virtue of subsection (1) above after the end of the period of limitation prescribed by section 14B of this Act.

Acknowledgment and part payment

Fresh accrual of action on acknowledgment or part payment

29.—(1) Subsections (2) and (3) below apply where any right of action (including a foreclosure action) to recover land or an advowson or any right of a mortgagee of personal property to bring a foreclosure action in respect of the property has accrued.

(2) If the person in possession of the land, benefice or personal property in question acknowledges the title of the person to whom the right of action has accrued—

    (a) the right shall be treated as having accrued on and not before the date of the acknowledgment; and

    (b) in the case of a right of action to recover land which has accrued to a person entitled to an estate or interest taking effect on the determination of an entailed interest against whom time is running under section 27 of this Act, section 27 shall thereupon cease to apply to the land.

(3) In the case of a foreclosure or other action by a mortgagee, if the person in possession of the land, benefice or personal property in question or the person liable for the mortgage debt makes any payment in respect of the debt (whether of principal or interest) the right shall be treated as having accrued on and not before the date of the payment.

(4) Where a mortgagee is by virtue of the mortgage in possession of any mortgaged land and either —

(a) receives any sum in respect of the principal or interest of the mortgage debt; or
(b) acknowledges the title of the mortgagor, or his equity of redemption;

an action to redeem the land in his possession may be brought at any time before the expiration of twelve years from the date of the payment or acknowledgment.

(5) Subject to subsection (6) below, where any right of action has accrued to recover —

(a) any debt or other liquidated pecuniary claim; or
(b) any claim to the personal estate of a deceased person or to any share or interest in any such estate;

and the person liable or accountable for the claim acknowledges the claim or makes any payment in respect of it the right shall be treated as having accrued on and not before the date of the acknowledgment or payment.

(6) A payment of a part of the rent or interest due at any time shall not extend the period for claiming the remainder then due, but any payment of interest shall be treated as a payment in respect of the principal debt.

(7) Subject to subsection (6) above, a current period of limitation may be repeatedly extended under this section by further acknowledgments or payments, but a right of action, once barred by this Act, shall not be revived by any subsequent acknowledgment or payment.

Formal provisions as to acknowledgments and part payments

30.—(1) To be effective for the purposes of section 29 of this Act, an acknowledgment must be in writing and signed by the person making it.

(2) For the purposes of section 29, any acknowledgment or payment —

(a) may be sent by the agent of the person by whom it is required to be made under that section; and
(b) shall be made to the person, or to an agent of the person, whose title or claim is being acknowledged or, as the case may be, in respect of whose claim the payment is being made.

Effect of acknowledgment or part payment on persons other than the maker or recipient

31.—(1) An acknowledgment of the title to any land, benefice, or mortgaged personalty by any person in possession of it shall bind all other persons in possession during the ensuing period of limitation.

(2) A payment in respect of a mortgage debt by the mortgagor or any other person liable for the debt, or by any person in possession of the mortgaged property, shall, so far as any right of the mortgagee to foreclose or otherwise to recover the property is concerned, bind all other persons in possession of the mortgaged property during the ensuing period of limitation.

(3) Where two or more mortgagees are by virtue of the mortgage in possession of the mortgaged land, an acknowledgment of the mortgagor's title or of his equity of redemption by one of the mortgagees shall only bind him and his successors and shall not bind any other mortgagee or his successors.

(4) Where in a case within subsection (3) above the mortgagee by whom the acknowledgment is given is entitled to a part of the mortgaged land and not to any ascertained part of the mortgage debt the mortgagor shall be entitled to redeem that part of the land on payment, with interest, of the part

of the mortgage debt which bears the same proportion to the whole of the debt as the value of the part of the land bears to the whole of the mortgaged land.

(5) Where there are two or more mortgagors, and the title or equity of redemption of one of the mortgagors is acknowledged as mentioned above in this section, the acknowledgment shall be treated as having been made to all the mortgagors.

(6) An acknowledgment of any debt or other liquidated pecuniary claim shall bind the acknowledgor and his successors but not any other person.

(7) A payment made in respect of any debt or other liquidated pecuniary claim shall bind all persons liable in respect of the debt or claim.

(8) An acknowledgment by one of several personal representatives of any claim to the personal estate of a deceased person or to any share or interest in any such estate, or a payment by one of several personal representatives in respect of any such claim, shall bind the estate of the deceased person.

(9) In this section "successor", in relation to any mortgagee or person liable in respect of any debt or claim, means his personal representatives and any other person on whom the rights under the mortgage or, as the case may be, the liability in respect of the debt or claim devolve (whether on death or bankruptcy or the disposition of property or the determination of a limited estate or interest in settled property or otherwise).

Fraud, concealment and mistake

Postponement of limitation period in case of fraud, concealment or mistake

32.—(1) Subject to subsections (3) and (4A) below, where in the case of any action for which a period of limitation is prescribed by this Act, either —

    (a) the action is based upon the fraud of the defendant; or

    (b) any fact relevant to the plaintiff's right of action has been deliberately concealed from him by the defendant; or

    (c) the action is for the relief from the consequences of a mistake;

the period of limitation shall not begin to run until the plaintiff has discovered the fraud, concealment or mistake (as the case may be) or could with reasonable diligence have discovered it.

References in this subsection to the defendant include references to the defendant's agent and to any person through whom the defendant claims and his agent.

(2) For the purposes of subsection (1) above, the deliberate commission of a breach of duty in circumstances in which it is unlikely to be discovered for some time amounts to deliberate concealment of the facts involved in that breach of duty.

(3) Nothing in this section shall enable any action —

    (a) to recover, or recover the value of, any property; or

    (b) to enforce any charge against, or set aside any transaction affecting, the property;

to be brought against the purchaser of the property or any person claiming through him in any case where the property has been purchased for valuable consideration by an innocent third party since the fraud or concealment or (as the case may be) the transaction in which the mistake was made took place.

(4) A purchaser is an innocent third party for the purposes of this section —

    (a) in the case of fraud or concealment of any fact relevant to the plaintiff's right of action, if he was not a party to the fraud or (as the case may be) to the concealment of that fact and did not at the time of the purchase know or have reason to believe that the fraud or concealment had taken place; and

    (b) in the case of mistake, if he did not at that time of the purchase know or have reason to believe that the mistake had been made.

(4A) Subsection (1) above shall not apply in relation to the time limit prescribed by section 11A(3) of this Act or in relation to that time limit as applied by virtue of section 12(1) of this Act.

(5) Sections 14A and 14B of this Act shall not apply to any action to which subsection (1)(b) above applies (and accordingly the period of limitation referred to in that subsection, in any case to which either of those sections would otherwise apply, is the period applicable under section 2 of this Act).

Discretionary extension of time limit for actions for libel or slander

Discretionary extension of time limit for actions for libel or slander

32A. Where a person to whom a cause of action for libel or slander has accrued has not brought such an action within the period of three years mentioned in section 4A of this Act (or, where applicable, the period allowed by section 28(1) as modified by section 28(4A)) because all or any of the facts relevant to that cause of action did not become known to him until after the expiration of that period, such an action —

(a) may be brought by him at any time before the expiration of one year from the earliest date on which he knew all the facts relevant to that cause of action; but
(b) shall not be brought without the leave of the High Court.

Discretionary exclusion of time limit for actions in respect of personal injuries or death

Discretionary exclusion of time limit for actions in respect of personal injuries or death

33.—(1) If it appears to the court that it would be equitable to allow an action to proceed having regard to the degree to which —

(a) the provisions of section 11 or 11A or 12 of this Act prejudice the plaintiff or any person whom he represents; and
(b) any decision of the court under this subsection would prejudice the defendant or any person whom he represents;

the court may direct that those provisions shall not apply to the action, or shall not apply to any specified cause of action to which the action relates.

(1A) The court shall not under this section disapply —

(a) subsection (3) of section 11A; or
(b) where the damages claimed by the plaintiff are confined to damages for loss of or damage to any property, any other provision in its application to an action by virtue of Part I of the Consumer Protection Act 1987.

(2) The court shall not under this section disapply section 12(1) except where the reason why the person injured could no longer maintain an action was because of the time limit in section 11 or subsection (4) of section 11A.

If, for example, the person injured could at his death no longer maintain an action under the Fatal Accidents Act 1976 because of the time limit in Article 29 in Schedule 1 to the Carriage by Air Act 1961, the court has no power to direct that section 12(1) shall not apply.

(3) In acting under this section the court shall have regard to all the circumstances of the case and in particular to —

(a) the length of, and the reasons for, the delay on the part of the plaintiff;
(b) the extent to which, having regard to the delay, the evidence adduced or likely to be adduced by the plaintiff or the defendant is or is likely to be less cogent than if the action had been brought within the time allowed by section 11, by section 11A or (as the case may be) by section 12;
(c) the conduct of the defendant after the cause of action arose, including the extent (if any) to which he responded to requests reasonably made by the plaintiff for information or inspection for the purpose of ascertaining facts which were or might be relevant to the plaintiff's cause of action against the defendant;
(d) the duration of any disability of the plaintiff arising after the date of the accrual of the cause of action;

(e) the extent to which the plaintiff acted promptly and reasonably once he knew whether or not the act or omission of the defendant, to which the injury was attributable, might be capable at that time of giving rise to an action for damages;

(f) the steps, if any, taken by the plaintiff to obtain medical, legal or other expert advice and the nature of any such advice he may have received.

(4) In a case where the person injured died when, because of section 11 or subsection (4) of section 11A, he could no longer maintain an action and recover damages in respect of the injury, the court shall have regard in particular to the length of, and the reasons for, the delay on the part of the deceased.

(5) In a case under subsection (4) above, or any other case where the time limit, or one of the time limits, depends on the date of knowledge of a person other than the plaintiff, subsection (3) above shall have effect with appropriate modifications, and shall have effect in particular as if references to the plaintiff included references to any person whose date of knowledge is or was relevant in determining a time limit.

(6) A direction by the court disapplying the provisions of section 12(1) shall operate to disapply the provisions to the same effect in section 1(1) of the Fatal Accidents Act 1976.

(7) In this section "the court" means the court in which the action has been brought.

(8) References in this section to section 11 or 11A include references to that section as extended by any of the preceding provisions of this Part of this Act or by any provision of Part III of this Act.

PART III. MISCELLANEOUS AND GENERAL

Application of Act and other limitation enactments to arbitrations

34.—(1) This Act and any other limitation enactment shall apply to arbitrations as they apply to actions in the High Court.

(2) Notwithstanding any term in an arbitration agreement to the effect that no cause of action shall accrue in respect of any matter required by the agreement to be referred until an award is made under the agreement, the cause of action shall, for the purposes of this Act and any other limitation enactment (whether in their application to arbitrations or to other proceedings), be deemed to have accrued in respect of any such matter at the time when it would have accrued but for that term in the agreement.

(3) For the purposes of this Act and of any other limitation enactment an arbitration shall be treated as being commenced —

(a) when one party to the arbitration served on the other party or parties a notice requiring him or them to appoint an arbitrator or to agree to the appointment of an arbitrator; or

(b) where the arbitration agreement provides that the reference shall be to a person named or designated in the agreement, when one party to the arbitration serves on the other party or parties a notice requiring him or them to submit the dispute to the person so named or designated.

(4) Any such notice may be served either —

(a) by delivering it to the person on whom it is to be served; or

(b) by leaving it at the usual or last-known place of abode in England and Wales of that person; or

(c) by sending it by post in a registered letter addressed to that person at his usual or last-known place of abode in England and Wales;

as well as in any other manner provided in the arbitration agreement.

(5) Where the High Court —

(a) orders that an award be set aside; or

(b) orders, after the commencement of an arbitration, that the arbitration agreement shall cease to have effect with respect to the dispute referred;

the court may further order that the period between the commencement of the arbitration and the date of the order of the court shall be excluded in computing the time prescribed by this Act or by any other limitation enactment for the commencement of proceedings (including arbitration) with respect to the dispute referred.

(6) This section shall apply to an arbitration under an Act of Parliament as well as to an arbitration pursuant to an arbitration agreement.

Subsections (3) and (4) above shall have effect, in relation to an arbitration under an Act, as if for the references to the arbitration agreement there were substituted references to such of the provisions of the Act or of any order, scheme, rules, regulations or byelaws made under the Act as relate to the arbitration.

(7) In this section —

(a) "arbitration", "arbitration agreement" and "award' have the same meanings as in Part I of the Arbitration Act 1950; and

(b) references to any other limitation enactment are references to any other enactment relating to the limitation of actions, whether passed before or after the passing of this Act.

New claims in pending actions: rules of court

35.—(1) For the purposes of this Act, any new claim made in the course of any action shall be deemed to be a separate action and to have been commenced —

(a) in the case of a new claim made in or by way of third party proceedings, on the date on which those proceedings were commenced; and

(b) in the case of any other new claim, on the same date as the original action.

(2) In this section a new claim means any claim by way of set-off or counterclaim, and any claim involving either —

(a) the addition or substitution of a new cause of action; or

(b) the addition or substitution of a new party;

and "third party proceedings" means any proceedings brought in the course of any action by any party to the action against a person not previously a party to the action, other than proceedings brought by joining any such person as defendant to any claim already made in the original action by the party bringing the proceedings.

(3) Except as provided by section 33 of this Act or by rules of court, neither the High Court nor any county court shall allow a new claim within subsection (1)(b) above, other than an original set-off or counter claim, to be made in the course of any action after the expiry of any time limit under this Act which would affect a new action to enforce that claim.

For the purposes of this subsection, a claim is an original set-off or an original counterclaim if it is a claim made by way of set-off or (as the case may be) by way of counterclaim by a party who has not previously made any claim in the action.

(4) Rules of court may provide for allowing a new claim to which subsection (3) above applies to be made as there mentioned, but only if the conditions specified in subsection (5) below are satisfied, and subject to any further restrictions the rules may impose.

(5) The conditions referred to in subsection (4) above are the following —

(a) in the case of a claim involving a new cause of action, if the new cause of action arises out of the same facts or substantially the same facts as are already in issue on any claim previously made in the original action; and

(b) in the case of a claim involving a new party, if the addition or substitution of the new party is necessary for the determination of the original action.

(6) The addition or substitution of a new party shall not be regarded for the purposes of subsection (5)(b) above as necessary for the determination of the original action unless either —

(a) the new party is substituted for a party whose name was given in any claim made in the original action in mistake for the new party's name; or

(b) any claim already made in the original action cannot be maintained by or against an existing party unless the new party is joined or substituted as plaintiff or defendant in that action.

(7) Subject to subsection (4) above, rules of court may provide for allowing a party to any action to claim relief in a new capacity in respect of a new cause of action notwithstanding that he had no title to make that claim at the date of the commencement of the action.

This subsection shall not be taken as prejudicing the power of rules of court to provide for allowing a party to claim relief in a new capacity without adding or substituting a new cause of action.

(8) Subsections (3) to (7) above shall apply in relation to a new claim made in the course of third party proceedings as if those proceedings were the original action, and subject to such other modifications as may be prescribed by rules of court in any case or class of case.

(9) ...

Equitable jurisdiction and remedies

36.—(1) The following time limits under this Act, that is to say —

(a) the time limit under section 2 for actions founded on tort;
(aa) the time limit under section 4A for actions for libel or slander;
(b) the time limit under section 5 for actions founded on simple contract;
(c) the time limit under section 7 for actions to enforce awards where the submission is not by an instrument under seal;
(d) the time limit under section 8 for actions on a specialty;
(e) the time limit under section 9 for actions to recover a sum recoverable by virtue of any enactment; and
(f) the time limit under section 24 for actions to enforce a judgment;

shall not apply to any claim for specific performance of a contract or for an injunction or for other equitable relief, except in so far as any such time limit may be applied by the court by analogy in like manner as the corresponding time limit under any enactment repealed by the Limitation Act 1939 was applied before 1st July 1940.

(2) Nothing in this Act shall affect any equitable jurisdiction to refuse relief on the ground of acquiescence or otherwise.

Application to the Crown and the Duke of Cornwall

37.—(1) Except as otherwise expressly provided in this Act, and without prejudice to section 39, this Act shall apply to proceedings by or against the Crown in like manner as it applies to proceedings between subjects.

(2) Notwithstanding subsection (1) above, this Act shall not apply to —

(a) any proceedings by the Crown for the recovery of any tax or duty or interest on any tax or duty;
(b) any forfeiture proceedings under the customs and excise Acts (within the meaning of the Customs and Excise Management Act 1979); or
(c) any proceedings in respect of the forfeiture of a ship.

In this subsection "duty" includes any debt due to Her Majesty under section 16 of the Tithe Act 1936, and "ship" includes every description of vessel used in navigation not propelled by oars.

(3) For the purposes of this section, proceedings by or against the Crown include —

(a) proceedings by or against Her Majesty in right of the Duchy of Lancaster;
(b) proceedings by or against any Government department or any officer of the Crown as such or any person acting on behalf of the Crown; and
(c) proceedings by or against the Duke of Cornwall.

(4) For the purpose of the provisions of this Act relating to actions for the recovery of land and advowsons, references to the Crown shall include references to Her Majesty in right of the Duchy of Lancaster; and those provisions shall apply to lands and advowsons forming part of the possessions of the Duchy of Cornwall as if for the references to the Crown there were substituted references to the Duke of Cornwall as defined in the Duchy of Cornwall Management Act 1863.

(5) For the purposes of this Act a proceeding by petition of right (in any case where any such proceeding lies, by virtue of any saving in section 40 of the Crown Proceedings Act 1947, notwithstanding the general abolition by that Act of proceedings by way of petition of right) shall be treated as being commenced on the date on which the petition is presented.

(6) Nothing in this Act shall affect the prerogative right of Her Majesty (whether in right of the Crown or of the Duchy of Lancaster) or of the Duke of Cornwall to any gold or silver mine.

Interpretation

38.—(1) In this Act, unless the context otherwise requires —

"action" includes any proceeding in a court of law, including an ecclesiastical court;

"land" includes corporeal hereditaments, tithes and rent-charges and any legal or equitable estate or interest therein, including an interest in the proceedings of the sale of land held upon trust for sale, but except as provided above in this definition does not include any incorporeal hereditament;

"personal estate" and "personal property" do not include chattels real;

"personal injuries" includes any disease and any impairment of a person's physical or mental condition, and "injury" and cognate expressions shall be construed accordingly;

"rent" includes a rentcharge and a rentservice;

"rentcharge" means any annuity or periodical sum of money charged upon or payable out of land, except a rent service or interest on a mortgage on land;

"settled land", "statutory owner" and "tenant for life" have the same meanings respectively as in the Settled Land Act 1925;

"trust" and "trustee" have the same meanings respectively as in the Trustee Act 1925; and

"trust for sale" has the same meaning as in the Law of Property Act 1925.

(2) For the purposes of this Act a person shall be treated as under a disability while he is an infant, or of unsound mind.

(3) For the purposes of subsection (2) above a person is of unsound mind if he is a person who, by reason of mental disorder within the meaning of the Mental Health Act 1983, is incapable of managing and administering his property and affairs.

(4) Without prejudice to the generality of subsection (3) above, a person shall be conclusively presumed for the purposes of subsection (2) above to be of unsound mind —

(a) while he is liable to be detained or subject to guardianship under the Mental Health Act 1983 (otherwise than by virtue of section 35 of 89); and

(b) while he is receiving treatment as an in-patient in any hospital within the meaning of the Mental Health Act 1983 or mental nursing home within the meaning of the Nursing Homes Act 1975 without being liable to be detained under the said Act of 1983 (otherwise than by virtue of section 35 of 89), being treatment which follows without any interval a period during which he was liable to be detained or subject to guardianship under the Mental Health Act 1959, or the said Act of 1983 (otherwise than by virtue of section 35 or 89) or by virtue of any enactment repealed or excluded by the Mental Health Act 1959.

(5) Subject to subsection (6) below, a person shall be treated as claiming through another person if he became entitled by, through, under, or by the act of that other person to the right claimed, and any person whose estate or interest might have been barred by a person entitled to an entailed interest in possession shall be treated as claiming through the person so entitled.

(6) A person becoming entitled to any estate or interest by virtue of a special power of appointment shall not be treated as claiming through the appointor.

(7) References in this Act to a right of action to recover land shall include references to a right to enter into possession of the land or, in the case of rentcharges and tithes, to distrain for arrears of rent or tithe, and references to the bringing of such an action shall include references to the making of such an entry or distress.

(8) References in this Act to the possession of land shall, in the case of tithes and rentcharges, be construed as references to the receipt of the tithe or rent, and references to the date of dispossession or discontinuance of possession of land shall, in the case of rent charges, be construed as references to the date of the last receipt of rent.

(9) References in Part II of this Act to a right of action shall include references to —

    (a) a cause of action;

    (b) a right to receive money secured by a mortgage or charge on any property;

    (c) a right to recover proceeds on the sale of land; and

    (d) a right to receive a share of interest in the personal estate of a deceased person.

(10) References in Part II to the date of the accrual of a right of action shall be construed —

    (a) in the case of an action upon a judgment, as references to the date on which the judgment became enforceable; and

    (b) in the case of an action to recover arrears of rent or interest, or damages in respect of arrears of rent or interest, as references to the date on which the rent or interest became due.

Saving for other limitation enactments

39. This Act shall not apply to any action or arbitration for which a period of limitation is prescribed by or under any other enactment (whether passed before or after the passing of this Act) or to any action or arbitration to which the Crown is a party and for which, if it were between subjects, a period of limitation would be prescribed by or under any such other enactment.

Transitional provisions amendments and repeals

40.—(1) Schedule 2 of this Act, which contains transitional provisions, shall have effect.

(2) The enactments specified in Schedule 3 to this Act shall have effect subject to the amendments specified in that Schedule, being amendments consequential on the provisions of this Act; but the amendment of any enactment by that Schedule shall not be taken as prejudicing the operation of section 17(2) of the Interpretation Act 1978 (effect of repeals).

(3) . . .

Short title, commencement and extent

41.—(1) This Act may be cited as the Limitation Act 1980.

(2) This Act, except section 35, shall come into force on 1st May 1981.

(3) Section 35 of this Act shall come into force on 1st May 1981 to the extent (if any) that the section substituted for section 28 of the Limitation Act 1939 by section 8 of the Limitation Amendment Act 1980 is in force immediately before that date; but otherwise section 35 shall come into force on such day as the Lord Chancellor may by order made by statutory instrument appoint, and different days may be appointed for different purposes of that section (including its application in relation to different courts of proceedings).

(4) The repeal by this Act of section 14(1) of the Limitation Act 1963 and the corresponding saving in paragraph 2 of Schedule 2 to this Act shall extend to Northern Ireland, but otherwise this Act does not extend to Scotland or to Northern Ireland.

SCHEDULES

SCHEDULE 1. PROVISIONS WITH RESPECT TO ACTIONS TO RECOVER LAND

Section 15(6), (7)

PART I. ACCRUAL OF RIGHTS OF ACTION TO RECOVER LAND

Accrual of right of action in case of present interests in land

1. Where the person bringing an action to recover land, or some person through whom he claims, has been in possession of the land, and has while entitled to the land been dispossessed or discontinued his possession, the right of action shall be treated as having accrued on the date of the dispossession or discontinuance.

2. Where any person brings an action to recover any land of a deceased person (whether under a will or on intestacy) and the deceased person —

   (a) was on the date of his death in possession of the land or, in the case of a rentcharge created by will or taking effect upon his death, in possession of the land charged; and
   (b) was the last person entitled to the land to be in possession of it;

the right of action shall be treated as having accrued on the date of his death.

3. Where any person brings an action to recover land, being an estate or interest in possession assured otherwise than by will to him, or to some person through whom he claims, and —

   (a) the person making the assurance was on the date when the assurance took effect in possession of the land or, in the case of a rentcharge created by the assurance, in possession of the land charged; and
   (b) no person has been in possession of the land by virtue of the assurance;

the right of action shall be treated as having accrued on the date when the assurance took effect.

Accrual of right of action in case of future interests

4. The right of action to recover any land shall, in a case where —

   (a) the estate or interest claimed was an estate or interest in reversion or remainder or any other future estate or interest; and
   (b) no person has taken possession of the land by virtue of the estate or interest claimed;

be treated as having accrued on the date on which the estate or interest fell into possession by the determination of the preceding estate or interest.

5.—(1) Subject to sub-paragraph (2) below, a tenancy from year to year or other period, without a lease in writing, shall for the purposes of this Act be treated as being determined at the expiration of the first year or other period; and accordingly the right of action of the person entitled to the land subject to the tenancy shall be treated as having accrued at the date on which in accordance with this sub-paragraph the tenancy is determined.

(2) Where any rent has subsequently been received in respect of the tenancy, the right of action shall be treated as having accrued on the date of the last receipt of rent.

6.—(1) Where —

   (a) any person is in possession of land by virtue of a lease in writing by which a rent of not less than ten pounds a years is reserved; and
   (b) the rent is received by some person wrongfully claiming to be entitled to the land in reversion immediately expectant on the determination of the lease; and
   (c) no rent is subsequently received by the person rightfully so entitled;

the right of action to recover the land of the person rightfully so entitled shall be treated as having accrued on the date when the rent was first received by the person wrongfully claiming to be so entitled and not on the date of the determination of the lease.

(2) Sub-paragraph (1) above shall not apply to any lease granted by the Crown.

Accrual of right of action in case of forfeiture or breach of condition

7.—(1) Subject to sub-paragraph (2) below, a right of action to recover land by virtue of a forfeiture or breach of condition shall be treated as having accrued on the date on which the forfeiture was incurred or the condition broken.

(2) If any such right has accrued to a person entitled to an estate or interest in reversion or remainder and the land was not recovered by virtue of that right, the right of action to recover the land shall not be treated as having accrued to that person until his estate or interest fell into possession, as if no such forfeiture or breach of condition had occurred.

Right of action not to accrue or continue unless there is adverse possession

8.—(1) No right of action to recover land shall be treated as accruing unless the land is in the possession of some person in whose favour the period of limitation can run (referred to below in this paragraph as "adverse possession"); and where under the preceding provisions of this Schedule any such right of action is treated as accruing on a certain date and no person is in adverse possession on that date, the right of action shall not be treated as accruing unless and until adverse possession is taken of the land.

(2) Where a right of action to recover land has accrued and after its accrual, before the right is barred, the land ceases to be in adverse possession, the right of action shall no longer be treated as having accrued and no fresh right of action shall be treated as accruing unless and until the land is again taken into adverse possession.

(3) For the purposes of this paragraph —

(a) possession of any land subject to a rentcharge by a person (other than the person entitled to the rentcharge) who does not pay the rent shall be treated as adverse possession of the rentcharge; and

(b) receipt of rent under a lease by a person wrongfully claiming to be entitled to the land in reversion immediately expectant on the determination of the lease shall be treated as adverse possession of the land.

(4) For the purpose of determining whether a person occupying any land is in adverse possession of the land it shall not be assumed by implication of law that his occupation is by permission of the person entitled to the land merely by virtue of the fact that his occupation is not inconsistent with the latter's present or future enjoyment of the land.

This provision shall not be taken as prejudicing a finding to the effect that a person's occupation of any land is by implied permission of the person entitled to the land in any case where such a finding is justified on the actual facts of the case.

Possession of beneficiary not adverse to others interested in settled land or
land held on trust for sale

9. Where any settled land or any land held on trust for sale is in the possession of a person entitled to a beneficial interest in the land or in the proceeds of sale (not being a person solely or absolutely entitled to the land or the proceeds), no right of action to recover the land shall be treated for the purposes of this Act as accruing during that possession to any person in whom the land is vested as tenant for life, statutory owner or trustee, or to any other person entitled to a beneficial interest in the land or the proceeds of sale.

PART II. MODIFICATION OF SECTION 15 WHERE CROWN OR CERTAIN
CORPORATIONS SOLE ARE INVOLVED

10 Subject to paragraph 11 below, section 15(1) of this Act shall apply to the bringing of an action to recover any land by the Crown or by any spiritual or eleemosynary corporation sole with the substitution for the reference to twelve years of a reference to thirty years.

11.—(1) An action to recover foreshore may be brought by the Crown at any time before the expiration of sixty years from the date mentioned in section 15(1) of this Act.

(2) Where any right of action to recover land which has ceased to be foreshore but remains in the ownership of the Crown accrued when the land was foreshore, the action may be brought at any time before the expiration of —

(a) sixty years from the date of accrual of the right of action; or
(b) thirty years from the date of the land ceased to be foreshore;

whichever period first expires.

(3) In this paragraph "foreshore" means the shore and bed of the sea and of any tidal water, below the line of the medium high tide between the spring tides and the neap tides.

12. Notwithstanding section 15(1) of this Act, where in the case of any action brought by a person other than the Crown or a spiritual or eleemosynary corporation sole the right of action first accrued to the Crown or any such corporation sole through whom the person in question claims, the action may be brought at any time before the expiration of —

(a) the period during which the action could have been brought by the Crown or the corporation sole; or
(b) twelve years from the date on which the right of action accrued to some person other than the Crown or the corporation sole;

whichever period first expires.

13. Section 15(2) of this Act shall apply in any case where the Crown or a spiritual or eleemosynary corporation sole is entitled to the succeeding estate or interest with the substitution —

(a) for the reference to twelve years of a reference to thirty years; and
(b) for the reference to six years of a reference to twelve years.

SCHEDULE 2. TRANSITIONAL PROVISIONS

Section 40(1)

1. Nothing in this Act shall affect the operation of section 4 of the Limitation Act 1963, as it had effect immediately before 1 January 1979 (being the date on which the Civil Liability (Contribution) Act 1978 came into force), in relation to any case where the damage in question occurred before that date.

2. The amendment made by section 14(1) of the Limitation Act 1963 in section 5 of the Limitation (Enemies and War Prisoners) Act 1945 (which provides that section 5 shall have effect as if for the words "in force in Northern Ireland at the date of the passing of this Act" there were substituted the words "for the time being in force in Northern Ireland") shall continue to have effect notwithstanding the repeal by this Act of section 14(1).

3. It is hereby declared that a decision taken at any time by a court to grant, or not to grant, leave under Part I of the Limitation Act 1963 (which, so far as it related to leave, was repealed by the Limitation Act 1975) does not affect the determination of any question in proceedings under any provision of this Act which corresponds to a provision of the Limitation Act 1975, but in such proceedings account may be taken of evidence admitted in proceedings under Part I of the Limitation Act 1963.

4.—(1) In section 33(6) of this Act the reference to section 1(1) of the Fatal Accidents Act 1976 shall be construed as including a reference to section 1 of the Fatal Accidents Act 1846.

(2) Any other reference in that section, or in section 12 or 13 of this Act, to the Fatal Accidents Act 1976 shall be construed as including a reference to the Fatal Accidents Act 1846.

5. Notwithstanding anything in section 29(7) of this Act or in the repeals made by this Act, the Limitation Act 1939 shall continue to have effect in relation to any acknowledgment or payment made before the coming into force of section 6 of the Limitation Amendment Act 1980 (which amended section 23 of the Limitation Act 1939 and made certain repeals in sections 23 and 25 of that Act so as to prevent the revival by acknowledgment or part payment of a right of action barred by that Act) as it had effect immediately before section 6 came into force.

6. Section 28 of the Limitation Act 1939 (provisions as to set-off or counterclaim) shall continue to apply (as originally enacted) to any claim by way of set-off or counterclaim made in an action to which section 35 of this Act does not apply, but as if the reference in section 28 to that Act were

a reference to this Act; and, in relation to any such action, references in this Act to section 35 of this Act shall be construed as references to section 28 as it applies by virtue of this paragraph.

7. Section 37(2)(c) of this Act shall be treated for the purposes of the Hovercraft Act 1968 as if it were contained in an Act passed before that Act.

8. In relation to a lease granted before the coming into force of section 3(2) of the Limitation Amendment Act 1980 (which substituted "ten pounds a year" for "twenty shillings" in section 9(3) of the Limitation Act 1939), paragraph 6(1)(a) of Schedule 1 to this Act shall have effect as if for the words "ten pounds a year" there were substituted the words "twenty shillings".

9.—(1) Nothing in any provision of this Act shall —

(a) enable any action to be brought which was barred by this Act or (as the case may be) by the Limitation Act 1939 before the relevant date; or
(b) affect any action or arbitration commenced before that date or the title to any property which is the subject of any such action or arbitration.

(2) In sub-paragraph (1) above "the relevant date" means —

(a) in relation to section 35 of this Act, the date on which that section comes into force in relation to actions of the description in question or, if section 8 of the Limitation Amendment Act 1980 (which substituted the provisions reproduced in section 35 for section 28 of the Limitation Act 1939) is in force immediately before 1st May 1981 in relation to actions of that description, the date on which section 8 came into force in relation to actions of that description; and
(b) in relation to any other provision of this Act, 1st August 1980 (being the date of coming into force of the remaining provisions of the Limitation Amendment Act 1980, apart from section 8).

SCHEDULE 3. CONSEQUENTIAL AMENDMENTS

Section 40(2)

1. ...

2. In section 21A of the Administration of Estates Act 1925 (debtor who becomes creditor's executor by representation or administrator to account for debt to estate) the reference in subsection (2) to the Limitation Act 1939 shall be construed as including a reference to this Act.

3.—12. ...

SCHEDULE 4

...

FOREIGN LIMITATION PERIODS ACT 1984

An Act to provide for any law relating to the limitation of actions to be treated, for the purposes of cases in which effect is given to foreign law or to determinations by foreign courts, as a matter of substance rather than as a matter of procedure. [24th May 1984]

BE IT ENACTED by the Queen's most Excellent Majesty, by and with the advice and consent of the Lords Spiritual and Temporal, and Commons, in this present Parliament assembled, and by the authority of the same, as follows: —

Application of foreign limitation law

1.—(1) Subject to the following provisions of this Act, where in any action or proceedings in a court in England and Wales the law of any other country falls (in accordance with rules or private international law applicable by any such court) to be taken into account in the determination of any matter —

(a) the law of that other country relating to limitation shall apply in respect of that matter for the purposes of the action or proceedings; and

(b) except where that matter falls within subsection (2) below, the law of England and Wales relating to limitation shall not so apply.

(2) A matter falls within this subsection if it is a matter in the determination of which both the law of England and Wales and the law of some other country fall to be taken into account.

(3) The law of England and Wales shall determine for the purposes of any law applicable by virtue of subsection (1)(a) above whether, and the time at which, proceedings have been commenced in respect of any matter; and, accordingly, section 35 of the Limitation Act 1980 (new claims in pending proceedings) shall apply in relation to time limits applicable by virtue of subsection (1)(a) above as it applies in relation to time limits under that Act.

(4) A court in England and Wales, in exercising in pursuance of subsection (1)(a) above any discretion conferred by the law of any other country, shall so far as practicable exercise that discretion in the manner in which it is exercised in comparable cases by the courts of that other country.

(5) In this section "law", in relation to any country, shall not include rules of private international law applicable by the courts of that country or, in the case of England and Wales, this Act.

Exceptions to s.1

2.—(1) In any case in which the application of section 1 above would to any extent conflict (whether under subsection (2) below or otherwise) with public policy, that section shall not apply to the extent that its application would so conflict.

(2) The application of section 1 above in relation to any action or proceedings shall conflict with public policy to the extent that its application would cause undue hardship to a person who is, or might be made, a party to the action or proceedings.

(3) Where, under a law applicable by virtue of section 1(1)(a) above for the purposes of any action or proceedings, a limitation period is or may be extended or interrupted in respect of the

absence of a party to the action or proceedings from any specified jurisdiction or country, so much of that law as provides for the extension or interruption shall be disregarded for those purposes.

(4) In section 2(1) of the Limitation (Enemies and War Prisoners) Act 1945 (which in relation to cases involving enemy aliens and war prisoners extends certain limitation periods), in the definition of "statute of limitation", at the end, there shall be inserted the words —

> "and, in a case to which section 1(1) of the Foreign Limitation Periods Act 1984 applies, so much of the law of any country outside England and Wales as applies by virtue of that Act".

Foreign judgments on limitation points

3. Where a court in any country outside England and Wales has determined any matter wholly or partly by reference to the law of that or any other country (including England and Wales) relating to limitation, then, for the purposes of the law relating to the effect to be given in England and Wales to that determination, that court shall, to the extent that it has so determined the matter, be deemed to have determined it on its merits.

Meaning of law relating to limitation

4.—(1) Subject to subsection (3) below, references in this Act to the law of any country (including England and Wales) relating to limitation shall, in relation to any matter, be construed as references to so much of the relevant law of that country as (in any manner) makes provision with respect to a limitation period applicable to the bringing of proceedings in respect of that matter in the courts of that country and shall include —

(a) references to so much of that law as relates to, and to the effect of, the application, extension, reduction or interruption of that period; and

(b) a reference, where under that law there is no limitation period which is so applicable, to the rule that such proceedings may be brought within an indefinite period.

(2) In subsection (1) above "relevant law", in relation to any country, means the procedural and substantive law applicable, apart from any rules of private international law, by the courts of that country.

(3) References in this Act to the law of England and Wales relating to limitation shall not include the rules by virtue of which a court may, in the exercise of any discretion refuse equitable relief on the grounds of acquiescence or otherwise; but, in applying those rules to a case in relation to which the law of any country outside England and Wales is applicable by virtue of section 1(1)(a) above (not being a law that provides for a limitation period that has expired), a court in England and Wales shall have regard, in particular, to the provisions of the law that is so applicable.

Application of Act to arbitrations

5. The references to any other limitation enactment in section 34 of the Limitation Act 1980 (application of limitation enactments to arbitration) include references to sections 1, 2 and 4 of this Act; and, accordingly, in subsection (5) of the said section 34, the reference to the time prescribed by a limitation enactment has effect for the purposes of any case to which section 1 above applies as a reference to the limitation period (if any) applicable by virtue of section 1 above.

Application to Crown

6.—(1) This Act applies in relation to any action or proceedings by or against the Crown as it applies in relation to actions and proceedings to which the Crown is not a party.

(2) For the purposes of this section references to an action or proceedings by or against the Crown include references to —

(a) any action or proceedings by or against Her Majesty in right of the Duchy of Lancaster;

(b) any action or proceedings by or against any Government department or any officer of the Crown as such or any person acting on behalf of the Crown;

(c) any action or proceedings by or against the Duke of Cornwall.

Short title, commencement, transitional provision and extent

7.—(1) This Act may be cited as the Foreign Limitation Periods Act 1984.

(2) This Act shall come into force on such day as the Lord Chancellor may by order made by statutory instrument appoint.

(3) Nothing in this Act shall —

(a) affect any action, proceedings or arbitration commenced in England and Wales before the day appointed under subsection (2) above; or

(b) apply in relation to any matter if the limitation period which, apart from this Act, would have been applied in respect of that matter in England and Wales expired before that day.

(4) This Act extends to England and Wales only.

ARBITRATION ACT 1996

Stay of legal proceedings

Stay of legal proceedings

9.—(1) A party to an arbitration agreement against whom legal proceedings are brought (whether by way of claim or counterclaim) in respect of a matter which under the agreement is to be referred to arbitration may (upon notice to the other parties to the proceedings) apply to the court in which the proceedings have been brought to stay the proceedings so far as they concern that matter.

(2) An application may be made notwithstanding that the matter is to be referred to arbitration only after the exhaustion of other dispute resolution procedures.

(3) An application may not be made by a person before taking the appropriate procedural step (if any) to acknowledge the legal proceedings against him or after he has taken any step in those proceedings to answer the substantive claim.

(4) On an application under this section the court shall grant a stay unless satisfied that the arbitration agreement is null and void, inoperative, or incapable of being performed.

(5) If the court refuses to stay the legal proceedings, any provision that an award is a condition precedent to the bringing of legal proceedings in respect of any matter is of no effect in relation to those proceedings.

Commencement of arbitral proceedings

Power of court to extend time for beginning arbitral proceedings, &c.

12.—(1) Where an arbitration agreement to refer future disputes to arbitration provides that a claim shall be barred, or the claimant's right extinguished, unless the claimant takes within a time fixed by the agreement some step —

   , (a) to begin arbitral proceedings, or
    (b) to begin other dispute resolution procedures which must be exhausted before arbitral proceedings can be begun,

the court may by order extend the time for taking that step.

(2) Any party to the arbitration agreement may apply for such an order (upon notice to the other parties), but only after a claim has arisen and after exhausting any available arbitral process for obtaining an extension of time.

(3) The court shall make an order only if satisfied —

    (a) that the circumstances are such as were outside the reasonable contemplation of the parties when they agreed the provision in question, and that it would be just to extend the time, or
    (b) that the conduct of one party makes it unjust to hold the other party to the strict terms of the provision in question.

(4) The court may extend the time for such period and on such terms as it thinks fit, and may do so whether or not the time previously fixed (by agreement or by a previous order) has expired.

(5) An order under this section does not affect the operation of the LImitation Acts (see section 13).

(6) The leave of the court is required for any appeal from a decision of the court under this section.

Application of Limitation Acts

13.—(1) The Limitation Acts apply to arbitral proceedings as they apply to legal proceedings.

(2) The court may order that in computing the time prescribed by the Limitation Acts for the commencement of proceedings (including arbitral proceedings) in respect of a dispute which was the subject matter —

   (a) of an award which the court orders to be set aside or declares to be of no effect, or
   (b) of the affected part of an award which the court orders to be set aside in part, or declares to be in part of no effect.

the period between the commencement of the arbitration and the date of the order referred to in paragraph (a) or (b) shall be excluded.

(3) In determining for the purposes of the Limitation Acts when a cause of action accrued, any provision that an award is a condition precedent to the bringing of legal proceedings in respect of a matter to which an arbitration agreement applies shall be disregarded.

(4) In this Part "the Limitation Acts" means —

   (a) in England and Wales, the Limitation Act 1980, the Foreign Limitation Periods Act 1984 and any other enactment (whenever passed) relating to the limitation of actions;
   (b) in Northern Ireland, the Limitation (Norther Ireland) Order 1989, the Foreign Limitation Periods (Northern Ireland) Order 1985 and any other enactment (whenever passed) relating to the limitation of actions.

Commencement of arbitral proceedings

14.—(1) The parties are free to agree when arbitral proceedings are to be regarded as commenced for the purposes of this Part and for the purposes of the Limitation Acts.

(2) If there is no such agreement the following provisions apply.

(3) Where the arbitrator is named or designated in the arbitration agreement, arbitral proceedings are commenced in respect of a matter when one party serves on the other party or parties a notice in writing requiring him or them to submit that matter to the person so named or designated.

(4) Where the arbitrator or arbitrators are to be appointed by the parties, arbitral proceedings are commenced in respect of a matter when one party serves on the other party or parties notice in writing requiring him or them to appoint an arbitrator or to agree to the appointment of an arbitrator in respect of that matter.

(5) Where the arbitrator or arbitrators are to be appointed by a person other than a party to the proceedings, arbitral proceedings are commenced in respect of a matter when one party gives notice in writing to that person requesting him to make the appointment in respect of that matter.

Extension of time for making award

50.—(1) Where the time for making an award is limited by or in pursuance of the arbitration agreement, then, unless otherwise agreed by the parties, the court may in accordance with the following provisions by order extend that time.

(2) An application for an order under this section may be made —

   (a) by the tribunal (upon notice to the parties), or
   (b) by any party to the proceedings (upon notice to the tribunal and the other parties),

but only after exhausting any available arbitral process for obtaining an extension of time.

(3) The court shall only make an order if satisfied that a substantial injustice would otherwise be done.

(4) The court may extend the time for such period and on such terms as it thinks fit, and may do so whether or not the time previously fixed (by or under the agreement or by a previous order) has expired.

(5) The leave of the court is required for any appeal from a decision of the court under this section.

Date of award

54.—(1) Unless otherwise agreed by the parties, the tribunal may decide what is to be taken to be the date on which the award was made.

(2) In the absence of any such decision, the date of the award shall be taken to be the date on which it is signed by the arbitrator or, where more than one arbitrator signs the award, by the last of them.

Challenge or appeal: supplementary provisions

70.—(1) The following provisions apply to an application or appeal under section 67, 68 or 69.

(2) An application or appeal may not be brought if the application or appellant has not first exhausted —

   (a) any available arbitral process of appeal or review, and
   (b) any available recourse under section 57 (correction of award or additional award).

(3) Any application or appeal must be brought within 28 days of the date of the award or, if there has been any arbitral process of appeal or review, of the date when the applicant or appellant was notified of the result of that process.

(4) If on an application or appeal it appears to the court that the award —

   (a) does not contain the tribunal's reasons, or
   (b) does not set out the tribunal's reasons in sufficient detail to enable the court property to consider the application or appeal.

the court may order the tribunal to state the reasons for its award in sufficient detail for that purpose.

(5) Where the court makes an order under subsection (4), it may make such further order as it thinks fit with respect to any additional costs of the arbitration resulting from its order.

(6) The court may order the applicant or appellant to provide security for the costs of the application or appeal, and may direct that the application or appeal be dismissed if the order is not complied with.

The power to order security for costs shall not be exercised on the ground that the applicant or appellant is —

   (a) an individual ordinarily resident outside the United Kingdom, or
   (b) a corporation or association incorporated or formed under the law of a country outside the United Kingdom, or whose central management and control is exercised outside the United Kingdom.

(7) The court may order that any money payable under the award shall be brought into court or otherwise secured pending the determination of the application or appeal, and may direct that the application or appeal be dismissed if the order is not complied with.

(8) The court may grant leave to appeal subject to conditions to the same or similar effect as an order under subsection (6) or (7).

This does not affect the general discretion of the court to grant leave subject to conditions.

Reckoning periods of time

78.—(1) The parties are free to agree on the method of reckoning periods of time for the purposes of any provision agreed by them or any provision of this Part having effect in default of such agreement.

(2) If or to the extent there is no such agreement, periods of time shall be reckoned in accordance with the following provisions.

(3) Where the act is required to be done within a specified period after or from a specified date, the period begins immediately after that date.

(4) Where the act is required to be done a specified number of clear days after a specified date, at least that number of days must intervene between the day on which the act is done and that date.

(5) Where the period is a period of seven days or less which would include a Saturday, Sunday or a public holiday in the place where anything which has to be done within the period falls to be done, that day shall be excluded.

In relation to England and Wales or Northern Ireland, a "public holiday" means Christmas Day, Good Friday or a day which under the Banking and Financial Dealings Act 1971 is a bank holiday.

Power of court to extend the time limits relating to arbitral proceedings

79.—(1) Unless the parties otherwise agree, the court may by order extend any time limit agreed by them in relation to any matter relating to the arbitral proceedings or specified in any provision of this Part having effect in default of such agreement.

This section does not apply to a time limit to which section 12 applies (power of court to extend time for beginning arbitral proceedings, &c.).

(2) An application for an order may be made —

    (a) by any party to the arbitral proceedings (upon notice to the other parties and to the tribunal), or

    (b) by the arbitral tribunal (upon notice to the parties).

(3) The court shall not exercise its power to extend a time limit unless it is satisfied —

    (a) that any available recourse to the tribunal, or to any arbitral or other institution or person vested by the parties with power in that regard, has first been exhausted, and

    (b) that a substantial injustice would otherwise be done.

(4) The court's power under this section may be exercised whether or not the time has already expired.

(5) An order under this section may be made on such terms as the court thinks fit.

(6) The leave of the court is required for any appeal from a decision of the court under this section.

DEFAMATION ACT 1996

Limitation

Limitation of actions: England and Wales

5.—(1) The Limitation Act 1980 is amended as follows.

(2) For section 4A (time limit for action for libel or slander) substitute —

"Time limit for actions for defamation or malicious falsehood

4A. The time limit under section 2 of this Act shall not apply to an action for —

(a) libel or slander, or

(b) slander of title, slander of goods or other malicious falsehood,

but no such action shall be brought after the expiration of one year from the date on which the cause of action accrued.".

(3) In section 28 (extension of limitation period in case of disability), for subsection (4A) substitute —

"(4A) If the action is one to which section 4A of this Act applies, subsection (1) above shall have effect —

(a) in the case of an action for libel or slander, as if for the words from 'at any time' to 'occurred)' there were substituted the words 'by him at any time before the expiration of one year from the date on which he ceased to be under a disability'; and

(b) in the case of an action for slander of title, slander of goods or other malicious falsehood, as if for the words 'six years' there were substituted the words 'one year'.".

(4) For section 32A substitute —

"Discretionary exclusion of time limit for actions for defamation or malicious falsehood

Discretionary exclusion of time limit for actions for defamation or malicious falsehood

32A.—(1) If it appears to the court that it would be equitable to allow an action to proceed having regard to the degree to which —

(a) the operation of section 4A of this Act prejudices the plaintiff or any person whom he represents, and

(b) any decision of the court under this subsection would prejudice the defendant or any person whom he represents,

the court may direct that that section shall not apply to the action or shall not apply to any specified cause of action to which the action relates.

(2) In acting under this section the court shall have regard to all the circumstances of the case and in particular to —

(a) the length of, and the reasons for, the delay on the part of the plaintiff;

(b) where the reason or one of the reasons for the delay was that all or any of the fact relevant to the cause of action did not become known to the plaintiff until after the end of the period mentioned in section 4A —

(i) the date on which any such facts did become known to him, and

(ii) the extent to which he acted promptly and reasonably once he knew whether or not the facts in question might be capable of giving rise to an action; and

(c) the extent to which, having regard to the delay, relevant evidence is likely —

(i) to be unavailable, or

(ii) to be less cogent than if the action had been brought within the period mentioned in section 4A.

(3) In the case of an action for slander of title, slander of goods or other malicious falsehood brought by a personal representative —

(a) the references in subsection (2) above to the plaintiff shall be construed as including the deceased person to whom the cause of action accrued and any previous personal representative of that person; and

(b) nothing in section 28(3) of this Act shall be construed as affecting the court's discretion under this section.

(4) In this section 'the court' means the court in which the action has been brought.".

(5) In section 36(1) (expiry of time limit no bar to equitable relief), for paragraph (aa) substitute —

"(aa) the time limit under section 4A for actions for libel or slander, or for slander of title, slander of goods or other malicious falsehood;".

(6) The amendments made by this section apply only to causes of action arising after the section comes into force.

Limitation of actions: Northern Ireland

6.—(1) The Limitation (Northern Ireland) Order 1989 is amended as follows.

(2) In Article 6 (time limit: certain actions founded on tort) for paragraph (2) substitute —

"(2) Subject to Article 51, an action for damages for —

(a) libel or slander; or

(b) slander of title, slander of goods or other malicious falsehood,

may not be brought after the expiration of one year from the date on which the cause of action accrued.".

(3) In Article 48 (extension of time limit, for paragraph (7) substitute —

"(7) Where the action is one to which Article 6(2) applies, paragraph (1) has effect —

(a) in the case of an action for libel and slander, as if for the words from 'at any time' to 'occurred' there were substituted the words 'by him at any time before the expiration of one year from the date on which he ceased to be under a disability'; and

(b) in the case of an action for slander of title, slander of goods or other malicious falsehood, as if for the words 'six years' there were substituted the words 'one year'.".

(4) For Article 51 substitute —

"Court's power to override time limit: actions for defamation or malicious falsehood

51.—(1) If it appears to the court that it would be equitable to allow an action to proceed having regard to the degree to which —

(a) the provisions of Article 6(2) prejudice the plaintiff or any person whom he represents; and

(b) any decision of the court under this paragraph would prejudice the defendant or any person whom he represents,

the court may direct that those provisions are not to apply to the action, or are not to apply to any specified cause of action to which the action relates.

(2) In acting under this Article the court is to have regard to all the circumstances of the case and in particular to —

(a) the length of, and the reasons for, the delay on the part of the plaintiff;

    (b) in a case where the reason, or one of the reasons, for the delay was that all or any of the facts relevant to the cause of action did not become known to the plaintiff until after the expiration of the period mentioned in Article 6(2) —

      (i) the date on which any such facts did become known to him, and

      (ii) the extent to which he acted promptly and reasonably once he knew whether or not the facts in question might be capable of giving rise to an action; and

    (c) the extent to which, having regard to the delay, relevant evidence is likely —

      (i) to be unavailable, or

      (ii) to be less cogent than if the action had been brought within the time allowed by Article 6(2).

(3) In the case of an action for slander of title, slander of goods or other malicious falsehood brought by a personal representative —

    (a) the references in paragraph (2) to the plaintiff shall be construed as including the deceased person to whom the cause of action accrued and any previous personal representative of that person; and

    (b) nothing in Article 48(3) shall be construed as affecting the court's discretion under this Article.

(4) In this Article 'the court' means the court in which the action has been brought.".

(5) The amendments made by this section apply only to causes of action arising after the section comes into force.

TRUSTS OF LAND AND APPOINTMENT OF TRUSTEES ACT 1996

SCHEDULE 4

Chapter	Short title	Extent of repeal
1980 c. 58.	The Limitation Act 1980.	In section 18— in subsection (1), the words ", including interests in the proceeds of the sale of land held upon trust for sale,", and in subsections (3) and (4), the words "(including a trust for sale)" and the words "or in the proceeds of sale". In section 38(1)— in the definition of "land", the words ", including an interest in the proceeds of the sale of land held upon trust for sale,", and the definition of "trust for sale". In Schedule 1, in Part I, in paragraph 9— the words "or in the proceeds of sale", the words "or the proceeds", and the words "or the proceeds of sale".

RULES OF THE SUPREME COURT

ORDER 1

Definitions

4.—(1) In these rules, unless the context otherwise requires, the following expressions have the meanings hereby respectively assigned to them, namely —

"*THE ACT*" means the Supreme Court Act 1981;

"an action for personal injuries" means an action in which there is a claim for damages in respect of personal injuries to the plaintiff or any other person or in respect of a person's death, and "personal injuries" includes any disease and any impairment of a person's physical or mental condition;

"cause book" means the book or other record kept in the Central Office, Chancery Chambers, the principal registry of the Family Division, the Admiralty and Commercial Registry and every district registry in which the letter and number of, and other details relating to, a cause or matter are entered;

"Central Office" means the central office of the Supreme Court;

"Chancery Chambers" means the offices of the Chancery Division;

"Chancery district registries" means the district registries of Birmingham, Bristol, Cardiff, Leeds, Liverpool, Manchester, Newcastle upon Tyne and Preston;

"chief master" means the Chief Chancery Master;

"circuit" means one of the six areas into which England and Wales are divided for the purposes of the conduct of judicial business;

"Crown Office" means the Crown Office and Associates' Department of the Central Office;

"FAX" means the making of a facsimile copy of a document by the transmission of electronic signals;

"folio" means 72 words, each figure being counted as one word;

"master" means a master of the Supreme Court other than a taxing master;

"notice of intention to defend" means an acknowledgment of service containing a statement to the effect that the person by whom or on whose behalf it is signed intends to contest the proceedings to which the acknowledgment relates;

"official referee" means a person nominated under section 68(1)(a) of the Act;

"Official Solicitor" means the Official Solicitor to the Supreme Court;

"officer" means an officer of the Supreme Court;

"originating summons" means every summons other than a summons in a pending cause or matter;

"pleading" does not include a petition, summons or Part One of a preliminary act;

"probate action" has the meaning assigned to it by Order 76;

receiver" includes a manager or consignee;

"senior master" means the Senior Master of the Queen's Bench Division;

"statement of the value of the action" means a statement showing —

(a) whether the value of the action (or, as the case may be, of the counterclaim) exceeds the sum for the time being specified in article 7(3) of the High Court and County

Courts Jurisdiction Order 1991 or, as the case may be, that it has no quantifiable value, and

(b) if it does not exceed that sum or if it has no quantifiable value, that by reason of one or more of the criteria mentioned in article 7(5) of the said Order the action is suitable for determination in the High Court;

"vacation" means the interval between the end of any of the sittings mentioned in Order 64, rule 1, and the beginning of the next sittings;

"value" in relation to an action, means the value as defined by articles 9 and 10 of the High Court and County Courts Jurisdiction Order 1991;

"writ" means a writ of summons.

(2) In these rules, unless the context otherwise requires, "the Court" means the High Court or any one or more judges thereof, whether sitting in court or in chambers or any master, the Admiralty Registrar or any registrar of the Family Division, or registrar of a district registry; but the foregoing provision shall not be taken as affecting any provision of these rules and, in particular, Order 32, rules 11, 14 and 23, by virtue of which the authority and jurisdiction of a master or any such registrar is defined and regulated.

(3) In these rules, unless the context otherwise requires any reference to acknowledging service of a document or giving notice of intention to defend any proceedings is a reference to lodging in the appropriate court office an acknowledgment of service of that document or, as the case may be, a notice of intention to defend those proceedings.

ORDER 5

Mode of beginning civil proceedings

1. Subject to the provisions of any Act and of these rules, civil proceedings in the High Court may be begun by writ, originating summons, originating motion or petition.

Proceedings which must be begun by writ

2. Subject to any provision of an Act, or of these rules, by virtue of which any proceedings are expressly required to be begun otherwise than by writ, the following proceedings must, notwithstanding anything in rule 4, be begun by writ, that is to say, proceedings —

(a) in which a claim is made by the plaintiff for any relief or remedy for any tort, other than trespass to land;

(b) in which a claim made by the plaintiff is based on an allegation of fraud;

(c) in which a claim is made by the plaintiff for damages for breach of duty (whether the duty exists by virtue of a contract or of a provision made by or under an Act or independently of any contract or any such provision) where the damages claimed consist of or include damages in respect of the death of any person or in respect of personal injuries to any person or in respect of damage to any property.

Proceedings which must be begun by originating summons

3. Proceedings by which an application is to be made to the High Court or a judge thereof under any Act must be begun by originating summons except where by these rules or by or under any Act the application in question is expressly required or authorised to be made by some other means.

This rule does not apply to an application made in pending proceedings.

Proceedings which may be begun by writ or originating summons

4.—(1) Except in the case of proceedings which by these rules or by or under any Act are required to be begun by writ or originating summons or are required or authorised to be begun by originating motion or petition, proceedings may be begun either by writ or by originating summons as the plaintiff considers appropriate.

(2) Proceedings —

(a) in which the sole or principal question at issue is, or is likely to be, one of the construction of an Act or of any instrument made under an Act, or of any deed, will, contract or other document, or some other question of law, or

(b) in which there is likely to be any substantial dispute of fact,

are appropriate to be begun by originating summons unless the plaintiff intends in those proceedings to apply for judgment under Order 14 or Order 86 or for any other reason considers the proceedings more appropriate to be begun by writ.

Proceedings to be begun by motion or petition

5. Proceedings may be begun by originating motion or petition if, but only if, by these rules or by or under any Act the proceedings in question are required or authorised to be so begun.

Right to sue in person

6.—(1) Subject to paragraph (2) and to Order 80, rule 2, any person (whether or not he sues as a trustee or personal representative or in any other representative capacity) may begin and carry on proceedings in the High Court by a solicitor or in person.

(2) Except as expressly provided by or under any enactment, a body corporate may not begin or carry on any such proceedings otherwise than by a solicitor.

ORDER 6

Duration and renewal of writ

8.—(1) For the purposes of service, a writ (other than a concurrent writ) is valid in the first instance —

(a) if an Admiralty writ *in rem*, for 12 months;

(b) where leave to serve the writ out of the jurisdiction is required under Order 11 or Order 75, rule 4, for 6 months,

(c) in any other case, for 4 months

beginning with the date of its issue.

(1A) A concurrent writ is valid in the first instance for the period of validity of the original writ which is unexpired at the date of issue of the concurrent writ.

(2) Subject to paragraph (2A), where a writ has not been served on a defendant, the Court may by order extend the validity of the writ from time to time for such period, not exceeding 4 months at any one time, beginning with the day next following that on which it would otherwise expire, as may be specified in the order, if an application for extension is made to the Court before that day or such later day (if any) as the Court may allow.

(2A) Where the Court is satisfied on an application under paragraph (2) that, despite the making of all reasonable efforts, it may not be possible to serve the writ within 4 months, the Court may, if it thinks fit, extend the validity of the writ for such period, not exceeding 12 months, as the Court may specify.

(3) Before a writ, the validity of which has been extended under this rule, is served, it must be marked with an official stamp showing the period for which the validity of the writ has been so extended.

(4) Where the validity of a writ is extended by order made under this Rule, the order shall operate in relation to any other writ (which original or concurrent) issued in the same action which has not been served so as to extend the validity of that other writ until the expiration of the period specified in the order.

ORDER 13

Proof of service of writ

7.—(1) Judgment shall not be entered against a defendant under this Order unless —

(a) the defendant has acknowledged service on him of the writ; or

(b) an affidavit is filed by or on behalf of the plaintiff proving due service of the writ on the defendant; or

(c) the plaintiff producers the writ indorsed by the defendant's solicitor with a statement that he accepts service of the writ on the defendant's behalf.

(2) Where, in an action begun by writ, an application is made to the Court for an order affecting a party who has failed to give notice of intention to defend, the Court hearing the application may require to be satisfied in such manner as it thinks fit that the party failed to give such notice.

(3) Where, after judgment has been entered under this Order against a defendant purporting to have been served by post under Order 10, rule 1(2)(a) the copy of the writ sent to the defendant is returned to the plaintiff through the post, undelivered to the addressee, the plaintiff, shall, before taking any step or further step in the action or the enforcement of the judgment either —

(a) make a request for the judgment to be set aside on the ground that the writ has not been duly served, or

(b) apply to the Court for directions.

(4) A request under paragraph (3)(a) shall be made by producing to an officer of the office in which the judgment was entered, and leaving with him for filing, an affidavit stating the relevant facts, and thereupon the judgment shall be set aside and the entry of the judgment and of any proceedings for its enforcement made in the book kept in the office for that purpose shall be marked accordingly.

(5) An application under paragraph (3)(b) shall be made *ex parte* by affidavit stating the facts on which the application is founded and any order or direction sought, and on the application the Court may —

(a) set aside the judgment; or

(b) direct that, notwithstanding the return of the copy of the writ, it shall be treated as having been duly served, or

(c) make such other order and give such other direction as the circumstances may require.

ORDER 15

Court may order separate trials, etc.

5.—(1) If claims in respect of two or more causes of action are included by a plaintiff in the same action or by a defendant in a counterclaim, or if two or more plaintiffs or defendants are parties to the same action, and it appears to the Court that the joinder of causes of action or of parties, as the case may be, may embarrass or delay the trial or is otherwise inconvenient, the Court may order separate trials or make such other order as may be expedient.

(2) If it appears on the application of any party against whom a counterclaim is made that the subject-matter of the counterclaim ought for any reason to be disposed of by a separate action, the Court may order the counterclaim to be struck out or may order it to be tried separately or make such other order as may be expedient.

Misjoinder and nonjoinder of parties

6.—(1) No cause or matter shall be defeated by reason of the misjoinder or nonjoinder of any party; and the Court may in any cause or matter determine the issues or questions in dispute so far as they affect the rights and interests of the persons who are parties to the cause or matter.

(2) Subject to the provisions of this rule, at any stage of the proceedings in any cause or matter the Court may on such terms as it thinks just and either of its own motion or on application —

(a) order any person who has been improperly or unnecessarily made a party or who has for any reason ceased to be a proper or necessary party, to cease to be a party;

(b) order any of the following persons to be added as a party, namely —

(i) any person who ought to have been joined as a party or whose presence before the Court is necessary to ensure that all matters in dispute in the cause or matter may be effectually and completely determined and adjudicated upon, or

(ii) any person between whom and any party to the cause or matter there may exist a question or issue arising out of or relating to or connected with any relief or remedy claimed in the cause or matter which in the opinion of the Court it would be just and convenient to determine as between him and that party as well as between the parties to the cause or matter.

(3) An application by any person for an order under paragraph (2) adding him as a party must, except with the leave of the Court, be supported by an affidavit showing his interest in the matters in dispute in the cause or matter or, as the case may be, the question or issue to be determined as between him and any party to the cause or matter.

(4) No person shall be added as a plaintiff without his consent signified in writing or in such other manner as may be authorised.

(5) No person shall be added or substituted as a party after the expiry of any relevant period of limitation unless either —

(a) the relevant period was current at the date when proceedings were commenced and it is necessary for the determination of the action that the new party should be added, or substituted, or

(b) the relevant period arises under the provisions of section 11 or 12 of the Limitation Act 1980 and the Court directs that those provisions should not apply to the action by or against the new party.

In this paragraph "any relevant period of limitation" means a time limit under the Limitation Act 1980 or a time limit which applies to the proceedings in question by virtue of the Foreign Limitation Periods Act 1984.

(6) Except in a case to which the law of another country relating to limitation applies, and the law of England and Wales does not so apply, the addition or substitution of a new party shall be treated as necessary for the purposes of paragraph (5)(a) if, and only if, the Court is satisfied that —

(a) the new party is a necessary party to the action in that property is vested in him at law or in equity and the plaintiff's claim in respect of an equitable interest in that property is liable to be defeated unless the new party is joined, or

(b) the relevant cause of action is vested in the new party and the plaintiff jointly but not severally, or

(c) the new party is the Attorney General and the proceedings should have been brought by relator proceedings in his name, or

(d) the new party is a company in which the plaintiff is a shareholder and on whose behalf the plaintiff is suing to enforce a right vested in the company, or

(e) the new party is sued jointly with the defendant and is not also liable severally with him and failure to join the new party might render the claim unenforceable.

Change of parties by reason of death, etc.

7.—(1) Where a party to an action dies or becomes bankrupt but the cause of action survives, the action shall not abate by reason of the death or bankruptcy.

(2) Where at any stage of the proceedings in any cause or matter the interest or liability of any party is assigned or transmitted to or devolves upon some other person, the Court may, if it thinks it necessary in order to ensure that all matters in dispute in the cause or matter may be effectually and completely determined and adjudicated upon, order that other person to be made a party to the cause or matter and the proceedings to be carried on as if he had been substituted for the first mentioned party.

An application for an order under this paragraph may be made *ex parte*.

(3) An order may be made under this rule for a person to be made a party to a cause or matter notwithstanding that he is already a party to it on the other side of the record, or on the same side but in a different capacity; but —

(a) if he is already a party on the other side, the order shall be treated as containing a direction that he shall cease to be a party on that other side, and

(b) if he is already a party on the same side but in another capacity, the order may contain a direction that he shall cease to be a party in that other capacity.

(4) The person on whose application an order is made under this rule must procure the order to be noted in the cause book, and after the order has been so noted that person must, unless the Court otherwise directs, serve the order on every other person who is a party to the cause or matter or who becomes or ceases to be a party by virtue of the order and serve with the order on any person who becomes a defendant a copy of the writ or originating summons by which the cause or matter was begun and of all other pleadings served in the proceedings and a form of acknowledgment of service in Form 14 or 15 in Appendix A, whichever is appropriate.

(5) Any application to the Court by a person served with an order made *ex parte* under this rule for the discharge or variation of the order must be made within 14 days after the service of the order on that person.

ORDER 16

Third party notice

1.—(1) Where in any action a defendant who has given notice of intention to defend —

    (a) claims against a person not already a party to the action any contribution or indemnity; or

    (b) claims against such a person any relief or remedy relating to or connected with the original subject-matter of the action and substantially the same as some relief or remedy claimed by the plaintiff; or

    (c) requires that any question or issue relating to or connected with the original subject-matter of the action should be determined not only as between the plaintiff and the defendant but also as between either or both of them and a person not already a party to the action;

then, subject to paragraph (2), the defendant may issue a notice in Form No. 20 or 21 in Appendix A, whichever is appropriate (in this Order referred to as a third party notice), containing a statement of the nature of the claim made against him and, as the case may be, either of the nature and grounds of the claim made by him or of the question or issue required to be determined.

(2) A defendant to an action may not issue a third party notice without the leave of the Court unless the action was begun by writ and he issues the notice before serving his defence on the plaintiff.

(3) Where a third party notice is served on the person against whom it is issued, he shall as from the time of service be a party to the action (in this Order referred to as a third party) with the same rights in respect of his defence against any claim made against him in the notice and otherwise as if he had been duly sued in the ordinary way by the defendant by whom the notice is issued.

Application for leave to issue third party notice

2.—(1) Application for leave to issue a third party notice may be made *ex parte* but the Court may direct a summons for leave to be issued.

(2) An application for leave to issue a third party notice must be supported by an affidavit stating —

    (a) the nature of the claim made by the plaintiff in the action;

    (b) the stage which proceedings in the action have reached;

    (c) the nature of the claim made by the applicant or particulars of the question or issue required to be determined, as the case may be, and the facts on which the proposed third party notice is based; and

    (d) the name and address of the person against whom the third party notice is to be issued.

Issue, service and acknowledgment of service, of third party notice

3.—(1) The order granting leave to issue a third party notice may contain directions as to the period within which the notice is to be issued.

(2) There must be served with every third party notice a copy of the writ or originating summons by which the action was begun and of the pleadings (if any) served in the action and a form of acknowledgment of service in Form No. 14 in Appendix A with such modifications as may be appropriate.

(3) The appropriate office for acknowledging service of a third party notice is the central office, except that, where the notice is issued in an action which is proceeding in the Chancery Division or a District Registry, or in an admiralty or commercial action which is not proceeding in a District Registry, the appropriate office is Chancery Chambers, the District Registry in question or the Admiralty and Commercial Registry, as the case may be.

(4) Subject to the foregoing provisions of this rule, the following provisions of these rules, namely, Order 6, rule 7(3) and (5), Order 10, Order 11, Order 12 and Order 75, rule 4, shall apply in relation to a third party notice and to the proceedings begun thereby as if —

(a) the third party notice were a writ and the proceedings begun thereby an action; and
(b) the defendant issuing the third party notice were a plaintiff and the person against whom it is issued a defendant in that action:

provided that in the application of Order 11, r. 1(1)(c) leave may be granted to serve a third party notice outside the jurisdiction on any necessary or proper party to the proceedings brought against the defendant.

Third party directions

4.—(1) If the third party gives notice of intention to defend, the defendant who issued the third party notice must, by summons to be served on all the other parties to the action, apply to the Court for directions.

(2) If no summons is served on the third party under paragraph (1) the third party may, not earlier than seven days after giving notice of intention to defend by summons to be served on all the other parties to the action, apply to the Court for directions or for an order to set aside the third party notice.

(3) On an application for directions under this rule the Court may —

(a) if the liability of the third party to the defendant who issued the third party notice is established on the hearing, order such judgment as the nature of the case may require to be entered against the third party in favour of the defendant; or
(b) order any claim, question or issue stated in the third party notice to be tried in such manner as the Court may direct; or
(c) dismiss the application and terminate the proceedings on the third party notice;

and may do so either before or after any judgment in the action has been signed by the plaintiff against the defendant.

(4) On an application of directions under this rule the Court may give the third party leave to defend the action, either alone or jointly with any defendant, upon such terms as may be just, or to appear at the trial and to take such part therein as may be just, and generally may make such orders and give such directions as appear to the Court proper for having the rights and liabilities of the parties most conveniently determined and enforced and as to the extent to which the third party is to be bound by any judgment or decision in the action.

(5) Any order made or direction given under this rule may be varied or rescinded by the Court at any time.

Default of third party, etc.

5.—(1) If a third party does not give notice of intention to defend or, having been ordered to serve a defence, fails to do so —

(a) he shall be deemed to admit any claim stated in the third party notice and shall be bound by any judgment (including judgment by consent) or decision in the action in so far as it is relevant to any claim, question or issue stated in that notice; and

(b) the defendant by whom the third party notice was issued may, if judgment in default is given against him in the action, at any time after satisfaction of that judgment and, with the leave of the Court, before satisfaction thereof, enter judgment against the third party in respect of any contribution or indemnity claimed in the notice, and, with the leave of the Court, in respect of any other relief or remedy claimed therein.

(2) If a third party or the defendant by whom a third party notice was issued makes default in serving any pleading which he is ordered to serve, the Court may, on the application by summons of that defendant or the third party, as the case may be, order such judgment to be entered for the applicant as he is entitled to on the pleadings or may make such other order as may appear to the Court necessary to do justice between the parties.

(3) The Court may at any time set aside or vary a judgment entered under paragraph (1)(b) or paragraph (2) on such terms (if any) as it thinks just.

Judgment between defendant and third party

7.—(1) Where in any action a defendant has served a third party notice, the Court may at or after the trial of the action or, if the action is decided otherwise than by trial, on an application by summons or motion, order such judgment as the nature of the case may require to be entered for the defendant against the third party or for the third party against the defendant.

(2) Where judgment is given for the payment of any contribution or indemnity to a person who is under a liability to make a payment in respect of the same debt or damage, execution shall not issue on the judgment without the leave of the Court until that liability has been discharged.

(3) For the purpose of paragraph (2) "liability" includes liability under a judgment in the same or other proceedings and liability under an agreement to which section 1(4) of the Civil Liability (Contribution) Act 1978 applies.

Claims and issues between a defendant and some other party

8.—(1) Where in any action a defendant who has given notice of intention to defend —

(a) claims against a person who is already a party to the action any contribution or indemnity; or

(b) claims against such a person any relief or remedy relating to or connected with the original subject-matter of the action and substantially the same as some relief or remedy claimed by the plaintiff; or

(c) requires that any question or issue relating to or connected with the original subject-matter of the action should be determined not only as between the plaintiff and himself but also as between either or both of them and some other person who is already a party to the action;

then, subject to paragraph (2) the defendant may, without leave, issue and serve on that person a notice containing a statement of the nature and grounds of his claim or, as the case may be, of the question or issue required to be determined.

(2) Where a defendant makes such a claim as is mentioned in paragraph (1) and that claim could be made by him by counterclaim in the action, paragraph (1) shall not apply in relation to the claim.

(3) No acknowledgment of service of such a notice shall be necessary if the person on whom it is served has acknowledged service of the writ or originating summons in the action or is a plaintiff therein, and the same procedure shall be adopted for the determination between the defendant by whom, and the person on whom, such a notice is served of the claim, question or issue stated in the notice as would be appropriate under this Order if the person served with the notice were a third party and (where he has given notice of intention to defend the action or is a plaintiff) had given notice of intention to defend the claim, question or issue.

(4) Rule 4(2) shall have effect in relation to proceedings on a notice issued under this rule as if for the words "7 days after giving notice of intention to defend" there were substituted the words "14 days after service of the notice on him."

Claims by third and subsequent parties

(9).—(1) Where a defendant has served a third party notice and the third party makes such a claim or requirement as is mentioned in rule 1 or rule 8, this Order shall, with the modification mentioned in paragraph (2) and any other necessary modifications, apply as if the third party were a defendant; and similarly where any further person to whom by virtue of this rule this Order applies as if he were a third party makes such a claim or requirement.

(2) The modification referred to in paragraph (1) is that paragraph (3) shall have effect in relation to the issue of a notice under rule 1 by a third party in substitution for rule 1(2).

(3) A third party may not issue a notice under rule 1 without the leave of the Court unless the action in question was begun by writ and he issues the notice before the expiration of 14 days after the time limited for acknowledging service of the notice issued against him.

Offer of contribution

10.—(1) If, at any time after he has acknowledged service, a party to an action, who stands to be held liable in the action to another party to contribute towards any debt or damages and which may be recovered against that other party in the action, makes (without prejudice to his defence) a written offer to that other party to contribute to a specified extent to the debt or damages, then, subject to paragraph (2) notwithstanding that he reserves the right to bring the offer to the attention of the Judge at the trial, the offer shall not be brought to the attention of the Judge until after all questions of liability and amount of debt or damages have been decided.

(2) Where the question of the costs of the issue of liability falls to be decided, that issue having been tried and an issue or question concerning the amount of the debt or damages remaining to be tried separately, any party may bring to the attention of the judge the fact that a written offer under paragraph (1) has or has not been made and the date (but not the amount) of such offer or of the first such offer if more than one.

Counterclaim by defendant

11. Where in any action a counterclaim is made by a defendant, the foregoing provisions of this Order shall apply in relation to the counterclaim as if the subject-matter of the counterclaim were the original subject-matter of the action, and as if the person making the counterclaim were the plaintiff and the person against whom it is made a defendant.

ORDER 18

Matters which must be specifically pleaded

8.—(1) A party must in any pleading subsequent to a statement of claim plead specifically any matter, for example, performance, release, the expiry of any relevant period of limitation, fraud or any fact showing illegality —

(a) which he alleges makes any claim or defence of the opposite party not maintainable; or
(b) which, if not specifically pleaded, might take the opposite party by surprise; or
(c) which raises issues of fact not arising out of the preceding pleading.

(2) Without prejudice to paragraph (1), a defendant to an action for possession of land must plead specifically every ground of defence on which he relies, and a plea that he is in possession of the land by himself or his tenant is not sufficient.

(3) A claim for exemplary damages or for provisional damages must be specifically pleaded together with the facts on which the party pleading relies.

(4) A party must plead specifically any claim for interest under section 35A of the Act or otherwise.

Striking out pleadings and indorsements

19.—(1) The Court may at any stage of the proceedings order to be struck out or amended any pleading or the indorsement of any writ in the action, or anything in any pleading or in the indorsement, on the ground that —

(a) it discloses no reasonable cause of action or defence, as the case may be, or

(b) it is scandalous, frivolous or vexatious; or

(c) it may prejudice, embarrass or delay the fair trial of the action; or

(d) it is otherwise an abuse of the process of the Court;

and may order the action to be stayed or dismissed or judgment to be entered accordingly, as the case may be.

(2) No evidence shall be admissible on an application under paragraph (1)(a).

(3) This rule shall, so far as applicable, apply to an originating summons and a petition as if the summons or petition, as the case may be, were a pleading.

ORDER 19

Default of defence: other claims

7.—(1) Where the plaintiff makes against a defendant or defendants a claim of a description not mentioned in rules 2 to 5, then, if the defendant or all the defendants (where there is more than one) fails or fail to serve a defence on the plaintiff, the plaintiff may, after the expiration of the period fixed by or under these rules for service of the defence, apply to the Court for judgment, and on the hearing of the application the Court shall give such judgment as the plaintiff appears entitled to on his statement of claim.

(2) Where the plaintiff makes such a claim as is mentioned in paragraph (1) against more than one defendant, then, if one of the defendants makes default as mentioned in that paragraph, the plaintiff may —

(a) if his claim against the defendant in default is severable from his claim against the other defendants, apply under that paragraph for judgment against that defendant, and proceed with the action against the other defendants; or

(b) set down the action on motion for judgment against the defendant in default at the time when the action is set down for trial, or is set down on motion for judgment, against the other defendants.

(3) An application under paragraph (1) must be by summons or motion.

ORDER 20

Amendment of writ or pleading with leave

5.—(1) Subject to Order 15, rules 6, 7 and 8 and the following provisions of this rule, the Court may at any stage of the proceedings allow the plaintiff to amend his writ, or any party to amend his pleading, on such terms as to costs or otherwise as may be just and in such manner (if any) as it may direct.

(2) Where an application to the Court for leave to make the amendment mentioned in paragraph (3), (4) or (5) is made after any relevant period of limitation current at the date of issue of the writ has expired, the Court may nevertheless grant such leave in the circumstances mentioned in that paragraph if it thinks it just to do so.

In this paragraph "any relevant period of limitation" includes a time limit which applies to the proceedings in question by virtue of the Foreign Limitation Periods Act 1984.

(3) An amendment to correct the name of a party may be allowed under paragraph (2) notwithstanding that it is alleged that the effect of the amendment will be to substitute a new party if the Court is satisfied that the mistake sought to be corrected was a genuine mistake and was not misleading or such as to cause any reasonable doubt as to the identity of the party intending to sue or, as the case may be, intended to be sued.

(4) An amendment to alter the capacity in which a party sues may be allowed under paragraph (2) if the new capacity is one which that party had at the date of the commencement of the proceedings or has since acquired.

(5) An amendment may be allowed under paragraph (2) notwithstanding that the effect of the amendment will be to add or substitute a new cause of action if the new cause of action arises out

of the same facts or substantially the same facts as a cause of action in respect of which relief has already been claimed in the action by the party applying for leave to make the amendment.

ORDER 46

When leave to issue any writ of execution is necessary

2.—(1) A writ of execution to enforce a judgment or order may not issue without the leave of the Court in the following cases, that is to say: —

    (a) where six years or more have elapsed since the date of the judgment or order;

    (b) where any change has taken place, whether by death or otherwise, in the parties entitled or liable to execution under the judgment or order;

    (c) where the judgment or order is against the assets of a deceased person coming to the hands of his executors or administrators after the date of the judgment or order, and it is sought to issue execution against such assets;

    (d) where under the judgment or order any person is entitled to relief subject to the fulfilment of any condition which it is alleged has been fulfilled;

    (e) where any goods sought to be seized under a writ of execution are in the hands of a receiver appointed by the Court or a sequestrator.

ORDER 59

Final and interlocutory orders

1A.—(1) For all purposes connected with appeals to the Court of Appeal, a judgment or order shall be treated as final or interlocutory in accordance with the following provisions of this rule.

(2) In this rule, unless the context otherwise requires —

    (a) "order" includes a judgment, decree, decision or direction;

    (b) references to an order giving specified directions for granting a specified form of remedy or relief shall include an order —

        (i) refusing to give such directions or grant such remedy or relief;

        (ii) giving such directions or granting such remedy or relief on terms;

        (iii) varying, suspending or revoking such an order, and

        (iv) determining an appeal from such an order.

(3) A judgment or order shall be treated as final if the entire cause or matter would (subject only to any possible appeal) have been finally determined whichever way the court below had decided the issues before it.

(4) For the purposes of paragraph (3), where the final hearing or the trial of a cause or matter is divided into parts, a judgment or order made at the end of any part shall be treated as if made at the end of the complete hearing or trial.

(5) Notwithstanding anything in paragraph (3), the following orders shall be treated as final —

    (a) an order for discovery of documents made in an action for discovery only;

    (b) an order granting any relief made at the hearing of an application for judicial review;

    (c) an order made on an originating summons under Order 85, rule 2(2)(b) or (c);

    (d) an order for the winding up of a company;

    (e) a decree absolute of divorce or nullity of marriage;

    (f) an order absolute for foreclosure;

    (g) an order as to costs made as part of a final judgment of order;

    (h) an order of committal.

(6) Notwithstanding anything in paragraph (3), but without prejudice to paragraph (5), the following judgments and orders shall be treated as interlocutory —

    (a) an order extending or abridging the period for the doing of any act;

    (b) an order for or relating to the transfer or consolidation of proceedings;

(c) an order for or relating to the validity, service (including service out of the jurisdiction) or renewal of a writ or other originating process;

(d) an order granting leave under section 139 of the Mental Health Act 1983 to bring proceedings against a person;

(e) an order for or relating to the amendment of an acknowledgment of service;

(f) any judgment in default or any "unless" order;

(g) an order for or relating to the joinder of causes of action;

(h) an order for or relating to the addition, substitution or striking out of parties;

(i) subject to Order 58, rule 7, an order granting relief by way of interpleader;

(j) an order for or relating to the service or amendment of any pleading;

(k) an order striking out an action or other proceedings or any pleading under Order 18, rule 19 or under the inherent jurisdiction of the court;

(l) an order dismissing or striking out an action or other proceedings for want of prosecution;

(m) an order staying proceedings or execution;

(n) an order for or relating to a payment into or out of court;

(o) an order for or relating to security for the costs of an action or other proceedings;

(p) subject to paragraph (5)(a), an order for or relating to the discovery or inspection of documents, including an order under Order 24, rule 7A(1) for the disclosure of documents before the commencement of proceedings;

(q) an order for or relating to the service of or answer to interrogatories;

(r) a judgment or order on admissions under Order 27, rule 3;

(s) an order granting an interlocutory injunction or for the appointment of a receiver;

(t) an order for or relating to an interim payment under Order 29;

(u) an order made under or relating to a summons for directions;

(v) an order directing a trial with a jury;

(w) an order for or relating to the fixing or adjournment of trial dates;

(x) an order directing a new trial or a re-hearing;

(y) an order relating to access to, or the custody, care, education or welfare of a minor whether in matrimonial, wardship, guardianship, custodianship or any other proceedings, or a certificate under section 41 of the Matrimonial Causes Act 1973;

(z) an order for or relating to ancillary relief in matrimonial proceedings, including a property adjustment order, an order for the payment of a lump sum and any other order making or relating to financial provision whether of a capital or income nature;

(aa) a judgment or order under Order 14, Order 14A or Order 86 or under Order 9, rule 14 of the County Court Rules 1981;

(bb) an order setting aside or refusing to set aside another judgment or order (whether such other judgment or order is final or interlocutory);

(cc) an order made for or relating to the enforcement of an earlier order (whether such earlier order is final or interlocutory) or giving further directions as to such an order and (without prejudice to the generality of the foregoing)—

(i) a garnishee order nisi or a garnishee order absolute;

(ii) a changing order nisi or a charging order absolute;

(iii) an order for the sale of any property by way of enforcement of an earlier order (whether such earlier order is final or interlocutory) or an order giving directions regarding any such sale, or an order designed to regulate or facilitate any such sale;

(dd) an order for or relating to the taxation of costs or the delivery, withdrawal or amendment of bills of costs;

(ee) without prejudice to paragraph (5)(d), an order made in the course of or by way of regulation of a liquidation and any other order ancillary to or consequential on a winding up order;

(ff) an order directing or otherwise determining an issue as to limitation of actions other than as part of a final judgment or order within the meaning of paragraph (3);

(gg) an order made on an originating summons under Order 85, rule 2, other than such an order as is mentioned in paragraph (5)(c);

(hh) an order made on an application under Order 82, rule 3A.

(7) Notwithstanding anything in paragraph (3) —

    (a) orders made on an appeal to the High Court under section 1(2) of the Arbitration Act 1979 shall be treated as final orders;

    (b) all other orders made in connection with or arising out of an arbitration or arbitral award shall be treated as interlocutory orders; without prejudice to the generality of the foregoing, such orders shall include —

        (i) orders made in connection with the appointment or removal of an arbitrator or umpire;

        (ii) orders made on or in connection with applications for an extension of time for commencing arbitration proceedings;

        (iii) orders setting aside an arbitral award or remitting the matter to an arbitrator or umpire (other than orders setting aside the award or remitting the matter made on an appeal in pursuance of the said section 1(2); and

        (iv) orders made on or in connection with applications for leave to enforce an award.

INDEX